The Hornbook

Dr. Johnson described the hornbook as "the first book of children, covered with horn to keep it unsoiled." Pardon's New General English Dictionary (1758) defined it as "A leaf of written or printed paper pasted on a board, and covered with horn, for children to learn their letters by, and to prevent their being torn and daubed."

It was used throughout Europe and America between the late 1400s and the middle 1700s.

Shaped like an old-fashioned butter paddle, the first hornbooks were made of wood. The paper lesson the child was to learn was fastened to the wooden paddle and covered with a piece of horn. The transparent strip of horn was made by soaking a cow's horn in hot water and peeling it away at the thickness of a piece of celluloid. The horn was necessary to protect the lesson from the damp and perhaps grubby hands of the child. Hornbooks commonly contained the alphabet, the vowels, and the Lord's Prayer. Later hornbooks were made of various materials: brass, copper, silver, ivory, bronze, leather, and stone.

As the art of printing advanced, the hornbook was supplanted by the primer in the book form we know today. Subsequently West Group developed its "Hornbook Series", a series of scholarly and well-respected one volume treatises on particular areas of law. Today they are widely used by law students, lawyers and judges.

BANK REGULATION

By

Michael P. Malloy, Ph.D.

Professor of Law
University of the Pacific
McGeorge School of Law

HORNBOOK SERIES®

WEST GROUP

ST. PAUL, MINN., 1999

COPYRIGHT © 1999 By WEST GROUP
            610 Opperman Drive
            P.O. Box 64526
            St. Paul, MN 55164–0526
            1–800–328–9352

ISBN 0–314–23865–4

*TEXT IS PRINTED ON 10% POST
CONSUMER RECYCLED PAPER*

*This book is dedicated to
my son
Michael Emil Malloy*

*

Preface

Depository institutions regulation is subject to a fast pace of change and development. In the past twenty years alone, for example, federal statutes governing this area have been broadly amended at least seven times. These legislative changes and the increasingly frequent intervention of the Supreme Court have repeatedly rearranged the furniture. In addition, the growing overlap in competition among depository institutions, insurance companies and securities firms has further complicated regulatory policy. As a result, we all remain students of the subject, no matter how long our experience. That may be one of the things that makes the regulation of depository institutions so fascinating and, at times, so frustrating. This book is intended to help law students satisfy their fascination with the subject without the frustration.

I thank my wife, Susie A. Malloy, for her encouragement, critique and inspiration. I also thank my student research assistants, Mr. Michael P. Battin, of the Fordham University Class of 1996; Mr. Edward Miklautsch, of the Fordham University Class of 1997; and Ms. Suzanne Uzelac, of the McGeorge Law School Class of 1998.

M.P.M.

*

Acknowledgements

Limited portions of certain chapters of this study have appeared in the form of reports and articles in scholarly publications, as indicated below. The material is used with permission of the following:

ADMINISTRATIVE CONFERENCE OF THE UNITED STATES, CONSULTANT'S REPORT ON ADJUDICATION PRACTICES AND PROCEDURES OF THE FEDERAL BANK REGULATORY AGENCIES (NOVEMBER 1987).

_____, CONSULTANT'S REPORT ON ADMINISTRATION OF THE SECURITIES EXCHANGE ACT OF 1934 BY THE FEDERAL BANK REGULATORY AGENCIES (OCTOBER 1990).

MICHAEL P. MALLOY, FUNDAMENTALS OF BANKING REGULATION (ASPEN LAW & BUSINESS: 1998).

Michael P. Malloy, *Balancing Public Confidence and Confidentiality: Adjudication Practices and Procedures of the Federal Bank Regulatory Agencies*, 61 Temple L. Rev. 723 (1988), *reprinted in* 4 BANKING L. ANTH. 631 (1988).

_____, *Bumper Cars: Themes of Convergence in International Regulation*, 60 Fordham L. Rev. S1 (Survey Issue 1992).

_____, *Can 10b-5 for the Banks? The Effect of an Antifraud Rule on the Regulation of Banks*, 61 Fordham L. Rev. S23 (Survey Issue 1993), *reprinted in* 8 Banking L. Anth. 257 (1994).

_____, *Depository Institutions Regulators*, *in* G. J. Edles & J. Nelson, Federal Regulatory Process: Agency Practices and Procedures (Prentice Hall Law & Business, 2d ed., 1989, revised).

_____, *Double, Double Toil and Trouble: Bank Regulatory Policy at Mid-Decade*, 63 Fordham L. Rev. 2031 (1995), *reprinted in* 9 BANKING L. ANTH. 269 (1995).

_____, *Foreword: . . . And Backward: Death and Transfiguration among the Savings Associations*, 59 Fordham L. Rev. S1 (Survey Issue 1991).

_____, *Nonbanks and Nondefinitions: New Challenges in Bank Regulatory Policy*, 10 Seton Hall Leg. J. 1 (1986), *reprinted in* 3 BANKING L. ANTH. 531 (1986-87).

_____, *Nothing to Fear but FIRREA Itself: Revising and Reshaping the Enforcement Process of Federal Bank Regulation*, 50 Ohio St. L.J. 1117 (1989), Copyright (C) 1990 The Ohio State University.

_____, *Public Disclosure as a Tool of Federal Bank Regulation*, 9 Ann. Rev. Banking L. 229 (1990).

_____, *The Regulation of Bank Brokerage Activities: Was Rule 3b-9 Benign?* 6 Ann. Rev. Banking L. 181 (1987).

_____, *Seeing the Light: Savings Associations Conversions and Regulatory Realignment*, 10 Ann. Rev. Banking L. 189 (1991).

_____, *The Sound of Two Hands Flapping: Insurance-Related Activities of National Banks*, 41 St. Louis U. L.J. 75 (1997).

_____, *State Change-in-Bank-Control Statutes: Does* MITE *Make Light of Recent Trends?*, 5 Ann. Rev. Banking L. 29 (1986).

_____, *The 12(i)'ed Monster: Administration of the Securities Exchange Act of 1934 by the Federal Bank Regulatory Agencies*, 19 Hofstra L. Rev. 269 (1990), *reprinted in*, 1992 Sec. L. Rev.

_____, *U.S. International Banking and the New Capital Adequacy Requirements: New, Old and Unexpected*, 7 Ann. Rev. Banking L. 75 (1988).

_____, *U.S. International Banking and Treasury's Foreign Assets Controls: Springing Traps for the Unwary*, 8 Ann. Rev. Banking L. 181 (1989).

_____, *U.S. International Banking Policy: Prospects and Problems in a New Millennium*, 15 Ann. Rev. Banking L. 277 (1996).

_____, *When You Wish Upon Winstar: Contract Analysis and the Future of Regulatory Action*, 42 St. Louis U. L.J. 409 (1998).

_____, *Written Statement of Views on D'Oench, Duhme* (Testimony before the Subcommittee on Oversight of Government Management of the Senate Committee on Governmental Affairs, January 31, 1995).

Michael P. Malloy & James T. Pitts, *Post-Mortem on Retail Repurchase Agreements: Where were the Regulators?* 3 Ann. Rev. Banking L. 89 (1984).

List of Figures

WESTLAW® Overview

Bank Regulation, by Michael P. Malloy, offers a detailed and comprehensive treatment of basic rules, principles and issues relating to the law of bank regulation. To supplement the information contained in this book, you can access Westlaw, a computer-assisted legal research service of West Group. Westlaw contains a broad array of legal resources, including case law, statutes, regulations, administrative decisions, expert commentary, current developments and various other types of information.

Learning how to use these materials effectively will enhance your legal research abilities. To help you coordinate the information in the book with your Westlaw research, this volume contains an appendix listing Westlaw databases, search techniques and sample problems.

THE PUBLISHER

*

Summary of Contents

———

*

Table of Contents

_____

*

BANK REGULATION

*

Chapter 1

THE REGULATED
ENVIRONMENT
OF BANKING

Table of Sections

§ 1.1   Introduction

Banking is a regulated industry. This obvious fact creates legal issues that do not exist for other enterprises. In addition, the regulated nature of the banking industry manifests itself in a variety of ways. First, banks and other bank-like entities are limited and controlled in their corporate and business activities by relatively specific statutory provisions. These activities are regulated not only by state law, but also by federal law. In this context, federal law extends far beyond disclosure requirements typical of federal securities regulation.[1] It includes substantive provisions of transactional and corporate law, including incorporation under federal law.[2]

Second, the degree of state and federal regulation is pervasive and thorough, extending to such issues as establishment of a corporation

---

§ 1.1

1. *See, e.g.*, 15 U.S.C.A. §§ 78*l*–78n, 78p (Securities Exchange Act of 1934 disclosure requirements for publicly traded companies).

2. *See, e.g.*, 12 U.S.C.A. §§ 21–22, 26–27 (authorizing establishment of national banking association).

1

intended to enter the industry, expansion into other geographic or product markets, merger with or acquisition of existing entities within the industry, recapitalization, or other reorganization of the entity. Each of these actions—and virtually any other activity undertaken by an entity within the industry—is subject to regulatory oversight or express approval of one or more of the regulators. Each step in the corporate and business life of these entities is subject to regulation.

Third, the industry is typified by a confusing array of specialized types of banking entities, and an equally formidable diversity of regulators. This situation is made even more complex by the fact that in any given corporate or business transaction, any one banking entity may find itself simultaneously subject to the regulatory authority of several of these regulators.[3]

Fourth, underlying the present policies applicable to banking and the current policy controversies affecting the industry is a long, often unstated, historical dialogue. This involves both legal and constitutional debate over the utility of banking and the proper role of state and federal regulation of the industry.

§ 1.2 History

Current bank regulatory policy is still rehearsing the historical controversies surrounding the development of banking and bank regulation. Banking has, of course, longstanding European precursors to the American experience,[1] but this book focuses on U.S. models of bank regulation.

§ 1.3 Early Federal Period

For two centuries, the history of U.S. bank regulation has been the tale of push and pull between federal and state authority, played out from one financial crisis to the next. The ascendancy of the first Bank of the United States and, after a brief hiatus, the second Bank of the United States (of *McCulloch v. Maryland*[1] fame) marked the first period of federal control.

The problem of establishing a coherent credit system for the fledgling United States of America was the initial impetus for the regulation of banking today. On 9 August 1790, the first Congress to meet under the Constitution requested that Treasury Secretary Alexander Hamilton study the financial condition of the new nation and make recommenda-

---

3. *See, e.g., Report of the Task Group on Regulation of Financial Services* 9 (1984) (discussing regulatory overlap).

§ 1.2

1. *See generally* 1 J. Gilbart, The History, Principles and Practice of Banking (Mi-

chie rev. 1893) (discussing European and colonial precursors).

§ 1.3

1. 17 U.S. (4 Wheat.) 316 (1819).

tions with a view to establishing public credit. Hamilton's report[2] concluded that a national bank should be chartered to support the credit market. The report, which turned out to be the opening move in a continuing constitutional controversy, focused almost exclusively on the instrumental effects of creating a national bank. The report argued that "public banks" had a clear utility in established commercial countries, and that utility could assist in the economic development of the new nation.

A bill based on Hamilton's proposal made its way through the Congress. It provided a 20–year charter for the Bank of the United States. The Bank was to have capital of $10 million, $2 million of which could be subscribed for by the federal government. There would be 25 directors. While foreign persons were not prohibited from ownership of the stock of the Bank, such persons could not vote their shares by proxy. The Bank would be limited to an interest rate of six percent on loans and discounts. In addition, it was prohibited from buying and selling real estate, except as it was acquired as foreclosed collateral.

The bill met with opposition from agrarian interests, who feared that the bank's operations would draw funds away from agriculture, increase speculation, and drive "specie" (gold and silver) out of the country. A constitutional dimension emerged to clothe these agrarian prejudices with principle. On 2 February 1791, James Madison opposed the bill in the House, claiming that the proposal was unconstitutional.[3]

Nevertheless, the bill passed. President Washington asked his cabinet officers for their views. On 15 February 1791, Secretary of State Thomas Jefferson delivered an opinion in opposition, essentially grounded on the constitutional aspects.[4] In his view, the power to create a bank, a corporate entity, had not been delegated to the federal government by the Constitution. It was not among the enumerated powers (e.g., taxation, borrowing, regulating commerce). Nor was it within either of the general powers (i.e., taxing to provide for the "general welfare," enacting laws "necessary and proper" for executing enumerated powers).

Attorney General Edmund Randolph had already registered opposition to the bill.[5] On 16 February 1791, the President wrote to Hamilton, enclosing the opinions of Jefferson and Randolph and requesting his views on the bill. In his reply of 23 February 1791, Hamilton for the first time directly addressed the constitutional dimensions of his proposal. His response served as the basic structure of the argument endorsed by the Supreme Court some 18 years later in *McCulloch*. Among other things, Hamilton argued:

2. *Treasury Report on a National Bank*, Dec. 13, 1790, 1 American State Papers 67, *reprinted in* Michael P. Malloy, Banking and Financial Services Law 6 (Carolina Academic Press: 1999).

3. 3 Annals of Cong. 1944 (1791).

4. *Reprinted in* 1 H.E. Krooss (ed.), Documentary History of Banking and Currency in the United States 147 (1969 ed.).

5. *Reprinted in* M. St. C. Clarke & D. A. Hall, Legislative and Documentary History of the Bank of the United States 86 (1832).

[T]his *general principle* is *inherent* in the very *definition* of government, and *essential* to every step of the progress to be made by that of the United States, namely: That every power vested in a government is in its nature *sovereign*, and includes, by *force* of the *term*, a right to employ all the *means* requisite and fairly applicable to the attainment of the *ends* of such power, and which are not precluded by restrictions and exceptions specified in the Constitution, or not immoral, or not contrary to the *essential ends* of political society. . . .

[N]ecessary often means no more than *needful, requisite, incidental, useful* or *conducive to*. It is a common mode of expression to say, that it is *necessary* for a government or a person to do this or that thing, when nothing more is intended or understood, than that the interests of the government or person require, or will be promoted by, the doing of this or that thing. . . .

A bank relates to the collection of taxes in two ways—*indirectly*, by increasing the quantity of circulating medium and quickening circulation which facilitates the means of paying[, and directly] by creating a *convenient species* of medium in which they are to be paid. . . .[6]

The President signed the bill. However, by the time its 20–year charter expired in 1811, Jefferson's party was in power, and there was no hope for renewal of the charter. The classic bank regulatory policy question had already been set, dressed up in basic constitutional terms: the extent to which the federal government could or should regulate banking. The terms of this question, which still incites controversy today, were first delineated in the dispute within President Washington's cabinet over the First Bank, but were essentially set in some of the earliest constitutional rulings of the Supreme Court. These concerned the status of the Second Bank of the United States.

Both before and after the demise of the First Bank, the number of state-chartered banks continued to grow through 1811, with no failures until 1809. From 1809 through the War of 1812, state banks—overextended, inexperienced and undercapitalized—frequently failed. The war left U.S. commercial and financial sectors in disarray. Even within Jefferson's party, support emerged for a central bank to stabilize the economy. Congress adopted a plan in 1816 for a Second Bank of the United States, which President Madison signed into law.

The new bank soon encountered hostility. State banks claimed that the Bank expanded the economy by liberal loans to the state banks during times of favorable financial conditions, but then triggered the collapse of these state banks by demands for repayment during the periods of financial difficulty.[7] Several states passed legislation to curb the activities of the Bank.[8] Maryland's law, taxing bank notes issued by

---

6. *Reprinted in* 1 Krooss at 152 (emphasis in original) (1969 ed.).

7. *See* R. C. H. Catterall, The Second Bank of the United States 27–65 (1902).

8. *See* Warre, The Supreme Court in

the Baltimore branch of the Bank, eventually precipitated the Supreme Court's decision in *McCulloch*. Constitutional law scholars celebrate the case as one of the first significant constitutional decisions of the Court, but of course it should actually be honored as one of the first significant bank regulatory law decisions. Writing for the Court in *McCulloch*, Chief Justice Marshall focused first on the question of whether Congress had power to incorporate a bank. He admitted that the power of establishing a bank or creating a corporation was not among the enumerated powers granted to the federal government under the Constitution.[9] This fact did not, however, exclude the possibility of "incidental or implied powers."[10] He proceeded by a process of inference, based in large part on Hamilton's constitutional argument:

> Although, among the enumerated powers of government, we do not find the word "bank" or "incorporation," we find the great powers to lay and collect taxes; to borrow money; to regulate commerce; to declare and conduct a war; and to raise and support armies and navies.... [I]t may with great reason be contended, that a government, entrusted with such ample powers, on the due execution of which the happiness and prosperity of the nation so vitally depends, must also be entrusted with ample means for their execution. The power being given, it is the interest of the nation to facilitate its execution.... [R]evenue is to be collected and expended, armies are to be marched and supported. The exigencies of the nation may require that the treasure raised in the north should be transported to the south, that raised in the east conveyed to the west, or that this order should be reversed.... [The Constitution] does not profess to enumerate the means by which the powers it confers may be executed; nor does it prohibit the creation of a corporation, if the existence of such a being be essential to the beneficial exercise of those powers. It is, then, the subject of fair inquiry, how far such means may be employed....[11]

In buttressing this inferential argument, Marshall also constructed a textual argument for federal power to intervene in economic policy through the incorporation of a bank. The basis of this argument was, of course, the "necessary and proper" clause of Article II. Marshall argued:

> But the constitution of the United States has not left the right of Congress to employ the necessary means for the execution of the powers conferred on the government to general reasoning. To its enumeration of powers is added that of making "all laws which shall be necessary and proper, for carrying into execution the foregoing powers, and all other powers vested by this constitution, in the government of the United States, or in any department thereof."
>
> ... [The word "necessary"] frequently imports no more than that one thing is convenient, or useful, or essential to another. To

United States History 505–506 (rev. ed. 1923).

9. 17 U.S. at 406.

10. *Id.*

11. *Id.* at 407–409.

employ the means necessary to an end, is generally understood as employing any means calculated to produce the end, and not as being confined to those single means, without which the end would be entirely unattainable. . . .

. . . The subject is the execution of those great powers on which the welfare of a nation essentially depends. It must have been the intention of those who gave these powers, to insure, as far as human prudence could insure, their beneficial execution. This could not be done by confining the choice of means to such narrow limits as not to leave it in the power of Congress to adopt any which might be appropriate and which were conducive to the end. . . .[12]

Essentially, it is for Congress to choose appropriate means for the accomplishment of powers and objectives entrusted to it under the Constitution. That being the case, Congress may decide that a public bank is an appropriate means for the nation's fiscal operations.[13]

Did it make a difference, however, that the bank was controlled by private investors, and hence was not literally a governmental instrumentality? This issue was raised by counsel in *McCulloch*, but skirted by the Court.[14] It was, however, raised squarely in *Osborn v. The Bank*,[15] in which Ohio officials had seized assets of the Bank for failure to pay the Ohio tax on in-state branches of banks chartered outside the state. In another opinion by Chief Justice Marshall, the Court finally expressed itself on the question. Marshall conceded that, if the bank were a private corporate entity "having private trade and private profit for its great end and principal object,"[16] it would be subject to individual state taxing power.[17] However, the bank is not such an entity. Marshall asserted that "[i]t has never been supposed that Congress could create such a corporation."[18]

The significance of *McCulloch* and *Osborn* to the development of constitutional theory is beyond dispute, but what do they tell us about the tensions inherent in the development of banking as a regulated industry in the United States? In the early stages of the history of U.S. bank regulation, arguments about the merits of federal bank regulatory policy were often couched in terms of constitutional theory. This was the case, for example, in President Jackson's July 1832 message vetoing the bill to recharter the Second Bank.[19] This was also the case in Chief Justice Chase's opinion in *Veazie Bank v. Fenno*,[20] upholding federal taxation of state banks. However, while the constitutional dimension of bank regulation may seem to have receded, the attitudes that fueled that debate, and seized upon constitutional rhetoric as a means of expression,

---

12. *Id.* at 411–415.

13. *Id.* at 422.

14. *See* Plous & Baker, *McCulloch v. Maryland: Right Principle, Wrong Case*, 9 Stan. L. Rev. 710 (1957) (discussing issues raised in *McCulloch*).

15. 22 U.S. (9 Wheat.) 738 (1824).

16. *Id.* at 859.

17. *Id.* at 859–860.

18. *Id.* at 860.

19. *Reprinted in* 2 H. E. Krooss at 21 (1983 ed.).

20. 75 U.S. (8 Wall.) 533 (1869).

continue to be felt. The result is a system of bank regulation that is in some respects irrational, redundant and often painfully indirect.

§ 1.4 State Law Primacy

The controversy that surrounded the birth of the Second Bank continued throughout its life.[1] In 1828, Andrew Jackson was elected to the presidency, the result of a coalition of small business people, agrarian interests, laborers, and others of the populist persuasion. In his 1829 message to the Congress, the new President expressed his opposition to the Bank, and indicated that he would oppose any extension of its charter, which was not due to expire until 1836. The Bank's supporters passed a rechartering bill in 1832, and the President vetoed the bill. His veto message to the Congress[2] may seem strange to the modern reader, unless the reader takes into account the fluidity of constitutional doctrine at this relatively early stage of U.S. history. Constitutional arguments aside, Jackson's message expressed in clear terms the populist bias against and suspicion of organized aggregations of economic power. The basic contours of that bias can still be recognized in current debate over bank regulatory policy.

Jackson expressed concern over the bank's monopoly of federal government business. He was bothered by the bank's concentration of economic power in the hands of "foreigners and . . . a few hundred of our citizens, chiefly of the richest class."[3] He also attacked the constitutionality of the bank, in the following terms:

> It is maintained by the advocates of the bank that its constitutionality in all its features ought to be considered as settled by precedent and by the decision of the Supreme Court. To this conclusion I cannot assent. Mere precedent is a dangerous source of authority, and should not be regarded as deciding questions of constitutional power except where the acquiescence of the people and the States can be considered as well settled. . . . There is nothing in precedent, therefore, which, if its authority were admitted, ought to weigh in favor of the act before me.[4]

The Congress failed to override the President's veto, and the Treasury Department began withdrawing U.S. Government funds from the Bank and placing them with state banks.[5] Distrusting bank notes, the Administration took steps to bring specie back into circulation. For example, the Administration announced in the July 1836 "Specie Circular" that only gold and silver would be accepted as payment in sales of

---

§ 1.4

1. *See* 1 Krooss at 653–655 (1969 ed.) (discussing political controversy surrounding Second Bank of the United States).

2. *Reprinted in* 2 Krooss at 21 (1983 ed.).

3. *Id.*

4. *Id.*

5. *See* 1 Krooss at 655–657 (1969 ed.) (discussing events following veto of rechartering bill).

public land. This naturally lead to the disparagement of all forms of paper money, including notes issued by strong, creditworthy banks.

With the eclipse of the Second Bank, a long period of state primacy in bank regulation set in, with disparate and inconsequential results. The emerging primacy of the state banks brought with it new problems for state governments. How were these institutions to be regulated? One of the first notable attempts at regulation during this period was in fact not governmental but private. Providing some of the protections of a central bank system, the so-called Suffolk system was instituted in Boston during the 1820s by a group of Boston banks. Suffolk Bank of Boston held deposits for outlying "country banks," the notes of which could be redeemed at Boston at their par value. To police this system and avoid instability due to over-issuance of bank notes, the Boston banks would accumulate large number of notes from country banks that were not participants in the system. These notes would be presented *en masse* to the nonparticipating country banks for payment. Faced with the possibility of these burdensome calls on their resources, many country banks were persuaded to join the Suffolk system.

The New York legislature established a New York Safety Fund System in 1829 which was, in many respects, like the federal deposit insurance system established in 1933. Under the New York system, banks seeking a charter to do business in New York were required to contribute .5 percent of the value of their capital to the safety fund. The fund was used to aid insolvent banks.

Over-issuance of state bank notes became a major problem. The 1837 depression, for example, was in part due to the over-issuance problem. Nevertheless, in the same year "free banking" statutes began to emerge, allowing for organization of state banks by general legislation, rather than by a special legislative act. In 1837, the legislature of Michigan enacted one of the first free banking acts and in 1838, the New York legislature enacted a free banking act. The free banking acts made it a condition of incorporation that the bank deposit securities with the state that could be used to pay off the bank's depositors in the event of a failure by the bank. Unfortunately, the quality of the securities deposited in fulfillment of this requirement was often questionable, and supervision of banks under the free banking systems was *laissez faire* in the extreme.

As the effects of the 1837 depression continued to be felt, the proliferation of banks created under the free banking statutes continued as well. The result was a wave of bank failures over a five-year period, wiping out hundreds of state banks.

In 1837 Martin Van Buren, close political adviser to Jackson, became president. Shaken in his confidence in the state banking systems, Van Buren backed a legislative proposal for an independent treasury system to hold all government deposits. The Independent Treasury Act was signed into law by Van Buren in 1840. The system of "subtreasuries" continued until subtreasury functions were transferred to the

Department of the Treasury and the Federal Reserve Banks after passage of the General Appropriations Act of May 1920. No major attempt at federalizing regulation of banking would occur until the crisis created by the Civil War.

§ 1.5   Civil War Developments

It required the national crisis of the Civil War before the federal government reentered bank regulation. Prosecution of the war required vast amounts of money and credit. State banks were one obvious source of that credit. By 1861, there were approximately 1,600 state-chartered banks,[1] but no central bank system to monitor credit, and no banks directly subject to federal supervision. Difficulties in financing the war were draining the nation's gold supply, and the gold standard was eventually abandoned as a result.[2] In 1861, Treasury Secretary Salmon P. Chase recommended the establishment of a national banking system. Under this system, national banks would be chartered by the federal government as commercial banks and would be authorized to issue bank notes secured by U.S. government bonds.[3] If Chase's plan were put into operation, it would thus ensure a market for federal debt.

Attempts were first made, however, to finance the war directly through the issuance of U.S. notes, without the captive distribution mechanism of a national bank system. By early 1862, Congress had authorized the issuance of $150 million in U.S. notes, the first of several such issuances.[4] These issuances were not adequate for the credit needs of the wartime budget, and by 1864 a national banking system was created on the model proposed by Chase. The emergence of this national bank system, which outlasted the crisis and became one of the central features of the contemporary bank regulatory system, also established the federal-state "dual banking system" that has been a characteristic of U.S. commercial banking ever since.

The National Currency Act was enacted in 1863,[5] and amended and reenacted as the National Bank Act ("NBA") in 1864.[6] The NBA created the position of the Comptroller of the Currency as an office within the Treasury Department.[7] The Comptroller was vested with the authority to issue national bank charters to groups of incorporators of at least five persons.[8] The system was originally intended to foster the captive market for U.S. bonds, since each newly chartered national bank was required to deliver to the Comptroller government bonds in an amount

---

§ 1.5

1. *See* 2 Krooss at 1261 (1969 ed.).

2. *See Veazie Bank v. Fenno,* 75 U.S. (8 Wall.) 533, 537 (1869) (discussing financial background leading to passage of National Bank Act).

3. *See* 1861 Annual Report of the Department of the Treasury, *reprinted* in Krooss at 1340–45 (1969 ed.).

4. *See Veazie Bank,* 75 U.S. at 537.

5. 12 Stat. 670 (1863).

6. 13 Stat. 111 (1864).

7. 12 U.S.C.A. § 2.

8. 12 U.S.C.A. § 21.

equal to $30,000 or one-third of its capital, whichever was greater. However, long after the need for this captive market had passed,[9] the system of federally chartered national banks persisted and the role of the Comptroller as administrator of national banks therefore continued to be significant.

As part of Chase's plan for financing the war, the legislation passed during the early 1860s imposed taxes on the capital and bank notes of commercial banks, state and national. The tax on state-chartered banks was an attempt on Chase's part to encourage them to convert to national charters. The Chase plan was challenged in *Veazie Bank v. Fenno*,[10] in which Chase, by then Chief Justice, wrote the majority opinion. The Court upheld the constitutionality of the tax,[11] but it did not directly address the constitutionality of the NBA to grant corporate charters to "national banks." This issue was finally addressed *en passant* in *Farmers' & Mechanics' National Bank v. Dearing*,[12] where the Supreme Court stated:

> The constitutionality of the act of 1864 is not questioned. It rests on the same principle as the act creating the second bank of the United States. The reasoning of Secretary Hamilton and of this court in *McCulloch v. Maryland* ... and in *Osborne v. The Bank of the United States* ..., therefore, applies. The national banks organized under the act are instruments designed to be used to aid the government in the administration of an important branch of the public service. They are means appropriate to that end. Of the degree of the necessity which existed for creating them Congress is the sole judge.[13]

Having accepted the constitutionality of the NBA, the Court went on to express the view that the national banks created under the Act's authority were to be accorded a degree of national favor.[14]

§ 1.6   Second Federal Period

The creation of a "national" banking system marked the beginning of the second federal period of U.S. bank regulation. This second distinct federal period would continue after the monetary panic of 1907, with the eventual establishment of the Federal Reserve System in 1913. However, federal involvement in bank regulation during this period, was at first

---

9. The requirement of a deposit of government bonds was revoked in 1913. *See* Act of December 23, 1913, § 17, 38 Stat. 268, *as amended*, Act of June 21, 1917, § 9, 40 Stat. 239.

10. 75 U.S. (8 Wall.) 533 (1869).

11. *Id.* at 549.

12. 91 U.S. (1 Otto) 29 (1875).

13. *Id.* at 33–34. *See Barnett Bank of Marion County, N.A. v. Nelson*, 517 U.S. 25, 42, 116 S.Ct. 1103, 1113 (1996) (*citing*

McCulloch and *Dearing* for proposition that National Bank Act is constitutional).

14. *Farmers' & Mechanics' Nat'l Bank v. Dearing*, 91 U.S. at 34. States now have explicit statutory authority to tax national banks. 12 U.S.C.A. § 548 ("For the purpose of any tax law enacted under the authority of ... any state, national bank shall be treated as a bank organized and existing under the laws of the State ... within which its principal office is located").

simply a matter of expediency. In its narrowest sense, of course, a national banking system *was* created by the enactment of the NBA, *i.e.*, authority was granted to the executive to charter banking businesses that were subject to federal law in their corporate structure, powers to do business and the like. However, in a broader sense, a "national" banking system surely entails more than the mere participation by the federal government as a competing incorporator of banks, along with the states. A consistent and coherent national policy for the regulation of banking would seem to be implied in the notion of a "national" banking system. The United States has been slow to achieve anything like that.

In the aftermath of the 1907 panic,[1] a National Monetary Commission was created in 1908 to investigate the causes of the panic and recommend remedial legislation.[2] The Commission eventually proposed the creation of a central banking system to monitor the monetary and credit functions of the nation's financial system.[3] As enacted into law, this central bank system, the Board of Governors of the Federal Reserve System ("the Fed") was also charged with supervision of the banks that became members of the Federal Reserve System.[4]

§ 1.7   Third Federal Period

A third federal period began in the aftermath of the 1929 stock market crash and the growing depression. This period established the complex structure of federal regulation more or less as we know it today.

The stock market crash of 1929, together with the accompanying nationwide series of bank failures through the mid–1930s, provided catastrophic evidence of the need for further improvements in the nation's bank regulatory system.[1] The resultant statutory improvements included, *inter alia*, the amendment of the Federal Reserve Act in June 1933, which established the Federal Deposit Insurance Corporation ("FDIC").[2] As is characteristic for U.S. bank regulation, however, even the catastrophe of the bank failures of the early 1930s did not lead to a comprehensive realignment of bank regulatory systems. Not only did the state banking systems continue along with the national banking system,

---

§ 1.6

1. For a discussion of the panic, see Ron Chernow, The House of Morgan 121–130 (Atlantic Monthly Press: 1990).

2. 35 Stat. 546 (1908).

3. H.R. Rep. No. 1593, 62d Cong., 3d Sess. (1912).

4. *See* Federal Reserve Act, § 11(a), 38 Stat. 261 (Dec. 23, 1913) (*currently codified at* 12 U.S.C.A. § 248(a)(1)) (providing for examination of member banks).

§ 1.7

1. On the congressional investigation of the causes of the market crash and bank failures, see 2 Michael P. Malloy, Banking Law and Regulation 7.16–7.28 (Aspen Law & Business: 1994 & Cum. Supp.).

2. *See* Act of June 16, 1933, ch. 89, § 8, 48 Stat. 168, *as amended*. This provision, originally codified at 12 U.S.C.A. § 264, was subsequently withdrawn from the Federal Reserve Act and recodified as the separate Federal Deposit Insurance Act, 12 U.S.C.A. ch. 16, in 1950. *See* Act of September 21, 1950, ch. 967, § 1, 64 Stat. 873.

but there was also no concerted attempt to exercise complete, preemptive federal regulatory authority over the activities of the existing state banks.

In the 1930s, and continuing until 1989, federal regulation of savings and loan associations ("S & Ls") was made the responsibility of the Federal Home Loan Bank Board ("FHLBB"), for federally chartered S & Ls, and the Federal Savings and Loan Insurance Corporation ("FSLIC"), for federally insured, state-chartered S & Ls.[3]

The National Credit Union Administration ("NCUA") is yet another legacy of the financial crisis that beset the country beginning in 1929. Unlike the federal regulatory systems imposed upon the troubled commercial banking and savings associations industries, however, the passage of the Federal Credit Union Act of 1934[4] was, at least on its face, not prompted by any systematic failure of credit unions.[5]

§ 1.8   Contemporary Developments

While the overall structure of U.S. bank regulation has changed remarkably little since the mid–1930s, the statutory interstices of that structure have grown increasingly complex, so much so that at times it seems that a major federal piece of omnibus bank legislation seems to come along almost every two years. In sections 1.9–1.11 we examine in detail the elements of the regulatory structure. For a general overview of contemporary developments, the reader may wish to review Figure 1–1, *infra.*

Figure 1–1

Contemporary Developments in U.S. Bank Regulation

```
1907   –monetary panic
1908   –Monetary Commission established

1913   –Federal Reserve Act

1919   –Edge Act (international banking corporations authorized)


1927   –McFadden Act (national bank branches authorized)
1929   –Collapse of stock market
1932   –Federal Home Loan Act (FHLBB established)
1933   ............................................................Banking Act of 1933 (deposit insurance;
1934   ............................National Housing Act        (limits on securities activities of banks)
1935   –Banking Act of 1935    (FSLIC established)         Securities Act of 1933
                    Securities Exchange Act of 1934        Home Owner's Loan Act (chartering of
                      (SEC established)                    federal S & Ls authorized)
                    Federal Credit Union Act
                    (federal credit union chartering)
1940   ............................................................Investment Company Act of 1940
                                                         Investment Advisers Act of 1940


1956   –Bank Holding Company Act
```

3. *See* Act of July 22, 1932, 47 Stat. 725 (enacting Federal Home Loan Bank Act); 12 U.S.C.A. §§ 1724–1730i (authorizing FSLIC), *repealed*, Financial Institutions Reform, Recovery, and Enforcement Act of 1989, § 407, 103 Stat. 183, 363 (1989).

4. 12 U.S.C.A. §§ 1751 *et seq.*

5. *See, e.g., Barany v. Buller*, 670 F.2d 726, 733 & n. 16 (7th Cir.1982).

1960   –Bank Merger Act
1962   –Bank Service Corporation Act (renamed Bank Service Company Act in 1996)
1964   –Securities Acts Amendments (banks & S & Ls to register under 1934 Act)
1966   ....Bank Merger Act Amendment
             Financial Institutions Supervisory Act
1968   –Savings and Loan Holding Company Amendments of 1967   Bank Holding Company Act Amendments
             Bank Interest Rates legislation
1970   –Bank Holding Company Act Amendments

1973   –Payment of Interest legislation
1974   ....Depository Institutions
1975   ....Banking and Interest   and Insurance legislation
1976   ....Bank Holding Company   Rates legislation
1977   –Community Reinvestment Act Tax Act of 1976
1978   ....International Banking Act
             Financial Institutions
1980   –S & L crisis begins to emerge   Regulatory and Interest
             Depository Institutions Deregulation and Monetary Control Act   Rate Control Act of 1978
1982   ....Garn–St Germain Depository
             Institutions Act
             international debt crisis emerges

1987   –Competitive Equality Banking Act
1989   –Financial Institutions Reform, Recovery,
             and Enforcement Act of 1989
1991   ....FDIC Improvements Act
             RTC Improvements Act
1994   ....Interstate Banking and Branching
             Efficiency Act
1996   –Economic Growth and Regulatory Paperwork Reduction Act   Community Development and
             Regulatory Improvement Act
1998   –Credit Union Membership Access Act

§ 1.9   Current Regulatory Environment

The environment in which depository institutions operate is defined by a complex set of regulators that charter, supervise, examine, and in many cases specifically approve or disapprove the activities in which the institutions engage. This environment is, then, decidedly regulatory in character.

Regulatory functions performed by the state and federal regulators may be divided into three broad categories:

(1) *Chartering and the administration of other, secondary entry restrictions.*[1] The chartering function is performed by the Comptroller of the Currency and the Director of the Office of Thrift Supervision ("OTS") among the federal regulators, and by various state regulators and regulatory bodies in each state. Secondary entry

§ 1.9

1. "Chartering" involves the establishment of an entity, corporate or otherwise, empowered to engage in the business of being a depository institution of a specified type. The "charter" is the certificate or articles of incorporation, or similar constitutive document. Unlike general business incorporation, chartering involves the review and substantive approval of a charter application by the regulatory official or body empowered by law to authorize an entity to operate as a depository institution. Chartering is, therefore a "primary entry restriction," *i.e.*, a restriction on free entry into the industry. "Secondary entry restrictions" limit the ability of a chartered institution to expand into other segments of the market of the industry (geographic or product). One such secondary entry restriction is the limitation on the power of chartered institutions to establish branch offices or operations. *See, e.g.*, 12 U.S.C.A. § 36 (restrictions on branching by national banks). Other secondary entry restrictions limit the ability of institutions to participate in certain collateral features of the regulatory system itself, such as deposit insurance or membership in the Federal Reserve System. Withholding some of these features, particularly deposit insurance, could have serious adverse effects on the ability of the institution to compete. *See* Scott, *In Quest of Reason: The Licensing Decisions of the Federal Banking Agencies*, 42 U. Chi. L. Rev. 235, 269–70 (1975) (discussing restrictions).

restrictions are administered by a variety of federal and state regulators.

(2) *Supervision.* The supervision of the activities of depository institutions involves not only the promulgation of regulations pursuant to statutory authority, but also the issuance of more or less formal interpretations of the statutory responsibilities imposed on these institutions and the practices that they should follow, through the use of circulars, memoranda, releases, and other publicly available guidance. The supervisory function also includes informal interpretive services provided by the agencies on a day-to-day basis, as well as the use of their statutory enforcement and investigative authority to inquire into cases of possible violations and abuses. Various federal regulators[2] as well as the state regulators exercise this supervisory function.

(3) *Examination.* The examination function is complementary to the supervisory function. On a periodic basis, whether or not violations or interpretive problems exist, depository institutions are subjected to on-site examination by the staffs of the regulators that supervise them.

A depository institution may be subject to the authority of more than one regulator.[3] Distributing primary responsibility for the supervisory and examination functions as to any type of depository institution is a task that is determined separately for each type of regulated activity. In addition, among the principal federal regulators—the Office of the Comptroller of the Currency ("OCC"), the Fed, the FDIC, and the OTS—regulatory responsibilities are usually distributed along the general lines of a now traditional statutory formula.[4]

National banks and District of Columbia banks are generally subject to supervision by the OCC.[5] State-chartered member banks of the

---

2. Principally, the following federal regulators exercise supervisory authority over depository institutions: the Office of the Comptroller of the Currency ("OCC"), the Board of Governors of the Federal Reserve System ("Fed"), the Federal Deposit Insurance Corporation ("FDIC"), the Office of Thrift Supervision ("OTS"), and the National Credit Union Administration ("NCUA"). The extent of their roles in this regard and the types of depository institutions subject to the supervisory authority of each are discussed in § 1.11, *infra*.

3. For example, a state-chartered commercial bank that has FDIC deposit insurance and is a member of the Federal Reserve System is of concern to its state chartering authority, the FDIC, and the Fed. A national bank, which is required to be a member of the Federal Reserve System and to carry FDIC insurance, is of

concern to the OCC, the Fed, and the FDIC.

4. *See, e.g.,* 12 U.S.C.A. § 1813(q) (defining "appropriate Federal banking agency" for purposes of Federal Deposit Insurance Act); 12 U.S.C.A. § 1828(c)(2) (defining "responsible agency" for purposes of prior written approval under Bank Merger Act); 12 U.S.C.A. § 1861(b)(1) (Bank Service Company Act; cross-reference to § 1813(q)); 15 U.S.C.A. § 78c(a)(34)(A) (defining "appropriate regulatory agency" for purposes of Securities Exchange Act of 1934, when used with respect to a "municipal securities dealer"). *Cf.* 15 U.S.C.A. § 78*l*(i) (distributing authority under Securities Exchange Act of 1934 with respect to securities issued by insured banks and savings associations).

5. 12 U.S.C.A. § 1813(q)(1).

Federal Reserve System are generally subject to supervision by the Fed[6] (and, of course, by a state regulator). The Fed is also the federal regulator of bank holding companies,[7] which may also be subject to state regulation.[8] State-chartered nonmember banks the deposits of which are insured by the FDIC are generally subject to supervision by the FDIC,[9] and by a state regulator. Savings associations are generally supervised by the OTS[10] and, if state-chartered, by a state regulator. The OTS is also the federal regulator of savings and loan holding companies,[11] which may also be subject to state regulation. Other depository institutions that are not insured by the FDIC are supervised by other regulators. Thus, state-chartered commercial banks and savings associations not insured by the FDIC are supervised by their state regulators. Federal credit unions are chartered and supervised by the NCUA. Federally insured, state-chartered credit unions are supervised by the NCUA and their state regulators. Uninsured, state-chartered credit unions are supervised by their state regulators. Figure 1–2, *infra*, illustrates these lines of authority.

Figure 1–2

Regulatory Lines of Authority

Institution	*Primary Regulator(s)*	*Other Regulators*
National Banks	OCC	Fed, FDIC
D.C. Banks	OCC	Fed, FDIC
State–Chartered Member Banks	Fed, State Regulator	FDIC, OCC[a]
State–Chartered Nonmember Insured Banks	FDIC, State Regulator	OCC,[a] Fed[b]
Federal Savings Associations	OTS	FDIC, OCC,[a] Fed[b]
State Savings Associations	OTS, State Regulator	FDIC, OCC,[a] Fed[b]
Uninsured State–Chartered Banks	State Regulator	OCC,[a] Fed[b]
Uninsured State–Chartered Savings Associations	State Regulator	OCC,[a] Fed[b]
Federal Credit Unions	NCUA	OCC,[a] Fed[b]
Insured State–Chartered Credit Unions	NCUA, State Regulator	OCC,[a] Fed[b]
Uninsured State–Chartered Credit Unions	State Regulator	OCC,[a] Fed[b]
Bank Holding Companies	Fed, State Regulator	OCC[c]
Savings and Loan Holding Companies	OTS, State Regulator	

a. As to transactions by the institution involving investment securities. 12 U.S.C.A. §§ 24 (Seventh), 378.

b. As to deposit reserves only. 12 U.S.C.A. § 461(b)(1)(A).

c. As to activities of national bank subsidiaries. *See American Ins. Ass'n v. Clarke*, 865 F.2d 278 (D.C.Cir.1988) (discussing role of OCC).

6. 12 U.S.C.A. § 1813(q)(2).

7. 12 U.S.C.A. § 1844.

8. 12 U.S.C.A. § 1848.

9. 12 U.S.C.A. § 1813(q)(3).

10. 12 U.S.C.A. § 1813(q)(4).

11. *Id.*

There are certain areas of regulation that apply not only to depository institutions but to all participants in the commercial and financial activities, such as antitrust and securities regulation. Here, the primary federal regulators of depository institutions have been given specialized responsibilities. In the area of antitrust law, for example, these regulators have been given the statutory responsibility to review certain transactions by depository institutions in advance of any action by the traditional antitrust regulator, the Department of Justice ("DOJ").[12] However, DOJ retains complete authority to review and regulate in the final analysis.[13]

In the area of securities regulation, the primary federal regulators of depository institutions have generally been given exclusive statutory responsibility at the federal level, preempting the usual authority of the Securities and Exchange Commission ("SEC").[14] However, this preemption does not include the enforcement of the antifraud provisions of the securities laws.[15] Nor does it include the regulation of the issuance of or trading in securities by any holding company of a depository institution. Such companies remain subject to the exclusive authority of the SEC at the federal level.

It should be obvious from this brief review that the structure of the regulatory environment is complex. For any one type of depository institution there may be only one regulator to whom the institution must answer, but the typical pattern is in fact usually more convoluted. The complexity of this regulatory structure has raised questions concerning the effectiveness of a regulatory system as fragmented as that governing the activities of depository institutions.[16] In terms of the development and implementation of overall regulatory policy for depository institutions, the structure is a bewildering network of overlapping lines of authority and regulatory interests, as can be seen from Figure 1–3, *infra*. In order to sort out some of these complexities, the next two sections identify the various types of depository institutions authorized by federal and state law and the corresponding federal regulators.

---

12. 12 U.S.C.A. § 1828(c) (Bank Merger Act).

13. 12 U.S.C.A. § 1828(c)(7).

14. *See, e.g.*, 15 U.S.C.A. § 78*l*(i) (authorizing primary regulators of depository institutions to administer Securities Exchange Act of 1934 with respect to securities of supervised institutions).

15. 15 U.S.C.A. §§ 77q, 78j.

16. *See, e.g., Report of the Task Group on Regulation of Financial Services* 9 (1984) ("Task Group Report"):

This fragmentation can impair the effectiveness of the regulatory system in maintaining safety and soundness, especially where ultimate responsibility for a particular program is not clearly identified. Impairment can also occur where the need to coordinate actions among too many different agencies and their field offices delays effective supervisory action.

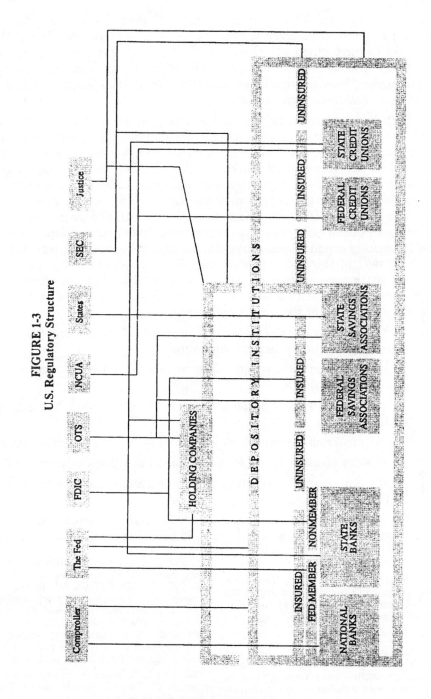

FIGURE 1-3
U.S. Regulatory Structure

§ 1.10   Regulated Entities

Until the 1960s, the financial services industry was typified by "distinct kinds of financial institutions, offering distinct financial products, generally in limited geographic areas."[1] Since then, the industry has experienced considerable blurring of the boundaries among the formerly distinct kinds of institutions.[2] There is now a wide range of "financial intermediaries"[3] (*e.g.*, commercial banks, savings associations, credit unions, finance companies, insurance companies, securities firms) in more or less direct competition.

With the increasing expansion beginning in 1980 of the powers of the once highly specialized savings associations (principally savings banks and S & Ls)[4] came a blurring of distinctions between these entities and full-service commercial banks. In this context, the concept of the "depository institution" has become a significant category in regulatory policy. While its factual significance was assured once distinctions based on differences in offered services became blurred, the technical legal significance of the term was not secured until 1980, with the passage of the Depository Institutions Deregulation and Monetary Control Act of 1980.[5] Title I of the Act, the Monetary Control Act of 1980 ("MCA"),[6] marked an important step in deregulation of the products offered by such institutions. Section 103 of the MCA[7] also contained a formal statutory definition of the term as including:

> (1) any commercial bank the deposits of which are federally insured or eligible for federal insurance;

> (2) any mutual savings bank which is federally insured or eligible for insurance;

> (3) any stock savings bank which is federally insured or eligible for insurance;

> (4) any credit union which is insured or eligible for insurance;

> (5) any member of the Federal Home Loan Bank System; and,

> (6) any savings association (such as an S & L, savings bank, and the like) that is insured or eligible for insurance.

The advantage of this definition, from the point of view of consistent formation of regulatory policy, is that it provides a legally cognizable,

---

§ 1.10

1. Report of the President, Geographic Restrictions on Commercial Banking in the United States 2 (Dep't of the Treasury, Jan. 1981) ("Report of the President").

2. *See id.*:

What was once a financial system consisting of highly segmented *geographic* markets has, for many kinds of banking services, been transformed into a competitive nationwide marketplace. What was once a segmented *product* market has been replaced by head-to-head competition between banks and various non-bank institutions; indeed, there is no longer a single service or product line offered exclusively by commercial banks.

(Emphasis in original.) *See also Marquette Nat'l Bank v. First of Omaha Serv. Corp.*, 439 U.S. 299, 317, 99 S.Ct. 540, 550 (1978) (noting credit market increasingly nationwide in scope). *But see United States v. Connecticut Nat'l Bank*, 418 U.S. 656, 94 S.Ct. 2788 (1974) (maintaining commercial banks and thrift institutions still distinct product markets for antitrust purposes).

3. The Task Group refers to this broad category as "financial service firms." *Task Group Report* at 16.

4. *See* Report of the President at 9–10.

5. Pub. L. No. 96–221, 94 Stat. 132 (March 31, 1980).

6. Pub. L. No. 96–221, tit. I.

7. 12 U.S.C.A. § 461(b)(1)(A).

generic category to cover a wide range of banking and bank-like institutions. Until the enactment of the Financial Institutions Reform, Recovery, and Enforcement Act of 1989 ("FIRREA"),[8] as a technical matter this generic concept was directly applicable only to regulatory policy with respect to reserve requirements, which are now fully subject to regulation by the Federal Reserve Board after an eight-year transitional period.[9] Even the technical acknowledgment of this generic concept resulted in at least a heightened awareness of its pertinence as a term of reference for regulatory policy.[10]

Ideally, then, regulatory issues should be resolved in terms of consistency and coherence with respect to the full spectrum of depository institutions taken as a class. For example, the Federal Deposit Insurance Act ("FDIA")[11] now generally refers to "insured depository institutions"[12] rather than "insured banks,"[13] moving federal regulation a step closer to a unified, functional system. Still, the distinct types of depository institutions remain subject to significantly differing regimes.

(a) *Commercial banks.* Commercial banks remain, in terms of percentage of financial assets held and in terms of the range of their products and services, the dominant category of depository institutions. They are to be distinguished from savings associations (savings banks and S & Ls), which—unlike commercial banks—are not empowered to offer the full range of banking services, including demand deposit accounts (*e.g.*, checking accounts) for business and personal use, savings[14] and time deposits, investment and loan services, and the like.[15] Despite this distinction between commercial and savings banks, the two types of entities (and, indeed, all of the depository institutions) do

---

8. Pub. L. No. 101–73, 103 Stat. 183 (1989).

9. *See* 12 U.S.C.A. § 461(b)(8).

10. *See, e.g.*, Garn–St Germain Depository Institutions Act of 1982, Pub. L. No. 97–320, 96 Stat. 14 (1982).

11. 12 U.S.C.A. §§ 1811 *et seq.*

12. For purposes of the FDIA, the term "depository institution" is defined to mean any "bank or savings institution." 12 U.S.C.A. § 1813(c). The term "savings association" is defined as a generic concept including federally chartered S & Ls and savings banks, state-chartered building and loan associations, S & Ls, homestead associations, cooperative banks (other than those that are "State banks" under 12 U.S.C.A. § 1813(a)(2)) and "any corporation (other than a bank) that the [FDIC] Board of Directors and the Director of the Office of Thrift Supervision jointly determine to be operating in substantially the same manner as a savings association." 12 U.S.C.A. § 1813(b).

13. *See* 12 U.S.C.A. § 1816 (factors to be considered in insurance applications; reference to "depository institution" rather than "bank"); § 1819 (corporate powers of FDIC; same); § 1822 (FDIC as receiver; same).

14. *See Franklin Nat'l Bank v. New York*, 347 U.S. 373, 74 S.Ct. 550 (1954) (commercial banks, though not "savings" institutions, may advertise "savings accounts").

15. Until recently, savings associations were prohibited from engaging in most of these activities, and were limited mainly to personal savings deposits and personal and home mortgage loans. The range of services that savings associations are permitted to offer has expanded dramatically since 1980. *See, e.g.*, Pub. L. No. 96–221, Title IV, 94 Stat. 151 (1980) (expanding transactional powers of savings associations). *See generally* Roster, *The Modern Role of Thrifts*, 18 Loy.-L.A. L. Rev. 1099 (1985). In practice, however, the traditional distinction between commercial banks and savings associations, based on extent of offered services, is still broadly accurate.

overlap services. What actually distinguishes them is the regulatory jurisdiction to which they are subject.

In *Franklin National Bank v. New York*,[16] the Supreme Court considered the authority of national banks (federally chartered commercial banks) to engage in "savings" account services offered by state savings banks. Under the New York Banking Law, New York prohibited the use of the word "savings" or its variants by any banks other than its own chartered savings banks and savings and loan associations. On the other hand, the federal government chartered national banks that were authorized to accept savings deposits.[17] Franklin National offered and advertised its savings accounts. The question therefore arose whether such advertisements violated New York law. The Court considered advertising as a permissible power incidental to the acceptance of the accounts.[18] The Court found no indication that Congress intended to make this phase of national banking subject to local restrictions, as it has done by express language in several other instances.[19] Accordingly, the Court held that the New York law was preempted by the NBA on the issue of permissible advertising of "savings" accounts.[20]

Franklin National notwithstanding, to what extent are national banks subject to state law? Except for situations in which federal statutes contain a contrary provision, national banks are fully subject to state laws, including those concerning collection of debts, transactions in commercial paper, bank deposits, contracts, and the like.[21]

Commercial banks should also be distinguished from investment banks, financial intermediaries whose business consists primarily of underwriting and distributing securities and acting as brokers and dealers in securities already distributed.[22] Since 1933, federal law has generally required that such activities be carried on by entities other than commercial banks and has prohibited most affiliations between commercial and investment banking entities.[23]

---

16.   347 U.S. 373, 74 S.Ct. 550 (1954).

17.   *Franklin*, 347 U.S. at 376, 74 S.Ct. at 553, *citing* R.S. § 5136, 12 U.S.C.A. § 24 (Seventh) (1952).

18.   *Id.* at 377–378.

19.   *Id.* at 378. In many situations, the National Bank Act refers a legal question over to the apposite state law rule. *See, e.g.*, 12 U.S.C.A. §§ 24 (Eighth) (contributions to charitable instrumentalities); 36(c) (intrastate branching); 85 (permissible rates of interest on loans).

20.   *Franklin, supra.* The preemption analysis utilized in the *Franklin* opinion was explicitly relied upon in the Supreme Court's decision in *Barnett Bank of Marion County, N.A. v. Nelson*, 517 U.S. 25, 116 S.Ct. 1103 (1996) (upholding statutory right of national banks to sell insurance under specified circumstances, despite contrary state law).

21.   *See First Nat'l Bank v. Kentucky*, 76 U.S. (9 Wall.) 353, 362 (1870) (noting that national banks "are subject to the laws of the State ... in their daily course of business"); *Davis v. Elmira Sav. Bank*, 161 U.S. 275, 283, 16 S.Ct. 502, 503–504 (1896); *McClellan v. Chipman*, 164 U.S. 347, 356–357, 17 S.Ct. 85, 87 (1896).

22.   For an historical review of the growth of the investment banking business in the United States, see *United States v. Morgan*, 118 F.Supp. 621, 635–55 (S.D.N.Y. 1953).

23.   12 U.S.C.A. §§ 24 (Seventh), 78, 377–378. The clarity of this separation of commercial and investment banking has been vigorously litigated. *See, e.g., Securities Indus. Ass'n v. Board of Governors*, 468 U.S. 137, 104 S.Ct. 2979 (1984) (rejecting Fed authorization of certain securities activities by commercial bank); *Securities In-*

Various attempts at an affirmative definition of "commercial bank" or "bank" have been attempted. The traditional definition defines a commercial bank as an institution whose business consists of discounting commercial paper,[24] accepting deposits (particularly demand deposits),[25] and making loans (particularly commercial loans).[26] More contemporary versions of the definition have stressed the demand deposit and commercial loan aspects only.[27]

(b) *Savings banks*. Savings banks are a relatively early form of the savings association, mainly found in the eastern portion of the United States.[28] They have traditionally been limited by statute to non-commercial deposit and lending activities. In the United States, savings banks have taken two distinct forms: (1) the mutual savings bank, which has no capital stock or stockholders and operates as a mutual association for the benefits of its "members" (*i.e.*, depositors); and, (2) the stock savings bank, of comparatively recent origin, which does operate as a corporate entity with stockholders distinct from depositors.[29] The former has a board of trustees rather than a board of directors, and its net earnings accrue to the mutual benefit of the members. The latter is managed as any other corporate entity. Until recently, both types of savings bank could be chartered only under state law. In 1982, the Garn–St Germain Depository Institutions Act authorized the conversion of state-chartered savings banks insured by the FDIC into federally chartered savings banks, under certain specified conditions.[30]

dus. Ass'n v. Board of Governors, 468 U.S. 207, 104 S.Ct. 3003 (1984) (upholding Fed authorization of acquisition of discount broker by bank holding company).

24. *Oulton v. German Sav. & Loan Soc'y*, 84 U.S. (17 Wall.) 109, 118 (1873); *In re Wilkins' Will*, 131 Misc. 188, 226 N.Y.S. 415 (1928).

25. *United States v. Philadelphia Nat'l Bank*, 374 U.S. 321, 326, 83 S.Ct. 1715, 1721 (1963).

26. *Wilshire Oil Co. v. Board of Governors*, 668 F.2d 732 (3d Cir.1981).

27. Statutory provisions have generally been somewhat vague on this issue, often containing no explicit definition of "bank" or "commercial bank" and apparently presupposing the common understanding of the term. *See, e.g.*, 12 U.S.C.A. § 24 (Seventh) (authorizing national banking association to exercise all powers "incidental to the business of banking"). One exception is the provision in the Bank Holding Company Act ("BHC Act") that adopts as one alternative the traditional definition of *bank* as an institution that accepts demand deposits and makes commercial loans. *See* 12 U.S.C.A. § 1841(c)(1)(B). However, this definition is only directly applicable to the BHC Act itself. *Id.*

28. *See Huntington v. National Savings Bank*, 96 U.S. (6 Otto.) 388, 395 (1878) (discussing statutory origin of savings banks in England; earliest existence in United States traced to 1834 Massachusetts statute). The savings and loan association (S & L) is the more prevalent type of savings association nationwide.

29. *See Dougherty v. Carver Fed. Sav. Bank*, 112 F.3d 613, 615 (2d Cir.1997) (discussing distinction between mutual and stock savings banks).

30. *See* 12 U.S.C.A. § 1464(*o*) (1988). Such a conversion is permitted only if it would not be "in contravention of State law." *Id.* § 1464(*o*)(1). *Cf. id.* § 1464(*o*)(2)(F) (providing for FDIC conversion of insured savings bank to prevent closing or to reopen previously closed savings bank, notwithstanding state law). After a year of effectiveness of this new provision, 143 federally chartered savings banks were in operation. *Task Group Report* at 22, n. 10. FIRREA continued authority for chartering of and conversion to the federal stock savings association form (including savings banks). FIRREA § 301, 103 Stat. at 282, 300–301 (*codified at* 12 U.S.C.A. § 1464(a), (*o*)) (providing chartering and conversion authority, respectively). FIRREA also provides for conversion, notwithstanding any

While their statutory powers have been expanded beyond traditional limits,[31] savings banks remain primarily consumer-oriented depository institutions. Savings banks have traditionally been viewed by the courts as *"quasi* benevolent"[32] or *"quasi* charitable and purely benevolent institutions."[33] The public policy embodied in the original statutes authorizing savings banks was that they were intended to encourage thrift among those of modest means.[34] In contemporary terms, however, savings banks represent one sector of the business of banking, and they operate, within the statutory limits on their powers, like other institutions within that business.

(c) *Savings and loan associations.* Savings and loan associations ("S & Ls"), or building and loan associations as they are called in some states, are the largest category of savings associations. Like savings banks, S & Ls were, until recently, generally limited by statute to the receipt of savings deposits and the making of consumer and mortgage loans. Since 1980, however, their powers have been expanded dramatically.

Since at least the 1930s, S & Ls could be either state or federally chartered. Like savings banks, S & Ls can be either mutual or stock in form. Conversions of mutual S & Ls into stock S & Ls increased through the 1980s as more S & Ls began to seek increased capital through public offerings of stock.[35]

Historically, S & Ls were intended to engage in much the same "thrift" activities that were mentioned with respect to savings banks. These traditional activities were essentially consumer-oriented and local in character.[36] Their "main [statutory] purpose ... is the financing of homes."[37] It was recognized at least by 1951 that S & Ls "do some of the same things which banks do, ... [b]ut they do not do a general banking business."[38] This perception may be less accurate in light of the expanded powers granted to S & Ls in 1980, but in practice S & Ls remain

---

other provision of law, of troubled state-chartered mutual savings banks into federally chartered stock savings banks under certain statutorily specified conditions. *Id.* at 301 (*codified at* 12 U.S.C.A. § 1464(p)).

31. *See, e.g., Connecticut Nat'l Bank,* 418 U.S. at 665–666, 94 S.Ct. at 2794–2795 (noting expanded role).

32. *Huntington v. National Savings Bank,* 96 U.S. (6 Otto.) at 394 (emphasis in original).

33. *Hannon v. Williams,* 34 N.J.Eq. 255, 258 (1881) (emphasis in original).

34. The original object of savings banks was said to be:

to receive and safely invest the savings of mechanics, laborers, servants, minors and others, thus affording to such persons the advantages of security and interest for their money, and in this way ameliorating the condition of the poor and laboring

classes by engendering habits of industry and frugality.

Id.

35. *Task Group Report* at 22 n.12.

36. *See, e.g.,* 12 U.S.C.A. § 1464(a) (authorizing federally chartered savings associations "for the deposit of funds and for the extension of credit for homes and other goods and services").

37. *State v. Minnesota Fed. Sav. & Loan Ass'n,* 218 Minn. 229, 239, 15 N.W.2d 568, 574 (1944).

38. *North Arlington Nat'l Bank v. Kearny Fed. Sav. & L. Ass'n,* 187 F.2d 564 (3d Cir.1951). *Cf. Connecticut Nat'l Bank,* 418 U.S. at 663–666, 94 S.Ct. at 2793–2795 (1974) (holding thrifts not part of banking market).

distinct from commercial banks. They are still charged with their original statutory purpose of fulfilling the community needs for local savings associations.

(d) *Credit unions*. Credit unions[39] may be either state or federally chartered.[40] The first credit union was organized in Germany in the mid–1800s.[41] St. Mary's Bank was the first credit union organized in the United States, chartered by Massachusetts shortly before the enactment of that state's general credit union statute, the first in the United States.[42] By the early 1930s, some 38 states had enacted credit union laws.[43] In 1932, Congress had passed a credit union statute for the District of Columbia,[44] and in 1934 the first federal credit union statute was enacted.[45]

Today credit unions are cooperative associations created to promote thrift among its members. The membership of a credit union is limited to individuals who have a "common bond" of association, occupation or residence in a well defined geographical area.[46] The nature of the common bond is usually identified in the charter of the credit union.

§ 1.11 Regulators

(a) *The Comptroller of the Currency*. The Comptroller of the Currency, the oldest extant federal bank regulator, is the administrator of the national banks chartered by him/her under the National Bank Act ("NBA").[1] The Comptroller and his/her Office ("OCC") constitute a bureau of the Department of the Treasury,[2] and the OCC is responsible for the administration of virtually all federal laws applicable to national banks, including all banks operating in the District of Columbia.[3]

The Comptroller, as the statutory official empowered by the NBA,[4] is given personal authority under the Act. In terms of organizational structure, the central office is the Washington, D.C., headquarters of the OCC. The field organization of the OCC consists of six district offices

39. For general discussion of the nature and operations of credit unions, see *State v. Minnesota Fed. Sav. & Loan Ass'n*, 218 Minn. 229, 15 N.W.2d 568 (1944).

40. For definitions of "federal credit union" and "state" or "state-chartered credit union" see 12 U.S.C.A. § 1752(1), (6).

41. *See Barany v. Buller*, 670 F.2d 726, 733 (7th Cir.1982) (discussing history of credit unions).

42. *La Caisse Populaire Ste.-Marie v. United States*, 425 F.Supp. 512, 515 (D.N.H. 1976), *aff'd*, 563 F.2d 505 (1st Cir.1977).

43. *See Barany*, 670 F.2d at 733.

44. *See* S. Rep. No. 555, 73d Cong., 2d Sess. 2 (1934) (discussing credit union statutes).

45. Pub. L. No. 73–467, 48 Stat. 1216 (1934).

46. *National Credit Union Admin. v. First Nat'l Bank & Trust Co.*, 522 U.S. 479, 118 S.Ct. 927 (1998). Legislation has expanded the common bond requirement, overriding *First National. See* Credit Union Membership Access Act, Pub. L. No. 105–219, Aug. 7, 1998, 112 Stat. 913 (1998) (codified at scattered sections of 12 U.S.C.A.)

§ 1.11

1. U.S.C.A. §§ 1 *et seq.*

2. 12 U.S.C.A. §§ 1, 2.

3. 12 U.S.C.A. § 1813(q)(1).

4. 12 U.S.C.A. §§ 2, 26.

covering the United States and its territories and dependencies.[5] In addition to the district offices, there are some 23 field offices located in major financial centers throughout the districts.[6]

The approval of the Comptroller is required for practically any significant action to be taken by a national bank, including among other things chartering, establishment of branches, changes in corporate control or in the structure of the organization.[7] In addition, the Comptroller has supervisory authority over the day-to-day activities of national banks, including loan and investment policies, trust activities, issuance of securities, and the like. These supervisory responsibilities are carried out, for the most part, through periodic on-site examinations of the banks by national bank examiners.

Courts have generally accorded a high degree of deference to the Comptroller's decisions under the NBA and other statutory authority.[8] In *Association of Data Processing Service Organizations v. Camp*,[9] the Supreme Court held that the Comptroller's decisions were subject to judicial review under the Administrative Procedure Act ("APA"). According to *Camp v. Pitts*,[10] the appropriate standard for this review is whether the Comptroller's actions are "arbitrary, capricious, an abuse of discretion, or otherwise not in accordance with law."[11] In applying that standard, the focal point is the extant administrative record, not a *de novo* record made by the reviewing court. However, neither the NBA nor the APA requires the Comptroller to hold a hearing or to make formal findings on the hearing record when passing on applications.[12] Hence, the APA "substantial evidence" test cannot be the appropriate standard of judicial review, since this standard is only appropriate in cases involving the review of findings on a hearing record.[13] Similarly, it is not open to a reviewing court to examine the administrative action *de novo* to decide whether the action was "unwarranted by the facts."[14]

5. 12 C.F.R. § 4.5(a).

6. 12 C.F.R. § 4.5(b).

7. *But cf. American Ins. Ass'n v. Clarke,* 865 F.2d 278 (D.C.Cir.1988) (discussing division of authority between OCC and Fed over certain corporate transactions).

8. *See generally* Scott, *In Quest of Reason: The Licensing Decisions of the Federal Banking Agencies,* 42 U. Chi. L. Rev. 235, 268 (1975) (noting limited judicial review of Comptroller's decisions).

9. 397 U.S. 150, 90 S.Ct. 827 (1970).

10. 411 U.S. 138, 93 S.Ct. 1241 (1973).

11. 5 U.S.C.A. § 706(2)(A); *Camp v. Pitts,* 411 U.S. at 142, 93 S.Ct. at 1244. *Cf. Washington v. Office of Comptroller of Currency,* 856 F.2d 1507, 1511 (11th Cir.1988) (*citing Camp*; reviewing denial of hearing on merger application on "arbitrary, capricious" standard).

12. *See, e.g.,* 12 U.S.C.A. § 26, which appears to contemplate an *ex parte* investigation by the Comptroller of charter applications. As to the APA, the requirement of a written statement of "findings and conclusions, and the reasons or basis therefor," 5 U.S.C.A. § 557(c)(3)(A), applies only to rulemaking proceedings, *id.* § 553, and to adjudications "required by statute to be determined on the record after opportunity for an agency hearing." *Id.* § 554(a). These APA requirements are not apposite to a charter application under the NBA, since the Act does not require agency hearings in that context. *Camp,* 411 U.S. at 141 n.3, 93 S.Ct. at 1243 n.3.

13. 5 U.S.C.A. § 706(2)(E). *See Camp,* 411 U.S. at 141, 93 S.Ct. at 1243 (discussing review standard).

14. 5 U.S.C.A. § 706(2)(F). *See Camp,* 411 U.S. at 141–142, 93 S.Ct. at 1244 (*citing Citizens to Preserve Overton Park v. Volpe,* 401 U.S. 402, 415, 91 S.Ct. 814 (1971)).

Camp has set the basic approach used in judicial review of all depository institutions regulators. *Camp* has widely been interpreted as severely limiting judicial review of the Comptroller's decisions.[15] Still, the case put to rest the traditional argument that the Comptroller's discretion in charter decisions was subject to no judicial review.[16] *Camp* also suggests that the Comptroller and other OCC officials may be required to submit proof in the form not only of affidavits, but also of testimony subject to cross-examination.[17] The ultimate remedy in such cases is to vacate the agency action and remand to the Comptroller for further consideration.[18] The burden on the party seeking even this limited relief is still particularly difficult to meet.[19]

(b) *The Board of Governors of the Federal Reserve System.* The Federal Reserve Act of 1913[20] created a system of federal reserve banks, each acting in effect as a central bank for its geographical region, and overseen by the Board of Governors of the Federal Reserve System ("the Fed") located in Washington, D.C. This "Federal Reserve System" consists of the Fed and its staff, the twelve Federal Reserve Banks, the Federal Open Market Committee ("FOMC"), the Federal Advisory Council ("FAC"), and the commercial banks which are members of the Federal Reserve System ("member banks"). The Fed, the twelve Reserve Banks and the FOMC have policymaking responsibilities.

The Fed is primarily charged with the responsibility of implementing monetary and credit policy applicable to the financial system and maintaining monetary and credit growth.[21] The Fed also administers federal laws concerning the reserves required to be held by all depository institutions against their deposits.[22]

The Fed does not perform a chartering function,[23] but it does have

15. *See, e.g.,* Scott at 265–268, and cases cited therein.

16. For examples of judicial statements suggesting that the Comptroller's discretionary determinations were beyond judicial review, see *Baltimore & O. R. Co. v. Smith*, 56 F.2d 799 (3d Cir.1932); *Cooper v. O'Connor*, 99 F.2d 135 (D.C.Cir.1938); *Myers v. Coffey*, 124 F.2d 396 (6th Cir.1941); *United States Nat'l Bank of La Grande v. Pole*, 2 F.Supp. 153 (D.Ore.1932). *Cf.* Stokes, *Public Convenience and Advantage in Applications for New Banks and Branches*, 74 Banking L.J. 921, 930 (1957) ("Well informed opinion is that there is no right of appeal from a decision of the Comptroller of the Currency."); Scott at 258 (noting Comptroller's arguments to this effect as late as mid–1960s).

17. *Camp* states:

If ... there was such a failure to explain administrative action as to frustrate effective judicial review, the remedy was not to hold a *de novo* hearing but ... to obtain from the agency, *either through affidavits or testimony, such additional*

explanation of the reasons for the agency decision as may prove necessary.

411 U.S. at 142–143, 93 S.Ct. at 1244 (emphasis added).

18. *Camp*, 411 U.S. at 143, 93 S.Ct. at 1244 (*citing Securities and Exch. Comm'n v. Chenery Corp.*, 318 U.S. 80, 63 S.Ct. 454 (1943)).

19. *See, e.g., Klanke v. Camp*, 327 F.Supp. 592, 593–594 (S.D.Tex.1971) (noting difficulties).

20. 38 Stat. 251 (1913) (codified at 12 U.S.C.A. §§ 221 *et seq.*).

21. *See, e.g.,* 12 U.S.C.A. §§ 225a, 461(b)(4)(A)(i).

22. 12 U.S.C.A. § 461. This authority was expanded to apply fully to the required reserves of all depository institutions by March 1988. 12 U.S.C.A. § 461(b)(8). *See* Pub. L. 96–221, Mar. 31, 1980, § 108, 94 Stat. 132, 141 (effective date provisions).

23. *But see* 12 U.S.C.A. § 611 (Fed chartering of "Edge Act" corporations, specializing in international and foreign banking).

supervisory and examination functions with respect to state-chartered member banks. In addition, certain specialized regulatory functions have also been given to it. For example, since 1956, the Fed has had primary responsibility for the administration of federal laws regulating the formation and operation of bank holding companies.[24] Since 1960, it has been charged with the administration of the Bank Merger Act in mergers in which the acquiring, assuming or resulting bank is a state-chartered member bank.[25] In addition, since 1964 the Fed has had responsibility for the administration of the Securities Exchange Act of 1934 ("1934 Act")[26] with respect to securities issued by state-chartered member banks.[27]

The Fed is a collegial body of seven members, appointed by the President with Senate confirmation.[28] Each member of the Fed is appointed for a term of fourteen years, staggered so that one member's term expires every two years.[29]

The Reserve Banks are separate quasi-governmental corporate entities, the stockholders of which are its member banks. Each Reserve Bank operates within its own geographic district. Each has a board of nine directors, classified according to statutory criteria.[30] Three are bankers elected by the reserve bank's member banks, three are nonbankers, representing the public but elected by the member banks "with due but not exclusive consideration to the interests of agriculture, commerce, industry, services, labor and consumers,"[31] and three are appointed by the Fed.[32] By designation of the Fed Chairman, one of the appointed directors serves as chairman of the Reserve Bank's board of directors, and another as deputy chairman.[33] The nine directors serve three-year terms, staggered so that the terms of three directors, one from each of class, expire each year.[34]

The FOMC consists of the seven Fed board members and five representatives from the Reserve Banks.[35] The legitimacy of the FOMC has been subjected to repeated, unsuccessful constitutional attacks, because of the selection of the five reserve bank representatives without appointment by the president and advice and consent of the Senate as

---

24. 12 U.S.C.A. §§ 1841 *et seq.*

25. 12 U.S.C.A. § 1828(c)(2)(B).

26. 15 U.S.C.A. §§ 78a *et seq.*

27. 15 U.S.C.A. § 78*l*(i).

28. 12 U.S.C.A. § 241.

29. 12 U.S.C.A. § 242.

30. 12 U.S.C.A. § 302.

31. 12 U.S.C.A. § 304.

32. 12 U.S.C.A. § 305. None of the three appointed directors may be a director, officer or employee of a bank. *Id.* § 303. However, the director designated by the Fed as chairman must "be a person of tested banking experience." *Id.* § 305.

33. *Id.* § 305.

34. *Id.* § 308.

35. *Id.* § 263(a). On the history, structure and operations of the FOMC, see *FOMC v. Merrill*, 443 U.S. 340, 343–347, 99 S.Ct. 2800, 2803–2805 (1979); *Committee for Monetary Reform v. Board of Governors*, 766 F.2d 538, 539–540 (D.C.Cir.1985); *Riegle v. FOMC*, 656 F.2d 873, 874–876 (D.C.Cir.), *cert. denied*, 454 U.S. 1082, 102 S.Ct. 636 (1981); *Reuss v. Balles*, 584 F.2d 461, 462–464 (D.C.Cir.), *cert. denied*, 439 U.S. 997, 99 S.Ct. 598 (1978).

provided in the Constitution's appointments clause.[36] One challenge, brought by a member of the U.S. House of Representatives, was held to lack standing to maintain the action either as a legislator or private bondholder.[37] A similar challenge, brought by a senator, was held not necessarily to fail on standing grounds,[38] but was dismissed under the court's equitable discretion to dismiss on the grounds that judicial action would improperly interfere with the legislative process.[39] A third challenge, brought by the Committee for Monetary Reform, a group of private businesses and individuals, was subsequently dismissed on alternative standing grounds.[40]

The latest challenge to the FOMC, again instituted by a senator, initially survived the standing question.[41] The district court declined to apply the doctrine of equitable discretion.[42] However, on the merits of the appointments clause challenge, the district court held that the selection of the five reserve bank representatives of the FOMC was constitutional, because open market trading activities could validly be delegated by Congress to private individuals.[43] On appeal, the D.C. Circuit affirmed, but on other grounds. The court rejected the district court's reading of the doctrine of equitable discretion.[44] Instead, the court relied upon the doctrine, in light of its understanding of the "separation-of-powers concerns informing the doctrine of equitable discretion."[45] The district court's opinion was vacated, and its dismissal of the action affirmed on the grounds that "if a legislator could obtain substantial relief from his fellow legislators through the legislative process itself, then it is an abuse of discretion for a court to entertain the legislator's action."[46]

The FOMC directs the Fed's purchases and sales of U.S. government securities and other obligations in the public securities markets (*i.e.*, the open market).[47] The activities of the FOMC are intended to affect the relative availability of credit in the banking system by direct participation in the market,[48] that is, by competing for liquid assets through sales of securities, or by infusing liquid assets into the system through purchases of securities.

---

36. U.S. Const. art. II, § 2, cl. 2.

37. *Reuss*, 584 F.2d at 469.

38. *See Riegle*, 656 F.2d at 877–879.

39. *Id*. at 881 (finding congressional plaintiff could obtain substantial relief from legislative colleagues).

40. *Committee for Monetary Reform*, 766 F.2d at 542–543 (failure to show economic harm caused by alleged constitutional violation); *id*. at 543–544 (separation-of-powers harm not involved where plaintiffs not directly subject to authority of challenged agency).

41. *Melcher v. Federal Open Market Committee*, 644 F.Supp. 510, 513–514 (D.D.C.1986), *affirmed on other grounds*,

836 F.2d 561 (D.C.Cir.1987), *cert. denied*, 486 U.S. 1042, 108 S.Ct. 2034 (1988).

42. *Melcher*, 644 F. Supp. at 514–517 (noting post-*Riegle* law of standing substantially changed in light of *Comm. for Monetary Reform*).

43. *Id*. at 522–523.

44. *Melcher*, 836 F.2d at 563–564.

45. *Id*. at 564.

46. *Id*. at 565 (footnote omitted). *See generally* Note, *The Federal Open Market Committee and the Sharing of Governmental Power with Private Citizens*, 75 Va. L. Rev. 111 (1989) (discussing case law).

47. 12 U.S.C.A. §§ 263(b), 355(2).

48. 12 C.F.R. § 270.3.

The FAC consists of one representative from each of the twelve Reserve Banks, selected by the boards of the Reserve Banks to serve one-year terms.[49] The FAC advises the Fed on current business conditions and makes recommendations concerning matters of concern to the Federal Reserve System as a whole.[50] These recommendations are advisory, and the FAC is not part of the supervisory apparatus of the System.

The member banks include all national banks in the continental United States,[51] as required by law,[52] and those state-chartered banks and trust companies which have chosen to apply for, and have received, membership.[53]

Much of the day-to-day supervisory and examination responsibilities of the Fed are carried out by the staff of the Fed and the Reserve Banks. The field organization of the Fed consists of the twelve Reserve Banks and the Federal Reserve Agents. Though the Reserve Banks are separate corporate entities, they do operate under the general supervision of the Fed. Thus, in many situations, the Reserve Banks will act as the Fed's field representatives in their respective districts and assist in the implementation, at the field level, of the Fed's regulations and policies.

Decisions by the Fed to grant or deny an application for membership, or to approve any proposed activity subject to its statutory authority, are committed to its discretion, and courts accord a significant degree of deference to the Fed's decisions.[54] Nevertheless, the Fed's decisions are subject, in accordance with *Camp* to judicial review under the APA, and its actions must be supported by adequate reasoning.[55] The standard of judicial review for the Fed's discretionary decisions is whether the Fed's actions are "arbitrary, capricious, an abuse of discretion, or otherwise not in accordance with law."[56] However, under the BHCA, the Fed's factual findings are reviewed under a "substantial evidence" standard.[57]

49. 12 U.S.C.A. § 261.

50. 12 U.S.C.A. § 262.

51. 12 U.S.C.A. § 221.

52. 12 U.S.C.A. § 222.

53. 12 U.S.C.A. § 321.

54. *See, e.g., Board of Governors v. Investment Co. Inst.,* 450 U.S. 46, 101 S.Ct. 973 (1981) (upholding Fed's authorization of holding company affiliates to act as investment advisers to closed-end investment companies); *Securities Industry Ass'n v. Board of Governors,* 468 U.S. 207, 104 S.Ct. 3003 (1984) (upholding Fed authorization of acquisition of discount brokerage firm by bank holding company); *First Bank & Trust Co. v. Board of Governors,* 605 F.Supp. 555 (D.Ky.1984) (upholding Fed's interpretation of application of deposit reserve provisions). *But see Securities Industry Ass'n v. Board of Governors,* 468 U.S. 137, 104 S.Ct. 2979

(1984) (*SIA I*) (rejecting Fed's "post hoc rationalizations" as "entitled to little deference").

55. *See, e.g., SIA I,* 468 U.S. at 143, 104 S.Ct. at 2982; *Alabama Ass'n of Ins. Agents v. Board of Governors,* 558 F.2d 729 (5th Cir.1977); *Georgia Ass'n of Independent Ins. Agents v. Board of Governors,* 533 F.2d 224 (5th Cir.1976).

56. 5 U.S.C.A. § 706(2)(A). *See Camp,* 411 U.S. at 142, 93 S.Ct. at 1244. *See also Investment Co. Inst. v. Board of Governors,* 551 F.2d 1270 (D.C.Cir.1977); *Marine Corp. v. Board of Governors,* 325 F.2d 960 (7th Cir.1963).

57. 12 U.S.C.A. § 1848. *See Bank of Boulder v. Board of Governors,* 535 F.2d 1221 (10th Cir.1976); *North Hills Bank v. Board of Governors,* 506 F.2d 623 (8th Cir. 1974); *Gravois Bank v. Board of Governors,* 478 F.2d 546 (8th Cir.1973).

(c) *The Federal Deposit Insurance Corporation*. Under the Federal Deposit Insurance Act ("FDIA"), state-chartered member banks[58] as well as national banks and federally chartered savings associations[59] are required to obtain deposit insurance from the FDIC. Federal deposit insurance is optional under the FDIA for state-chartered nonmember banks and savings associations. In fact, however, virtually all state-chartered banks have opted for FDIC insurance.

The primary statutory mandate of the FDIC is to provide deposit insurance to depository institutions qualifying for insurance coverage under the FDIA. The statutory policy behind the act is discussed in *FDIC v. Philadelphia Gear Corp.*[60] in the following terms:

> Congress' purpose in creating the FDIC was clear. Faced with virtual panic [after the 1929 stock market collapse], Congress attempted to safeguard the hard earnings of individuals against the possibility that bank failures would deprive them of their savings. Congress passed the 1933 provisions "[i]n order to provide against a repetition of the present painful experience in which a vast sum of *assets and purchasing power* is 'tied up.' " S. Rep. No. 77, 73d Cong., 1st Sess., 12 (1933) (emphasis added). The focus of Congress was therefore upon ensuring that a deposit of "hard earnings" entrusted by individuals to a bank would not lead to a tangible loss in the event of a bank failure.[61]

Today the FDIC administers a Bank Insurance Fund ("BIF") for deposits of insured banks,[62] and a Savings Association Insurance Fund ("SAIF") for deposits of savings associations.[63]

It is the responsibility of the FDIC to pay off depositors of insured institutions that are closed without sufficient assets to satisfy claims of depositors, to the extent of FDIA insurance coverage,[64] and to act as receiver for national banks and federally chartered savings associations in receivership,[65] and for state institutions in receivership where the FDIC has been appointed by the appropriate state regulatory authority.[66] The authority of the FDIC includes not only receivership powers, but also powers to take remedial action to prevent formal closing of an insured bank.[67]

In terms of judicial review, there has been relatively little reported

---

58. 12 U.S.C.A. § 329.

59. *See, e.g.*, 12 U.S.C.A. § 222.

60. 476 U.S. 426, 106 S.Ct. 1931 (1986).

61. *Id.* at 432–433, 106 S.Ct. at 1935.

62. 12 U.S.C.A. § 1821(a)(4)–(5).

63. 12 U.S.C.A. § 1821(a)(4), (6). The Economic Growth and Regulatory Paperwork Reduction Act (EGRPR Act), Pub. L. No. 104–208, title II, 110 Stat. 3009 (1996) (codified at scattered sections of 5, 12, 15, 26, 42 U.S.C.A.), provided for the merger of the FDIC insurance funds into a new De-

posit Insurance Fund (DIF), if there were no more savings associations by 1 January 1999. EGRPR Act, § 2704 (establishing DIF; repealing inconsistent provisions; making other technical and conforming amendments).

64. 12 U.S.C.A. § 1821(f).

65. *Id.* § 1821(c).

66. *Id.* § 1821(e).

67. *See, e.g., id.* § 1823(c).

litigation challenging the FDIC's insurance decisions.[68] The FDIC's decisions are committed to the agency's discretion.[69] Nevertheless, the FDIC's administrative discretion is subject to judicial review as to whether or not it had acted in a manner that was arbitrary, capricious, an abuse of discretion or otherwise not in accordance with law.[70]

(d) *The Office of Thrift Supervision.* The Office of Thrift Supervision ("OTS") is the successor to the Federal Home Loan Bank Board ("FHLBB") and the Federal Savings and Loan Insurance Corporation ("FSLIC"), at least with respect to the federal chartering, regulation and supervision of savings associations.[71] The Director of the OTS ("DOTS") is the "appropriate Federal banking agency" with respect to any savings association or any savings and loan holding company.[72]

Among other things, the DOTS has the authority to charter federal savings associations[73] and is responsible for the examination, safe and sound operation and regulation of such entities.[74] The DOTS has specific enforcement authority with respect to the chartering and permitted activities of federally chartered savings associations,[75] as well as general enforcement authority under the provisions of section 8 of the FDIA.[76]

The DOTS is authorized to issue regulations as he or she determines to be appropriate to carry out statutory responsibilities.[77] The DOTS is also responsible for prescribing uniform accounting and disclosure standards for savings associations.[78] The DOTS has exclusive power and jurisdiction to appoint a conservator or receiver for a federally chartered savings association.[79] The DOTS is also authorized to promulgate regulations for the reorganization, consolidation, liquidation and dissolution of savings associations, for mergers between insured savings associations,[80] and for savings associations in conservatorship or receivership and the conduct thereof.[81] In addition, under statutorily specified grounds, the

---

68. *But cf. Magellsen v. Federal Deposit Insurance Corporation,* 341 F.Supp. 1031 (D.Mont.1972) (involving unsuccessful challenge); *James v. F.D.I.C.,* 231 F.Supp. 475 (W.D.La.1964); *Freeling v. F.D.I.C.,* 221 F.Supp. 955 (W.D.Okla.1962), *affirmed,* 326 F.2d 971 (10th Cir.1963).

69. *See, e.g., Magellsen, supra.*

70. *Cf. Camp, supra* note 10; *Association of Data Processing Service Organizations, supra* note 9.

71. 112 U.S.C.A. § 1462a(a). For discussion of the FHLBB and the FSLIC, and the transition to the OTS in 1989, see *Olympic Federal Savings and Loan Ass'n v. Director, Office of Thrift Supervision,* 732 F.Supp. 1183 (D.D.C.1990), *appeal rendered moot,* 903 F.2d 837 (D.C.Cir.1990).

72. 212 U.S.C.A. § 1813(q)(4).

73. 312 U.S.C.A. § 1464(a).

74. 412 U.S.C.A. § 1463(a)(1). On examinations, see 12 U.S.C.A.

§ 1464(d)(1)(B). As to safety and soundness supervision, the Home Owner's Loan Act specifies that "[a]ll regulations and policies of the [DOTS] governing safe and sound operation of savings associations ... shall be no less stringent than those established by the Comptroller of the Currency for national banks." 12 U.S.C.A. § 1463(c).

75. 512 U.S.C.A. § 1464(d)(1)(A).

76. 612 U.S.C.A. § 1818.

77. 712 U.S.C.A. § 1463(a)(2).

78. 812 U.S.C.A. § 1463(b)(1).

79. 912 U.S.C.A. § 1464(d)(2)(E).

80. 012 U.S.C.A. § 1828(c)(8).

81. 112 U.S.C.A. § 1464(d)(3)(A). In cases where the FDIC is the conservator or receiver, DOTS regulations must be consistent with regulations prescribed by the FDIC. 12 U.S.C.A. § 1464(d)(3)(B).

DOTS has the power and jurisdiction to appoint a conservator or receiver for an insured state-chartered savings association.[82]

Despite significant structural changes introduced in 1989,[83] much of the substance of federal regulation of the thrift industry remains in large part the same.[84] Hence, the prior case law examining the authority of the FHLBB continues to be pertinent, at least by analogy, to questions concerning the authority of the DOTS.[85]

(e) *The National Credit Union Administration.* Federal credit unions are granted their charters by the authority of the National Credit Union Administration ("NCUA").[86] The federal credit union system is an integrated system of regulation in which the chartering, insuring, supervisory and "central bank" functions are all the responsibility of the NCUA and its constitutive units.

Insurance of the accounts of credit union members, both state and federally chartered, is provided by the Administrator of the NCUA. Insurance is required for federally chartered credit unions, voluntary in the case of state-chartered credit unions.

Since 1978, the National Credit Union Central Liquidity Facility ("CLF") has assisted credit unions experiencing liquidity problems by granting them loans. Such liquidity assistance is a central bank function. Within the credit union system, it is performed by the CLF, a unit of the NCUA.

The NCUA consists of the NCUA Board, located in Washington, D.C., six regional offices, and the CLF.[87] The NCUA Board is a collegial body of three members.[88] They are appointed by the President with the confirmation of the Senate.[89] The term of each member is six years, staggered so that one member's term expires every two years.[90] One member is designated by the President as Chairman of the NCUA Board, and one as Vice Chairman.[91]

The members of the NCUA Board also serve as the Board of Directors of the CLF.[92] The Board of Directors is assisted in managing the CLF by the President of the CLF, appointed by the Board, and the

---

82. 212 U.S.C.A. § 1464(d)(2)(C). Written approval of the state official with jurisdiction over the insured association, indicating that one or more of the statutory grounds exists, is generally necessary for the exercise of this authority by the DOTS. 12 U.S.C.A. § 1464(d)(2)(D)(i). *But cf.* 12 U.S.C.A. § 1464(d)(2)(D)(ii) (authority of DOTS to proceed with appointment under certain circumstances).

83. Financial Institutions Reform, Recovery, and Enforcement Act of 1989 ("FIRREA"), Pub. L. No. 101–73, 103 Stat. 183 (1989).

84. *See* FIRREA, §§ 401(f) (savings provisions relating to FSLIC), 401(g) (savings provisions relating to FHLBB), 401(h)-(i)

(continuation under DOTS of orders, resolutions, determinations and regulations of FSLIC and FHLBB), 402(a)-(b) (continuation and coordination of certain regulations).

85. *Cf., e.g., Federal Home Loan Bank Bd. v. Rowe,* 284 F.2d 274 (D.C.Cir.1960) (upholding FHLBB chartering decision).

86. 612 U.S.C.A. § 1753.

87. 712 C.F.R. § 790.2.

88. 812 U.S.C.A. § 1752a(b).

89. 912 U.S.C.A. § 1752a(b).

90. 012 U.S.C.A. § 1752a(c).

91. 112 U.S.C.A. § 1752a(b).

92. 212 U.S.C.A. § 1795b.

NCUA staff.[93] The CLF is also assisted in its operations by "central credit unions,"[94] CLF member credit unions designated as "Agent members."[95] When acting as Agent members, these central credit unions function as rough equivalents of the Federal Reserve Banks, performing "central bank" services on a regional basis for credit unions that do not have direct access to the CLF.[96]

The range of discretionary decisions committed to the NCUA is rather broad. Judicial review of these discretionary decisions is "necessarily limited."[97] The reasoning of *Camp* has been held applicable to these discretionary decisions.[98] Accordingly, the standard of judicial review for such decisions is whether the NCUA's action is "arbitrary, capricious, an abuse of discretion or otherwise not in accordance with law."[99]

(f) *State Regulators*. State regulators of depository institutions play a major role as chartering authorities for commercial banks, savings associations and credit unions within their respective jurisdictions.[100] They also supervise and examine these state-chartered institutions.[101] Today few states provide deposit insurance under state law.[102]

The organizational structures of the state regulators are varied. However, certain general characteristics can be identified. Two basic patterns are evident. A bare majority of the states uses a relatively specialized regulator to supervise all or specified types of depository institutions.[103] The regulator may be an individual "commissioner,"

93. 312 U.S.C.A. § 1795f(a).

94. *See* 12 C.F.R. § 725.2(d) (defining "central credit union" as credit union primarily serving other credit unions).

95. *See* 12 C.F.R. § 790.2(d)(1). Regular and Agent membership in the CLF requires, *inter alia*, subscription to CLF capital stock. 12 C.F.R. §§ 725.3(a)(2), 725.4(a)(2).

96. 612 C.F.R. § 790.2(d)(1).

97. *Nat. Alliance of Postal and Fed. Emp. v. Nickerson*, 424 F.Supp. 323, 325–326 (D.D.C.1976), *citing Rowe*, 284 F.2d at 277–278; *Sterling National Bank of Davie v. Camp*, 431 F.2d 514, 516 (5th Cir.1970). *Cf. Massachusetts Credit Union Share Ins. Corp. v. NCUA*, 693 F.Supp. 1225 (D.D.C. 1988) (examining state-chartered credit union insurance cooperative advertisement of "federally insured" accounts).

98. *Nat. Alliance of Postal and Fed. Emp.*, 424 F. Supp. at 326, *citing Camp* and *Overton Park*.

99. 5 U.S.C.A. § 706(2)(A). *See National Alliance of Postal and Fed. Emp.*, 424 F. Supp. at 326–328. *See also Camp*, 411 U.S. at 142, 93 S.Ct. at 1244.

100. Within the District of Columbia, most roles typically performed by state reg-

ulatory authorities have been performed by federal regulators. Thus, the Comptroller of the Currency exercises general authority to charter, examine and supervise banks in the District. D.C. Code Ann. §§ 26–101, 26–102, 26–103(b) (1981). The OTS has performed these functions with respect to savings associations in the District. D.C. Code §§ 26–103(c), 26–504(a)–(b), 26–505. *Cf.* D.C. Code §§ 26–601, 26–602 (NCUA approval of credit union conversions).

101. Because of their role in the examination of depository institutions, the view of state regulators is represented within the Federal Financial Institutions Examination Council ("FFIEC"), which coordinates federal examination policies. *See* 12 U.S.C.A. § 3306 (mandating state liaison with FFIEC). In addition, since 1996 state banking views must be represented on the FDIC Board of Directors. 12 U.S.C.A. § 1812(a)(1)(C) (requiring appointment of one FDIC director with "State bank supervisory experience").

102. *See generally* H.R. Rep. No. 99–175, 99th Cong., 1st Sess. 17, 22 (1985) (discussing deposit insurance).

103. *See, e.g.*, Ala. Code §§ 5–2A–1 *et seq.* (applying to all institutions); Ariz. Rev. Stat. Ann. §§ 6–110 *et seq.* (financial insti-

"superintendent" or similar official, operating independently or with the advice or general oversight of a board or commission. Alternatively, the regulator may be a collegial body—a "department," "board" or similar body—with an individual official designated as chair or chief executive officer.

A substantial minority of states places regulatory authority for all or specified types of depository institutions in an official or collegial body that is a constituent unit of a larger, less specialized department or division of the state government.[104] The larger department or division may have overall responsibility for corporations, commerce and industry, or the like.

tutions); Ark. Stat. Ann. §§ 67–101, 67–201 (banks); Cal. Fin. Code §§ 200, 210–217 (establishing Commissioner of Financial Institutions and Department of Financial Institutions).

104. *See,* *e.g.,* Alaska Stat. §§ 06.05.005–06.05.075 (concerning banks, S & Ls); Ark. Stat. Ann. §§ 23–35–201—23–35–207, 23–37–207—23–37–214 (S & Ls,

credit unions); Cal. Fin. Code §§ 14200–14210 (credit unions, Commissioner, Department of Corporations); Colo. Rev. Stat. §§ 11–2–101—11–2–122, 11–23–117—11–23–125, 11–30–106—11–30–124, 11–44–101—11–44–123 (all institutions); La. Rev. Stat. Ann. §§ 6:101–6:103 (financial institutions).

Chapter 2

ENTRY RULES

Table of Sections

§ 2.1 Introduction

In this chapter we examine basic rules that govern initial entry into the industry of depository institutions. The typical entry event is the "chartering" or establishment of the entity. In this regard the chapter looks in succession at the rules applicable to the chartering of national and state banks, of federal and state savings associations, and of federal and state credit unions.

We then turn our attention to typical secondary entry restrictions that accompany chartering. The chapter examines deposit insurance, which as a practical matter is a necessity for almost all depository institutions. The chapter also examines bank membership in the Federal Reserve System, which is optional in the case of state-chartered banks.

Conversions represent another form of "entry." What is involved here is not entry into the industry itself, but rather the transfer from one jurisdictionally distinct sector of the industry (*e.g.*, state-chartered banks) into another jurisdictional sector (*e.g.*, national banks), or the transfer from one form of organization (*e.g.*, a mutual savings association) to another form of organization (*e.g.*, a stock savings association). The chapter considers both types of conversions, known respectively as charter conversions and conversions of form.

§ 2.2   Chartering

In the choice of a charter, the overall goal is to identify a jurisdiction that has sufficiently acceptable (*i.e.*, "permissive") rules with respect to the business objectives, expectations, and proposed activities of the institution that are of particular importance to the organizers. However, unlike general business incorporation, chartering of a depository institution is not "free-floating" with respect to the incorporating jurisdiction. The common corporate practice of incorporating in one state (*e.g.*, Delaware) and operating the business in another state or states is virtually unknown within the depository institutions industry (except for interstate banking, discussed in Chapter 4). The chartering state expects to exercise a significant degree of supervision over institutions seeking charters from it.

Choice of a charter involves two levels of analysis. First, there is the choice of the type of charter itself, that is, commercial bank, savings association, or credit union. Second, there is a choice of federal or state charter. There are, of course, differences among the powers of the various types of depository institutions. However, within each type of institution, differences in powers between federally and state-chartered institutions have been minimized.[1]

Nevertheless, some significant differences remain. One obvious difference is that a national bank is required to be a member of the Federal Reserve System, whereas membership of state-chartered banks is voluntary.[2] Membership in the Federal Reserve System carries with it additional burdens, such as cost of membership. This fact may influence the choice of a national or state charter.[3] Of far greater importance, howev-

---

§ 2.2

1. The significance of the differences between state and federally chartered institutions has diminished due to the prevalence of FDIC deposit insurance, which is a virtual necessity for state-chartered banks and savings associations. *See* Helen A. Garten, *Devolution and Deregulation: The Paradox of Financial Reform*, 14 Yale L. & Pol'y Rev. 65, 79 n.72 (1996) ("the potential loss of deposits to insured national banks ... may make federal deposit insurance a less costly option for many banks"). Hence, federal supervision and regulation (at least by the FDIC) will be unavoidable regardless of the choice of chartering authority. *See, e.g.*, Michael P. Malloy, *Seeing the Light: Savings Association Conversions and Federal Regulatory Realignment*, 10 Ann. Rev. Banking L. 189 (1991) (arguing that federal regulation based on FDIC deposit insurance substantially realigned scope of federal jurisdiction). In addition, since there is a relatively high degree of coordination among federal bank regulators on supervisory matters, there should not be radical differences on most issues between the federal regulation of national bank activities and of state-chartered FDIC-insured bank activities. *See, e.g.*, 12 U.S.C.A. § 3301 (mandating uniform principles and standards for federal bank examinations).

2. 12 U.S.C.A. § 222.

3. Such differences may be reduced by the fact that deposit reserve requirements administered by the Fed are now to be applied to all depository institutions, regardless of source of charter. 12 U.S.C.A. § 461.

er, is the fact that membership will also subject the proposed bank to other federal banking statutes expressly applicable to member banks.[4]

§ 2.3 National Banks

Chartering of national banks (or "national banking associations,"[1] as the 1864 statutory language puts it) is within the authority of the Comptroller of the Currency. This authority is derived primarily from the National Bank Act ("NBA") itself,[2] as well as from the Federal Deposit Insurance Act ("FDIA").[3] In addition, the Office of the Comptroller of the Currency ("OCC") is required by the Community Reinvestment Act ("CRA") to assess a proposed bank's anticipated ability to meet the credit needs of the bank's proposed community, including low- and moderate-income neighborhoods, to the extent consistent with the safe and sound operation of the bank.[4]

In reviewing a charter application, the Comptroller must consider primarily the following statutory factors[5] as reflected in the application's operating plan:

(1) *Future earnings prospects*. The operating plan included in the application must demonstrate that the proposed bank can reasonably expect to achieve and sustain profitability in the market to be served by the proposed bank.[6]

(2) *Character of proposed management*. The NBA requires organization of a national bank by five or more natural persons, who individually enter into the articles of association for the proposed bank.[7] The character of the organizers and executive management of the proposed bank is subject to scrutiny.[8]

---

4. *See, e.g.*, 12 U.S.C.A. § 377 (prohibiting affiliations between "member banks" and securities firms).

§ 2.3

1. 12 U.S.C.A. § 21.

2. 12 U.S.C.A. §§ 21, 22, 26, 27.

3. *See* 12 U.S.C.A. §§ 1814 *et seq.* It has been persuasively argued by Professor Scott that the standards under which the Comptroller exercises his broad discretion with respect to the decision to grant or deny charter applications are to be found in the FDIA, rather than the NBA, the latter being relatively silent on this question. *See* Kenneth Scott, *In Quest of Reason: The Licensing Decisions of the Federal Banking Agencies*, 42 U. Chi. L. Rev. 235, 238–240 (1975). *But see Sterling Nat'l Bank of Davie v. Camp*, 431 F.2d 514, 516 (5th Cir.1970), *cert. denied*, 401 U.S. 925, 91 S.Ct. 879 (1971) (noting longstanding recognition of "vast discretion" of Comptroller). *See also City Nat'l Bank v. Smith*, 513 F.2d 479 (D.C.Cir.1975); *Warren Bank v. Camp*, 396 F.2d 52 (6th Cir.1968); *Webster Groves Trust Co. v. Saxon*, 370 F.2d 381 (8th Cir. 1966) (discussing Comptroller's discretion). *See generally* C. Westbrook Murphy, *What Reason for the Quest?: A Response to Professor Scott*, 42 U. Chi. L. Rev. 299 (1975) (criticizing Scott). Nevertheless, the Comptroller's current regulations explicitly acknowledge the FDIA as one of the statutory sources of his authority with respect to approving the organization of national banks. *See* 12 C.F.R. § 5.20(a).

4. *See* 12 U.S.C.A. §§ 2901 *et seq.*

5. *See* 12 U.S.C.A. § 1816.

6. 12 C.F.R. § 5.20(f)(2)(i)(D), (h)(2).

7. 12 U.S.C.A. § 21.

8. 12 C.F.R. § 5.20(f)(2)(i)(A)–(B), (g)(2), (h)(3). *See, e.g., Connelly v. Comptroller*, 876 F.2d 1209 (5th Cir.1989) (rejecting proposed president of proposed national bank because of past performance; qualified immunity defense of individual regulators upheld).

(3) *Adequacy of capital structure.* The minimum capital requirements set forth in the NBA relate to the size of the community in which the bank will be located.[9] These requirements, last amended in 1933,[10] are completely impractical in light of current economic conditions.[11] In fact, OCC regulations have established a higher minimum capital requirement.[12]

(4) *Convenience and needs of community.* This somewhat elusive standard, at issue in *Camp v. Pitts*,[13] is now discussed in the OCC regulations as "community service."[14] Historically, the lack of an articulated statutory standard in this regard had been a problem,[15] and by the 1920s many states had begun incorporating an explicit "convenience and needs" standard in their banking statutes.[16] Since 1933, the "convenience and needs" standard has been a usual feature of both state and federal law.[17] The standard has sometimes been interpreted to restrict entry into the industry significantly.[18] At other times, it has been interpreted very loosely, in a manner intended to foster competition in the market.[19] This concept is reinforced by the OCC requirement that "the organizing group . . . submit a statement that demonstrates its plans to achieve CRA objectives."[20] Under current OCC regulations, the organizing group is required to "evaluate the banking needs of the community, including its consumer, business, nonprofit, and government sectors."[21] The application's operating plan "must demonstrate how the

---

9. 12 U.S.C.A. § 51.

10. *See* Banking Act of 1933, § 17(a), 48 Stat. 185 (1933) (*codified at* 12 U.S.C.A. § 51).

11. For example, under the literal terms of 12 U.S.C.A. § 51, a national bank could be organized in San Francisco with a minimum required capital of $200,000. *Id.*

12. *See* 12 C.F.R. § 5.20(f)(2)(i)(C), (h)(4) (regulatory capital). The FDIA requires the Comptroller to consider "the adequacy of [the proposed bank's] capital structure." 12 U.S.C.A. § 1816. This determination is clearly committed to the discretion of the regulator. *See generally Magellsen v. Federal Deposit Ins. Corp.*, 341 F.Supp. 1031 (D.Mont.1972) (noting discretion of FDIC). Hence, whatever the implications of the NBA minimum capital standard, the FDIA capital adequacy standard remains a matter for administrative discretion. A national bank applicant thus could be denied a charter in light of the FDIA, even if the NBA were read narrowly to deny discretion to the Comptroller with respect to capital requirements. *Cf. United States v. Shively*, 715 F.2d 260 (7th Cir. 1983), *cert. denied*, 465 U.S. 1007, 104 S.Ct. 1001 (involving loss of deposit insurance by national bank). *See generally Edwards v. First Bank of Dundee*, 534 F.2d 1242 (7th Cir. 1976) (concerning jurisdiction of district court to

review Comptroller's administration of FDIA provisions).

13. 411 U.S. 138, 93 S.Ct. 1241 (1973).

14. 12 C.F.R. § 5.50(h)(5).

15. *See, e.g., Speer v. Dossey*, 177 Ky. 761, 198 S.W. 19 (1917) (discussing convenience and needs problem).

16. *See generally* Note, *Bank Charter, Branching, Holding Company and Merger Laws: Competition Frustrated*, 71 Yale L.J. 502 (1962) (discussing problem).

17. *See* Banking Act of 1933, § 8, 48 Stat. 168 (1933) (*codified at* 12 U.S.C.A. § 264) (containing "convenience and needs" standard in § 264(g)), *recodified at* 12 U.S.C.A. § 1816, Act of September 21, 1950, ch. 967, 64 Stat. 873 (1950).

18. *Cf., e.g., Hempstead Bank v. Smith*, 540 F.2d 57 (2d Cir.1976) (involving national bank branch application under 12 U.S.C.A. § 36).

19. *Cf., e.g., United States v. Third Nat'l Bank in Nashville*, 390 U.S. 171, 88 S.Ct. 882 (1968) (involving "convenience and needs" defense under Bank Merger Act).

20. 12 C.F.R. § 5.50(h)(5)(ii).

21. 12 C.F.R. § 5.50(h)(5)(i).

proposed bank [will] respond[] to those needs consistent with the safe and sound operation of the bank."[22] In addition, since community support is important to the long-term success of a bank, the OCC regulations require the organizing group to "include plans for attracting and maintaining community support."[23]

(5) *Financial history and condition of the bank.* In the case of a proposed bank, there is, of course, no available data in this regard. In the case of an application sponsored by a bank holding company, however, or by an organizing group affiliated with an extant institution, the financial history and condition of the holding company or affiliate institution will be subject to analysis and evaluation.[24]

(6) *Compliance with applicable laws.* Approval of the application requires compliance with laws applicable to national banks. For example, the NBA requires that, prior to issuing a certificate of authority to commence business, the Comptroller "shall examine . . . generally whether [the national bank] has complied with all the provisions of this chapter required to entitle it to engage in the business of banking."[25] The application must also meet the requirements of the FDIA, including "whether or not [the bank's] corporate powers are consistent with the purposes" of the FDIA.[26]

Compliance with the NBA itself is, of course, an obvious prerequisite for the national bank in formation to attain its corporate status.[27] As with general business corporations, there is a possibility that preformation activities may be questioned under the corporate law doctrine of *ultra vires* activities. *McCormick v. Market Nat. Bank*[28] illustrates this problem as it existed prior to contemporary OCC regulations. In that case, a national bank in organization had signed a lease for its business premises prior to final approval. The NBA required that "no such association shall transact any business, except such as is incidental and necessarily preliminary to its organization, until it has been authorized by the Comptroller of the Currency to commence the business of banking."[29]

The question facing the Court in *McCormick* was whether the national bank was bound by the lease, according to its provisions. The lessee bank contended that the lease was not incidental and necessarily preliminary to the organization of the corporation, and therefore did not bind the bank. The Court agreed with the bank. Upon filing its articles of association and its organization certificate with the Comptroller, the bank became a corporate entity, but it had not been authorized by the Comptroller to commence the business of banking. Until it was authorized, the NBA forbade the corporation to "transact any business"

---

22. *Id.*

23. 12 C.F.R. § 5.50(h)(5)(iii).

24. *See* 12 C.F.R. § 5.50(g)(5) (discussing sponsor's experience and support).

25. 12 U.S.C.A. § 26.

26. 12 U.S.C.A. § 1816.

27. *See* 12 C.F.R. § 5.50(e)(1) (discussing NBA requirements for organization of national bank).

28. 165 U.S. 538, 17 S.Ct. 433 (1897).

29. Rev. Stat. § 5136.

whatever, "except such as is incidental and necessarily preliminary" to its organization. The exception would include "electing directors and officers, receiving subscriptions and payments for shares, procuring a corporate seal, and a book for recording its proceedings, temporarily hiring a room, and contracting any small debts incidental to the completion of its organization."[30] It would not include the lease in question.

This restricted approach to the corporate powers of a national bank in organization continued into the 1930s.[31] However, the clause relied upon by *McCormick* in reaching such a decision was omitted from Section 16 of the Banking Act of 1933, as recodified.[32] The Act, popularly known as the Glass–Steagall Act, amended the NBA provision without including in its revised language the language relied upon by the Court in *McCormick*. The House Judiciary Subcommittee on the Revision of the Laws concluded that the effect was to repeal the unnumbered paragraph, and it was excluded from subsequent codified editions of the federal laws.[33]

It would be possible to read post-*McCormick* cases like *Wise v. Citizens National Bank at Brownwood*[34] as endorsing the proposition that the paragraph is still in effect, but the current statute and applicable regulations do not support this reading. The current OCC regulations resolve situations like those in *Wise* and *McCormick* by controlling the process of chartering more closely.[35] The regulations acknowledge the *statutory* procedure for chartering—preparing and filing the incorporating documents—but the *regulatory* procedures for chartering—authorization to commence business—are layered over these statutory requirements.[36]

The regulations also include the separate approval stages of "preliminary approval"[37] and "final approval."[38] Preliminary approval involves a decision by the OCC to permit an organizing group to proceed with *the organization* of the proposed national bank. Typically, preliminary approval is subject to specified conditions that an applicant must satisfy before the OCC will grant final approval.[39] Final approval occurs when the proposed bank has satisfied the condition and the OCC *issues* a charter certificate and *authorizes* a national bank to open for business.[40] As a practical matter, therefore, it is unlikely that a bank in organization would proceed into transactions such as those involved in *McCormick* or *Wise* at a time when those activities would have been *ultra vires*.

---

30. *McCormick*, 165 U.S. at 549, 17 S.Ct. at 436.

31. *See, e.g.*, *Wise v. Citizens Nat'l Bank at Brownwood*, 107 S.W.2d 715 (Tex.Civ. App.1937) (finding employment of executive for national bank in organization to be *ultra vires*).

32. 12 U.S.C.A. § 24 (Seventh).

33. *See* 12 U.S.C.A. § 24 note.

34. *See Wise v. Citizens Nat'l Bank at Brownwood*, 107 S.W.2d 715 (Tex.Civ.App. 1937).

35. 12 C.F.R. § 5.20(e), (i).

36. *See* 12 C.F.R. § 5.20(i) (setting forth regulatory procedures).

37. 12 C.F.R. § 5.20(d)(7).

38. 12 C.F.R. § 5.20(d)(3).

39. 12 C.F.R. § 5.20(d)(7), (i)(5)(i).

40. 12 C.F.R. § 5.20(d)(3), (i)(5)(iii).

However, there is no explicit statutory basis in the NBA for the two stages of "approval" established by the regulations.[41]

§ 2.4 State Banks

Commercial banking under state authority requires the granting of a charter from an appropriate state official or agency in accordance with the terms and conditions of the pertinent state statute.[1] The specifics of the chartering process vary broadly from state to state, in keeping with the variety of regulatory structures employed by the states. The chartering decision may be committed to the judgment of a single official, a collegial body, or some combination of the two. In practice, state chartering procedures for the formation of a commercial bank bear obvious similarities to the federal procedures.[2]

§ 2.5 Federal Savings Associations

The procedures available for the formation of savings associations[1] are similar to those available for commercial banks. There are, however, some important differences. For example, savings associations may be formed as mutual or stock entities.

Federal chartering of savings associations is within the authority of the Office of Thrift Supervision ("OTS"). Chartering is approved under OTS regulations, "giving primary consideration [to] the best practices of thrift institutions in the United States."[2] A charter may be granted only upon the satisfaction of the following statutory conditions:

> (1) the persons to whom the charter is to be issued are of good character and responsibility;

> (2) in the judgment of the Director of the OTS, necessity exists for such an institution in the community to be served;

> (3) there is a reasonable probability of the association's usefulness and success; and

---

41. *But cf.* 12 U.S.C.A. §§ 24 (satisfaction of NBA formal filing requirements creates corporate entity); 27 (certificate of authority to commence banking).

§ 2.4

1. *See, e.g., Oliphant v. Carthage Bank*, 224 Miss. 386, 80 So.2d 63 (1955) (discussing chartering).

2. *See* MICHAEL P. MALLOY, BANKING LAW & REGULATION 2.38–2.39, FIGURE 2–1 (ASPEN LAW & BUSINESS: 1994 & CUM. SUPP.) (providing finding aid for state bank chartering procedures).

§ 2.5

1. Under the Financial Institutions Reform, Recovery, and Enforcement Act of 1989 ("FIRREA"), Pub. L. No. 101–73, 103 Stat. 183 (1989), the term "savings association" is now used as the generic concept including, *inter alia*, federally chartered savings and loan associations and savings banks, state-chartered savings and loan associations, building and loan associations, and similar institutions. *See* FIRREA § 204(b), 103 Stat. at 190–191 (*codified at* 12 U.S.C.A. § 1813(b)) (definition of "savings association" for purposes of FDIA).

2. 12 U.S.C.A. § 1464(a). The OTS has promulgated regulations governing the chartering of savings associations. *See* 12 C.F.R. pts. 543, 552 (setting forth OTS chartering regulations).

(4) the institution can be established without undue injury to properly conducted existing local thrift and home financing institutions.[3]

On receiving its charter, a federal savings association automatically becomes a member of the Federal Home Loan Bank in the district in which the association is located (or, if convenience requires and the OTS approves, in an adjoining district).[4]

§ 2.6   State Savings Associations

State chartering procedures for savings associations bear obvious similarities to the federal procedures, with many individual variations among the state statutory provisions.[1] For example, California law presents a unified model of regulation of "savings associations."[2] In contrast, New York law presents a typical example of the traditional approach, separating savings and loan association chartering[3] from savings bank chartering.[4] The statutory trend, manifested in the California statute, is towards a unitary system regulating the formation of any and all institutions that are generically referred to as "associations" or "savings associations."

§ 2.7   Federal Credit Unions

This section examines briefly the federal procedures available for the formation of a credit union.[1] Under the Federal Credit Union Act ("FCUA"),[2] any seven or more individuals may form a federal credit union in accordance with the provisions of the FCUA.[3] The organizers must present an organization certificate, in duplicate, to the Board of the National Credit Union Administration ("NCUA").[4] Among other things,

---

3. 12 U.S.C.A. § 1464(e)(1)–(4).

4. 12 U.S.C.A. § 1464(f). Newly chartered federal savings associations must qualify for membership in same manner under the Home Loan Bank Act as other members. *Id.* On membership, see 12 U.S.C.A. § 1424(a).

§ 2.6

1. For analysis of the different state statutory provisions for chartering of savings associations, see MICHAEL P. MALLOY, BANKING LAW & REGULATION 2.68–2.69, 2.71, FIGURES 2–3, 2–4 (1994 & CUM. SUPP).

2. *See* Cal. Fin. Code §§ 5000 *et seq.*

3. N.Y. Banking Law §§ 375 *et seq.*

4. N.Y. Banking Law §§ 230 *et seq.*

§ 2.7

1. On federal policies and procedures with respect to credit union chartering, see 63 Fed. Reg. 71,998 (1998) (*codified at* 12 C.F.R. § 701.1) (federal credit union chartering, field of membership modifications, and conversion rules; incorporating by reference NCUA Interpretive Ruling and Policy Statement 99–1) (hereinafter "IRPS 99–1").

2. 12 U.S.C.A. §§ 1751 *et seq.*

3. 12 U.S.C.A. § 1753.

4. 12 U.S.C.A. § 1754. The Board of the NCUA is also responsible for the insurance of member accounts of federally chartered credit unions (mandatory insurance) and state-chartered credit unions (optional insurance), on a pattern similar in all material respects to that administered by the FDIC. 12 U.S.C.A. §§ 1781–1783. *Cf. Massachusetts Credit Union Share Ins. Corp. v. National Credit Union Admin.*, 693 F.Supp. 1225 (D.D.C.1988) (holding state-chartered credit union insurance cooperative lacked standing to challenge NCUA regulation concerning advertisement of "federally in-the certificate is required to include information concerning the proposed field of membership of the credit union, specified in detail.[5]

Membership in a federal credit union is "limited to groups having a common bond of occupation or association, or to groups within a well-defined neighborhood, community, or rural district."[6] The NCUA interpretation of this "common bond" requirement[7] allowed multiple groups—each of which independently shares a common bond—to join together to form a credit union, if all occupational groups "are located within a well defined area." This interpretation was rejected by the Supreme Court as inconsistent with statutory language.[8] Legislation has overridden *First National* and now explicitly allows chartering of a "multiple common-bond credit union."[9]

The NCUA Board is required to undertake an appropriate investigation to determine if the proposed credit union meets the following approval factors: (1) conformity of the organization certificate with the provisions of the FCUA;[10] (2) general character and fitness of the subscribers;[11] and, (3) economic advisability of establishing the proposed credit union.[12]

§ 2.8   State Credit Unions

State chartering procedures for the formation of credit unions are similar to the federal procedures. However, there are many individual variations.[1] For example, New York law[2] follows the traditional approach to credit union chartering, similar to the Federal Credit Union Act. By contrast, California law provides for an incorporation procedure, similar to general business incorporation.[3]

sured" accounts). In addition, through its Central Liquidity Facility ("CLF"), it performs such "central bank" functions as acting as lender of last resort to CLF member credit unions experiencing liquidity problems. 12 U.S.C.A. §§ 1795b–1795c, 1795e–1795f.

5. 12 U.S.C.A. § 1753(5).

6. 12 U.S.C.A. § 1759. On the common bond requirement, see generally *La Caisse Populaire Ste.-Marie v. United States*, 425 F.Supp. 512 (D.N.H.), *aff'd*, 563 F.2d 505 (1st Cir.1977); *Board of Directors and Officers, Forbes Federal Credit Union v. National Credit Union Admin.*, 477 F.2d 777 (10th Cir.1973), *cert. denied*, 414 U.S. 924, 94 S.Ct. 233; *National Alliance of Postal and Fed. Employees v. Nickerson*, 424 F.Supp. 323 (D.D.C.1976).

7. NCUA Interpretive Ruling and Policy Statement 82–1, 47 Fed. Reg. 16,775 (1982).

8. *National Credit Union Admin. v. First Nat'l Bank & Trust Co.*, 522 U.S. 479, 118 S.Ct. 927 (1998).

9. Credit Union Membership Access Act, Pub. L. No. 105–219, § 101, Aug. 7, 1998, 112 Stat. 913, 914–916 (1998) (codified at 12 U.S.C.A. § 1759(a)–(e)) (CU-

MAA). The NCUA has implemented the provisions of the CUMAA. *See e.g.*, 63 Fed. Reg. 65,532 (1998) (*codified at* 12 C.F.R. Pt. 708a) (conversion of insured credit unions to mutual savings banks effective 27 November 1998); 63 Fed. Reg. 71,998 (1998) (*codified at* 12 C.F.R. Pt. 701) (federal credit union chartering, field of membership modifications, and conversion rules, incorporating IRPS 99–1 by reference, effective 1 January 1999).

10. 12 U.S.C.A. § 1754(1).

11. 12 U.S.C.A. § 1754(2).

12. 12 U.S.C.A. § 1754(3). *See generally National Alliance of Postal and Fed. Employees v. Nickerson*, 424 F.Supp. 323 (D.D.C.1976) (discussing requirements).

§ 2.8

1. *See* MICHAEL P. MALLOY, BANKING LAW AND REGULATION §§ 2.83–2.84, FIGURE 2–5 (1994 & CUM. SUPP.) (identifying state statutory provisions for credit union chartering).

2. N.Y. Banking Law §§ 450 *et seq.*

3. Cal. Corp. Code §§ 7110 *et seq.*; Cal. Fin. Code §§ 14100 *et seq.*

§ 2.9   Secondary Entry Restrictions

In the following sections we examine two important forms of secondary entry restriction. These restrictions limit the ability of depository institutions to participate in certain features of the regulatory system itself. One such restriction is eligibility for federal deposit insurance. Withholding deposit insurance could have serious adverse effects on the ability of the institution to compete in the deposit market.[1]

The second restriction is eligibility for membership in the Federal Reserve System. As a practical matter, this concerns only commercial banks.[2] Compared to the virtual necessity of deposit insurance, this is not a critical concern for banks, but it is nonetheless a requirement for all national banks.[3] Thus, eligibility and maintenance of Fed membership is a necessary precondition to their operation.

§ 2.10   Deposit Insurance

As a matter of federal law, deposit insurance is generally not required for commercial banks that are not members of the Federal Reserve System.[1] As a matter of fact, however, federal deposit insurance is virtually a necessity for all depository institutions.[2] Even for those banks that are required to be FDIC-insured (national banks and state member banks), prior to 1991 there was usually no separate approval process undertaken by the FDIC itself. The Federal Deposit Insurance Corporation Improvement Act of 1991 ("FDICIA")[3] provides that a specific application to, and approval by, the FDIC is required for FDIC insurance of the deposits of all depository institutions.[4]

Every national member bank[5] that receives or will receive non-trust

---

§ 2.9

1. *See generally* Kenneth Scott, *In Quest of Reason: The Licensing Decisions of the Federal Banking Agencies*, 42 U. Chi. L. Rev. 235, 269–70 (1975) (discussing restrictions).

2. Savings associations may be eligible for membership in the Federal Home Loan Bank System. *See* 12 U.S.C.A. § 1424(a) (providing for FHLBS membership).

3. *See* 12 U.S.C.A. § 282 (requiring Fed membership for national banks).

§ 2.10

1. 12 U.S.C.A. § 1815(a). However, state-chartered banks that are subsidiaries of bank holding companies, and banks that are themselves holding companies of other banks, are generally required by the Bank Holding Company Act to be FDIC-insured. 12 U.S.C.A. § 1842(e).

2. *See* Helen A. Garten, *Devolution and Deregulation: The Paradox of Financial Reform*, 14 Yale L. & Pol'y Rev. 65, 79 n.72 (1996) ("the potential loss of deposits to insured national banks ... may make federal deposit insurance a less costly option for many banks").

3. FDICIA, Pub. L. No. 102–242, 105 Stat. 2236 (Dec. 19, 1991).

4. 12 U.S.C.A. § 1815(a).

5. National banks located in U.S. territories are not required to become members of the Federal Reserve System. 12 U.S.C.A. §§ 282, 1813(d)–(e), 1815(a). However, a national nonmember bank that receives or will receive non-trust fund deposits, and that subsequently opts to become a member fund deposits is required to obtain FDIC deposit insurance.[6] The situation of state-chartered banks is more complicated. If a state-chartered nonmember bank opts to obtain FDIC insurance—as virtually all such banks do[7]—it must obtain the approval of the Board of Directors of the FDIC.[8] If a state-chartered bank opts to become a member of the Federal Reserve System, FDIC insurance requirements are automatically imposed.[9] If a state-chartered bank is converted into a national member bank, the requirement of FDIC insurance is automatically imposed, in the same way in which FDIC insurance is required for *de novo* national member banks.[10]

In each of the situations described above, an application to and examination by the FDIC is required, with approval of the application by the FDIC Board of Directors.[11] However, if a state-chartered insured bank subsequently becomes a member of the Federal Reserve System, it is not required to reapply for FDIC insurance; its status as an FDIC-insured bank continues despite subsequent acceptance of Fed membership.[12] Similarly, if a state-chartered, FDIC-insured bank subsequently converts to a national charter, its insurance continues without a new application.[13]

The deposit insurance system for savings associations has been subjected to a number of significant changes in recent years. Throughout the 1970s and 1980s, the deposit system of the Federal Savings and Loan Insurance Corporation ("FSLIC") was becoming increasingly burdened, not only by crises precipitated by savings associations failures, but also, ironically, by the rapid growth of the savings industry in certain states.[14] Thus, in 1985 the now defunct Federal Home Loan Bank Board announced that it had stopped granting deposit insurance for *de novo* state-chartered S & L's in such states as California, Florida, and Texas, which were the sites of dramatic industry expansion.[15]

The situation was exacerbated by the fact that the now defunct FSLIC insurance fund itself was in the midst of a major financial crisis, reflecting the critical condition of the savings industry generally. Despite a $10.8 billion dollar recapitalization of the FSLIC in August 1987 in response to the savings industry crisis, by March 1988 it was apparent that another significant capital infusion might be required.[16]

bank, is required to be FDIC insured. *Id.* § 1814(b).

6. *Id.* § 1814(b).

7. *See* Report of the Task Group on Regulation of Financial Services 18 n. 6 (1984).

8. 12 U.S.C.A. § 1815(a).

9. *Id.* § 1814(b).

10. *Id.* § 1814(b).

11. *Id.* § 1815(a).

12. *Id.* § 1814(b).

13. *Id.* The same is true for a state-chartered, FDIC-insured bank that results from a merger or consolidation between FDIC-insured banks or between an FDIC-insured bank and an uninsured bank. *Id.*

14. *See, e.g.,* Wynter, *Bank Board Stops Granting Insurance For S & Ls in California, Florida, Texas,* Wall St. J., June 17, 1985, at 7, col. 1 (describing problems of FSLIC system).

15. *Id.*

16. *See, e.g.,* Nash, *F.S.L.I.C.'s 2d Bailout Is Studied,* N.Y. Times, March 7, 1988, at D1, col. 1 (noting insufficiency of $10.8 billion fund over next three years, in light of continuing losses at insolvent S & Ls).

The Financial Institutions Reform, Recovery, and Enforcement Act of 1989 ("FIRREA") mandated the immediate abolition of the FSLIC,[17] and gave the FDIC responsibility for insurance of deposits of savings associations.[18] The FDIC now administers a Bank Insurance Fund ("BIF"), formerly the Permanent Insurance Fund, with respect to deposits of insured banks,[19] and a Savings Association Insurance Fund ("SAIF"), replacing the functions of the FSLIC.[20] FIRREA also established an FSLIC Resolution Fund, to wind up the affairs of the FSLIC.[21]

Further changes in the federal deposit insurance system were mandated by FDICIA. The principal features of the legislation in this regard are as follows. First, the FDICIA created the requirement for specific application and approval of deposit insurance, even in the case of a national bank or a state member bank.[22]

Second, new rules were imposed on depository institutions that were not insured by the FDIC.[23] Private deposit insurers are now required to obtain an annual audit from an independent auditor, using generally accepted auditing standards.[24] The private insurer is required to provide copies of the annual audit report to depository institutions insured by it.[25] The insurer must also provide copies to the appropriate state supervisors of the insured depository institutions.[26]

The depository institutions must provide copies of the annual audit report upon request to any current or prospective customer.[27] In addition, every depository institution that is not insured by the FDIC is required to include a conspicuous notice on specified documentation[28] stating that it "is not federally insured, and that if the institution fails, the Federal Government does not guarantee that depositors will get back their money."[29] The institution must display a notice to the effect that it is not federally insured in all its advertising and at each place where it

17. FIRREA, § 401(a)(1), 103 Stat. at 354.

18. FIRREA § 205(1), 103 Stat. at 194 (*codified at* 12 U.S.C.A. § 1814(a)). The FDIC amended its deposit insurance provisions, pursuant to Section 402(c)(3) of FIRREA, to provide for uniform deposit insurance regulations for deposits in all federally insured depository institutions, including savings associations formerly insured by the now defunct FSLIC. *See* 55 Fed. Reg. 20,-111 (1990) (*codified at* 12 C.F.R. Pt. 330; removing 12 C.F.R. Pt. 331, §§ 386.1(a)-(c), 386.2–386.13, Appendix).

19. FIRREA § 211(3), 103 Stat. at 218–219 (*codified at* 12 U.S.C.A. § 1821(a)(4)-(5)).

20. FIRREA, § 211(3), 103 Stat. at 218–220 (*codified at* 12 U.S.C.A. § 1821(a)(4), (6)).

21. FIRREA, § 215, 103 Stat. at 252–254 (*codified at* 12 U.S.C.A. § 1821a).

22. FDICIA, § 115(a) (*codified at* 12 U.S.C.A. § 1815(a)).

23. FDICIA, § 151(a)(1), (b) (*codified at* 12 U.S.C.A. § 1831t).

24. 12 U.S.C.A. § 1831t(a)(1).

25. *Id.* § 1831t(a)(2)(A)(i). The copies must be provided not later than 14 days after completion of the audit. *Id.*

26. *Id.* § 1831t(a)(2)(A)(ii). The copies must be provided not later than seven days after completion of the audit. *Id.*

27. *Id.* § 1831t(a)(2)(B).

28. The statement must appear on all periodic account statements, signature cards, passbook, certificate of deposit, or similar instrument evidencing a deposit. *Id.* § 1831t(b)(1).

29. *Id.*

receives deposits.[30] Depositors of such institutions must sign a written statement acknowledging that "the institution is not federally insured, and that if the institution fails, the Federal Government does not guarantee that depositors will get back their money."[31]

A depository institution that is not a bank and that lacks federal deposit insurance (*e.g.*, an uninsured savings association or uninsured credit union[32]) is prohibited from using the mails or any instrumentality of interstate commerce to receive or facilitate receiving deposits, with certain exceptions.[33] First, an institution whose state chartering authority has determined that it meets all the eligibility requirements for federal deposit insurance is excepted from the prohibitions.[34] Second, the Federal Trade Commission, in consultation with the FDIC, is authorized to except the institution from the prohibition.[35]

Third, the FDICIA required the establishment of a risk-based assessment system for federal deposit insurance.[36] The FDIC has promulgated regulations implementing the risk-based system.[37]

In September 1996, the president signed into law the Economic Growth and Regulatory Paperwork Reduction Act ("EGRPR Act").[38] The Act makes a number of significant changes to the structure of regulation of depository institutions, and also refines or reduces the regulatory requirements applicable to such institutions in a wide variety of statutory provisions. Of particular note in the present context are the EGRPR Act's amendments to the deposit insurance system.

The EGRPR Act imposes a special assessment on insured depository institutions holding SAIF-insured deposits in order to recapitalize the ailing SAIF.[39] It also provided for the merger of the BIF and SAIF into a new Deposit Insurance Fund ("DIF"), if there were no more savings associations by 1 January 1999,[40] which did not happen.

§ 2.11   Federal Reserve Membership

For national banks, membership in the Federal Reserve System is generally mandatory.[1] For state-chartered banks,[2] membership is option-

---

30. *Id.* § 1831t(b)(2).

31. *Id.* § 1831t(b)(3).

32. *Id.* § 1831t(f)(3).

33. *Id.* § 1831t(e)(1).

34. *Id.* The state chartering authority's determination that the institution is eligible for federal deposit insurance does not bind or otherwise affect the authority of the FDIC or the NCUA in making such a determination. *Id.* § 1831t(e)(2).

35. *Id.* § 1831t(e)(1).

36. *Id.* § 1817(b).

37. *See* 57 Fed. Reg. 45,263 (1992) (*codified at* 12 C.F.R. Pt. 327) (promulgating transitional risk-based assessment system); 58 Fed. Reg. 34,357 (1993) (*codified at* 12 C.F.R. Pt. 327) (establishing new risk-based

assessment system; limited changes to transitional system).

38. Pub. L. No. 104–208, title II, 110 Stat. 3009 (1996) (*codified at* scattered sections of 5, 12, 15, 26, 42 U.S.C.A.).

39. EGRPR Act, § 2702 (*to be codified at* 12 U.S.C.A. § 1817 note).

40. EGRPR Act, § 2704.

§ 2.11

1. 12 U.S.C.A. § 282. *See generally United States v. Davenport*, 266 Fed. 425 (W.D.Tex.1920) (discussing Fed membership). *But cf.* 12 U.S.C.A. §§ 1813(e),

---

2. See note 2 on page 47.

al,[3] subject to approval of an application for membership by the Fed.[4] Similarly, if a national bank converts into a state-chartered bank, Fed membership of the converted institution is optional.[5]

In the case of a merger or consolidation of a national bank with a state-chartered nonmember bank in which the state-chartered bank survives or results, Fed membership of the surviving or resulting institution is optional.[6] If the state-chartered bank participating in the merger or consolidation had been a member bank, then its Fed membership will continue in the surviving or resulting bank.[7]

The Fed has asserted the authority to condition approval of an application for membership, as public interest requires, in its judgment.[8] Fed decisions on membership are rarely challenged, and are unlikely to be successful, given the typical judicial deference given such decisions. One such challenge did reach the Supreme Court in *Eccles v. Peoples Bank of Lakewood Village*,[9] but was disposed of without reaching the merits. The bank had sought Fed membership, but its application was rejected.[10] On a request for reconsideration, the Fed stated that favorable action depended on a showing that the Transamerica Corporation, a bank holding company, did not have, and was not intended to have, any interest in the bank.[11] The condition having been satisfied, the Fed granted membership, subject to certain specified conditions, including the following:

> If, without prior written approval of the Board of Governors of the Federal Reserve System, Transamerica Corporation, or any unit of the Transamerica group, including Bank of America National Trust and Savings Association, or any holding company affiliate or any subsidiary thereof, acquires, directly or indirectly, through the mechanism of extension of loans for the purpose of acquiring bank

1814(b) (concerning national nonmember banks).

2. *See* 12 C.F.R. § 208.1(a) (defining "State bank"). Fed membership is also available to mutual savings banks. 12 U.S.C.A. § 333. *See also Hiatt v. United States*, 4 F.2d 374 (7th Cir.1924), *cert. denied*, 268 U.S. 704, 45 S.Ct. 638 (1925) (concerning trust company Fed membership); *Louisville Bridge Comm'n v. Louisville Trust Co.*, 258 Ky. 846, 81 S.W.2d 894 (1935).

3. *Fidelity–Philadelphia Trust Co. v. Hines*, 337 Pa. 48, 10 A.2d 553 (1940).

4. 12 U.S.C.A. § 321. On the constitutionality of the statutory provision for membership of state-chartered banks in the Federal Reserve System, see *Hiatt*, 4 F.2d 374. The Fed has promulgated detailed regulations governing applications for, and conditions of, Fed membership of state-chartered banks. 12 C.F.R. Pt. 208. On the validity of these regulations and of conditions of membership imposed thereunder,

see *Continental Bank & Trust Co. of Salt Lake City, Utah v. Woodall*, 239 F.2d 707 (10th Cir.1957), *cert. denied*, 353 U.S. 909, 77 S.Ct. 663; *Eccles v. Peoples Bank of Lakewood Village, Cal.*, 333 U.S. 426, 68 S.Ct. 641 (1948), *reh'g denied*, 333 U.S. 877, 68 S.Ct. 900.

5. 12 U.S.C.A. § 321.

6. *Id.* § 321.

7. *Id.*

8. *See, e.g., Eccles, supra* (conditioning approval of membership on restriction of control by holding company); *Continental Bank and Trust Co., supra* (noting longstanding Fed rules relating to conditions of membership of state banking institutions).

9. 333 U.S. 426, 68 S.Ct. 641 (1948), *reh'g denied*, 333 U.S. 877, 68 S.Ct. 900.

10. *Eccles*, 333 U.S. at 427, 68 S.Ct. at 642.

11. *Id.*

stock, or in any other manner, any interest in such bank, other than such as may arise out of the usual correspondent bank relationships, such bank, within 60 days after written notice from the Board of Governors of the Federal Reserve System, shall withdraw from membership in the Federal Reserve System.[12]

Some time thereafter, Transamerica acquired just over 10 percent of the outstanding stock of the bank, without its prior knowledge. The bank advised the Fed of this fact, but requested that it be relieved of the condition quoted above.[13] The Fed refused to do so, though it was not clear that the Fed intended to enforce the condition in the absence of the exercise of control by Transamerica.[14]

When the Fed's position was challenged, the D.C. District Court in an unreported opinion held that the bank was bound by the condition on which it had accepted membership.[15] The D.C. Circuit reversed, characterizing the condition as "only as a statement that, if the Board of Governors should determine, after hearing, that Transamerica's ownership of the bank's shares has resulted in a change for the worse in the character of the bank's personnel, in its banking policies, in the safety of its deposits, or in any other substantial way, it may require the bank to withdraw from the Federal Reserve System."[16]

Since this was a declaratory judgment action, the Supreme Court was of the view that, "[e]specially where governmental action is involved, courts should not intervene unless the need for equitable relief is clear, not remote or speculative."[17] The Court noted that the Fed, "having imposed the condition to safeguard [the bank's] independence, disavows any action to terminate the Bank's membership, so long as the Bank maintains the independence on which it insists."[18] In light of the existing uncertainty regarding any future enforcement of the condition, the Court held that injunctive relief would be inappropriate.[19]

Despite the ambiguity of the result in *Eccles*, currently it is not unusual to find that a regulator has attached conditions to its approval of an application. Unlike the situation at the time *Eccles* was decided, violation of such a condition is now explicitly identified as one of the grounds for an administrative cease and desist order under the FDIA.[20] The use of general approval conditions has been particularly important in, for example, capital adequacy supervision.[21] Although the regulators'

---

12. *Id*. at 427–428, 68 S.Ct. at 642.

13. *Id*. at 428. 68 S.Ct. at 643.

14. *Id*.

15. *Id*. at 428–429, 68 S.Ct. at 643.

16. *Id*. at 429, 68 S.Ct. at 643.

17. *Id*. at 431, 68 S.Ct. at 644.

18. *Id*. at 432, 68 S.Ct. at 644.

19. *Id*. at 435, 68 S.Ct. at 645.

20. *See* 12 U.S.C.A. § 1818(b)(1) (providing for initiation of cease and desist proceedings for violation of "any condition imposed in writing by the agency in connection with the granting of any application or other request by the depository institution").

21. *See, e.g., Board of Governors v. First Lincolnwood Corp.*, 439 U.S. 234, 99 S.Ct. 505 (1978) (conditioning approval of bank holding company formation on adequacy of capital); *Kaneb Servs., Inc. v. Federal Sav. & Loan Ins. Corp.*, 650 F.2d 78 (5th Cir. 1981) (upholding condition on savings and loan holding company approval).

authority to enforce strict capital adequacy standards has occasionally been challenged,[22] it is now a significant, legislatively confirmed feature of contemporary depository institution regulation.

While the field of Fed membership may be limited to national and state-chartered banks (including savings banks), this does not affect the scope of the Fed's jurisdiction over deposit reserves. The Fed directly supervises the deposit reserve requirements for all depository institutions, not just member banks.[23]

§ 2.12   Conversions

In this section, we examine depository institution "conversions," quasi-entry transactions in which a formal change occurs in the nature of the charter that leaves the type of depository institution essentially unaffected. There are two distinct kinds of conversion. The first, a "conversion of charter," is similar to a change in the state of incorporation in general corporate law.[1] In the depository institutions context, however, the *situs* of the institution remains the same; what changes is the statutory source of the charter. Reincorporation and charter conversion are contrasted in Figure 2–1, *infra*.

FIGURE 2-1
Reincorporation v. Charter Conversion

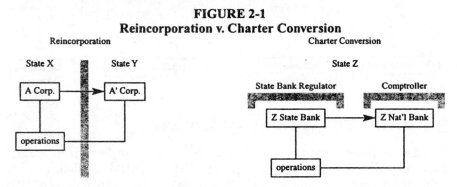

Because of the dual regulatory system under which depository institutions operate, a bank might convert from a national to a state charter, or from a state to a national charter, but the geographical *situs* of the institution—and that of its operations—remains unchanged. The

---

22. *See, e.g., MCorp Fin., Inc. v. Board of Governors*, 900 F.2d 852 (5th Cir.1990) (challenging, *inter alia*, Fed authority to impose capital conditions on holding company; distinguishing *First Lincolnwood*), *aff'd in part and rev'd in part on other grounds*, 502 U.S. 32, 112 S.Ct. 459 (1991); *First Nat'l Bank of Bellaire v. Comptroller of the Currency*, 697 F.2d 674 (5th Cir.1983) (challenging OCC authority to enforce capital adequacy requirements; subsequently reversed by legislative amendment, 12 U.S.C.A. § 3907). *But cf. Kaneb Servs., Inc.*, 650 F.2d 78 (upholding FSLIC authority to impose capital conditions on holding company).

23.   12 U.S.C.A. § 461(b).

§ 2.12

1. *See* H. G. Henn & J. R. Alexander, Law of Corporations 179 & n. 9 (3d ed. 1983) (discussing reincorporation).

type of institution also remains essentially unchanged (*e.g.*, a commercial bank), but the primary regulator having jurisdiction over the institution would change (*e.g.*, from the Comptroller to a state banking official).[2]

The second type of conversion, a "conversion of form," is similar to a corporate reorganization or recapitalization in the general corporate law context.[3] However, in the depository institutions context, the conversion involves a change from a mutual form of organization and ownership to a stock form.[4] The conversion does not change the primary regulator of the institution, unless the conversion of form is accompanied by a charter conversion. Recapitalization and conversion of form are contrasted in Figure 2–2, *infra*.

FIGURE 2-2
Recapitalization v. Conversion of Form

§ 2.13 Conversion of Charter

The requirements for conversion of charter from federal to state or state to federal differ. Conversions of charter should be distinguished from the related process of merger between state- and federally chartered depository institutions.[1]

A fundamental question of jurisdiction is at issue in a conversion of charter. The result of the process is the relinquishment of jurisdiction over the depository institution by one chartering authority and the

---

2. Accordingly, this type of conversion may be described as a "jurisdictional conversion." *See, e.g.*, Wisc. Stat. Ann. § 215.57 (concerning "jurisdictional conversion," state to federal charter).

3. *See* HENN & ALEXANDER at 1011–18.

4. This type of conversion may be described as an "organizational conversion." *See, e.g.*, Wisc. Stat. Ann. § 215.58 (concerning "organizational conversion," mutual to stock).

§ 2.13

1. *See, e.g., Federal Home Loan Bank Bd. v. Elliott*, 386 F.2d 42 (9th Cir.1967), *cert. denied*, 390 U.S. 1011, 88 S.Ct. 1260 (1968) (noting conversion requirements and procedures exclusive of requirements and procedures applicable to mergers); *Opdyke v. Security Sav. & Loan Co.*, 99 N.E.2d 84 (Ohio App. 1951), *aff'd*, 157 Ohio St. 121, 105 N.E.2d 9 (1952).

acquisition of such authority by another. Hence, the interrelationship between the interested federal and state chartering authorities involved in this process is particularly important.[2] The authority of one regulator to approve the conversion over the objections of the chartering regulator of the converting institution has raised serious questions of competing federal and state authority.[3]

The courts have reacted in varying ways to this issue in cases under the NBA[4] and the Home Owners' Loan Act ("HOLA").[5] It has long been established, for example, that the NBA could authorize the Comptroller to approve the conversion of a state-chartered bank to a national bank charter, even in the absence of approval by the state chartering authority.[6]

In a similar situation, involving a state-chartered savings and loan association seeking approval from the Federal Home Loan Bank Board of a conversion to a federal charter, the Supreme Court held, in *Hopkins Fed. Savings & Loan Association v. Cleary*,[7] that to the extent that HOLA, as amended in 1934, permitted conversion of state-chartered associations in contravention of state law, it was "an unconstitutional encroachment upon the reserved powers of the states" under the Tenth Amendment of the U.S. Constitution.[8] Justice Cardozo's opinion has never been overruled.

The Court distinguished the situation in *Hopkins Fed. Savings* from its earlier decision in *Casey v. Galli*[9] on several grounds. Among other things, the constitutional question at issue in *Hopkins Fed. Savings* had not been raised in *Casey*. This distinction does not seem very satisfying. As the *Hopkins Fed. Savings* Court characterized it, the precise issue raised in *Casey* was whether "the change from one form of association to another was to be condemned as *ultra vires*."[10] Is it to be assumed that a serious issue of constitutionality under the Tenth Amendment would not have affected the *Casey* Court's analysis of the *ultra vires* question, or that the Court would not have raised the issue *sua sponte*? In some question-begging *dicta*, the *Hopkins Fed. Savings* Court suggested that distinctions might "conceivably exist between the power of Congress in respect of [commercial] banks ... and its power in respect of [savings] associations...."[11] It is difficult to imagine what those distinctions might be.[12] In any event, under current federal statutes, the general rule

---

2. *See, e.g., Hopkins Fed. Sav. & Loan Ass'n v. Cleary*, 296 U.S. 315, 56 S.Ct. 235 (1935) (involving state to federal conversion); *Federal Home Loan Bank Bd. v. Greater Del. Valley Federal Sav. and Loan Ass'n*, 277 F.2d 437 (3d Cir.1960) (federal to state conversion).

3. *Hopkins Fed. Savings, supra.*

4. 12 U.S.C.A. §§ 1 *et seq.*

5. *Id.* §§ 1461 *et seq.*

6. *Casey v. Galli*, 94 U.S. (4 Otto) 673 (1876).

7. 296 U.S. 315, 56 S.Ct. 235 (1935).

8. 296 U.S. at 335, 56 S.Ct. at 240.

9. 94 U.S. (4 Otto) 673 (1876).

10. *Hopkins Fed. Savings*, 296 U.S. at 342–343, 56 S.Ct. at 243.

11. 296 U.S. at 343, 56 S.Ct. at 243–244.

12. *Cf. Veazie Bank v. Fenno*, 75 U.S. (8 Wall.) 533, 549–555 (1869) (Nelson, J., dissenting) (arguing that federal government lacked power to deprive states of power to issue commercial banking franchises, citing Tenth Amendment).

is that a conversion of a state-chartered depository institution to a federal charter must be in conformity with state law.[13]

The apparent disparity in the treatment of state-to-federal conversions under the NBA (in light of *Casey*) and under HOLA (in light of *Hopkins Fed. Savings*) is no longer a practical consideration, since the NBA had already been amended, prior to *Hopkins Fed. Savings*, to require that such state-to-national bank conversions "not be in contravention of the State law."[14] That condition is currently contained in the NBA.[15] A similar condition is imposed on conversion of a national-to-state bank charter.[16] OTS regulations also generally require compliance with applicable state law as a condition of approval of a conversion of a state-chartered savings association to a federal charter.[17]

FIRREA generally subjects conversions of savings associations to regulations prescribed by the OTS.[18] Despite *Hopkins Fed. Savings*, however, the OTS is authorized by FIRREA, *notwithstanding any other provision of law*, to approve conversion of a mutual savings association into a federal stock savings association or federal stock savings bank if the OTS determines that severe financial conditions exist that threaten the stability of the association to be converted, and that the conversion is likely to improve the financial condition of the association.[19] Such action by the OTS is also authorized where the FDIC has contracted to provide financial assistance to the association.[20] These conversions are also authorized if intended to assist an institution in receivership.[21] The question naturally arises whether this authority is consistent with *Hopkins Fed. Savings*. In fact, the Tenth Amendment, relied upon so heavily by *Hopkins Fed. Savings*, may have since been virtually overwhelmed by the Commerce Clause authority of Congress to make laws, in which case decisions limiting federal regulatory power based upon the amendment may simply be *hors de combat*.[22] One is tempted to think of *Hopkins Fed. Savings* as having fallen into desuetude.[23]

---

13. *See, e.g.*, 12 U.S.C.A. § 35 (NBA provision); *id.* § 1464(i) (HOLA provision). *But cf. id.* § 1464(p) (providing for emergency savings and loan association conversions notwithstanding contrary law).

14. Act of December 23, 1913, § 8, 38 Stat. 258 (1913) (*codified at* 12 U.S.C.A. § 35).

15. *See* 12 U.S.C.A. § 35 (governing state-to-federal conversions of commercial banks).

16. *See* 12 U.S.C.A. § 214c. *Cf. Ellis v. State Nat'l Bank of Ala.*, 434 F.2d 1182 (5th Cir.1970), *cert. denied*, 402 U.S. 973, 91 S.Ct. 1661 (1971) (concerning state law limitations on bank merger).

17. *See, e.g.*, 12 C.F.R. §§ 543.9(c)(2), 552.2–6.

18. 12 U.S.C.A. § 1464(i)(1).

19. *Id.* § 1464(p)(2)(A).

20. *Id.* § 1464(p)(2)(B).

21. *Id.* § 1464(p)(2)(C).

22. *See* Van Alstyne, *The Second Death of Federalism*, 83 Mich. L. Rev. 1709 (1985) (discussing Tenth Amendment jurisprudence); Field, *Garcia v. San Antonio Metropolitan Transit Authority: The Demise of a Misguided Doctrine*, 99 Harv. L. Rev. 84 (1985) (same).

23. *But cf. Garcia* v. *San Antonio Metro. Transit Auth.*, 469 U.S. 528, 586, 105 S.Ct. 1005, 1036 (1985) (O'Connor, J., dissenting) (citing *Hopkins* with approval).

§ 2.14 Changes of Charter from Federal to State

Conversion of a national bank to a state charter in the state in which the bank is located requires an affirmative vote representing at least two-thirds of each class of its capital stock.[1] Shareholders of the converting bank are entitled to dissenters' appraisal rights.[2] Shareholders wishing to exercise these rights must vote against the conversion, or give notice of dissent in writing to the bank at or prior to the shareholders' meeting called to approve the conversion.[3] Shareholders who qualify for dissenters' appraisal rights are entitled to receive the value of their shares in cash, if and when the conversion is consummated, upon written request to the resulting state-chartered bank. This written request must be made within 30 days of the conversion, and it must be accompanied by the surrender of stock certificates.

Upon conversion, the resulting state-chartered bank may be admitted to membership in the Federal Reserve System by the Fed.[4] If the resulting bank does not obtain Fed membership, the stock of the Federal Reserve Bank owned by the converted national bank must be canceled and repaid.[5] If the resulting bank is an FDIC-insured, nonmember bank, and it will have less capital stock or surplus than the converting bank, an FDIC application may be required for consent to convert.[6]

A federal savings association may convert into a state savings association or savings bank,[7] organized under the laws of the state in which the principal office of the association is located, if the following conditions are met: (1) The state must permit conversions of state savings associations or savings banks into federal savings associations;[8] (2) The conversion is approved on the requisite vote, in person or by proxy, of members or stockholders of the association in accordance with state law, but in no event by less than 51 percent of the votes cast at the members' or stockholders' meeting.[9] The approval must comply with any other requirements reciprocally equivalent to the requirements of state law for conversion of a state chartered institution into a federal savings association;[10] (3) The requisite notice of the meeting must be given;[11] (4) If the converted institution is mutual in form, in any dissolution after the conversion the members or shareholders must share on a mutual basis in the assets of the association in exact proportion to their relative

§ 2.14

1. 12 U.S.C.A. § 214a.

2. *Id.* § 214a(b).

3. *Id.*

4. *Id.* § 321.

5. *Id.* §§ 287, 321.

6. 12 C.F.R. § 303.3(c).

7. *See generally Federal Home Loan Bank Bd. v. Greater Del. Valley Fed. Sav. & Loan Ass'n,* 277 F.2d 437 (3d Cir.1960) (concerning FHLBB challenge to statutory conversion of federal savings and loan asso-

ciation to state charter as legally ineffective, per prior statutory language).

8. 12 U.S.C.A. § 1464(i)(3)(A)(i).

9. *Id.* § 1464(i)(3)(A)(ii)(I)-(II).

10. *Id. See Federal Home Loan Bank Bd. v. Greater Del. Valley Fed. Sav. & Loan Ass'n,* 277 F.2d 437 (3d Cir.1960) (interpreting prior statutory language).

11. *See* 12 U.S.C.A. § 1464(i)(3)(A)(iii) (notice requirements under HOLA).

share or account credits;[12] and, (5) If the converted institution is stock in form, in any dissolution after the conversion the stockholders must share on an equitable basis in the assets of the association.[13] The conversion is effective on the date that all provisions of the HOLA have been fully complied with, and the state in which the savings association is located has issued the new charter.[14]

A converted savings association remains subject to the authority of the OTS.[15] Insurance of the converted savings association's accounts may be terminated in connection with the conversion, so long as the termination is effected consistent with applicable law and regulations.[16]

Conversion of a federal credit union to a state charter is subject to the following conditions specified in the FCUA. (1) A majority of the directors of the converting federal credit union must first approve the conversion and set a date for a vote by the members on the conversion.[17] (2) The conversion must be approved by a majority vote of the members voting on the proposal.[18] (3) A verified statement of the results of that vote must be filed with the NCUA within 10 days of the vote.[19] (4) Within 90 days of the vote, the converting credit union must take all necessary action under applicable state law to become a state-chartered credit union.[20] (5) Finally, within 10 days of receipt of the state charter, the converted credit union must file a copy thereof with the NCUA.[21] At that point, the converted credit union is no longer subject to any of the provisions of the FCUA.[22]

The Credit Union Membership Access Act ("CUMAA")[23] now allows a peculiar form of cross-industry conversion. Under specified circumstances, an insured credit union may convert to a mutual savings association charter.[24] Such a conversion does not require the prior approval of the NCUA.[25] A proposal for the conversion must be approved by a majority of the directors of the insured credit union and by a majority of the members of the credit union.[26]

---

12. *Id*. § 1464(i)(3)(A)(iv).

13. *Id*. § 1464(i)(3)(A)(v).

14. *Id*. § 1464(i)(3)(A)(vi).

15. *Id*. § 1464(i)(3)(B)(i)-(ii).

16. *Id*. § 1464(i)(3)(B)(iii).

17. *Id*. § 1771(a)(1).

18. *Id*.

19. *Id*. § 1771(a)(2).

20. *Id*. § 1771(a)(3).

21. *Id*.

22. *Id*. § 1771(a)(4).

23. Pub. L. No. 105–219, Aug. 7, 1998, 112 Stat. 913 (1998) (codified at scattered sections of 12 U.S.C.A.).

24. CUMAA, § 202(3) (codified at 12 U.S.C.A. § 1785(2)).

25. 12 U.S.C.A. § 1785(2)(A). However, notice to the NCUA Board is required. *Id*. § 1785(2)(D). The NCUA is also required to "administer" the required vote of the members of the insured credit union seeking to convert. *Id*. § 1785(2)(G)(ii). The vote must be verified by the federal or state agency that would have jurisdiction over the converted institution. *Id*.

26. *Id*. § 1785(2)(B). If the NCUA or the federal or state agency that would have jurisdiction over the converted institution does not approve of the methods by which the member vote is taken, the member vote must be taken again, "as directed by the

State regulatory policy has an interest in the conversion of federally chartered depository institutions into state-chartered institutions. Approaches to state regulation of such conversions varies. For example, New York law permits conversion of a national bank to a state charter provided that the conversion complies with federal law and the state statutory requirements governing conversions.[27] Similarly, a federal savings association with its place of business in New York is authorized to convert to a state charter.[28] These conversions require approval at a duly noticed shareholders meeting by an affirmative vote representing two-thirds of the book value of all outstanding shares or three-fourths of the outstanding shares represented at the meeting.[29] Similar provisions apply to the conversion of a federal credit union to a state charter.[30]

In contrast, California law presents a relatively more progressive model. California permits conversion of national banks to state charters with the approval of the Commissioner of Financial Institutions (formerly the Superintendent of Banks).[31] In granting approval, the Commissioner must be satisfied that the converting bank has complied with disclosure requirements, and has met general requirements applicable to conversion.[32] Upon conversion, the resulting bank is deemed to be the successor corporate entity of the converting national bank for all purposes.[33]

Conversions of federally chartered savings associations to state charters have been regulated under California's Unitary Savings Association Law.[34] Federal associations are permitted to convert into state-chartered savings associations in accordance with the requirements and procedures set forth in the Law.[35]

California also provides for cross-industry conversions, *i.e.*, conversions from one type of depository institution (*e.g.*, a commercial bank) to another type of depository institution (*e.g.*, a savings association), under its Depository Corporation Sale, Merger, and Conversion Law.[36]

[NCUA] or the agency." *Id.* § 1785(2)(G)(ii).

27. N.Y. Banking Law § 136(1).

28. N.Y. Banking Law § 136(2).

29. *Id.*

30. N.Y. Banking Law § 480–a.

31. Cal. Fin. Code § 4941(a). An amendment to the California law, effective 1 July 1997, abolished the office of the Superintendent of Banks and the State Banking Department and the office of the Commissioner and the Department of Savings and Loan, transferring their powers to the Commissioner of Financial Institutions and the Department of Financial Institutions. Cal. Stats. 1996, ch. 1064, §§ 28.5, 29.5 (*codified at* Cal. Fin. Code §§ 200, 210–217).

32. Cal. Fin. Code §§ 4942–4945.

33. Cal. Fin. Code § 4950.

34. Cal. Fin. Code §§ 5000 *et seq.*

35. Cal. Fin. Code § 5709.

36. Cal. Fin. Code §§ 4800 *et seq.* On the effect of other savings association and banking laws on the Depository Corporation Sale, Merger, and Conversion Law, see Cal. Fin. Code § 4827. These cross-industry conversion provisions create a third category of conversions, in addition to conversions from state to federal or federal to state charter and conversions from mutual to stock organization. The third category is cross-industry conversion from one type of state-chartered depository institution to another type of state-chartered depository institution. *See* Cal. Fin. Code §§ 4920 *et seq.* (concerning cross-industry conversions of state depository corporations). However, certain cross-industry conversions have been prohibited under the Law. Conversions of state-chartered banks to mutual savings associations, federally or state-char-

California law also provides for conversion of federal credit unions to state charters.[37] A federal credit union can convert under California law, upon the recommendation of its board of directors, by complying with the requirements of the FCUA and obtaining a certificate of authorization to act as a credit union under California law.[38]

§ 2.15 Change of Charter from State to Federal

The National Bank Act ("NBA") authorizes the Comptroller to approve conversions of state banks to national charters on the following conditions.[1] The converting bank must have sufficient unimpaired capital to have allowed its chartering as a national bank.[2] The conversion must be approved by an affirmative vote of shareholders representing not less than 51 percent of the capital stock of the converting bank. The NBA requires that the name of the resulting national bank contain the word "national." The NBA also expressly requires that the conversion "not be in contravention of the State law."[3]

Conversion of any state savings association that is, or is eligible to become, a member of a federal home loan bank into a federal savings association, and any accompanying conversion from mutual to stock or stock to mutual form,[4] is subject to regulations prescribed by the OTS.[5] Further, any federal savings association may change its designation from a federal savings association to a federal savings bank, or *vice versa.*[6]

Conversion of a state savings bank that is a member of the BIF into a federal savings bank is permitted, subject to the provisions of the amended Home Owners' Loan Act ("HOLA")[7] and pursuant to regulations promulgated by the OTS.[8] The OTS is authorized to provide for the organization, incorporation, operation, examination, and regulation of

---

tered, are not permitted. Cal. Fin. Code § 4825(a). Likewise, conversions of state-chartered mutual savings associations to state commercial banks are prohibited, Cal. Fin. Code § 4825(b), as are conversions of federal or state mutual savings associations to state-chartered commercial banks and *vice versa.* Cal. Fin. Code § 4825(c)-(d). In addition, a savings association has been prohibited from converting into a commercial bank, if the ownership of the converting savings association, as ownership of the resulting bank, would be prohibited by the restrictions on interstate bank holding companies under the Douglas Amendment to the Bank Holding Company Act of 1956 (BHCA). Cal. Fin. Code § 4826. *See* 12 U.S.C.A. § 1842(d) (1992) (setting forth former interstate holding company restrictions). The BHCA interstate restrictions were removed in September 1994.

37. Cal. Fin. Code §§ 15350 *et seq.*

38. Cal. Fin. Code § 15350. *See* Cal. Fin. Code §§ 14100 *et seq.* (formation of state-chartered credit union).

§ 2.15

1. 12 U.S.C.A. § 35.

2. *Id.*

3. *Id. See generally Marion Nat'l Bank v. Saxon,* 261 F.Supp. 373 (N.D.Ind.1966); *Traverse City State Bank v. Empire Nat'l Bank,* 228 F.Supp. 984 (W.D.Mich.1964).

4. Conversion of any savings association from mutual to stock or stock to mutual form is prohibited except in accordance with regulations promulgated by the OTS. 12 U.S.C.A. § 1464(i)(2)(A).

5. *Id.* § 1464(i)(1).

6. *Id.* § 1464(i)(2)(C).

7. *Id.* § 1464(*o*)(2)(B)-(E).

8. *Id.* § 1464(*o*)(1).

such converted savings banks.[9] The converted savings bank continues to be a BIF member until such time as it changes its status to membership in the SAIF.[10]

Section 125 of the Federal Credit Union Act ("FCUA")[11] provides for the conversion of a state-chartered credit union to a federal charter.[12] Such conversions require approval of the NCUA.[13] They are treated by the NCUA like an initial application for a federal charter, "including mandatory on-site examination by NCUA."[14] Approval is conditioned on the following factors. (1) There must be compliance with all applicable state law requirements.[15] (2) The institution must file with the NCUA satisfactory proof of such compliance.[16] (3) The institution must file with the NCUA an organization certificate, as required under the FCUA.[17]

State practice varies. For example, New York law freely permits conversions of state-chartered banks to national bank charters.[18] These conversions do not require the approval of any state authority.[19] The proposed conversion must be approved by a vote of stockholders representing at least two-thirds of the stock of the converting bank and must be effected in the manner provided by federal law.

State-chartered savings associations are also permitted to convert to a federal charter, subject to procedures imposed by the New York statute.[20] The conversion must be approved at a duly noticed meeting of shareholders,[21] by an affirmative vote representing at least two-thirds of the book value of all outstanding shares,[22] or at least three-fourths of the book value of the outstanding shares represented at the meeting.[23] Similar state law provisions apply to conversions of state-chartered credit unions to federal charters.[24]

A more progressive model is provided by California law, which freely permits state-chartered banks to convert to national bank charters, so long as the converting bank complies with all conversion requirements of federal law.[25] The resulting national bank is deemed to be the successor corporate entity of the converting state-chartered bank.[26] The resulting bank may be required to file a report with the Commissioner of Finan-

---

9. *Id.*

10. *Id.* § 1464(*o*)(2)(A).

11. *Id.* § 1771.

12. 12 U.S.C.A. § 1771(b). For interpretive guidance with respect to such conversions, see 54 Fed. Reg. 31,165, 31,179–31,-180 (1989) (NCUA Interpretive Ruling and Policy Statement No. 89–1).

13. *Id.* § 1771(b)(2).

14. 54 Fed. Reg. at 31,179.

15. *Id.* § 1771(b)(1)(A).

16. *Id.* § 1771(b)(1)(B).

17. *Id.* § 1771(b)(1)(C). *See id.* § 1753 (setting forth organization certificate requirement).

18. N.Y. Banking Law § 137.

19. N.Y. Banking Law § 137(1).

20. N.Y. Banking Law § 409.

21. *See* N.Y. Banking Law § 409 (notice requirements).

22. N.Y. Banking Law § 409(a).

23. N.Y. Banking Law § 409(b).

24. *See* N.Y. Banking Law § 480–b (credit union conversions).

25. Cal. Fin. Code § 4961(a).

26. Cal. Fin. Code § 4940, 4963.

cial Institutions detailing the conversion.[27] The converting bank must surrender its certificate of authority to do a banking business to the Commissioner for cancellation.[28]

Conversions of state-chartered savings associations to federal charters are regulated under California's unitary Savings Association Law.[29] State-chartered savings associations have been permitted to convert into federally chartered savings associations in accordance with the requirements and procedures set forth in the Law.[30]

California also provides for cross-industry conversions, *i.e.*, conversions from one type of depository institution (*e.g.*, a commercial bank) to another type of depository institution (*e.g.*, a savings association), under its Depository Corporation Sale, Merger, and Conversion Law.[31]

In cross-industry state-to-federal conversions, California law also permits conversion of a state-chartered bank to a federally chartered savings association.[32] Conversion of a state-chartered savings association to a national bank is also permitted.[33]

California law provides for conversion of a state-chartered credit union to a federal charter.[34] A state-chartered credit union can convert under California law, on the recommendation of its board of directors, by an affirmative vote of a majority of the members of the credit union.[35] Within ten days of the vote, the credit union is required to file with the Commissioner a verified certificate containing a copy of the minutes of the members' meeting or a copy of the written ballot and results of the vote, together with a statement that the proposed conversion has been approved.[36] A copy of the certificate must be filed with the Secretary of State.[37]

§ 2.16 Conversion of Form

This section examines the other major type of depository institution conversion, the conversion from one organization form, the mutual institution, to another, the stock institution. The main focus is upon savings associations, such as savings and loan associations and savings banks, which may be organized in mutual form. Accordingly, particular attention is given to the applicable provisions of Home Owners' Loan Act ("HOLA").[1]

---

27. Cal. Fin. Code § 4964(b).

28. Cal. Fin. Code § 4964(a).

29. Cal. Fin. Code §§ 5000 *et seq.*

30. Cal. Fin. Code § 5700.

31. Cal. Fin. Code §§ 4800 *et seq.* On the effect of other savings association and banking laws on the Depository Corporation Sale, Merger, and Conversion Law, see Cal. Fin. Code § 4827. *See also supra* § 2.14, note 36 (discussing California cross-industry conversion provisions).

32. Cal. Fin. Code § 4961(b).

33. *Id.*

34. Cal. Fin. Code §§ 15300 *et seq.*

35. Cal. Fin. Code § 15301.

36. Cal. Fin. Code § 15302. *See also* Cal. Fin. Code § 15303 (certificate as presumptive evidence).

37. 7Cal. Fin. Code § 15302.

§ 2.16

1. 112 U.S.C.A. § 1464(i). *See generally York v. Federal Home Loan Bank Bd.*, 624 F.2d 495 (4th Cir.1980), *cert. denied*, 449 U.S. 1043, 101 S.Ct. 621 (concerning conversion from federal mutual to federal stock savings association).

For various reasons, conversions of form have become increasingly prevalent in recent years. One reason is that conversion to the stock form of ownership may offer the institution an opportunity to attract new capital from the investing public, rather than from mutual depositors. Also, the conversion may facilitate reorganization into a holding company pattern of ownership.[2] Finally, during the 1980s, the organizational conversion played an important role in the rehabilitation of savings associations in danger of default.[3] Conversion from mutual to stock form of organization may be the first step in a reorganization or private sale of a mutual savings association which, as it begins to return to profitability, has particular needs for a capital infusion.[4]

HOLA provides general authority for the conversion from mutual to stock form of any savings association converting to a federal charter.[5] In addition, consistent with the purposes of the HOLA, the OTS has been authorized, notwithstanding any other provision of law, (1) to approve or (in the case of a federal savings association) require conversion of a mutual savings association or an FDIC-insured federal mutual savings bank into a federal stock savings association or federal stock savings bank; (2) to charter a federal stock savings association or federal stock savings bank to acquire the assets of such a mutual institution; or (3) to charter a federal stock savings association or federal stock savings bank to merge with such a mutual institution.[6]

Such a conversion is authorized only if any one of the three following conditions is met: (1) The conversion can be authorized or required if the OTS determines that severe financial conditions exist that threaten the stability of the association to be converted, and that the conversion is likely to improve the financial condition of the association.[7] (2) The conversion can be authorized or required if the FDIC has contracted to provide assistance to the association under Section 13 of the FDIA.[8] (3) The conversion can be authorized or required if it is intended to assist an institution in receivership.[9]

---

2. However, since 1987, authority has existed in federal law for the establishment of a mutual holding company as well. *See* 12 U.S.C.A. § 1730a(s) (1988) (providing for mutual holding companies). Section 1730a was repealed in 1989. *See* Financial Institutions Reform, Recovery, and Enforcement Act of 1989, Pub. L. No. 101–73, § 407, 103 Stat. 183, 363 (1989) ("FIRREA") (repealing § 1730a). Mutual holding companies are now governed by Section 10 of HOLA, as amended by FIRREA. 12 U.S.C.A. § 1467a(*o*), *as amended*, FIRREA § 301, 103 Stat. at 336–338.

3. *See, e.g.,* Berg, *State Savings Banks Thriving*, N.Y. Times, Feb. 7, 1987, at 33. col. 3 (discussing role of conversions).

4. This factor has been an underlying motive of the sudden rise of the federal stock savings bank authorized since 1982.

See Pub. L. No. 97–320, § 121, 96 Stat. 1479–1480 (1982) (*codified at* 12 U.S.C.A. § 1464(p)), *as amended*, FIRREA § 301, 103 Stat. at 301.

5. 12 U.S.C.A. § 1464(i)(1).

6. 12 U.S.C.A. § 1464(p)(1).

7. *Id.* § 1464(p)(2)(A).

8. *Id.* § 1464(p)(2)(B). *See id.* § 1823 (FDIA Section 13, providing for financial assistance to institutions in default or in danger of default under specified circumstances).

9. *Id.* § 1464(p)(2)(C). The authority of the OTS to force a conversion of a state-chartered mutual savings association to a federal stock savings association, notwithstanding contrary state law, was upheld in *Smallwood v. Office of Thrift Supervision*, 925 F.2d 894 (6th Cir.1991). The court ex-

A federal savings bank chartered under these provisions would have the same authority and be subject to the same restrictions that would apply if it had been chartered as a federal savings bank under any other provision of HOLA.[10] Furthermore, it can engage in any investment, activity, or operation that the converting institution was engaged in, if the latter was a federal savings bank, or would have been authorized to engage in if the latter had converted to a federal charter.[11]

pressed the view that "FIRREA and its legislative history demonstrates [*sic*] an unmistakable purpose to insure that Federal authority is paramount regarding the maintenance of the solvency of the Federal deposit insurance system, and therefore that § 5(p) [of HOLA, 12 U.S.C.A. § 1464(p)] impliedly preempts state laws that could impede the authority of the [OTS] to approve or deny conversions." *Smallwood*, 925 F.2d at 898.

10. 12 U.S.C.A. § 1464(p)(3).

11. *Id.*

Chapter 3

BRANCHING

Table of Sections

---

§ 3.1   Introduction

Establishment of a branch[1] is one means by which a depository institution can enter another geographic segment of the industry market. This is subject to an approval process similar to the one that applies to chartering. Branches are normally considered to be geographically distinct outlets of one institutional entity. Functionally, however, other institutional structures or arrangements may operate as "branches" of a single enterprise. For example, in "chain banking," separately operating banks may be interrelated through common stock control,[2] interlocking directorates,[3] or other similar control devices. The members of the chain functionally act like branches, but to the extent that they are independently structured and operated, they are not subject to the legal princi-

---

§ 3.1

1. On the meaning of the term "branch," *see, e.g.,* 12 U.S.C.A. § 36(j) (defining the term for purposes of National Bank Act ("NBA")). *See also First Nat'l Bank in Plant City v. Dickinson,* 396 U.S. 122, 90 S.Ct. 337 (1969); *Independent Bankers Ass'n of Am. v. Smith,* 534 F.2d 921 (D.C.Cir.), *cert. denied,* 429 U.S. 862, 97 S.Ct. 166 (1976) (interpreting and applying NBA definition).

2. There are statutory limitations on common control through stock ownership of depository institutions. *See* 12 U.S.C.A. § 1817(j) (Change in Bank Control Act). *Cf.* 12 U.S.C.A. § 1467a (regulating holding companies of savings associations); §§ 1841 *et seq.* (regulating holding companies of banks).

3. There are statutory limitations on management interlocks between otherwise unaffiliated depository institutions. *See* 12 U.S.C.A. §§ 3201 *et seq.*

ples applicable to branches.[4] To the extent that the independence of the chain members is open to question, however, these principles may be applied to them by their regulator.[5]

Common control exerted by a holding company enterprise over constituent operating subsidiaries is often referred to as "group banking." Group banking differs from chain banking in the formality of the control relationship. However, group banking is as vulnerable in principle as chain banking to the possibility that the regulator may consider it to be an impermissible evasion of branch banking regulation.[6] Before the enactment of federal law in 1994 permitting interstate branch banking,[7] this concern over group banking was an important issue for state regulators.[8]

This chapter focuses on restrictions on traditional branch banking. As a general rule, within any state, both state-chartered and federally chartered depository institutions have the power to branch. Where a state statute prohibits or restricts state banks from intrastate branching, national banks located in that state are subject to the same branching rules.[9]

This chapter first considers the regulatory principles that apply to intrastate branching by national banks. It then provides a brief survey of state law restrictions on intrastate branching. Thereafter, the chapter considers savings association branching and credit union branching, and concludes with analysis of the 1994 federal legislation authorizing interstate branching.

§ 3.2 National Bank Branching

A key provision of the National Bank Act ("NBA") authorizes the establishment of intrastate branches of national banks, with the approval of the Comptroller, to the extent that "such establishment and operation are at the time expressly authorized to State banks by the law of the State in question.... "[1] In addition, the branch is permitted to be established outside the city in which the principal office of the national bank is located only if state statutory law permits such branching by state banks "affirmatively and not merely by implication or recognition."[2] Establishment of the branch is also subject to capital require-

---

4. *See National State Bank, Elizabeth, N.J. v. Howell*, 49 N.J. 330, 230 A.2d 377 (1967).

5. *See Bank of N. Am. v. State Banking Bd.*, 468 S.W.2d 529 (Tex. 1971).

6. *See, e.g., Commercial Nat'l Bank of Little Rock v. Board of Governors*, 451 F.2d 86 (8th Cir.1971); *Whitney Natl. Bank in Jefferson Parish v. James*, 189 So.2d 430 (La. 1966).

7. Pub. L. No. 103–328, 108 Stat. 2338 (1994) (*codified at* scattered sections of 12 U.S.C.).

8. *See, e.g., Commercial Nat'l Bank of Little Rock v. Board of Governors*, 451 F.2d 86 (8th Cir.1971); *Whitney Nat'l Bank in Jefferson Parish v. James*, 189 So.2d 430 (La. 1966).

9. 12 U.S.C.A. § 36(c).

§ 3.2

1. 12 U.S.C.A. § 36(c)(1).

2. *Id.* § 36(c)(2).

ments that would apply to a state bank application for a branch.[3] In addition, until 1996, the aggregate capital of the bank and its branches was required to be at least equal to the aggregate minimum required capital for the establishment of the bank and each of its branches as separate national banks.[4]

§ 3.3   Policy of Competitive Equality

The NBA provision concerning branching was enacted in 1927 as part of the McFadden Act.[1] According to its chief sponsor, Representative McFadden, the provision was intended "to restore as nearly as possible the equilibrium between state and national banks within the Federal Reserve System."[2] Prior to this enactment, several states allowed branch banking for state chartered institutions; national banks could not compete effectively in those jurisdictions without converting from federal to state charters. The McFadden Act authorized the Comptroller of the Currency to allow national banks to establish branch offices in any state that permitted branching for state chartered institutions, but only under the same terms and conditions.[3]

In *First National Bank of Logan v. Walker Bank & Trust Co.*,[4] the Supreme Court considered how specifically this requirement was to be interpreted and applied in assessing the legality of the Comptroller's decisions approving branching applications of two Utah-based national banks. *Walker Bank* viewed the NBA branching provision as fundamentally controlled by a policy of "competitive equality" between state and national banks with respect to branching.

The Utah branching statute prohibited Utah banks, with certain exceptions, from branching except through the acquisition of an existing bank that had been in operation for not less than five years.[5] The two applicant national banks had sought to establish *de novo* branches.[6] In upholding the Comptroller's approval of these applications over competitor challenge,[7] one district court had found "express authority" for state

---

3. *See First-Citizens Bank & Trust Co. v. Camp*, 409 F.2d 1086 (4th Cir.1969) (applying "solvency of the branch" test under state law).

4. *Id.* § 36(h), *repealed*, Pub. L. No. 104–208, § 2204, 110 Stat. 3009 (Sept. 30, 1996).

§ 3.3

1. For discussion of the legislative history of the McFadden Act with respect to its branching provisions, see *Clarke v. Securities Indus. Ass'n*, 479 U.S. 388, 404–408, 107 S.Ct. 750, 759–762 (1987); *First Nat'l Bank of Logan v. Walker Bank & Trust Co.*, 385 U.S. 252, 256–260, 87 S.Ct. 492, 495–497 (1966); *Cheshire Nat'l Bank v. Smith*, 427 F.Supp. 277, 279–280 (D.N.H.1977).

2. 68 Cong. Rec. 1296 (1924) (remarks of Cong. McFadden).

3. 12 U.S.C.A. § 36(c).

4. 385 U.S. 252, 87 S.Ct. 492 (1966).

5. Utah Code Ann., tit. 7, ch. 3, § 6 (1965 Supp.).

6. *Walker Bank*, 385 U.S. at 254, 87 S.Ct. at 493.

7. Competing banks in the area where a proposed national bank branch is to be established have standing to object to the branch application, but there is no indication that the Comptroller need give notice to competing banks. *See Community Bank of Washtenaw v. Smith*, 378 F.Supp. 235 (E.D.Mich.1974) (holding failure to notify not denial of due process).

bank branching in general, and would not apply the specific conditions that would have attached to a branch application of a state bank.[8] In other words, the court interpreted Section 36 as "referencing over" to state law on *whether* a national bank could branch, and possibly *where*, but not as to *how* it might branch. The Court of Appeals reversed, holding that Section 36(c) created a policy of "competitive equality" between state and national banks, which required "reference over" to all pertinent provisions of state branching law.[9] In the other application, another district court "imposed all of the restrictions of ... Utah law on the establishment of national banks and the Court of Appeals for the District of Columbia Circuit affirmed."[10]

On *certiorari*, the Supreme Court endorsed this broad policy of competitive equality, arguing:

> It appears clear from ... the legislative history of § 36(c)(1) and (2) that Congress intended to place national and state banks on a basis of "competitive equality" insofar as branch banking was concerned. Both sponsors of the applicable banking Acts, Representative McFadden and Senator Glass, so characterized the legislation. It is not for us to so construe the Acts as to frustrate this clearcut purpose so forcefully expressed by both friend and foe of the legislation at the time of its adoption. To us it appears beyond question that the Congress was continuing its policy of equalization [of state and national banks] first adopted in the National Bank Act of 1864.... [11]

In response, the Comptroller tried to parse the NBA provision narrowly, as mandating reference over to state law "only as to 'whether' and 'where' branches may be located and not the 'method' by which this is effected."[12] The Court refused to read the section and its legislative history so narrowly. It explained:

> We believe that where a State allows branching only by taking over an existing bank, it expresses as much "whether" and "where" a branch may be located as does a prohibition or a limitation to the home office municipality. As to the restriction being a "method," we have concluded that since it is part and parcel of Utah's policy, it

---

8. *Walker Bank*, 385 U.S. at 255, 87 S.Ct. at 494.

9. *Id. But see First Nat'l Bank of Smithfield v. Saxon*, 352 F.2d 267 (4th Cir.1965) (holding *contra*).

10. *Walker Bank*, 385 U.S. at 256, 87 S.Ct. at 495.

11. 385 U.S. at 261, 87 S.Ct. at 497.

12. *Id*. Ironically, the Comptroller successfully made essentially the same argument as to U.S. branching by foreign banks in *Conference of State Bank Supervisors v. Conover*, 715 F.2d 604 (D.C.Cir.1983), *cert.* denied, 466 U.S. 927, 104 S.Ct. 1708 (1984). The D.C. Circuit rejected application of Section 36–like limitations to the Comptroller's decision to license federal branches of foreign banks without "reference over" to state law restrictions on state licensing of such branches. Unlike the legislative policy that informed *Walker Bank, Conference* was guided in its decision by the policy of "national treatment" of foreign banks that informed the International Banking Act of 1978, 12 U.S.C.A. §§ 3101 *et seq*.

was absorbed by the provisions of §§ 36(c)(1) and (2), regardless of the tag placed upon it.[13]

Hence, whether, where, and how national banks may branch intrastate are all questions subject to reference over to applicable state law embodied in Section 36(c). This policy of "competitive equality" has been extended to such issues as whether the needs of the community in which a proposed national bank branch would operate were sufficiently served by existing branches.[14] Failure to follow explicitly such a state law requirement would render the Comptroller's decision in contravention of law.[15] The level of this analysis descends to a minute level of detail, including such issues as whether or not the Comptroller's approval properly determined, for example, that the proposed site of a branch was a "town" within the meaning of applicable state law.[16]

Some modest limitations on the "reference over" analysis under Section 36(c) have been recognized by the courts. A state statutory requirement that prohibits a branch in any city or town in which its principal place of business is located, except by acquiring an existing bank, apparently does not prevent the Comptroller from authorizing a national bank to acquire existing *branches* of another national bank in exchange for its existing branches.[17] The congressional policy of competitive equality can be read to authorize exchange of branches under the NBA if state banks are able to exchange branches under state banking law.[18] Alternatively, where a state restricts branching into the "home office" location of another bank, the Comptroller may still authorize a national bank branch in a home office location, if the national bank relocates *its* home office to the site of the proposed branch.[19] In addition, if a particular state has no explicit statutory provisions for branching of state-chartered banks, but does have such provisions for other depository institutions, such as state savings associations, then the Comptroller may authorize branching by national banks in the state.[20]

§ 3.4   Meaning of "Branch"

One issue that has been the source of considerable controversy is the meaning of "branch" for purposes of the NBA. The federal statutory

---

13. *Walker Bank*, 385 U.S. at 262, 87 S.Ct. at 497.

14. *Hempstead Bank v. Smith*, 540 F.2d 57 (2d Cir.1976).

15. *Id.*

16. *First Union Bank & Trust Co. v. Heimann*, 600 F.2d 91 (7th Cir.1979) (applying Indiana branch banking requirement, Ind. Code § 28–1–17). *See also American Bank & Trust Co. v. Saxon*, 373 F.2d 283 (6th Cir.1967); *Peoples Bank of Trenton v. Saxon*, 373 F.2d 185 (6th Cir.1967); *Security Bank v. Saxon*, 298 F.Supp. 991 (E.D.Mich.1968); *Marion Nat'l Bank v. Van Buren Bank*, 418 F.2d 121, 124 (7th Cir. 1969); *First Nat'l Bank of Crown Point v. Camp*, 463 F.2d 595 (7th Cir.1972); *Albion Nat. Bank v. Department of Fin. Insts.*, 171 Ind.App. 211, 355 N.E.2d 873 (1976).

17. *State ex rel. Edwards v. Heimann*, 633 F.2d 886, 889–890 (9th Cir.1980) (noting Section 36(c) reference to establishment and operation of "new branches").

18. *Id.* (*citing Seattle Trust & Sav. Bank v. Bank of Ca.*, 492 F.2d 48, 52 (9th Cir.), *cert. denied*, 419 U.S. 844, 95 S.Ct. 77 (1974); *Dakota Nat'l Bank & Trust v. First Nat'l Bank*, 554 F.2d 345, 355 (8th Cir.), *cert. denied*, 434 U.S. 877, 98 S.Ct. 229 (1977)).

19. *Ramapo Bank v. Camp*, 425 F.2d 333 (3d Cir.1970), *cert. denied*, 400 U.S. 828, 91 S.Ct. 57 (applying 12 U.S.C.A. §§ 30, 36).

20. *Department of Banking v. Clarke*, 809 F.2d 266 (5th Cir.), *cert. denied*, 483 U.S. 1010, 107 S.Ct. 3240 (1987).

definition provides in part that a branch is "any branch bank, branch office, branch agency, additional office, or any branch place of business located in any State or Territory of the United States or in the District of Columbia at which deposits are received, or checks paid, or money lent."[1] Despite the fact that the NBA provides its own definition for this concept, in *First National Bank in Plant City v. Dickinson*[2] the Supreme Court interpreted the term in light of the policy of "competitive equality" that it had previously held to be the basic principle embodied in the NBA branching provision.[3] The end result, counterintuitive as it may seem, was that armored cars and deposit drop boxes were interpreted to be branches.

The situs of the national bank in *Plant City* was Florida, which prohibited all branch banking by state chartered banks, and hence by all national banks as well.[4] The Comptroller permitted the bank to operate an armored car messenger service and an off-premises receptacle for the receipt of packages containing cash or checks for deposit.[5] The Comptroller's letters authorizing the services contained explicit requirements that deposits received through these services not become bank liabilities until actually in the hands of the bank teller at the office of the bank, and that checks cashed for customers be deemed paid at the bank when the cash was handed to the messenger, not when delivered to the customer by the armored car teller.[6] The Florida Bank Comptroller challenged the services, arguing that Florida unequivocally prohibited off-premises banking of any kind.[7] Thus, the question was whether the services constituted the establishment and operation of a "branch." In the Court's view, this question was governed by federal law.[8] Nevertheless, the Court invoked the policy of competitive equality in resolving the issue. The Court explained:

> The policy of competitive equality is ... firmly embedded in the statutes governing the national banking system. The mechanism of referring to state law is simply one designed to implement that congressional intent and build into the federal statute a self-executing provision to accommodate to changes in state regulation....

> Although the definition [of branch] may not be a model of precision, in part due to its circular aspect, it defines the minimum content of the term "branch"; by use of the word "include" the definition suggests a calculated indefiniteness with respect to the other limits of the term. However, the term "branch bank" at the

---

§ 3.4

1. 12 U.S.C.A. § 36(j).

2. 396 U.S. 122, 90 S.Ct. 337 (1969).

3. *First Nat'l Bank of Logan v. Walker Bank & Trust Co.*, 385 U.S. 252, 87 S.Ct. 492 (1966).

4. *Plant City*, 396 U.S. at 124–125, 90 S.Ct. at 339.

5. 396 U.S. at 125–126, 90 S.Ct. at 339.

6. 396 U.S. at 126, 90 S.Ct. at 339.

7. 396 U.S. at 130–131. 90 S.Ct. at 342.

8. 396 U.S. at 133–134, 90 S.Ct. at 343.

very least includes any place for receiving deposits or paying checks or lending money apart from the chartered premises; it may include more. It should be emphasized that, since § 36(f) [currently codified as § 36(j)] is phrased in the disjunctive, the offering of any one of the three services mentioned in that definition will provide the basis for finding that "branch" banking is taking place. Thus not only the taking of deposits but also the paying of checks or the lending of money could equally well provide the basis for such a finding....

Because the purpose of the statute is to maintain competitive equality, it is relevant in construing "branch" to consider, not merely the contractual rights and liabilities created by the transaction, but all those aspects of the transaction that might give the bank an advantage in its competition for customers. Unquestionably, a competitive advantage accrues to a bank that provides the service of receiving money for deposit at a place away from its main office; the convenience to the customer is unrelated to whether the relationship of debtor and creditor is established at the moment of receipt or somewhat later....

Since the putative deposits are in fact "received" by a bank facility apart from its chartered place of business, we are compelled, in construing § 36(f), to view the place of delivery of the customer's cash and checks accompanied by a deposit slip as an "additional office, or * * * branch place of business * * * at which deposits are received."...[9]

The broad sweep of *Plant City*'s approach to the meaning of the term "branch" caused its own complications. Rather than the simple dichotomy of things that were "branches" and things that were not, *Plant City* created a banking world in which there was a middle category of things that *might* be "branches" in some rarified sense. In this realm, "common sense" was no longer the guide.[10]

---

9.   396 U.S. at 133, 135–137, 90 S.Ct. at 343–345.

10.   Justice Douglas in dissent in *Plant City* invoked common sense as a guide to his decision:

It will come as a shock, where common sense is the guide, to learn that an armored car picking up merchants' cash boxes and checks is a branch bank. Conceivably a bank could use an armored car as a place of business by stationing it at designated places during designated hours for opening accounts, receiving, deposits, making loans, and the like. But no armored car was so used in these cases.

... The opinion of the Court leaves the impression that the McFadden Act created "competitive equality" between national and state banks across the board. But as we stated in the *Walker Bank* case, that Act "intended to place national

and state banks on a basis of 'competitive equality' *insofar as branch banking was concerned." Id.*, at 261. (Italics added.) There was no other or additional overriding principle of "competitive equality" that limited off-premises services of national banks to those that state banks could provide.

Among those off-premises activities of national banks was the furnishing of armored car messenger services, which, we are advised by the Comptroller of the Currency, antedated by many years the 1927 McFadden Act. One can read the legislative history of the Act without finding any hint that Congress was providing "competitive equality" as respects armored car messenger services....

... Certainly the Comptroller, who is the supervisory agent for policing § 36, has some authority to define "deposits"

§ 3.5 *Plant City* and the Emergence of New Technologies

One major difficulty that arose in the wake of *Plant City* concerned the newly emerging technology of customer-bank communication terminals, or ATMs ("automated transfer machines"), as they are now generally known.[1] In the face of *Plant City*, the Comptroller approved the use of ATMs, relying upon precisely the sort of rationale that was rejected by the Supreme Court in the case of armored cars and drop boxes.

Following *Plant City*, many federal courts had occasion to reaffirm the preeminence of "reference over" to state law with respect to branching. In *First National Bank v. Camp*,[2] the District of Columbia Circuit held that, in considering a branch application, the Comptroller was not bound by an opinion of a state administrative officer interpreting state law. However, the court also emphasized that the Comptroller was bound by the statute law of the state. In *Driscoll v. Northwestern National Bank*,[3] the Eighth Circuit expressed concern over the Comptroller's determination that a national bank could maintain a group of walk-up television tellers, where a state bank would be limited to one, and remanded the case to the Comptroller for further consideration.

Several district courts were confronted with the question whether ATMs of various types were "branches" within the meaning of Section 36. In *Independent Bankers v. Camp*,[4] the District of Oregon held that, in the absence of a specific state statute authorizing state banks to install and operate ATMs, Section 36(c) prohibited their establishment by national banks. In *Colorado ex rel. State Bank Board v. First National Bank*,[5] the District of Colorado held that an electronic facility was a "branch" within the meaning of Section 36, because it received deposits, not because it paid checks or lent money. In *Illinois ex rel. Lignoul v. Continental Illinois National Bank & Trust Co.*,[6] the Northern District of Illinois held that "the functions performed by [ATMs], both unmanned and manned, constitute making a deposit or lending money within the meaning of 12 U.S.C.A. § 36(f) [now codified at § 36(j)] . . . [but that] cash withdrawals as presently effectuated by ATMs do not constitute cashing checks."[7] Other district courts in the meantime came

as used in § 36(f) [currently codified as § 36(j)], and this case affords no excuse for disparaging him.

396 U.S. at 138–140, 90 S.Ct. at 345–346.

§ 3.5

1. Despite considerable litigation, discussed *infra*, this question was not definitively resolved by the Congress until 1996, with the amendment of Section 36(j) (formerly 36(f)) by Pub. L. No. 104–208, § 2205(a), 110 Stat. 3009 (Sept. 30, 1996) (*codified at* 12 U.S.C.A. § 36(j)).

2. 465 F.2d 586 (D.C.Cir.1972).

3. 484 F.2d 173 (8th Cir.1973).

4. 357 F.Supp. 1352 (D.Or.1973).

5. 394 F.Supp. 979 (D.Colo.1975).

6. 409 F.Supp. 1167 (N.D.Ill.1975).

7. *Id.* at 1181. In September 1994, § 36(f) was redesignated as "36(j)." *See* Pub. L. No. 103–328, § 102(b) (1)(A), 108 Stat. 2349, 2352 (Sept. 29, 1994) (redesignating former § 36(f) as 36(j)), *as amended*, Pub. L. No. 104–208, § 2205(a), 110 Stat. 3009 (Sept. 30, 1996) (*codified at* 12 U.S.C.A. § 36(j)).

up with conflicting answers on the question of whether ATMs were branches.[8]

The definitive challenge to the Comptroller's authorization of national bank ATMs came in *Independent Bankers Association of America v. Smith* ("*Independent Bankers*").[9] There the D.C. Circuit held that ATMs were "branches" within the meaning of Section 36 of the National Bank Act, because all ATMs—whether on-line directly to the bank or independent—perform at least one of the three specified branch services ("deposits . . . received, checks paid, or money lent"). In so holding, the court relied explicitly on *Plant City* and its application of the "competitive equality" policy to the federal definition of "branch."[10] Several circuits quickly followed the reasoning in *Independent Bankers* and held that similar electronic devices established by national banks were "branches," and thus subject to federal and state restrictions on branch banking.[11]

Following the decision in *Independent Bankers*, the Comptroller abandoned its previous position.[12] Thereafter, it seemed clear "that when a national bank makes use of [an ATM], it is engaging in 'branch banking,' at least where the [ATM] is located away from the bank's main business premises."[13]

However, in *State Bank of Fargo v. Merchants' National Bank & Trust*,[14] the Eighth Circuit confronted a curious conceptual problem that arose out of the uneasy fit between Section 36(c) and the actions that several states had taken in response to the Comptroller's original position on ATMs. In North Dakota, public policy with respect to branch banking had been restrictive, and North Dakota banks were generally not permitted to engage in off-premises operations. As of 1975, the powers of state banks in North Dakota law did not include the operation of ATMs. The Comptroller's original position on ATMs caused understandable concern among state banks, which feared competition with national banks using ATMs. In response, the North Dakota Legislature adopted legislation in 1975 that permitted state banks to provide electronic services to its customers "to the same extent that other financial institutions chartered and regulated by any agency of the federal government are permitted to provide such services within this state."[15] Howev-

---

8. *Kostman v. First Nat'l Bank*, 405 F.Supp. 733 (E.D.Mo.1975) (holding ATMs to be branches); *Oklahoma ex rel. State Banking Bd. v. Utica Nat'l Bank & Trust Co.*, 409 F.Supp. 71 (N.D.Okla.1975) (*contra*).

9. 534 F.2d 921 (D.C.Cir.), *cert. denied*, 429 U.S. 862, 97 S.Ct. 166 (1976).

10. *Id.* at 928–930.

11. *Illinois ex rel. Lignoul v. Continental Ill. Nat'l Bank and Trust Co.*, 536 F.2d 176 (7th Cir.), *cert. denied*, 429 U.S. 871, 97 S.Ct. 184 (1976); *Missouri ex rel. Kostman v. First Nat'l Bank in St. Louis*, 538 F.2d 219 (8th Cir.), *cert. denied*, 429 U.S. 941, 97 S.Ct. 357 (1976); *Colorado ex rel. State Banking Bd. v. First Nat'l Bank of Fort Collins*, 540 F.2d 497 (10th Cir.1976), *cert. denied*, 429 U.S. 1091, 97 S.Ct. 1102 (1977).

12. 41 Fed. Reg. 48,333 (1976).

13. *State Bank of Fargo v. Merchants Nat'l Bank & Trust*, 593 F.2d 341, 344 (8th Cir.1979).

14. *Id.*

15. N.D. Cent. Code § 6–03–02(8).

er, the legislation explicitly provided that an ATM was not considered a "branch."[16]

Consider the position of competing state and national banks in North Dakota following the 1976 decision in *Independent Bankers*. A national bank ATM could only be authorized if it complied with Section 36(c), that is, if state law "expressly authorized to State banks"[17] or authorized "affirmatively and not merely by implication or recognition"[18] such *branches*. But under state law, ATMs, though authorized, were not "branches."

Did this mean, in light of *Independent Bankers*, that ATMs could not be authorized for national banks operating in North Dakota?[19] At the time that the State Bank of Fargo challenged the Comptroller's authorization of ATMs to Merchants National Bank & Trust in 1977, federal savings and loan associations and federal credit unions were being permitted to operate ATMs, known as remote service units ("RSUs").[20] Apparently, this situation would be enough to authorize state banks to operate ATMs, but not as "branches" under North Dakota law. What, then, of national banks in the state? The Eighth Circuit construed the interplay of federal law and the North Dakota statute to permit the Comptroller under Section 36(c) to authorize Merchants National Bank & Trust to maintain and operate its Fargo ATMs as "branches."[21]

This case may represent vengeance upon Judge Wilkey's hypothetical in *Independent Bankers*. Law professors endure all sorts of abuse about the unrealistic nature of their hypotheticals, no matter how elegant they (always) are. Yet consider Judge Wilkey's famous hypothetical from *Independent Bankers*:

> Suppose, for example, that the national bank in *Plant City* is now receiving deposits, paying checks, and lending money through the agency of several [ATMs], rather than an armored car and a shopping center receptacle. Florida prohibits all branch banking by state chartered banks, and we will assume that since *Plant City* there has been only the following change in Florida banking law: According to a recent state administrative opinion or ruling interpreting state law, [ATMs] are not considered "branches" for purposes of state law. Because under these assumed facts Florida statute law does not specifically and affirmatively grant to state banks the authority to

---

16. This was a prevalent problem among a large number of states that authorized state bank ATMs but explicitly did not define them as "branches." *See Independent Bankers Ass'n of N.Y. v. Marine Midland Bank*, 757 F.2d 453, 461 n. 4 (2d Cir.1985) (noting that many states did not classify ATMs as "branches").

17. 12 U.S.C.A. § 36(c)(1).

18. *Id.* § 36(c)(2).

19. Fighting the hypothetical, the D.C. Circuit in *Independent Bankers* had simply denied that this situation would present a

practical problem. *Independent Bankers*, 534 F.2d at 948 n. 104.

20. *State Bank of Fargo v. Merchants Nat'l Bank & Trust Co. of Fargo*, 451 F.Supp. 775, 784 n. 14 (D.N.D.1978). Furthermore, at the time of the district court's decision in 1978, federal credit unions were still being permitted to use RSUs. *Id.* at 790 nn.32–33.

21. *State Bank of Fargo*, 593 F.2d at 344–346.

establish and operate [ATMs] without complying with the state's anti-branching statute, narrow interpretation of section 36(c) could prevent the Comptroller from approving national bank [ATMs] in Florida. We reject this narrow construction of section 36(c) for two reasons. First, as Judge MacKinnon recognized in *First Nat'l Bank v. Camp*, 465 F.2d at 597, the Comptroller can consider and follow the Florida administrative opinion or ruling interpreting the state's branching laws so long as that opinion does not violate the anti-branching standard imposed by the statute law of the state. Second, this narrow reading of section 36(c) would resurrect the precise form of competitive inequality which the McFadden Act was designed to cure. . . . By manipulating their banking statutes and administrative rulings, the states would again be able to secure a competitive advantage for state banks in the field of branching, *i.e.*, under this narrow reading of section 36(c) national bank [ATMs] would be subject to the state's anti-branching statute while state bank [ATMs] would be exempt under a permissive opinion or ruling issued by the state's banking commissioner. We refuse to frustrate legislative intent by adopting this narrow reading of section 36(c)'s language.[22]

What Judge Wilkey failed to realize, of course, was that: (1) the problem was not hypothetical, but reflected the emerging practice of many states with respect to ATMs;[23] and (2) the dilemma presented by his hypothetical problem arose not because of a "narrow reading" the language of the federal statute, but because of the broad sweep of his interpretation of that language.

In *Independent Bankers Association of New York v. Marine Midland Bank*,[24] the Second Circuit confronted yet another interpretive problem left over in the fallout of *Independent Bankers*. If a third party (whether another bank or, in *Marine Midland*, a nonbank) installs an ATM, and makes it available to depositors of a national bank, must that national bank first comply with Section 36(c)? In the typical situation, the ATM is controlled and maintained by the third party, and as to participating banks, it is a shared ATM. However, while it may be clear under *Independent Bankers* that the shared ATM is a "branch" for purposes of Section 36, is it Marine Midland's branch?

The Comptroller took the position that an ATM is not a "branch" of a national bank unless it owns or rents the ATM.[25] Thus, the narrow legal question presented by *Marine Midland* was what the language of Section 36 meant by the phrase "establish and operate" a "branch." The *Independent Bankers* opinion appeared to focus on the relation between "establishing" and "owning or renting."[26] Ultimately, the *Marine Mid-*

---

22. *Independent Bankers*, 534 F.2d at 948 n. 104.

23. *See Independent Bankers Ass'n of New York*, 757 F.2d at 461 n. 4 (noting that many states did not classify ATMs as "branches").

24. *Id*.

25. 12 C.F.R. § 5.31(b) (1985).

26. *See Independent Bankers*, 534 F.2d at 941, 946 n. 98, 951.

land court deferred to the Comptroller's interpretation of Section 36 as a "reasonable construction."[27]

In 1996 Congress brushed up against the implications of the *Plant City* interpretation of "branch" without going to the heart of the matter. The definition of "branch" was amended to read as follows:

> The term "branch" as used in this section shall be held to include any branch bank, branch office, branch agency, additional office, or any branch place of business located in any State or Territory of the United States or in the District of Columbia at which deposits are received, or checks paid, or money lent. *The term "branch", as used in this section, does not include an automated teller machine or a remote service unit.*[28]

Despite this resolution of the question posed by *Independent Bankers* concerning the status of ATMs, the consequences of the decisions in *Plant City* and *Independent Bankers*—creating the middle category of things that might or might not be "branches"—remain untouched by the 1996 amendment of Section 36. When some other new technology or technique emerges[29] that intuitively is not a "branch" if "common sense is the guide,"[30] the broad and counterintuitive interpretation of *Plant City* is still the definitive guidance on the subject.

§ 3.6 Possible Relaxed Approach to the *Plant City* Analysis

The Supreme Court did not reconsider the implications of *Plant City* until 1987, when it decided *Clarke v. Securities Industry Association*,[1] which concerned the legality of the Comptroller's approval of national bank establishment or purchase of discount brokerage subsidiaries. While the case principally affected the scope of Glass–Steagall Act restrictions on securities activities of banks,[2] one argument raised by the Securities Industry Association was that offices of a discount brokerage operation of a national bank would constitute "branches" under the broad concept laid out in *Plant City*. The Comptroller had concluded that the discount brokerage offices would not constitute "branches" because, among other things, no defined branching functions would be performed there.[3] The brokerage operation would provide margin lending, but loan approval would take place at the bank's chartered offices. The brokerage operation would maintain interest-bearing customer balances, but the

---

27. *Marine Midland Bank*, 757 F.2d at 462.

28. 12 U.S.C.A. § 36(j) (emphasis added).

29. *See, e.g.,* Guenther, *Citicorp Skips Computer In New Home–Banking Plan*, Wall St. J., Feb. 28, 1990, at B1, col. 5 (discussing banking at home by means of telephone-like device provided by bank).

30. *Plant City*, 396 U.S. at 138, 90 S.Ct. at 345 (Douglas, J., dissenting).

§ 3.6

1. 479 U.S. 388, 107 S.Ct. 750 (1987).

2. 12 U.S.C.A. §§ 24 (Seventh), 377–378.

3. *Clarke*, 479 U.S. at 391, 107 S.Ct. at 753.

Comptroller believed "that these accounts differ sufficiently in nature from ordinary bank accounts that Discount Brokerage would not be engaged in receiving deposits."[4]

In one respect, the Court's response in *Clarke* was consistent with *Plant City*. Both cases essentially swept aside or ignored the technical issues presented and disposed of the question before it with a dose of legislative history. After twisting and turning through legislative history arguments on both sides of the question, the Court concluded that Congress did not intend to subject a bank's conduct of a securities business to the branching restrictions.[5] How, then, can this decision be squared with the rather broad reading given to the definition of "branch" in *Plant City*? Basically, by ignoring the implications of that decision. To accomplish this, the Court introduced a new interpretive gloss on the federal definition of "branch." The Court's opinion explained:

> The Comptroller reasonably interprets the statute as requiring "competitive equality" *only in core banking functions*, and not in all incidental services in which national banks are authorized to engage. We are not faced today with the need to decide whether there are core banking functions beyond those explicitly enumerated in § 36(f); it suffices, to decide this case, to hold that the operation of a discount brokerage service is not a core banking function.[6]

This conclusion embodies a very odd reading of the scope of *Plant City* and an even odder characterization of the issue presented in *Clarke*. The Court in *Plant City* does not make use of the "core banking functions" terminology; the Court simply applies the NBA definition of "branch" for purposes of Section 36. Nor is there any sense in characterizing the issue before the Court in *Clarke* as a question of whether "operation of a discount brokerage service is . . . a core banking function."[7] The question should be whether a discount brokerage's margin lending and holding of free credit balances (*i.e.*, deposits) caused it to be considered a "branch." The Court's reconstruction of the issues before it is particularly apparent in a footnote in which the Court suggests, hypothetically:

> If the "competitive equality" principle were carried to its logical extreme, the ability of a national bank to carry on an incidental activity such as the safe-deposit business would be limited to the same extent as a state bank's ability to do so under state law.

4. 479 U.S. at 391–392, 107 S.Ct. at 753 (footnote omitted).

5. 479 U.S. at 409, 107 S.Ct. at 762. It should be noted that pre–1927 activities thereafter caught by the federal definition of "branch" were well recognized by Congress in passing the McFadden Act. Prior to the passage of the McFadden Act, for example, national banks operated "agencies" and other "offices," limited to such activities as deposit taking or certain check transactions. On the pre–1927 operations of such offices, see *Cheshire Natl. Bank v. Smith*, 427 F.Supp. 277 (D.N.H.1977). These operations, captured by the broad definition of "branch" contained in former Section 36(f), were grandfathered by Section 36(a).

6. *Clarke*, 479 U.S. at 409, 107 S.Ct. at 762 (emphasis added; footnote omitted).

7. *Id.*

However, as we have noted, the legislative history of the McFadden Act rather clearly indicates that Congress intended national banks to be able to carry on a safe-deposit business without locational restrictions.[8]

Only if the safe deposit business involved "deposits ... received, or checks paid, or money lent"[9] would this issue be raised. Under *Plant City*, the fact that the issue would involve a "safe-deposit business"—or a brokerage business—should be as irrelevant as the fact that an armored car or a dropbox was being used. That this fact is not irrelevant may suggest that the Court is no longer comfortable with the competitive equality principle, which had already been "carried to its logical extreme" in *Plant City* itself. We may expect to see some continued relaxation in judicial approaches to the application of the *Plant City* rationale, as the courts struggle to make sense of the broad implications of that case.

§ 3.7   State Bank Branching

As discussed in § 3.3, *supra*, national banks are, to a significant extent, subject to the same restrictions on branching that apply to state banks in the same state of operation, through the "reference over" provisions of the NBA.[1] However, certain state banks will also be subject to conditions and restrictions on branching under federal statutory law.

This indirect effect occurs through the jurisdiction of the Federal Reserve Board over state member banks and the jurisdiction of the FDIC over state nonmember insured banks. Section 9 of the Federal Reserve Act[2] provides for branching by state member banks to the same extent permissible to national banks. Similarly, the Federal Deposit Insurance Act subjects state nonmember insured banks to prior approval by the FDIC before a branch bank can be established.[3] The FDIC's determination in this regard will be based upon the same factors that the FDIC considers in deciding whether or not to insure a principal office.[4]

Nevertheless, for the most part, the substantive restrictions on state bank branching are a matter of state law, and they can vary considerably from state to state. The latest trend in state branching policy has been to link state bank powers (including, in some cases, the ability to branch) to permissible national bank powers.[5] A majority of states now appear to have adopted such a "wild card" approach to the scope of state bank powers.

8. 479 U.S. at 409 n. 23, 107 S.Ct. at 762 n. 23.

9. 12 U.S.C.A. § 36(j).

§ 3.7

1. 12 U.S.C.A. § 36(c).

2. *Id.* § 321.

3. *Id.* § 1828(d).

4. *See id.* §§ 1816, 1828(d).

5. *See, e.g., State Bank of Fargo v. Merchants Nat'l Bank & Trust*, 593 F.2d 341 (8th Cir.1979) (discussing N.D. Cent. Code § 6–03–02(8)). *See also* Henry N. Butler, *The Competitive Equality Doctrine and the Demise of Intrastate Bank Branching Restrictions*, 55 Tenn. L. Rev. 703 (1988) (discussing "wild card" state banking statutes).

§ 3.8   Savings Association Branching

Savings association branching is not subject to the strictures applicable to national banks under Section 36(c).[1] However, savings associations are required to obtain approval from their regulator before establishing and operating branches.[2] For example, in the case of federally chartered savings associations, Section 5 of HOLA[3] makes no reference to branching. From the beginning, the Federal Home Loan Bank Board ("FHLBB") and its successor, the OTS, have taken the position that the agency has statutory power to authorize branches,[4] and this position has been upheld.[5] HOLA is still largely silent on the subject,[6] except for interstate branching rules applicable to savings associations.[7]

§ 3.9   Credit Union Branching

In an interpretive ruling and policy statement published in July 1989,[1] the NCUA took a markedly different approach to branching from

---

§ 3.8

1. *State Bank of Fargo v. Merchants Nat'l Bank & Trust*, 593 F.2d 341 (8th Cir.1979).

2. *See generally* Kenneth E. Scott, *In Quest of Reason: The Licensing Decisions of the Federal Banking Agencies*, 42 U. Chi. L. Rev. 235, 239–242 (1975) (contrasting branch approval processes of Comptroller and FHLBB, predecessor to Office of Thrift Supervision).

3. 12 U.S.C.A. § 1464.

4. 12 C.F.R. § 545.92 (authorizing branch offices). Establishment of a drive-in or pedestrian office opened in conjunction with an approved branch or home office requires no additional approval from the OTS. *Id.* § 545.92(g).

5. *See, e.g., Independent Bankers Ass'n v. Federal Home Loan Bank Bd.*, 557 F.Supp. 23 (D.D.C.1982) (upholding FHLBB policy statements allowing federally regulated savings and loan associations to acquire or open branch offices in states other than association's home state as exempt from APA notice and comment requirements under 5 U.S.C.A. § 553).

6. *But see* 12 U.S.C.A. § 1464(m)(1), which provides:

(m) Branching

(1) In general

(A) No savings association incorporated under the laws of the District of Columbia or organized in the District or doing business in the District shall establish any branch or move its principal of-

fice or any branch without the Director's prior written approval.

(B) No savings association shall establish any branch in the District of Columbia or move its principal office or any branch in the District without the Director's prior written approval.

For purposes of Section 1464(m)(1), "branch" is defined to mean:

any office, place of business, or facility, other than the principal office as defined by the Director [of the Office of Thrift Supervision], of a savings association at which accounts are opened or payments are received or withdrawals are made, or any other office, place of business, or facility of a savings association *defined by the Director as a branch within the meaning of such sentence.*

12 U.S.C.A. § 1464(m)(2) (emphasis added). Thus, unlike NBA, HOLA specifically allows the OTS to define the scope of the term "branch" for these purposes. *Compare* 12 U.S.C.A. § 36(j) (NBA definition of "branch"), *with* 12 U.S.C.A. § 1464(m)(2) (HOLA definition).

7. 12 U.S.C.A. § 1464(r). *See* 12 C.F.R. § 556.5 (interstate branching by federal savings associations generally permitted). Interstate branching is subject to prior approval by the OTS. 12 C.F.R. §§ 545.92, 556.5(c).

§ 3.9

1. 54 Fed. Reg. 31,165 (1989). The NCUA has retained this policy with respect that expressed in *Independent Bankers Association v. Smith*.[2] In discussing its policy with respect to chartering of a federal credit union to serve a combination of distinct occupational and associational groups (a "multiple-group charter"),[3] the NCUA has stated that, "[f]or chartering purposes, 'branch office' means any office of a Federal credit union where an employee accepts payment on shares and disburses loans. *An ATM or similar cash disbursing machine does not qualify as a 'branch office.'*"[4]

§ 3.10   Interstate Branching

The Riegle–Neal Interstate Banking and Branching Efficiency Act of 1994 ("IBBEA")[1] has authorized interstate geographic expansion by banks, without regard to artificial barriers to interstate expansion heretofore imposed by the branching provisions of state law and the NBA.[2] IBBEA permits interstate branching directly, through the establishment of *de novo* interstate branches.[3]

The Comptroller of the Currency is authorized by the IBBEA to approve the establishment and operation of *de novo* interstate national bank branches.[4] This authority is available only if the host state[5] has enacted legislation, applicable equally to all banks, that expressly per-

to ATMs in the revised version of its rules. *See* 63 Fed. Reg. 71,998, 72,002 (1998) (*codified at* 12 C.F.R. Pt. 701) (discussing IRPS 99–1, replacing previous IRPS 89–1 but retaining ATM policy).

2. 534 F.2d 921 (D.C.Cir.), *cert. denied*, 429 U.S. 862, 97 S.Ct. 166 (1976).

3. Multigroup charters were invalidated as unauthorized under the Federal Credit Union Act in *National Credit Union Admin. v. First Nat'l Bank & Trust Co.*, 522 U.S. 479, 118 S.Ct. 927 (1998). Subsequent legislation has overridden *First National*. Credit Union Membership Access Act, Pub. L. No. 105–219, § 101(2), Aug. 7, 1998, 112 Stat. 913, 914–917 (1998) (codified at 12 U.S.C.A. § 1759(b)-(e)).

4. 54 Fed. Reg. at 31,170 (emphasis added). The status of bank ATMs has been made consistent with the NCUA approach by statute. The Economic Growth and Regulatory Paperwork Reduction Act, Pub. L. No. 104–208, § 2204 (a), 110 Stat. 3009 (1996) (*codified at* 12 U.S.C.A. § 36(j)), eliminated ATMs from the federal definition of "branch" for purposes of the National Bank Act.

§ 3.10

1. Pub. L. No. 103–328, 108 Stat. 2338 (Sept. 29, 1994) ("IBBEA").

2. *See, e.g.*, 12 U.S.C.A. § 36(c) (limiting branching by national banks). *Cf. First Nat'l Bank of Logan v. Walker Bank & Trust Co.*, 385 U.S. 252, 87 S.Ct. 492 (1966) (construing § 36(c)); *First Nat'l Bank in Plant City v. Dickinson*, 396 U.S. 122, 90 S.Ct. 337 (1969), 396 U.S. 122, 90 S.Ct. 337 (considering meaning of "branch" for purposes of § 36(c)).

3. IBBEA § 103, 108 Stat. at 2352 (*codified at* 12 U.S.C.A. §§ 36(g), 1828(d)(4)).

4. For these purposes, "*de novo* branch" is defined to mean a national bank branch that

(i) is originally established by the national bank as a branch; and

(ii) does not become a branch of such bank as a result of—

(I) the acquisition by the bank of an insured depository institution or a branch of an insured depository institution; or

(II) the conversion, merger, or consolidation of any such institution or branch.

12 U.S.C.A. § 36(g)(3)(A)(i)-(ii).

5. For these purposes, "host state" is defined to mean "with respect to a bank, a State, other than the home State of the bank, in which the bank maintains, or seeks to establish and maintain, a branch." *Id.* § 36(g)(3)(C).

mits all out-of-state banks to establish branches in the state.[6] Almost all states have acted to allow interstate branching into their respective jurisdictions in some form.[7] Arkansas, Colorado, Iowa, Kansas, Missouri, and Texas have either refrained from authorizing interstate branching into their respective jurisdictions or have explicitly prohibited such branching.[8]

Approval of a *de novo* interstate national bank branch is subject to the same requirements and conditions applicable to interstate merger transactions concerning state filing requirements,[9] community reinvestment,[10] and adequacy of capital and management.[11] In addition, each *de novo* interstate national bank branch is subject to state and federal antitrust laws[12] and to limitations on the operation of additional branches,[13] to the same extent that such laws and limitations would apply to a branch resulting from an interstate merger transaction.[14]

The FDIC is authorized by the IBBEA to approve *de novo* interstate branches of insured state nonmember banks, subject to rules corresponding to those applicable to interstate national bank branches.[15] That is, approval of interstate branches of insured state nonmember banks requires state legislation expressly permitting such branches.[16] FDIC approval is also subject to compliance of the interstate branch with state filing requirements, community reinvestment, and adequacy of capital and management applicable to interstate merger transactions.[17] Finally, state and federal antitrust laws and limitations on the operation of additional branches also apply to these interstate branches.[18]

Following the creation of an interstate branching operation under the IBBEA, a bank might consider consolidating its operations to eliminate unnecessary or unprofitable branches. The effect on a low- or moderate-income areas[19] served by such a branch could be seriously

---

6. *Id.* § 36(g)(1)(A)(i)-(ii).

7. 4 Fed. Banking L. Rep. (CCH) ¶ 45-651.

8. Source: BNA Banking Daily; individual state codes. These states have either explicitly opted out of the IBBEA, have otherwise prohibited interstate branching into their respective jurisdictions, or have no statutory provision with respect to interstate branches.

9. *See* 12 U.S.C.A. § 1831u(b)(1).

10. *See id.* § 1831u(b)(3).

11. *Id.* § 36(g)(2)(A). *See id.* § 1831u(b)(4) (setting forth capital and management adequacy requirement).

12. *Id.* § 1831u(c).

13. *Id.* § 1831u(d)(2).

14. *Id.* § 36(g)(2)(B).

15. *Id.* § 1828(d)(4).

16. *Compare id.* § 36(g)(1) (NBA provision), *with id.* § 1828(d)(4)(A) (corresponding FDIA provision).

17. *Compare id.* § 36(g)(1)(B), (2)(A) (NBA provision), *with id.* § 1828(d)(4)(A)(ii), (B)(i) (corresponding FDIA provision).

18. *Compare id.* § 36(g)(2)(B) (NBA provision), *with id.* § 1828(d)(4)(B)(ii) (corresponding FDIA provision).

19. For these purposes, the term "low- or moderate-income area" is defined to mean

a census tract for which the median family income is—

(i) less than 80 percent of the median family income for the metropolitan statistical area (as designated by the Director of the Office of Management and Budget) in which the census tract is located; or

(ii) in the case of a census tract which is not located in a metropolitan statistical area, less than 80 percent of the median family income for the State in which the census tract is located, as determined adverse. The IBBEA requires interstate banks to comply with branch closure notice requirements of the Federal Deposit Insurance Act.[20] If a person from an affected area submits a written request to the appropriate federal banking agency (including a statement of specific reasons for the request and a discussion of the adverse effect of the closing on the availability of banking services in the area)[21] and the agency concludes that the request is not frivolous,[22] the agency is required to consult and meet with community leaders and other appropriate parties

> to explore the feasibility of obtaining adequate alternative facilities and services for the affected area, including the establishment of a new branch by another depository institution, or the establishment of a community development credit union, following the closing of the branch.[23]

However, no action by the agency in this regard affects the authority of the bank to close the branch, so long as it meets the generally applicable provisions with respect to branch closure notice.[24] The bank still controls the timing of the branch closing.[25]

The IBBEA requires the banking agencies to promulgate implementing regulations that include guidelines ensuring that interstate branches of an out-of-state bank reasonably help to meet the credit needs of the communities within the host state where the branches are located.[26] The regulations must also require that, not later than one year after establishment or acquisition of an interstate branch in a host state, the branch must be appreciably serving the credit needs of its local community.[27] If the appropriate agency determines that the bank's level of lending in the host state is less than half the average of total loans in the host state relative to total deposits for all banks for which the interstate bank's host state is the home state, the agency must then review the loan portfolio of the bank to determine if it is reasonably helping to meet the credit needs of the communities served in the host state.[28]

If the agency determines that the bank is not meeting this responsibility, it may order the interstate branch to be closed, unless the bank provides reasonable assurances, to the agency's satisfaction, that it has an acceptable plan reasonably designed to help the credit needs of the local community.[29] In addition, the bank is prohibited from opening any new interstate branch in the host state, unless it provides such reasonable assurances.[30]

without taking into account family income in metropolitan statistical areas in such State.
Id. § 1831r–1(d)(4)(B)(i)-(ii).

20. *Id*. § 1831r–1(d)(1) (subjecting interstate banks to notice requirement of § 1831r–1(b)(2)).

21. *Id*. § 1831r–1(d)(2)(A)(i)–(ii).

22. *Id*. § 1831r–1(d)(2)(B).

23. *Id*. § 1831r–1(d)(2).

24. *Id*. § 1831r–1(d)(3).

25. *Id*.

26. *Id*. § 1835a note.

27. IBBEA, § 109(c)(1).

28. IBBEA, § 109(c)(1)(A).

29. IBBEA, § 109(c)(1)(B)(i). *See* IBBEA, § 109(c)(3) (procedures applicable to branch closing).

30. IBBEA, § 109(c)(1)(B)(ii).

Of course, the traditional approach to ensuring local community involvement by banks has been to condition approval of bank regulatory applications on adequate performance by the applicant under the Community Reinvestment Act of 1977 ("CRA").[31] The IBBEA amended the CRA to provide specific rules for CRA evaluation of banks with interstate branches.[32] A bank with domestic branches in two or more states must be evaluated by its federal regulator under the CRA not only on its entire record of performance,[33] but also on a state-by-state basis,[34] and on a separate basis, for each multistate metropolitan area served by branches in different states within the area.[35]

31. 12 U.S.C.A. §§ 2901 *et seq.*

32. *Id.* § 2906(d)-(e).

33. *See id.* § 2906(a)-(c), (d)(1)(A).

34. *Id.* § 2906(d)(1)(B). On the required content of these state-by-state evaluations, see *id.* § 2906(d)(3).

35. *Id.* § 2906(d)(2). *Cf. id.* § 2906(b)(1)(B) (requiring separate presentations for each metropolitan area in which a regulated depository institution maintains a domestic branch).

Chapter 4

CONTROL TRANSACTIONS

Table of Sections

---

§ 4.1   Introduction

Regulatory concerns over the exercise of control have steadily increased since the 1950s, and the area is now one primarily governed by statutory solutions. This chapter considers federal statutory and regulatory efforts specifically intended to supervise acquisitions and other changes in control of depository institutions.

It may be useful, as a preliminary matter, to consider the meaning of the concept of "control." This term has a diverse range of general and technical meanings. Regulatory concepts of "control" reflect the notion, first advanced by Berle and Means,[1] that corporate control is exercised

§ 4.1

1. *See* A. A. BERLE & G. MEANS, THE
MODERN CORPORATION AND PRIVATE PROPERTY
69–70 (1932) (establishing concept).

80

by the individual or group having actual power, directly or indirectly, to select the directors, or otherwise to dictate, directly or indirectly, the management and policies of the corporation. The obvious problem is, of course, how to identify situations involving "indirect" dictation of management and policies.

The federal change-in-control statute, examined later in this chapter, deals with this problem by defining the concept of "control" as "the power, directly or indirectly, to direct the management or policies ... or to vote 25 per centum of any class of voting securities."[2] The Bank Holding Company Act ("BHCA")[3] contains a similar, but more elaborate, version of this definition of "control."[4] It defines the concept primarily in terms of (1) direct or indirect ownership of at least 25 percent of any class of voting securities;[5] or (2) control "in any manner" of the election of a majority of the directors or trustees.[6] In addition, the BHCA adds an explicit statutory device for an administrative determination that a company "directly or indirectly exercises a controlling influence over the management or policies of [a] bank."[7]

The federal securities laws provide other, more specialized concepts of "control."[8] The concept is used more as a trigger for the imposition of disclosure duties[9] or secondary liability[10] than as the basis for direct, substantive regulation of the control relationship itself,[11] as is the case under bank regulatory law.

2. 12 U.S.C.A. § 1817(j)(8)(B). On the concept of "control" under Section 1817(j), see *Federal Deposit Ins. Corp. v. D'Annunzio*, 524 F.Supp. 694 (N.D.W.Va.1981).

3. 12 U.S.C.A. §§ 1841 *et seq.*

4. The federal savings and loan holding company ("SLHC") provisions, 12 U.S.C.A. § 1467a, contain a definition of "control" that is in all material respects identical to that contained in the BHCA.

5. 12 U.S.C.A. § 1841(a)(2)(A).

6. *Id.* § 1841(a)(2)(B).

7. *Id.* § 1841(a)(2)(C). On the meaning of "control" for purposes of the BHCA, see *Huston v. Board of Governors*, 758 F.2d 275 (8th Cir.1985).

8. For discussion of "control" with respect to securities regulation, see *Chromalloy Am. Corp. v. Sun Chem. Corp.*, 611 F.2d 240 (8th Cir.1979) (discussing influence as element of "control"); *FMC Corp. v. Boesky*, 727 F.Supp. 1182 (N.D.Ill.1989), *aff'd sub nom. In re Ivan F. Boesky Sec. Litig.*, 36 F.3d 255 (2d Cir.1994) (finding recapitalization not involving change in control of corporation). *Graphic Sciences, Inc. v. International Mogul Mines Ltd.*, 397 F.Supp. 112 (D.D.C.1974) (discussing realities of commerce as determinative of control).

9. *See, e.g.*, 15 U.S.C.A. § 78p(a) (requiring disclosure of insider securities purchases).

10. *See, e.g.*, 12 U.S.C.A. § 78t(a) (concerning secondary liability of "controlling person").

11. *But cf.* 15 U.S.C.A. § 78c(a)(18) (including "person directly or indirectly controlling, controlled by, or under common control with such broker or dealer" within meaning of term "person associated with a broker or dealer"); *Id.* § 78c(a)(21) (including "person directly or indirectly controlling, controlled by, or under common control with such member" within term "person associated with a member"); *Id.* § 78c(a)(32) (including "person directly or indirectly controlling [municipal securities dealer's] activities or controlled by the municipal securities dealer in connection with such activities" within term "person associated with a municipal securities dealer"); *Id.* § 78c(a)(45) (including "person directly or indirectly controlling, controlled by, or under common control with ... government securities broker or government securities dealer" within term "person associated with a government securities broker or government securities dealer").

§ 4.2 Holding Company Acquisitions

Holding company acquisition of a depository institution may involve the establishment of a new holding company enterprise or the expansion of an existing one. The use of the holding company structure is a dominant trend in the corporate law and practice of depository institutions. The creation of such a structure typically occurs in one of three circumstances, as illustrated in Figure 4–1, *infra*. In many cases, a depository institution may "spin up" a holding company of its own. The formation of the holding company amounts to a reorganization of the corporate structure of a preexisting enterprise.[1]

FIGURE 4-1
Creating the Holding Company Structure

In other cases, a company may emerge as a holding company of a depository institution through the *de novo* chartering of a depository institution subsidiary.[2] Finally, a holding company enterprise may emerge or expand through the acquisition of a preexisting, independent depository institution.[3] In these last two situations, the process of formation of the holding company enterprise may be viewed as a method of entry into the regulated industry by the holding company. In general, the statutory requirements applicable to the process of formation of a

---

§ 4.2

1. E.g., *Board of Governors v. First Lincolnwood Corp.*, 439 U.S. 234, 99 S.Ct. 505 (1978) (providing example of spin up establishment of bank holding company).

2. *See, e.g., Deerbrook State Bank v. Conover*, 568 F.Supp. 696 (N.D.Ill.1983) (involving challenge to chartering of 31 national banks by Dimension Financial Corp.). *See also Board of Governors v. Dimension Fin. Corp.*, 474 U.S. 361, 106 S.Ct. 681 (1986) (upholding acquisitions despite contrary Fed regulations). *Cf. Synovus Fin. Corp., v. Board of Governors*, 952 F.2d 426 (D.C.Cir.1991) (finding no Fed authority over "acquisition" by relocation of subsidiary bank from one state to another); *State of Idaho, Dep't of Fin. v. Clarke*, 994 F.2d 1441 (9th Cir.1993) (declining to follow *Synovus*).

3. *See, e.g., Commercial Nat'l Bank of Little Rock v. Board of Governors*, 451 F.2d 86 (8th Cir.1971) (involving challenge to acquisition of preexisting bank by one-bank holding company); *Centerre Bancorporation v. Kemper*, 682 F.Supp. 459 (E.D.Mo.1988).

holding company enterprise do not make appreciable distinctions between reorganization- and entry-motivated acquisitions.

Essentially, holding company formation or expansion involves some form of corporate reorganization or acquisition following typical acquisition methods. Tax consequences aside, the most obvious and straightforward method for forming the holding company system would be the purchase of the outstanding stock of the subject institution by the prospective holding company, or in the alternative, the exchange of short-term debt instruments issued by the holding company in exchange for the voting stock of the subject institution. The purchase or exchange would, however, be a taxable event for the institution's former shareholders.

In order to make the transaction more attractive to the institution's shareholders, therefore, the prospective holding company will structure it as a corporate reorganization that is not considered a taxable transaction under the Internal Revenue Code,[4] thus postponing indefinitely the recognition of taxable gain. Three principal alternative methods of reorganization have been frequently utilized in this regard.[5] First, a statutory merger or consolidation may involve the merger of the target bank with a "phantom bank" subsidiary of the holding company. The merger itself would be governed by the Bank Merger Act ("BMA").[6] Typically, the merger itself would require approval of a two-thirds majority of the shareholders of the target. Second, a stock-for-stock exchange between the prospective holding company and the shareholders of the target institution could be used, with the target becoming a subsidiary of the holding company. Third, the acquisition could involve purchase of the assets and assumption of liabilities of the target institution by the prospective holding company. Typically, the consideration paid for the assets of the target institution will then be distributed by the former target to its shareholders, with liquidation of the institution to follow upon that event. Formal shareholder approval of the sale of assets may be required, but dissenters' appraisal rights are usually not available.

§ 4.3   Bank Holding Company Act

The Bank Holding Company Act ("BHCA")[1] is the product of congressional concern that economic concentration could lead to conflicts of interest, self-dealing, involuntary tying arrangements, and generally to a derogation of competition.[2] Bank holding company regulation at the federal level is uniformly administered by the Fed, without regard to the status of a holding company's subsidiary banks, whether they are nation-

---

4. *See* 26 U.S.C.A. §§ 351 *et seq.*

5. *Id.* § 368(a)(1).

6. 12 U.S.C.A. § 1828(c).

§ 4.3

1. 12 U.S.C.A. §§ 1841 *et seq.*

2. *Cf. Hearings on H.R. 6778 Before the House Comm. on Banking and Currency,* 91st Cong., 1st Sess., pt. 1, at 20–26 (1969) (discussing bank holding company regulation).

al, state member, or state nonmember insured banks.[3]

The BHCA pursues three regulatory objectives. First, it provides authority for the Fed to regulate the formation and expansion of bank holding companies.[4] Second, it prohibits, with specified exceptions, diversification of bank holding companies into nonbanking or nonfinancial sectors.[5] Third, the act seeks to contain the tendency of bank holding companies to restrict competition.[6] In this chapter we focus primarily on BHCA restrictions that are concerned with the first and third objectives of the act.

The BHCA does not regulate the formation of the bank holding company as a business entity since the company will be organized and incorporated under state law, typically a general business corporation statute.[7] However, when the company seeks to acquire control over a bank,[8] or over an existing bank holding company, the BHCA intervenes, requiring prior approval by the Fed of the acquisition of control.[9]

The BHCA prohibits, absent prior Fed approval, any action taken that causes any company to become a bank holding company.[10] In addition, bank holding companies are subject to a number of prohibitions with respect to their acquisition of control over any additional bank or any other bank holding company. Thus, bank holding companies are prohibited from taking any of the following actions, absent prior Fed approval: (1) Any action that would cause a bank to become a bank holding company subsidiary.[11] (2) Acquisition of direct or indirect ownership or control of any voting shares of any bank by a bank holding company if, after the acquisition, the company would own or control more than five percent of the voting shares of the bank.[12] (3) Acquisition

---

3. State bank holding company regulation is not preempted by federal bank holding company regulation. 12 U.S.C.A. § 1846(a). See *Northeast Bancorp, Inc. v. Board of Governors*, 472 U.S. 159, 168–173, 105 S.Ct. 2545, 2550–2553 (1985) (discussing state authority to regulate bank holding companies in light of 12 U.S.C.A. § 1842(d)).

4. 12 U.S.C.A. § 1842.

5. *Id*. § 1843. Regulation of nonbanking activities of bank holding companies will be discussed in Chapter 6, *infra*.

6. See 12 U.S.C.A. §§ 1842(c)(1)(A)–(B) (anticompetitive factors in approval of bank holding company acquisition); 1843(c)(8) (competitive factors in "proper incident" test for "closely related" nonbanking activities); 1971–1976 (antitying provisions).

7. *But cf. Northeast Bancorp v. Board of Governors*, 849 F.2d 1499, 1505 n. 11 (D.C.Cir.1988) (referring to § 1842 applicants as seeking "a bank holding company charter").

8. See 12 U.S.C.A. § 1841(c) (defining "bank" for purposes of BHCA). The fact that a "bank" is in formation, and not yet operating, does not deprive the Fed of authority to act on a simultaneous bank holding company application. See, e.g., *First State Bank of Clute, Tex. v. Board of Governors*, 553 F.2d 950 (5th Cir. 1977); *Gravois Bank v. Board of Governors*, 478 F.2d 546 (8th Cir.1973).

9. 12 U.S.C.A. § 1842(a).

10. *Id*. § 1842(a)(1). See generally *Marshall & Ilsley Corp. v. Heimann*, 652 F.2d 685 (7th Cir.1981), cert. denied, 455 U.S. 981, 102 S.Ct. 1489; *First Nat'l Bank of Homestead v. Watson*, 363 F.Supp. 466 (D.D.C.1973) (discussing § 1842).

11. 12 U.S.C.A. § 1842(a)(2).

12. *Id*. § 1842(a)(3). See generally *First Nat'l Bank in Billings v. First Bank Stock Corp.*, 306 F.2d 937 (9th Cir.1962) (discussing § 1842).

of all or substantially all of the assets of a bank by the bank holding company or any nonbanking subsidiary of the company.[13] (4) Merger or consolidation with any other bank holding company.[14]

Any company or bank holding company seeking to engage in any of these specified transactions must therefore submit an application[15] to the Fed for its prior approval.[16] Upon receipt of such an application, the Fed is required to give notice to the Comptroller of the Currency (if the target bank is a national bank or a D.C. bank), or to the appropriate state supervisor (if the target bank is state-chartered).[17] The Comptroller or state supervisor is afforded an opportunity thereby to submit "views and recommendations" with respect to the transaction that is the subject of the application, generally within 30 days of the date of notice.[18]

At the conclusion of any hearing on an application, the Fed is required to grant or deny the application, by order, on the basis of the record made at the hearing.[19] If the Fed fails to act on a BHCA application within 91 days of submission of the complete record on the application, the application is deemed to be granted.[20]

13. 12 U.S.C.A. § 1842(a)(4). *See generally South Dakota v. National Bank of S.D., Sioux Falls,* 335 F.2d 444 (8th Cir.1964), *cert. denied,* 379 U.S. 970, 85 S.Ct. 667 (discussing § 1842).

14. 12 U.S.C.A. § 1842(a)(5).

15. *See id.* § 1842(a) (mandating prior approval).

16. *See id.* § 1842(a), (b).

17. *Id.* § 1842(b)(1).

18. *See, e.g., First Lincolnwood Corp. v. Board of Governors,* 560 F.2d 258 (7th Cir. 1977), *rev'd,* 439 U.S. 234, 99 S.Ct. 505 (1978); *Whitney Nat'l Bank in Jefferson Parish v. Bank of New Orleans & Trust Co.,* 379 U.S. 411, 85 S.Ct. 551 (1965) (involving views of appropriate supervisor). If the Fed advises the Comptroller or the state supervisor that an emergency exists requiring expeditious action, then the notice period is shortened to 10 days. 12 U.S.C.A. § 1842(b)(1). Furthermore, if the Fed determines that it must act immediately to prevent probable failure of the target bank or bank holding company, it may dispense with the notice requirements, or require that "views and recommendations" be submitted immediately. *Id.* On the effects of comments by the appropriate supervisor, see generally *Farmers and Merchants Bank of Las Cruces v. Board of Governors,* 567 F.2d 1082 (D.C.Cir.1977); *Grandview Bank & Trust Co. v. Board of Governors,* 550 F.2d 415 (8th Cir.), *cert. denied,* 434 U.S. 821, 98 S.Ct. 64 (1977); *Bank of Boulder v. Board of Governors,* 535 F.2d 1221 (10th Cir.1976); *Commercial Nat'l Bank of Little Rock v. Board of Governors,* 451 F.2d 86

(8th Cir.1971); *Kirsch v. Board of Governors,* 353 F.2d 353 (6th Cir.1965); *First Wisc. Bankshares Corp. v. Board of Governors,* 325 F.2d 946 (7th Cir.1963); *Northwest Bancorporation v. Board of Governors,* 303 F.2d 832 (8th Cir.1962).

19. 12 U.S.C.A. § 1842(b)(1).

20. *Id.* The 91–day period does not begin to run until the Fed has received all final material needed for its decision. *See First Lincolnwood Corp. v. Board of Governors,* 546 F.2d 718 (7th Cir.1976), *reh'g,* 560 F.2d 258 (1977), *rev'd on other grounds,* 439 U.S. 234, 99 S.Ct. 505 (1978); *Tri–State Bancorporation, Inc. v. Board of Governors,* 524 F.2d 562 (7th Cir.1975). A Fed request for further information on a relevant issue with respect to a BHCA application before it may "retrigger" the 91–day period. *See Central Wisc. Bankshares, Inc. v. Board of Governors,* 583 F.2d 294 (7th Cir.1978). In addition, the 91–day period may not begin to run until at least the close of the public comment period following the Fed's publication of notice in the Federal Register. *See Republic of Tex. Corp. v. Board of Governors,* 649 F.2d 1026 (5th Cir.1981). Oral argument on facts already in Fed's possession is not part of the "complete record" for the purpose of tolling the 91–day period. *See North Lawndale Economic Dev. Corp. v. Board of Governors,* 553 F.2d 23 (7th Cir.1977). Likewise, Fed staff reports and recommendations are not part of the "complete record" for this purpose. *See Tri–State Bancorporation, Inc., supra.*

Factors the Fed considers when reviewing a BHCA application are as follows:

(1) *Monopolization.* The application should be disapproved if the proposed transaction would result in a monopoly, or would be in furtherance of a combination or conspiracy to monopolize or to attempt to monopolize the business of banking in any part of the United States.[21]

(2) *Anticompetitiveness.* The application should be disapproved if the effect of the proposed transaction in any section of the country would be substantially to lessen competition, or to tend to create a monopoly, or would be in any other manner in restraint of trade, unless the Fed finds that these anticompetitive effects "are clearly outweighed in the public interest by the probable effect of the transaction in meeting the convenience and needs of the community to be served."[22]

(3) *Traditional Banking Factors.*[23] The Fed must take into consideration the financial[24] and managerial resources[25] of the company or companies and bank(s) concerned; the future prospects of the company or companies and bank(s) concerned;[26] and, the convenience and needs of the community to be served.[27]

21. 12 U.S.C.A. § 1842(c)(1)(A).

22. *Id.* § 1842(c)(1)(B). *See generally Wyoming Bancorporation v. Board of Governors*, 729 F.2d 687 (10th Cir.1984); *Republic of Tex. Corp. v. Board of Governors*, 649 F.2d 1026; *Mercantile Tex. Corp. v. Board of Governors*, 638 F.2d 1255 (5th Cir.1981); *Mid–Nebraska Bancshares, Inc. v. Board of Governors*, 627 F.2d 266 (D.C.Cir.1980); *First State Bank of Clute, Tex. v. Board of Governors*, 553 F.2d 950 (5th Cir. 1977); *Orbanco, Inc. v. Security Bank of Oregon*, 371 F.Supp. 125 (D.Or.1974) (concerning anticompetitiveness). On hearing requirements generally, see *Northeast Bancorp v. Board of Governors*, 849 F.2d 1499, 1505 n. 11 (D.C.Cir.1988) (rejecting argument that hearing was required before Fed refusal to allow participation in management by person subject to removal order, *per* 12 U.S.C.A. § 1818(e)(5), (j)).

23. 12 U.S.C.A. § 1842(c)(2). These factors are traditional criteria throughout federal bank regulatory policy. *See Bank of Boulder v. Board of Governors*, 535 F.2d 1221 (10th Cir.1976).

24. *See generally Board of Governors v. First Lincolnwood Corp.*, 439 U.S. 234, 99 S.Ct. 505 (1978); *Northeast Bancorp v. Board of Governors*, 849 F.2d 1499; *Grandview Bank & Trust Co. v. Board of Governors*, 550 F.2d 415 (8th Cir.), *cert. denied*, 434 U.S. 821, 98 S.Ct. 64 (1977); *Western Bancshares, Inc. v. Board of Governors*, 480 F.2d 749 (10th Cir.1973). As to applications

for the formation of a one-bank holding company specifically, the Fed is prohibited from applying any policy or practice that would result in the rejection of an one-bank holding company application "solely because the transaction ... involves a bank stock loan which is for a period of not more than twenty-five years." 12 U.S.C.A. § 1842(c)(4). However, other unsatisfactory financial arrangements in connection with such an application may be the basis of Fed rejection of a one-bank holding company application. *Id.* In addition, in considering one-bank holding company applications involving bank stock loans with a maturity of 12 or more years, on a case-by-case basis, the Fed may not approve such applications if it believes that the safety or soundness of the subject bank would be jeopardized thereby. *Id.*

25. *See generally First Lincolnwood Corp., supra; Northeast Bancorp, supra; Grandview Bank, supra; Western Bancshares, supra.* By statute, consideration of managerial resources must include "consideration of the competence, experience, and integrity of the officers, directors, and principal shareholders of the company or bank." 12 U.S.C.A. § 1842(c)(5).

26. *See generally Grandview Bank, supra.*

27. *See generally County Nat'l Bancorporation v. Board of Governors*, 654 F.2d 1253 (8th Cir.1981); *Northwest Bancorporation, supra.*

(4) *Supervisory Factors.* The Fed is required to disapprove an application if the applicant company fails to provide adequate assurances that it will make information available on the operations or activities of the company and its affiliates, as the Fed deems appropriate to determine and enforce compliance with the BHCA;[28] or, in the case of an application involving a foreign bank, if the foreign bank is not subject to comprehensive supervision or regulation on a consolidated basis by the bank's home country authorities.[29]

Any party aggrieved[30] by an order of the Fed[31] under the BHCA is entitled to judicial review of the order in the federal court of appeals in the circuit in which the party has its principal place of business, or before the D.C. Circuit.[32] A petition must be filed before the appropriate circuit court within 30 days of the entry of the Fed order in question.[33] The jurisdiction of the courts of appeals in the first instance is exclusive.[34] Generally, federal district courts have no jurisdiction over matters involving the BHCA.[35]

A copy of the petition is required to be transmitted by the clerk of the court to the Fed.[36] The Fed is then required to file with the court the record made before it.[37] In reviewing the factual findings in the Fed's

---

28. 12 U.S.C.A. § 1842(c)(3)(A).

29. *Id.* § 1842(c)(3)(B).

30. A "party aggrieved" generally would be required to have presented an objection to the Fed in the application proceedings. *See, e.g., Bank of Commerce v. Smith,* 513 F.2d 167 (10th Cir.1975); *First Nat'l Bank of St. Charles v. Board of Governors,* 509 F.2d 1004 (8th Cir.1975); *But cf. Northeast Bancorp,* 849 F.2d at 1504 (questioning whether court could review Fed refusal to allow participation in management by person subject to removal order, *per* 12 U.S.C.A. § 1818(e)(5), (j)). A "party aggrieved" would not include a target bank that did not participate in the application proceedings before the Fed. *See, e.g., Blackstone Valley Nat'l Bank v. Board of Governors,* 537 F.2d 1146 (1st Cir.1976). On the meaning of "party aggrieved" for these purposes, see generally *Jones v. Board of Governors,* 79 F.3d 1168 (D.C.Cir.1996); *State of Idaho, Dep't of Finance v. Clarke,* 786 F.Supp. 885 (D.Idaho 1992), *aff'd,* 994 F.2d 1441 (9th Cir.1993); *Synovus Fin. Corp. v. Board of Governors,* 952 F.2d 426 (D.C.Cir. 1991).

31. Only a final order approving (or denying) an application triggers judicial review under the BHCA. *See Executive Nat'l Bank v. Board of Governors,* 889 F.2d 556 (5th Cir.1989); *BankAmerica Corp. v. Board of Governors,* 596 F.2d 1368 (9th Cir.1979). *But cf. Investment Co. Inst. v. Board of Governors,* 551 F.2d 1270 (D.C.Cir.1977); *National Ass'n of Ins. Agents v. Board of Governors,* 489 F.2d 1268 (D.C.Cir.1974).

The Comptroller's preliminary action in authorizing the creation of the new target bank is not the final subject of review in this context. *See Whitney Nat'l Bank supra; Bank of Boulder, supra. But see American Ins. Ass'n v. Clarke,* 865 F.2d 278 (D.C.Cir. 1988) (discussing *Whitney*).

32. 12 U.S.C.A. § 1848.

33. *Id.*

34. *Id. See, e.g., Association of Data Processing Serv. Orgs., Inc. v. Board of Governors,* 745 F.2d 677 (D.C.Cir.1984); *Wyoming Bancorporation v. Board of Governors,* 729 F.2d 687 (10th Cir.1984); *Nehring v. First DeKalb Bancshares, Inc.,* 692 F.2d 1138 (7th Cir.1982); *BankAmerica Corp. v. Board of Governors,* 596 F.2d 1368 (9th Cir.1979); *Kirsch v. Board of Governors,* 353 F.2d 353 (6th Cir.1965). *Cf. Investment Co. Inst. v. Board of Governors,* 551 F.2d 1270 (D.C.Cir.1977).

35. *See, e.g., Nehring, supra; Memphis Trust Co. v. Board of Governors,* 584 F.2d 921 (6th Cir.1978). *Cf. Mid Am. Bancorporation, Inc. v. Board of Governors,* 523 F.Supp. 568 (D.Minn.1980); *Investment Co. Inst., supra; American Bank of Tulsa v. Smith,* 503 F.2d 784 (10th Cir.1974). *Cf. NoDak Bancorporation v. Clarkson,* 471 N.W.2d 140 (N.D.1991) (finding minority shareholder's state law cause of action preempted).

36. 12 U.S.C.A. § 1848.

37. *Id.*

order, the court is required to apply a substantial evidence standard.[38] As to questions of law, the standard of judicial review is whether the Fed's action was arbitrary, capricious, an abuse of discretion or not otherwise in accordance with law.[39] The Fed's determinations are usually accorded great weight by reviewing courts.[40]

§ 4.4 Home Owners' Loan Act

Savings and loan holding companies have grown considerably and now represent an important alternative for expansion of savings association activities and the further concentration of financial and economic power in the savings association sector.[1] The savings and loan holding company provisions[2] of the HOLA broadly parallel the BHCA. This section examines the restrictions and procedures imposed on the formation of savings and loan holding companies.

The language of the savings and loan holding company provisions is quite similar to that of the BHCA,[3] and parallels in judicial treatment of the two acts are therefore understandable. The alternative structures available for formation and expansion of a savings and loan holding company are substantially similar to those available for formation or expansion of a bank holding company.[4] The tax treatment of these

38. *Id. See generally Association of Data Processing Serv. Orgs., Inc. v. Board of Governors*, 745 F.2d 677 (D.C.Cir.1984); *Wyoming Bancorporation v. Board of Governors*, 729 F.2d 687 (10th Cir.1984); *Bank of Boulder, supra; North Hills Bank v. Board of Governors*, 506 F.2d 623 (8th Cir.1974); *Gravois Bank v. Board of Governors*, 478 F.2d 546 (8th Cir.1973).

39. *See, e.g., Association of Data Processing Serv. Orgs., Inc. v. Board of Governors*, 745 F.2d 677 (D.C.Cir.1984); *Wyoming Bancorporation v. Board of Governors*, 729 F.2d 687 (10th Cir.1984); *Investment Co. Inst., supra; Marine Corp. v. Board of Governors*, 325 F.2d 960 (7th Cir.1963). *Cf. First Wisc. Bancshares Corp. v. Board of Governors*, 325 F.2d 946 (7th Cir.1963).

40. *See Association of Data Processing Serv. Orgs., Inc. v. Board of Governors*, 745 F.2d 677 (D.C.Cir.1984); *Wyoming Bancorporation v. Board of Governors*, 729 F.2d 687 (10th Cir.1984); *First Lincolnwood Corp., supra; Grandview Bank, supra; Commercial Nat'l Bank of Little Rock v. Board of Governors*, 451 F.2d 86 (8th Cir.1971).

§ 4.4

1. Sen. Rep. No. 810, *reprinted in* 1959 U.S. Code Cong. and Admin. News 2883.

2. 12 U.S.C.A. § 1467a.

3. A bank holding company acquiring control of a savings association or of a sav-

ings and loan holding company may be subject to the BHCA but not the savings and loan holding company provisions. Thus, prior approval under the savings and loan holding company provisions is not required

> in connection with the control of a savings association, . . . acquired by a bank holding company that is registered under, and subject to, the Bank Holding Company Act of 1956, or any company controlled by such bank holding company.

Id. § 1467a(e)(1)(B)(iii).

4. One major difference between the two concerns the treatment of "spin ups" resulting in the creation of a holding company for a single depository institution. Such a transaction, if involving control of a bank, is fully subject to prior Fed approval under the BHCA. *Id.* § 1842(a). If involving control of a savings association, however, the result is not parallel under the HOLA. Prior approval is not required

> in connection with the control of a savings association, . . . acquired in connection with a reorganization in which a person or group of persons, having had control of a savings association for more than 3 years, vests control of that association in a newly formed holding company subject to the control of the same person or group of persons. . . .

Id. § 1467a(e)(1)(B)(ii).

alternative structures for formation of a savings and loan holding company will also be quite similar to that applicable to formation of a bank holding company.[5] Until the mid 1980s, however, special tax treatment was given to acquisitions and reorganizations involving financially troubled thrift institutions.[6] With the enactment of the Tax Reform Act of 1986,[7] this special treatment was repealed, generally effective as to transactions after December 31, 1988.[8]

The savings and loan holding company provisions require registration of a savings and loan holding company with the OTS,[9] within 90 days of becoming a savings and loan holding company.[10] Absent prior written approval of the OTS, savings and loan holding companies are prohibited from engaging, directly or indirectly, in any of the following activities:

> (1) acquisition or retention of control of a savings association or a savings and loan holding company in violation of the savings and

---

5. *See generally* 26 U.S.C.A. §§ 351 *et seq. Cf.* 12 U.S.C.A. § 1730a(e)(4) (1988) (concerning loss of certain tax benefits under prior legislation).

6. *See* 26 U.S.C.A. § 597 (1982) (excluding FSLIC financial assistance from income; basis reduction requirement).

7. Pub. L. No. 99–514, 99th Cong., 2d Sess. (Oct. 22, 1986).

8. *Id.* § 904(b)(1), (c)(2)(A). *See also* 26 U.S.C.A. § 597 (providing early termination of special reorganization rules for financial institutions; treatment of transactions involving federal financial assistance).

9. For these purposes, a savings and loan holding company is defined as "any company which directly or indirectly controls a savings association or controls any other company which is a[n SLHC]." 12 U.S.C.A. § 1467a(a)(1)(D)(i). On the meaning of "control" for these purposes, see *id.* § 1467a(a)(2). The term "company" is defined for these purposes to include:

> any corporation, partnership, trust, joint-stock company, or similar organization, but does not include the Federal Deposit Insurance Corporation, the Resolution Trust Corporation, any Federal home loan bank, or any company the majority of the shares of which is owned by the United States or any State, or by an instrumentality of the United States or any State.

Id. § 1467a(a)(1)(C). A "savings association," control of which may trigger the application of the savings and loan holding company provisions, is defined to include "a savings bank or cooperative bank which is deemed by the Director [of the Office of Thrift Supervision] to be a savings association . . . ." *Id.* § 1467a(a)(1)(A). The term "savings and loan holding company" does not include the following:

> (1) a bank holding company that is registered under, and subject to, the BHCA, and any company directly or indirectly controlled by such a bank holding company (other than a savings association);

> (2) a company that owns or controls voting shares of a savings association or a savings and loan holding company acquired in connection with underwriting of securities, if the shares are held for a period of time (generally not exceeding 120 days) necessary to permit their sale on a reasonable basis; and,

> (3) certain trusts with specified termination periods (other than a pension, profit-sharing, shareholders voting or business trust).

Id. § 1467a(a)(1)(D)(ii), (a)(3)(A)–(B). In addition, a savings and loan holding company is not deemed to control a savings association or another savings and loan holding company solely by reason of purchase of shares in a "qualified stock issuance," if the purchase is approved by the Director, unless the acquiring savings and loan holding company owns, controls or has the power to vote (or holds proxies representing) in the aggregate, directly and indirectly, more than 15 percent of the voting shares of the association or savings and loan holding company. *Id.* § 1467a(a)(4). On qualified stock issuances (limited to undercapitalized associations and savings and loan holding companies) and their approval, see *id.* § 1467a(q).

10. *Id.* § 1467a(b)(1). The OTS is given authority to extend, upon application, the loan holding company provisions;[11]

(2) acquisition, by merger, consolidation or purchase of assets, of another savings association or a savings and loan holding company, or the acquisition of all or substantially all the assets of any such association or savings and loan holding company;[12]

(3) acquisition or retention of any voting shares of a nonsubsidiary savings association or savings and loan holding company[13] or (in the case of a multiple savings and loan holding company[14]) acquisition or retention of more than five percent of the voting shares of any nonsubsidiary company engaged in any business activity other than those permitted to a multiple savings and loan holding company itself;[15] and

(4) acquisition or retention of control of an uninsured institution.[16]

In addition, the savings and loan holding company provisions prohibit any other company from acquiring direct or indirect control of one or more savings associations without prior written approval of the OTS.[17] Approval by the OTS may not be given if the OTS finds "the financial and managerial resources and future prospects of the company and association . . . to be such that the acquisition would be detrimental to the association or the insurance risk of the Savings Association Insurance Fund or Bank Insurance Fund."[18] However, approval is not required for control of a savings association acquired by devise under the terms of a will creating a trust that is itself excluded from the Act's definition of "savings and loan holding company."[19] Approval is also not required where control of a savings association is acquired in connection with a reorganization in which a holding company is "spinning up" from an association that has been controlled for more than three years by a person or group of persons who will control the holding company upon completion of the reorganization.

As with the BHCA—though stated in a slightly different order—a proposed acquisition of control subject to prior approval under the

time within which a savings and loan holding company must register. See id.

11. Id. § 1467a(e)(1)(A)(i).

12. Id. § 1467a(e)(1)(A)(ii).

13. See id. § 1467a(a)(1)(G) (defining "subsidiary" by reference to 12 U.S.C.A. § 1813).

14. For these purposes, a multiple savings and loan holding company is defined as "any savings and loan holding company which directly or indirectly controls 2 or more savings associations." Id. § 1467a(a)(1)(E).

15. Id. § 1467a(e)(1)(A)(iii). On activities permitted to multiple savings and loan holding companies, see id. § 1467a(c)(2).

On the exceptions to this prohibition, see id. § 1467a(e)(1)(A)(iii)(I)–(VIII).

16. Id. § 1467a(e)(1)(A)(iv). Retention of control is permitted for one year, and, upon application, the OTS may extend this period of retention for no more than three successive one-year periods. Id. The term "uninsured institution" is defined for these purposes to mean "any depository institution the deposits of which are not insured by the Federal Deposit Insurance Corporation." Id. § 1467a(a)(1)(B).

17. Id. § 1467a(e)(1)(B).

18. Id.

19. Id. § 1467a(e)(1)(B)(i). On the exclusion of certain trusts from the definition savings and loan holding company provisions is to be reviewed in light of the following considerations:

(1) *Traditional factors.* The OTS must take into consideration the financial and managerial resources and future prospects of the company and association involved, the effect of the acquisition on the association, the insurance risk to the Savings Association Insurance Fund ("SAIF") or the Bank Insurance Fund ("BIF"), and the convenience and needs of the community to be served.[20]

(2) *Monopolization.* The acquisition must be disapproved if it would result in a monopoly or would be in furtherance of a combination or conspiracy to monopolize or to attempt to monopolize the savings association business in any part of the United States.[21]

(3) *Anticompetitiveness.* The acquisition must be disapproved if it *may* have the effect in any section of the country of substantially lessening competition, or of tending to create a monopoly, or would in any other manner be in restraint of trade, "unless [the OTS] finds that the anticompetitive effects of the proposed acquisition are clearly outweighed in the public interest by the probable effect of the acquisition in meeting the convenience and needs of the community to be served."[22]

(4) *Supervisory Factors.* The OTS is required to disapprove an application if the company fails to provide adequate assurances that it will make information available on the operations or activities of the company and its affiliates, as the OTS deems to be appropriate to determine and enforce compliance with the HOLA;[23] or, in the case of an application involving a foreign bank, if the foreign bank is not subject to comprehensive supervision or regulation on a consolidated basis by the bank's home country authorities.[24]

Since 1987, the predecessor to the savings and loan holding company provisions provided specifically for the formation of mutual holding companies by the reorganization of a mutual insured institution.[25] An institution could effect such a reorganization by chartering an "interim savings institution," the stock of which would be wholly-owned by the mutual institution,[26] at which time the mutual institution would transfer a substantial part of its assets and liabilities[27] to the interim institution.[28] The plan of reorganization was required to be approved by a majority of

of "savings and loan holding company," see *id.* § 1467a(a)(3)(B).

20. *Id.* § 1467a(e)(2).

21. *Id.* § 1467a(e)(2)(A).

22. *Id.* § 1467a(e)(2)(B).

23. *Id.* § 1467a(e)(2)(C).

24. *Id.* § 1467(e)(2)(D).

25. Competitive Equality Banking Act ("CEBA"), Pub. L. No. 100–86, § 107(a), 101 Stat. 552 (1987) (*codified at* 12 U.S.C.A. § 1730a(s)). *Cf.* CEBA, § 107(b), *codified at* 12 U.S.C.A. § 1842(g) (providing for reorganization of mutual savings or cooperative bank to form mutual bank holding compa-

ny). These provisions of the savings and loan holding company were repealed in August 1989. Financial Institutions Reform, Recovery, and Enforcement Act ("FIRREA"), Pub. L. No. 101–73, § 407, 103 Stat. 183, 363 (1989).

26. *See* 12 U.S.C.A. § 1730a(s)(1)(A) (1988).

27. On retention of capital assets at the holding company level, see *id.* § 1730a(s)(3)(D). Transferred liabilities were required to include all insured liabilities. *See id.* § 1730a(s)(1)(B).

28. *Id.* § 1730a(s)(1). Notice of the planned reorganization was required to be the mutual institution's board of directors[29] and, if they exercised voting rights, by a majority of the account holders and obligors of the institution.[30] The permitted activities of such a mutual holding company were rather limited, consisting of little more beyond holding the stock of the subsidiary mutual institution.[31] In 1989, the Financial Institutions Reform, Recovery, and Enforcement Act ("FIRREA") continued to grant the OTS authority to approve reorganization of mutual savings associations into the mutual holding company form.[32]

The savings and loan holding company provisions do not regulate the formation of the savings and loan holding company as a business entity. However, when such an entity seeks to acquire control over a savings association, or over a savings and loan holding company, the savings and loan holding company provisions intervene at that stage of "formation," requiring prior approval by the OTS of the acquisition of control.[33] The OTS is required to render its decision on any such application within 90 days of submission of the complete record on the application.[34] Before approving an application, the OTS is required to request from the Attorney General a report on the competitive factors involved in the proposed acquisition,[35] and to consider any such report in its evaluation of the application.[36] In contrast to the situation under the BHCA, the role of the Attorney General, and of the federal antitrust laws in general, under the savings and loan holding company provisions is rather limited.[37]

Any party aggrieved[38] by an order of the OTS under the savings and loan holding company provisions is entitled to judicial review of the

---

given to the FSLIC 60 days prior to the chartering and transfer of assets and liabilities. *Id.* § 1730a(s)(3)(A). FSLIC review was similar to that provided under the Change in Savings and Loan Control Act, *id.* § 1730(q), with any FSLIC disapproval action required within 60 days (and an extension period of 30 days), on specified statutory grounds. *Id.* § 1730a(s)(3)(C) (1988).

29. *Id.* § 1730a(s)(2)(A).

30. *Id.* § 1730a(s)(2)(B). In any event, persons with ownership rights in the mutual institution had the same ownership rights in the mutual holding company. *See id.* § 1730a(s)(4).

31. *See id.* § 1730a(s)(5), (6).

32. *See* FIRREA, § 301, 103 Stat. at 336–338 (*codified at* 12 U.S.C.A. § 1467a(*o*)).

33. 12 U.S.C.A. § 1467a(e).

34. *Id.* § 1467a(e)(2). *See, e.g., Fidelity Fin. Corp. v. Federal Sav. & Loan Ins. Corp.*, 359 F.Supp. 324 (N.D.Cal.1973) (decision under prior statutory provision). *Cf. Nasser v. Federal Home Loan Bank Bd.*, 723 F.2d 1437 (9th Cir.1984).

35. *Id.* § 1467a(e)(2). On the consideration of anticompetitive effects involved in a proposed acquisition undertaken by the OTS's predecessor agency, see generally *Fort Worth Nat'l Corp. v. Federal Sav. & Loan Ins. Corp.*, 469 F.2d 47 (5th Cir.1972); *Fidelity Fin. Corp., supra.*

36. 12 U.S.C.A. § 1467a(e)(2). Any such report must be rendered within 30 days. *Id.*

37. *See, e.g., id.* 1467a(k)(2), which provides as follows:

Nothing contained in [the savings and loan holding company provisions], other than [an acquisition approved under subsection (e)(2) or the emergency acquisitions provisions of 12 U.S.C.A. § 1823], shall be interpreted or construed as approving any act, action, or conduct which is or has been or may be in violation of existing law, nor shall anything herein contained constitute a defense to any action, suit, or proceeding pending or hereafter instituted on account of any act, action, or conduct in violation of the antitrust laws.

38. For these purposes, a state may be a "party aggrieved" in cases where the OTS is required to consult with state supervisory order in the federal court of appeals in the circuit in which the party has its principal place of business, or before the D.C. Circuit.[39] A petition must be filed before the appropriate circuit court within 30 days of the issuance of the OTS order in question.[40] The jurisdiction of the courts of appeals in the first instance is exclusive.[41] Generally, federal district courts have no jurisdiction over such petitions.[42]

A copy of the petition is required to be transmitted by the clerk of the court to the OTS.[43] The OTS is then required to file with the court the record made before it.[44] The court's review is subject to the Administrative Procedure Act,[45] by express reference in the savings and loan holding company provisions.[46] Unlike the more explicit and specific language in the BHCA,[47] the savings and loan holding company provisions do not indicate whether, in reviewing any factual findings or assumptions in the OTS order, a court is required to apply a substantial evidence standard.[48] As to nonfactual issues, however, it may be assumed that the standard of judicial review is whether the OTS action was arbitrary, capricious, an abuse of discretion or not otherwise in accordance with law.[49]

§ 4.5　 State Holding Company Law

State supervisory officials have an express role to play in the review of bank holding company applications under the BHCA.[1] In addition, state authority to supervise formation or expansion of bank holding companies is expressly preserved from preemption by the BHCA.[2]

officials in "emergency acquisitions." *See Hartigan v. Federal Home Loan Bank Bd.*, 746 F.2d 1300 (7th Cir.1984) (involving predecessor to savings and loan holding company provisions). A frustrated bidder for a financially troubled savings association, but not a trade association of competing commercial banks, may also be a "party aggrieved." *See id.*

39. 12 U.S.C.A. § 1467a(j).

40. *Id.*

41. *Cf., e.g., Fort Worth Nat'l Corp. v. Federal Sav. & Loan Ins. Corp.*, 469 F.2d 47 (5th Cir.1972) (discussing corresponding provision of predecessor to savings and loan holding company provisions).

42. *Cf., e.g., North Am. Sav. Ass'n v. Federal Home Loan Bank Bd.*, 755 F.2d 122 (8th Cir.1985); *Independent Bankers Ass'n v. Federal Home Loan Bank Bd.*, 557 F.Supp. 23 (D.D.C.1982); *Fidelity Fin. Corp. v. Federal Sav. & Loan Ins. Corp.*, 359 F.Supp. 324 (N.D.Cal.1973) (discussing corresponding provision of predecessor to savings and loan holding company provisions).

43. 12 U.S.C.A. § 1467a(j).

44. *Id. See also* 28 U.S.C.A. § 2112.

45. *See* 5 U.S.C.A. §§ 701 *et seq.*

46. *See* 12 U.S.C.A. § 1467a(j).

47. *See id.* § 1848 (subjecting factual findings to "substantial evidence" standard of judicial review).

48. *Cf. North Am. Sav. Ass'n, supra.*

49. *Cf. id.*

§ 4.5

1. *See* 12 U.S.C.A. § 1842(b)(1) (providing for notice to and comment from state supervisor). *But cf. North Hills Bank v. Board of Governors*, 506 F.2d 623 (8th Cir. 1974) (discussing role of state supervisor).

2. *See* 12 U.S.C.A. § 1846(a) (reservation of rights to states). *See Security Nat'l Bank & Trust Co. v. First W. Va. Bancorp., Inc.*, 166 W.Va. 775, 277 S.E.2d 613 (1981), *appeal dismissed*, 454 U.S. 1131, 102 S.Ct. 986 (1982). *See also Heritage Fin. Servs. Corp. v. Commonwealth Bancshares Corp.*, Pa. Ct. Common Pleas No. 4504 Equity, *reprinted in* [1988–1989 Transfer Binder] Fed. Banking L. Rep. (CCH) ¶ 87,302 (April 22, 1988) (Section 1846 allows state banking department jurisdiction for preapproval

The BHCA explicitly reserves to the states the exercise of "such powers and jurisdiction which [they] now ha[ve] or may hereafter have with respect to companies, banks, [bank holding companies], and subsidiaries thereof."[3] This reservation is merely preservative and does not broaden the permissible scope of state regulation beyond the general strictures of, for example, the Commerce Clause of the U.S. Constitution.[4] Thus, it is permissible for a state to prohibit the formation of bank holding companies.[5] State regulation may also reasonably limit the degree of entry permitted to bank holding companies, rather than prohibit them outright,[6] subject to federal law concerning interstate bank holding company acquisitions (discussed in §§ 4.6–4.8, *infra*). State regulation of bank holding companies may affect holding companies seeking to control national as well as state-chartered banks.[7]

Prior to the 1994 passage of federal legislation governing interstate bank holding company acquisitions,[8] a regional interstate model had already emerged as the dominant approach of state regulation. A growing number of states were adopting statutes permitting out-of-state bank holding companies located in states within a specified region to operate a bank within their respective borders. In 1985, the New England regional banking arrangement was upheld by the Supreme Court, in a unanimous decision, in *Northeast Bancorp, Inc. v. Board of Governors*,[9] as against challenges based upon then-applicable BHCA restrictions on interstate acquisitions, known as the Douglas Amendment to the BHCA,[10] as well as, *inter alia*, the Commerce Clause. In this regard, the Court emphasized that the BHCA reflected congressional "policies of community control and local responsiveness of banks."[11] However, the importance of

---

of a resident bank holding company acquisition of stock of another bank holding company). However, interstate bank holding company acquisitions are now governed by federal law. 12 U.S.C.A. § 1842(d). On the role preserved to the states, prior to the change in federal law regarding interstate acquisitions, see generally *Whitney Nat'l Bank in Jefferson Parish v. Bank of New Orleans & Trust*, 379 U.S. 411, 85 S.Ct. 551 (1965); *Iowa Indep. Bankers v. Board of Governors*, 511 F.2d 1288 (D.C.Cir.1975), *cert. denied*, 423 U.S. 875, 96 S.Ct. 144. *But cf. Independent Community Bankers Ass'n v. Board of Governors*, 838 F.2d 969 (8th Cir.1988) (finding restrictive South Dakota statute allowing limited entry by out-of-state bank holding companies in violation of Commerce Clause).

3. 12 U.S.C.A. § 1846(a).

4. U.S. Const. art. 1, § 8, cl. 3. *See BT Inv. Managers, Inc. v. Lewis*, 461 F.Supp. 1187 (N.D.Fla.1978), *aff'd in part, vacated in part on other grounds*, 447 U.S. 27, 100 S.Ct. 2009 (1980); *Independent Community Bankers Ass'n, supra. But see Northeast Bancorp, Inc. v. Board of Governors*, 849

F.2d 1499 (D.C.Cir.1988) (upholding Connecticut bank holding company statute). *Cf. Sears, Roebuck and Co. v. Brown*, 806 F.2d 399 (2d Cir.1986).

5. *See, e.g., Commercial Nat'l Bank of Little Rock v. Board of Governors*, 451 F.2d 86 (8th Cir.1971).

6. *See Northeast Bancorp, Inc., supra* (permitting regional interstate banking compacts). *But see Independent Community Bankers Ass'n, supra.*

7. *See Security Nat'l Bank & Trust Co., supra; Braeburn Sec. Corp. v. Smith*, 15 Ill.2d 55, 153 N.E.2d 806 (1958), *appeal dismissed*, 359 U.S. 311, 79 S.Ct. 876 (1959).

8. Riegle–Neal Interstate Banking and Branching Efficiency Act of 1994, Pub. L. No. 103–328, 108 Stat. 2338 (Sept. 29, 1994).

9. 472 U.S. 159, 105 S.Ct. 2545 (1985).

10. 12 U.S.C.A. § 1842(d) (1988).

11. *Northeast Bancorp, Inc.*, 472 U.S. at 169, 105 S.Ct. at 2551.

state policy in this regard has been minimized by the emergence of federal rules on interstate acquisitions.

§ 4.6   Interstate Acquisitions

A dramatic development in bank holding company interstate practice occurred in September 1994, with the enactment of the Riegle–Neal Interstate Banking and Branching Efficiency Act of 1994 ("IBBEA").[1] The IBBEA permits geographic expansion by banks without regard to the artificial barriers to interstate expansion heretofore imposed by the Douglas Amendment[2] to the BHCA and by the branching provisions of state law and the National Bank Act ("NBA").[3]

§ 4.7   Bank Holding Company Acquisitions

As of 29 September 1995, the Fed has been authorized to approve BHCA applications for acquisition of control of out-of-state banks "without regard to whether such transaction is prohibited under the law of any State."[1] This authority is limited to acquisitions by banks that are adequately capitalized and adequately managed.[2] Permitted "acquisitions" include acquisition of a *de novo* bank chartered to establish a presence of the acquiring bank holding company within the target state.[3]

Specified state law restrictions affecting interstate acquisitions continue in effect. First, the Fed is generally not permitted to approve an acquisition that would contravene applicable state statutory law requiring a bank to be in existence for a minimum period of time before acquisition.[4] The Fed may approve such an acquisition if the target bank has been in existence for at least five years, notwithstanding any longer minimum period in the statutory law of the host state.[5]

Second, state law requirements that a portion of the assets of a target bank be held available for call by a state-sponsored housing entity

---

§ 4.6

1. Pub. L. No. 103–328, 108 Stat. 2338 (Sept. 29, 1994).

2. 12 U.S.C.A. § 1842(d) (1988).

3. *See, e.g.*, 12 U.S.C.A. § 36(c) (NBA provision limiting branching by national banks to branching permitted to state banks in same state). *See generally First Nat'l Bank of Logan v. Walker Bank & Trust Co.*, 385 U.S. 252, 87 S.Ct. 492 (1966) (construing § 36(c)); *First Nat'l Bank in Plant City v. Dickinson*, 396 U.S. 122, 90 S.Ct. 337 (1969) (meaning of "branch" for purposes of § 36(c)).

§ 4.7

1. 12 U.S.C.A. § 1842(d)(1)(A).

2. *Id.* "Adequately capitalized" means "a level of capitalization [that] meets or exceeds all applicable Federal regulatory capital standards." *Id.* § 1841(*o*)(1). The term "adequately managed" is undefined by the IBBEA.

3. *See, e.g., id.* § 1842(d)(1)(A), (C) (acquisitions of "shell banks" included within new rules).

4. *Id.* § 1842(d)(1)(B)(i). For these purposes, a "shell" or "phantom" bank, created to be controlled by the acquiring bank holding company and to receive an existing target bank, is deemed to have been in existence for as long as the target bank has been. *Id.* § 1842(d)(1)(C).

5. *Id.* § 1842(d)(1)(B)(ii).

remain applicable to such acquisitions, if four conditions are met: (1) State law must not have the effect of discriminating against out-of-state banks, bank holding companies and their subsidiaries.[6] (2) State law must have been in effect prior to September 29, 1994.[7] (3) The FDIC has not made a determination that compliance with the state law would result in an unacceptable risk to the BIF or SAIF.[8] (4) Finally, the "appropriate Federal banking agency"[9] of the target bank has not made a determination that compliance with the state law would place the bank in an unsafe or unsound condition.[10]

Third, certain nationwide and statewide concentration limits apply to the newly-authorized interstate bank holding company acquisitions:

(1) The Fed is not permitted to approve an interstate acquisition if the applicant[11] controls, or would control upon consummation of the acquisition, more than 10 percent of the total amount of deposits of insured depository institutions in the United States.[12]

(2) As to acquisitions other than initial entry into the target state, the Fed is not permitted to approve an acquisition if, immediately before the proposed acquisition, the applicant controls an insured depository institution or any branch of such an institution in the home state of the target bank, or in any host state in which the target bank maintains a branch; and, upon consummation of the proposed acquisition the applicant would control 30 percent or more of the total amount of deposits of insured depository institutions in any such state.[13] The nationwide and statewide concentration provisions do not affect the authority of any state to limit, by statute, regulation, or order, the percentage of the total amount of deposits of insured depository institutions in the state held or controlled by a bank, bank holding company, and subsidiaries thereof.[14]

---

6. *Id.* § 1842(d)(1)(D)(i).

7. *Id.* § 1842(d)(1)(D)(ii).

8. *Id.* § 1842(d)(1)(D)(iii).

9. For these purposes, the term "appropriate Federal banking agency" has the same meaning as in Section 3 of the FDIA, 12 U.S.C.A. § 1813(q). IBBEA, § 101(c), 108 Stat. at 2341 (*codified at* 12 U.S.C.A. § 1841(n)).

10. 12 U.S.C.A. § 1842(d)(1)(D)(iv).

11. For these purposes, the "applicant" would include all insured depository institutions that are affiliates of the applicant bank holding company. *Id.* § 1842(d)(2)(A).

12. *Id.* "Deposit" has the same meaning as in Section 3(*l*) of the FDIA, 12 U.S.C.A. § 1813(*l*). 12 U.S.C.A. § 1842(d)(2)(E). *See generally FDIC v. Philadelphia Gear Corp.*, 476 U.S. 426, 106 S.Ct. 1931 (1986) (construing the term "deposit" under § 1813(*l*)).

13. 12 U.S.C.A. § 1842(d)(2)(B)(i)–(ii). IBBEA provides certain exceptions to the statewide concentration restriction. The acquisition will be permitted if there is state deposit cap limitation that permits a bank or bank holding company (and affiliates thereof) to control a greater percentage of total deposits in the target state. *Id.* § 1842(d)(2)(D)(i). Alternatively, the acquisition will be permitted if it is approved by the appropriate state bank supervisor of the host state, and the applicable standard of approval does not have the effect of discriminating against out-of-state banks, bank holding companies and subsidiaries thereof. *Id.* § 1842(d)(2)(D)(ii).

14. *Id.* § 1842(d)(2)(C). These state deposit caps are given effect so long as they do not discriminate against out-of-state banks, bank holding companies and subsidiaries thereof. *Id.*

Approval of interstate acquisitions are fully subject to compliance with the Community Reinvestment Act ("CRA").[15] The Fed must also take into account the record of the applicant bank holding company in complying with applicable state community reinvestment laws.[16]

Similarly, approval of interstate acquisitions are fully subject to applicable antitrust laws.[17] The Fed must also take into account the applicability of any similar state anticompetitive laws.[18]

An exception exists for acquisitions of banks in default or in danger of default. Notwithstanding the restrictions discussed above, the Fed may approve an interstate acquisition of one or more banks in default or in danger of default,[19] or an interstate acquisition as to which financial assistance is provided by the FDIC under Section 13(c) of the FDIA.[20]

§ 4.8　Effects on State Authority

Prior to the enactment of the IBBEA, the BHCA generally did not affect the authority of states to regulate banks and bank holding companies subject to their jurisdiction.[1] Aside from preempting state authority to prohibit interstate bank holding company acquisitions, the IBBEA not only confirms state authority over bank holding companies, but also explicitly provides that nothing in the Act is to be construed as affecting the authority of states and their political subdivisions to subject banks, bank holding companies, foreign banks, and affiliates thereof to state taxation.[2]

Pre–IBBEA, questions sometimes arose as a matter of state law over whether or not a depository institution subsidiary of a bank holding company could undertake transactions as an agent for an affiliate institution.[3] The IBBEA resolves these questions, as a natural extension of its authorization of interstate acquisitions by bank holding companies.

A bank subsidiary is generally permitted to "receive deposits, renew time deposits, close loans, service loans, and receive payments on loans and other obligations as an agent for a depository institution affiliate."[4]

---

15. *Id.* § 1842(d)(3)(A). *See id.* §§ 2901 *et seq.* (CRA requirements).

16. *Id.* § 1842(d)(3)(B).

17. *Id.* § 1842(d)(4)(A).

18. *Id.* § 1842(d)(4)(B).

19. *Id.* § 1842(d)(5)(A).

20. *Id.* § 1842(d)(5)(B).

§ 4.8

1. *See* 12 U.S.C.A. § 1846 (1988) (pre-IBBEA BHCA provision; state authority preserved), *redesignated by* IBBEA, § 101(b)(1), 108 Stat. at 2341 (*codified at* 12 U.S.C.A. § 1846(a)).

2. 12 U.S.C.A. § 1846(b). This state authority is confirmed "to the extent that such tax or tax method is otherwise permis-

sible by or under the Constitution of the United States or other Federal law." *Id. See also* IBBEA, § 111 (*codified at* 12 U.S.C.A. § 1811 note) (restating existing law with respect to state taxation of banking enterprises).

3. The issue might involve, for example, whether the institution was, in effect, acting as a branch of its affiliate rather than simply as an agent. *See, e.g., Commercial Nat'l Bank of Little Rock v. Board of Governors,* 451 F.2d 86 (8th Cir.1971) (discussing use of bank as functional branch of affiliated bank).

4. 12 U.S.C.A. § 1828(r)(1). The question may be raised whether the list of permitted agency activities is intended to be exclusive. According to the IBBEA, the list

A bank acting in this capacity "shall not be considered to be a branch of the affiliate."[5] Any such agency relationship must be consistent with safe and sound banking practices, and all applicable regulations of any appropriate federal banking agency.[6]

Similarly, an insured savings association that was an affiliate of a bank on 1 July 1994, is permitted to act as agent for the bank in the same manner as an insured bank affiliate could act.[7] However, the agency activities must be conducted only: (1) in a state in which the bank is not prohibited from operating a branch,[8] and the savings association maintained an office or branch and conducted business as of 1 July 1994;[9] or (2) in a state in which the bank is not expressly prohibited from operating a branch under a state law prohibiting inter-state bank mergers,[10] and the savings association maintained a main office and conducted business as of that date.[11] Any such agency relation-ship must be consistent with safe and sound banking practices, and all applicable regulations of any appropriate federal banking agency.[12]

Certain prohibitions apply to agency activities of depository institu-tions. The institution may not conduct on an agency basis any activity prohibited to it as principal under any applicable federal or state law.[13] Correspondingly, the institution, as principal, may not authorize an agent to conduct any activity on its behalf that it is prohibited from conducting under applicable federal or state law.[14]

§ 4.9 SLHC Acquisitions

The savings and loan holding company provisions[1] of the HOLA restrict the OTS from approving a proposed acquisition that would result in the formation of an interstate multiple savings and loan holding company.[2] The OTS may approve such acquisitions in any of the follow-ing situations:

> (1) Pursuant to emergency acquisition provisions,[3] the company or an insured institution subsidiary thereof is authorized to acquire control of an insured institution subsidiary in the additional state or states in question, or is authorized to operate a home or branch

---

is not to be construed as limiting the au-thority of the bank to act in such a capacity "under any other provision of law." *Id.* § 1828(r)(4)(A).

5. *Id.* § 1828(r)(2). However, if the bank acts in an agency capacity under another provision of law, the IBBEA does not affect the question of whether or not the bank so acting is to be considered a branch of the principal. *See id.* § 1828(r)(4)(B).

6. *Id.* § 1828(r)(5).

7. *Id.* § 1828(r)(6).

8. *Id.* § 1828(r)(6)(A)(i).

9. *Id.* § 1828(r)(6)(A)(ii).

10. *Id.* § 1828(r)(6)(B)(i). *See* IBBEA, § 102(a), 108 Stat. at 2343 (*codified at* 12 U.S.C.A. § 1831u(a)(2)) (state election to prohibit interstate merger transactions).

11. 12 U.S.C.A. § 1828(r)(6)(B)(ii).

12. *Id.* § 1828(r)(5).

13. *Id.* § 1828(r)(3)(A).

14. *Id.* § 1828(r)(3)(B).

§ 4.9

1. 12 U.S.C.A. § 1467a.

2. *Id.* § 1467a(e)(3).

3. *See id.* § 1823(k).

office there.[4]

(2) The company controls an insured institution subsidiary that already operated a home or branch office in the additional state or states in question as of 5 March 1987.[5]

(3) The statute laws of the state in which the target insured institution is located "specifically authorize ... by language to that effect and not merely by implication" that an insured institution chartered by that state can be acquired by an insured institution chartered by the state in which the acquiring insured institution or savings and loan holding company is located, or by a holding company that controls such a state-chartered insured institution.[6]

§ 4.10   Mergers and Consolidations

Both bank holding company formations and bank mergers involve some form of acquisition activity directed at a target bank. The typical acquisition methods, discussed in the holding company context and illustrated in Figure 4–1, *supra*, are therefore equally pertinent in the present context.

The following sections begin with an examination of the corporate law of mergers and consolidation of commercial banks and then consider the corresponding rules for savings associations. Mergers of depository institutions are also subject to the Bank Merger Act ("BMA").[1] In addition, depository institutions are affected by the 1994 federal statutory amendments authorizing interstate mergers.

Strictly speaking, a "consolidation" involves the business combination of two or more corporate entities into a new, third entity, with the termination of the corporate existence of the two prior entities.[2] The consolidation need not involve all of the assets and liabilities of the parties to the transaction.[3] In contrast, a "merger" continues the corporate existence of one of the parties to the transaction, now possessed of assets and liabilities of the merged party, with the termination of the corporate existence of the latter.[4] Figure 4–2, *infra*, illustrates the basic structures of the typical acquisition transactions, all of which are subject to regulatory oversight.   SLP5

---

4. *Id.* § 1467a(e)(3)(A).

5. *Id.* § 1467a(e)(3)(B).

6. *Id.* § 1467a(e)(3)(C).

§ 4.10

1. 12 U.S.C.A. § 1828(c).

2. *See, e.g., United States v. Philadelphia Nat'l Bank*, 374 U.S. 321, 83 S.Ct. 1715 (1963); *Braak v. Hobbs*, 210 N.C. 379, 186 S.E. 500 (1936); *Collinsville Nat'l Bank v. Esau*, 74 Okla. 45, 176 P. 514 (1918).

3. *Cf. Dauphin Deposit Trust Co. v. Myers*, 388 Pa. 444, 130 A.2d 686 (1957); *Personal Credit Plan v. Kling*, 130 N.J.Eq. 41, 20 A.2d 704 (1941); *Seattle–First Nat'l Bank v. Spokane County*, 196 Wash. 419, 83 P.2d 359 (1938).

4. *See, e.g., Philadelphia Nat'l Bank, supra. Cf. Exchange Bank of Commerce v. Meadors*, 199 Okla. 10, 184 P.2d 458 (1947).

FIGURE 4-2
Typical Acquisition Structures

§ 4.11 National Bank Transactions

Merger, consolidation, and purchase/assumption transactions[1] between banks are subject to a range of restrictions. Foremost among these are: (1) the prior approval requirement of the BMA;[2] (2) the application of the general federal antitrust laws to such transactions, regardless of prior BMA approval;[3] and, (3) in the case of transactions involving banks subject to the Securities Exchange Act of 1934,[4] the application of the proxy disclosure rules.[5] In addition, as to transactions involving national

---

§ 4.11

1. These three are treated as equivalents for purposes of the BMA. *See* 12 U.S.C.A. § 1828(c)(2) (referring to all three).

2. *Id.* § 1828(c).

3. *See id.* § 1828(c)(6)–(8) (applying federal antitrust laws to transactions approved by BMA).

4. 15 U.S.C.A. §§ 78a *et seq. See generally* 2 MICHAEL P. MALLOY, BANKING LAW AND REGULATION § 6.2 (1994 & CUM. SUPP.) (discussing 1934 Act).

5. 15 U.S.C.A. § 78n(a).

banks, certain provisions of the National Bank Act ("NBA")[6] will govern the approval, terms, and conditions of any such transaction.

(a) *Consolidations*. The NBA requires that the consolidation of any national bank with any other national bank or state-chartered bank under a national bank charter be approved by the Comptroller of the Currency.[7] The capital stock of the resulting national bank must be "not less than that required under existing law for the organization of a national bank in the place in which it is located."[8] Capital stock to be issued under the consolidation agreement is not subject to preemptive rights of the shareholders of the predecessor banks.[9] The consolidated bank will be liable for all liabilities of its predecessors.[10]

The consolidation may be effected "on such terms and conditions as may be lawfully agreed upon by a majority of the board of directors of each [national bank] or [state-chartered] bank proposing to consolidate."[11] The agreement must be ratified and confirmed by the affirmative vote of shareholders representing at least two-thirds of the capital stock outstanding of each bank.[12] At least 10 days prior to the meeting, notice must also be sent to each shareholder of record by certified or registered mail.[13]

If the consolidation is approved by the necessary majorities and subsequently approved by the Comptroller, a shareholder of the predecessor banks is entitled to dissenters appraisal rights for all shares held at the time the consolidation is approved by the Comptroller.[14] To qualify for these rights, the shareholder must either: (1) have voted against the consolidation at the shareholders' meeting; or (2) have given notice of dissent from the plan of consolidation, in writing, at or prior to the meeting to the presiding officer.[15] In order to exercise these rights, the shareholder must make a written request to the consolidated national bank within 30 days of the date of consummation of the consolidation, accompanied by the surrender of the shareholder's stock certificates.[16]

---

6. 12 U.S.C.A. §§ 1 *et seq.*

7. *Id.* § 215(a).

8. *Id.* § 215(b).

9. *Id.* § 215(g).

10. *Id.* § 215(b). *See generally First Nat'l Bank in Oklahoma City v. Harris*, 27 F.2d 117 (8th Cir.1928); *U.S. Fidelity & Guar. Co. v. Citizens' Nat'l Bank*, 13 F.2d 213 (D.N.M.1924) (interpreting prior provision).

11. 12 U.S.C.A. § 215(a).

12. *Id.* In the case of a state-chartered bank involved in such a proposed consolidation, the NBA provides for an affirmative vote "by a greater proportion of such capital stock in the case of such State bank if the laws of the State where it is organized so require." *Id.*

13. *Id.* § 215(a). Shareholder notice need not be sent to shareholders "who specifically waive notice." *Id.* In the case of state-chartered banks involved in such a consolidation, the shareholders thereof must be given "any additional notice … which may be required by the laws of the State where [the state-chartered bank] is organized." *Id.*

14. *Id.* § 215(b).

15. *Id.* Failure to comply with the procedures specified in the NBA may destroy the dissenting appraisal rights. *See, e.g., Hiatt v. Peddy*, 73 F.2d 235 (5th Cir.1934) (interpreting prior provision).

16. 12 U.S.C.A. § 215(b).

The value of the shares must be determined as of the effective date of the consolidation.[17] Appraisal of this value is made by a committee of three persons: (1) one person selected by the vote of the dissenting shareholders representing the majority of the stock entitled to payment in cash; (2) one selected by the directors of the consolidated national bank; and (3) one selected by the other two members of the committee.[18] The valuation agreed upon by a majority of the committee governs.[19] A dissenting shareholder dissatisfied with the valuation may appeal to the Comptroller within five days of notice of the appraised value of the shares.[20] The Comptroller has authority to require a reappraisal to be made that is final and binding as to the value of the shares.[21]

If for any reason any member of the appraisal committee has not been selected within 90 days of the date of the consummation of the consolidation, or if the committee fails to determine the value of the shares of dissenting shareholders, the Comptroller is authorized to make a final and binding appraisal, upon the written request of an interested party.[22]

In August 1988, the OCC issued a bulletin explaining the methods of valuation that it used in estimating the value of the shares of a bank involved in a conversion, merger, or consolidation.[23] The objective of the appraisal process is "to arrive at a fair estimate of the value of a bank's shares."[24] In fulfilling this objective, the OCC will select, in light of the particular facts of the case, an appropriate method or combination of methods to determine share value.[25] The OCC methodology essentially applies the traditional Delaware weighted block method.[26]

The primary method consulted is the market value method. If the shares are sufficiently traded, and prices are available from direct

---

17. *Id.* § 215(c). *Cf. Central–Penn. Nat'l Bank of Philadelphia v. Portner*, 201 F.2d 607 (3d Cir.1953), *cert. denied*, 346 U.S. 815, 74 S.Ct. 26 (purchase of shares by "dissenter" after announcement of consolidation agreement).

18. 12 U.S.C.A. § 215(c).

19. *Id.*

20. *Id.*

21. *Id.*

22. *Id.* § 215(d). The NBA requires that the Comptroller's expenses be paid by the consolidated national bank. *See id.* The NBA provides, however, that

[t]he appraisal of such shares of stock in any State bank shall be determined in the manner prescribed by the law of the State in such cases, rather than as provided in [12 U.S.C.A. § 215], if such provision is made in the State law; and no such consolidation shall be in contravention of the law of the State under which such bank is incorporated.

Id. For a useful analysis of dissenters' appraisals handled by the OCC, see Austin &

Nigem, *Dissenters' Appraisals Revisited*, 106 Banking L.J. 246 (1989). *See also Lewis v. Clark* [sic], 911 F.2d 1558, 1561–1564 (11th Cir.1990) (discussing Comptroller's appraisal methods with approval).

23. OCC Banking Bulletin 88–22, *reprinted in* [1988–1989 Transfer Binder] Fed. Banking L. Rep. ¶ 70,195 (Sept. 9, 1988). For a discussion of the Comptroller's appraisal methods, see *Lewis*, 911 F.2d at 1561–1564.

24. OCC Banking Bulletin 88–22, at 46,-191.

25. *Id.*

26. *See, e.g.*, Note, *Valuation of Dissenters Stock*, 79 Harv. L. Rev. (1966); Note, *Elements in Valuation of Corporate Stock*, 55 Mich. L. Rev. 689 (1957) (discussing valuation methods). *But cf. Weinberger v. UOP, Inc.*, 457 A.2d 701, 712–714 (Del. 1983) (rejecting traditional weighted block method as exclusive valuation methodology).

quotations from the WALL STREET JOURNAL or a market maker, those price quotations "are considered in determining market value."[27] If either no market value is readily available, or the available market value is "not well established"[28] then other methods of estimating value will be used.[29]

Another method is the investment value method. This requires "an assessment of the value to investors of a share in the future earnings of the target bank."[30] An average price/earnings ratio of peer group banks having similar earnings potential to the target bank is applied to the estimated earnings per share of the target.[31] Difficulty may arise in selecting the peer group, which is generally based on location, size, and earnings patterns. Where the state in which the target is located provides a sufficient number of potential peer group banks, the price/earnings ratio assigned to such banks can be readily applied to the target. However, if there are too few comparable independent banks in a comparable location, then the pool of banks from which a peer group is selected is broadened by including one-bank bank holding companies in a comparable location, or by selecting banks in a less comparable location (including adjacent states) with similar earnings patterns.[32]

A third method of valuation is the book value method. The OCC, however, has expressed some reservations about the use of this method. Book value "is based on historical acquisition costs of the bank's assets[] and does not reflect investors' perceptions of the value of the bank as a going concern."[33] Accordingly, the OCC tends to use a variant, "adjusted book value."[34] The utility of the adjusted book value is impaired to the extent that a sufficient peer group of comparably situated banks are not readily available. However, the OCC expressly rejects the use of unadjusted book value of the target bank as a basis for valuation.[35]

If more than one method of valuation is employed, the resulting values will be weighted to reach the overall valuation of the target bank.[36] The relative weight given to each resulting value will be "based

---

27. OCC Banking Bulletin 88–22, at 46,-191.

28. *Id*. Typically, this would occur if the shares are thinly traded, raising questions about the representativeness of the historical quotations available.

29. *Id*.

30. *Id*.

31. *Id*. Though the OCC Bulletin does not expressly so state, the investment value method normally involves application of the price/earnings ratio to an average—typically, a five-year average—of estimated earnings. *See, e.g., In re Olivetti Underwood Corp.*, 246 A.2d 800 (Del.Ch.1968).

32. OCC Banking Bulletin 88–22, at 46,-191.

33. *Id*. Similar reservations are often expressed in the case law concerning the cogency of the asset value method. *See, e.g.,*

Swanton v. State Guar. Corp., 42 Del.Ch. 477, 215 A.2d 242 (1965).

34. "Adjusted book value" may be described as follows:

> Adjusted book value is calculated by multiplying the book value of the target bank's assets per share [by] the average market price to book value ratio of comparable banking organizations. The average market price to book value ratio measures the premium or discount to book value which investors attribute to shares of similarly situated banking organizations.

OCC Banking Bulletin 88–22, at 46,191.

35. *See id*. ("As a rule, the OCC does not place any weight on 'unadjusted book value' ").

36. *Id*.

on how accurately the given method is believed to represent market value."[37] The weighting assigned to the various resulting values will reflect the Comptroller's judgment of the credibility of the respective methods employed. For example, where the earnings patterns of the target bank have been irregular, or may reflect in given years certain unusual (and probably nonrecurring) developments in such years, it is likely that the value resulting from application of the investment value method would receive a relatively lower weight than, for example, the value resulting from the market value method. On the other hand, thinness in the trading market of the target bank's shares may lower the weight that might otherwise be assigned to the value resulting from application of the market value method.

Contrary to developments in the general corporate law with respect to valuation,[38] the OCC does not contemplate the use of other, less traditional methods of valuation in arriving at the fair value of the shares of a target bank. While recognizing that purchase premiums do exist in the merger and consolidation context, the OCC will not consider them in arriving at the value of shares.[39]

(b) *Mergers*. A merger between a national bank and another national bank or a state-chartered bank under the national bank charter of the surviving bank also requires approval of the OCC under the NBA.[40] The merger agreement must specify, *inter alia*, the amount of capital stock of the surviving national bank and the stock that will be outstanding on completion of the merger,[41] in an amount not less than would be required for the chartering of a national bank in the place where the surviving bank is located.[42] The agreement must also specify the amount of stock to be allocated, if any, and cash to be paid, if any, to the target bank shareholders.[43] The NBA also requires that the merger agreement provide that the surviving bank shall be liable for all liabilities of the target bank.[44]

The merger agreement must be approved in writing by a majority of the board of directors of each national bank or state-chartered bank participating in the merger.[45] The agreement must be ratified and confirmed by the affirmative vote of the shareholders of each participating bank representing at least two-thirds of its capital stock outstand-

---

37. *Id.*

38. *See, e.g., Weinberger v. UOP, Inc.,* 457 A.2d at 712–714 (Del. 1983) (rejecting traditional weighted block method as exclusive valuation methodology).

39. OCC Banking Bulletin 88–22, at 46,-192.

40. 12 U.S.C.A. § 215a(a). *See generally Nehring v. First DeKalb Bancshares, Inc.,* 692 F.2d 1138 (7th Cir.1982). For two successful challenges to merger approvals by minority shareholders, see *Lewis,* 911 F.2d at 1560–1561 (invalidating take-out merger; lack of statutory authority cited); *Bloom-*

ington Nat'l Bank v. Telfer, 916 F.2d 1305 (7th Cir.1990) (invalidating reorganization plan involving buy-back of stock at depressed price; lack of statutory authority cited).

41. 12 U.S.C.A. § 215a(a)(3).

42. *Id.*

43. *Id.* Capital stock to be issued under the merger agreement is not subject to preemptive rights of the shareholders of the merging banks. *See id.* § 215a(g).

44. *Id.* § 215a(a)(4).

45. *Id.* § 215a(a)(1).

ing.[46] Notice of the meeting must be sent to each shareholder of record, at least 10 days prior to the meeting, by certified or registered mail.[47]

If the merger is approved by the necessary majorities and is subsequently approved by the Comptroller, a shareholder of a target bank is entitled to dissenters appraisal rights for all shares held at the time the Comptroller approves the merger.[48] To qualify for these rights, the shareholder must either: (1) have voted against the merger at the shareholders' meeting; or (2) have given notice of dissent from the plan of merger, in writing, at or prior to the meeting to the presiding officer.[49] To exercise these rights, the shareholder must make a written request to the surviving national bank within 30 days of the date of consummation of the merger, accompanied by the surrender of the shareholder's stock certificates.[50]

The value of the shares is determined as of the effective date of the merger.[51] Appraisal is made by a committee of three persons: (1) one person selected by the vote of the dissenting shareholders representing the majority of the stock entitled to payment in cash; (2) one selected by the directors of the surviving national bank; and (3) one selected by the other two members of the committee.[52] The valuation agreed upon by a majority of the committee governs.[53] Any dissenting shareholder dissatisfied with this valuation may appeal to the Comptroller within five days of notice of the appraised value of the shares.[54] The Comptroller has authority for a reappraisal, which is final and binding as to the value of the shares.[55] If for any reason any one of the members of the appraisal committee has not been selected within 90 days of the date of the consummation of the consolidation, or if the committee fails to determine the value of the shares of dissenting shareholders, the Comptroller is authorized to make a final and binding appraisal, upon the written request of an interested party.[56]

46. *Id.* § 215a(a)(2). *See generally Rogers v. First Nat'l Bank of St. George*, 297 F.Supp. 641 (D.S.C.1969), *aff'd and remanded*, 410 F.2d 579 (4th Cir.) In the case of a state-chartered bank involved in such a proposed merger, the NBA provides for an affirmative vote "by a greater proportion of such capital stock in the case of a State bank if the laws of the State where it is organized so require." 12 U.S.C.A. § 215a(a)(2).

47. 12 U.S.C.A. § 215a(a)(2). This notice need not be sent to those shareholders who have specifically waived notice. *Id.* In the case of a state-chartered bank involved in such a merger, any additional notice must be given that "may be required by the laws of the State where it is organized." *Id.*

48. *Id.* § 215a(b).

49. *Id.*

50. *Id.*

51. 12 U.S.C.A. § 215a(c).

52. *Id.* § 215a(c)(1)–(3).

53. *Id.* § 215a(c).

54. *Id.*

55. *Id.*

56. 12 U.S.C.A. § 215a(d). The NBA requires that the Comptroller's expenses be paid by the surviving national bank. *Id.* The NBA provides, however, that

> [t]he appraisal of such shares of stock in any State bank shall be determined in the manner prescribed by the law of the State in such cases, rather than as provided in [12 U.S.C.A. § 215a], if such provision is made in the State law; and no such merger shall be in contravention of the law of the State under which such bank is incorporated.

Id. 215a(d). *See Beerly v. Department of Treasury*, 768 F.2d 942 (7th Cir.1985), *cert. denied*, 475 U.S. 1010, 106 S.Ct. 1184 (1986) (dissenter's appraisal rights under

The valuation methods that apply to consolidation apply to mergers as well,[57] and so the OCC valuation procedures in the consolidation context apply directly to the case of mergers as well.

§ 4.12   State Bank Transactions

State law restrictions on mergers and acquisitions involving depository institutions vary considerably from state to state.[1] These restrictions coexist with corresponding federal restrictions, and, in merger transactions involving both federally and state-chartered institutions, compliance with both applicable federal and state law restrictions may be required before such a transaction may be consummated.[2]

§ 4.13   Savings Associations

Prior to the enactment of the Financial Institutions Reform, Recovery, and Enforcement Act ("FIRREA"),[1] mergers and acquisitions involving savings associations were not subject to any specific federal regulatory statute corresponding to the BMA[2] requiring prior regulatory approval of savings association mergers. On the other hand, unlike bank mergers, mergers involving savings associations were subject to the prior notification and filing requirements of the Hart–Scott–Rodino Antitrust Improvements Act.[3] After FIRREA, savings associations are now subject to regulations of the OTS that directly regulate merger transactions[4] and to the requirements of the BMA.[5] In addition, savings association mergers

---

12 U.S.C.A. § 215a). *See generally* Austin & Nigem, *Dissenters' Appraisals Revisited,* 106 Banking L.J. 246 (1989) (analysis of dissenters' appraisals handled by the OCC). Despite the apparent finality of the appraisal remedy, two cases have allowed minority shareholders to challenge the approval of mergers on the merits. *See Lewis v. Clark* [*sic*], 911 F.2d 1558, 1560–1561 (11th Cir. 1990), *reh'g denied,* 972 F.2d 1351 (11th Cir.1991) (invalidating take-out merger); *Bloomington Nat'l Bank,* 916 F.2d at 1308–1310 (invalidating reorganization plan involving buy-back of stock). *But see NoDak Bancorporation v. Clarke,* 998 F.2d 1416 (8th Cir.1993) (finding no inconsistency with NBA in minority shareholders forced to accept only cash in exchange for acquired shares).

57. *See* OCC Banking Bulletin 88–22, at 46,191.

§ 4.12

1. *See generally* 3 Michael P. Malloy, Banking Law and Regulation § 9.5 (1994 & Cum. Supp.) (discussing state law restrictions on mergers).

2. *But cf.* McKenna, *Federal Preemption of State Anti–Trust Law in Transactions of*

Federally Chartered Banks, 58 Conn. B. J. 355 (1984).

§ 4.13

1. Pub. L. No. 101–73, 103 Stat. 183 (1989).

2. *See* 12 U.S.C.A. § 1828(c) (1988) (pre-FIRREA BMA applicable only to banks).

3. *See* 15 U.S.C.A. § 18a, *as amended,* FIRREA, § 1214, 103 Stat. at 529 (*codified at* 15 U.S.C.A. § 18a(c)(7)–(8)) (exempting from requirements, *inter alia,* holding company acquisitions subject to approval under 12 U.S.C.A. § 1467a(e) and savings association acquisitions subject to approval under § 1464 or § 1828).

4. *See, e.g.,* 12 C.F.R. §§ 546.1–546.3, 563.22, 571.5.

5. See 12 U.S.C.A. § 1828(c), *as amended,* FIRREA, §§ 201(a)(1), 221(2)(A)–(D), 103 Stat. 183, 187, 266–267 (1989) (*codified at* 12 U.S.C.A. § 1828(c)(2)(C)–(D), (c)(3), (c)(4), (c)(6), (c)(7), (c)(9); *repealing* 12 U.S.C.A. § 1828(c)(12)).

are generally subject to the Sherman Act[6] and the Clayton Act.[7]

§ 4.14   Bank Merger Act

As originally enacted in May 1960,[1] the BMA did not focus on anticompetitiveness with respect to bank mergers and acquisitions. Indeed, it was not clear from the language of the 1960 version what the relationship was, if any, between the BMA and federal antitrust laws generally. In any event, the BMA had had little appreciable effect on the fevered pace of bank mergers. In the meantime, the Justice Department began to challenge bank mergers under the antitrust laws, particularly Section 7 of the Clayton Act,[2] despite the fact that federal banking agencies had approved the mergers under the BMA. In *United States v. Philadelphia National Bank*,[3] the Supreme Court held that Section 7 of the Clayton Act was applicable to bank mergers.[4]

Philadelphia National had argued that the acquisition, structured as a statutory merger, was in fact a purchase of assets, to which the Clayton Act would not apply.[5] In response, the Justice Department argued that the statutory merger was essentially a stock acquisition fully subject to Section 7 of the Clayton Act. In the Court's view,

> [b]oth positions ... have merit; a merger fits neither category neatly. Since the literal terms of § 7 thus do not dispose of our question, we must determine whether a congressional design to embrace bank mergers is revealed in the history of the statute....
>
> ... Congress contemplated that ... the entire range of corporate amalgamations, from pure stock acquisitions to pure assets acquisitions, [would be] within the scope of § 7. Thus, the stock-acquisition and assets-acquisition provisions, *read together*, reach mergers, which fit neither category perfectly but lie somewhere between the two ends of the spectrum.... So construed, the specific exception for acquiring corporations not subject to the FTC's jurisdiction excludes from the coverage of § 7 only assets acquisitions by such corporations when not accomplished by merger.... [6]

6. 15 U.S.C.A. §§ 1 *et seq. See* 12 U.S.C.A. § 1828(c)(7)(B) (applying Sherman Act to, *inter alia*, savings association mergers).

7. 15 U.S.C.A. §§ 12 *et seq. See* 12 U.S.C.A. § 1828(c)(7) (applying federal antitrust laws to, *inter alia*, savings association mergers).

§ 4.14

1. Pub. L. No. 86–463, 79 Stat. 437 (1960) (*codified at* 12 U.S.C.A. § 1828(c)).

2. 15 U.S.C.A. § 18.

3. 374 U.S. 321, 83 S.Ct. 1715 (1963).

4. 374 U.S. at 352, 83 S.Ct. at 1736. The Court did not go on to the question of whether the merger in question was also prohibited by the Sherman Act. 374 U.S. at 324, 83 S.Ct. at 1720. On the applicability of the Sherman Act, see *infra* this section.

5. Section 7 of the Clayton Act only reached assets acquisitions undertaken by a person subject to FTC jurisdiction, but banks were not subject to that jurisdiction. 15 U.S.C.A. § 18.

6. *Philadelphia Nat'l Bank*, 374 U.S. at 337, 342, 83 S.Ct. at 1727, 1730 (emphasis in original).

The enactment of the BMA was not intended to displace the general antitrust laws to the extent that they were otherwise applicable.[7] In assessing the lawfulness of the proposed merger under Section 7 of the Clayton Act, the Court refused to accept affirmative justifications of an anticompetitive merger based on, *inter alia*, the benefits that the merger might confer upon the affected banking community.[8]

Similarly, in *United States v. First National Bank & Trust Co. of Lexington*,[9] the Court held that such mergers were also subject to the Sherman Act.[10] In both *Philadelphia National Bank* and *First National Bank*, the Court went on to apply traditional antitrust analysis, without regard to the "convenience and needs" of the community to be served by the surviving bank.[11]

An amended BMA was enacted in February 1966.[12] As further amended in 1989, the BMA applies to any insured depository institution[13] that intends to: (1) merge or consolidate with an uninsured

---

7. 374 U.S. at 350–355, 83 S.Ct. at 1734–1737.

8. *See* 374 U.S. at 370–372, 83 S.Ct. at 1745–1746. Among other things, Philadelphia National had argued:

> Philadelphia needs a bank larger than it now has in order to bring business to the area and stimulate its economic development.... [The Court was] clear, however, that a merger the effect of which "may be substantially to lessen competition" is not saved because, on some ultimate reckoning of social or economic debits and credits, it may be deemed beneficial. A value choice of such magnitude is beyond the ordinary limits of judicial competence, and in any event has been made for us already, by Congress when it enacted the amended § 7.

374 U.S. at 371, 83 U.S. at 1745, *quoting* 15 U.S.C.A. § 18.

9. 376 U.S. 665, 84 S.Ct. 1033 (1964).

10. 376 U.S. at 667, 84 S.Ct. at 1034. However, with the Court's decision in *Philadelphia Nat'l Bank* opening the way to Clayton Act challenges to bank mergers, the government would rarely rely in the future, as it had in *First Nat'l Bank*, solely on Sherman Act arguments. 376 U.S. at 673, 84 S.Ct. at 1038 (Harlan, J., dissenting).

11. *See, e.g.*, *Philadelphia Nat'l Bank*, 374 U.S. at 371, 83 S.Ct. at 1746 (Clayton Act "proscribed anticompetitive mergers, the benign and the malignant alike").

12. Pub. L. No. 89–356, 80 Stat. 7 (1966) (codified at 12 U.S.C.A. § 1828(c)). The FIRREA has amended the BMA in light in the significant changes in the federal regulatory structure. The FDIC is identified as the "responsible agency" for approval with respect to covered mergers and acquisitions "if the acquiring, assuming, or resulting bank is to be a State non-member insured bank (except a District [of Columbia] bank) or a savings bank supervised by the Director of Thrift Supervision." FIRREA, § 221(2)(A), 103 Stat. at 266–267 (codified at 12 U.S.C.A. § 1828(c)(2)(C)). In addition, insured savings associations are now brought under the jurisdiction of the BMA, FIRREA, § 201(a)(1), 103 Stat. at 187 (codified at 12 U.S.C.A. § 1828), and the OTS is identified as the "responsible agency" for approval with respect to covered mergers and acquisitions "if the acquiring, assuming, or resulting institution is to be a savings association." FIRREA, § 221(2)(A), 103 Stat. at 266–267 (codified at 12 U.S.C.A. § 1828(c)(2)(D)).

13. From 1982 to 1989, the BMA did not apply to a merger transaction involving an insured federal savings bank unless the resulting depository institution would have been an insured bank other than a federal savings bank. Pub. L. No. 97–320, § 113(n), 96 Stat. 1474 (1982) (codified at 12 U.S.C.A. § 1828(c)(12)). Section 504(b)(1) of the Competitive Equality Banking Act of 1987, Pub. L. No. 100–86, 101 Stat. 552, 632 (1987), further amended this provision to read as follows:

> The provisions of this subsection shall not apply to any transaction where the acquiring, assuming, or resulting institution is an insured Federal savings bank or an institution insured by the [FSLIC], except that any insured bank involved in the transaction shall notify the [FDIC] in writing at least 30 days prior to consummation of the transaction and, if any ap-

depository institution;[14] (2) assume liability to pay deposits in, or similar liabilities of, such an institution;[15] or, (3) transfer assets to such an institution in consideration of the assumption of liabilities for any deposits in the insured depository institution.[16] Any such transaction requires the prior written approval of the FDIC under the BMA.[17]

The BMA also applies to any insured depository institution that intends to "merge or consolidate with any other insured depository institution or, either directly or indirectly, acquire the assets of, or assume liability to pay any deposits" in any other insured depository institution.[18] All such transactions require the prior written approval under the BMA of the appropriate banking agency (including, as to savings associations, the OTS).[19]

When a BMA application is filed with the appropriate banking agency,[20] notice of the proposed acquisition generally must be published prior to the approval of the acquisition, in a form approved by the appropriate banking agency,[21] at appropriate intervals during the period of regulatory consideration[22] of the application.[23] The decision whether or not to grant a hearing on the application is within the discretion of the agency.[24]

Before acting on the application, the appropriate banking agency generally must request reports on the competitive factors involved in the proposed acquisition from the Attorney General and from each of the other three banking agencies.[25] The reports generally must be furnished within 30 calendar days of the request.[26]

proval by the [FHLBB] or the [FSLIC] is required in connection therewith, such approving authority shall provide the [FDIC] with notification of the application for approval, consult with the [FDIC] before disposing of the application, and shall provide notification to the [FDIC] of the determination with respect to said application.

12 U.S.C.A. § 1828(c)(12) (1988). With the inclusion of all insured depository institutions (including savings associations) under the jurisdiction of the BMA, this provision was repealed by the FIRREA. FIRREA, § 221(2)(B), 103 Stat. at 267.

14. 12 U.S.C.A. § 1828(c)(1)(A).

15. *Id.* § 1828(c)(1)(B). A 1978 amendment of this provision expressly included "liabilities which would be 'deposits' except for the proviso in [12 U.S.C.A. §] 1813(*l*)(5)," concerning deposits payable only at off-shore offices of a bank, within the coverage of this subsection of the BMA. Pub. L. No. 95–630, § 306, 92 Stat. 3677 (1978) (codified at 12 U.S.C.A. § 1828(c)(1)(B)).

16. 12 U.S.C.A. § 1828(c)(1)(C).

17. *Id.* § 1828(c)(1).

18. *Id.* § 1828(c)(2).

19. *Id.* § 1828(c)(2)(A)–(D).

20. *Id.* § 1828(c)(1), (2).

21. *Id.* § 1828(c)(3)(A)–(B).

22. The "period of regulatory consideration" will generally be 30 days, unless an emergency exists, in which case the period is 10 days. 12 U.S.C.A. § 1828(c)(3)(C), (4).

23. *Id.* § 1828(c)(3).

24. *See Washington v. Office of Comptroller of Currency*, 856 F.2d 1507, 1511–1512 (11th Cir.1988), *citing* 12 C.F.R. § 5.10(b)(3).

25. 12 U.S.C.A. § 1828(c)(4). This requirement is dispensed with if the appropriate banking agency finds that it must act on the application immediately, so as to prevent the probable default of one of the depository institutions involved in the merger. *Id.*

26. *Id.* This period is shortened to 10 days when the requesting agency advises the Attorney General and the other three agencies that an emergency exists that requires expeditious action on the application. *Id.* The request requirement can be dis-

If upon completion of its review of the application the appropriate agency approves the proposed acquisition, it is required to notify the Attorney General immediately of this decision.[27] Generally, an approved acquisition may not be consummated before 30 calendar days after the date of approval.[28] However, if the approving agency had requested agency reports during its review of the application on an emergency basis within 10 days, rather than 30 days, of its request,[29] then the acquisition may be consummated after the fifth calendar day following the approval.[30] If the approving agency had dispensed with agency reports because of the danger of probable default of one of the depository institutions involved in the acquisition,[31] then the acquisition may be consummated immediately upon its approval.[32]

In reviewing the transaction, the appropriate agency must consider the following statutory factors:

(1) *Monopolization.* The agency cannot approve a proposed transaction that would result in a monopoly, or that would be in furtherance of any combination or conspiracy to monopolize or to attempt to monopolize the business of banking in any part of the United States.[33]

(2) *Anticompetitiveness.* The agency cannot approve a proposed transaction the effect of which in any section of the country[34] may be substantially to lessen competition,[35] or to tend to create a monopo-

---

pensed with entirely if the appropriate agency determines that it must act immediately to prevent probable failure of one of the banks or savings associations involved in the transaction. *Id.*

27. *Id.* § 1828(c)(6).

28. *Id.*

29. *See id.* § 1828(c)(4) (concerning emergency requests).

30. *Id.* § 1828(c)(6).

31. *See id.* § 1828(c)(4) (concerning immediate action to prevent default).

32. *Id.* § 1828(c)(6).

33. *Id.* § 1828(c)(5)(A).

34. On the delineation of the geographic market, see generally *United States v. Long Island Jewish Med. Ctr.*, 983 F.Supp. 121 (E.D.N.Y.1997) (delineating geographic market for hospital) *Federal Trade Comm'n v. Freeman Hosp.*, 69 F.3d 260 (8th Cir. 1995) (same); *United States v. Mercy Health Servs.*, 902 F.Supp. 968 (N.D.Iowa 1995) (same), *vacated as moot*, 107 F.3d 632 (8th Cir.1997); *United States v. Gillette Co.*, 828 F.Supp. 78 (D.D.C.1993) (concerning market for pens); *Ansell Inc. v. Schmid Labs., Inc.*, 757 F.Supp. 467 (D.N.J.1991), *aff'd*, 941 F.2d 1200 (concerning nationwide market for condoms); *United States v. Country Lake Foods, Inc.*, 754 F.Supp. 669 (D.Minn.

1990) (delineating geographic market for milk); *United States v. M. P. M., Inc.*, 397 F.Supp. 78 (D.Colo.1975); *United States v. Phillipsburg Nat'l Bank & Trust Co.*, 399 U.S. 350, 90 S.Ct. 2035 (1970); *Southwest Mississippi Bank v. Federal Deposit Ins. Corp.*, 499 F.Supp. 1 (D.Miss.1979); *Washington Mut. Sav. Bank v. Federal Deposit Ins. Corp.*, 347 F.Supp. 790 (W.D.Wash. 1972), *aff'd* 482 F.2d 459 (9th Cir.1973). The burden of proof on the issue of delineation of the geographic market is plaintiff's. *Country Lake Foods, Inc., supra.*

35. On the effects of a proposed transaction on competition, see generally *New York v. Kraft Gen. Foods, Inc.*, 926 F.Supp. 321 (S.D.N.Y.1995); *Mercy Health Servs., supra*; *Bon-Ton Stores, Inc. v. May Dep't Stores Co.*, 881 F.Supp. 860 (W.D.N.Y.1994); *SCFC ILC, Inc. v. Visa U.S.A. Inc.*, 819 F.Supp. 956 (D.Utah 1993), *aff'd in part & rev'd in part*, 36 F.3d 958 (10th Cir.1994), *cert. denied sub nom. MountainWest Fin. Corp. v. Visa U.S.A., Inc.*, 515 U.S. 1152, 115 S.Ct. 2600 (1995); *United States v. Gillette Co.*, 828 F.Supp. 78 (D.D.C.1993); *Federal Trade Comm'n v. University Health, Inc.*, 938 F.2d 1206 (11th Cir.1991); *United States v. Baker Hughes Inc.*, 908 F.2d 981 (D.C.Cir. 1990); *United States v. Marine Bancorporation, Inc.*, 418 U.S. 602, 94 S.Ct. 2856 (1974); *Washington Mut. Sav. Bank v. Fed-*

ly, or that in any other manner would be in restraint of trade.[36] However, in a departure from *Philadelphia National Bank*,[37] the BMA permits approval of such a transaction if the agency finds that its anticompetitive effects "are clearly outweighed in the public interest by the probable effect of the transaction in meeting the convenience and needs of the community to be served."[38]

(3) *Traditional Banking Factors.* The agency must take into consideration the financial and managerial resources and the future prospects of the existing and proposed institutions, and the convenience and needs of the community to be served.[39]

Approval under the BMA does not shield the proposed transaction from attack by the Attorney General as violative of federal antitrust law.[40] However, any action brought by the Justice Department under the

eral Deposit Ins. Corp., 482 F.2d 459 (9th Cir.1973). On the burden of proof with respect to anticompetitive effects, see *United States v. United Tote, Inc.*, 768 F.Supp. 1064 (D.Del.1991).

36. 12 U.S.C.A. § 1828(c)(5)(B). On the determination of the "line of commerce" affected by the possible anticompetitive effects of the proposed transaction, see generally *Long Island Jewish Med. Ctr., supra* (concerning hospitals); *Community Publishers, Inc. v. Donrey Corp.*, 892 F.Supp. 1146 (W.D.Ark.1995) (concerning small town newspapers); *Appraisers Coalition v. Appraisal Inst.*, 845 F.Supp. 592 (N.D.Ill.1994) (concerning appraisal services); *Bon-Ton Stores, Inc., supra* (concerning submarkets); *Federal Trade Comm'n v. Alliant Techsystems Inc.*, 808 F.Supp. 9 (D.D.C.1992) (servicing of 120 millimeter ammunition rounds); *Ansell Inc., supra* (concerning cross-elasticity of demand in condom market); *United States v. Connecticut Nat'l Bank*, 418 U.S. 656, 94 S.Ct. 2788 (1974) (thrift institutions excluded); *Washington Mut. Sav. Bank, supra* (same); *United States v. First Nat'l Bank of Jackson*, 301 F.Supp. 1161 (D.Miss.1969) (*contra*); *United States v. Crocker–Anglo Nat'l Bank*, 277 F.Supp. 133 (N.D.Cal.1967). Complainant bears the burden of proof on the issue of delineation of the product market. *United States v. Engelhard Corp.*, 970 F.Supp. 1463 (M.D.Ga.1997).

37. *See* 374 U.S. at 371, 83 S.Ct. at 1745–1746 (rejecting convenience and needs defense).

38. 12 U.S.C.A. § 1828(c)(5)(B). On the convenience and needs defense, see generally *Marine Bancorporation, supra*; *Phillipsburg Nat'l Bank & Trust Co., supra*; *United States v. Third Nat'l Bank in Nashville*, 390 U.S. 171, 88 S.Ct. 882 (1968); *United States v. First Nat'l Bank of Md.*, 310 F.Supp. 157

(D.Md.1970); *United States v. Provident Nat'l Bank*, 280 F.Supp. 1 (E.D.Pa.1968); *Crocker-Anglo Nat'l Bank, supra.*

39. 12 U.S.C.A. § 1828(c)(5). On the balancing of anticompetitive and banking factors, see generally *Phillipsburg Nat'l Bank, supra*; *Third Nat'l Bank in Nashville, supra*; *United States v. First City Nat'l Bank of Houston*, 386 U.S. 361, 87 S.Ct. 1088 (1967).

40. *See* 12 U.S.C.A. § 1828(c)(7)(A). *See First City Nat'l Bank of Houston, supra* (involving Justice Department challenge despite Comptroller's approval); *United States v. Citizens & Southern Nat'l Bank*, 339 F.Supp. 1143 (N.D.Ga.1972) (same; FDIC's approval). The BMA does not alter the antitrust rules generally applicable in determining whether a proposed acquisition would be violative of the antitrust laws. *See Third Nat'l Bank in Nashville, supra*; *Philadelphia Nat'l Bank, supra.* There has been some dispute whether the language of the BMA restricts the Justice Department to Sections 1 and 2 of the Sherman Act and Section 7 of the Clayton Act, or whether the DOJ may draw upon the federal antitrust laws generally. *Compare United States v. Provident Nat'l Bank*, 259 F.Supp. 373 (E.D.Pa.1966), *with United States v. Manufacturers Hanover Trust Co.*, 240 F.Supp. 867 (S.D.N.Y.1965); *United States v. First Nat'l Bank & Trust Co. of Lexington*, 208 F.Supp. 457 (E.D.Ky.1962), *rev'd on other grounds*, 376 U.S. 665, 84 S.Ct. 1033 (1964). The better view is that the action is based upon the antitrust laws, not the BMA, but with the additional "convenience and needs" defense provided by the BMA. *See, e.g., First City Nat'l Bank of Houston, supra*; *United States v. County Nat'l Bank of Bennington*, 330 F.Supp. 155 (D.Vt. 1971).

antitrust laws arising out of an approved acquisition must be commenced prior to the earliest time at which the acquisition could be consummated under the BMA.[41] Commencement of the action automatically stays the effectiveness of the agency approval of the proposed acquisition,[42] although the court has authority to remove the stay by specific order.[43]

§ 4.15   Interstate Mergers

As of June 1, 1997,[1] under the Riegle–Neal Interstate Banking and Branching Efficiency Act of 1994 ("IBBEA"), the responsible federal agencies[2] are generally permitted to approve interstate merger transactions under the BMA between insured banks with different home states, regardless of state law prohibitions. This authority is subject to election by the home state of a merging bank to enact a law expressly prohibiting merger transactions involving out-of-state banks.[3] Any such state law must be applicable to all out-of-state banks.[4] State election has no effect on merger transactions approved before the effective date of the state law.[5]

The responsible federal agency (OCC, Fed, or OTS) is generally not permitted to approve an interstate merger that would contravene applicable state statutory law requiring a bank to be in existence for a minimum period of time before a merger.[6] However, the agency may approve such a merger if the target bank has been in existence for at least five years, notwithstanding any longer minimum period specified in the statutory law of the host state.[7]

---

41.   12 U.S.C.A. § 1828(c)(7)(A).

42.   *Id.*

43.   *Id.*

§ 4.15

1. Interstate merger approvals by the responsible federal agency were permitted prior to June 1, 1997, if the home state of each bank involved in the transaction had already elected to permit interstate mergers. 12 U.S.C.A. § 1831u(a)(3)(A). The state law had to apply equally to all out-of-state banks, *id.* § 1831u(a)(3)(A)(i), and it had to expressly permit such transactions with all out-of-state banks. *Id.* § 1831u(a)(3)(A)(ii).

In early merger situations, the host state was permitted under the IBBEA to impose certain conditions on instate branches of the resulting bank in an interstate merger transaction. *Id.* § 1831u(a)(3)(B). Such conditions could not have the effect of discriminating against out-of-state banks, bank holding companies, or subsidiaries thereof. *Id.* § 1831u(a)(3)(B)(i). The restriction against discriminatory conditions would not apply to a nationwide reciprocal treatment requirement. *Id.* § 1831u(a)(3)(B)(i). The imposition of the conditions must not otherwise be preempted by federal law. *Id.*

§ 1831u(a)(3)(B)(ii). Finally, any such conditions must lapse after May 31, 1997. *Id.* § 1831u(a)(3)(B)(iii).

2. For these purposes, the "responsible agency" means the Comptroller, if the acquiring bank is a national bank or a District of Columbia bank; the Fed is the "responsible agency" if the bank is a state member bank (other than a District of Columbia bank); the FDIC, if the bank is a state nonmember insured bank (other than a District of Columbia bank or a savings bank supervised by the OTS); and the OTS, if the acquiring institution is a savings association. *Id.* § 1828(c)(2)(A)–(D).

3. *Id.* § 1831u(a)(2)(A)(ii).

4. *Id.* § 1831u(a)(2)(A)(i).

5. *Id.* § 1831u(a)(2)(B).

6. *Id.* § 1831u(a)(5)(A). For these purposes, a "shell" or "phantom" bank, created to be controlled by the acquiring bank holding company and to receive an existing target bank, is deemed to have been in existence for as long as the target bank has been in existence. *Id.* § 1831u(a)(6).

7. *Id.* § 1831u(a)(5)(B).

Under IBBEA, an interstate merger transaction may involve the acquisition of a branch[8] of an insured bank without the acquisition of the entire target bank.[9] Such acquisitions will be permitted only if the law of the state in which the target branch is located permits out-of-state banks to acquire a branch without acquisition of the entire target bank.[10]

Essentially the same rules apply to a consolidation involving a national bank.[11] There is now express authority for a consolidation or merger by a national bank with an out-of-state bank, if the consolidation or merger is approved pursuant to the interstate merger transaction provisions.[12] This authority was not available for any consolidation or merger before June 1, 1997, unless the home state of each bank involved in the transaction had an early interstate merger transaction provision.[13]

Any interstate merger involving insured depository institutions is subject to the application and approval requirements of the BMA.[14] In addition, IBBEA requires compliance with certain state filing requirements.[15] Material failure to comply with these state filing requirements bars approval of the BMA application.[16] A bank that files a BMA application for an interstate merger transaction must comply with filing requirements of any host state of the resulting bank, so long as the requirements do not have the effect of discriminating against out-of-state banks, bank holding companies, or subsidiaries thereof.[17] The filing requirements must also be similar in effect to any requirement imposed by the host state on out-of-state nonbanking corporations engaging in business in the host state.[18] The applicant must submit a copy of the BMA application to the state bank supervisor of the host state.[19]

In addition, certain nationwide and statewide concentration limits will apply to interstate merger transactions, except for transactions involving only affiliated banks.[20] First, the responsible federal agency is not permitted to approve an interstate merger transaction if the resulting bank[21] would control upon consummation of the transaction more than 10 percent of the total amount of deposits of insured depository

---

8. Where an interstate transaction involves acquisition of a branch of an insured bank, without acquisition of the bank itself, the branch will be treated as an insured bank, the home state of which is the state in which the branch is located. *Id.* § 1831u(a)(4)(B).

9. *Id.* § 1831u(a)(4)(A).

10. *Id.*

11. *See* IBBEA, § 102(b)(4), 108 Stat. at 2351–2352 (codified at 12 U.S.C.A. §§ 215, 215a–1).

12. 12 U.S.C.A. § 215a–1(a).

13. *Id.* § 215a–1(b). *See id.* § 1831u(a)(3) (state early interstate merger transaction provision).

14. *See id.* § 1828(c).

15. *See id.* § 1831u(b)(1).

16. *Id.* § 1831u(b)(1)(B).

17. *Id.* § 1831u(b)(1)(A)(i)(I).

18. *Id.* § 1831u(b)(1)(A)(i)(II). In other words, the filing requirement applicable to the out-of-state bank must essentially be similar to generally applicable corporate law provisions requiring registration of foreign corporations doing business within the state. *See, e.g.,* N.Y. Bus. Corp. Law art. 13 (foreign corporations).

19. 12 U.S.C.A. § 1831u(b)(1)(A)(ii).

20. *Id.* § 1831u(b)(2)(E).

21. For these purposes, the "applicant" would include all insured depository institutions that are affiliates of the resulting bank. *Id.* § 1831u(b)(2)(A).

institutions in the United States.[22] Second, as to transactions other than initial entry into the host state, the agency is not permitted to approve a transaction if: (1) any bank involved in the transaction has a branch in any state in which any other bank involved in the transaction has a branch;[23] and, (2) upon consummation, the resulting bank would control 30 percent or more of the total amount of deposits of insured depository institutions in any such state.[24] These concentration provisions do not affect state authority to limit the percentage of the total amount of deposits of insured depository institutions in the state held or controlled by any bank, bank holding company, and subsidiaries thereof.[25]

Approval of an interstate merger is subject to the following considerations identified in the IBBEA:

(1) If the merger would give the resulting bank a branch or bank affiliate in a state in which the acquiring bank had no branch or bank affiliate, the responsible federal agency must apply the Community Reinvestment Act ("CRA") in its consideration of the application.[26] It must take into account the most recent written CRA evaluation of any bank that would be an affiliate of the resulting bank.[27] The agency must also take into account the record of any applicant bank in complying with applicable state community reinvestment laws.[28]

(2) The responsible federal agency must take into account adequacy of capital and management. The agency is permitted to approve an interstate merger transaction only if each bank involved is adequately capitalized as of the date on which the application is filed.[29] It must also determine that the resulting bank will continue to be adequately capitalized and adequately managed upon consummation of the transaction.[30]

(3) Interstate transactions remain fully subject to applicable antitrust laws.[31] The agency must also take into account the applicability of any similar state anticompetitive laws.[32]

A general exception exists for interstate merger transactions involving banks in default or in danger of default. In these situations IBBEA

---

22. *Id.* § 1831u(b)(2)(E).

23. *Id.*

24. *Id.* § 1831u(b)(2)(B)(ii). However, the transaction will be permitted if a state deposit cap limitation (*see* text, *infra*; 12 U.S.C.A. § 1831u(b)(2)(C)) permits a bank or bank holding company (and affiliates thereof) to control a greater percentage of total deposits. 12 U.S.C.A. § 1831u(b)(2)(D)(i). The transaction will also be permitted if approved by the appropriate state bank supervisor of the host state under a standard that does not have the effect of discriminating against out-of-state banks, bank holding companies, and subsidiaries thereof. *Id.* § 1831u(b)(2)(D)(ii).

25. 12 U.S.C.A. § 1831u(b)(2)(C). These state deposit caps are given effect so long as they do not discriminate against out-of-state banks, bank holding companies, and subsidiaries thereof. *Id.*

26. *Id.* § 1831u(b)(3)(A).

27. *Id.* § 1831u(b)(3)(B).

28. *Id.* § 1831u(b)(3)(C).

29. *Id.* § 1831u(b)(4)(A).

30. *Id.* § 1831u(b)(4)(B).

31. *Id.* § 1831u(c)(2)(A).

32. *Id.* § 1831u(c)(2)(B).

waives the following requirements: (1) state election to prohibit interstate merger transactions; (2) branch acquisition provisions; (3) state law provisions concerning required minimum years of existence prior to merger; (4) compliance with state filing requirements; (5) concentration limits; (6) community reinvestment compliance; and (7) adequacy of capital and management.[33] The responsible federal agency may approve an application for an interstate merger in which one or more banks in default or in danger of default are involved, or as to which financial assistance is provided by the FDIC under Section 13(c) of the Federal Deposit Insurance Act ("FDIA").[34]

If the interstate merger transaction is approved, the charters of all banks involved, except for the resulting bank, must be surrendered, upon request, to the federal or state chartering authority.[35] Subject to the approval of the appropriate federal banking agency, the resulting bank may retain and operate, as a main office or branch, any office that any bank involved in the transaction was operating immediately before the merger transaction.[36] In addition, after consummation of the transaction, the resulting bank is permitted to establish, acquire, or operate additional branches at any location where any involved bank could have done so under federal or state law, if it had not been involved in the transaction.[37]

§ 4.16 Effect on Branch Ownership and Control

One effect of the interstate merger transaction provisions will be to create new interstate patterns of branch ownership and control. The IBBEA therefore includes certain conforming amendments to other provisions of federal law concerning branches.

Domestic branching by national banks is governed by the NBA.[1] IBBEA amends the NBA on this point in several respects.[2] A national bank that results from an interstate merger transaction is permitted to maintain and operate a branch in a host state, in accordance with the interstate merger transaction provisions.[3] Effective June 1, 1997, a national bank generally may acquire, establish, or operate a branch in a host state (including a host state in which it already has a branch) only if

---

33. *Id.* § 1831u(e).

34. *See id.* § 1823(c) (financial assistance under FDIA).

35. *Id.* § 1831u(b)(5).

36. *Id.* § 1831u(d)(1). However, IBBEA has required the federal banking agencies to promulgate regulations prohibiting any out-of-state bank from using any authority to engage in interstate branching primarily for the purpose of deposit production. *Id.* § 1835a.

37. *Id.* § 1831u(d)(2).

§ 4.16

1. 12 U.S.C.A. § 36.

2. *See id.* § 36(d)–(f), (h)–(*l*).

3. *Id.* § 36(d). However, IBBEA required the federal banking agencies to promulgate regulations prohibiting any out-of-state bank from using any authority to engage in interstate branching primarily for the purpose of deposit production. *Id.* § 1835a.

authorized by the amended NBA, the emergency acquisition provisions of the FDIA,[4] or the new interstate merger transactions provision.[5] If a national bank relocates its main office from one state to another after May 31, 1997,[6] the bank may retain and operate its branches within its former home state only to the extent that the bank would be authorized to acquire, establish, or commence operation of a branch in such a state.[7]

In general, any host-state branch of an out-of-state national bank will be subject to host state laws concerning community reinvestment, consumer protection, fair lending, and establishment of intrastate branches to the same extent as a state-chartered bank would be.[8] However, this rule does not apply if federal law preempts the application of any such state law to a national bank.[9] The rule also does not apply if the Comptroller of the Currency determines that application of any such state law would have a discriminatory effect on the national bank branch, as compared to its effect on branches of state-chartered banks.[10] All other laws of the host state, except for the application or administration of any tax or method of taxation, apply to the in-state branches of an out-of-state national bank to the same extent such laws would apply if the in-state branch were itself a national bank with its main office in the host state.[11]

The FDIA has also been amended to apply to branches of state nonmember banks in host states rules that correspond to those applicable to branches of national banks in host states.[12] Thus, such state nonmember banks will be subject to corresponding exclusive rules with respect to the acquisition, establishment, and operation of host state branches,[13] retention of branches upon out-of-state relocation of the main office,[14] and applicability of host state law to the activities of the in-

---

4. *See id.* § 1823(f), (k).

5. *Id.* § 36(e)(1).

6. *Cf. id.* § 30(c) (coordinating NBA relocation provision with new § 36(e)(2) governing retention of branches).

7. *Id.* § 36(e)(2). In determining whether the national bank would have been authorized "to acquire, establish or commence to operate" such a branch, the provision contemplates a situation in which:

    (1) the bank had no branches in the former home state (*i.e.*, where it had previously operated only a main office in the former home state); or,

    (2) the branch resulted from either an interstate merger transaction under section 1831u, or a transaction after May 31, 1997, pursuant to which the bank received financial assistance from the FDIC under section 1823(c).

Id. § 36(e)(2)(A)–(B).

8. *Id.* § 36(f)(1)(A). Enforcement of these state laws with respect to national

bank branches is the responsibility of the Comptroller of the Currency, not the applicable state authority. *Id.* § 36(f)(1)(B).

9. *Id.* § 36(f)(1)(A)(i). This provision does not affect the generally applicable legal standards with respect to preemption of the application of state law to national banks. *Id.* § 36(f)(3). On notice requirements for federal bank agency decisions preempting state law, see *id.* § 43.

10. *Id.* § 36(f)(1)(A)(ii).

11. *Id.* § 36(f)(2).

12. *Id.* §§ 1828(d)(3), 1831a(j).

13. *Compare id.* § 36(e)(1), *as amended* (NBA provision), *with id.* § 1828(d)(3)(A) (corresponding FDIA provision applicable to state nonmember banks).

14. *Compare id.* § 36(e)(2), *as amended* (NBA provision), *with id.* § 1828(d)(3)(B) (corresponding FDIA provision applicable to state nonmember banks).

state branch.[15] In addition, the FDIA has been amended to prohibit an in-state branch of an out-of-state state nonmember bank from conducting any activity that is not permissible for a state-chartered bank in the host state.[16]

§ 4.17   State Authority

The interstate merger transaction provisions do not affect the authority of any state or political subdivision thereof to adopt, apply, or administer any tax or method of taxation to any bank, bank holding company, foreign bank, or any affiliate thereof.[1] However, the tax or tax method must be one that is otherwise permissible under the U.S. Constitution or other federal law.[2] In addition, in the case of an in-state branch of an out-of-state bank resulting from an interstate merger transaction, the value of the bank's shares may be subjected to any bank shares tax of the host state or its political subdivisions, on a proportional basis.[3]

As to supervisory concerns, under IBBEA the states retain the authority to supervise, regulate, and examine their respective state-chartered banks.[4] In addition, IBBEA also does not limit the right of a state to determine the authority of its state-chartered banks to establish and maintain branches.[5] A host state may also impose notification or reporting requirements on branches of out-of-state banks.[6]

Furthermore, the interposition of IBBEA does not necessarily preempt previously imposed conditions on and commitments of out-of-state banks by host states.[7] If, in connection with approval of a pre-IBBEA acquisition of a bank by an out-of-state bank holding company, the home state of the target bank imposed conditions or the company made commitments to the home state, the state may continue to enforce those conditions or commitments.[8] Indeed, the state may enforce the conditions or commitments to the same extent even with respect to an affiliated successor company that controls an in-state bank or branch as a result of an interstate merger transaction.[9]

---

15. *Compare id.* § 36(f)(1)(A), *as amended* (NBA provision), *with id.* § 1831a(j)(1) (corresponding FDIA provision applicable to state nonmember banks).

16. *Id.* § 1831a(j)(2).

§ 4.17

1. 12 U.S.C.A. § 1831u(c)(1)(A).

2. *Id.*

3. *Id.* § 1831u(c)(1)(B).

4. *Id.* § 1831u(c)(3)(B).

5. *Id.* § 1831u(c)(3)(A).

6. *Id.* § 1831u(c)(4). Such requirements must not discriminate against out-of-state banks or bank holding companies. *Id.*

§ 1831u(c)(4)(A). They may be subject to preemption by federal laws other than the IBBEA on the same subject. *See id.* § 1831u(c)(4)(B) (permitting states to impose notification and reporting requirements if "not preempted by any Federal law").

7. *See id.* § 1831u(d)(3) (rules governing prior conditions and commitments). On notice requirements for federal bank agency decisions preempting state law, see *id.* § 43.

8. *Id.* § 1831u(d)(3)(A)–(B).

9. *Id.* § 1831u(d)(3).

§ 4.18   Change-in-Control Transactions

In the area of control transactions, the difference between the regulated industry and other sectors is often merely a matter of degree. Mergers and acquisitions are, after all, generally subject to a potentially significant degree of regulation. Similarly, interlocking directorates of depository institutions may be subject to a significant degree of restriction and regulation,[1] and yet there are also restrictions on interlocks under generally applicable federal antitrust law.[2]

However, acquisitions in the depository institution sector are not only subjected to antitrust review and securities disclosure requirements, but also to substantive review on the merits. The pervasiveness of regulation is particularly marked when we consider acquisitions of control of depository institutions, undertaken by individuals through stock purchases, not involving publicly-traded corporate entities. Such acquisitions would rarely if ever attract antitrust analysis or securities disclosure requirements. Yet they remain subject to a significant degree of substantive review on the merits under change-in-control requirements in depository institutions law.

§ 4.19   Change in Bank Control Act

The Change in Bank Control Act ("CBCA")[1] was enacted in 1978 to provide the "statutory authority . . . needed to give financial institution regulators authority over . . . transfers"[2] of control by individuals.[3] An acquisition of control by any person of an existing FDIC-insured depository institution or of a holding company[4] is subject to the CBCA's

---

§ 4.18

1. *See, e.g.,* 12 U.S.C.A. §§ 3201 *et seq.* (Depository Institutions Management Interlocks Act).

2. 15 U.S.C.A. § 19. *See generally Bankamerica Corp. v. United States,* 462 U.S. 122, 103 S.Ct. 2266 (1983) (discussing interlock provision of Clayton Act; holding provision inapplicable to bank holding company/insurance company interlock).

§ 4.19

1. 12 U.S.C.A. § 1817(j).

2. H.R. Rep. No. 1383, 95th Cong., 1st Sess. (1978), *reprinted in,* 1978 U.S. Code Cong. & Admin. News 9273, 9292.

3. On changes in control, see generally *Sletteland v. Federal Deposit Ins. Corp.,* 924 F.2d 350 (D.C.Cir.1991); *Citibank Fed. Sav. Bank v. Federal Deposit Ins. Corp.,* 836 F.Supp. 3 (D.D.C.1993). A persuasive case has been made for the proposition that the

statute is not intended to grant a private right of action. *See Indiana Nat'l Corp. v. Rich,* 712 F.2d 1180 (7th Cir.1983) (reviewing CBCA legislative history); *Quaker City Nat'l Bank v. Hartley,* 533 F.Supp. 126 (S.D.Ohio 1981) (rejecting *First Alabama, infra*). *But see First Alabama Bancshares, Inc. v. Lowder,* [1981 Transfer Binder] Fed. Sec. L. Rep. (CCH) ¶ 98,015 (N.D. Ala. 1981) (finding private right of action); *Mid-Continent Bancshares, Inc. v. O'Brien,* [1981 Transfer Binder] Fed. Sec. L. Rep. (CCH) ¶ 98,734 (E.D. Mo. 1981) (relying on *First Alabama*); *CityFed Fin. Corp. v. Federal Home Loan Bank Bd.,* 615 F.Supp. 1122 (D.D.C.1985) (interpreting prior statutory language; finding SLHC to be "party aggrieved").

4. By its own terms, the CBCA applied to acquisitions of control of FDIC-insured depository institutions, but it defined "insured depository institution" for these purposes to include "any depository institution holding company" and any other company relatively passive disapproval process.[5] The scope of the CBCA was significantly expanded in 1989, with the passage of the Financial Institutions Reform, Recovery, and Enforcement Act ("FIRREA").[6] As amended, the CBCA now applies to insured depository institutions rather than insured banks.[7] The OTS is the "appropriate Federal banking agency" for these purposes with respect to savings associations.[8]

The CBCA prohibits any person,[9] directly or indirectly or through or in concert with one or more other persons, from acquiring "control"[10] of an insured depository institution or holding company through the purchase, assignment, transfer, pledge, or other disposition of the target's voting stock, unless: (1) the person has given prior notice to the "appropriate Federal banking agency;" and, (2) the agency has not disapproved the acquisition within the statutory time period.[11]

that controls an insured depository institution. 12 U.S.C.A. § 1817(j)(18)(A)–(B).

5. *See id.* § 1817(j)(1) (affirmative regulatory approval of change in control not required).

6. Pub. L. No. 101–73, 103 Stat. 183 (1989), §§ 201(a)(1), 201(b), 208(8)-(13), 905(c), 907(d), 103 Stat. at 187–188, 213, 460, 468–469 (codified at 12 U.S.C.A. § (j)(2)(A), (j)(2)(D), (j)(7)(F), (j)(15), (j)(16)–(18)).

7. *See* FIRREA, § 201(a)(1), 103 Stat. at 187 (codified at 12 U.S.C.A. § 1817).

8. 12 U.S.C.A. § 1813(q)(4).

9. For these purposes, "person" is defined to mean "an individual or a corporation, partnership, trust, association, joint venture, pool, syndicate, sole proprietorship, unincorporated organization, or any other form of entity not specifically listed herein." *Id.* § 1817(j)(8)(A). *But cf. id.* § 1817(j)(17) (acquisitions subject to 12 U.S.C.A. §§ 1467a, 1828(c), 1842 not subject to CBCA).

10. For these purposes, the term "control" is defined to mean "the power, directly or indirectly, to direct the management or policies of an insured depository institution or to vote 25 per centum or more of any class of voting securities of an insured depository institution." *Id.* § 1817(j)(8)(B) On the meaning of "control" under the CBCA, see *Zinman v. Federal Deposit Ins. Corp.*, 567 F.Supp. 243 (E.D.Pa.1983); *Citizens First Bancorp v. Harrell*, 559 F.Supp. 867 (W.D.Ky.1982); *Southeast Banking Corp. v. Adler*, [1982–1983 Transfer Binder] Fed. Sec. L. Rep. (CCH) ¶ 99,183 (S.D. Fla. 1982); *Riggs Nat'l Bank v. Allbritton*, 516 F.Supp. 164, 179 (D.D.C.1981).

11. 12 U.S.C.A. § 1817(j)(1). For these purposes, the "appropriate Federal banking agency" is defined to mean:

(1) the Comptroller of the Currency, in the case of any national banking association, any District [of Columbia] bank, or any Federal branch or agency of a foreign bank;

(2) the Board of Governors of the Federal Reserve System, in the case of—

(A) any State member insured bank (except a District bank),

(B) any branch or agency of a foreign bank with respect to any provision of the Federal Reserve Act which is made applicable under the International Banking Act of 1978[, 12 U.S.C.A. §§ 3101 *et seq.*],

(C) any foreign bank which does not operate an insured branch,

(D) any agency or commercial lending company other than a Federal agency,

(E) supervisory or regulatory proceedings arising from the authority given to the Board of Governors under section 7(c)(1) of the International Banking Act of 1978, including such proceedings under the Depository Institutions Supervisory Act, and

(F) any bank holding company and any subsidiary of a bank holding company (other than a bank);

(3) the Federal Deposit Insurance Corporation in the case of a State nonmember insured bank (except a District bank), or a foreign bank having an insured branch; and

(4) the Director of the Office of Thrift Supervision in the case of any savings association or any savings and loan holding company.

Id. § 1813(q)(1)–(4). As to the statutory time period for disapproval of changes in control, the appropriate federal banking

The CBCA requires that, except as otherwise provided by regulation, the CBCA notice filed by the acquiring party must contain the following information:

(A) The identity, personal history, business background and experience of each person by whom or on whose behalf the acquisition is to be made, including his material business activities and affiliations during the past five years, and a description of any material pending legal or administrative proceedings in which he is a party and any criminal indictment or conviction of such person by a State or Federal court.

(B) A statement of the assets and liabilities of each person by whom or on whose behalf the acquisition is to be made, as of the end of the fiscal year for each of the five fiscal years immediately preceding the date of the notice, together with related statements of income and source and application of funds for each of the fiscal years then concluded, all prepared in accordance with generally accepted accounting principles consistently applied, and an interim statement of the assets and liabilities for each such person, together with related statements of income and source and application of funds, as of a date not more than ninety days prior to the date of the filing of the notice.

(C) The terms and conditions of the proposed acquisition and the manner in which the acquisition is to be made.

(D) The identity, source and amount of the funds or other consideration used or to be used in making the acquisition, and if any part of these funds or other consideration has been or is to be borrowed or otherwise obtained for the purpose of making the acquisition, a description of the transaction, the names of the parties, and any arrangements, agreements, or understandings with such persons.

(E) Any plans or proposals which any acquiring party making the acquisition may have to liquidate the bank, to sell its assets or merge it with any company or to make any other major change in its business or corporate structure or management.

agency generally has 60 days from the submission of a CBCA notice to decide whether to disapprove the change in control. *Id.* § 1817(j)(1). In the agency's discretion, this time period may be extended "for an additional 30 days during which such a disapproval may issue." *Id.* The period of disapproval "may be extended not to exceed 2 additional times for not more than 45 days each time," *id.*, but on the explicit condition that

(A) the agency determines that any acquiring party has not furnished all the information [required under 12 U.S.C.A. § 1817(j)(6), discussed *infra*];

(B) in the agency's judgment, any material information submitted is substantially inaccurate;

(C) the agency has been unable to complete the investigation of an acquiring party under paragraph (2)(B) because of any delay caused by, or the inadequate cooperation of, such acquiring party; or

(D) the agency determines that additional time is needed to investigate and determine that no acquiring party has a record of failing to comply with the requirements of [31 U.S.C.A. §§ 5311–5324].

12 U.S.C.A. § 1817(j)(1)(A)–(D).

(F) The identification of any person employed, retained, or to be compensated by the acquiring party, or by any person on his behalf, to make solicitations or recommendations to stockholders for the purpose of assisting in the acquisition, and a brief description of the terms of such employment, retainer, or arrangement for compensation.

(G) Copies of all invitations or tenders or advertisements making a tender offer to stockholders for purchase of their stock to be used in connection with the proposed acquisition.

(H) Any additional relevant information in such form as the appropriate Federal banking agency may require by regulation or by specific request in connection with any particular notice.[12]

Upon receipt of the notice, the appropriate agency must "within a reasonable period of time" publish the name of the target and each proposed acquiring person and solicit public comment, before the agency's final consideration of the notice, on the proposed change in control, particularly from persons in the geographic area in which the target is located.[13] If the target institution is state-chartered, the agency must forward a copy of the notice to the appropriate state supervisory agency.[14] In any event, the agency determination of whether or not to disapprove the acquisition may be based on any of the following statutory factors:

(A) the proposed acquisition of control would result in a monopoly or would be in furtherance of any combination or conspiracy to monopolize or to attempt to monopolize the business of banking in any part of the United States;

(B) the effect of the proposed acquisition of control in any section of the country may be substantially to lessen competition or to tend to create a monopoly or the proposed acquisition of control would in any other manner be in restraint of trade, and the anticompetitive effects of the proposed acquisition of control are not clearly outweighed in the public interest by the probable effect of the transaction in meeting the convenience and needs of the community to be served;[15]

(C) the financial condition of any acquiring person is such as might jeopardize the financial stability of the bank or prejudice the

---

12. 12 U.S.C.A. § 1817(j)(6)(A)–(H).

13. *Id.* § 1817(j)(2)(D)(i)–(ii). Each of these requirements is eliminated if the agency makes a written determination that the required disclosure or solicitation would seriously threaten the safety or soundness of the target bank. *Id.* § 1817(j)(2)(D).

14. *Id.* § 1817(j)(2)(A). In such cases, the agency must give the state agency 30 days to submit its views and recommendations with respect to the proposed acquisition. *Id.* However, in situations in which the agency must act immediately to prevent

probable failure of the target, the agency may dispense with notice to the state agency, or require that the agency's views and recommendations be submitted immediately. *Id.* The federal agency receiving CBCA notice must also immediately furnish a copy of the notice to the other "appropriate Federal banking agencies." *Id.* § 1817(j)(11).

15. On the convenience and needs concept, see *United States v. Central State Bank*, 564 F.Supp. 1478 (W.D.Mich.1983).

interests of the depositors of the bank;[16]

(D) the competence, experience, or integrity of any acquiring person or of any of the proposed management personnel indicates that it would not be in the interest of the depositors of the bank, or in the interest of the public to permit such person to control the bank;[17]

(E) any acquiring person neglects, fails, or refuses to furnish the appropriate Federal banking agency all the information required by the appropriate Federal banking agency; or

(F) the appropriate Federal banking agency determines that the proposed transaction would result in an adverse effect on the Bank Insurance Fund or the Savings Association Insurance Fund.[18]

If the agency disapproves a proposed transaction, it must notify the acquiring party in writing of the disapproval within three days after the decision to disapprove is made.[19] Within 10 days of receipt of this notification, the acquiring party may request an APA hearing[20] on the proposed acquisition.[21] At the conclusion of the hearing, the agency is required to approve or disapprove the proposed acquisition by order, on the basis of the hearing record.[22]

If the agency issues an order of disapproval after hearing on the record, the acquiring party may obtain judicial review of the order in the U.S. court of appeals for the circuit in which the home office of the target is located, or in the U.S. Court of Appeals for the District of Columbia.[23] The agency is required to certify and file promptly in the court the record upon which the disapproval was based.[24] However, despite the existence of a certified record on an APA hearing, the specified standard of judicial review is whether the findings of the agency are "arbitrary or capricious or ... violate procedures established by [the CBCA]."[25]

The agency may issue a written notice of its intention not to disapprove the acquisition prior to the expiration of the notice period.[26] In any event, if the acquisition of control is not disapproved by the

---

16. The CBCA explicitly requires the agency to conduct an investigation of financial ability. 12 U.S.C.A. § 1817 (j)(2)(B)(i). On the agencies' investigative and enforcement authority for these purposes, see *id.* § 1817(j)(15).

17. The CBCA explicitly requires the agency to conduct an investigation of competence, experience, and integrity. *Id.* § 1817(j)(2)(B)(i). On the agencies' investigative and enforcement authority for these purposes, see *id.* § 1817(j)(15).

18. *Id.* § 1817(j)(7)(A)–(F). The CBCA requires the agency to make an independent determination of the accuracy and completeness of information in the submitted notice. *Id.* § 1817(j)(2)(B)(ii).

19. *Id.* § 1817(j)(3).

20. *See* 5 U.S.C.A. § 554.

21. 12 U.S.C.A. § 1817(j)(4). All issues are to be determined on the record, with the length of the hearing determined by the agency. *See id.*

22. *Id.*

23. *Id.* § 1817(j)(5). On judicial review under the savings association predecessor statute to the CBCA, see *Investors Sav. Ass'n v. Federal Sav. & Loan Ins. Corp.,* 583 F.Supp. 974 (S.D.Tex.1984).

24. 12 U.S.C.A. § 1817(j)(5).

25. *Id.*

26. *Id.* 1817(j)(1)(D).

agency and a change in control results, the target is required to report promptly to the agency "any changes or replacement of its [CEO] or any director occurring in the next twelve-month period."[27] The report must include a statement of past and current business and professional affiliations of the new CEO or directors.

§ 4.20 State   Change-in-Control   Provisions

There is a wide divergence in state regulatory approaches to changes in control.[1] However, several distinct trends can be identified among the various approaches taken by states, together with a range of hybrids.[2] A small number of states have tended to require little or no regulatory oversight of such transactions.[3] A few others generally follow a "pure notification" model, requiring formal notification to the supervisory authorities upon a change in control.[4] Beginning in the 1980s, however, the predominant trend among the states by a narrow margin was one that followed the prior notice approach of the federal CBCA,[5] prohibiting acquisition of control or consummation of a control transaction in the absence of prior regulatory review.[6]

At the other extreme, the second most prominent model for change-in-control regulation at the state level was one that prohibited, in the absence of approval by the state supervisor, tender offers for, requests or invitations for tenders of, or offers to exchange securities for, any voting securities of a bank.[7] In some cases, these provisions were so restrictive, that they could raise questions of federal preemption because of possible conflicts between state bank regulatory law and, for example, the federal securities law provisions concerning the conduct of tender offers for the securities of registered companies.[8]

---

27. *Id*. § 1817(j)(12).

§ 4.20

1. For extended discussion of state change-in-control provisions, see 1 MICHAEL P. MALLOY, BANKING LAW AND REGULATION §§ 4.5–4.5.3 (1994 & CUM. SUPP.).

2. *See id.* § 4.5.1, Figures 4.1–4.2.

3. *See, e.g.*, Del. Code Ann. tit. 5, §§ 821–826; Me. Rev. Stat. Ann. tit. 9–B, §§ 1011–1019; N.M. Stat. Ann. § 58–1–64.

4. *See, e.g.*, Kan. Stat. Ann. § 9–903.

5. 12 U.S.C.A. § 1817(j).

6. See, e.g., Ala. Code § 5–5A–44; Ark. Stat. § 06.05.327; N.Y. Banking Law § 143–b(1); 19 R.I. Stat. Ann. §§ 19–8–1— 19–8–9. For an application of one such statute, see *Alvarez-Stelling v. Siebert*, 98 Misc.2d 1055, 415 N.Y.S.2d 378 (1979).

7. *See, e.g.*, Cal. Fin. Code § 701(a).

8. *Cf., e.g., Great W. United Corp. v. Kidwell*, 577 F.2d 1256 (5th Cir.1978), *rev'd on venue grounds sub nom. Leroy v. Great W. United Corp.*, 443 U.S. 173, 99 S.Ct. 2710 (1979) (Idaho antitakeover statute); *Edgar v. MITE Corp.*, 457 U.S. 624, 102 S.Ct. 2629 (1982) (Illinois anti-takeover statute). *See generally* 1 MALLOY, *supra*, § 4.5.3 (discussing interaction between state change-in-control statutes and federal securities law).

Chapter 5

TRANSACTIONAL RULES

Table of Sections

§ 5.1 Introduction

As a practical matter state and national banks appear to be equally and entirely subject to state laws governing collection of debts, transactions in commercial paper, bank deposits, contracts, and the like. For national banks, however, there is one important exception to this rule. Federal law, primarily that administered by the Office of the Comptroller of the Currency ("OCC"), defines the rights and obligations of

124

national banks as corporate entities.[1] It is this balance of generally applicable state transactional law and fundamental, federal corporate law that defines the framework in which banks operate. Attempts by state authority to intrude into the fundamental governance of federally chartered depository institutions have generally been held to be constitutionally preempted.[2] Hence, it has long been accepted that national banks

> are subject to the laws of the State, and are governed in their daily course of business far more by the laws of the State than of the Nation. . . . It is only when the state law incapacitates the banks from discharging their duties to the government that it becomes unconstitutional.[3]

However, federal law has come to play an increasingly important role in the powers of depository institutions, state and federal, to engage in particular types of transactions. There are a number of reasons for this development.

First, and most importantly, despite the dual nature of the depository institutions industry, it has become markedly federalized, primarily due to the fact that virtually all depository institutions are subject to federal supervision through the federal deposit insurance system. Hence, despite occasional suggestions that the dual system should be modified, the fact is that the system has already been significantly modified over time, due to the prevalence of federal deposit insurance.

Second, at a technical level, standards of conduct in transactions are subject to a distinctive federal regime. The authority of state-chartered banks to engage in activities not permitted to national banks has been significantly curtailed by the enactment of the Federal Deposit Insurance Corporation Improvements Act ("FDICIA").[4] With certain specified exceptions, FDICIA generally requires that insured state banks not engage in any type of activity not permissible for national banks.[5] Hence, in the sections that follow, the emphasis will be on regulation at the federal level, focusing primarily on national banks.

In general, when examining the powers of any depository institution to engage in particular types of transactions, one must keep in mind that

§ 5.1

1. *See, e.g.*, 12 U.S.C.A. § 24 (concerning powers of national banking associations). *See also Easton v. Iowa*, 188 U.S. 220, 23 S.Ct. 288 (1903) (recognizing sole power of Congress to define powers of national banks); *Bullard v. National Eagle Bank*, 85 U.S. (18 Wall.) 589 (1873); *Coon v. Smith*, 4 F.Supp. 960 (E.D.Ill.1933).

2. *See, e.g., Franklin Nat'l Bank v. New York*, 347 U.S. 373, 74 S.Ct. 550 (1954) (preempting state law governing advertisement of accounts in light of national bank powers under 12 U.S.C.A. § 24); *Fidelity Fed. Sav. & Loan Ass'n v. De la Cuesta*, 458 U.S. 141, 102 S.Ct. 3014 (1982) (preempting state law governing due-on-sale clauses applicable to savings associations).

3. *First Nat'l Bank v. Kentucky*, 76 U.S. (9 Wall.) 353, 362 (1870). *See also Davis v. Elmira Sav. Bank*, 161 U.S. 275, 283, 16 S.Ct. 502, 503 (1896); *McClellan v. Chipman*, 164 U.S. 347, 356–357, 17 S.Ct. 85, 87 (1896).

4. Pub. L. No. 102–242, 105 Stat. 2236 (Dec. 19, 1991) (codified at scattered sections of 12 U.S.C.A.).

5. FDICIA, § 303 (*codified at* 12 U.S.C.A. § 1831a).

these institutions remain creatures of their constitutive statutes. This principle has traditionally been interpreted by the courts as defining the limits of the institution's power to engage in transactions.[6] Banks generally have authority only to exercise express statutory powers and powers necessarily incident to such express powers.[7] Typical express powers include the power to adopt a corporate seal;[8] to make contracts;[9] to sue and be sued;[10] to elect and appoint executive management;[11] to adopt bylaws;[12] and, to carry on the business of banking.[13]

Carrying on the business of banking—in effect the theme of this chapter—has become a complicated undertaking. The statutory language that supports it is complex. In the case of national banks, the language begins simply enough, with the mandate that a national bank has the power "[t]o exercise by its board of directors or duly authorized officers or agents, subject to law, all such incidental powers as shall be necessary to carry on the business of banking."[14] This seems inverted; the statute

---

6. *See, e.g., City of Yonkers v. Downey,* 309 U.S. 590, 60 S.Ct. 796 (1940) (using statutory provisions as measure of bank's powers); *Texas & Pac. Ry. v. Pottorff,* 291 U.S. 245, 54 S.Ct. 416, (1934), *amended sub nom. Texas & Pac. Ry. v. First Nat'l Bank of El Paso, Tex.,* 291 U.S. 649, 54 S.Ct. 525, *reh'g denied sub nom. Texas & Pac. Ry. v. Pottorff,* 292 U.S. 600, 54 S.Ct. 627 (using statutory provisions as measure of bank's powers); *First Nat'l Bank of St. Louis v. Missouri,* 263 U.S. 640, 44 S.Ct. 213 (1924) (limiting national banks to express statutory powers and necessary incidental powers); *Easton v. Iowa,* 188 U.S. 220, 23 S.Ct. 288 (1903); *California Sav. Bank v. Kennedy,* 167 U.S. 362, 17 S.Ct. 831 (1897) (limiting banks to express statutory powers and necessary incidental powers); *Logan County Nat'l Bank v. Townsend,* 139 U.S. 67, 11 S.Ct. 496 (1891) (limiting national banks to express statutory powers and necessary incidental powers); *Kimen v. Atlas Exch. Nat'l Bank of Chicago,* 92 F.2d 615 (7th Cir.1937), *cert. denied sub nom. Awotin v. Healy,* 303 U.S. 650, 58 S.Ct. 746 (1938); *Berylwood Inv. Co. v. Graham,* 43 Cal. App.2d 659, 111 P.2d 467 (1941); *Commonwealth Trust Co. v. First–Second Nat'l Bank,* 260 Pa. 223 103 A. 598 (Pa. 1918), *cert. denied,* 246 U.S. 675, 38 S.Ct. 425.

7. *Williams v. Merchants' Nat'l Bank of St. Cloud,* 42 F.2d 243 (D.Minn.1930); *Suburban Trust Co. v. Nat'l Bank of Westfield,* 211 F.Supp. 694 (D.N.J.1962); *Bank of California v. Portland,* 157 Or. 203, 69 P.2d 273 (1937), *cert. denied,* 302 U.S. 765, 58 S.Ct. 476.

8. 12 U.S.C.A. § 24 (First).

9. 12 U.S.C.A. § 24 (Third). On the power to make contracts, see *G.H. Crawford Co. v. Dixon,* 22 F.Supp. 636 (E.D.S.C. 1938). Specific types of contracts may, however, be prohibited by other statutory provisions. *See, e.g., Kimen, supra* (invalidating repurchase agreement as guaranty); *Awotin v. Atlas Exch. Nat'l Bank of Chicago,* 295 U.S. 209, 55 S.Ct. 674 (1935) (same).

10. 12 U.S.C.A. § 24 (Fourth). On the power to sue and be sued, see *Miller v. King,* 223 U.S. 505, 32 S.Ct. 243 (1912); *Casey v. Adams,* 102 U.S. (12 Otto) 66 (1880); *Kennedy v. Gibson,* 75 U.S. (8 Wall.) 498 (1869). This power would preempt any state law requirement of a certificate to sue as "foreign corporation." *Indiana Nat'l Bank v. Roberts,* 326 So.2d 802 (Miss.1976).

11. 12 U.S.C.A. § 24 (Fifth).

12. 12 U.S.C.A. § 24 (Sixth). On the use of this express power, see *Western Nat'l Bank v. Armstrong,* 152 U.S. 346, 14 S.Ct. 572 (1894) (concerning credits and obligations under bylaws); *Rankin v. Tygard,* 198 F. 795 (8th Cir.1912) (considering effect of invalid provision on remainder of bylaws); *McKee & Co. v. First Nat'l Bank,* 265 F.Supp. 1 (S.D.Cal.1967), *aff'd,* 397 F.2d 248 (9th Cir.1968) (discussing general power to adopt bylaws; bylaw specifying residence requirements for directors); *Bath Sav. Inst. v. Sagadahoc Nat'l Bank,* 89 Me. 500, 36 A. 996 (1897) (upholding bylaw imposing lien on bank stock of debtor).

13. 12 U.S.C.A. § 24 (Seventh).

14. *Id.*

expressly grants the incidental powers before the express powers of which they are incidental are even specified. There follows a disjointed list of five activities that appear to represent "the business of banking,"[15] though the text does not so identify them:

> by discounting and negotiating promissory notes, drafts, bills of exchange, and other evidences of debt; by receiving deposits; by buying and selling exchange, coin, and bullion; by loaning money on personal security; and by obtaining, issuing, and circulating notes.... [16]

By a later amendment of the section, we are told that "[t]he business of dealing in securities and stock by the association shall be limited to purchasing and selling such securities and stock without recourse, solely upon the order, and for the account of, customers, and in no case for its own account, and [a national bank] shall not underwrite any issue of securities or stock,"[17] with certain exceptions with respect to eligible "investment securities."

§ 5.2   Lending

Commercial banks generally have the broadest lending powers, both as to types of loans and extensions of credit and as to types of borrowers.[1] Lending is, however, subject to statutory and regulatory limitations with respect to, for example, lending limits, certain specified limitations on loans to insiders, prohibitions on involuntary tying, and traditional usury prohibitions.

Note that the Federal Deposit Insurance Corporation Improvements Act ("FDICIA"),[2] enacted in December 1991, has changed certain selective aspects of the regulation of lending activities. First, FDICIA has had a direct impact on activities of insured state banks. With certain specified exceptions, FDICIA generally requires that insured state banks not engage in any type of activity not permissible for national banks.[3]

---

15. *See, e.g., First Nat'l Bank v. Nat'l Exch. Bank*, 92 U.S. (2 Otto) 122 (1875) (construing language not as limitation on incidental powers, but as description of "banking").

16. 12 U.S.C.A. § 24 (Seventh). On discounting and negotiating, see *National Bank v. Johnson*, 104 U.S. (14 Otto) 271 (1881); *National Bank of the Republic v. Price*, 65 Utah 57, 234 P. 231 (1923). *Cf. Cooper v. National Bank of Savannah*, 21 Ga.App. 356, 94 S.E. 611 (1917), *aff'd sub nom. Evans v. National Bank of Savannah*, 251 U.S. 108, 40 S.Ct. 58 (1919) (holding power to discount includes power to take interest in advance). On the power to accept deposits, see *Eastern Townships Bank v. Vermont Nat'l Bank*, 22 F. 186 (D. Vt. 1884). On the power to make loans, see

First Nat'l Bank v. Harris, 27 F.2d 117 (8th Cir.1928); *Murphy v. Hanna*, 37 N.D. 156 164 N.W. 32 (1917).

17. 12 U.S.C.A. § 24 (Seventh). On the meaning of "without recourse" for these purposes, see *Awotin, supra*; *Genessee Trustee Corp. v. Smith*, 102 F.2d 125 (6th Cir.1939).

§ 5.2

1. *See, e.g.*, 12 U.S.C.A. § 24 (Seventh) (authorizing lending by national banks).

2. Pub. L. No. 102–242, 105 Stat. 2236 (Dec. 19, 1991) ("FDICIA") (codified at scattered sections of 12 U.S.C.A.).

3. FDICIA, § 303 (codified at 12 U.S.C.A. § 1831a).

Second, FDICIA requires the agencies to adopt uniform regulations restricting real estate lending by prescribing standards for such extensions of credit in accordance with certain general principles specified in the act.[4] FDICIA also recodified the statutory provisions restricting extensions of credit to insiders of depository institutions.[5]

§ 5.3   Federal Lending Limits

Federal lending limits restrict the total amount of loans and extensions of credit[1] by a national bank[2] to any one person[3] at any one time in an amount equal to a statutorily specified percentage of total unimpaired capital and surplus[4] of the bank.[5] This is a common and traditional regulatory device of state and federal law,[6] which is intended to ensure the safety and soundness of banks by preventing excessive concentrations of lending to one person (or to related persons that are financially dependent).[7] This device also has the effect of promoting diversification of loans and equitable access to banking services.[8]

4. FDICIA, § 304(a) (codified at 12 U.S.C.A. § 1828(*o*)). *See also* FDICIA, § 304(b) (codified at 12 U.S.C.A. § 371(a)) (conforming amendment to Federal Reserve Act).

5. FDICIA, § 306(a) (codified at 12 U.S.C.A. § 375b). Restrictions on transactions with affiliates and insiders apply to insured nonmember insured banks as well as member banks. FDICIA, § 306(k) (codified at 12 U.S.C.A. § 1828(j)). Corresponding rules apply to savings associations. FDICIA § 306(i)–(j) (codified at 12 U.S.C.A. §§ 1468(b)(1), 1972(2)(H)(i)). Existing transactions are not affected by these new rules. FDICIA § 306(n).

§ 5.3

1. For these purposes, the term "loans and extensions of credit" is defined to include the following:

> all direct or indirect advances of funds to a person made on the basis of any obligation of that person to repay the funds or repayable from specific property pledged by or on behalf of the person and, to the extent specified by the Comptroller of the Currency, such term shall also include any liability of a national banking association to advance funds to or on behalf of a person pursuant to a contractual commitment.

12 U.S.C.A. § 84(b)(1). *See, e.g., Anderson v. Akers*, 9 F.Supp. 151 (W.D.Ky.1934) (construing purported "investment" by national bank in rubber company as "obligation" subject to lending limits).

2. On federal lending limits applicable to savings associations, see 12 C.F.R. §§ 560.93, 560.100–560.101.

3. For these purposes, the term "person" is defined to include "an individual, sole proprietorship, partnership, joint venture, association, trust, estate, business trust, corporation, sovereign government or agency, instrumentality, or political subdivision thereof, or any similar entity or organization." 12 U.S.C.A. § 84(b)(2).

4. On calculation of capital and surplus for these purposes, see *Jaynes v. First Nat'l Bank of Ketchikan, Alaska*, 236 F.2d 258 (9th Cir.1956).

5. 12 U.S.C.A. § 84(a).

6. *See Northway Lanes v. Hackley Union Nat'l Bank & Trust Co.*, 334 F.Supp. 723 (W.D.Mich.1971), *aff'd*, 464 F.2d 855 (6th Cir.) (contrasting state and federal lending limits).

7. *See Valente v. Dennis*, 437 F.Supp. 783 (E.D.Pa.1977) (discussing purposes of lending limits); *Huff v. Union Nat'l Bank of Oakland*, 173 F. 333 (N.D. Cal. 1909). *See also* 12 C.F.R. § 32.1(b) (discussing purpose of lending limit regulations).

8. *Valente, supra.*

The applicable lending limit will vary depending upon whether or not the loan is fully secured by readily marketable collateral. If it is not, the applicable lending limit is fifteen percent.[9] If it is, the applicable limit is ten percent.[10] This ten percent limit is in addition to and separate from the basic fifteen percent limit.[11] Hence, because the second limit is *in addition* to the first limit, working carefully with these two limits a bank may lend a total amount to one person equal to 25 percent of the bank's unimpaired capital and surplus.[12] However, because the second limit is *separate from* the first limit, the two limits are not simply aggregated.[13] A loan that is not fully collateralized by readily marketable collateral cannot benefit from the second limit,[14] even though total lending to the borrower is less than 25 percent of unimpaired capital and surplus. Figure 5–1, *infra*, illustrates the parameters of the federal lending limits.

FIGURE 5-1
Parameters of Federal Lending Limits

National Bank *A*

Total unimpaired capital and surplus = $1,000,000
84(a)(1) Limit = $ 150,000
84(a)(2) Limit = $ 100,000

Case 1:
No Loans to Borrower Fully Collateralized by Readily Marketable Collateral

---

9. 12 U.S.C.A. § 84(a)(1). For discussion of the implications of § 84(a)(1) for a national bank and its holding company, see *Marx v. Centran Corp.*, 747 F.2d 1536 (6th Cir.1984), *cert. denied*, 471 U.S. 1125, 105 S.Ct. 2656 (1985).

10. 12 U.S.C.A. § 84(a)(2).

11. *Id.*

12. See 12 C.F.R. § 32.3(a) (providing that national bank's total outstanding loans and extensions of credit to any one borrower "may not exceed 15 percent of the bank's capital and surplus, plus an additional 10 percent of the bank's capital and surplus").

13. *See* 12 C.F.R. § 32.2(a) (providing that amount exceeding 15 percent general limit must be "fully secured by readily marketable collateral").

14. *See* 12 C.F.R. § 32.2(a), which provides in pertinent part:

To qualify for the additional 10 percent limit, the bank must perfect a security interest in the collateral under applicable law and the collateral must have a current market value at all times of at least 100 percent of the amount of the loan or extension of credit that exceeds the bank's 15 percent general limit.

Case 2:

Some Loans to Borrower Fully Collateralized by Readily Marketable Collateral

Case 3:

All Loans to Borrower Fully Collateralized by Readily Marketable Collateral

Thus, if National Bank *A* had no loans or extensions of credit outstanding to a particular borrower that qualified for the additional lending limit of ten percent, it would be absolutely limited to $150,000 in total outstanding loans and extensions to that borrower (Figure 5–1, Case 1). However, to the extent that some of the loans and extensions qualified, Bank *A* could utilize the aggregate limit of $250,000 per borrower in virtually any combination of qualifying and nonqualifying loans and extensions, so long as the nonqualifying portion did not exceed the $150,000 limit (Figure 5–1, Case 2). This means, of course, that even if all loans and extensions to the borrower were qualifying, Bank *A* would still be limited to the $250,000 aggregate amount (Figure 5–1, Case 3).

The lending limits provisions also include a range of specified exceptions.[15] These contain their own special lending limits or other conditions, and are separate from and in addition to the generally applicable limits.

The Office of the Comptroller of the Currency ("OCC") has statutory authority to administer and carry out the purposes of the National Bank Act ("NBA") lending limits through promulgation of rules and regulations,[16] including "rules or regulations to define or further define

---

15.   12 U.S.C.A. § 84(c).

16.   12 U.S.C.A. § 84(d)(1).

terms" used in the statutory provisions.[17] The Comptroller has issued extensive rules in this regard.[18] The NBA also gives the Comptroller the authority to establish limits or requirements other than those specified in the lending limit provisions for particular classes or categories of loans or extensions of credit,[19] but the Comptroller generally has not done so.

Finally, the NBA gives the Comptroller the express authority "to determine when a loan putatively made to a person shall for purposes of [NBA lending limits] be attributed to another person."[20] The Comptroller's lending limit regulations contain detailed "combination rules" in this regard.[21] Whether viewed as "attribution" or "combination" of loans and extensions of credit, this is a process that has long been applied by the Comptroller in administering the NBA lending limits.[22]

It is a longstanding rule that directors are directly responsible for supervision of a national bank's compliance with its lending limits.[23] Directors who participate or acquiesce in a violation of the lending limits are subject to liability for losses to the bank that result from the loans or extensions of credit.[24] This liability may include contribution for another executive officer's violation of the lending limits.[25] Both direct and derivative actions may be available to shareholders of the bank involved[26] or its holding company.[27] However, no such action is available to the borrower,[28] and as between bank and borrower, violation of the lending limits does not render the loan or extension of credit void or unenforceable.[29]

---

17. *Id.*

18. *See* 12 C.F.R. Pt. 32 (setting forth Comptroller's lending limit rules).

19. 12 U.S.C.A. § 84(d)(1).

20. *Id.* § 84(d)(2). For cases construing combination rules prior to the 1982 amendment of the statute to provide more explicit authority, see *Hughes v. Reed*, 46 F.2d 435 (10th Cir. 1931); *Keller, supra.* The 1982 amendments and the implementing regulations would have had a significant effect on the analysis in cases like *Keller.* First, and most obviously, the post–1982 general lending limit is fifteen percent, not ten percent as it was at the time *Keller* was decided. Second, the statutorily authorized combination rules of 12 C.F.R. § 32.5 would have applied. (However, as in *Keller,* 12 C.F.R. § 32.5(d)(1) would have required parent control of more than 50 percent of the stock of the subsidiary for combination purposes.) Third, the "common enterprise" test of 12 C.F.R. § 32.5(c) would have governed the analysis in the case. Fourth, in any event no more than 50 percent of the national bank's unimpaired capital and surplus could have been lent to any one corporate group under 12 C.F.R. § 32.5(d)(1).

21. 12 C.F.R. § 32.5.

22. *See, e.g., First Nat'l Bank of Barron v. Strimling,* 308 Minn. 207, 241 N.W.2d 478 (1976) (applying lending limits to loan obtained by one borrower on behalf of another).

23. *See, e.g., Atherton v. Anderson,* 99 F.2d 883 (6th Cir.1938); *Anderson v. Gailey,* 33 F.2d 589 (D.Ga.1929) (discussing director responsibility). *See also* 12 U.S.C.A. § 93 (providing for director liability for certain violations).

24. *Cockrill v. Cooper,* 86 F. 7 (8th Cir. 1898); *Federal Deposit Ins. Corp. v. Mapp's Executor,* 184 Va. 970, 37 S.E.2d 23 (1946).

25. *Cache Nat'l Bank v. Hinman,* 626 F.Supp. 1341 (D.Colo.1986).

26. *See Harmsen v. Smith,* 542 F.2d 496 (9th Cir.1976) (requiring knowing violation by bank directors).

27. *Marx, supra.*

28. *Valente, supra; Municipal Leasing Sys., Inc. v. Northhampton Nat'l Bank of Easton,* 382 F.Supp. 968 (E.D.Pa.1974).

29. *Union Gold–Mining Co. of Colo. v. Rocky Mtn. Nat'l Bank of Central City,* 96 U.S. (6 Otto) 640 (1877); *First Am. Nat'l Bank of Iuka v. Alcorn, Inc.,* 361 So.2d 481 (Miss.1978).

§ 5.4   Limitations on Types of Loans

Loans to directors, officers, principal shareholders, and affiliates are subject to special statutory restrictions.[1] On their own terms, these provisions apply only to "member banks," *i.e.*, national and state-chartered member banks. However, provisions of the Federal Deposit Insurance Act[2] and the Home Owners' Loan Act[3] make these provisions applicable to nonmember insured banks and savings associations, respectively.

§ 5.5   Extensions of Credit to Directors, Executive Officers, and Principal Shareholders

As a general rule, a member bank[1] is prohibited from making an extension of credit[2] to any of its insiders[3] (*i.e.*, its directors, executive officers,[4] and principal shareholders[5]), or to any related interest of an insider,[6] except to the extent specifically permitted by statute.[7] A member bank is permitted to extend credit to its insiders, or to related interests, if the credit is made on substantially the same terms (including interest rates and collateral requirements), as those prevailing at the

§ 5.4

1. *Cf.* 12 U.S.C.A. § 376 (prohibiting payment of preferential rate of interest by member bank to director, officer, attorney, or employee); § 1972(2) (prohibiting tying between bank extending credit to insider of another bank and insider's own bank).

2. 12 U.S.C.A. § 1828(j)(1)–(2). *See Fitzpatrick v. Federal Deposit Ins. Corp.*, 765 F.2d 569 (6th Cir.1985) (discussing § 1828(j)(2)).

3. 12 U.S.C.A. § 1468(a)-(b).

§ 5.5

1. For these purposes, the term "member bank" includes a subsidiary of a member bank. 12 U.S.C.A. § 375b(9)(E).

2. For these purposes, the term "extension of credit" is defined as follows:

A member bank extends credit by making or renewing any loan, granting a line of credit, or entering into any similar transaction as a result of which a person becomes obligated (directly or indirectly, or by any means whatsoever) to pay money or its equivalent to the bank.

Id. § 375b(9)(D)(i). However, the Fed is authorized by regulation to "make exceptions to clause (i) for transactions that the [Fed] determines pose minimal risk." *Id.* § 375b(9)(D)(ii).

3. *See also id.* § 375b(8) (treating directors, executive officers, and principal shareholders of certain affiliates insiders of member bank for purposes of § 375b).

4. For these purposes, the term "executive officer" is defined to mean a person who "participates or has authority to participate (other than as a director) in major policymaking functions of [a] company or bank." 12 U.S.C.A. § 375b(9)(C). *See generally Bullion v. Federal Deposit Ins. Corp.*, 881 F.2d 1368 (5th Cir.1989) (discussing meaning of term).

5. For these purposes, the term "principal shareholder" is defined to mean:

any person that directly or indirectly, or acting through or in concert with one or more persons, owns, controls, or has the power to vote more than 10 percent of any class of voting securities of a member bank or company.

12 U.S.C.A. § 375b(9)(F)(i). The term does not include a company of which the member bank is a subsidiary. *Id.* § 375b(9)(F)(ii).

6. For these purposes, the term "related interest" of a person is defined to mean:

(i) any company controlled by that person; and

(ii) any political or campaign committee that is controlled by that person or the funds or services of which will benefit that person.

Id. § 375b(9)(G)(i)-(ii).

7. *Id.* § 375b(1). *See generally Fitzpatrick, supra* (discussing private right of action for violations); *Marx, supra*; *Lode v. Leonardo*, 557 F.Supp. 675 (N.D.Ill.1982). While the prohibitions and restrictions in time for comparable transactions by the bank with persons who are not insiders.[8] Such credits must not involve more than the normal risk of repayment or present other unfavorable features.[9] Furthermore, in making such extensions of credit, the bank must follow credit underwriting procedures that are no less stringent than those applicable to comparable transactions by the bank with persons who are not insiders.[10]

A member bank also may extend credit to an insider and related interests in an aggregate amount that exceeds amounts prescribed by regulation only if the following two conditions are met: (1) The credit must be approved in advance by a majority vote of the bank's entire board of directors;[11] and, (2) The insider must abstain from participating, directly or indirectly, in the deliberations or voting on the extension of credit.[12]

Moreover, a member bank may extend credit to an insider or a related interest only if the aggregate extensions of credit to the insider would not exceed the NBA lending limits[13] on loans to a single borrower.[14] In addition, as a general rule, a member bank may extend credit to an insider or related interest if aggregate extensions of credit to all insiders and related interests is in an amount that would not exceed the bank's unimpaired capital and unimpaired surplus.[15] The Fed is authorized by statute to prescribe by regulation a more stringent limit.[16] In addition, it may make exceptions for member banks with less than $100 million in deposits if it determines that the exceptions are important to avoid constricting the availability of credit in small communities or to attract directors to such banks.[17]

---

section 375b are generally targeted at the member bank, the section also provides that

> No executive officer, director, or principal shareholder shall knowingly receive (or knowingly permit any of that person's related interests to receive) from a member bank, directly or indirectly, any extension of credit not authorized under this section.

12 U.S.C.A. § 375b(7).

8. 12 U.S.C.A. § 375b(2)(A)(i). *But cf. id.* § 375b(2)(B), which provides:

> Nothing in this paragraph shall prohibit any extension of credit made pursuant to a benefit or compensation program—
>
> (i) that is widely available to employees of the member bank; and
>
> (ii) that does not give preference to any officer, director, or principal shareholder of the member bank, or to any related interest of such person, over other employees of the member bank.

See generally Bullion, supra (discussing prohibition against preferential terms).

9. 12 U.S.C.A. § 375b(2)(A)(ii). *See generally Bullion, supra* (discussing requirement).

10. 12 U.S.C.A. § 375b(2)(A)(iii).

11. *Id.* § 375b(3)(A).

12. *Id.* § 375b(3)(B).

13. *Id.* § 84.

14. *Id.* § 375b(4). For these purposes, the NBA lending limits apply to a state-chartered member bank as if it were a national bank. *Id.*

15. *Id.* § 375b(5)(A).

16. *Id.* § 375b(5)(B). *See, e.g.,* 12 C.F.R. § 215.1(b)(2) (limiting member bank extension of credit to any insider or affiliate thereof in aggregate amount not exceeding $500,000, except as specifically approved by Fed).

17. 12 U.S.C.A. § 375b(5)(C). The aggregate amount of all outstanding extensions of credit to a bank's insiders and

As a general rule, a member bank is not permitted to allow overdrafts in deposit accounts of its *directors* and *executive officers*.[18] There are, however, two exceptions to this prohibition: (1) The bank may allow overdraft protection, in the form of a written preauthorized, interest-bearing extension of credit specifying a method of repayment;[19] and, (2) The bank may allow sweep arrangements, in the form of a written preauthorized transfer of funds from another account of the director or officer at the bank.[20]

§ 5.6   Loans to Executive Officers

As a general rule, no member bank is permitted to extend credit in any manner to any of its own executive officers.[1] No executive officer of any member bank is permitted to become indebted to the bank, except through an extension of credit that the bank is specifically authorized to make by statute.[2] Furthermore, even an authorized extension of credit must be promptly reported to the board of directors of the bank.[3]

Such extensions of credit can be made only if they meet the following requirements: (1) The bank must be authorized to make such an extension of credit to borrowers other than its officers;[4] (2) The credit must be on terms no more favorable than those afforded other borrowers;[5] (3) The borrowing officer must submit a detailed current financial statement;[6] and, (4) The credit must be granted on the condition that it becomes due and payable on demand of the bank at any time when the officer is indebted to any other banks on account of mortgage, educational, or general limit loans in an aggregate amount greater than the amount of credit of the same category that could be extended to the officer by his or her own bank.[7]

A member bank may make a mortgage loan to an executive officer if, at the time the loan is made, the following two conditions are met: (1) The loan must be secured by a first lien on a dwelling that will be used

---

related interests cannot exceed an amount equal to 200 percent of the bank's unimpaired capital and unimpaired surplus. *Id.* *See* 12 C.F.R. § 215.4(d)(2)(i)–(ii) (providing exceptions for member banks with deposits of less than $100,000,000).

18.   12 U.S.C.A. § 375b(6)(A).

19.   *Id.* § 375b(6)(B)(i).

20.   *Id.* § 375b(6)(B)(ii).

§ 5.6

1.   12 U.S.C.A. § 375a(1). *See generally First Nat'l Bank of Bellaire v. Comptroller of the Currency*, 697 F.2d 674 (5th Cir.1983) (interpreting prior version of statute). This provision does not prohibit an executive officer of a member bank from endorsing or guaranteeing, for the protection of the bank, any loan or other asset previously acquired by the bank in good faith, or from incurring any indebtedness to the bank for the purpose of protecting the bank against loss or giving financial assistance to it. 12 U.S.C.A. § 375a(7).

2.   12 U.S.C.A. § 375a(1).

3.   *Id.*

4.   *Id.* § 375a(1)(A).

5.   *Id.* § 375a(1)(B).

6.   *Id.* § 375a(1)(C).

7.   *Id.* § 375a(1)(D). Whenever an executive officer of a member bank becomes indebted to any other bank for mortgage, educational or general limit loans in an aggregate amount greater than the aggregate amount of credit of the same category that could lawfully be extended to the executive officer by his or her own bank, the officer is required to make a written report to the board of directors of the bank, stat-by the officer as his or her residence;[8] and, (2) No other mortgage loan by the bank to the officer can be outstanding.[9] In addition, a member bank may make extensions of credit to any executive officer of the bank to finance the education of the children of the officer.[10]

A member bank may also make "general limit" loans, extensions of credit not otherwise specifically authorized by statute, to any executive officer of the bank in an amount prescribed in a regulation of the member bank's "appropriate Federal banking agency."[11] Aside from these loans, however, a member bank is prohibited from extending credit to a partnership in which one or more of its executive officers are partners, having either individually or together a majority interest.[12]

§ 5.7   Affiliate Transactions

Transactions with bank affiliates,[1] including loans and extensions of credit, are subject to restrictions expressed as percentages of capital and

ing the date and amount of each such extension of credit, the security therefor, and the purposes for which the proceeds have been or are to be used. *Id.* § 375a(6).

8. *Id.* § 375a(2)(A).

9. *Id.* § 375a(2)(B).

10. *Id.* § 375a(3).

11. *Id.* § 375a(4). For regulations of the appropriate federal regulator with respect to insider and affiliate transactions, see, *e.g.*, 12 C.F.R. §§ 31.1–31.2, Appendices A, B (setting forth OCC regulations applicable to national banks), *id.* Pt. 215 (setting forth Fed regulations applicable to member banks); *id.* §§ 349.1–349.4 (setting forth FDIC regulations applicable to state-chartered, FDIC-insured banks).

12. 12 U.S.C.A. § 375a(5).

§ 5.7

1. For these purposes, an "affiliate" of a member bank is defined to mean the following:

(A) any company that controls the member bank and any other company that is controlled by the company that controls the member bank;

(B) a bank subsidiary of the member bank;

(C) any company—

(i) that is controlled directly or indirectly, by a trust or otherwise, by or for the benefit of shareholders who beneficially or otherwise control, directly or indirectly, by trust or otherwise, the member bank or any company that controls the member bank; or

(ii) in which a majority of its directors or trustees constitute a majority of the persons holding any such office with the

member bank or any company that controls the member bank;

(D)(i) any company, including a real estate investment trust, that is sponsored and advised on a contractual basis by the member bank or any subsidiary or affiliate of the member bank; or

(ii) any investment company with respect to which a member bank or any affiliate thereof is an investment advisor as defined in [15 U.S.C.A. § 80a–2(a)(20)]; and

(E) any company that [the Fed] determines by regulation or order to have a relationship with the member bank or any subsidiary or affiliate of the member bank, such that covered transactions by the member bank or its subsidiary with that company may be affected by the relationship to the detriment of the member bank or its subsidiary. . . .

12 U.S.C.A. § 371c(b)(1). *See, e.g., Northwest Nat'l Bank, Fayetteville, Ark. v. United States Dep't of the Treasury,* 917 F.2d 1111 (8th Cir.1990) (discussing affiliation of banks through direct and indirect ownership of stock by director). On the meaning of "control" for these purposes, see 12 U.S.C.A. § 371c(3)(A). *See also Greenberg v. Board of Governors,* 968 F.2d 164 (2d Cir. 1992) (discussing "control"). The statute explicitly identifies certain entities as *not* being considered an "affiliate" for these purposes. These entities are:

(A) any company, other than a bank, that is a subsidiary of a member bank, unless a determination is made under [12 U.S.C.A. § 371c(b)(1)(E), *supra*] not to exclude such subsidiary company from the definition of affiliate;

(B) any company engaged solely in holding the premises of the member bank;

surplus.[2] Thus, a member bank and its subsidiaries may engage in a covered transaction[3] with an affiliate[4] only if: (1) the aggregate amount of covered transactions of the member bank and its subsidiaries with any one affiliate does not exceed ten percent of the capital stock and surplus of the member bank;[5] and, (2) the aggregate amount of covered transactions of the member bank and its subsidiaries with all affiliates does not exceed twenty percent of the capital stock and surplus of the member bank.[6] Specified collateral requirements apply to affiliate loans.[7] Required collateral that is subsequently retired or amortized must be replaced by additional eligible collateral, as necessary to keep the percentage of the collateral value, relative to the amount of the outstanding loan or other obligation, equal to the minimum percentage required at the inception of the transaction.[8]

In addition, a member bank and its subsidiaries are prohibited from purchasing a low-quality asset[9] from an affiliate.[10] Finally, covered trans-

---

(C) any company engaged solely in conducting a safe deposit business;

(D) any company engaged solely in holding obligations of the United States or its agencies or obligations fully guaranteed by the United States or its agencies as to principal and interest; and

(E) any company where control results from the exercise of rights arising out of a bona fide debt previously contracted, but only for the period of time specifically authorized under applicable State or Federal law or regulation or, in the absence of such law or regulation, for a period of two years from the date of the exercise of such rights or the effective date of this Act, whichever date is later, subject, upon application, to authorization by [the Fed] for good cause shown of extensions of time for not more than one year at a time, but such extensions in the aggregate shall not exceed three years.
12 U.S.C.A. § 371c(b)(2).

2. 12 U.S.C.A. § 371c(a).

3. For these purposes, the term "covered transaction" is defined to mean the following:

(A) a loan or extension of credit to the affiliate;

(B) a purchase of or an investment in securities issued by the affiliate;

(C) a purchase of assets, including assets subject to an agreement to repurchase, from the affiliate, except such purchase of real and personal property as may be specifically exempted by the [Fed] by order or regulation;

(D) the acceptance of securities issued by the affiliate as collateral security for a loan or extension of credit to any person or company; or

(E) the issuance of a guarantee, acceptance, or letter of credit, including an endorsement or standby letter of credit, on behalf of an affiliate.
Id. § 371c(b)(7).

4. For these purposes, a transaction by a member bank with any person is deemed to be a transaction with an affiliate to the extent that the proceeds of the transaction are used for the benefit of, or are transferred to, the affiliate. *Id.* § 371c(a)(2).

5. *Id.* § 371c(a)(1)(A).

6. *Id.* § 371c(a)(1)(B).

7. *See Fitzpatrick v. Federal Deposit Ins. Corp.*, 765 F.2d 569 (6th Cir.1985) (discussing collateral requirements).

8. 12 U.S.C.A. § 371c(c)(2).

9. For these purposes, the term "low-quality asset" is defined to mean an asset that falls into one of the following categories:

(A) an asset classified as "substandard", "doubtful", or "loss" or treated as "other loans especially mentioned" in the most recent report of examination or inspection of an affiliate prepared by either a Federal or State supervisory agency;

(B) an asset in a nonaccrual status;

(C) an asset on which principal or interest payments are more than thirty days past due; or

(D) an asset whose terms have been renegotiated or compromised due to the deteriorating financial condition of the obligor.
Id. § 371c(b)(10).

10. *Id.* § 371c(a)(3). The prohibition does not apply if the bank or subsidiary, actions and exempt transactions[11] are required to be on terms and conditions consistent with safe and sound banking practices.[12]

The restrictions on affiliate transactions are subject to a series of exemptions, except for the requirement[13] that transactions be on terms and conditions that are consistent with safe and sound banking practices.[14] These include exemptions for affiliated interbank transactions;[15] deposit transactions involving affiliated banks;[16] credits for uncollected items, such as checks and drafts;[17] certain loans fully secured by U.S. issued or guaranteed obligations;[18] purchasing securities issued by an affiliated service company;[19] purchasing certain readily marketable loans and assets from an affiliate;[20] and, repurchasing certain loans and assets permissibly sold to an affiliate.[21]

There are also statutory restrictions that focus on the substance of affiliate transactions, rather than percentage limitations.[22] A member bank and its subsidiaries may engage in covered transactions[23] and certain other specified transactions[24] with an affiliate[25] only on terms and under circumstances that are substantially the same, or at least as favorable to such bank or its subsidiary, as those prevailing at the time for comparable transactions with or involving other nonaffiliated companies.[26] Furthermore, in the absence of comparable transactions, such a bank and its subsidiaries are permitted to engage in such transactions on

---

pursuant to an independent credit evaluation, committed itself to purchase the asset *before* the asset was acquired by the affiliate. *Id.*

11. *I.e.*, transactions exempt under subsection 12 U.S.C.A. § 371c(d). *See* discussion of § 371c(d) *infra*.

12. 12 U.S.C.A. § 371c(a)(4). *See, e.g., Senior Unsecured Creditors' Comm. of First RepublicBank Corp. v. Fed. Deposit Ins. Corp.*, 749 F.Supp. 758 (N.D.Tex.1990) (discussing safety and soundness of guaranty issued by subsidiary banks).

13. 12 U.S.C.A. § 371c(a)(4).

14. *Id.* § 371c(d).

15. *Id.* § 371c(d)(1).

16. *Id.* § 371c(d)(2).

17. *Id.* § 371c(d)(3).

18. *Id.* § 371c(d)(4).

19. *Id.* § 371c(d)(5).

20. *Id.* § 371c(d)(6).

21. *Id.* § 371c(d)(7).

22. *See, e.g., id.* § 371c–1 (setting forth restrictions on transactions with affiliates).

23. For these purposes, the term "covered transaction" has the same meaning as in § 371c, not including any transaction exempt under § 371c(d). *Id.* § 371c–1(d)(3). On the meaning of "covered transaction,"

see *supra* note 3 (setting forth statutory definition).

24. In addition to "covered transactions," these other transactions are specified by statute as follows:

(B) The sale of securities or other assets to an affiliate, including assets subject to an agreement to repurchase.

(C) The payment of money or the furnishing of services to an affiliate under contract, lease, or otherwise.

(D) Any transaction in which an affiliate acts as an agent or broker or receives a fee for its services to the bank or to any other person.

(E) Any transaction or series of transactions with a third party—

(i) if an affiliate has a financial interest in the third party, or

(ii) if an affiliate is a participant in such transaction or series of transactions.

12 U.S.C.A. § 371c–1(a)(2)(B)-(E).

25. For the purposes of this provision, a transaction by a member bank or its subsidiary with any person is deemed to be a transaction with an affiliate of the bank if any of the proceeds of the transaction are used for the benefit of or transferred to the affiliate. *Id.* § 371c–1(a)(3).

26. *Id.* § 371c–1(a)(1)(A). These terms and circumstances include similar credit standards. *Id.*

terms and under circumstances that in good faith would be offered to, or would apply to, such transactions with nonaffiliated companies.[27]

Certain types of transactions are prohibited by statute.[28] A member bank and its subsidiaries are prohibited from purchasing as fiduciary any securities or other assets from an affiliate, unless the purchase is permitted (1) under an instrument creating the fiduciary relationship; (2) by a court order; or, (3) by the law of the jurisdiction governing the fiduciary relationship.[29] Furthermore, whether it is acting as a principal or as a fiduciary, a member bank or its subsidiary is prohibited from *knowingly* purchasing or otherwise acquiring, during the existence of any underwriting or selling syndicate, any security if a principal underwriter of the security is an affiliate of the bank.[30]

§ 5.8 Tying Arrangements

Under federal law, certain involuntary tying arrangements involving loans are prohibited.[1] While these prohibitions have their analogs in antitrust law,[2] they are distinct from antitrust insofar as they do not require a showing of adverse effects on competition or other restraint of trade to be actionable.[3] Nor do the anti-tying prohibitions require a showing of the relative degree of control exercised by the bank over the tying, or of a minimum amount of commerce.[4]

A bank[5] is prohibited from extending credit,[6] leasing or selling

27. *Id.* § 371c–1(a)(1)(B). These terms and conditions include similar credit standards. *Id.*

28. *Id.* § 371c–1(b).

29. *Id.* § 371c–1(b)(1)(A).

30. *Id.* § 371c–1(b)(1)(B). This prohibition does not apply if the purchase or acquisition has been approved, before the securities are initially offered for sale to the public, by a majority of those directors of the bank who are not officers or employees of the bank or of any affiliate thereof. *Id.* § 371c–1(b)(2).

§ 5.8

1. 12 U.S.C.A. § 1972. Despite the title of the section, the substantive provisions of Section 1972 speaks in terms of "conditioning" or "requiring," rather than "tying." Nevertheless, the case law and literature usually characterizes the prohibited activity under the section as "tying." On the meaning and application of the term "tying" for these purposes, see *Doe v. Norwest Bank of Minnesota, N.A.*, 107 F.3d 1297 (8th Cir. 1997); *Kenty v. Bank One, Columbus, N.A.*, 92 F.3d 384 (6th Cir.1996); *Gushi Bros. Co. v. Bank of Guam*, 28 F.3d 1535 (9th Cir. 1994); *Sanders v. First Nat'l Bank & Trust Co. in Great Bend*, 936 F.2d 273 (6th Cir. 1991); *Graue Mill Dev. Corp. v. Colonial*

Bank & Trust Co. of Chicago, 927 F.2d 988 (7th Cir.1991); *McGee v. First Fed. Sav. & Loan Ass'n of Brunswick*, 761 F.2d 647 (11th Cir.1985), *cert. denied*, 474 U.S. 905, 106 S.Ct. 273.

2. *See, e.g., Kenty, supra* (discussing relation of anti-tying provisions to Sherman Act prohibitions of anticompetitive tying arrangements); *Swerdloff v. Miami Nat'l Bank*, 584 F.2d 54 (5th Cir.1978) (discussing purposes of anti-tying provisions); *New England Co. v. Bank of Gwinnett County*, 891 F.Supp. 1569 (N.D.Ga.1995) (contrasting general antitrust law and anti-tying provisions); *Alpine Elec. Co. v. Union Bank*, 776 F.Supp. 486 (W.D.Mo.1991), *aff'd*, 979 F.2d 133 (8th Cir.1992) (discussing purposes of anti-tying provisions); *Shulman v. Continental Bank*, 513 F.Supp. 979 (E.D.Pa. 1981) (same); *Freidco of Wilmington, Delaware, Ltd. v. Farmers Bank*, 499 F.Supp. 995 (D.Del.1980) (same).

3. *Gage v. First Fed. Sav. & Loan Ass'n of Hutchinson, Kan.*, 717 F.Supp. 745 (D.Kan.1989).

4. *Id.*

5. On the meaning of the term "bank" for these purposes, see *Flintridge Station Assocs. v. American Fletcher Mortgage Co.*,

6. See note 6 on page 139.

property of any kind, or furnishing any service,[7] or fixing or varying the consideration for any of these financial services, on the condition that the customer[8] obtain some additional credit, property, or service from the bank, other than a loan, discount, deposit, or trust service.[9] In addition, the bank cannot tie such financial services to a requirement that the customer obtain some additional credit, property, or service from the bank holding company of the bank, or from another subsidiary of its holding company.[10]

Nor can the customer be required to provide additional credit, property, or service to the bank, other than that related to, and usually provided in connection with, a loan, discount, deposit, or trust service.[11] Similarly, the customer cannot be required to provide additional credit, property, or service to the holding company of the bank, or to another subsidiary of the holding company.[12]

Finally, the bank cannot prohibit or restrict the customer from obtaining some other credit, property, or service from a competitor of the bank, its holding company, or any subsidiary of the holding company, other than as a reasonable condition or requirement imposed in a credit transaction to assure the soundness of the credit.[13]

761 F.2d 434 (7th Cir.1985); *Nordic Bank PLC v. Trend Group, Ltd.*, 619 F.Supp. 542 (S.D.N.Y.1985).

6. On the meaning of "extending credit" for these purposes, see *Amerifirst Props., Inc. v. Federal Deposit Ins. Corp.*, 880 F.2d 821 (5th Cir.1989); *Boulevard Bank Nat. Ass'n v. Adams Newspapers, Inc.*, 787 F.Supp. 122 (E.D.Mich.1992); *Nordic Bank PLC, supra*; *Dannhausen v. First Nat'l Bank of Sturgeon Bay*, 538 F.Supp. 551 (E.D.Wis.1982).

7. On the meaning of "furnishing a service" for these purposes, see *Shulman, supra*.

8. On the meaning of the term "customer" for these purposes, see *Swerdloff, supra*; *Hargus v. First Nat'l Bank in Port Lavaca*, 666 F.Supp. 111 (S.D.Tex.1987), *aff'd*, 835 F.2d 286 (5th Cir.).

9. 12 U.S.C.A. § 1972(1)(A). On the meaning and application of the term "additional credit, property or service," see *Integon Life Ins. Corp. v. Browning*, 989 F.2d 1143 (11th Cir.1993); *Gulf States Land & Dev. Co. v. Premier Bank N.A.*, 956 F.2d 502 (5th Cir.1992); *Bieber v. State Bank of Terry*, 928 F.2d 328 (9th Cir.1991); *Palermo v. First Nat'l Bank and Trust Co. of Oklahoma City*, 894 F.2d 363 (10th Cir.1990); *Tose v. First Pennsylvania Bank, N.A.*, 648 F.2d 879 (3d Cir.1981), *cert. denied*, 454 U.S. 893, 102 S.Ct. 390; *B.C. Recreational Ind. v. First Nat'l Bank of Boston*, 639 F.2d 828 (1st Cir.1981); *Duryea v. Third Northwestern Nat'l Bank of Minneapolis*, 606 F.2d 823 (8th Cir.1979); *Hargus, supra*; *Federal Deposit Ins. Corp. v. Eagle Props., Ltd.*, 664 F.Supp. 1027 (W.D.Tex.1985); *Pappas v. NCNB Nat'l Bank of North Carolina*, 653 F.Supp. 699 (M.D.N.C.1987); *Sharkey v. Security Bank & Trust Co.*, 651 F.Supp. 1231 (D.Minn.1987); *Nordic Bank PLC, supra*; *Freidco, supra*.

10. 12 U.S.C.A. § 1972(1)(B).

11. *Id.* § 1972(1)(C). On the issue of whether a bank demand for additional security is a usual banking practice for these purposes, see *New England Co., supra*; *Quintana v. First Nat'l Bank of Santa Fe*, 851 F.Supp. 407 (D.N.M.1994), *rev'd*, 64 F.3d 670 (10th Cir.1995). On what constitutes a "traditional banking practice" for these purposes, see *Alpine Elec. Co., supra*; *Gulf States, supra*; *Sanders, supra*; *Bieber, supra*; *McCoy v. Franklin Sav. Ass'n*, 636 F.2d 172 (7th Cir.1980); *Mid-State Fertilizer Co. v. Exchange Nat'l Bank of Chicago*, 693 F.Supp. 666 (N.D.Ill.1988), *aff'd*, 877 F.2d 1333 (7th Cir.1989); *Federal Deposit Ins. Co. v. Linn*, 671 F.Supp. 547 (N.D.Ill. 1987); *Continental Ill. Bank & Trust Co. v. Windham*, 668 F.Supp. 578 (E.D.Tex.1987), *reconsideration denied*, 685 F.Supp. 152 (E.D.Tex.1988); *Nordic Bank PLC, supra*; *Bank of Am. Nat'l Trust & Sav. Ass'n v. Hotel Rittenhouse Assocs.*, 595 F.Supp. 800 (E.D.Pa.1984); *Peterson v. Wells Fargo Bank*, 556 F.Supp. 1100 (N.D.Cal.1981).

12. 12 U.S.C.A. § 1972(1)(D).

13. *Id.* § 1972(1)(E).

The Fed has the authority, by regulation or order, to permit exceptions to these five prohibitions, as it considers not contrary to the purposes of the anti-tying provisions.[14] The Fed currently has three exceptions to the tying restrictions.[15] (1) A bank may extend credit, lease or sell property of any kind, or furnish any service, or fix or vary the consideration for any of these financial services, on the condition or requirement that a customer obtain a loan, discount, deposit, or trust service from an affiliate of the bank, or provide to an affiliate of the bank some additional credit, property, or service that the bank could require to be provided to itself pursuant to the anti-tying provisions.[16] (2) A bank may vary the consideration for any financial service or group of services based on a customer's maintaining a combined minimum balance in certain products specified by the bank if the bank offers deposits, and of which are eligible under this rule; and, balances in deposits count at least as much as nondeposits toward the minimum balance required by the bank.[17] (3) A bank may engage in any transaction with a customer if that customer is a corporation, business, or other person (other than an individual) that is incorporated, chartered, or otherwise organized outside the United States and has its principal place of business outside the United States; or, the customer is an individual who is a citizen of a foreign country and is not resident in the United States.[18]

Any of these exceptions terminates if the Fed finds that the arrangement results in anti-competitive practices.[19] The eligibility of a bank to operate under any of these exceptions also terminates upon a finding by the Fed that its exercise of this authority is resulting in anti-competitive practices.[20]

A person "injured in his business or property" by reason of a violation of these prohibitions may sue in any U.S. district court in which the defendant resides or is found or has an agent, without regard to the amount in controversy.[21] Plaintiff is entitled to recover treble damages and costs and reasonable attorneys' fees in such an action.[22] Injunctive relief for threatened loss or damages is also available, under traditional equitable principles for injunctive relief and under the statutory rules governing such proceedings.[23] In such actions, preliminary injunctions may issue on execution of a bond against damages for an injunction improvidently granted and a showing that the danger of irreparable loss or damage is immediate.[24]

---

14. *Id.* § 1972(1).
15. 12 C.F.R. § 225.7(b).
16. *Id.* § 225.7(b)(1).
17. *Id.* § 225.7(b)(2).
18. *Id.* § 225.7(b)(3).
19. *Id.* § 225.7(c).
20. *Id.*
21. 12 U.S.C.A. § 1975.

22. *Id.* Attorneys' fees are apparently not available to a bank successfully defending against a counterclaim based on the anti-tying provisions. *Cohen v. United Am. Bank of Central Fla.*, 83 F.3d 1347 (11th Cir.1996) (interpreting Florida law).

23. 12 U.S.C.A. § 1976.

24. Id.

§ 5.9 Usury Rules

Statutory usury provisions, limiting the amount of interest that may be charged on a loan or extension of credit, appear in both federal and state law.[1] Federal law is peculiar in this regard because, under certain circumstances, it references over to state law to determine the maximum allowable interest rate.[2]

The rates of interest permitted under the National Bank Act present a somewhat complex series of alternatives. The series of alternative rates is illustrated in Figure 5–2, *infra.* They represent entirely distinct tests, and, according to *Tiffany v. National Bank of Missouri,*[3] it is the purpose of the statute to treat national banks as "national favorites"[4] in this regard, so that they are entitled to use the most favored rate available under the statute, whether the rate is derived from the NBA directly or from state law.[5]

Nevertheless, the rate, even if *derived* from state law, is governed by federal law.[6] Hence, if a national bank is operating an *interstate* credit

§ 5.9

1. For analysis of the state law provisions that restrict the interest that may be charged, see 6 Fed. Banking L. Rep. (CCH) ¶¶ 64,052–64,053.

2. 12 U.S.C.A. § 85.

3. 85 U.S. (18 Wall.) 409 (1873).

4. Despite the "national favorites" formulation of *Tiffany,* some courts have spoken of Section 85 in terms of national banks achieving "competitive equality" with other lenders in their respective states. *See, e.g., Roper v. Consurve, Inc.,* 578 F.2d 1106 (5th Cir.1978), *aff'd sub nom. Deposit Guar. Nat'l Bank v. Roper,* 445 U.S. 326, 100 S.Ct. 1166 (1980), *reh'g denied,* 446 U.S. 947, 100 S.Ct. 2177 *on remand sub nom. Roper v. Consurve, Inc.,* 777 F.Supp. 508 (D.Miss.1990), *aff'd,* 932 F.2d 965 (5th Cir.), *cert. denied,* 502 U.S. 861, 112 S.Ct. 181 (1991); *First Nat'l Bank in Mena v. Nowlin,* 509 F.2d 872 (8th Cir.1975); *Brown v. First Nat'l City Bank,* 503 F.2d 114 (2d Cir.1974); *Hiatt v. San Francisco Nat'l Bank,* 361 F.2d 504 (9th Cir.1966), *cert. denied,* 385 U.S. 948, 87 S.Ct. 323, *reh'g denied,* 385 U.S. 1021, 87 S.Ct. 702 (1967); *United Missouri Bank of Kansas City, N.A. v. Danforth,* 394 F.Supp. 774 (W.D.Mo. 1975); *Monongahela Appliance Co. v. Community Bank & Trust, N.A.,* 393 F.Supp. 1226 (N.D.W.Va.1975), *aff'd,* 532 F.2d 751 (4th Cir.1976), *cert. denied,* 425 U.S. 960, 96 S.Ct. 1742; *Meadow Brook Nat'l Bank v. Recile,* 302 F.Supp. 62 (D.La.1969).

Cases like *Northway Lanes v. Hackley Union Nat'l Bank & Trust Co.,* 334 F.Supp. 723 (W.D.Mich.1971), *aff'd,* 464 F.2d 855 (6th Cir.1972), endorse the full implications of *Tiffany* in favoring national banks over competing state banks in the application of usury provisions. If we accept the *Tiffany* preference in favor of national banks, then the "reference over" required by Section 85 is intended not to ensure "competitive equality," but rather to ensure the greatest available advantage to the national bank. Reasonable people may differ about the answer here, but *Nowlin* does not appear to be reconcilable with *Tiffany,* which seems to counsel a policy of competitive *advantage* in favor of national banks.

Northway and *Nowlin* represent a fundamental clash at a number of levels. *Northway* gives national banks the best of both worlds. If a specialized state rate is to the national bank's advantage, then that rate applies, but as calculated under federal rules, not state rules. Hence, under longstanding (but arguably outdated) federal rules, the *nominal* rate could be applied by discounting (*i.e.,* taking the interest up front, even though this would mean that the *effective* rate applied to the loan is higher than the permitted rate. The *Nowlin* court, reinterpreting section 85 in light of later "competitive equality" notions, finds this objectionable. Read in this fashion, *Nowlin* argues, Section 85 leaves the national bank at a competitive advantage over state banks working with the same rate. The better authority appears to be that which remains true to *Tiffany.*

5. *Daggs v. Phoenix Nat'l Bank,* 177 U.S. 549, 20 S.Ct. 732 (1900); *Union Nat'l Bank of Chicago v. Louisville, N.A. & C. Ry. Co.,* 163 U.S. 325, 16 S.Ct. 1039 (1896); *Ray v. American Nat'l Bank & Trust Co. of Chattanooga,* 443 F.Supp. 883 (E.D.Tenn. 1978).

card business, for example, the maximum rate to be charged is still the rate of the state in which the *bank* is located, if that is the highest permissible rate under the federal statute.[7]

6. *Marquette Nat'l Bank of Minneapolis v. First of Omaha Serv. Corp.*, 439 U.S. 299, 99 S.Ct. 540 (1978); *Schuyler Nat'l Bank v. Gadsden*, 191 U.S. 451, 24 S.Ct. 129 (1903); *Barnet v. Muncie Nat'l Bank*, 98 U.S. (8 Otto) 555 (1878); *Farmers' & Mechanics' Nat'l Bank v. Dearing*, 91 U.S. (1 Otto) 29 (1875); *Ray, supra*; *American Auto. Ins. Co. v. Albert*, 102 F.Supp. 542 (D.Minn.1952). This does not necessarily preempt other state claims related to the loan or extension of credit. *See, e.g., Hunter v. Beneficial Nat'l Bank USA*, 947 F.Supp. 446 (M.D.Ala. 1996) (involving state law fraud claims). *But cf. Basile v. H & R Block, Inc.*, 897 F.Supp. 194 (E.D.Pa.1995) (preempting claim under state unfair trade practices and consumer protection act).

7. *Smiley v. Citibank (South Dakota) N.A.*, 517 U.S. 735, 116 S.Ct. 1730 (1996); *Marquette Nat'l Bank, supra*; *Tikkanen v. Citibank (South Dakota) N.A.*, 801 F.Supp. 270 (D.Minn.1992). *See also Cades v. H & R Block, Inc.*, 43 F.3d 869 (4th Cir.1994), *cert. denied*, 515 U.S. 1103, 115 S.Ct. 2247 (1995) (permitting use of home-state rate for out-of-state loan); *Fisher v. First Nat'l Bank of Chicago*, 538 F.2d 1284 (7th Cir. 1976), *cert. denied*, 429 U.S. 1062, 97 S.Ct. 786 (1977) (involving out-of-state revolving credit at higher home-state rate). *But cf. Meadow Brook Nat'l Bank, supra* (finding loan made in Louisiana by New York bank subject to law of state of transaction); *Haas v. Pittsburgh Nat'l Bank*, 60 F.R.D. 604 (W.D.Pa.1973) (same).

The Supreme Court's June 1996 decision in *Smiley* follows up on *Marquette* by considering whether late charges should be included within the meaning of the term "interest" for purposes of Section 85. If they should be (as the Court ultimately decides that they are), then the statutory decision of the *home* state of the bank—here, South Dakota—to authorize such a higher permissible rate of interest trumps the attempt of the transaction state—here, California—to prohibit certain late charges on credit cards. The key to the decision is the Court's deference to the Comptroller's interpretation of Section 85 as including such charges. That being established, the *Marquette* analysis takes hold, and the enhanced rate can be "exported" by the home state of the bank. The combined practical effect of *Marquette* and *Smiley* is that usury policy with respect to credit card transactions will be equalized nationally, in accordance with the most liberal home state policy. Since national bank credit card operations will migrate to the liberal home states, like South Dakota, banks in other home states will not have the same flexibility in pricing credit card services unless either: (1) they also migrate to liberal home states (robbing their current home states of influence over credit card operations); or (2) their current home states also liberalize their credit card policies to retain such business within their jurisdiction.

One possible implication of *Marquette Nat'l Bank* in the merger context (*see generally supra* §§ 4.10–4.14 (discussing bank merger law)) is that it could lead to the delineation of a larger geographic market for certain products, such as credit cards. This might be an advantage to the bank, if it results in dilution of its apparent market share. On the other hand, it may place two merging banks from different states within the same broad geographic market for these purposes.

FIGURE 5-2
Usury Rates: National Bank Act Alternatives

A national bank "may take, receive, reserve, and charge on any loan or discount made, or upon any notes, bills of exchange, or other evidence of debt" interest at a rate allowed by the laws of the state where it is located.[8] In the alternative, the bank may charge interest at a maximum rate of one percent above the discount rate on 90–day commercial paper in effect at the Federal Reserve Bank in the district where it is located, "whichever may be the greater, and no more."[9]

Second, in situations in which the state provides a different rate for banks organized under state law, that rate "shall be allowed" for national banks within the state.[10] However, if some other financial institution is given a more favorable rate under state law, the NBA has been interpreted to allow national banks to use that higher rate.[11]

Third, if no rate is fixed by the laws of the state, a national bank is limited to a maximum rate of seven percent, or one percent above the discount rate on 90–day commercial paper in effect at its Federal Reserve Bank, "whichever may be the greater."[12]

Fourth, for a national bank branch outside of the United States and the District of Columbia, the maximum rate is that "allowed by the laws of the country; territory, dependency, province, dominion, insular possession, or other political subdivision where the branch is located."[13]

Federal law specifies its own penalties for charging interest at a usurious rate, even if the applicable maximum rate for national banks is derived from state law.[14] There is apparently no *de minimis* defense to a

---

8. 12 U.S.C.A. § 85. Elsewhere the section explicitly indicates that "such interest may be taken in advance." *Id. See, e.g., Evans v. National Bank of Savannah,* 251 U.S. 108, 40 S.Ct. 58 (1919) (permitting upfront discounting of short-term note, despite fact that effective rate of interest charged would thereby exceed the nominal rate permitted); *National Bank v. Johnson,* 104 U.S. (14 Otto) 271 (1881) (recognizing no difference between loan and discount for purposes of § 85); *Northway Lanes, supra* (permitting reserving of interest in advance). *But cf. First Nat'l Bank in Mena, supra* (rejecting reserving in advance as permissible method of calculation). Other methods of calculating interest, though using the nominal rate permitted, may still violate the statute based on the effective rate charged. *See, e.g., American Timber & Trading Co. v. First Nat'l Bank of Oregon,* 511 F.2d 980 (9th Cir.1973), *cert. denied,* 421 U.S. 921, 95 S.Ct. 1588 (1975) (involving use of 360–day computation of interest). The maximum allowable state rate referenced over by the statute includes any exceptions to that rate permitted by state law. *Monongahela Appliance Co., supra.* In defining "interest" for purposes of calculating the maximum allowable rate under state law, the bank may include other charges permitted by local state law. *See, e.g., Smiley, supra* (including late-payment fees). It does not matter whether or not state lenders are in fact charging the maximum al-

lowable rate, but only that rate is legally available. *United Missouri Bank, supra.*

9. 12 U.S.C.A. § 85. On the use of the 90–day discount rate, see *Kimball v. Nat'l Bank of N. Am.,* 468 F.Supp. 1069 (E.D.N.Y.), *aff'd,* 614 F.2d 1288 (2d Cir. 1979).

10. 12 U.S.C.A. § 85.

11. *Northway Lanes, supra* (referring to rate for savings and loan associations). *But cf. United States v. Palmer,* 28 F.Supp. 936 (S.D.N.Y.1939) (limiting national banks to rate for state banks and trust companies, not industrial banks).

12. 12 U.S.C.A. § 85.

13. *Id.*

14. 12 U.S.C.A. § 86. *See generally Schuyler Nat'l Bank, supra* (discussing penalty provision); *Farmers' & Mechanics' Nat'l Bank, supra* (invalidating application of higher state penalty to national bank); *Beatrice Prod. Credit Ass'n v. Vieselmeyer,* 376 F.Supp. 1391 (D.Neb.1973) (noting penalties governed by federal law); *First Nat'l Bank in Mena, supra* (same); *American Auto. Ins. Co., supra* (same). This does not preempt possible state law penalties for other claims based on state law. *See, e.g., Hunter, supra. But cf. Watson v. First Union Nat'l Bank of South Carolina,* 837 F.Supp. 146 (D.S.C.1993) (arguing for complete preemption).

penalty action under the NBA.[15] The validity of the underlying contract is not affected, however, by the penalties imposed by the NBA.[16]

When knowingly done,[17] taking, receiving, reserving, or charging a usurious rate is "deemed a forfeiture of the entire interest."[18] If the usurious rate has been paid,[19] the debtor (or the legal representative[20] thereof) may recover from the national bank twice the amount of the interest paid.[21] A two-year limitation on such actions applies, calculated from the time the usurious transaction occurred.[22]

§ 5.10   Deposits

Depository institutions have express statutory authority to take

---

15. *Citizens' Nat'l Bank of Kansas City v. Donnell*, 195 U.S. 369, 25 S.Ct. 49 (1904).

16. *Oates v. First Nat'l Bank of Montgomery*, 100 U.S. (10 Otto) 239 (1879).

17. On the *mens rea* requirement of this provision, see *Wheeler v. Union Nat'l Bank of Pittsburg*, 96 U.S. (6 Otto) 268 (1877) (discussing requirement); *American Timber & Trading Co., supra* (same); *McAdoo v. Union Nat'l Bank of Little Rock, Ark.*, 535 F.2d 1050 (8th Cir.1976) (same).

18. 12 U.S.C.A. § 86. *See Brown v. Marion Nat'l Bank of Lebanon, Ky.*, 169 U.S. 416, 18 S.Ct. 390 (1898) (discussing forfeiture provision); *Barnet, supra* (same); *Anderson v. Hershey*, 127 F.2d 884 (6th Cir.1942) (same). *But cf. Wheeler v. Union Nat'l Bank of Pittsburg*, 96 U.S. (6 Otto) 268 (1877) (disfavoring forfeiture unless facts clearly established).

19. If the interest has been paid, it cannot be reapplied to principal to avoid the double penalty provision. *Walsh v. Mayer*, 111 U.S. 31, 4 S.Ct. 260 (1884). *But cf. Danforth v. Nat'l State Bank*, 48 F. 271 (3d Cir.1891) (allowing unallocated payments to be applied to principal). Rollover of a previous note does not in itself constitute a payment of the usurious interest for purposes of this penalty provision. *First Nat'l Bank v. Lasater*, 196 U.S. 115, 25 S.Ct. 206 (1905); *National Bank of Daingerfield v. Ragland*, 181 U.S. 45, 21 S.Ct. 536 (1901).

20. On the meaning of the term "legal representative" for these purposes, see *Louisville Trust Co. v. Kentucky Nat'l Bank*, 87 F. 143 (D.Ky.1898) (including assignee for benefit of creditors); *Barnet, supra* (excluding indorser of bill of exchange).

21. 12 U.S.C.A. § 86. *See McCollum v. Hamilton Nat'l Bank of Chattanooga*, 303 U.S. 245, 58 S.Ct. 568 (1938) (applying "knowingly" requirement to double penalty provision); *Talbot v. First Nat'l Bank of Sioux City*, 185 U.S. 172, 22 S.Ct. 612

(1902) (discussing double penalty provision); *First Nat'l Bank of Lake Benton v. Watt*, 184 U.S. 151, 22 S.Ct. 457 (1902) (applying double penalty to entire interest paid, not only to usurious portion); *Anderson, supra* (discussing double penalty provision).

Class actions may be appropriate for certain issues with respect to double penalty actions. *American Timber & Trading Co., supra. See also Cosgrove v. First & Merchants Nat'l Bank*, 68 F.R.D. 555 (E.D.Va. 1975) (involving cash advance fees); *Partain v. First Nat'l Bank of Montgomery*, 59 F.R.D. 56 (M.D.Ala.1973) (limiting class to current holders of credit cards issued by bank). *But cf. Landau v. Chase Manhattan Bank, N.A.*, 367 F.Supp. 992 (S.D.N.Y.1973) (denying class action treatment); *Koos v. First Nat'l Bank of Peoria*, 358 F.Supp. 890 (S.D.Ill.1973), *aff'd*, 496 F.2d 1162 (7th Cir. 1974) (same).

22. 12 U.S.C.A. § 86. *See M. Nahas & Co., Inc. v. First Nat'l Bank of Hot Springs*, 930 F.2d 608 (8th Cir.1991) (discussing limitation provision in light of subsequent state legislation); *First Nat'l Bank of Birmingham v. Daniel*, 239 F.2d 801 (5th Cir. 1956) (discussing effect of two-year limitation provision on double penalty provision). *See generally McCarthy v. First Nat'l Bank*, 223 U.S. 493, 32 S.Ct. 240 (1912) (beginning limitation period from date of payment of usurious interest); *National Bank of Daingerfield, supra* (rejecting view that rollover of previous note starts limitation period); *Panos v. Smith*, 116 F.2d 445 (6th Cir.1940) (discussing effect of rollovers of notes on running of limitation period); *Cronkleton v. Hall*, 66 F.2d 384 (8th Cir. 1933) (starting limitation period on first payment of interest); *Louisville Trust Co., supra* (starting limitation period with respect to discounted note at full payment of note or its renewals).

deposits.[1] In the case of commercial banks like national banks, this power typically extends to all types of deposits, including demand deposits, time deposits, and deposits for all types of depositors whether individuals, business entities, nonprofit organizations, or governmental.[2] While the deposit-taking activities of other depository institutions have generally been limited to time and savings deposits of individuals,[3] the emergence of NOW accounts and other modern developments gradually blurred the distinctions between the different types of financial institutions with respect to deposit-taking.[4] Currently the range of deposits and depositors that these institutions, and particularly savings associations, may service has expanded significantly.[5]

§ 5.11 Deposit Insurance

One of the distinctive features of deposit-taking in the post-Depression United States has been the availability of federal deposit insurance. Today the reach of the deposit insurance regime is broad in two important respects. First, all depository institutions are eligible in principle for federal deposit insurance, either through the FDIC,[1] or through the NCUA.[2] Second, the concept of what constitutes a "deposit" for purposes of federal deposit insurance is markedly broader than our ordinary application of the term.[3]

The first point is illustrated by the breadth of coverage of the FDIA, as recently amended, to include a wide range of institutions within the scope of its eligibility, and its broadened impact on uninsured deposits as well. Under the Federal Deposit Insurance Corporation Improvements Act ("FDICIA"),[4] FDIC insurance of deposits of any depository institution now generally requires a specific application to and approval by the FDIC.[5] New rules also apply to depository institutions that are not insured by the FDIC.[6] Private deposit insurers are required to obtain an

§ 5.10

1. *See, e.g.,* 12 U.S.C.A. § 24(Seventh) (national banks); 1464 (federal savings associations); 1757 (federal credit unions).

2. 12 U.S.C.A. § 24 (Seventh).

3. *See, e.g.,* 12 U.S.C.A. §§ 1464, 1757 (1968).

4. *See La Caisse Populaire St.-Marie (St. Mary's Bank) v. United States,* 425 F.Supp. 512 (D.N.H.1976) (discussing changes).

5. *See, e.g.,* 12 U.S.C.A. § 1464(b). For permissible deposits of federal credit unions (known as "shares"), see *id.* § 1757(6).

§ 5.11

1. 12 U.S.C.A. §§ 1813(c)(1), 1815 (providing for FDIC deposit insurance for "depository institutions," defined as banks and savings associations).

2. *Id.* §§ 1781–1789 (providing for NCUA deposit insurance for credit unions).

3. *See id.* § 1813(*l*) (defining "deposit" for purposes of FDIA).

4. Pub. L. No. 102–242, 105 Stat. 2236 (Dec. 19, 1991) (codified at scattered sections of 12 U.S.C.A.).

5. FDICIA, § 115(a) (codified at 12 U.S.C.A. § 1815(a)).

6. *See* FDICIA, § 151(a)(1), (b) (codified at 12 U.S.C.A. § 1831t), *as amended,* Riegle Community Development and Regulatory Improvement Act of 1994 ("CDRIA"), Pub. L. No. 103–325, § 340(a), 108 Stat. 2160, 2237–2238 (Sept. 23, 1994) (codified at 12 U.S.C.A. § 1831t(b)(3)) (simplified disclosure for existing depositors). *See also* CDRIA, § 304(b), 108 Stat. at 2238 (codified at 12 U.S.C.A. § 1831t note) (effective date).

annual audit from an independent auditor, using generally accepted auditing standards.[7] The audit must include a determination by the auditor of whether or not the private insurer follows generally accepted accounting principles, and whether or not it has set aside sufficient reserves for losses.[8] A nonbank depository institution lacking federal deposit insurance is prohibited from using the mails or any instrumentality of interstate commerce to receive or facilitate receiving deposits, with certain exceptions.[9] The FDICIA also required the establishment of a risk-based assessment system for federal deposit insurance.[10]

The second point is illustrated by *Federal Deposit Insurance Corp. v. Philadelphia Gear Corp.*,[11] which considered whether the term "deposit" under the FDIA was sufficiently broad to include a standby letter of credit backed by a contingent promissory note. Both the majority and the dissent in *Philadelphia Gear* acknowledged the very broad language and potential scope of the definition of "deposit" in the FDIA, which as amended, states:

> The term "deposit" means ... the unpaid balance of money or its equivalent received or held by a bank or savings association in the usual course of business and for which it has given or is obligated to give credit, either conditionally or unconditionally, to a commercial, checking, savings, time, or thrift account, or which is evidenced by its certificate of deposit, thrift certificate, investment certificate, certificate of indebtedness, or other similar name, or a check or draft drawn against a deposit account and certified by the bank or savings association, or a letter of credit or a traveler's check on which the bank or savings association is primarily liable: Provided, That, without limiting the generality of the term "money or its equivalent", any such account or instrument must be regarded as evidencing the receipt of the equivalent of money when credited or issued in exchange for checks or drafts or for a promissory note upon which the person obtaining any such credit or instrument is primarily or secondarily liable, or for a charge against a deposit account, or in settlement of checks, drafts, or other instruments forwarded to such bank or savings association for collection.[12]

To a significant extent, of course, this definitional concept is circular. At base, "deposit" represents a credit relationship in favor of a person dealing with a bank, "in the usual course of [the bank's] business and for which it has given or is obligated to give credit," but since deposit-taking (along with lending) *is* a bank's usual course of business, this barely delineates the concept. Presumably, "deposit" does not include a bank's account outstanding for window washing services, or for rent on its business premises, or for other similar undertakings. Howev-

7. 12 U.S.C.A. § 1831t(a)(1).
8. *Id.*
9. *Id.* § 1831t(e)(1).
10. FDICIA, § 302 (codified at 12 U.S.C.A. § 1817(b)). *Cf.* 12 C.F.R. Pt. 330 (FDIC deposit insurance coverage regulations).
11. 476 U.S. 426, 106 S.Ct. 1931 (1986).
12. 12 U.S.C.A. § 1813(*l*)(1).

er, any credit created in favor of a person dealing with the bank *qua* bank is potentially within this broad definition.

Philadelphia Gear focused on the "purpose behind the insurance of deposits in general, and especially in the [FDIA] section defining deposits as 'money or its equivalent,' [as] the protection of assets and hard earnings entrusted to a bank."[13] Applying its understanding of the significance of the term "money or its equivalent"—as understood against the background of this purpose—the Court concluded that the "purpose [was] not furthered by extending deposit insurance to cover a standby letter of credit backed by a contingent promissory note, which involves no surrender of assets or hard earnings to the custody of the bank."[14]

Justice Marshall, in a dissenting opinion joined by Justices Blackmun and Rehnquist, acknowledged the "considerable common sense backing the Court's opinion,"[15] but could not find the qualifications that the Court wanted to read into the definition of "deposit" in the statutory language itself.[16] That definition explicitly included letters of credit within the scope of the term, and the instruments in question clearly fit within the concepts of a note and a "letter of credit" for purposes of, for example, the Uniform Commercial Code ("UCC").[17]

However, it is misleading to focus on whether or not the instrument involved is governed, as a matter of transactional law, by Article 5 of the UCC.[18] Rather, the question is whether the arrangement represents the kind of obligation or instrument covered by the language of the FDIA definition of "deposit," as informed by its legislative history, which is not necessarily coterminous with its treatment in the UCC in any event.

§ 5.12 Reserve Requirements

With the enactment of the Depository Institutions Deregulation and Monetary Control Act of 1980,[1] all depository institutions, including savings associations and credit unions generally became subject to the deposit reserve requirements administered by the Fed.[2] The complex

---

13. *Philadelphia Gear Corp.*, 476 U.S. at 435, 106 S.Ct. at 1936.

14. *Id.*

15. 476 U.S. at 440, 106 S.Ct. at 1939 (Marshall, J., dissenting).

16. 476 U.S. at 440–441, 106 S.Ct. at 1939.

17. 476 U.S. at 442, 106 S.Ct. at 1940. *See generally* UCC §§ 3–104(1), 5–117 (dealing with notes and letters of credit, respectively).

18. *Cf. First Empire Bank–New York v. Federal Deposit Ins. Corp.*, 572 F.2d 1361 (9th Cir.1978), *cert. denied*, 439 U.S. 919,

99 S.Ct. 293, *appeal after remand*, 634 F.2d 1222 (9th Cir.1980), *cert. denied*, 452 U.S. 906, 101 S.Ct. 3032 (1981) (dealing with treatment of letters of credit by FDIC in failing bank situation).

§ 5.12

1. *See* Pub. L. No. 96–221, tit. I, § 103, 94 Stat. 133 (1980) (codified *at* 12 U.S.C.A. § 461(b)), *as amended*, Financial Institutions Reform, Recovery, and Enforcement Act of 1989 ("FIRREA"), Pub. L. No. 101–73, § 744(i)(2), 103 Stat. 183, 439 (1989).

2. *See* 12 U.S.C.A. § 461(b)(1), (b)(2)-(4). *See also* 12 C.F.R. Pt. 204 (setting forth Fed's Regulation D reserve requirements).

transitional period generally ended in September 1987,[3] so that currently all depository institutions, whether or not federally chartered or insured, became fully subject to the Fed's deposit reserve requirements.

Hence, all depository institutions are currently subject to the Fed's Regulation D concerning deposit reserve requirements.[4] These regulations cover the technical issues of computation and maintenance of reserves.[5] They also provide for necessary transitional adjustments of reserves when depository institutions merge.[6]

Most issues that might be raised under the reserve requirements have been mechanized outside of the lawyer's normal scope, *e.g.*, the calculation of reserves, which is normally prepared on detailed Fed forms. Nevertheless, there are certain aspects of importance from a legal and policy point of view that should be noted. Foremost among these is the scope of the current reserve requirements. The statutory provisions mandating Fed jurisdiction over reserves of all depository institutions represent a rather dramatic jurisdictional assertion.[7] The provisions sweep within direct federal jurisdiction the reserve requirements applicable to all depository institutions *eligible for* federal deposit insurance, not just those actually insured by the FDIC.[8]

§ 5.13   Interest Rates

Traditionally, the rate of interest that depository institutions could pay on deposits was restricted.[1] Pursuant to changes in federal statute beginning in 1980,[2] however, interest rate limitations were gradually eliminated with the transitional process completed by March 31, 1986.[3]

§ 5.14   Brokered Deposits

The practice of brokering deposits, in which an intermediary consolidates funds of prospective depositors and negotiates *en bloc* with a depository institution for a jumbo rate for placement of the consolidated deposit,[1] represents a danger for depository institutions that may be in

---

3. *See* 12 U.S.C.A. § 461(b)(8). *Cf.* 12 C.F.R. § 204.4.

4. 12 C.F.R. Pt. 204.

5. 12 C.F.R. §§ 204.2–204.3, 204.9. *See also id.* § 204.5 (concerning authority to impose emergency reserve requirements, not currently in use); 204.6 (concerning authority to impose supplemental reserve requirements, not currently in use).

6. *Id.* § 204.4.

7. 12 U.S.C.A. § 461(b)(1)(A), (c).

8. *Id.* § 461(b)(1)(A).

§ 5.13

1. *See, e.g.*, 12 C.F.R. Pt. 208 (1979) (restricting interest rates under Fed Regulation Q).

2. 12 U.S.C.A. §§ 3501 *et seq.*

3. *Id.* Elimination of interest rate limitation on insured credit union shares was effected by regulatory action by the NCUA in 1982. 47 Fed. Reg. 17,979 (1982) (codified at 12 C.F.R. § 701.35).

§ 5.14

1. For a curious early case involving a "solicitor" of deposits for a national bank, see *Case v. First Nat'l Bank of City of Brooklyn*, 109 N.Y.S. 1119, 59 Misc. 269 (Sup. Ct. 1908) (finding the practice permissible, on a one-year basis, under 12 U.S.C.A. § 24 (Third), (Seventh)).

danger of default. These institutions are particularly vulnerable to overbidding on the consolidated deposits, since they often desperately need the working liquidity that the deposits would offer. Since these deposits tend to be particularly rate sensitive, they are also relatively volatile; they will follow the bidding-up of rates to other institutions, thus leaving the vulnerable depository with an immediate liquidity crisis. As a result, the practice of brokering deposits was also a serious problem for deposit insurers like the FDIC and the now defunct FSLIC.

Attempts to deal with this problem at the regulatory level, for example, by treating such deposits as defined FDIA "deposits" only up to $100,000 per broker, were struck down in *FAIC Securities v. Federal Deposit Insurance Corp.*[2] as unauthorized by the statute. In response, the Financial Institutions Reform, Recovery, and Enforcement Act of 1989 ("FIRREA")[3] established a statutory scheme of regulation for brokered deposits,[4] which is essentially based upon supervision of these activities as a matter of "safe and sound banking" under the FDIA,[5] an approach neither tried by the FDIC nor addressed by *FAIC Securities*. The end result is probably the equivalent of the result under the approach invalidated in the case: troubled institutions are excluded from the brokered deposit market.

Currently, the FDIC rules provide for three distinct tiers of depository institutions within the scheme of regulation of brokered deposits.[6] First, a "well capitalized" insured depository institution (*e.g.*, one with capital equal to at least ten percent of its risk-weighted assets[7]) may solicit and accept, renew or roll over any brokered deposit without restriction.[8]

Second, an "adequately capitalized" insured depository institution (*e.g.*, one with capital equal to eight to ten percent of assets[9]) may not accept, renew or roll over any brokered deposit, unless it has been granted a waiver by the FDIC.[10] However, an adequately capitalized insured depository institution that has been granted a waiver may not pay an effective yield on any such deposit which, at the time the deposit is accepted, renewed or rolled over, exceeds by more than 75 basis points

---

2. 768 F.2d 352 (D.C.Cir.1985).

3. Pub. L. No. 101–73, § 744(i)(2), 103 Stat. 183, 439 (1989) (codified at scattered sections of 12 U.S.C.A.).

4. 12 U.S.C.A. § 1831f.

5. 12 U.S.C.A. § 1818(b).

6. 12 C.F.R. § 337.6.

7. *See   id.   §§* 325.103(b)(1), 337.6(a)(3)(i) (discussing "well capitalized" institution).

8. *Id.* § 337.6(b)(1).

9. *Id.* §§ 325.103(b)(2), 337.6(a)(3)(i).

10. *Id.* § 337.6(b)(2)(i). Waivers are available on a case-by-case basis, as follows:

The FDIC may, on a case-by-case basis and upon application by an adequately capitalized insured depository institution, waive the prohibition on the acceptance, renewal or rollover of brokered deposits upon a finding that such acceptance, renewal or rollover does not constitute an unsafe or unsound practice with respect to such institution. The FDIC may conclude that it is not unsafe or unsound and may grant a waiver when the acceptance, renewal or rollover of brokered deposits is determined to pose no undue risk to the institution. Any waiver granted may be revoked at any time by written notice to the institution.

Id. § 337.6(c).

(1) the effective yield paid on deposits of comparable size and maturity in such institution's normal market area for deposits accepted from within its normal market area; or (2) the national rate[11] paid on deposits of comparable size and maturity for deposits accepted outside the institution's normal market area.[12]

Third, an "undercapitalized" insured depository institution (*e.g.*, one with capital equal to less than eight percent of assets[13]) may not accept, renew or roll over any brokered deposit.[14] An undercapitalized insured depository institution may not solicit deposits by offering an effective yield that exceeds by more than 75 basis points the prevailing effective yields on insured deposits of comparable maturity in its normal market area, or in the market area in which the deposits are being solicited.[15]

§ 5.15　Tying Arrangements

As noted previously,[1] the anti-tying provisions prohibit involuntary tying of bank products and services in specified instances. In addition, the provisions prohibit a bank that maintains a correspondent account in the name of another bank from making an extension of credit to an executive officer or director of, or to a significant insider of,[2] the other bank, or to any related interest of such person, except on specified conditions.[3] The extension of credit must be made on substantially the same terms (including interest rates and collateral requirements) as those prevailing at the time for comparable transactions with other persons.[4] In addition, the extension of credit may not involve more than the normal risk of repayment or present other unfavorable features.[5]

Furthermore, a bank is generally prohibited from opening a correspondent account at another bank, if the other bank has an outstanding extension of credit in favor of an executive officer or director of, or significant insider of, the bank wishing to open the account, or to any related interest of such person.[6] Again, the opening of the correspondent

---

11. For these purposes, the national rate is considered to be:

    (1) 120 percent of the current yield on similar maturity U.S. Treasury obligations; or

    (2) In the case of any deposit at least half of which is uninsured, 130 percent of such applicable yield.

Id. § 337.6(b)(2)(ii).

12. *Id.* § 337.6(b)(2)(ii)(A)-(B).

13. *Id.* § 325.103(b)(3), 337.6(a)(3)(i).

14. *Id.* § 337.6(b)(3)(i).

15. *Id.* § 337.6(b)(3)(ii).

§ 5.15

1. *See supra* § 5.8 (discussing anti-tying provisions as applied to lending activities).

2. The statutory formulation for this "significant insider" is "any person who directly or indirectly or acting through or in concert with one or more persons owns, controls, or has the power to vote more than 10 per centum of any class of voting securities of, such other bank." 12 U.S.C.A. § 1972(2)(A).

3. *Id.* § 1972(2)(A).

4. *Id.* § 1972(2)(A).

5. *Id.*

6. *Id.* § 1972(2)(B). *See also id.* § 1972(2)(D).

account will be permitted if the existing extension of credit was made on substantially the same terms (including interest rates and collateral requirements) as those prevailing at the time for comparable transactions with other persons, and the credit does not involve more than the normal risk of repayment or present other unfavorable features.[7]

Civil money penalties may be assessed for violation of these prohibitions of the anti-tying provisions.[8] The civil money penalty provision does not itself create a private right of action.[9] However, private civil actions for treble damages[10] and injunctive relief against threatened loss or damage[11] are authorized elsewhere in the anti-tying provisions.

§ 5.16   Guarantees and Letters of Credit

It may be reasonably argued that the regulatory law and lore surrounding the treatment of third-party guarantees and letters of credit represent the triumph of form over substance. Starting with the proposition that national banks lacked the statutory authority to issue third-party guarantees,[1] the courts and the regulators have fashioned a series of end-runs and near-misses around this proposition, which typically continues to be cited as a starting point for analysis. The trend in the cases appears to suggest that, even if a transaction is for all economic purposes a third-party guarantee, calling it something else (*e.g.*, a standby letter of credit) will suffice to escape the basic proposition that third-party guarantees are unauthorized.

§ 5.17   Guarantees

The judicial treatment of third-party guarantees exhibits much ambiguity and is generally unsatisfying from an analytical point of view. Since the courts originally decided that national banks lacked the power to issue third-party guarantees,[1] the project of the case law developments has generally been to find ways to back away from that position. Hence, the courts are often quite willing to distinguish the arrangement under

---

7. *Id.* § 1972(2)(B).

8. *Id.* § 1972(2)(F).

9. *Baggett v. First Nat'l Bank of Gaines-ville*, 117 F.3d 1342 (11th Cir.1997).

10. 12 U.S.C.A. § 1975.

11. *Id.* § 1976.

§ 5.16

1. *See, e.g., Federal Intermediate Credit Bank of Omaha v. L'Herisson*, 33 F.2d 841 (8th Cir.1929) (holding national bank may not lend its credit); *Border Nat'l Bank of Eagle Pass, Tex. v. American Nat'l Bank of San Francisco*, 282 F. 73 (5th Cir.1922), *error dismissed and cert. denied*, 260 U.S. 732, 43 S.Ct. 96 (noting that guaranty by

national bank is *ultra vires*); *C.E. Healey & Son v. Stewardson Nat'l Bank*, 285 Ill.App. 290, 1 N.E.2d 858 (1936) (finding no power in national bank to guarantee).

§ 5.17

1. *See, e.g., Federal Intermediate Credit Bank of Omaha v. L'Herisson*, 33 F.2d 841 (8th Cir.1929) (holding national bank may not lend its credit); *Border Nat'l Bank of Eagle Pass, Tex. v. American Nat'l Bank of San Francisco*, 282 F. 73 (5th Cir.1922), *error dismissed and cert. denied*, 260 U.S. 732, 43 S.Ct. 96 (noting that guaranty by national bank is *ultra vires*); *C.E. Healey & Son v. Stewardson Nat'l Bank*, 285 Ill.App. 290, 1 N.E.2d 858 (1936) (finding no power in national bank to guarantee).

consideration from a forbidden third-party guarantee—even when "guarantee" language is explicitly used by the bank, as in *Border National Bank of Eagle Pass, Texas v. American National Bank of San Francisco*.[2]

While the proposition that national banks cannot issue third-party guarantees is often stated quite baldly, it is in fact subject to many refinements and qualifications. Thus, a guaranty issued by a bank in the furtherance of its own rights or incidental to a transaction in which it has an interest is authorized.[3] Guarantees may also be validly issued in favor of a failing bank in order to protect the banking business of the guaranteeing banks.[4] Likewise, a national bank may indorse or guarantee negotiable paper in connection with its transfer or discount,[5] in the ordinary course of the bank's business.[6]

Current regulatory policy expressly permits the use of third-party guarantees, whether styled as a guaranty, surety on an indemnity bond, or otherwise, subject to certain conditions.[7] The national bank must have a substantial interest in the performance of the underlying transaction involved,[8] or the transaction must be for the benefit of a customer from whom the bank obtains a segregated deposit sufficient to cover the bank's total potential liability.[9] Essentially, these conditions create a situation likely to enhance the safety and soundness of a bank's practice in issuing third-party guarantees.

§ 5.18 Documentary Letters of Credit

Issuance and confirmation of documentary letters of credit are incidental powers of a bank in which the transaction itself is governed by state law. Currently, Article 5 of the Uniform Commercial Code covers these transactions.[1] These activities are permissible even if the bank has

---

2. *Border Nat'l Bank, supra. See also Federal Deposit Ins. Corp. v. Freudenfeld*, 492 F.Supp. 763 (E.D. Wis. 1980) (finding that letter of credit, even if impermissible guaranty, can only be challenged by federal government).

3. *Second Nat'l Bank of Parkersburg, W. Va. v. U.S. Fidelity & Guar. Co.*, 266 F. 489 (4th Cir.1920), *appeal dismissed*, 254 U.S. 660, 41 S.Ct. 10; *Dunn v. McCoy*, 113 F.2d 587 (3d Cir.1940); *American Nat'l Bank v. National Wall–Paper Co.*, 77 F. 85 (8th Cir.1896).

4. *McCoy v. Adams*, 29 F.Supp. 815 (E.D.Pa.1939).

5. *People's Bank v. Manufacturers' Nat'l Bank*, 101 U.S. (11 Otto) 181 (1879); *Farmers' & Miners' Bank v. Bluefield Nat'l Bank*, 11 F.2d 83 (4th Cir.1926), *cert. denied*, 271 U.S. 669, 46 S.Ct. 483; *Hanover Nat'l Bank v. Burlingame First Nat'l Bank*, 109 F. 421 (8th Cir.1901); *Bowen v. Needles Nat'l Bank*, 94 F. 925 (9th Cir.1899), *cert. denied*, 176 U.S. 682, 20 S.Ct. 1024 (1900);

Commercial Nat'l Bank v. Pirie, 82 F. 799 (8th Cir.1897).

6. *Barron v. McKinnon*, 179 F. 759 (D. Mass. 1910) (finding guarantee not in ordinary course of business of banking).

7. 12 C.F.R. § 7.1017.

8. 12 C.F.R. § 7.1017(a).

9. *Id.* § 7.1017(b). The segregated deposit can include collateral. It should have a market value equal to the bank's exposure and be cash or specified liquid securities, or it should have a market value equal to 110 percent of the bank's exposure and be composed of obligations of a State or political subdivision of a State. *Id.* § 7.1017(b)(1)–(3).

§ 5.18

1. *Prudential Ins. Co. of Am. v. Marquette Nat'l Bank of Minneapolis*, 419 F.Supp. 734 (D.Minn.1976). *See also American Ins. Ass'n v. Clarke*, 865 F.2d 278, 282 (D.C.Cir.1988) (discussing characteristics of characterized what it is doing as a "guaranty."[2] The primary regulatory concern here is that the bank's practices in issuing and confirming letters of credit are conducted in a safe and sound manner.[3]

§ 5.19   Standby Letters of Credit

Standby letters of credit operate, in terms of their economic reality, are third-party guarantees, yet to the extent they are structured as letters of credit, they share the legal treatment of documentary letters of credit.[1] Because of their dual nature as functional guarantees and as letters of credit, standby letters of credit raise some peculiar issues concerning their proper treatment for regulatory purposes; this problem is discussed in Chapter 9, *infra.*[2]

§ 5.20   Real Property

The power of banks to hold real property, aside from a headquarters and branches, was traditionally limited because of concerns about the need for liquidity, the dangers of land speculation, and the fear of large aggregations of economic power that banks' control of land naturally exacerbated in an agrarian society.[1] An additional complication for national banks arose from the fact that the original provision of the NBA dealing with real property[2] did not permit the taking of a mortgage interest in a transaction extending credit, but only to secure a debt previously contracted. Positive authority for real estate holdings did not enter the federal statutes until the 20th century, permitting contemporaneous mortgages under specified conditions.[3]

However, courts resisted voiding of lending transactions on the basis of the existence of an impermissible mortgage, instead limiting the remedy of voidability to the chartering authority.[4] *Ultra vires* notwith-

letters of credit as incidental activities of national banks); *United Bank Ltd. v. Cambridge Sporting Goods Corp.*, 41 N.Y.2d 254, 360 N.E.2d 943, 392 N.Y.S.2d 265 (1976) (discussing documentary letters of credit under applicable state law); *Maurice O'Meara Co. v. National Park Bank of New York*, 239 N.Y. 386, 146 N.E. 636 (1925) (same).

2. *Border Nat'l Bank of Eagle Pass, Tex. v. American Nat'l Bank of San Francisco*, 282 F. 73 (5th Cir.1922), *error dismissed and cert. denied*, 260 U.S. 732, 43 S.Ct. 96.

3. 12 C.F.R. § 7.1016(b).

§ 5.19

1. *Legality of Guaranty Letters of Credit*, [1974 Transfer Binder] Fed. Banking L. Rep. (CCH) ¶ 96,301 (July 1, 1974); *American Ins. Ass'n v. Clarke*, 865 F.2d 278, 282 (D.C.Cir.1988) (comparing documentary and standby letters of credit); *Federal De-*

posit Ins. Corp. v. Freudenfeld, 492 F.Supp. 763 (E.D. Wisc. 1980) (discussing standby letters of credit).

2. *See infra* § 9.21 (discussing regulatory policy concerning standby letters of credit).

§ 5.20

1. *Union National Bank v. Matthews*, 98 U.S. (8 Otto) 621, 626 (1878); *First Nat'l Bank of Bellaire v. Comptroller of the Currency*, 697 F.2d 674, 681 (5th Cir.1983) (quoting *Matthews*).

2. 12 U.S.C.A. § 29. For a modern case interpreting and applying this provision, see *First Nat'l Bank of Bellaire, supra.*

3. 12 U.S.C.A. § 371.

4. *Kerfoot v. Farmers' & Merchants' Bank*, 218 U.S. 281, 31 S.Ct. 14 (1910); *National Bank v. Whitney*, 103 U.S. (13 Otto) 99 (1880); *Matthews, supra.*

standing, where a bank has already enjoyed the benefits of an executed real estate transaction—*e.g.*, occupation of leased premises—the courts have had little difficulty in requiring payment by the bank for the benefit received.[5]

The original NBA provision, as amended, generally limits the power of a national bank to purchase, own, and convey real property to the following specified purposes: (1) It may do so to the extent "necessary for its accommodation in the transaction of its business."[6] (2) It may accept mortgages on real property "in good faith by way of security for debts previously contracted."[7] (3) It may accept conveyance of real estate "in satisfaction of debts previously contracted in the course of its dealings."[8] (4) It may purchase real estate at sales, "under judgments, decrees, or mortgages held by [it], or [it may] purchase to secure debts due to it."[9]

By its own terms, these provisions give no authority for taking of a mortgage contemporaneous with the making of a real estate loan. Furthermore, under these provisions, national banks are generally not permitted to hold any real estate under mortgage, or the title and possession of any real estate purchased to secure any debts due to it, for longer than five years.[10]

This restrictive situation is ameliorated by a provision of the Federal Reserve Act ("FRA") dealing with real estate loans.[11] Among other things, the FRA authorizes national banks to make real estate loans secured by liens on interests in real estate, subject to any requirements that the Comptroller may prescribe.[12] The Comptroller has consolidated regulatory provisions drawing on the authority of both the NBA and the FRA provision.[13]

---

5. *Houston v. Drake*, 97 F.2d 863 (9th Cir.1938).

6. 12 U.S.C.A. § 29 (First).

7. *Id.* § 29 (Second).

8. *Id.* § 29 (Third).

9. *Id.* § 29 (Fourth).

10. *Id.* § 29. However, upon application, the Comptroller may approve possession of such real property for a longer period, not to exceed an additional five years, if one of the following conditions is met: (1) the bank must have made a good faith attempt to dispose of the real property within the original five-year period; or, (2) disposal of the real property within the original five-year period would be detrimental to the bank. *Id.* § 29(1)-(2). The Comptroller may also approve expenditure of funds by the bank for the development and improvement of the property, subject to conditions and limitations imposed by the Comptroller in his discretion. *Id.* § 29. Limited grandfathering of certain property holdings is also provided, as follows:

Notwithstanding the five-year holding limitation of this section or any other provision of this chapter, any national [bank that] on October 15, 1982, held, directly or indirectly, real estate, including any subsurface rights or interests therein, that since December 31, 1979, had not been valued on the books of such association for more than a nominal amount, may continue to hold such real estate, rights, or interests for such longer period of time as would be permitted a State chartered bank by the law of the State in which the association is located if the aggregate amount of earnings from such real estate, rights, or interests is separately disclosed in the annual financial statements of the association.

Id.

11. 12 U.S.C.A. § 371.

12. *Id.* § 371(a).

13. 12 C.F.R. §§ 5.37 (requiring application for investment in bank premises); 7.1000 (providing interpretive guidance

§ 5.21   Trust Powers

Approval of the formation of a commercial bank does not necessarily include an inherent grant of authority to engage in trust activities. Under one statutory model, this authority must be specifically granted by the chartering authority.[1] Other statutes may authorize exercise of such powers by either a bank or trust company at the applicant's option, subject to approval by the appropriate regulator,[2] or by a bank or trust company limited to fiduciary activities.[3] Nevertheless, most commercial banks apply for and obtain those powers, typically incorporating the trust activities within a trust department or division of the bank itself.

For national banks, the NBA authorizes the Comptroller to grant trust powers to national banks.[4] The NBA limits the availability of trust powers for national banks by reference over to state law; the Comptroller may only grant trust powers if, and to the extent that, the state of a national bank's locality permits such powers to state-chartered entities.[5] In passing upon applications for trust powers, the Comptroller may consider the following factors: (1) the amount of capital and surplus of the applicant bank;[6] (2) the needs of the community to be served;[7] and, (3) any other facts and circumstances that seem appropriate to the Comptroller.[8]

In the 1970s, the OCC initiated a policy of chartering a national bank limited to the exercise of trust powers only, and the policy was challenged as outside the authority of the Comptroller under the NBA.[9] However, in the interim, Congress amended the NBA specifically to ratify such charters.[10] Hence, it is now clear that national banks limited

with respect to national bank ownership of property).

§ 5.21

1. *See, e.g.*, 12 U.S.C.A. § 92a (authorizing approval of trust powers for national bank).

2. Cal. Fin. Code §§ 1500, 1500.1 (specifying prerequisites for engaging in trust business).

3. 12 U.S.C.A. § 27; N.Y. Banking Law §§ 94, 96.

4. 12 U.S.C.A. § 92a(a).

5. *Id. See St. Louis County Nat'l Bank v. Mercantile Trust Co. Nat'l Ass'n*, 548 F.2d 716 (8th Cir.1976), *cert. denied*, 433 U.S. 909, 97 S.Ct. 2975 (1977) (applying "local law" requirement); *American Trust Co., Inc. v. South Carolina Bd. of Bank Control*, 381 F.Supp. 313 (D.S.C.1974) (discussing "local law" requirement).

6. 12 U.S.C.A. § 92a(i). Specifically, the Comptroller may consider "whether or not

such capital and surplus is sufficient under the circumstances of the case.... " *Id.* Despite the permissive tone of the language of Section 92a(i), the Comptroller is specifically prohibited from issuing a trust powers permit "to any national [bank] having a capital and surplus less than the capital and surplus required by State law of State banks, trust companies, and corporations exercising such powers." *Id.*

7. *Id.*

8. *Id.* For discussion of the Comptroller's implementing regulations, see 1 MICHAEL P. MALLOY, BANKING LAW AND REGULATION § 2.2.4.1 (1994 & CUM. SUPP.).

9. *National State Bank of Elizabeth, N.J. v. Smith*, 591 F.2d 223 (3d Cir.1979).

10. Pub. L. No. 95–630, § 1504, 92 Stat. 3713 (1978) (codified at 12 U.S.C.A. § 27(a)), which provided that

A [national bank], to which the Comptroller of the Currency has heretofore issued or hereafter issues [a] certificate to trust powers may be chartered by the OCC.[11] Charter applications for such banks resemble those for any *de novo* national bank.

The trust activities of commercial banks are governed by principles of the law of trusts, as they would affect any fiduciary. Overlaying the operation of these principles, however, is a system of federal regulation of trust activities.[12] The Comptroller will in the first instance supervise and examine the trust departments and activities of national banks;[13] the Fed will do the same for state member banks,[14] the FDIC for state nonmember insured banks,[15] and the OTS for savings associations.[16]

§ 5.22　Incidental Powers

Since state-chartered insured banks are significantly limited in their activities to those permissible for national banks,[1] the scope of national bank incidental powers has become increasingly important for all participants in the depository institutions industry. The concept of incidental powers, in fact, serves as the authority for many traditional banking activities.

With ever greater frequency, however, it is also the basis for many nontraditional activities. There are certain inherent analytical difficulties here. In large part, what constitutes a "traditional" banking activity for these purposes is whatever banks have historically done, beyond the core functions of deposit-taking and lending. Attempts can be made to organize this group of activities under a generic concept such as "incidental powers," but problems arise in that regard.

First of all, it is not at all clear that certain traditional banking powers necessarily fit under this concept at all. (For example, is the issuance of letters of credit an "incidental power?" Trust activities?) Second, in its contemporary guise, the "incidental powers" approach has resulted in the prospective addition of new powers that are in no realistic sense banking powers at all.

The "incidental powers" concept has often been used as the justification for the prospective addition of new powers that we might not

[of authority to commence banking], is not illegally constituted solely because its operations are or have been required by the Comptroller of the Currency to be limited to those of a trust company and activities related thereto.

11. *Cf.* OCC Trust Interpretation No. 175, *reprinted in*, [1988–1989 Transfer Binder] Fed. Banking L. Rep. (CCH) ¶ 84,942 (Oct. 21, 1988) (concerning separation of national bank's trust department into national trust company); OCC Interpretive Letter No. 436, *reprinted in*, [1988–1989 Transfer Binder] Fed. Banking L. Rep. (CCH) & 85,660 (Aug. 19, 1988) (permitting establishment of limited national trust company affiliated with investment adviser and registered broker-dealer).

12. For a case exploring this overlay of state substantive law and federal supervisory rules, see *Humane Soc'y of Austin and Travis County v. Austin Nat'l Bank*, 531 S.W.2d 574 (Tex.1975), *cert. denied*, 425 U.S. 976, 96 S.Ct. 2177 (1976).

13. 12 C.F.R. Pt. 9.

14. *See, e.g.*, Board of Governors, Division of Banking Supervision and Regulation, Memorandum SR–83–2 (SA) (Jan. 11, 1983), *reprinted in*, 4 Fed. Banking L. Rep. (CCH) ¶ 37–659.

15. 12 C.F.R. Pt. 330.

16. 12 C.F.R. Pt. 550.

§ 5.22

1. 12 U.S.C.A. § 1831a.

think of intuitively as banking powers. Yet, in the framework of the NBA,[2] incidental powers could be viewed as a natural and integral part of banking powers. Indeed, if we take seriously the notion that a bank is a creature of its enabling statute, so that "powers not conferred . . . are denied,"[3] then we must find a way to locate "new" powers within the statutory concept of incidental powers.

An initial question concerns the character of the incidental powers provision. Is it a limiting concept, or an enabling concept? Early cases seem to be ambiguous on this issue.[4] One might suggest that a court inclined towards a "limiting" characterization is more likely to withhold power, particularly for an activity that is not historically one performed by banks, whereas a court that is inclined towards an "enabling" characterization may be more likely to recognize a power.[5] Yet cases that speak of incidental powers as those "convenient and useful in connection with the performance of one of [a] bank's established activities" may just as well refuse to recognize a particular activity as an incidental power.[6] Similarly, is there a practical difference between the view that an incidental power must be directly related to an express power,[7] and one that insists that an incidental power may simply be convenient and useful in connection with established activities?[8]

The fact is that none of the formulations of the incidental powers concept that float through the cases has added any precision to what is essentially a case-by-case inquiry. *Arnold Tours, Inc. v. Camp*[9] clears away some of the underbrush by providing some relatively unprovocative examples of incidental powers, but it speaks successively about the incidental powers concept as "directly related to one or another of a national bank's express powers,"[10] as bearing a "great similarity" to an express power,[11] and as "virtually identical to" an express power.[12] Obviously, these varying formulations could lead to rather different results in a close case.

Ultimately, each of these formulations leads us back to the same question: what is the power incidental *to*, or "directly related *to*," or

---

2. 12 U.S.C.A. § 24 (Seventh).

3. *Texas & Pac. Ry. v. Pottorff*, 291 U.S. 245, 253, 54 S.Ct. 416, 417 (1934), *amended sub nom. Texas & Pac. Ry. v. First Nat'l Bank of El Paso, Tex.*, 291 U.S. 649, 54 S.Ct. 525, *reh'g denied sub nom. Texas & Pac. Ry. v. Pottorff*, 292 U.S. 600, 54 S.Ct. 627.

4. *See, e.g., First Nat'l Bank v. Nat'l Exch. Bank*, 92 U.S. (2 Otto) 122 (1875) (finding incidental power to compromise contested claim, while speaking of incidental powers concept as limiting).

5. *See, e.g., M & M Leasing Corp. v. Seattle First Nat'l Bank*, 563 F.2d 1377 (9th Cir.1977), *cert. denied*, 436 U.S. 956, 98 S.Ct. 3069 (1978) (upholding lease financing as incidental power, with certain exceptions).

6. *See, e.g., Arnold Tours, Inc. v. Camp*, 472 F.2d 427 (1st Cir.1972) (disapproving operation of travel agency under incidental powers doctrine).

7. *See, e.g., Arnold Tours, Inc., supra* (using both the "directly related" and the "convenient and useful" formulations).

8. *See, e.g., M & M Leasing Corp., supra* (upholding lease financing as incidental power, while citing *Arnold Tours* with approval).

9. 472 F.2d 427 (1st Cir.1972).

10. Id. at 431.

11. *Id.*

12. *Id.* at 432.

bearing a "great similarity *to*," or "virtually identical *to*"? The short answer is "the business of banking."[13] But what is the "business of banking" for these purposes? The long answer, or one version, is presented by *M & M Leasing Corp. v. Seattle First National Bank*.[14] The business of banking is *represented* by the series of express powers mentioned in the same section of the NBA,[15] but this does not necessarily freeze banking powers in a single historical moment. Opting for a fluid approach that seeks to identify functional equivalence between express statutory powers and challenged incidental powers, the court noted:

> [T]he National Bank Act did not freeze the practices of national banks in their nineteenth century forms.... [W]hatever the scope of [incidental] powers may be, we believe the powers of national banks must be construed so as to permit the use of new ways of conducting the very old business of banking.[16]

"Functional equivalence" or "interchangeability" would appear to open up incidental powers analysis to include a connection between an express power and an asserted incidental power based, not on a weak causal or supportive link between the two ("convenient or useful" to the exercise of the express power), but rather an independent connection of practical equivalence or identity between the two powers.[17]

To the extent that incidental powers analysis remains a case-by-case inquiry, Figure 5–3, *infra*, is an illustrative, selective list of activities held to be within the incidental powers concept.

Figure 5–3

Incidental Powers: Selected Examples

Incidental Power	*Authority*
Acceptance of assignment of judgment for collection	*Miller v. King*, 223 U.S. 505, 32 S.Ct. 243 (1912).
Agent for depositor or customer	*Wylie v. Northhampton Nat'l Bank*, 119 U.S. 361, 7 S.Ct. 268 (1886); *Brooklyn Nat'l Bank of*

13. 12 U.S.C.A. § 24 (Seventh).

14. 563 F.2d 1377 (9th Cir.1977), *cert. denied*, 436 U.S. 956, 98 S.Ct. 3069 (1978).

15. 12 U.S.C.A. § 24 (Seventh). *See NationsBank of North Carolina, N.A. v. Variable Annuity Life Ins. Co.*, 513 U.S. 251, 115 S.Ct. 810 (1995) (interpreting express powers mentioned in § 24 (Seventh) as not exclusive).

16. *M & M Leasing Corp.*, 563 F.2d at 1382.

17. *See, e.g., NationsBank of North Carolina, N.A., supra* (reading "business of banking" in NBA as open-ended term of art, to be fleshed out through functional analysis); *American Ins. Ass'n v. Clarke*,

865 F.2d 278 (D.C.Cir.1988) (suggesting "functional equivalence" test for incidental powers). The *Clarke* opinion rejects the "convenient or useful" formulation of the test of incidental powers as being "a narrow and artificially rigid view of both the business of banking and the [NBA]." *Id*. at 281. To the contrary, the opinion recognizes the municipal bond insurance business as an incidental part of the business of banking, because it is "sufficiently similar to credit services routinely performed by banks," *id*. at 282, and is "functionally equivalent to the issuance of a standby letter of credit, a device long recognized as within the business of banking." *Id*.

Incidental Power	Authority
	New York v. Keystone Bond & Mortgage Co., 150 Misc. 571, 268 N.Y.S. 485 (N.Y.Sup.1933); *Bock v. First Nat'l Bank*, 123 Kan. 304, 255 P. 68 (1927).[18]
Annuities, variable, sale of	*NationsBank of North Carolina, N.A. v. Variable Annuity Life Ins. Co.*, 513 U.S. 251, 115 S.Ct. 810 (1995).
Assignment or sale of judgment	*Emory v. Joice*, 70 Mo. 537 (1879).
Bill of lading, purchase of	*Citizens' Bank & Trust Co. v. Harpeth Nat'l Bank of Franklin*, 120 Miss. 505, 82 So. 329 (1919).[19]
Borrowing	*Wyman v. Wallace*, 201 U.S. 230, 26 S.Ct. 495 (1906); *Frenzer v. Wallace*, 201 U.S. 244, 26 S.Ct. 498 (1906); *Aldrich v. Chemical Nat'l Bank*, 176 U.S. 618, 20 S.Ct. 498 (1900); *Auten v. U.S. Nat'l Bank*, 174 U.S. 125, 19 S.Ct. 628 (1899).
Borrowing, Interbank	*Armstrong v. Chemical Nat'l Bank*, 83 F. 556 (6th Cir.1897).
Certification of checks	*Merchants' Nat'l Bank v. State Nat'l Bank*, 77 U.S. (10 Wall.) 604 (1870); *Fidelity & Deposit Co. of Md. v. National Bank of Commerce of Dallas*, 48 Tex. Civ.App. 301, 106 S.W. 782 (1907) (limiting power).
Charge-backs	*Bryant v. Williams*, 16 F.2d 159 (E.D.N.C.1926).
Check protection	*Thompson v. St. Nicholas Nat'l Bank*, 113 N.Y. 325, 21 N.E. 57 (1889), *aff'd*, 146 U.S. 240, 13 S.Ct. 66 (1892).
Collection of judgment on behalf of depositor	*Miller v. King*, 223 U.S. 505, 32 S.Ct. 243 (1912).
Collection of negotiable instruments	*Logan County Nat'l Bank v. Townsend*, 139 U.S. 67, 11 S.Ct. 496 (1891); *Brandenburg v. First Nat'l Bank of Casselton*,

18. *But cf. Pollock v. Lumbermen's Nat'l Bank of Portland*, 86 Or. 324, 168 P. 616 (1917) (denying power to negotiate loan for another); *Hotchkin v. Third Nat'l Bank of Syracuse*, 219 Mass. 234, 106 N.E. 974 (1914) (acting as broker for sale of stock *ultra vires*).

19. *But cf. First Nat'l Bank of Mifflintown v. First Nat'l Bank of New Kensington*, 247 Pa. 40, 92 A. 1076 (1915) (finding no power to purchase bills of lading, in contrast to purchase of sight drafts).

Incidental Power	*Authority*
	48 N.D. 176, 183 N.W. 643 (1921); *Hanson v. Heard*, 69 N.H. 190, 38 A. 788 (1897).
Compromise of debts	*First Nat'l Bank v. National Exchange Bank*, 92 U.S. (2 Otto) 122 (1875).
Data processing services	*National Retailers Corp. of Ariz. v. Valley Nat'l Bank of Ariz.*, 604 F.2d 32 (9th Cir.1979) (limiting services).
Debt cancellation contracts	*First Nat'l Bank of Eastern Ark. v. Taylor*, 907 F.2d 775 (8th Cir. 1990), *cert. denied*, 498 U.S. 972, 111 S.Ct. 442.
Debt, evidences of, sale of	*First Nat'l Bank v. Hartford*, 273 U.S. 548, 47 S.Ct. 462 (1927).
Electronic interbank communications systems, operation of	*State of Oklahoma ex rel. State Banking Bd. v. Bank of Okla.*, 409 F.Supp. 71 (N.D.Okla. 1975).
Financial advice	*Norwest Bank of Minn. Nat'l Ass'n v. Sween Corp.*, 916 F.Supp. 1494 (D.Minn.1996), *aff'd in part and remanded in part*, 118 F.3d 1255 (8th Cir. 1997).
Individual Retirement Accounts, management of	*Investment Co. Inst. v. Clarke*, 793 F.2d 220 (9th Cir.1986), *cert. denied*, 479 U.S. 939, 107 S.Ct. 422.
Investment securities, purchase and sale of	*City Nat'l Bank v. McCann*, 193 Ark. 967, 106 S.W.2d 195 (1937).
Lease financing	*M & M Leasing Corp. v. Seattle First Nat'l Bank*, 563 F.2d 1377 (9th Cir.1977), *cert. denied*, 436 U.S. 956, 98 S.Ct. 3069 (1978).
Mortgage, agreements and compromises concerning	*Morris v. Third Nat'l Bank*, 142 F. 25 (8th Cir.1905), *cert. denied*, 201 U.S. 649, 26 S.Ct. 762 (1906); *Guth v. First Nat'l Bank*, 137 Wash. 280, 242 P. 42 (1926); *Security Nat'l Bank v. Home Nat'l Bank*, 106 Kan. 303, 187 P. 697 (1920).
Mortgage pass-through certificates, sale of	*Securities Indus. Ass'n v. Clarke*, 885 F.2d 1034 (2d Cir. 1989), *cert. denied*, 493 U.S. 1070, 110 S.Ct. 1113 (1990).

Incidental Power	Authority
Mortgage, sale of	*First Nat'l Bank v. Hartford,* 273 U.S. 548, 47 S.Ct. 462 (1927).
Municipal bond insurance	*American Ins. Ass'n v. Clarke,* 656 F.Supp. 404 (D.D.C.1987), *aff'd,* 865 F.2d 278 (D.C.Cir. 1988).
Pension fund, creation of	*Heinz v. National Bank of Commerce of St. Louis,* 237 F. 942 (8th Cir.1916).
Pledged property, acceptance of as security	*California Nat. Bank v. Kennedy,* 167 U.S. 362, 17 S.Ct. 831 (1897); *Thompson v. St. Nicholas Nat'l Bank,* 146 U.S. 240, 13 S.Ct. 66 (1892); *Crescent City Nat'l Bank v. Case,* 99 U.S. (9 Otto) 628 (1878); *Hayward v. Eliot Nat'l Bank,* 96 U.S. (6 Otto) 611 (1877); *First Nat'l Bank v. National Exchange Bank,* 92 U.S. (2 Otto) 122 (1875).
Pledged property, sale of	*Merchants' Nat'l Bank v. State Nat'l Bank,* 77 U.S. (10 Wall.) 604 (1870).
Pledged property, transfer of	*U.S. Securities Corp. v. Exchange Nat'l Bank of Shreveport,* 15 La.App. 23, 130 So. 818 (1930).
Pledging assets for deposits	*Lewis v. Fidelity & Deposit Co. of Md.,* 292 U.S. 559, 54 S.Ct. 848 (1934);[20] *Nebraska v. First Nat'l Bank,* 88 F. 947 (D. Neb. 1898).[21]
Real property, maintenance of	*Cooper v. Hill,* 94 F. 582 (8th Cir.1899).
Rediscounting	*Auten v. U.S. Nat'l Bank,* 174 U.S. 125, 19 S.Ct. 628 (1899); *U.S. Nat'l Bank v. First Nat'l Bank,* 79 F. 296 (8th Cir.1897).
Resale of mortgages	*First Nat'l Bank v. City of Hartford,* 273 U.S. 548, 47 S.Ct. 462 (1927).

20. *But cf. City of Marion, Ill. v. Sneeden,* 291 U.S. 651, 54 S.Ct. 557 (1934) (limiting pledge to public deposits of United States).

21. *But cf. Texas & Pac. Ry. Co. v. Pottorff,* 291 U.S. 245, 54 S.Ct. 416 (1934), *amended sub nom. Texas & Pac. Ry. v. First Nat'l Bank of El Paso, Tex.,* 291 U.S. 649, 54 S.Ct. 525, *reh'g denied sub nom. Texas & Pac. Ry. v. Pottorff,* 292 U.S. 600, 54 S.Ct. 627; *Griffin v. Royall,* 70 F.2d 103 (4th Cir.1934) (same); *Third Nat'l Bank and Trust Co. of Scranton v. McMahon,* 17 F.Supp. 869 (M.D.Pa.1937) (same).

Incidental Power	*Authority*
Safe deposit and other "special deposits"	*Colorado Nat'l Bank of Denver v. Bedford,* 310 U.S. 41, 60 S.Ct. 800 (1940); *First Nat'l Bank of Carlisle, Pa. v. Graham,* 100 U.S. (10 Otto) 699 (1879); *Cooper v. National Bank of Savannah,* 21 Ga.App. 356, 94 S.E. 611 (1917), *aff'd sub nom. Evans v. National Bank of Savannah,* 251 U.S. 108, 40 S.Ct. 58 (1991); *U.S. Shipping Bd. Emcy. Fleet Corp. v. Atlantic Corp.,* 5 F.2d 529 (D.Mass. 1925), *error dismissed,* 16 F.2d 27 (1st Cir.1926).
Savings deposits, advertisement of	*Franklin Nat'l Bank v. New York,* 347 U.S. 373, 74 S.Ct. 550 (1954).
Seed grain lien, acceptance of	*First Nat'l Bank of Parker v. Peavy Elevator Co.,* 10 S.D. 167, 72 N.W. 402 (S.D. 1897).
Setoff	*Lawrence v. Lincoln County Trust Co.,* 123 Me. 273, 122 A. 765 (1923).[22]
Stock, acquisition of by foreclosure of pledge	*First Nat'l Bank v. Federal Land Bank of Louisville,* 93 Ind.App. 15, 177 N.E. 462 (1931); *McBoyle v. Union Nat'l Bank,* 162 Cal. 277, 122 P. 458 (1911).
Stock, acquisition of in settlement of claim	*First Nat'l Bank v. National Exchange Bank,* 92 U.S. (2 Otto) 122 (1875).
Taxes, payment of on behalf of depositor	*Clement Nat'l Bank v. Vermont,* 231 U.S. 120, 34 S.Ct. 31 (1913).
Thrift bonds, sale of	*Adams v. Compo Bond Corp.,* 282 F. 894 (S.D.N.Y.1922).
Title, warrant of	*Farmers' & Miners' Bank v. Bluefield Nat'l Bank,* 11 F.2d 83 (4th Cir.1926), *cert. denied,* 271 U.S. 669, 46 S.Ct. 483.

§ 5.23   Bank Service Companies

The establishment or acquisition of a bank service company subsidiary or affiliate represents another method by which a bank may diversify into nonbanking activities. Analysis of the authority of the bank to

---

22. *But cf. Appleton v. National Park Bank of N.Y.,* 122 Misc. 248, 202 N.Y.S. 516 (N.Y.Sup.1924) (allowing no setoff where subject note not matured). *Contra Parker v. First Nat'l Bank,* 96 Okla. 70, 220 P. 39 (Okla. 1923).

diversify in this fashion under the Bank Service Company Act ("BSCA"),[1] does not differ greatly from that applied to its direct exercise of incidental powers.[2] Nonbanking competitors have standing to challenge such activities.[3]

An FDIC-insured bank has the authority under the BSCA to invest an amount not more than ten percent of its paid in and unimpaired capital and unimpaired surplus in a bank service company.[4] However, the amount invested must not exceed five percent of the bank's total assets.[5] The company may perform any and all of the following services exclusively for depository institutions: (1) check and deposit sorting and posting; (2) computation and posting of interest and other credits and charges; (3) preparation and mailing of checks, statements, notices, and similar items; and, (4) any other clerical, bookkeeping, accounting, statistical, or similar functions performed for a depository institution.[6]

Beyond these rather modest services, a bank service company may offer a wide range of services to the public—except deposit-taking[7]—subject to a complex set of requirements and limitations,[8] discussed below. The service company, and any person performing contracted-out services for the company, are also subject to regulation and periodic examination by the appropriate federal regulator of the principal investor of the company.[9]

§ 5.23

1. 12 U.S.C.A. §§ 1861 *et seq.* The Act was originally known as the Bank Service Corporation Act, and only authorized the creation of a corporate subsidiary of a national bank. The Act was amended in 1996 to authorize bank service "companies" to be organized as limited liability partnerships. *See* Economic Growth and Regulatory Paperwork Reduction Act, Pub. L. No. 104–208, title II, § 2613, 110 Stat. 3009 (1996) (codified at 12 U.S.C.A. §§ 1861–1867) (renaming Bank Service Corporation Act as Bank Service Company Act; authorizing bank service companies to organize as limited liability partnerships; conforming amendments).

2. *Arnold Tours v. Camp*, 400 U.S. 45, 91 S.Ct. 158 (1970) (incidental powers analysis applied to activities under § 4 of BSCA).

3. *Association of Data Processing Serv. Orgs. v. Camp*, 397 U.S. 150, 90 S.Ct. 827 (1970); *Arnold Tours, supra.*

4. 12 U.S.C.A. § 1862. A "bank service company" by definition includes a limited liability company. *Id.* § 1861(b)(2)(B). Authorization of limited liability companies as a permitted form of organization of the bank service company is significant, since under prior case law, national banks had been held to be legally incapable of entering into a partnership agreement. *See, e.g., First Nat'l Bank v. Stokes*, 134 Ark. 368,

203 S.W. 1026 (1918); *Pronger v. Old Nat'l Bank*, 20 Wash. 618, 56 P. 391 (1899); *Cameron v. First Nat'l Bank*, 34 S.W. 178 (Tex.Civ.App.1896).

5. 12 U.S.C.A. § 1862.

6. *Id.* § 1863.

7. *See id.* § 1864(a) (prohibiting deposit-taking by bank service companies).

8. *Id.* §§ 1864–1866.

9. *Id.* § 1867(a), (c). The principal investor is required to inform the appropriate federal regulator of any contracting-out within 30 days of entry into the contract or performance, whichever occurs first. *Id.* § 1867(c)(2). For these purposes, the BSCA uses the term "appropriate Federal banking agency," which is defined to have the same meaning as the term is given in 12 U.S.C.A. § 1813(q). In other words, the appropriate regulator is the Comptroller of the Currency, in the case of a national bank; the Fed, in the case of a state-chartered member bank; and the FDIC, in the case of a state-chartered, insured nonmember bank. *Id.* The agencies are authorized to issue regulations and orders necessary to administer the BSCA, to carry out its purposes, and to prevent evasions. *Id.* § 1867(d).

The service company is subject to the administrative enforcement powers of 12 U.S.C.A. § 1818 to the same extent as if it were an insured bank. *Id.* § 1867(b).

If the company confines itself to services performed in the state in which its shareholders or members are located[10]—and all insured bank shareholders or members must be located in the same state[11]—then investment of an insured bank is permitted with prior notice to the bank's appropriate federal regulator.[12] The following services may be performed. (1) *Where the shareholder or member is a state bank*: The company may perform services that the state bank is permitted to perform under state law, at locations where the bank would be authorized to perform them under state law.[13] (2) *Where the shareholder or member is a national bank*: The company may perform services that the national bank is permitted to perform under federal law, at locations where the bank would be authorized to perform them under federal law.[14] (3) *Where the shareholders or members are state and national banks*: The company may perform services that both the national bank and the state bank are permitted to perform under federal and state law respectively, at locations where either bank would be authorized to perform them under federal and state law respectively.[15]

Notwithstanding these or any other provision of law,[16] a company may offer any service (except deposit-taking) that the Fed has determined to be a "closely related" activity under the Bank Holding Company Act ("BHCA")[17] at *any* geographic location.[18] However, an insured bank may not invest in a service company performing any such service, nor may the company perform such a service, without the prior approval of the Fed.[19]

Prior approval of the Fed, and approval of prior notice by any appropriate federal regulator, is subject to the following factors:

> the financial and managerial resources and future prospects of the bank or banks and bank service company involved, including the financial capability of the bank to make a proposed investment under this chapter, and possible adverse effects such as undue concentration of resources, unfair or decreased competition, conflicts of interest, or unsafe or unsound banking practices.[20]

10. *Id.* § 1864(b)(1).

11. *Id.* § 1864(b)(2).

12. *Id.* § 1865(a).

13. *Id.* § 1864(c).

14. *Id.* § 1864(d).

15. *Id.* § 1864(e).

16. With the exception of limitations on interstate branching. *Id.* § 1864(f).

17. *Id.* § 1843(c)(8).

18. *Id.* § 1864(f).

19. *Id.* § 1865(b).

20. *Id.* § 1865(c). In addition, bank service companies are prohibited from "unreasonably discriminat[ing] in the provision of any services ... to any depository institu-tion" that is not a shareholder or member, on the basis that the institution is in competition with an institution that is a shareholder or member. *Id.* § 1866. However, the following exceptions apply to this nondiscrimination rule:

(1) it shall not be considered unreasonable discrimination for a bank service company to provide services to a nonstockholding or nonmember institution only at a price that fully reflects all of the costs of offering those services, including the cost of capital and a reasonable return thereon; and

(2) a bank service company may refuse to provide services to a nonstockholding or nonmember institution if comparable services are available from another source

Failure on the part of the regulatory agency to act on a prior notice or application for prior approval within 90 days of submission of a complete notice or application is deemed to be approval.[21]

If the bank that owns or controls the service company is itself a subsidiary of a holding company, then the bank subsidiary's control of the nonbanking activity constitutes "indirect" control of the activity by the holding company, and is therefore subject to the BHCA.[22] Direct or indirect control of the service company by a bank holding company may require approval under the BHCA.[23]

On the other hand, a service corporation owned directly by a bank holding company, rather than by a bank subsidiary is not a "bank service company" for purposes of the BSCA.[24] For service companies owned or controlled by subsidiary banks, the BSCA applies.[25]

§ 5.24   Securities Activities

The securities sector is one area of the financial services industry that has exhibited significant crossover of depository institutions.[1] Depository institutions may also be securities market professionals, that is, persons who underwrite, purchase, sell, and otherwise deal in securities in the securities markets. These activities have been significantly limited, until relatively recently, by the Glass–Steagall Act,[2] but these limitations have been progressively eroded by administrative interpretation and court decisions.

This section focuses on the Glass–Steagall Act, since it has been the major concern of much recent litigation and congressional consideration. However, to be understood adequately, securities activities of depository institutions need to be seen in conjunction with the overall federal policy on securities regulation, which in part applies to depository institutions, as well as to all other securities issuers and securities professionals. In

---

at competitive overall costs, or if the providing of services would be beyond the practical capacity of the service company. *Id.* § 1866(1)–(2).

21. *Id.* § 1865(d).

22. 12 C.F.R. §§ 225.101(c), 225.102 (interpreting indirect bank holding company control through subsidiaries). *See* 12 U.S.C.A. § 1843 (BHCA provision governing holding company control of nonbanking activities). *See also American Ins. Ass'n v. Clarke,* 865 F.2d 278 (D.C.Cir.1988) (discussing indirect holding company "control" of bank subsidiary's controlled subsidiary operations).

23. 12 C.F.R. § 225.115(c)(3)–(4), (d).

24. *Id.* § 225.115(b)(2). Accordingly, only Section 5 of the BSCA applies to such service corporations.

25. *Id.* § 225.115(c)(2).

§ 5.24

1. Note that the discussion in this section focuses primarily on the effect of Sections 16 and 21 of the Glass–Steagall Act, 12 U.S.C.A. § 24 (Seventh), 378, on depository institutions. Restrictions may also apply to an enterprise of which a depository institution is a subsidiary or affiliate, under Section 20 of the Glass–Steagall Act, *id.* § 377, and Section 4(c) of the Bank Holding Company Act ("BHCA"), *id.* § 1843(c). The interaction of these two provisions is discussed Chapter 6, *infra.* For more detailed treatment of securities activities of depository institutions, see 2 MICHAEL P. MALLOY, BANKING LAW AND REGULATION §§ 7.3–7.3.10.3 (1994 & CUM. SUPP.).

2. 48 Stat. 162 (1933) (codified at scattered sections of 12 U.S.C.A.).

Chapter 7, *infra*, this subject is discussed from the perspective of securities regulation.

The Glass–Steagall Act was enacted in the wake of the financial crisis that burgeoned during the period from 1929 to 1933. As *Investment Company Institute v. Camp*[3] explained, during the 1920s close affiliation between investment and commercial banks resulted in a great potential for harm in the activities of each. The congressional solution was a radical break between the two, in many situations involving divestiture of the investment banking affiliates of major commercial banks.[4] In the years since its enactment in 1933, and particularly since the 1960s, banks and bank regulators have been crossing over into investment banking and the securities business with increasing vigor. Until relatively recently, however, this was a slow development.

Congress has also assisted this development, although perhaps inadvertently. Section 16, one of the key provisions of the Glass–Steagall Act,[5] has been amended repeatedly to allow more and more exceptions to the basic rule that depository institutions are generally prohibited from underwriting, purchasing and dealing in securities.[6]

Reviewing the key provisions of Glass–Steagall,[7] one can see that the limitations on the securities activities overlap for national banks,[8] member banks,[9] and "financial institutions" generally.[10] It may be useful to

3. 401 U.S. 617, 91 S.Ct. 1091 (1971).

4. *See United States v. Morgan*, 118 F.Supp. 621, 646 (S.D.N.Y.1953):

Institutions which had previously engaged both in commercial and deposit banking on the one hand and investment banking on the other were required to elect prior to June 16, 1934, which of the two functions they would pursue to the exclusion of the other. This resulted in the complete elimination of the commercial banks and trust companies from the investment banking business; and the various bank affiliates were dissolved and liquidated.

On the basis of the Glass–Steagall Act, the Court in *Investment Company Institute* therefore held that the Comptroller's regulations permitting a national bank to market "participations" in a collective investment fund, 12 C.F.R. Pt. 9 (1963), were prohibited. A second generation of the Comptroller's regulations was promulgated in 1982, authorizing "common trust funds," 12 C.F.R. § 9.18(a)(1), (collective investment and reinvestment of funds contributed to a common trust fund maintained by a national bank) and "collective investment funds," *id.* § 9.18(a)(2) (collective investment in a fund consisting solely of assets of retirement, pension, profit-sharing, stock bonus or other trusts exempt from federal income taxation). These regulations were upheld despite a challenge under the Glass–Steagall Act. *Investment Co.*

Inst. v. Conover, 790 F.2d 925 (D.C.Cir. 1986), *cert. denied sub nom. Investment Co. Inst. v. Clarke*, 479 U.S. 939, 107 S.Ct. 421; *accord, Investment Co. Inst. v. Clarke*, 789 F.2d 175 (2d Cir.1986), *cert. denied*, 479 U.S. 940, 107 S.Ct. 422; *Investment Co. Inst. v. Clarke*, 793 F.2d 220 (9th Cir.1986), *cert. denied*, 479 U.S. 939, 107 S.Ct. 422.

5. 12 U.S.C.A. § 24 (Seventh). For an interesting interpretation of the meaning and applicability of 12 U.S.C.A. § 24(Seventh), see *NationsBank of North Carolina, N.A. v. Variable Annuity Life Ins. Co.*, 513 U.S. 251, 115 S.Ct. 810 (1995).

6. *See, e.g.*, 12 C.F.R. Pt. 1 (interpreting and applying investment securities provisions of 12 U.S.C.A. § 24 (Seventh)). *See also* 2 MICHAEL P. MALLOY, BANKING LAW AND REGULATION §§ 7.3–7.3.2.3 (1994 & CUM. SUPP.) (discussing investment securities activities of depository institutions).

7. 12 U.S.C.A. §§ 24, 78, 377, 378.

8. *See id.* § 24 (Seventh) (restricting securities activities of national banks).

9. *See id.* §§ 78, 377 (prohibiting certain interlocks and affiliations of member banks). In addition, 12 U.S.C.A. § 335 expressly imposes the same limitations on state member banks that apply to national banks.

10. *See id.* § 378 (prohibiting certain securities activities of "financial institutions").

take a walk through these statutory provisions. As currently applicable, there are actually five sections of the Glass–Steagall Act that are relevant. The first is Section 16,[11] which provides for, *inter alia*, the regulation of investment activities of national banks.[12]

The second relevant section is Section 32,[13] which provides that:

> No officer, director, or employee of any corporation or unincorporated association, no partner or employee of any partnership, and no individual, primarily engaged in the issue, flotation, underwriting, public sale, or distribution, at wholesale or retail, or through syndicate participation, of stocks, bonds, or other similar securities, shall serve at the same time as an officer, director, or employee of any member bank *except in limited classes of cases in the Board of Governors of the Federal Reserve System may allow such service by general regulations when in the judgment of the said Board it would not unduly influence the investment policies of such member bank or the advice it gives its customers regarding investments.*[14]

The italicized language in the quotation was the result of a 1935 amendment of the section.[15] Section 32 broadens the scope of the Glass–Steagall Act provisions to include all Fed member banks, whether national or state-chartered. In contrast, Section 16 on its own terms applies only to national banks. However, other provisions of the Glass–Steagall Act have had the effect of expanding the reach of Section 16 at least as far as Section 32. Thus, section 5(c) of the Act imposed the Section 16 limitations on "purchasing, selling, underwriting, and holding of investment securities and stock," applicable to national banks, on all Fed member banks.[16]

Two provisions complete the separation of commercial and investment banking originally contemplated by Senator Glass. Under Section 20 of the Glass–Steagall Act,[17] affiliations between member banks and any organization "engaged principally in the issue, flotation, underwriting, public sale, or distribution at wholesale or retail or through syndicate participation of stocks, bonds, debentures, notes, or other securities" are prohibited.[18] The attention of many administra-

---

11. *Id.* § 24 (Seventh).

12. *See* 12 C.F.R. Pt. 1.

13. *Id.* § 78.

14. *Id.* (emphasis added).

15. *See generally Board of Governors v. Agnew*, 329 U.S. 441, 67 S.Ct. 411 (1947) (interpreting § 32); *United States v. Brown*, 381 U.S. 437, 85 S.Ct. 1707 (1965). For an interpretation of the scope and applicability of the prohibitions of Section 32, OCC Interpretive Letter No. 436, July 19, 1988, *reprinted in*, [1988–89 Transfer Binder] Fed. Banking L. Rep. (CCH) ¶ 85,660 (Aug. 19, 1988) (finding interlock between investment adviser and affiliated limited national trust company not prohibited by Section 32).

16. 12 U.S.C.A. § 335. For an interpretation of the applicability of Section 5(c), see 54 Fed. Reg. 7180 (1989) (codified at 12 C.F.R. § 208.124).

17. *Id.* § 377.

18. *Id.* § 377. *See generally Agnew, supra.*

tive interpretations of this section has focused upon what it means for an organization to be "principally" engaged in the securities activities specified.[19]

Finally, under Section 21, it became unlawful, as of June 16, 1934,

[f]or *any person*, firm, corporation, association, business trust, or other similar organization, *engaged in the business of* issuing, underwriting, *selling*, or distributing, *at wholesale or retail*, or through syndicate participation, *stocks, bonds, debentures, notes, or other securities*, to engage at the same time to any extent whatever in the business of receiving deposits subject to check or to repayment upon presentation of a passbook, certificate of deposit, or other evidence of debt, or upon request of the depositor.... [20]

This provision, which might raise serious questions concerning the legality of traditional bank securities activities, was modified in 1935, definitively mooting these questions. The original prohibition was qualified by the following proviso:

[T]he provisions of this paragraph shall not prohibit *national banks or State banks or trust companies (whether or not members of the Federal Reserve System) or other financial institutions or private bankers* from dealing in, underwriting, purchasing, and selling investment securities to the extent permitted to national banking associations by the provisions of [12 U.S.C.A. § 24]....[21]

This language has the effect of broadening the scope of Section 16 to reach all depository institutions and financial intermediaries, limiting them to the securities activities permitted to national banks under Section 16 of the Act.[22] This restriction on securities activities of "financial institutions" would seem to be the broadest of the Glass–Steagall Act provisions. Overall, Fed member banks, whether national or state-chartered, are subject to all of these provisions, either by direct reference to such entities in the pertinent provision,[23] or by cross-reference in the

---

19. *See, e.g., J.P. Morgan & Co. Inc./ The Chase Manhattan Corp./Bankers Trust New York Corp./Citicorp/Security Pacific Corp.*, 75 Fed. Res. Bull. 192 (1989); *Citicorp/J.P. Morgan & Co./Bankers Trust New York Corp.*, 73 Fed. Res. Bull. 473 (1987). *See also Canadian Imperial Bank of Commerce, The Royal Bank of Canada, Barclays PLC and Barclays Bank PLC*, 76 Fed. Res. Bull. 158 (1990) (applying earlier orders to Section 20 subsidiaries of foreign banks). *See also J & W. Seligman Trust Co., N.A.*, Fed. Banking L. Rep. (CCH) ¶ 99,463 (1983); *Dreyfus Nat'l Bank and Trust Co.*, Fed. Banking L. Rep. (CCH) ¶ 99,464 (1983); *Financial Servs. Corp. of the Midwest*, 63 Fed. Res. Bull. 948 (1977). *See also* OCC Interpretive Letter No. 436 (private placement activities of investment adviser affiliated with limited national trust compa-

ny do not constitute "issue, flotation, underwriting" prohibited by section 20; investment adviser not "engaged principally" in prohibited securities activities).

20. 12 U.S.C.A. § 378(a)(1) (emphasis added).

21. *Id.* § 378(a)(1) (emphasis added).

22. For an interpretation of the applicability of this prohibition to the activities of an insured state nonmember bank, see FDIC Advisory Opinion 83–20, *reprinted in* [1988–1989 Transfer Binder] Fed. Banking L. Rep. (CCH) ¶ 81,194 (Feb. 3, 1989) (application of prohibition of Section 21 to bank's operation of collective investment pool).

23. *See* 12 U.S.C.A. §§ 78, 377.

pertinent provision to the restrictions applicable to national banks under section 16 of the Act.[24] However, the reach of the Glass–Steagall Act extends to *all* national and state-chartered banks by limiting securities activities of such entities to those permitted to national banks under section 16.[25] Indeed, as the language quoted above indicates, all "financial institutions" that receive demand or savings deposits are subject to the restrictions of section 16 on investment activities.[26] The interrelationships among these prohibitions is illustrated in Figure 5–4, *infra*.

---

24. *See id.* §§ 335, 378.

25. *See id.* § 378.

26. *See id.* § 378(a)(1).

FIGURE 5-4
Scope of Glass–Steagall Prohibitions

Independent National Banks
Independent Member Banks

Affiliations & Interlocks
Permitted under § 20

Banking Affiliates

National Banks
Member Banks
Nonmember Banks

Bank Holding Companies

Nonmember Banks
Savings Associations
Credit Unions
Other Institutions Receiving Deposits

Bank-Eligible Securities Activities
Permitted under §§ 16, 21

Affiliate engaged principally
in bank-eligible securities activities
(§ 20 subsidiary)

Unaffiliated Nonbanking Firms
engaged principally
in securities activities

Bank-Ineligible Securities Activities
Permitted under § 20 (See *infra* § 6.02[C])

Judicial interpretation of the scope the Glass–Steagall Act has been increasingly favorable to involvement by depository institutions in securities activities. As congressional modernization of the Glass–Steagall prohibitions continues to elude policymakers,[27] the courts have become ever more tolerant of bank inroads into the securities business. The contrasts in judicial attitudes over time are striking.

At the turn of the century, well before Glass–Steagall, judicial pronouncements rejecting securities powers for banks were unequivocal.[28] Similarly, for almost 50 years following the enactment of Glass–Steagall, courts took a relatively strict approach to the separation of banking and securities.[29] As Glass–Steagall has become viewed as more and more anachronistic, however, the courts have begun to relax their view of the precise contours of that separation.

Thus, the courts have permitted private placement of short-term notes.[30] They have upheld the Comptroller's second version of collective investment regulations,[31] despite the clear language of a prior Supreme Court decision to the contrary.[32] Courts have permitted bank in-house operation of securities brokerage services without registration as a broker under the Securities Exchange Act of 1934.[33] Similar developments have occurred in the bank holding company context, discussed in Chapter 6, *infra*. Figure 5–5, *infra*, provides selected examples of judicial interpretations under the Glass–Steagall Act permitting certain securities activities.

Figure 5–5

Glass–Steagall: Selected Judicial Interpretations

Security Activity	*Authority*
Annuities, variable, sale of	*NationsBank of North Carolina, N.A. v. Variable Annuity Life Ins. Co.*, 513 U.S. 251, 115 S.Ct. 810 (1995).
Brokerage services	*Clarke v. Securities Indus. Ass'n*, 479 U.S. 388, 107 S.Ct. 750 (1987); *American Bankers Ass'n v. Securities Exchange Comm'n*, 804 F.2d 739 (D.C.Cir. 1986).

27. R. Christian Bruce, *House Leaders Reach Compromise on Financial Services Modernization*, BNA Banking Daily (March 11, 1998) at D2 (reporting in slow progress of latest Glass–Steagall reform proposals).

28. *See, e.g., California Nat'l Bank v. Kennedy*, 167 U.S. 362, 17 S.Ct. 831 (1897) (allowing *ultra vires* defense, even where bank received benefits from stock purchases).

29. *See, e.g., Investment Co. Inst. v. Camp*, 401 U.S. 617, 91 S.Ct. 1091 (1971) (rejecting Comptroller's collective investment regulations).

30. *Securities Indus. Ass'n v. Board of Governors*, 468 U.S. 137, 104 S.Ct. 2979

(1984), *on remand*, 807 F.2d 1052 (D.C.Cir. 1986), *cert. denied*, 483 U.S. 1005, 107 S.Ct. 3228 (1987) (holding placement of commercial paper by member banks permissible under section 16).

31. *See supra* note 4 (discussing *Investment Co. Institute v. Conover* and related cases). *See also* 12 C.F.R. § 9.18 (establishing OCC collective investment regulations).

32. *Investment Co. Inst., supra* (striking previous version of OCC collective investment regulations).

33. *American Bankers Ass'n v. Securities and Exch. Comm'n*, 804 F.2d 739 (D.C.Cir.1986).

Security Activity	Authority
Collective investment funds	*Investment Co. Inst. v. Conover*, 790 F.2d 925 (D.C.Cir.1986), *cert. denied sub nom. Investment Co. Inst. v. Clarke*, 479 U.S. 939, 107 S.Ct. 421; *Investment Co. Inst. v. Clarke*, 789 F.2d 175 (2d Cir.1986), *cert. denied*, 479 U.S. 940, 107 S.Ct. 422; *Investment Co. Inst. v. Clarke*, 793 F.2d 220 (9th Cir. 1986), *cert. denied*, 479 U.S. 939, 107 S.Ct. 422.
Commercial paper, distribution of	*Securities Indus. Ass'n v. Board of Governors*, 807 F.2d 1052 (D.C.Cir.1986), *cert. denied*, 483 U.S. 1005, 107 S.Ct. 3228 (1987).
Investment advisory services	*Board of Governors v. Investment Co. Inst.*, 450 U.S. 46, 101 S.Ct. 973 (1981).
Investment securities, purchase and sale of	*Marx v. Centran Corp.*, 747 F.2d 1536 (6th Cir.1984), *cert. denied*, 471 U.S. 1125, 105 S.Ct. 2656 (1985); *City Nat'l Bank v. McCann*, 193 Ark. 967, 106 S.W.2d 195 (1937).
Mortgage pass-through certificates, sale of	*Securities Indus. Ass'n v. Clarke*, 885 F.2d 1034 (2d Cir. 1989), *cert. denied*, 493 U.S. 1070, 110 S.Ct. 1113 (1990).
Stock of bank, dealing in	*Oppenheimer v. Harriman Nat'l Bank & Trust Co.*, 301 U.S. 206, 57 S.Ct. 719 (1937).
Stock transfers in connection with reorganization	*Independent Bankers Ass'n of Ga. v. Board of Governors*, 516 F.2d 1206 (D.C.Cir.1975).

The proposed Financial Services Act of 1998[34] was intended to overhaul the U.S. financial services system, with significant effects for securities activities of financial institutions. The principal features of the bill included the following. The bill would have revised the permissible activities of subsidiaries of national banks.[35] It also provided authority for national banks to underwrite certain specified municipal bonds.[36] Finally, it would have established a new regulatory regime for bank investment company activities.[37]

The bill was also intended to provide "appropriate functional regulation of insurance activities," rather than overlapping regulation depend-

34. H.R. 10, 105th Cong., 2d Sess. (1998).

35. H.R. 10, § 121.

36. *Id.* § 181.

37. *Id.* §§ 211–225.

ing upon an institution's primary regulator.[38] The Acting Comptroller had criticized the bill's provisions on insurance regulation as a bad result for banks, arguing that insurance sales provisions of the bill "would effectively insulate State rules that discriminate against banks and place significant, unfair and anticompetitive restrictions on banks' ability to sell insurance."[39]

At the last possible moment, the bill failed to reach a Senate vote, largely through the opposition of Senator Gramm to community reinvestment provisions in the bill.[40] Ironically, Gramm, as the new Chair of the Senate Banking Committee, indicated that he expects to send a financial services reform bill to the floor by the end of February 1999.[41] In fact, two competing bills have already been introduced in the House reviving the congressional debate on financial services reform, including securities activities.[42] At this writing, it is too early to tell what, if anything, will result from this latest congressional consideration of securities activities of depository institutions, but two competing approaches are being given consideration.

A bill sponsored by Representative James A. Leach, the Chair of the House Banking Committee,[43] would allow holding company affiliates, but not direct subsidiaries of banks, to engage in a wide range of new *financial* activities (including securities activities), not including commercial activities. The bill would require a one-time demonstration of CRA compliance for new activities. Apparently, the Fed favors this bill over competing proposals, particularly since it requires new nonbanking activities to be conducted through holding company affiliates subject to Fed supervision.[44]

A bill sponsored by Representative John J. LaFalce, the ranking Democrat on the Committee,[45] would allow a wide range of new activities for bank subsidiaries, except for real estate investment and insurance underwriting. In addition, the bill would allow holding companies to engage in commercial (*i.e.*, nonfinancial) activities, not exceeding fifteen percent of a company's annual consolidated gross revenues. On CRA

---

38. *Id.* § 1(b)(4). *See also id.* §§ 301–316 (concerning state regulation of insurance).

39. *Financial Services Reform: Backers of Financial Services Measure Hoping for Markup in Senate Committee*, BNA Banking Daily, Sept. 10, 1998, at D2 (quoting Sept. 9, 1998, letter from Acting Comptroller Williams to Financial Institutions Insurance Association).

40. *See* Dean Anason, *New Senate Banking Chief Aims To Move Reform Bill Next Month*, Am. Banker, Jan. 13, 1999, at 1, col. 2 (characterizing Gramm as "lawmaker most responsible for killing financial reform").

41. *Id.*

42. *See* R. Christian Bruce, *Financial Services Execs Back Leach Bill; Rubin*

Lends Support to LaFalce Measure, 31 Sec. Reg. L. Rep. 205 (Feb. 12, 1999) (describing competing bills to revive financial services reform).

43. H.R. 10, 106th Cong., 1st Sess. (1999).

44. *See* Barbara A. Rehm, *Fed Under Pressure To Give Ground in Turf War with Treasury*, Am. Banker, Feb. 22, 1999, at 4 (discussing opposing positions of Treasury and Fed on reform proposals); Dean Anason, *Regulators At a Standoff Over Reform Differences*, Am. Banker, Feb. 24, 1999, at 1 (same).

45. H.R. 665, 106th Cong., 1st Sess. (1999).

compliance, the bill would require that satisfactory CRA ratings be maintained as a condition of continued operation of new activities. Apparently, the Treasury Department favors this bill over the Leach measure.[46]

Senator Gramm introduced his version of financial services reform on 16 March 1999.[47] The bill would allow national banks with less than $1 billion in assets to underwrite securities and insurance through direct subsidiaries, but larger banks would be required to engage in these activities through holding company affiliates. The barrier between banking and commercial activities would gradually be lowered, eventually permitting up to 25 percent of bank's revenues to be earned from nonfinancial activities, and permitting a commercial firm to derive up to 25 percent of its revenues from a bank subsidiary. Tentatively, the Gramm proposal remains generally opposed to CRA compliance requirements.[48] The Treasury Department promptly voiced strong opposition to the Gramm proposal, particularly to the extent that it would weaken CRA requirements.[49]

With intensely competing positions being taken within the Congress and between Fed and the Treasury,[50] it is as yet unclear whether an acceptable compromise position can be reached, and what its terms might be.[51] Nevertheless, the reform agenda has already begun to advance in both the House and Senate banking committees.[52]

§ 5.25 Insurance Activities

Banks, and particularly national banks, have made significant inroads into the insurance industry.[1] *NationsBank of North Carolina v.*

46. See Bruce, *supra*.

47. See Jaret Seiberg, *Early March Votes Seen On Financial Reform Bill*, Am. Banker, Feb. 17, 1999, at 1 (reporting on Gramm bill).

48. Seiberg, *supra*, at 2.

49. See Dean Anason, *Insurance Groups Join Treasury in Knocking Gramm's Reform Plan*, Am. Banker, Feb. 19, 1999, at 2.

50. See Anason, *Regulators At a Standoff, supra* (discussing opposing positions).

51. See Dean Anason, *House Compromise on Reform Offers a Solution to Turf War*, Am. Banker, Mar. 2, 1999, at 1 (discussing possible compromise proposals).

52. See, e.g., Dean Anason, *House Panel Would Require ATM Owners to Disclose Fees*, Am. Banker, Mar. 11, 1999, at 2, col. 1 (reporting on progress of financial services reform bill in House Banking Committee).

§ 5.25

1. See, e.g., NationsBank of North Carolina v. Variable Annuity Life Insurance Co., 513 U.S. 251, 115 S.Ct. 810 (1995)

(approving national bank offering of variable annuities); *Barnett Bank of Marion County, N.A. v. Nelson*, 517 U.S. 25, 116 S.Ct. 1103 (1996) (approving national bank insurance agency activities). For a discussion of the longstanding issues between commercial banking and insurance services, see Schweitzer & Halbrook, *Insurance Activities of Banks and Banks Holding Companies: A Survey of Current Issues and Regulations*, 29 Drake L. Rev. 743 (1979/1980); Hemmer, *Insurance Underwriting Activities of BHC's*, 100 Banking L.J. 700 (1983); Note, *The Merger of Banking and Insurance: Will Congress Close the South Dakota Loophole?*, 60 Notre Dame L. Rev. 762 (1985); Malloy, *The Sound of Two Hands Flapping: Insurance–Related Activities of National Banks*, 41 St. Louis U. L.J. 75 (1997).

Variable Annuity Life Insurance Co.[2] upheld the Comptroller's authorization[3] of the brokerage of variable annuities[4] by national banks as an incidental power. *Barnett Bank of Marion County, N.A. v. Nelson,*[5] upheld insurance agency powers of national banks under a specialized section of the National Bank Act (NBA).[6] *NationsBank* and *Barnett Bank* are significant as part of a broader range of developments expanding the involvement of banking enterprises in insurance services. Despite the modest limitations on bank holding company involvement in insurance services suggested by *Alabama Ass'n of Ins. Agents v. Board of Governors,*[7] a range of insurance activities were later imbedded in the amended Bank Holding Company Act[8] as closely related to banking, and as such permissible in principle for bank holding companies.[9] The Court's decision in *NationsBank* extended the reach of national banks into insurance services by upholding the Comptroller's authorization of sales of variable annuities as an "incidental power" under the NBA.[10] In this perspective, *Barnett Bank* confirms the direction and quickens the speed of the march of commercial banks into insurance services. It remains to be seen whether Congress will undertake any significant changes in this area.

2. *Supra* note 1.

3. 12 C.F.R. § 5.34 (1996).

4. For these purposes, an "annuity" may be understood as follows:

Annuities are contracts under which the purchaser makes one or more premium payments to the issuer in exchange for a series of payments, which continue either for a fixed period or for the life of the purchaser or a designated beneficiary. When a purchaser invests in a "variable" annuity, the purchaser's money is invested in a designated way and payments to the purchaser vary with investment performance. In a classic "fixed" annuity, in contrast, payments do not vary.

NationsBank, 513 U.S. at 254, 115 S.Ct. at 812.

5. *Supra* note 1.

6. 12 U.S.C.A. § 92.

7. 533 F.2d 224 (5th Cir. 1976), *amended*, 558 F.2d 729 (1977), *cert. denied*, 435 U.S. 904, 98 S.Ct. 1448 (1978) (questioning authorization by Federal Reserve of general insurance agency activities by bank holding companies).

8. 12 U.S.C.A. § 1843(c)(8)(A)–(G).

9. *But cf. id.* § 1843(c)(8) ("closely related" activity subject to showing that activity is "proper incident" of banking).

10. 12 U.S.C.A. § 24 (Seventh).

Chapter 6

HOLDING COMPANY ACTIVITIES

Table of Sections

§ 6.1 Introduction

As a general rule, holding companies are expected to limit their activities to ownership and control of banks[1] (in the case of bank holding companies) or of savings associations[2] (in the case of savings and loan holding companies). However, an extensive set of statutory provisions provide exemptions from this general rule. This chapter examines the effect of those exemptive provisions on the activities of holding companies.

§ 6.2 Bank Holding Company Act

Sections 6.2–6.5 focus on the Bank Holding Company Act ("BHCA") provisions governing nonbanking activities of holding companies,[1] as implemented by the Fed.[2] However, at the outset we should note the relationship between the Comptroller's power to approve incidental powers (including the acquisition or creation of a bank subsidiary to engage in incidental powers) under the National Bank Act ("NBA")[3] and

§ 6.1

1. 12 U.S.C.A. § 1843(a)(1)–(2), (b).

2. 12 U.S.C.A. § 1467a(c)(1).

§ 6.2

1. 112 U.S.C.A. §§ 1843–1844, 1848.

2. *See, e.g.,* 12 C.F.R. §§ 225.2, 225.21–225.28.

3. 12 U.S.C.A. § 24 (Seventh).

the Fed's power to approve direct or indirect control of nonbanking activities under the BHCA.[4]

If a national bank proposes to conduct an activity as an "incidental power" in a wholly owned subsidiary, but the subsidiary is "indirectly controlled" by the bank's own holding company parent, does the Comptroller get to approve the activity, or must it also (or first) be approved by the Fed? As the D.C. Circuit's opinion in *American Insurance Association v. Clarke*[5] illustrates, this has been a particularly complex inquiry.[6] Essentially, the Fed has exclusive jurisdiction to interpret and apply the BHCA.[7] If the Comptroller, in applying the NBA, must interpret the BHCA, its interpretation is not entitled to deference, since the Comptroller is not charged with administration of that statute.[8] Hence, in "exceptional circumstances," the Comptroller may be required to defer his *final* approval under the NBA pending completion of the Fed's review under the BHCA.[9]

What seems clear from *American Insurance Association* is that the BHCA *does* apply to the acquisition of a nonbanking subsidiary by a national bank that is itself owned by a bank holding company, since the holding company is prohibited from acquiring "direct *or indirect* ownership or control of any voting shares of any company which is not a bank," unless an exception applies.[10] Hence, in cases that present a "substantial" question under the BHCA, "analysis must be undertaken by the [Fed] in the first instance."[11]

4. *Id.* § 1843(a)(1)–(2), (c).

5. 865 F.2d 278 (D.C.Cir.1988).

6. The D.C. Circuit's first opinion, *American Ins. Ass'n v. Clarke*, 854 F.2d 1405 (D.C.Cir.1988), was later withdrawn, and its superseding opinion was itself later modified. *American Ins. Ass'n*, 865 F.2d 278.

7. *See generally Whitney Nat'l Bank v. Bank of New Orleans & Trust Co.*, 379 U.S. 411, 85 S.Ct. 551 (1965).

8. *Department of the Treasury v. Federal Labor Relations Auth.*, 837 F.2d 1163, 1167 (D.C.Cir.1988) (citing cases).

9. *Whitney Nat'l Bank*, 379 U.S. at 426 n.7, 85 S.Ct. at 560 n. 7. *Whitney Nat'l Bank* has been interpreted to require the Comptroller to defer the issuance of a bank charter pending completion of the Fed's BHCA review when the transaction in question presents a "substantial" question under the BHCA. *American Bank of Tulsa v. Smith*, 503 F.2d 784, 789 (10th Cir.1974).

10. *See, e.g.,* 12 U.S.C.A. § 1843(a)(1) (emphasis added). *See also Security Pacific Corp.*, 72 Fed. Res. Bull. 800, 801 (1986)

(acquisition of voting shares by subsidiary bank of bank holding company treated as acquisition by bank holding company and thus subject to § 1843); *Merchants Nat'l Corp.*, 73 Fed. Res. Bull. 876, 880 (1987) (same), *vacated in part on other grounds sub nom. Independent Ins. Agents of Am. v. Board of Governors*, 838 F.2d 627 (2d Cir. 1988). *But cf. Citicorp v. Board of Governors*, 589 F.2d 1182 (2d Cir.1979), *cert. denied*, 442 U.S. 929, 99 S.Ct. 2860 (finding BHCA inapplicable to bank insurance subsidiary).

11. *American Ins. Ass'n*, 865 F.2d at 285. However, on rehearing, the D.C. Circuit concluded that "the facts of this case do not present the 'exceptional circumstances' that would warrant our reaching the merits of the AIA's contention that the challenged acquisition is prohibited by the BHCA." *Id.* at 288. This issue was left to possible future petition by the American Insurance Association to the Fed. *Id.* at 287.

§ 6.3　Structure of the Statute

The Bank Holding Company Act ("BHCA") generally prohibits direct and indirect acquisition by a bank holding company of a company that is not a bank.[1] However, the typical question is whether or not a proposed acquisition of a nonbanking company meets the requirements of one of the exemptions specified in the BHCA.[2] Aside from some transitional and grandfathering exemptions,[3] there are 14 principal exemptions to the nonbanking prohibition.[4] The scope of each of these exemptions is illustrated in Figure 6–1, *infra*.

Figure 6–1

BHCA: Principal Exemptions of Nonbanking Activities

12 U.S.C.A.	*Exempted Activity*
§ 1843(c)(1)	providing intra-company services; conducting safe deposit business; liquidating assets acquired from the parent holding company or banking subsidiaries, or acquired from any other source prior to becoming a bank holding company
§ 1843(c)(2)	holding shares acquired in satisfaction of a debt previously contracted (shares must be disposed of within two years, plus extensions granted by Fed)
§ 1843(c)(3)	acquiring shares from subsidiary requested to dispose of shares by federal or state examining authority (holding company must dispose of shares within two years)
§ 1843(c)(4)	holding or acquiring shares by bank in good faith in a fiduciary capacity[5]
§ 1843(c)(5)	holding "bank eligible" shares; *i.e.*, "investment securities" eligible for investment by national banks under 12 U.S.C.A. § 24(Seventh)
§ 1843(c)(6)	holding not more than five percent of the outstanding voting shares of any company
§ 1843(c)(7)	holding shares of any investment company that is not a bank holding company and is not engaged in any business other than investing in securities (securities held by the investment company not to involve more than five percent of the outstanding voting shares of any company)

§ 6.3

1. 12 U.S.C.A. § 1843(a)(1)–(2). On acquisitions of savings associations by bank holding companies, see 12 U.S.C.A. § 1843(i). *See Citicorp v. Board of Governors*, 589 F.2d 1182 (2d Cir.1979), *cert. denied*, 442 U.S. 929, 99 S.Ct. 2860 (discussing nature of prohibition).

2. 12 U.S.C.A. § 1843(c).

3. 12 U.S.C.A. § 1843(c)(i)–(ii). *Cf. Patagonia Corp. v. Board of Governors*, 517 F.2d 803 (9th Cir.1975) (discussing grandfathering under § 1843).

4. 12 U.S.C.A. § 1843(c)(1)–(14).

5. This exemption does not cover shares held under a trust that itself constitutes a "company" for BHCA purposes For these purposes, "company" is defined in 12 U.S.C.A. § 1841(b). *See also id.* § 1841(g)(2)–(3) (stating exceptions).

12 U.S.C.A.	*Exempted Activity*
§ 1843(c)(8)	holding shares of any company the activities of which the Fed has determined to be *so closely related* to banking or managing or controlling banks as to be a *proper incident* thereto; holding of shares of company involved in insurance permitted is subject to specific limitations;[6] emergency acquisitions of savings institutions is allowed under an expedited approval process
§ 1843(c)(9)	holding shares of or conducting activities by a company organized under laws of foreign country, with a majority of its business conducted outside the United States (application of the exemption must not be substantially at variance with the purposes of BHCA and must be in the public interest)
§ 1843(c)(10)	holding shares lawfully acquired and owned prior to May 9, 1956, by a bank that is bank holding company, or by its wholly owned subsidiary
§ 1843(c)(11)	holding shares owned directly or indirectly by a company that became a bank holding company under 1970 BHCA amendments, of a company that engages only in activities permissible for a bank holding company or subsidiaries (shares must have been owned as a subsidiary on June 30, 1968)[7]
§ 1843(c)(12)	ten-year transitional exemption generally allowing company that became a bank holding company under 1970 BHCA amendments, or its subsidiary, to retain shares if within ten years it ceases to be a bank holding company, divests shares,[8] or ceases activities not authorized under § 1843 (must comply with other conditions prescribed by Fed)[9]
§ 1843(c)(13)	holding shares of or conducting activities by, a company that does no U.S. business except incident to international or foreign business (application of the exemption must not be substantially at variance with the purposes of BHCA and must be in the public interest)
§ 1843(c)(14)	holding shares of an export trading company whose acquisition or formation by bank holding company has not been disapproved by Fed (the investment,

6. On insurance activities of bank holding companies, see *National Ass'n of Cas. & Sur. Agents v. Board of Governors*, 856 F.2d 282 (D.C.Cir.1988), *reh'g denied*, 862 F.2d 351, *cert. denied*, 490 U.S. 1090, 109 S.Ct. 2430 (1989); *Florida Ass'n of Ins. Agents, Inc. v. Board of Governors*, 591 F.2d 334 (5th Cir.1979); *Alabama Ass'n of Ins. Agents v. Board of Governors*, 533 F.2d 224 (5th Cir.1976), *amended*, 558 F.2d 729 (5th Cir.1977), *cert. denied*, 435 U.S. 904, 98 S.Ct. 1448 (1978); *Independent Bankers Ass'n of Ga. v. Board of Governors*, 516 F.2d 1206 (D.C.Cir.1975); *National Ass'n of Ins. Agents, Inc. v. Board of Governors*, 489 F.2d 1268 (D.C.Cir.1974). *See also* Michael P. Malloy, *The Sound of Two Hands Flapping: Insurance–Related Activities of National Banks*, 41 St. Louis U. L.J. 75 (1997).

7. *Cf.* 12 U.S.C.A. § 1843(d) (providing special exemption for certain companies that controlled one bank prior to 1 July 1968).

8. *Cf. id.* § 1843(e) (providing generally for divestiture of non exempted shares).

9. *Cf. id.* § 1843(d).

12 U.S.C.A.	*Exempted Activity*
	direct or indirect, must not exceed five percent of holding company's consolidated capital and surplus)

As a practical matter, the key exemptive provision has proven to be the "closely related" exemption.[10] Textually, the language of the exemption seems to present one "test" with two integrated elements;[11] the question is whether a nonbanking activity is "so closely related to banking or managing or controlling banks as to be a proper incident thereto."[12] The provision later explains:

> In determining whether a particular activity is a proper incident to banking or managing or controlling banks the [Fed] shall consider whether its performance by an affiliate of a holding company can reasonably be expected to produce benefits to the public, such as greater convenience, increased competition, or gains in efficiency, that outweigh possible adverse effects, such as undue concentration of resources, decreased or unfair competition, conflicts of interests, or unsound banking practices. In orders and regulations under this subsection, the [Fed] may differentiate between activities commenced de novo and activities commenced by the acquisition, in whole or in part, of a going concern.[13]

In practice, the "closely related" provision has been read and applied as two distinct tests; namely, (1) whether a proposed activity is closely related; and (2) whether its public benefits outweigh its adverse effects.[14] Taken as two separate tests, supportive information on one "test"—for example, the high degree of public benefits to be derived from bank holding company involvement in the activity—cannot influence the outcome under the other.[15]

As to the first, "closely related" test, the details of that inquiry have been set by *National Courier Association v. Board of Governors.*[16] The court endorsed a tripartite test, since broadly accepted, as follows:

> The [Fed] must ... articulate the ways in which banking activities and the proposed activities are assertedly connected, and must determine, not arbitrarily or capriciously, that the connections

---

10. *Id.* § 1843(c)(8). On the relation of the "closely related" exemption to the other exemptions in § 1843(c), see 12 C.F.R. § 225.123(a)–(c). On the scope of the "closely related" exemption, see, *e.g., id.* §§ 225.126–225.127.

11. *See National Courier Ass'n v. Board of Governors,* 516 F.2d 1229, 1232 (D.C.Cir. 1975) (referring to two "issues" under § 1843(c)(8)).

12. 12 U.S.C.A. § 1843(c)(8).

13. *Id.*

14. *Securities Indus. Ass'n, supra; Independent Ins. Agents of Am., Inc. v. Board of*

Governors, 658 F.2d 571 (8th Cir.1981), *reh'g denied,* 664 F.2d 177, *appeal after remand,* 736 F.2d 468 (8th Cir.1984); *Association of Bank Travel Bureaus, Inc. v. Board of Governors,* 568 F.2d 549 (7th Cir. 1978).

15. *See, e.g., Alabama Ass'n of Ins. Agents, supra,* (refusing to allow alleged "public benefits" of bank holding company involvement in insurance influence outcome on "closely related" inquiry).

16. 516 F.2d 1229 (D.C.Cir.1975).

are close. As to what kinds of connections may qualify, at the following seems to us within the statutory intent:

    1.   Banks have in fact provided the proposed services.

    2.   Banks generally provide services that are operationally or functionally so similar to the proposed services as to equip them particularly well to provide the proposed service.

    3.   Banks generally provide services that are so integrally related to the proposed service as to require their provision in a specialized form.[17]

The statute itself provides the elements of the second test, a balancing of public benefits and adverse effects.[18] Since these are interpreted as two separate "tests," judicial inquiry into the public benefits issue will not occur unless the activity in question first passes the closely related test.[19]

    The "closely related" test is one that is susceptible to resolution outside of the context of a specific case.[20] In fact the Fed's regulations identify a series of activities that are, in its view, closely related.[21] However, the "public benefits" test is on its own terms one that must be performed in context on a case-by-case basis.[22]

    Despite the availability of the exemptions, if the Fed has reasonable cause to believe that the continuation of any nonbanking activity by a bank holding company constitutes a serious risk to the financial safety, soundness, or stability of a subsidiary bank of the company, or is otherwise inconsistent with sound banking principles, the BHCA, or other statutory authority, the Fed may order the company or its non-bank subsidiary to terminate the activity or divest the subsidiary.[23] The Fed's authority is subject to the requirement of due notice and opportunity for a hearing.[24] The Fed must also consider the views of the Comptroller (if the subsidiary bank is a national bank) or the FDIC and the appropriate state supervisory authority (if the subsidiary bank is a insured nonmember bank).[25] The Fed may enforce any order under this procedure by application to the U.S. district court in whose jurisdiction

---

17. *National Courier Ass'n*, 516 F.2d at 1237. *See Association of Data Processing Serv. Orgs. v. Board of Governors*, 745 F.2d 677 (D.C.Cir.1984) (applying test).

18. 12 U.S.C.A. § 1843(c)(8). *See supra* text at note 13 (quoting public benefits test of § 1843(c)(8)). *See also Securities Indus. Ass'n, supra*; *American Land Title Ass'n v. Board of Governors*, 892 F.2d 1059 (D.C.Cir.1989); *Alabama Ass'n of Ins. Agents*, 533 F.2d at 246–252 (applying public benefits test); *Independent Bankers Ass'n of Ga., supra* (discussing required balancing).

19. *Securities Indus. Ass'n, supra*; *BankAmerica Corp. v. Board of Governors*, 491 F.2d 985 (9th Cir.1974).

20. *See, e.g., National Courier Ass'n*, 516 F.2d at 1233–1234 (discussing closely related test).

21. 12 C.F.R. § 225.28(b) (listing activities determined by regulation to be permissible under § 1843(c)(8)).

22. *See, e.g., National Courier Ass'n*, 516 F.2d at 1233 (discussing public benefits test as "one which normally must be resolved upon specific facts").

23. 12 U.S.C.A. § 1844(e)(1). Divestiture may be by sale or *pro rata* distribution of the subsidiary's shares to shareholders of the bank holding company. *Id.*

24. *Id.*

25. *Id.*

the holding company is located.[26] The procedure does not apply in the case of a nonbanking subsidiary of a bank (indirectly controlled by the bank's holding company).[27]

Any person aggrieved by an order of the Fed under the BHCA may obtain judicial review in the U.S. court of appeals in any circuit in which the person has a principal place of business, or in the D.C. Circuit.[28] Petition for review must be filed within 30 days after entry of the Fed's order.[29] The standard of judicial review with respect to Fed action under the BHCA is generally whether the action was arbitrary, capricious, an abuse of discretion, or otherwise not in accordance with law.[30] However, the Fed's factual findings under the act are conclusive only if supported by substantial evidence.[31]

The proposed Financial Services Act of 1998[32] was intended to overhaul the U.S. financial services system, including permissible holding company activities. Among other things, the bill would have allowed affiliations among banks, securities firms, and insurance companies through "financial holding companies" that would be regulated by the Fed.[33] In that regard, the stated purposes of the bill included "enhance[d] competition in the financial services industry, in order to foster innovation and efficiency,"[34] and "reduc[tion] and, to the maximum extent practicable, ... eliminat[ion of] the legal barriers preventing affiliation among depository institutions, securities firms, insurance companies, and other financial service providers."[35]

At the last possible moment, the bill failed to reach a Senate vote, largely through the opposition of Senator Gramm to community reinvestment provisions in the bill.[36] A new set of financial services reform bills, including one sponsored by Senator Gramm, is now under consideration.[37] The Gramm proposal includes provisions requiring national banks with more than $1 billion in assets to underwrite securities and insurance through holding company affiliates subject to Fed supervision, rather than through direct subsidiaries.[38] Competing bills take differing

---

26. *Id.* § 1844(e)(2).

27. *Id.* § 1844(e)(1).

28. 12 U.S.C.A. § 1848. On the options available to a "party aggrieved," see *BankAmerica Corp. v. Board of Governors*, 596 F.2d 1368 (9th Cir.1979).

29. 12 U.S.C.A. § 1848. *See Memphis Trust Co. v. Board of Governors*, 584 F.2d 921 (6th Cir.1978) (discussing filing requirement and exclusive jurisdiction of courts of appeal).

30. *See, e.g., Securities Indus. Ass'n v. Board of Governors*, 468 U.S. 207, 104 S.Ct. 3003 (1984) (upholding Fed action under standard); *NCNB Corp. v. Board of Governors*, 599 F.2d 609 (4th Cir.1979).

31. 12 U.S.C.A. § 1848. On application of the substantial evidence standard of review, see *Association of Data Processing Serv. Orgs. v. Board of Governors*, 745 F.2d 677 (D.C.Cir.1984); *Independent Bankers Ass'n of Ga., supra*: *American Bancorporation, Inc. v. Board of Governors*, 509 F.2d 29 (8th Cir.1974).

32. H.R. 10, 105th Cong., 2d Sess. (1998).

33. H.R. 10, §§ 111–117.

34. *Id.* § 1(b)(1).

35. *Id.* § 1(b)(5).

36. *See supra* at 174 (discussing Gramm opposition to Financial Services Act).

37. *See id.* at 174–175 (discussing competing reform proposals).

38. *See* Jaret Seiberg, *Early March Votes Seen On Financial Reform Bill*, Am. Banker, Feb. 17, 1999, at 1 (reporting on Gramm bill).

positions on this issue. A bill sponsored by Representative James A. Leach, the Chair of the House Banking Committee, would allow holding company affiliates, but not direct subsidiaries of banks, to engage in a wide range of new *financial* activities (including securities activities), not including commercial activities.[39] A bill sponsored by Representative John LaFalce, the ranking Democrat on the Committee, would allow a wide range of new activities for direct bank subsidiaries, except for real estate investment and insurance underwriting, while holding companies would be allowed to engage in commercial (*i.e.,* nonfinancial) activities, not exceeding fifteen percent of a company's annual consolidated gross revenues.[40] With intensely competing positions being taken within the Congress and between Fed and the Treasury,[41] it is as yet unclear whether an acceptable compromise position can be reached, and what its terms might be.[42] Nevertheless, the reform agenda has already begun to advance in both the House and Senate banking committees.[43]

§ 6.4   Structure of the Regulations

The current regulations mirror the structure of the statute, but they are skewed in favor of the statute's application in practice. For example, while the statute gives formally equivalent status to all of the exemptions, the regulations emphasize the role of the closely related exemption and almost trivializes the others.[1] The structure is illustrated in Figure 6–2, *infra.*

39. H.R. 10, 106th Cong., 1st Sess. (1999).

40. H.R. 665, 106th Cong., 1st Sess. (1999).

41. *See* Dean Anason, *Regulators At a Standoff Over Reform Differences,* Am. Banker, Feb. 24, 1999, at 1 (discussing opposing positions).

42. *See* Dean Anason, *House Compromise on Reform Offers a Solution to Turf War,* Am. Banker, Mar. 2, 1999, at 1 (discussing possible compromise proposals).

43. *See, e.g.,* Dean Anason, *House Panel Would Require ATM Owners to Disclose Fees,* Am. Banker, Mar. 11, 1999, at 2, col. 1 (reporting on progress of financial services reform bill in House Banking Committee).

§ 6.4

1. *See, e.g.* 12 C.F.R. § 225.21(a):

(a) Prohibited nonbanking activities and acquisitions. Except as provided in § 225.22 ..., a bank holding company or a subsidiary may not engage in, or acquire or control, directly or indirectly, voting securities or assets of a company engaged in, any activity other than:

(1) Banking or managing or controlling banks and other subsidiaries authorized under the [BHCA]; and

(2) An activity that the [Fed] determines to be so closely related to banking, or managing or controlling banks as to be a proper incident thereto, including any incidental activities that are necessary to carry on such an activity, if the bank holding company has obtained the prior approval of the Board for that activity in accordance with the requirements of this regulation.

In fact, of course, § 225.21(a)(1) collapses into 14 words, the provisions of 12 U.S.C.A. § 1843(a)(1)–(2), while § 225.21(a)(2) memorializes 12 U.S.C.A. § 1843(c)(8). The other 13 exemptions of § 1843(c) are picked up by various paragraphs of 12 C.F.R. § 225.22. *But see* 12 U.S.C.A. § 1843(j)(1)(A) (requiring written notice and often prior approval for closely related activities).

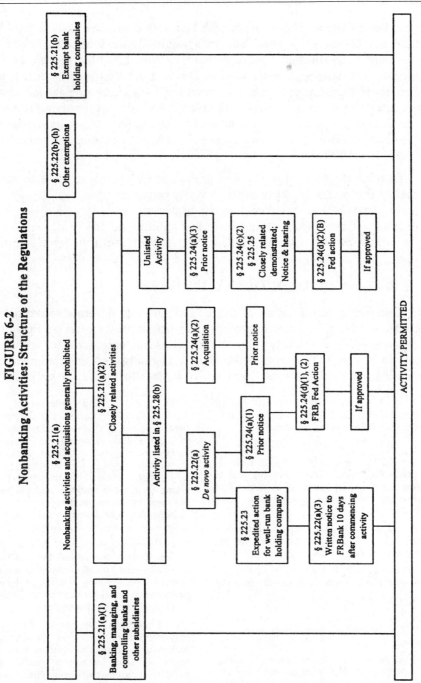

FIGURE 6-2
Nonbanking Activities: Structure of the Regulations

Both the statute and the implementing regulations provide for a limited period of time for action on an application (or "notice," in current Fed practice).[2] In general, a notice is deemed approved 60 days after filing of a complete notice with the Fed, unless the Fed acts on the

2. *Cf. BankAmerica Corp. v. Board of Governors*, 596 F.2d 1368 (9th Cir.1979)   (discussing statutory objective of prompt consideration of applications).

notice before the end of that period.[3] The period may be extended for an additional 30 days by the Fed, with additional extensions subject to agreement with the bank holding company that has filed the notice.[4] In addition, if a hearing is requested or the Fed determines that a hearing is warranted,[5] the period may be extended for a time not exceeding 91 days after the hearing record is complete.[6] For notices involving nonlisted activities (*i.e.*, activities not listed in the regulations as being closely related to banking[7]), the Fed has the authority to extend the period for an additional 90 days.[8]

In reviewing a notice, the Fed is required by the statute to consider whether the public benefits of the activity outweigh the possible adverse effects.[9] In addition, the Fed has the statutory authority to disapprove any notice if the bank holding company submitting the notice neglects, fails, or refuses to furnish all the information required by the Fed.[10]

§ 6.5   Permissible Activities

Through a combination of formal rulemaking, administrative determinations based on specific notices, and litigation concerning Fed policies, a core list of "closely related" activities has emerged. For the most part, it is codified in the Fed's BHCA regulations,[1] and refined and amended from time to time. Figure 6–3, *infra*, illustrates the current list

---

3. 12 U.S.C.A. § 1843(j)(1)(C)(i). *See* 12 C.F.R. § 225.25(b)(1) (providing for approval through failure to act on notice).

4. 12 U.S.C.A. § 1843(j)(1)(C)(ii).

5. *See* 12 C.F.R. § 225.25(a)(2) (providing that Fed "shall order a hearing only if there are disputed issues of material fact that cannot be resolved in some other manner").

6. 12 U.S.C.A. § 1843(j)(1)(C)(iii). *See* 12 C.F.R. § 225.25(a)(3) (providing for extension of period for hearing).

7. *See* 12 C.F.R. § 225.28(b) (listing activities predetermined to be closely related).

8. 12 U.S.C.A. § 1843(j)(1)(E).

9. 12 U.S.C.A. § 1843(j)(2)(A). *See* 12 C.F.R. § 225.26, which provides in part as follows:

(a) In general. In evaluating a notice . . . the Fed shall consider whether the notificant's performance of the activities can reasonably be expected to produce benefits to the public (such as greater convenience, increased competition, and gains in efficiency) that outweigh possible adverse effects (such as undue concentration of resources, decreased or unfair competition, conflicts of interest, and unsound banking practices).

(b) Financial and managerial resources. Consideration of the factors in paragraph (a) of this section includes an evaluation of the financial and managerial resources of the notificant, including its subsidiaries and any company to be acquired, the effect of the proposed transaction on those resources, and the management expertise, internal control and risk-management systems, and capital of the entity conducting the activity.

(c) Competitive effect of *de novo* proposals. Unless the record demonstrates otherwise, the commencement or expansion of a nonbanking activity *de novo* is presumed to result in benefits to the public through increased competition. . . .

(e) Conditional approvals. The Fed may impose conditions on any approval, including conditions to address permissibility, financial, managerial, safety and soundness, competitive, compliance, conflicts of interest, or other concerns to ensure that approval is consistent with the relevant statutory factors and other provisions of the [BHCA].

10. 12 U.S.C.A. § 1843(j)(2)(B).

§ 6.5

1. 12 C.F.R. § 225.28(b).

of closely related activities. Although the inclusion of a particular activity in the list creates certain procedural advantages in the processing of a notice,[2] it does not predetermine the outcome of a notice.[3] The public benefits of the proposed activity, outweighing its possible adverse affects, must still be demonstrated on a case-by-case basis.[4]

Figure 6–3
Activities Predetermined to be Closely Related[5]

12 C.F.R.	Activity
§ 225.28(b)(1)	extending credit and servicing loans
§ 225.28(b)(2)	activities related to extending credit (*e.g.*, property appraising; arranging financing; check-guaranty services; collection agency services; credit bureau services; asset management; acquiring debt in default; real estate settlement servicing)
§ 225.28(b)(3)	leasing personal or real property, under specified circumstances
§ 225.28(b)(4)	operating nonbank depository institutions, including industrial banks and savings associations
§ 225.28(b)(5)	trust company functions
§ 225.28(b)(6)	financial and investment advisory activities
§ 225.28(b)(7)	transactional services as agent for customer investments (*e.g.*, securities brokerage;[6] private placement services; futures commission merchant, under specified circumstances; services with respect to swaps and similar transactions); permitted activities do not include selling "bank-ineligible" securities[7] at the order of a customer that is the issuer of the securities, selling bank-ineligible securities in a transaction where the company has a contractual agreement to place the securities as agent of the issuer, or acting as a principal in a transaction involving a bank-ineligible security for which the company or any of its affiliates acts as underwriter (during the period of the underwriting or for 30 days thereafter) or dealer
§ 225.28(b)(8)	investment transactions as principal (*e.g.*, underwriting and dealing in government obligations and money market instruments; investing and trading activities involving foreign exchange, forward con-

2. *See, e.g.,* 12 C.F.R. §§ 225.22(a), 225.24(a)(1)–(2) (concerning treatment of notices involving listed activities).

3. *Independent Bankers Ass'n of Ga. v. Board of Governors,* 516 F.2d 1206 (D.C.Cir.1975).

4. 12 C.F.R. § 225.26(a). *Cf. Independent Bankers Ass'n of Ga., supra* (emphasizing right of interested parties to full adjudicatory hearing).

5. *Source:* 12 C.F.R. § 225.28(b).

6. *See Securities Indus. Ass'n v. Board of Governors,* 468 U.S. 207, 104 S.Ct. 3003 (1984) (upholding Fed position).

7. A bank-ineligible security is any security that a national or state member bank is not permitted to underwrite or deal in under 12 U.S.C.A. §§ 24 and 335.

12 C.F.R.	*Activity*
	tracts, options, futures, options on futures, swaps, and similar contracts, under specified circumstances; buying and selling bullion, and related activities)
§ 225.28(b)(9)	management consulting and counseling activities (*e.g.*, employee benefits consulting services; career counseling services)
§ 225.28(b)(10)	support services such as courier services, under specified circumstances;[8] (printing and selling MICR-encoded items)
§ 225.28(b)(11)	insurance agency and underwriting, under specified circumstances[9]
§ 225.28(b)(12)	community development activities, including financing and investment activities, advisory activities
§ 225.28(b)(13)	money orders, savings bonds, and traveler's checks
§ 225.28(b)(14)	data processing, under specified circumstances[10]

The Fed has gradually expanded securities underwriting by "Section 20 subsidiaries,"[11] that is, nonbanking subsidiaries of bank holding companies that engage in both "bank-eligible" securities underwriting[12] and "bank-ineligible" securities underwriting.[13] The only clear statutory limitation on these subsidiaries appears to be the requirement under Section 20 of the Glass–Steagall Act[14] that the bank affiliates not be "engaged principally" in bank-ineligible securities activities.[15] In addi-

8. *Cf. National Courier Ass'n v. Board of Governors*, 516 F.2d 1229 (D.C.Cir.1975) (approving certain courier services); *Cameron Fin. Corp. v. Board of Governors*, 497 F.2d 841 (4th Cir.1974) (discussing courier services spun off from holding company).

9. *See* 12 U.S.C.A. § 1843(c)(8)(A)–(G) (providing statutory limits on insurance activities of bank holding companies). *See also National Ass'n of Cas. & Sur. Agents v. Board of Governors*, 856 F.2d 282 (D.C.Cir. 1988), *reh'g denied*, 862 F.2d 351, *cert. denied*, 490 U.S. 1090, 109 S.Ct. 2430 (1989) (discussing § 1843(c)(8)(D)). *Cf. Florida Ass'n of Ins. Agents, Inc. v. Board of Governors*, 591 F.2d 334 (5th Cir.1979) (interpreting prior statutory language); *Alabama Ass'n of Ins. Agents v. Board of Governors*, 533 F.2d 224 (5th Cir.1976), *amended*, 558 F.2d 729 (5th Cir.1977), *cert. denied*, 435 U.S. 904, 98 S.Ct. 1448 (1978); *Independent Bankers Ass'n of Ga. v. Board of Governors*, 516 F.2d 1206 (D.C.Cir.1975); *National Ass'n of Ins. Agents, Inc. v. Board of Governors*, 489 F.2d 1268 (D.C.Cir.1974). *See generally* Michael P. Malloy, *The Sound of Two Hands Flapping: Insurance–Related Activities of National Banks*, 41 St. Louis U. L.J. 75 (1997) (discussing insurance activities).

10. *See National Courier Ass'n, supra; Association of Data Processing Serv. Orgs. v. Board of Governors*, 745 F.2d 677 (D.C.Cir.1984).

11. *I.e.*, nonbanking subsidiaries of bank holding companies that engage in securities underwriting and related activities consistent with Section 20 of the Glass–Steagall Act, 12 U.S.C.A. § 377. Section 20 limits the affiliations of member banks with securities firms "engaged principally" in specified securities activities.

12. *I.e.*, purchasing, underwriting and dealing in securities that banks are permitted to underwrite (typically government-issued or guaranteed debt securities) in accordance with Section 16 of the Glass–Steagall Act, 12 U.S.C.A. § 24 (Seventh).

13. For discussion of the development of the Fed policy, see 2 MICHAEL P. MALLOY, BANKING LAW AND REGULATION § 7.2.2 N.20 (1994 & Cum. Supp.).

14. 12 U.S.C.A. § 377.

15. *See, e.g., J.P. Morgan & Co. Inc./ The Chase Manhattan Corp./Bankers Trust New York Corp./Citicorp/Security Pacific Corp.*, 75 Fed. Res. Bull. 192 (1989); *Citicorp/J.P. Morgan & Co./Bankers Trust New* tion, however, in successive orders beginning in 1987, the Fed established a series of prudential restrictions, or "firewalls," as conditions for approval of such affiliations under the BHCA.[16] The restrictions were "designed to prevent securities underwriting and dealing risks from being passed from a section 20 subsidiary to an affiliated insured depository institution ..., and to mitigate the potential for conflicts of interest, unfair competition, and other adverse effects that may arise from the affiliation of commercial and investment banks."[17]

In August 1997, the Fed modified the prudential limitations established in the previous orders permitting a nonbank subsidiary of a bank holding company to underwrite and deal in securities.[18] This change was effective October 27, 1997.[19] The modifications eliminated those restrictions that the Fed now considers unduly burdensome or unnecessary in light of other laws or regulations, and consolidated the remaining restrictions in a series of eight operating standards. The Fed concluded that a narrower set of restrictions would still be consistent with safety and soundness, while improving operating efficiencies at Section 20 subsidiaries. The currently applicable limitations are illustrated in Figure 6–4, *infra*.

Figure 6–4
Section 20 Subsidiaries: Prudential Limitations

12 C.F.R.	*Prudential Limitation*
§ 225.200(b)(1)	adequacy of capital (on a fully consolidated basis)
§ 225.200(b)(2)	internal controls, including appropriate limits on exposure, with respect to participation by subsidiary banks, savings associations, branches or agencies in transactions underwritten or arranged by a Section 20 affiliate
§ 225.200(b)(3)	interlocks restriction, to less than majority on each respective board within the holding company
§ 225.200(b)(4)	customer disclosure, to Section 20 subsidiary customers and to bank, thrift, branch or agency customers
§ 225.200(b)(5)	intra-day credit extension to a Section 20 subsidiary by affiliated bank, thrift, branch, or agency on market terms consistent with affiliate loans provisions of Federal Reserve Act[20]
§ 225.200(b)(6)	restriction on funding by affiliated bank, thrift, branch, or agency of purchases of securities during underwriting period

York Corp., 73 Fed. Res. Bull. 473 (1987). *See also Canadian Imperial Bank of Commerce/The Royal Bank of Canada, Barclays PLC/Barclays Bank PLC*, 76 Fed. Res. Bull. 158 (1990) (applying earlier orders to Section 20 subsidiaries of foreign banks).

16. 12 U.S.C.A. § 1843(c)(8).

17. 62 Fed. Reg. 45,295, 45,295 (1997).

18. 62 Fed. Reg. 45,295 (1997) (codified at 12 C.F.R. § 225.200).

19. 62 Fed. Reg. at 45,295.

20. On statutory restrictions on loans to affiliates, see *supra* § 5.7.

12 C.F.R.	Prudential Limitation
§ 225.200(b)(7)	concurrent reporting to appropriate Federal Reserve Bank required to parallel required reports to NASD, other self-regulatory organizations, and Securities and Exchange Commission[21]
§ 225.200(b)(8)	restrictions on foreign bank with a Section 20 affiliate, and on any branch or agency thereof, with respect to loans and extensions of credit, and with respect to advertisement concerning obligations of the Section 20 affiliate

§ 6.6   Home Owners' Loan Act

The savings and loan holding company provisions of the Home Owners' Loan Act ("HOLA")[1] generally parallel the Bank Holding Company Act "(BHCA)" provisions, although there are some significant differences. Figure 6–5, *infra*, gives a schematic comparison of the two sets of provisions.

Figure 6–5
Holding Company Activities: BHCA and HOLA

Provision	BHCA Section	HOLA Section
General prohibition on non-banking/non-S & L activities	§ 1843(a)	§ 1467a(c)(1), (4)
Treatment of share certificates	§ 1843(b)	
Exceptions	§ 1843(c)	§ 1467a(c)(2)
Special organizations	§ 1843(c)(i)	[§ 1467a(c)(2)(F), (4)]
Family companies	§ 1843(c)(ii)	[§ 1467a(c)(2)(F), (4)]
Special services	§ 1843(c)(1)	§ 1467a(c)(2)(A), (C), (D), (F), (4)
Debt previously contracted	§ 1843(c)(2)	§ 1467a(c)(2)(F), (4)
Divesting subsidiaries	§ 1843(c)(3)	§ 1467a(c)(2)(C), (F), 4
Fiduciary activities	§ 1843(c)(4)	§ 1467a(c)(2)(E), (F), (4)
Investment securities	§ 1843(c)(5)	§ 1467a(c)(2)(F), (4)
Five percent holdings	§ 1843(c)(6)	§ 1467a(c)(2)(F), (4)
Diversified investment company	§ 1843(c)(7)	§ 1467a(c)(2)(F), (4)
Closely related activities	§ 1843(c)(8)	§ 1467a(c)(2)(B), (F), (4)
Foreign corporation	§ 1843(c)(9)	§ 1467a(c)(2)(F), (4)

21. *Per* 17 C.F.R. § 240.17a–11 (capitalization reports).

§ 6.6

1. 12 U.S.C.A. § 1467a.

Provision	BHCA Section	HOLA Section
Grandfathered bank subsidiary	§ 1843(c)(10)	[§ 1467a(c)(2)(F), (4)]
Grandfathered 1970 activities	§ 1843(c)(11)	[§ 1467a(c)(2)(F), (4)]
Transition for 1970 companies	§ 1843(c)(12)	[§ 1467a(c)(2)(F), (4)]
Foreign-based company activities	§ 1843(c)(13)	§ 1467a(c)(2)(F), (4), (7)
Export trading company	§ 1843(c)(14)	§ 1467a(c)(2)(F), (4)
Qualified stock issuance		§ 1467a(b)(4), (c)(2)(G)
Unitary stock issuance		§ 1467a(c)(3)(A)
Qualified thrift lender holding companies		§ 1467a(c)(3)(B)
Bank holding companies		§ 1467a(c)(B), (t)
Grace period for compliance		§ 1467a(c)(5)
Special provisions for 1987 amendments		§ 1467a(c)(6)
Judicial review	§ 1848	§ 1467a(j)
Mutual holding companies		§ 1467a(o)(5), (6)

One important structural difference is that the HOLA incorporates by reference activities approved by the Fed for bank holding companies.[2] These activities are authorized for savings and loan holding companies unless the Office of Thrift Supervision ("OTS") prohibits or limits such an activity by regulation for savings and loan holding companies.[3] However, BHCA-authorized activities still require the prior approval of the OTS.[4]

In reviewing an application for approval of such activities, the OTS is required to consider the following statutory factors: (1) Whether the performance of the activity described in the application by the company or the subsidiary can reasonably be expected to produce benefits to the public (such as greater convenience, increased competition, or gains in efficiency) that outweigh possible adverse effects of such activity (such as undue concentration of resources, decreased or unfair competition, conflicts of interest, or unsound financial practices).[5] (2) The managerial resources of the companies involved.[6] (3) Finally, the adequacy of the financial resources, including capital, of the companies involved.[7]

Unlike the situation under the BHCA, the HOLA exempts from regulation the non-savings association activities of any holding company

---

2. *Id.* § 1467a(c)(2)(F)(i).

3. *Id.*

4. *Id.* § 1467a(b)(4)(A).

5. *Id.* § 1467a(c)(4)(B)(i).

6. *Id.* § 1467a(c)(4)(B)(ii).

7. *Id.* § 1467a(c)(4)(B)(iii).

that controls only one savings association.[8] This exemption is available so long as the savings association subsidiary is a "qualified thrift lender"[9]—in effect, an association specializing to a significant degree in traditional savings association activities of home mortgage lending and savings deposits.[10]

Alternatively, the exemption is available for a holding company controlling more than one savings association, on the following conditions.[11] (1) All or all but one of the savings association subsidiaries must have been acquired initially by the holding company, or an individual controlling the company, either in an FDIC-assisted transaction,[12] an emergency acquisition,[13] or an FSLIC-approved acquisition;[14] or in an acquisition in which capital assistance to the savings association was continued under the FDIA.[15] (2) All of the savings association subsidiaries must be qualified thrift lenders.[16]

One final set of differences between the BHCA and HOLA provisions concerns the applicability of HOLA to certain entities. First, upon application, a savings bank or cooperative bank[17] may be treated as a savings association for purposes of the holding company provisions of the HOLA, if the OTS determines that the bank is a qualified thrift lender.[18] Second, a bank holding company subject to the BHCA, or a company controlled by such a bank holding company, is exempt from the HOLA provisions.[19]

§ 6.7   Structure of the Regulations

The structure of the regulations implementing the HOLA provisions[1] roughly tracks the structure of the statute. Figure 6–6, *infra*, illustrates the structure of the regulations.

8. *Id.* § 1467a(c)(3)(A).

9. *Id.*

10. *See id.* § 1467a(m) (establishing qualified thrift lender test).

11. *Id.* § 1467a(c)(3)(B).

12. *Id.* § 1823(c) (providing for FDIC "open bank" assistance).

13. *Id.* § 1823(k) (providing for FDIC-approved emergency acquisitions).

14. *Id.* § 1467a(c)(3)(B)(i)(I). *See* 12 U.S.C.A. § 1730a(m) (1988) (providing since repealed emergency acquisitions authority for now abolished FSLIC).

15. 12 U.S.C.A. § 1467a(c)(3)(B)(i)(II). *See id.* § 1823(i) (concerning purchase of

"net worth certificates" from troubled depository institution by FDIC as support for institution's capital position).

16. *Id.* § 1467a(c)(3)(B)(ii).

17. *See id.* § 1813(h) (defining "cooperative bank").

18. *Id.* § 1467a(*l*)(1). However, failure to maintain qualified thrift lender status will disqualify the bank for treatment as such a lender (and, hence, as a savings association for these purposes) for a period of five years. *Id.* § 1467a(*l*)(2).

19. *Id.* § 1467a(t).

§ 6.7

1. 12 C.F.R. Pt. 584.

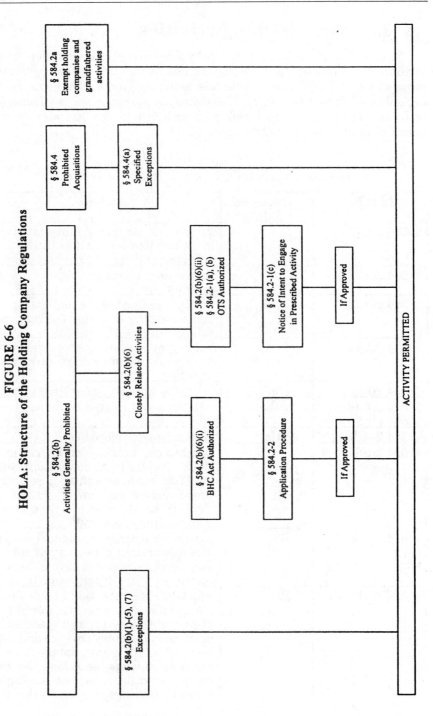

FIGURE 6-6

HOLA: Structure of the Holding Company Regulations

§ 6.8 Permissible Activities

A core list of prescribed or permissible activities is codified in the various provisions of the OTS regulations.[1] In addition, the regulations incorporate by reference permissible activities under the Fed's BHCA regulations.[2] Figure 6–7, *infra*, illustrates these prescribed or permissible activities. However, certain activities included in the list may require notice or application and OTS approval.

Figure 6–7
HOLA: Prescribed or Permitted Activities

12 C.F.R.	Required Filing	Activity
§ 584.2(b)(1)		furnishing or performing management services for savings association subsidiary
§ 584.2(b)(2)		conducting insurance agency or escrow business
§ 584.2(b)(3)		holding, managing, or liquidating assets owned by or acquired from subsidiary savings association
§ 584.2(b)(4)		holding or managing properties used or occupied by subsidiary savings association
§ 584.2(b)(5)		acting as trustee under deed of trust
§ 584.2(b)(6)(i), § 584.2(b)(6)(ii)	Application[3]	BHCA closely related activities
§ 584.2–1(b)	Notice[4]	HOLA closely related activities
§ 584.2(b)(7)		purchasing, holding, or disposing of stock acquired in connection with qualified stock issuance, if prior approval for acquisition is granted by the OTS (in the case of a savings and loan holding company)[5]
§ 584.2–1(d)		service or activity conducted by service corporation subsidiary of subsidiary savings association, if service corporation has legal power to do so
§ 584.4(a)		acquisition or retention of more than five percent of voting stock or shares of nonsubsidiary savings association, or of nonsubsidiary savings and loan holding company, or, in the case of multiple savings and loan holding company (other than an exempted multiple savings and loan holding

§ 6.8

1. 12 C.F.R. §§ 584.2(b)(1)–(7), 584.2–1(b), 584.4(a)(1)–(7).

2. *Id.* § 584.2–2(a). *Cf.* Figure 6–3, *supra* (identifying predetermined "closely related" activities under BHCA).

3. 12 C.F.R. § 584.2–2.

4. *Id.* § 584.2–1(c).

5. *Per id.* § 574.8.

12 C.F.R.	Required Filing	Activity
		company[6]); acquisition or retention of more than five percent of voting shares of nonsubsidiary company engaged in specified business activities if the voting shares acquired or retained are held as a bona fide fiduciary or in other specified limited or temporary capacity

§ 6.9   State Law

By its own terms, the BHCA reserves to the states the right to exercise jurisdiction over bank holding companies.[1] Presumably, under this authority states laws could be *more* restrictive than the BHCA on the question of the scope of nonbanking activities of bank holding companies,[2] but it is doubtful whether a state could expand the permissible nonbanking activities of a bank holding company beyond the limits established by the BHCA. Hence, the BHCA effectively defines the outer limits of nonbanking activities of bank holding companies.

6. *Per id.* § 584.2a(a)(ii).

§ 6.9

1. 12 U.S.C.A. § 1846(a), which provides:

No provision of this chapter shall be construed as preventing any State from exercising such powers and jurisdiction which it now has or may hereafter have with respect to companies, banks, bank holding companies, and subsidiaries thereof.

See Security Nat'l Bank & Trust Co. v. First W. Va. Bancorp., Inc., 166 W.Va. 775, 277 S.E.2d 613 (1981), *appeal dismissed,* 454 U.S. 1131, 102 S.Ct. 986 (1982) (finding state authority not preempted).

2. *Cf., e.g., Commercial Nat'l Bank of Little Rock v. Board of Governors,* 451 F.2d 86 (8th Cir.1971) (finding state free to prohibit formation of bank holding companies).

Chapter 7

SECURITIES REGULATION

Table of Sections

§ 7.1 Introduction

This chapter deals with two interrelated areas of concern: (1) the regulation of depository institutions as issuers of securities, a topic usually neglected in the literature;[1] and, (2) the regulation (or restriction) of depository institutions as *participants* in the securities markets, an area still dominated by considerations of the Glass–Steagall Act.[2]

Aside from regulatory restrictions on securities activities, banks and other depository institutions are also subject to securities regulation, like

---

§ 7.1

1. *But see* 1 MICHAEL P. MALLOY, THE CORPORATE LAW OF BANKS 367–544 (1988) (providing seminal study of securities regulation of depository institutions); Michael P. Malloy, *Public Disclosure as a Tool of Federal Bank Regulation*, 9 Ann. Rev. Banking L. 229 (1990) (discussing implications of disclosure-oriented securities regulation on depository institutions); Michael P. Malloy, *The 12(i)'ed Monster: Administration of the Securities Exchange Act of 1934 by the Federal Bank Regulatory Agencies*, 19 Hofstra L. Rev. 269 (1990) (criticizing regulators).

2. On the Glass–Steagall Act restrictions on participation of depository institutions in the securities market, see *supra* § 5.24.

196

other issuers and traders in securities. However, as issuers, they are not fully subject to the Securities Act of 1933 ("1933 Act"),[3] the federal regulatory statute generally applicable to the issuance of securities.[4] In addition, until 1964, the generally applicable SEC regulations[5] governing periodic disclosure and trading in securities in the secondary market were also, as a practical matter, inapplicable to bank- and thrift-issued securities.[6] In 1964, banks and savings associations with publicly traded securities became subject to the requirements of the Securities Exchange Act of 1934 ("1934 Act"),[7] but these requirements are administered in their case *not* by the SEC, but by their respective primary federal banking regulators.[8]

Depository institutions may also be securities market professionals—enterprises that underwrite, purchase, sell, and otherwise deal in securities—subject to the limits of the Glass–Steagall Act. However, banks acting as market professionals are rarely subject to SEC supervision of their activities in that capacity.[9]

§ 7.2   Issuance of Securities

Issuance of securities in a public offering, involving the use of interstate instrumentalities, normally is subject to regulation by the SEC under the 1933 Act.[1] However, bank- and thrift-issued securities are exempt from the registration requirements of the 1933 Act.[2]

Section 3(a)(2) of the 1933 Act exempts any security issued by a "bank" from the registration requirements of the act.[3] Section 3(a)(5) exempts any security issued by a savings and loan association, building and loan association, cooperative bank, homestead association, or similar thrift institution.[4] The reason for these exemptions appears to be that Congress assumed that depository institutions would be adequately supervised by their primary federal and state regulators, making application of the 1933 Act requirements unnecessary.[5] However, on its own

---

3. 15 U.S.C.A. §§ 77a *et seq.*

4. *See* 12 U.S.C.A. § 77c(a)(2), (5) (exempting bank- and thrift-issued securities from registration requirements of Securities Act of 1933).

5. 15 C.F.R. Pt. 240.

6. *See* 2 MICHAEL P. MALLOY, BANKING LAW AND REGULATION § 6.2.1 (1994 & CUM. SUPP.) (discussing pre–1964 scope of SEC regulations).

7. 15 U.S.C.A. §§ 78a *et seq.*

8. *Id.* § 78*l*(i).

9. *See infra* §§ 7.13–7.19 (discussing regulation of securities market activities of depository institutions).

§ 7.2

1. 15 U.S.C.A. §§ 77a *et seq.*

2. 15 U.S.C.A. § 77c(a)(2), (5). *See Dougherty v. Carver Fed. Sav. Bank*, 112 F.3d 613, 617, 619 (2d Cir.1997) (discussing exemption).

3. "Bank" for these purposes means "any national bank, or any banking institution organized under the laws of any State, territory, or the District of Columbia, the business of which is substantially confined to banking and is supervised by the State or territorial banking commission or similar official." 15 U.S.C.A. § 77c(a)(2).

4. 15 U.S.C.A. § 77c(a)(5)(A). An institution must be "supervised and examined by State or Federal authority having supervision over such institution" to qualify for the exemption. *Id.*

5. *See* MICHAEL P. MALLOY, BANKING LAW AND REGULATION §§ 5.2.1–5.2.2 (1994 & CUM. SUPP.) (discussing exemption and legislative history of 1933 Act).

terms, the general antifraud provision of the 1933 Act[6] applies to *any* security, exempted or not.[7]

§ 7.3 Regulatory Parallels to the 1933 Act

The Office of the Comptroller of the Currency ("OCC") and the Office of Thrift Supervision ("OTS") administer parallel systems of securities regulation for issuance of bank- and thrift-issued securities into the public market. Taken as a whole, the parallel systems that apply to depository institutions are broader than that of the 1933 Act, and many of their elements are informed primarily by policy concerns peculiar to the depository institutions regulators: namely, maintenance of safety and soundness of the depository institutions sector, not protection of investors and stability of the securities markets.

§ 7.4 Securities Disclosure Requirements

The first element of each parallel system is in fact concerned with adequate disclosure to investors in bank- and thrift-issued securities. Each is, in most respects, virtually identical to the SEC's regulations under the 1933 Act,[1] but is also based upon the general statutory authority of each regulator to supervise the capital of institutions subject to their respective authority.[2]

These disclosure requirements can be illustrated by the regulations of the OCC. (The OTS has a corresponding set of regulations requiring material disclosure in the issuance of securities by savings associations subject to its supervision.[3]) As regulator of national banks, the Comptroller has promulgated detailed Securities Offering Disclosure Rules that require material disclosure in connection with the issuance of securities by national banks.[4] These regulations generally require that any direct or indirect offer or sale by a national bank of any security[5] issued by it be made through the use of an "offering circular" filed with and declared effective by the Comptroller.[6] Like the 1933 Act requirements applicable

---

6. 15 U.S.C.A. § 77q.

7. *See Dougherty*, 112 F.3d at 619 (stating that common stock of savings bank not exempt from antifraud provisions of 1933 and 1934 Acts).

§ 7.4

1. *Compare, e.g.*, 17 C.F.R. Pt. 230 (SEC 1933 Act regulations), *with* 12 C.F.R. Pts. 16 (OCC securities disclosure regulations); 563g (OTS securities disclosure regulations).

2. 12 U.S.C.A. §§ 57 (concerning capital of national banks); 1464 (concerning savings associations). *See, e.g.*, 42 Fed. Reg. 2200 (1977) (promulgating Comptroller regulations, *citing* 12 U.S.C.A. § 57 as statutory authority).

3. 12 C.F.R. Pt. 563g.

4. *Id.* Pt. 16.

5. The regulations define "security" to mean:

any common stock, preferred stock, or other equity security, or right to subscribe to any of the foregoing, or subordinated note or debenture. The term "security" shall not include any deposit loan, participation, letter of credit or other form of bank indebtedness incurred in the ordinary course of business.

Id. § 16.2(d).

6. *Id.* § 16.3(a)

to non-bank issuers,[7] the offering circular requirements contemplate three separate stages in the process leading to distribution of securities: (1) prior to filing the circular, offers and sales are prohibited;[8] (2) between filing and the effective date of the circular, offers to sell, but not sales, may be made through underwriters, under certain conditions;[9] and (3) after the effective date of the offering circular, offers and sales of the securities may generally be made.[10] The effective period of the offering circular is generally six months.[11]

What is notable about the OCC and OTS regulations is the degree to which they resemble, and in many respects directly incorporate, the coordinate provisions of the regulations promulgated by the SEC under the 1933 Act. Securities disclosure would appear to be "an area of unnecessary duplication of government resources."[12] In an effort to promote more consistent functional regulation of financial services generally and to streamline unnecessary regulatory controls, the Task Group on Regulation of Financial Services made the recommendation that "[t]he registration requirements of the [1933 Act] should be made applicable to publicly offered securities of banks and thrifts (but not deposit instruments)."[13] However, the Task Group would have allowed the Federal Home Loan Bank Board ("FHLBB"), the predecessor to the OTS, to continue to exercise securities jurisdiction over the conversion of savings associations banks from the mutual to the stock form of organization.[14]

In addition, the Task Group would have left such jurisdiction with the FHLBB with respect to "other matters involving the safety and soundness of [Federal Savings and Loan Insurance Corporation ("FSLIC")] insured thrift institutions [*i.e.*, savings associations] or affecting the operations of the [FSLIC]."[15] The Task Group offered no cogent reason why it would split off securities jurisdiction for conversions. As to the retention of this jurisdiction by the FHLBB with respect to safety and soundness matters and FSLIC operations, the Task Group argued:

> The issuance of securities by thrift institutions sometimes differs from securities offerings by other financial institutions because

---

7. *See* 15 U.S.C.A. § 77e (setting forth 1933 Act registration requirements).

8. *Compare* 12 C.F.R. § 16.3(a)-(b), *with* 15 U.S.C.A. § 77e(a), (c).

9. *Compare* 12 C.F.R. § 16.3(b), *with* 15 U.S.C.A. § 77e(b)(1), (c). The conditions are: (1) prior authorization must be obtained from the Comptroller, 12 C.F.R. § 16.3(b)(1), and an appropriate "preliminary offering circular" must be used, *id.* § 16(b); (2) prior to consummation of the actual sale, a copy of the offering circular as finally effective, must be furnished to each purchaser, *id.* § 16.3(b)(2).

10. *Compare* 12 C.F.R. § 16.3(a), (e), *with* 15 U.S.C.A. § 77e.

11. 12 C.F.R. § 16.3(e).

12. REPORT OF THE TASK GROUP ON REGULATION OF FINANCIAL SERVICES 93 (1984) ("TASK GROUP REPORT").

13. TASK GROUP REPORT at 91. In light of the Supreme Court's holding in *Marine Bank v. Weaver*, 455 U.S. 551, 102 S.Ct. 1220 (1982), that a bank-issued certificate of deposit was not a "security" for purposes of the 1934 Act, 15 U.S.C.A. §§ 78a *et seq.*, it seems doubtful whether the parenthetical limitation in the quoted text is necessary.

14. TASK GROUP REPORT at 91.

15. *Id.*

of the unique mortgage-related nature of many types of thrift securities. For example, thrifts issue a variety of securities that represent interests in pools of mortgages, or that are collateralized by mortgages. Thrifts also have developed other debt and equity financing techniques that use mortgage-related securities that have been obtained in exchange for mortgages in their portfolio.

> While other types of firms issue mortgage-backed securities that are registered with the SEC under the 1933 Act, such issuances by thrifts are unique because the mortgages backing such securities issued by thrifts may directly affect the assets available to the FSLIC in the event of insolvency or have other direct impacts on safety and soundness. Therefore, the FHLBB should have authority to limit securities offerings by thrift institutions that would adversely affect thrift safety and soundness or the FSLIC [insurance] fund.[16]

This distinction between savings associations and other issuers is unconvincing. Realignment of securities disclosure regulation under the administration of the SEC does not have any impact upon regulatory considerations such as safety and soundness and the integrity of the FSLIC's deposit insurance fund. Since securities regulation is disclosure-oriented, not primarily substantive, it is a weak argument to assert that the FHLBB needs to retain disclosure regulation authority in order to "to limit [certain] securities offerings by thrift institutions." Such direct authority does not exist under the federal securities laws; it remains with the regulator of the substantive activities of the depository institution in question.[17]

§ 7.5 Minimum Capital Requirements

The second element in the parallel system of securities regulation that applies to the issuance of securities by depository institutions is concerned with minimum capital requirements for entry into the depository institutions industry. Minimum capital requirements relate to safety and soundness of *de novo* depository institutions. NBA minimum capital requirements are calculated in relation to the size of the community in which a proposed national bank is to be located.[1] However, these requirements top out at $200,000 in capital for the largest metropolitan area, and are simply archaic. The Comptroller routinely requires much more in minimum capital, generally not less than $1 million.

The NBA also requires that a national bank have a paid-in surplus equal to 20 percent of capital before it will be authorized to commence business.[2] The requirement may be waived for state banks converting to

---

16. *Id.* at 93.

17. *See, e.g.,* 12 U.S.C.A. §§ 57, 1464 (providing general supervisory authority over capital of national banks and savings associations); *id.* §§ 1818(b)(1), 3907(b) (providing enforcement authority with re-

spect to capital of insured depository institutions).

§ 7.5

1. 12 U.S.C.A. § 51.

2. *Id.*

a national charter.[3] Since this amounts to no more than $40,000 for a bank proposed for the largest metropolitan areas, it is obviously a negligible requirement.

The Fed also imposes minimum capital requirements for Fed membership.[4] To be eligible for membership, state-chartered banks must possess capital and surplus adequate for their assets and deposit liabilities and other obligations.[5]

For state-chartered banks to be eligible for deposit insurance, adequacy of capital is also a requirement.[6]

§ 7.6   Regulation of Capital Formation

The third element in the parallel system of securities regulation that applies to the issuance of securities by depository institutions regulates the process of capital formation itself. Capital formation by a depository institution is subject to prior approval by its chartering agency—on the merits of the securities offering planned by the institution—quite apart from any applicable public disclosure requirements imposed in connection with the issuance of securities. The practice of the agencies varies. In the case of national banks, for example, the NBA permits the issuance of common stock,[1] and, since 1933, preferred stock,[2] with the approval of the Comptroller.

What is the relationship between securities disclosure requirements and capital formation requirements? Capital formation requires merit review of the proposed issuance on the merits. And yet the two federal chartering agencies require in their respective offering circular rules that the circular include a boldface disclaimer to the effect that:

THESE SHARES HAVE NOT BEEN APPROVED OR DISAPPROVED BY THE OFFICE OF THRIFT SUPERVISION NOR HAS SUCH OFFICE PASSED UPON THE ACCURACY OR ADEQUACY OF THIS OFFERING CIRCULAR. ANY REPRESENTATION TO THE CONTRARY IS UNLAWFUL.[3]

If the issuance has been approved by the agency under capital formation rules, how can it require this kind of disclaimer under its securities disclosure rules? Essentially, *Dougherty v. Carver Federal Savings Bank*[4] has taken the position that there is no relationship between the securities disclosure and merit review (capital formation) aspects of securities regulation applicable to depository institutions. While this position may underplay the significance of merit review, it

---

3. *Id.*

4. *See Continental Bank & Trust Co. of Salt Lake City v. Woodall*, 239 F.2d 707 (10th Cir.1957), *cert. denied*, 353 U.S. 909, 77 S.Ct. 663 (1957) (upholding Fed membership requirements).

5. 12 C.F.R. Pt. 208.

6. 12 U.S.C.A. § 1816.

§ 7.6

1. 12 U.S.C.A. § 51.

2. *Id.* § 51a.

3. 12 C.F.R. § 563b.102 Item 3 (1994) (OTS rules). *See also* 12 C.F.R. § 16.7(c), Item 1(d) (OCC rules).

4. 112 F.3d 613 (2d Cir.1997).

does have the result of leaving it open to investors to proceed to appropriate remedies for, *e.g.*, securities fraud, notwithstanding the merit review process.[5]

§ 7.7 Securities Exchange Act of 1934

Until 1964, the Securities Exchange Act did not cover over-the-counter securities (*i.e.*, securities not listed on a national securities exchange)[1] except for the antifraud provisions of Section 10(b),[2] which covers all securities, whether listed or not.[3] As a matter of fact, most, if not all, bank-issued securities fell into this over-the-counter category, and hence they were not generally subject to the 1934 Act.

Based on a special study performed by the SEC,[4] Congress decided to bring over-the-counter securities—and specifically, bank-issued securities—under the 1934 Act.[5] The bank regulators resisted this change in the law.[6] Their efforts were unsuccessful, but the bank regulators did extract one significant concession: they were granted administrative authority over the 1934 Act provisions that applied to depository institutions, with one important exception. With respect to securities issued by banks and savings associations, the registration,[7] reporting,[8] proxy,[9] tender offer[10] and insider reporting provisions[11] of the 1934 Act are administered by the depository institutions regulatory agencies, not by the SEC.[12] Section 12(i) of the 1934 Act,[13] added in 1964, contains a statutory mandate that, within 60 days of any amendments to pertinent SEC rules, these regulatory agencies issue regulations substantially similar to those issued by the SEC, unless such regulations would not be

---

5. *Id.*

§ 7.7

1. *See, e.g.,* 15 U.S.C.A. § 78*l*(a) (1960) (applying registration requirements of 1934 Act to securities listed on national securities exchange).

2. 15 U.S.C.A. § 78j(b).

3. *See, e.g., id.* § 78j(b) (authorizing SEC to promulgate rules with respect to securities fraud). *See also* 17 C.F.R. § 240.10b–5 (establishing generally applicable antifraud prohibition). *See generally Dougherty v. Carver Fed. Sav. Bank,* 112 F.3d 613, 619 (2d Cir.1997) (stating that common stock of savings bank not exempt from antifraud provisions of 1933 and 1934 Acts).

4. *Report of the Special Study of the Securities Markets of the Securities and Exchange Commission,* H.R. Doc. No., 95, 88th Cong., 1st Sess. (1963).

5. *See* 15 U.S.C.A. § 78*l*(g) (subjecting publicly traded securities to registration requirements of 1934 Act).

6. *See, e.g., Letter from the Federal Reserve Board to the Chairman, House Interstate and Foreign Commerce Committee,* June 21, 1963, *reprinted in* H.R. Rep. No. 1418, 88th Cong., 1st Sess. (1963). *See also Reports on Bank Securities Activities of the Securities and Exchange Commission,* 95th Cong., 1st Sess. 307–8 (1977).

7. 15 U.S.C.A. § 78*l*.

8. *Id.* § 78m.

9. *Id.* § 78n.

10. *Id.* § 78n(d), (f).

11. *Id.* § 78p.

12. *Id.* § 78*l*(i). *See* Michael P. Malloy, *The 12(i)'ed Monster: Administration of the Securities Exchange Act of 1934 by the Federal Bank Regulatory Agencies,* 19 Hofstra L. Rev. 269 (1991) (discussing § 78*l*(i) and its implementation by depository institution regulators).

13. 15 U.S.C.A. § 78*l*(i).

"necessary or appropriate in the public interest or for the protection of investors."[14]

Despite this statutory mandate, by the end of the 1980s, the regulatory agencies were generally at least one year, and often as much as seven years, behind in adopting appropriate analogs to SEC amendments,[15] with one longstanding exception: the FHLBB (and, since 1989, its successor, the OTS), whose 1934 Act regulations simply incorporate by reference the SEC regulations.[16] Hence, neither the FHLBB nor the OTS has never had occasion to amend this section. In 1988, the Fed followed the FHLBB's lead, and converted to an incorporation-by-reference approach as well.[17] The Fed was later joined by the OCC,[18] and, in February 1997, by the FDIC.[19]

If the federal bank and saving association regulators are simply incorporating 1934 Act rules into their own regulations, one might reasonably ask what the point is in delegating authority to them under Section 12(i). The SEC administers the 1934 Act with respect to bank and savings and loan holding companies,[20] and it could do the same directly with respect to banks and savings associations. In any event, with respect to antifraud violations involving securities issued by banks and savings associations, only the SEC has the authority to bring action for violations of Section 10(b) of the 1934 Act.[21]

§ 7.8　Capital Adequacy

A fourth element in the parallel system of securities regulation that applies to the issuance of securities by depository institutions represents the most recent development in this regard. It concerns the supervision of capital adequacy of existing institutions (usually measured in a ratio to the assets of the institutions). Recently, the regulators have increased their attention to capital adequacy of depository institutions. If inadequate capital maintenance constitutes an "unsafe and unsound practice,"[1] the bank regulators have broad statutory authority progressively to define and remedy capital inadequacy.[2] This authority was questioned

---

14. *Id.*

15. *See* Malloy, *The 12(i)'ed Monster, supra* (reviewing performance of regulatory agencies under § 12(i)).

16. 12 C.F.R. § 563d.1.

17. *See id.* § 208.16.

18. *See id.* Pt. 11 (incorporating SEC 1934 Act rules into OCC rules).

19. *See* 62 Fed. Reg. 6852 (1997) (*codified at* 12 C.F.R. Pt. 335) (incorporating 1934 Act rules into FDIC rules).

20. *See* 15 U.S.C.A. § 78*l*(i) (limiting delegation to regulatory agencies to securities of banks and savings associations, not holding companies thereof).

21. *See* 15 U.S.C.A. §§ 78j(b), 78*l*(i) (providing no delegated authority to regula-

tory agencies with respect to antifraud violations). *Cf. Peoples Bank of Danville v. Williams,* 449 F.Supp. 254 (W.D.Va.1978) (discussing antifraud provision). *But cf.* 12 U.S.C.A. § 1818(b)(1) (providing administrative enforcement authority to regulatory agencies for "violations of law").

§ 7.8

1. *See* 12 U.S.C.A. §§ 1818(b)(1), 3907(b) (providing enforcement authority with respect to "unsafe and unsound" practices).

2. 12 U.S.C.A. §§ 1818(b)(1), 3907(b). *Cf., e.g., Groos Nat'l Bank v. Comptroller of the Currency,* 573 F.2d 889 (5th Cir.1978); *First Nat'l Bank of Eden v. Department of the Treasury,* 568 F.2d 610 (8th Cir.1978).

in *First National Bank of Bellaire v. Comptroller of the Currency*,[3] but the authority was confirmed by congressional action.[4]

The International Lending Supervision Act ("ILSA"),[5] enacted in 1983, requires each agency to "cause banking institutions to achieve and maintain adequate capital by establishing minimum levels of capital for such banking institutions."[6] What constitutes "adequate capital" remains a question within the discretion of the agencies, and ILSA explicitly gives them authority to establish capital adequacy levels as they deem "necessary or appropriate in light of the particular circumstances of the banking institution."[7]

In a legislative reversal of *Bellaire*, ILSA also provides that the failure of a bank to maintain prescribed capital adequacy levels may be deemed to constitute an unsafe and unsound practice.[8] Failure to maintain capital adequacy may also lead to the issuance of a directive requiring the bank to submit and comply with a capital plan to reform capital levels.[9] Pursuant to their statutory authority, the federal bank regulators have developed specific capital adequacy policies.

The regulators have progressively focused their attention on refining their capital adequacy policies to take into account, in an explicit way, the relative degrees of risk among the various elements composing the assets of depository institutions, and to define more precisely the elements of "capital." This effort has become more particularly directed at the establishment of convergent capital adequacy regimes among the United States and it major trading partners.

The regulators had freely admitted that their pre–1992 rules did not adequately or efficiently realize the capital adequacy goals of ILSA.[10] The new approach attempts to quantify and account for, *within* the capital ratio, financial factors that significantly affect capital adequacy, but that are not necessarily apparent from the face of the balance sheet.[11]

Guidelines for international convergence of capital measurement and capital standards developed by the Basle Committee on Banking

Similar authority exists in the bank holding company context. *See Board of Governors v. First Lincolnwood Corp.*, 439 U.S. 234, 99 S.Ct. 505 (1978).

3. 697 F.2d 674 (5th Cir.1983)

4. Pub. L. No. 98–181, tit. IX, § 908, 97 Stat. 1280 (1983) (codified at 12 U.S.C.A. § 3907).

5. 12 U.S.C.A. §§ 3901 *et seq.*

6. *Id.* § 3907(a)(1).

7. *Id.* § 3907(a)(2).

8. *Id.* § 3907(b)(1).

9. *See id.* § 3907(b)(2). Such directives and plans submitted pursuant to such directives are enforceable to the same extent as an effective and outstanding final cease and desist order under Section 8(b) of the Federal Deposit Insurance Act, *id.* § 1818(b). *See id.* § 3907(b) (2)(B)(ii).

10. For example, in issuing its 1985 capital adequacy regulations, the OCC acknowledged that the minimum capital ratio rules did not rigorously account either for differences in a given bank's balance sheet composition or for the presence of off-balance-sheet activities. *See* 50 Fed. Reg. 10,207, 10,214 (1985) (so stating). The OCC therefore announced its intention to give further consideration to alternatives for incorporating risk-related criteria into its capital adequacy rules. *Id.*

11. *See generally* 2 MICHAEL P. MALLOY, BANKING LAW AND REGULATION 5.99–5.112 (1994 & CUM. SUPP.) (discussing capital adequacy guidelines).

Regulations and Supervisory Practices[12] set forth "the details of the agreed framework for measuring capital adequacy and the minimum standard to be achieved that the national supervisory authorities represented on the Committee intend to implement in their respective countries."[13] The basic focus of this multilateral framework is "assessing capital in relation to credit risk (the risk of counterparty failure)."[14] However, the framework acknowledges that "other risks, notably interest rate risk and the investment risk on securities, need to be taken into account by supervisors in assessing overall capital adequacy."[15]

The multilateral framework consists of a minimum required ratio of certain specified constituents of capital to risk-weighted assets. "Capital" has two types of constituents: (1) "core capital;"[16] and (2) "supplementary capital."[17] Core capital, the so-called Tier 1 of capital elements, consists of: (a) equity capital;[18] and (b) disclosed reserves from post-tax earnings.[19]

Tier 1 capital elements are the only ones common to the banking systems of all the countries represented on the Committee.[20] Nevertheless, a number of other significant elements of capital are often recognized. The framework therefore identified two tiers of capital elements. The Tier 1 elements must account for at least 50 percent of a bank's capital base for purposes of the risk-weighted ratio.[21] Constituents of supplementary capital, the so-called Tier 2 of capital elements, may be included for these purposes, up to an amount equal to the amount of

---

12. *See* FINAL REPORT FOR INTERNATIONAL CONVERGENCE OF CAPITAL MEASUREMENT AND CAPITAL STANDARDS, *reprinted in* 1 Fed. Banking L. Rep. (CCH) ¶ 5403 (July 29, 1988) ("FINAL REPORT").

13. FINAL REPORT at 3309.

14. *Id.*

15. *Id.* The agencies have since released guidance with respect to interest rate risk. 61 Fed. Reg. 33,166 (1996) (OCC, FRS, and FDIC joint policy statement providing guidance on sound practices for managing interest rate risk). *See also* 62 Fed. Reg. 68,064 (1997) (codified at 12 C.F.R. Pts. 3, 208, 225, 325) (amending market risk provisions in risk-based capital standards); 63 Fed. Reg. 30,369 (1998) (codified at 12 C.F.R. pt. 225) (amending Tier 1 leverage ratio for bank holding companies; incorporating market risk capital rule into leverage standard). *See generally* FDIC, *Differences in Capital and Accounting Standards Among the Federal Banking and Thrift Agencies*, *reprinted in*, 63 Fed. Reg. 20,633 (1998) (discussing treatment of capital adequacy by federal agencies).

16. *See* FINAL REPORT at 3309. (discussing "core capital"). *See generally id.* at 3316, Annex 1 (defining capital included in the capital base after transitional period).

17. *See id.* at 3310–3311 (discussion of "supplementary capital").

18. The term "equity capital" is defined for these purposes as "[i]ssued and fully paid ordinary shares/common stock and non-cumulative perpetual preferred stock (but excluding cumulative preferred stock)." *Id.* at 3310 n.2. *See also id.* at 3316, Annex 1, § D(i) (definition of "Tier 1" capital elements). In the case of consolidated accounts, Tier 1 capital would also include the minority interests in the equity of subsidiaries of the bank which are less than wholly owned. *Id.*

19. *Id.* at 3310. For these purposes, disclosed reserves are those "created or increased by appropriations of retained earnings or other surplus, *e.g.* share premiums, retained profit, general reserves and legal reserves." *Id.* (footnote omitted). "Retained profit" may include (in the discretion of the national supervisory authorities) allocations to or from reserve, during the course of the year, from current year retain profit. *Id.* n.2. Tier 1 does not include revaluation reserves. *Id.*

20. *Id.* at 3310.

21. *See id.*

Tier 1 capital elements.[22] Supplementary capital consists of: (1) undisclosed reserves;[23] (2) revaluation reserves;[24] (3) general provisions or loan loss reserves;[25] (4) certain hybrid debt capital instruments;[26] and (5) subordinated term debt.[27]

22. *Id.*

23. *Id.* (discussion of undisclosed reserves). *See also id.* at 3316, Annex 1, § D(ii)(a) (defining capital included in capital base). Inclusion of undisclosed reserves in the capital base is contemplated by the framework only to the extent permitted by local legal and accounting regimes. *Id.* at 3310. In any event, undisclosed reserves are included in supplementary capital only to the extent they "have been passed through the profit and loss account and [have been] accepted by [a] bank's supervisory authorities." *Id.*

24. *Id.* at 3310–3311 (discussion of revaluation reserves). *See also id.* at 3316, Annex 1, § D(ii)(b) (defining capital included in capital base). Inclusion of revaluation reserves in the capital base is contemplated by the framework only to the extent permitted by local regulatory and accounting rules. Revaluation reserves, whether arising from a formal revaluation or from a "latent revaluation" (a notional additional to capital of hidden values with respect to securities carried at historic cost), may be included in the capital base only if "the assets are considered by the supervisory authority to be prudently valued, fully reflecting the possibility of price fluctuations and forced sale." *Id.* at 3310–3311. In addition, latent revaluation reserves are subject to a substantial discount reflecting, for example, market volatility and any tax effect of realization of the gain. *Id.* at 3311. The framework indicates that a 55 percent discount on the difference between historical cost book value and current market value has been agreed to be appropriate in this regard. *See id.*

25. *Id.* at 3311 (discussing general provisions/general loan loss reserves). *See also id.* at 3316, Annex 1, § D(ii)(c) (defining capital included in the capital base). Reserves against identified losses or with respect to "demonstrable deterioration in the value of particular assets" are not included in this category. *Id.* at 3311. What constitutes a "general" reserve or provision for these purposes is, of course, not always easy to determine. The framework indicates that during the transitional period under the framework, it intends to attempt "to clarify the distinction made in member countries between those elements which should conceptually be regarded as part of capital and those which should not qualify." *Id. See*

also id. at 3315, 3320 (discussing transitional arrangements). However, in the event that an agreed clarification cannot be achieved, in situations where nominally "general" reserves or provisions might include amounts reflecting lower valuations for assets or latent but unidentified losses, the amount qualifying as supplementary capital would be phased down by the end of the transition to constitute no more than 1.25 percent (or up to 2 percent during exceptional and temporary periods) of supplementary capital. *Id.* at 3311.

26. *Id.* at 3311 (discussing "hybrid debt capital instruments"). *See also id.* at 3316–3317, Annex 1, § D(ii)(d) (defining capital included in capital base). Generally, this category includes elements that "combine certain characteristics of equity and certain characteristics of debt." *Id.* at 3311. Characteristics vary from country to country, but to be included the instruments should exhibit the following specifications:

* they are *unsecured, subordinated and fully paid-up*;

* they are *not redeemable* at the initiative of the holder or without prior consent of the supervisory authority;

* they are *available to participate in losses* without the bank being obliged to cease trading (unlike conventional subordinated debt); [and]

* although the capital instrument may carry an obligation to pay interest that cannot permanently be reduced or waived (unlike dividends on ordinary share holders' equity), *it should allow service obligations to be deferred* (as with cumulative preference shares) where the profitability of the bank would not support payment.

Id. at 3316–3317 (emphasis in original). Such instruments as mandatory convertible debt instruments (in U.S. practice), perpetual debt and preference shares (in U.K. practice), long-term preferred shares (in Canadian practice), *titres participatifs* and *titres subordonnes a duree indeterminee* (in French practice), or *Genussscheine* (in German practice) would qualify for inclusion in this category of Tier 2 capital. *See id.* at 3311.

27. *Id.* at 3311 (discussing subordinated term debt). *See also id.* at 3317, Annex 1,

The eligible constituents of Tier 1 and Tier 2 capital are subject to certain deductions under the framework.[28] The amount of goodwill must be deducted from the figure for Tier 1 capital.[29] The amount of investments in unconsolidated banking and financial subsidiaries, if any,[30] must be deducted from the total capital base.[31] The Committee considered, but ultimately rejected, requiring deduction of banks' holdings of capital issued by other banks or depository institutions.[32] Nevertheless, the framework does reflect the agreement that individual supervisory authorities retain the discretion to require such deductions.[33] If no deduction is applied, then the full value of such holdings must be included in assessing capital adequacy of the holding bank.[34]

The framework endorses a risk-weighted approach to the assets denominator of the capital-assets ratio utilized in assessing capital adequacy.[35] The framework establishes a relatively simplified methodology for risk-weighting, with only five basic risk weights being employed.[36] The basic methodology effectively captures only credit risk.[37] It is left to the discretion of individual supervisory authorities to decide whether to attempt to account for more methodologically difficult types of risk, such as investment risk, interest rate risk, exchange rate risk, or concentration risk.[38] Furthermore, the individual supervisory authorities also retain discretion to supplement the framework's risk-weighted methodology with "other methods of capital measurement,"[39] such as capital-assets ratios. Furthermore, to account for country transfer risk, the Committee ultimately adopted an approach that applied differing risk

§ D(ii)(e) (defining capital included in the capital base). This category includes "conventional unsecured subordinated debt capital instruments with a minimum original fixed term to maturity of over five years and limited life redeemable preference shares." *Id.* at 3317. Such instruments are not normally available to cover the losses of an issuing bank that continues trading; they are viewed as having "significant deficiencies as constituents of capital in view of their fixed maturity and inability to absorb losses except in liquidation." *Id.* at 3311. Hence, these instruments may be included only up to an amount equal to 50 percent of the total amount of core capital, and they are subject to a cumulative discount or amortization of twenty percent per year during the last five years of maturity "to reflect the diminishing value of these instruments as a continuing source of strength." *Id.* at 3317.

28. *See id.* at 3311–3312.

29. *Id.* at 3311.

30. The framework generally assumes as the normal practice that subsidiaries will be consolidated for the purpose of assessing capital adequacy. *See id.* However, "[w]here this is not done, deduction is essential to prevent multiple use of the same capital resources in different parts of [a banking] group." *Id.*

31. *Id.* at 3311–3312.

32. *See id.* at 3312.

33. *Id.* Conceivably, these discretionary policies may require deduction of the amount of all such holdings, holdings to the extent that they exceed some determined limit in relation to the holding bank's or the issuing bank's capital, or on a case-by-case basis. *Id.* The framework also reflects the agreement that, "in applying these policies, member countries [should] consider that reciprocal cross-holdings of bank capital designed artificially to inflate the capital position of the banks concerned should not be permitted." *Id.*

34. *Id.* at 3312.

35. *See id.*

36. *See id.* at 3317, Annex 2 (risk weights by category of on-balance-sheet asset).

37. *Id.* at 3312.

38. *Id.*

39. *Id.*

weights to defined groups of countries.[40]

The framework also recognizes the importance of bringing off-balance-sheet risk into the analysis of capital adequacy (*e.g.*, contingent letter of credit exposure).[41] Off-balance-sheet risk is brought within the framework by conversion into appropriate credit risk equivalents.[42]

Some uncertainty remained about the appropriate approach to interest rate and exchange rate related items, such as swaps, options, and futures.[43] As to these contingencies, the framework takes the position that special treatment is necessary, "because banks are not exposed to credit risk for the full face value of their contracts, but only to the cost of replacing the cash flow if the counterparty defaults."[44]

Once the credit equivalent amounts of such contingencies have been calculated, the amounts are to be weighted in accordance with the risk weights applicable to the category of counterparties involved. However, in anticipation of the fact that most counterparties in the market for such contingencies, particularly long-term contracts, "tend to be first-class names,"[45] the FINAL REPORT reflects general agreement that such contingencies will be assigned a 50 percent risk weight, rather than the 100 percent risk weight that might otherwise be applicable.[46]

The final element in the risk-weighted methodology, as with any capital-assets ratio requirement, is the required minimum level of the

---

40. *Id.* at 3313:

[T]he Committee has concluded that a defined group of countries should be adopted as the basis for applying differential weighting coefficients[.] The framework also recognizes the importance of and that this group should be full members of the OECD [Organization for Economic Cooperation and Development] or countries which have concluded special arrangements with the [International Monetary Fund] associated with the Fund's General Arrangements to Borrow....

... This decision has the following consequences for the weighting structure. Claims on central governments within the OECD will attract a zero weight (or a low weight if the national supervisory authority elects to incorporate interest rate risk); and claims on OECD non-central government public-sector entities will attract a low weight.... Claims on central governments and central banks outside the OECD will also attract a zero weight (or a low weight if the national supervisory authority elects to incorporate investment risk), provided such claims are denominated in the national currency and funded by liabilities in the same currency....

... As regards the treatment of interbank claims, in order to preserve the efficiency and liquidity of the international interbank market[,] there will be no differentiation between short-term claims on banks incorporated within or outside the OECD. However, the Committee draws a distinction between ... short-term placements with other banks ... and ... longer-term cross-border loans to banks which are often associated with particular transactions and carry greater transfer and/or credit risks. A 20 per cent [*sic*] weight will therefore be applied to claims on all banks, wherever incorporated, with a residual maturity of up to an[d] including one year; longer-term claims on OECD incorporated banks will be weighted at 20 per cent [*sic*]; and longer-term claims on banks incorporated outside the OECD will be weighted at 100 percent.

41. *See id.* at 3314 (discussing treatment of off-balance-sheet obligations).

42. *See id.* at 3317–3319, Annex 3 (establishing credit conversion factors for off-balance-sheet items).

43. *See id.* at 3314.

44. *Id.*

45. *Id.* at 3319.

46. *Id.* However, some member countries have apparently reserved the right to apply the full 100 percent risk weight. *See id.* n. 9.

ratio. The framework adopted a target standard ratio of eight percent, of which core capital must constitute at least four percent.[47] This target ratio was fully applicable by year-end 1992.[48]

In brief, the risk-weighted methodology is applied as follows:

(1) Identification of Tier 1 capital elements must be made, with the amount of goodwill deducted from the gross amount of Tier 1 capital.

(2) Tier 2 capital elements must be identified. The total of Tier 2 capital may be included for ratio purposes only up to an amount equal to the amount of Tier 1 capital. Furthermore, among the Tier 2 capital elements, subordinated term debt is limited to a maximum of 50 percent of the amount of Tier 1 elements, and certain amounts for general provisions or general loan loss reserves are generally limited to an amount equal to 1.25 percent of risk-weighted assets.

(3) From the total capital base (Tier 1 plus eligible Tier 2), there must be deducted any investments in unconsolidated banking and finance subsidiaries of the banking enterprise under consideration. Furthermore, in the discretion of the individual supervisory authorities, investments in the capital of other banks and depository institutions may also be required to be deducted from the total capital base.

The result of these first three steps yields the numerator of the risk-weighted ratio.

(4) The on-balance-sheet assets must be weighted according to the general categories of risk set forth in Annex 2 of the FINAL REPORT. (Figure 7–1, *infra*, illustrates the risk weights by asset category.)

Figure 7–1

Risk Weights by Category of On–Balance–Sheet Asset

Risk Weight	*Category of Assets*
0%	Cash[49]
	Claims on central governments and central banks denominated in national currency and funded in that currency
	Other claims on OECD[50] central governments[51] and central banks

---

47. *Id.* at 3314.

48. *Id.* at 3314–3315.

49. Includes (at national discretion) gold bullion held in own vaults or on an allocated basis to the extent backed by bullion liabilities.

50. The OECD comprises countries which are full members of the OECD or which have concluded special lending ar-

rangements with the International Monetary Fund ("IMF") associated with the IMF General Arrangements to Borrow.

51. Some member countries intend to apply weights to securities issued by OECD central governments to take account of investment risk. These weights would, for example, be ten percent for all securities or ten percent for those maturing in up to one

Risk Weight	Category of Assets
0, 10, 20, or 50%[53]	Claims collateralized by cash or OECD central-government securities or guaranteed by OECD central governments[52]
	Claims on domestic public-sector entities, excluding central government, and loans guaranteed by such entities
20%	Claims on multilateral development banks[54] and claims guaranteed by or collateralized by securities issued by such banks
	Claims on banks incorporated in the OECD and loans guaranteed by OECD incorporated banks
	Claims on banks incorporated in countries outside the OECD with a residual maturity of up to one year and loans with a residual maturity of up to one year guaranteed by banks incorporated in countries outside the OECD
	Claims on non-domestic OECD public-sector entities, excluding central government, and loans guaranteed by such entities
	Cash items in process of collection
50%	Loans fully secured by mortgage on residential property that is or will be occupied by the borrower or that is rented
100%	Claims on the private sector
	Claims on banks incorporated outside the OECD with a residual maturity of over one year
	Claims on central governments outside the OECD (unless denominated in national currency—and funded in that currency—see above)
	Claims on commercial companies owned by the public sector
	Premises, plant, and equipment and other fixed assets
	Real estate and other investments (including non-consolidated investment participations in other companies)
	Capital instruments issued by other banks (unless deducted from capital)

year and twenty percent for those maturing in over one year.

52. Commercial loans partially guaranteed by these bodies will attract equivalent low weights on that part of the loan that is fully covered. Similarly, loans partially collateralized by cash or securities issued by OECD central governments and multilateral development banks will attract low weights on that part of the loan which is fully covered.

53. In the discretion of individual supervisory authorities.

54. *I.e.*, International Bank for Reconstruction and Development; Inter–American Development Bank; Asian Development Bank; African Development Bank; European Investment Bank. Claims on other multilateral development banks of which G–10 countries are shareholding members may, at national discretion, also attract a twenty percent weight.

Risk Weight	Category of Assets
	All other assets

(5) Off-balance-sheet items must be converted to their credit equivalents. (Figure 7–2, *infra*, illustrates the credit conversion factors.) The credit equivalent amounts are then risk-weighted in accordance with the generally applicable rules governing risk weighting.

Figure 7–2
Credit Conversion Factors for Off–Balance–Sheet Items

Factor	Type of Instrument[55]
100%	Direct credit substitutes, *e.g.*, general guarantees of indebtedness (including standby letters of credit serving as financial guarantees for loans and securities) and acceptances (including endorsements with the character of acceptances)
50%	Certain transaction-related contingent items (*e.g.*, performance bonds, bid bonds, warranties, and standby letters of credit related to particular transactions)
20%	Short-term self-liquidating trade-related contingencies (such as documentary credits collateralized by the underlying shipments)
100%	Sale and repurchase agreements and asset sales with recourse,[56] where the credit risk remains with the bank
100%	Forward asset purchases, forward deposits, and partly-paid shares and securities, that represent commitments with certain drawdown
50%	Note issuance facilities and revolving underwriting facilities
50%	Other commitments (*e.g.*, formal standby facilities and credit lines) with an original[57] maturity of over one year
0%	Similar commitments with an original maturity of up to one year, or that can be unconditionally canceled at any time

55. "Member countries will have some limited discretion to allocate particular instruments into [the above] items ... according to the characteristics of the instrument in the national market." FINAL REPORT, Annex 3.

56. These items are to be weighted according to the type of asset and not according to the type of counterparty with whom the transaction has been entered into. Reverse repos (*i.e.*, purchase and resale agreements—where the bank is the receiver of the asset) are to be treated as collateralized loans, reflecting the economic reality of the transaction. The risk is therefore to be measured as an exposure to the counterparty. Where the asset temporarily acquired is a security that attracts a preferential risk weighting, this would be recognized as collateral and the risk weighting would be reduced accordingly.

57. *But see* FINAL REPORT at 3319 n.5.

(6) The denominator of the risk-weighted ratio, total risk-weighted assets, is derived by adding the risk-weighted on-balance-sheet amounts to the risk-weighted credit equivalents of the off-balance-sheet items. The ratios of Tier 1 capital to total risk-weighted assets and of total capital (Tier 1 plus eligible Tier 2 amounts) to total risk-weighted assets are then calculated and assessed in relation to the required minimum ratios under the framework.

§ 7.9   Capital Supervision as a Central Focus of Federal Bank Regulatory Policy under the FDICIA

"Capital supervision," the use of capital adequacy ratios for supervisory purposes, has become a central focus of current federal bank regulatory policy. This is mainly the result of three developments: (1) the emergence of the international capital adequacy guidelines; (2) the issuance in February 1991 of a study by the Department of the Treasury that advanced certain recommendations to strengthen capital supervision of banks;[1] and, (3) the enactment of the Federal Deposit Insurance Corporation Improvement Act of 1991 ("FDICIA") in December 1991.[2]

FDICIA includes a series of provisions intended to improve supervision of insured depository institutions, with a significant emphasis on capital supervision as a primary tool. For example, it adopted a general rule requiring annual on-site examinations of all insured depository institutions,[3] effective one year after enactment (December 19, 1991). However, well-capitalized and well-managed institutions, with total assets of less than $100 million and with no recent change in control, are exempt from this rule. They are to be examined only every 18 months.[4]

The FDICIA generally requires "prompt corrective action"[5] intended to "resolve the problems of insured depository institutions at the least possible long-term loss to the deposit insurance fund,"[6] including the imposition of capital requirements.[7]

§ 7.9

1. *See* U.S. DEPARTMENT OF THE TREASURY, MODERNIZING THE FINANCIAL SYSTEM: U.S. TREASURY DEPARTMENT RECOMMENDATIONS FOR SAFER, MORE COMPETITIVE BANKS (FEBRUARY 1991), *reprinted in* Fed. Banking L. Rep. (CCH) No. 1377, Part II (Feb. 14, 1991) ("MODERNIZATION STUDY").

2. Pub. L. No. 102–242, 105 Stat. 2236 (Dec. 9, 1991) (codified at scattered sections of 12 U.S.C.A.).

3. FDICIA, § 111(a) (codified at 12 U.S.C.A. § 1820(d) (1)-(3)).

4. FDICIA, §§ 111(a) (codified at 12 U.S.C.A. § 1820(d) (4)). *But see* FDICIA, § 111(c) (transition rule).

5. FDICIA, § 131 (codified at 12 U.S.C.A. § 1831o(a) (2)).

6. *Id.* (codified at 12 U.S.C.A. § 1831o(a)(1)).

7. *Id.* (codified at 12 U.S.C.A. § 1831o(c)-(f), (h)-(i), (k), (n)). These rules do not apply to depository institutions in conservatorship, or to bridge banks the stock of which is owned only by the FDIC. *Id.* (codified at 12 U.S.C.A. § 1831o(j)). The

On the subject of safety and soundness of insured depository institutions, the FDICIA authorizes federal banking agencies to impose more stringent treatment of capital of institutions that are in an unsafe and unsound condition or are engaged in an unsafe and unsound practice.[8]

§ 7.10   Market Activities

In the remainder of this chapter, we examine some of the principal market activities of depository institutions. It should be kept in mind that this is an open-ended set of activities, since the principal sources of authority in this regard, Section 16 of the Glass–Steagall Act[1] and Section 4(c)(8) of the Bank Holding Company Act ("BHCA"),[2] do not limit the incidental powers of banks or the closely related activities of bank holding companies, respectively, to specified activities. As a result, this is an area of remarkable growth for diversification of banking enterprises into related nonbanking activities. Nevertheless, the activities highlighted in the following sections remain of continuing importance.

§ 7.11   Broker–Dealer Activities

Discount brokerage services are one area in the securities sector where banks have become active. It would seem that here the results may be similar both under Sections 16 and 21 of the Glass–Steagall Act,[1] and under Section 20 of the act.[2] In 1982, the Comptroller abandoned a longstanding interpretation—that Section 16 of the Glass–Steagall Act limited bank brokerage activities to current customers of traditional banking services—by allowing a national bank to establish a subsidiary to offer retail discount brokerage services to any customer at branch offices of the bank.[3] The Comptroller's decision was upheld in *Securities*

---

act also contains provisions requiring the periodic review and improvement of applicable capital standards. *See* FDICIA, § 305.

8. FDICIA, § 131(a) (codified at 12 U.S.C.A. § 1831o (g)).

§ 7.10

1. 12 U.S.C.A. § 24 (Seventh). *See also* 61 Fed. Reg. 60,342, 60,374–60,379 (1996) (codified at 12 C.F.R. §§ 5.34–5.36) (amending OCC rules, policies, and procedures for corporate activities; establishing rules for operating subsidiaries, service companies, and other equity investments of national banks, *per* 12 U.S.C.A. § 24(Seventh)).

2. 12 U.S.C.A. § 1843(c)(8). *See also* 12 U.S.C.A. §§ 1861–1867 (authorizing bank service companies). *Cf.* 61 Fed. Reg. at 60,-377–60,379 (1996) (codified at 12 C.F.R. § 5.35(f)(5)) (amending OCC rules, policies, and procedures for corporate activities; re-

quiring Fed approval of certain service companies of national banks, *per* Bank Service Company Act ("BSCA") and § 4(c)(8) of BHCA).

§ 7.11

1. 12 U.S.C.A. §§ 24 (Seventh), 378 (governing activities of banks and other financial institutions). *See supra* § 5.24 (discussing Glass–Steagall Act §§ 16 and 21 as applied to national banks and member banks).

2. 12 U.S.C.A. § 377 (governing affiliations between member banks and securities firms). *See supra* § 6.5 (discussing Glass–Steagall Act § 20 as applied to bank holding companies).

3. *In re Security Pacific Nat'l Bank*, reprinted in [1982–1983 Transfer Binder] Fed. Banking L. Rep. (CCH) ¶ 99,284 (Aug. 26, 1982), at 86,255.

Industry Association v. Comptroller of Currency.[4] The Comptroller subsequently made clear that his new interpretation of Section 16 applied to brokerage activities undertaken directly by a bank itself, in addition to those of a bank subsidiary.[5]

As to affiliations governed by Section 20 of the Glass–Steagall Act, bank service companies[6] also are authorized by the Bank Service Company Act ("BSCA")[7] to engage in discount brokerage activities.[8] However, a bank's investment in a bank service company is limited to not more than 10 percent of its paid-in and unimpaired capital and unimpaired surplus, and not more than 5 percent of its total assets may be invested in such a company.[9] Engaging in this activity would require prior approval of either the Comptroller[10] or the Fed.[11] Approval would be based upon a consideration of

> the financial and managerial resources and future prospects of the bank or banks and [company] involved, including the financial capability of the bank to make a proposed investment ... , and possible adverse effects such as undue concentration of resources, unfair or decreased competition, conflicts of interest, or unsafe or unsound banking practices.[12]

Furthermore, discount brokerage services are also permitted by a nonbanking subsidiary of a bank holding company. In *Securities Industry Association v. Board of Governors* ("*SIA II*"),[13] the Supreme Court allowed an affiliation between a broker (registered with the SEC) and a bank holding company (and, hence, indirectly an affiliation with a commercial bank).

If a banking enterprise operated a brokerage service through a separately incorporated affiliate, the brokerage affiliate would be required to register with the SEC.[14] However, banks themselves are not covered by the definitions of "broker"[15] and "dealer"[16] in the 1934 Act,

---

4. 577 F.Supp. 252 (D.D.C.1983), *aff'd,* 758 F.2d 739 (D.C.Cir.1985) (per curiam), *cert. denied sub nom. Securities Indus. Ass'n v. Comptroller of Currency,* 474 U.S. 1054, 106 S.Ct. 790 (1986), *cert. granted on other grounds and aff'd sub nom. Clarke v. Securities Indus. Ass'n,* 479 U.S. 388, 107 S.Ct. 750 (1987).

5. *See, e.g.,* Comptroller of the Currency Opinion Letter No. 363 (May 23, 1986); *see also* 50 Fed. Reg. 31,605 (Aug. 5, 1985) (withdrawing proposed rule requiring national bank engaging in discount brokerage services to do so through nonbanking subsidiary).

6. *See supra* § 5.23 (discussing bank service companies).

7. 12 U.S.C.A. §§ 1861–1865.

8. *See* 12 U.S.C.A. § 1864(f) (authorizing bank service company to engage in any activity "permissible for a bank holding company" under 12 U.S.C.A. § 1843(c)(8)).

9. 12 U.S.C.A. § 1862.

10. *See* 12 C.F.R. § 5.35(f)(1)-(4) (establishing rules for approval of service companies of national banks, *per* BSCA).

11. 12 U.S.C.A. § 1865(b). *See* 12 C.F.R. § 5.35(f)(5) (requiring Fed approval of certain service companies of national banks, *per* BSCA and § 4(c)(8) of BHCA).

12. 12 U.S.C.A. § 1865(c).

13. 468 U.S. 207, 104 S.Ct. 3003 (1984).

14. *See* 15 U.S.C.A. § 78o (authorizing supervision of broker-dealers by SEC).

15. *See* 15 U.S.C.A. § 78c(a)(4), which reads:

> When used in this title, unless the context otherwise requires—

> (4) The term "broker" means any person engaged in the business of effecting transactions in securities for the account of others, *but does not include a bank.*

---

16. See note 16 on page 215.

and so would not be subject to supervision by the SEC in that regard. Hence, if a bank established its discount brokerage service in house, the question arises whether the service would be treated as a separate entity by the SEC (and thus subject to SEC supervision). In *American Bankers Association v. Securities and Exchange Commission*,[17] the D.C. Circuit held that a bank's brokerage services are not subject to SEC supervision. The SEC's Rule 3b–9, challenged in *American Bankers*, in effect required banks that wished to conduct a discount brokerage business either to register as broker-dealers under the 1934 Act, to conduct brokerage activities through a separate securities subsidiary registered under the 1934 Act, or to confine their involvement to participation in a networking arrangement.[18]

Prior to the promulgation of Rule 3b–9, it appeared clear that banks themselves were not required to register as broker-dealers under the 1934 Act since they were expressly excluded from the definitions of "broker" and "dealer" under the 1934 Act. Thus, the alternatives that were available to banks and were in use to varying degrees prior to the promulgation of the rule included the unregistered conduct of discount brokerage services in house, as well as separate subsidiaries and networking arrangements.

From a technical point of view, Rule 3b–9 was a further definitional refinement of the term "bank" as used in excluding "banks" from the statutory definitions of "broker" and "dealer." As finally adopted, the rule stated that the term, as used in the "bank exclusion," did *not* include any bank that either (1) "publicly solicits brokerage business for

---

(Emphasis added). The term "bank" is defined for these purposes to mean:

(A) a banking institution organized under the laws of the United States, (B) a member bank of the Federal Reserve System, (C) any other banking institution, whether incorporated or not, doing business under the laws of any State or of the United States, a substantial portion of the business of which consists of receiving deposits or exercising fiduciary powers similar to those permitted to national banks ... , and which is supervised and examined by State or Federal authority having supervision over banks, and which is not operated for the purpose of evading the provisions of this title, and (D) a receiver, conservator, or other liquidating agent of any institution or firm included in clauses (A), (B), or (C) of this paragraph.

Id. § 78c(a)(6). The SEC has taken the position that the term "bank" as used in this context does not include savings and loan associations ("S & L's"), and they therefore cannot rely on the exclusion of "banks" from the definition of "broker." *See* Securities Exchange Act Release No. 22205, 50 Fed. Reg. 28,385, 28,389 n. 34 (1985) (codified at 17 C.F.R. § 240.3b–9) (citing *Savings Ass'n Inv. Sec. Servs.*, [1982 Transfer Binder] Fed. Sec. L. Rep. (CCH) ¶ 77,228).

16. *See* 15 U.S.C.A. § 78c(a)(5), which reads:

When used in this title, unless the context otherwise requires—

(5) The term "dealer" means any person engaged in the business of buying and selling securities for his own account, through a broker or otherwise, *but does not include a bank*, or any person insofar as he buys or sells securities for his own account, either individually or in some fiduciary capacity, but not as a part of a regular business.

(Emphasis added.) For the definition of "bank" for these purposes, see preceding note, *supra*. S & L's do not qualify for the bank exclusion from the definition of "dealer." *Cf. id.*

17. 804 F.2d 739 (D.C.Cir.1986).

18. 15 C.F.R. § 240.3b–9.

which it receives transaction-related compensation;"[19] (2) receives direct or indirect transaction-related compensation for brokerage services provided to "trust, managing agency or other accounts to which the bank provides advice;"[20] or, (3) "deals in or underwrites securities."[21]

If a bank's in-house securities activities triggered one of these three categories, then the "bank exclusion" would not apply to that bank, and it could therefore be included under the definitions of "broker" and "dealer" in the 1934 Act. The result would be that, short of abandoning the activities altogether, the bank would be required either: (1) to register as a broker-dealer in accordance with Section 15 of the 1934 Act;[22] (2) to spin off the activities into an operating subsidiary, into a bank service company, or into a bank holding company affiliate, any of which would then register as a broker-dealer; or, (3) to restrict its securities activities to those excepted or exempted from the coverage of the rule.

In *American Bankers*, the SEC confronted the difficulty of explaining how authority could exist to bring banks within the registration requirement of Section 15 of the 1934 Act in the face of the very clear statutory language of the "bank exception." The provisions of Section 3(a)(4) and (5) of the 1934 Act clearly exclude "banks," as defined in

---

19. Rule 3b–9(a)(1). For these purposes, the rule defined "transaction-related compensation" as "monetary profit to the bank in excess of cost recovery for providing brokerage execution services." Rule 3b–9(d). Hence, paragraph (a)(1) had the effect of returning "accommodation" services to their earlier restriction to cost-only trading on behalf of bank customers.

20. Rule 3b–9(a)(2). The rule did not specify the kind of investment "advice" that would render trust, managing agency and other accounts to be covered under the rule. However, the SEC indicated that such advice would include "individualized advice as well as investment seminars and research on particular securities or groups of securities that is disseminated generally to [such] accounts." SEC Release No. 22205, at 28,390.

21. Rule 3b–9(a)(3). The category of activities that triggered the requirement of registration as a broker-dealer was a rather narrow one. "Underwriting," as used in the rule, was interpreted by the SEC (*see* Release No. 22205, at 28,391) to be consistent with the definition of "underwriter" in the Securities Act of 1933 ("the 1933 Act"), which reads in pertinent part as follows:

any person who has purchased from an issuer with a view to, or offers or sells for an issuer in connection with, the distribution of any security, or participates or has a direct or indirect participation in any such undertaking, or participates or has a

participation in the direct or indirect underwriting of any such undertaking.…

15 U.S.C.A. § 77b(11). The Glass–Steagall Act significantly limits the underwriting and dealing activities of commercial banks. *See generally* Bevan, *et al.*, *Corporate Securities Underwriting and Broker–Dealer Services by Banks*, 2 Ann. Rev. Banking L. 111 (1983). The SEC did not express any views on whether the activities specified by Rule 3b–9(a)(3) would constitute "underwriting" for purposes of the Glass–Steagall Act (*see* SEC Release No. 22205, at 28,392 & n.58), but it is likely that the term would be interpreted to carry the same meaning in either context. Hence, it may be argued that a commercial bank's in-house dealing and underwriting activities would be limited to those permitted by the Glass–Steagall Act, primarily U.S. Government-issued or guaranteed obligations, and direct obligations issued or guaranteed by states and their political subdivisions, agencies and instrumentalities. If that argument were sustained, then for the most part the bank's underwriting and dealing would only involve securities that were exempted under the 1934 Act. *See* 15 U.S.C.A. § 78c(a) (12), (29). However, Rule 3b–9(b)(1) exempted transactions in such securities from the application of the rule. *See* SEC Release No. 22205, at 28,391–28,392. Accordingly, the impact of paragraph (a)(3) of the rule was likely to have been relatively limited.

22. *See* 15 U.S.C.A. § 78o(a)(1).

Section 3(a)(6), from the definition of "broker" and "dealer." The SEC argument rested in large part on the "context clause" that introduces the definitional provisions of Section 3 of the 1934 Act. This prefatory language states that defined terms have the meaning assigned in the definitional provisions, "unless the context otherwise requires."[23] While the *context* of the context clause itself (*i.e.*, a preface to a series of statutory definitions) might suggest that the reader is to focus upon the textual context of the statute in which the terms are used, the Supreme Court had taken the position in *Marine Bank v. Weaver*,[24] that the extra-statutory context of the transaction under consideration is to be consulted in construing terms of art used in the federal securities laws.[25] Accordingly, it may be argued that one must therefore examine the context of events surrounding bank involvement in broker-dealer activities.

Examined in this light, it was clear that the "context" had changed dramatically. Bank involvement in securities brokerage was significantly limited from the time of the enactment of the 1934 Act until at least the late 1970s, but the extra-statutory context had changed dramatically in this regard during the 1980s.[26] Hence, it may be argued, the "context" required, particularly in terms of the 1934 Act's goal of investor protection and fair competition among market participants, that the terms "broker" and "dealer" be interpreted to include banks significantly involved securities brokerage.

In light of these policy purposes, reference may also be made to Section 3(b) of the 1934 Act,[27] a statutory source of rulemaking authority relied upon by the SEC in promulgating the rule.[28] This provision grants the SEC power "by rules and regulations to define technical trade, accounting, and other terms used in this title, *consistently with the provisions and purposes*" of the 1934 Act.[29] However, the relationship of this general grant of authority to define terms to the specific statutory definitions contained in the same section was problematic.

Despite the flexibility that the cases interpreting the "context clause" have imported into those statutory definitions, the case law has not gone so far as to countenance an administrative amendment to an explicit statutory definition.[30] Furthermore, there remained serious question whether the SEC's general power to define terms was adequate authority to effect such an administrative amendment in the explicit and

---

23. *Id.* § 78c(a).

24. 455 U.S. 551, 102 S.Ct. 1220 (1982).

25. *Cf. Securities and Exch. Comm'n v. Variable Annuity Life Ins. Co. of Am.*, 359 U.S. 65, 79 S.Ct. 618 (1959) ("*VALIC*"). *But cf. American Bankers Ass'n*, 804 F.2d at 753–754 (rejecting application of *VALIC*).

26. *See* SEC Release No. 22205, at 28,-393.

27. 15 U.S.C.A. § 78c(b).

28. *See* SEC Release No. 22205, at 28,-392.

29. 15 U.S.C.A. § 78c(b) (emphasis added).

30. *See, e.g., Marine Bank, supra. Cf. Board of Governors v. Dimension Fin. Corp.*, 474 U.S. 361, 106 S.Ct. 681 (1986) (rejecting Fed's attempt to amend statutory definition of "bank" administratively).

straightforward statutory language of the "bank exception."[31]

This is not to say that the "bank exception," under present circumstances, is still warranted on its own merits. The question is, rather, whether it is for the SEC or Congress to address shortcomings in the scheme of broker-dealer regulation that has emerged as a result of changes in the degree of bank involvement in recent years. As the Supreme Court stated, in response to a strikingly similar argument advanced by the Fed in *Dimension Financial*, if the definitional provisions of the statute make it "fall[] short of providing safeguards desirable or necessary to protect the public interest, that is a problem for Congress, and not the [Fed] or the courts, to address."[32] *American Bankers* observed that

> [t]he SEC never attempted to apply its broker-dealer regulations to banks that engaged in profitless accommodation transactions. Nor did the SEC attempt to regulate banks as broker-dealers after either the 1957 or the 1974 revisions in the Comptroller's interpretation. The dramatic surge of banks into the discount brokerage business, resulting from the post–1980 administrative reinterpretation of Glass–Steagall, however, prompted the SEC to subject banks engaging in brokerage business to the same broker-dealer regulation as nonbank brokers.[33]

Furthermore, in the court's view, "[a]s far as the statutory definition of bank is concerned ... Rule 3b–9 directly conflicts with the language of the 1934 Act."[34] The court took the position that the "[r]elevant legislative history confirms that Congress intended to preclude SEC regulation of institutions meeting the statutory definition of 'bank' in order to avoid duplicative regulation."[35]

In reviewing the Supreme Court decision in *VALIC*, the *American Bankers* court found what it took to be "crucial distinctions" between *VALIC* and the present case. The former involved a variable annuity contract that contained markedly distinct features from a traditional fixed-dollar annuity contract. Thus, it was open to argue that variable annuity contracts were not "insurance" within the meaning of the 1933 Act. In contrast, the banks brought within the broker-dealer registration requirements by Rule 3b–9 were clearly within the statutory definition of "bank" in the 1934 Act. Furthermore, the undefined statutory term

---

31. *Cf. Securities and Exch. Comm'n v. National Sec., Inc.*, 393 U.S. 453, 466, 89 S.Ct. 564, 571–572 (1969) (meaning of "sale" in federal securities law); *FAIC Sec., Inc. v. United States*, 768 F.2d 352 (D.C.Cir. 1985) (meaning of "deposit" as applied to brokered deposits under federal banking law). In recent years, the courts have repeatedly emphasized the primacy of plain and unambiguous language in federal statutes. *See, e.g., Landreth Timber Co. v. Landreth*, 471 U.S. 681, 105 S.Ct. 2297 (1985) (meaning of "stock" in federal securities law); *Securities Indus. Ass'n v. Board of Governors*, 468 U.S. 137, 104 S.Ct. 2979 (1984) (meaning of "security" in Glass–Steagall Act and federal securities law); *Dimension Fin., supra* (meaning of "commercial loan" and "demand deposit" in BHCA).

32. *Dimension Financial*, 474 U.S. at 374, 106 S.Ct. at 689.

33. *American Bankers Ass'n*, 804 F.2d at 742 (footnote omitted).

34. *Id.* at 744.

35. *Id.* at 744–745.

"insurance" was "sufficient[ly] imprecis[e]" to permit interpretive fine-tuning, whereas the "bank exclusion" of the 1934 Act involves "unambiguous statutory language." Furthermore, the court saw the extra-statutory approach precluded by the Supreme Court's decision in *Dimension Financial*. There the Supreme Court refused to uphold the Fed's attempt to readjust the BHCA definition of "bank" to draw "nonbank banks" within the BHCA.[36]

Had the rule been upheld, it would have applied to over 1,000 banks,[37] and undoubtedly many of these banks would not have opted for the in-house brokerage alternative in order to avoid direct regulation by the SEC. Instead, they would have chosen either the networking alternative or the separate securities subsidiary. Ironically, this is quite close to the choices that the FDIC has already in effect mandated,[38] and what the Comptroller would have mandated[39] had he not withdrawn his proposal in light of the SEC's 3b–9 initiative.[40]

§ 7.12 Investment Management

The two ends of the spectrum of commercial bank involvement in sponsoring and advising investment companies are occupied by the Supreme Court's decisions in *Investment Company Institute v. Camp* ("*ICI I*")[1] and *Board of Governors v. Investment Company Institute* ("*ICI II*").[2] *ICI I* established the basic framework that has been used in interpreting the prohibitions of securities activities in Glass–Steagall Act in judicial decisions since the case was decided in 1971.[3] It also established the premise that commercial banks are generally prohibited from sponsoring open-end investment companies, also known as mutual funds,[4] which are continuous issuers of redeemable securities. Since open-end investment companies are defined in terms of certain of their key functions (*e.g.*, continuous issuance and redemption of securities), rather than by a mere formal label, this case has fostered the continuing concern in the analysis of securities-related activities of banks that the bank might be inadvertently involved in the sponsorship of an activity which is, functionally, an open-end investment company.[5]

On the other hand, *ICI II*, distinguishing itself from *ICI I*, held that

---

36. *American Bankers Ass'n*, 804 F.2d at 752.

37. *See SEC Release on Rule Stating When Banks Must Register as Brokers*, 17 Sec. Reg. & L. Rep. 1235 (1985).

38. *See* 49 Fed. Reg. 46,722 (1984) (codified at 12 C.F.R. § 337.4). *See also* 51 Fed. Reg. 880 (1986) (extending time for compliance); 51 Fed. Reg. at 45,755 (same).

39. *See* 49 Fed. Reg. 15,089 (1984) (to be codified at 12 C.F.R. §§ 5.52, 12.6).

40. *See* 50 Fed. Reg. 31,605 (1985) (withdrawing proposal).

§ 7.12

1. 401 U.S. 617, 91 S.Ct. 1091 (1971).

2. 450 U.S. 46, 101 S.Ct. 973 (1981).

3. *See, e.g., supra* § 5.24 (discussing *ICI I*).

4. On the definition of "open-end investment company," see 15 U.S.C.A. § 80a–5(a)(1).

5. *Cf., e.g.,* Michael P. Malloy & James T. Pitts, *Post-Mortem on Retail Repurchase Agreements: Where Were the Regulators*, 3 Ann. Rev. Banking L. 89, 102, 114 (1984) (discussing implications of investment company definition for bank activities).

the affiliation prohibition of the Glass–Steagall Act[6] did not bar a bank holding company from control of a nonbanking subsidiary that acted as an investment adviser[7] to a closed-end investment company,[8] which issues (nonredeemable) securities only from time to time as capital needs dictate. As a result, a closed-end investment company would not be "engaged principally" in the issuance of securities, a key feature that would trigger the affiliation prohibition of the Act.[9] The Court suggested, though it did not decide, that advising a closed-end investment company would not necessarily be prohibited to Fed member banks that undertook the service directly.[10] A similar result would be expected in the case of savings and loan associations and nonmember, state-chartered banks, which, not being "member banks," are not subject to the Glass–Steagall Act's affiliation prohibition by its own terms.[11]

Continuing member bank involvement with mutual funds has re-emerged, but generally within the confines established by *ICI I*. For example, the OCC indicated in March 1985 that a national bank would be permitted to offer investment services to its customers, in which the bank would execute customer orders to buy and sell shares in tax-exempt mutual funds.[12] While the service contemplated bank use of continuing facilities at the mutual funds involved,[13] as well as fee income from the funds,[14] the primary activity of the bank was analogized to bank discount brokerage services previously approved by the OCC.[15] Other proposed services, such as the provision of information on current yields and values, immediate cash credits for redemptions, and automatic purchases and redemptions (including customer-predetermined "sweeps" of accounts), were also considered by the OCC to be authorized banking activities.[16] The OCC found no danger of the "subtle hazards" identified by *ICI I* as the intended target of the prohibitions of the Glass–Steagall Act.[17]

---

6. 12 U.S.C.A. § 377.

7. On the definition of "investment adviser," see 15 U.S.C.A. § 80b–2(a)(11).

8. *ICI II*, 450 U.S. at 66–67, 101 S.Ct. at 986–987.

9. *See* 450 U.S. at 63–64, 101 S.Ct. at 985–986.

10. *See* 450 U.S. at 59–60, 62–63, 101 S.Ct. at 983, 984–985.

11. *See* 12 U.S.C.A. § 377 (prohibited affiliations between investment firms and member banks). *See also* FDIC Advisory Opinion FDIC–83–14 (Oct. 11, 1983), *reprinted in* [1988–1989 Transfer Binder] Fed. Banking L. Rep. (CCH) ¶ 81,159 (Feb. 10, 1989) (permitting state nonmember insured bank discount brokerage service to act as agent for customers in purchase of units of closed-end mutual fund). *Cf.* FDIC Advisory Opinion FDIC 83–20 (Nov. 17, 1983), *reprinted in* [1988–1989 Transfer Binder] Fed. Banking L. Rep. (CCH) ¶ 81,-

194 (Feb. 3, 1989), at 55,310 (applying prohibition of Section 21 to insured state nonmember bank's operation of collective investment pool).

12. OCC Interpretive Letter No. 332, [1984–85 Transfer Binder] Fed. Banking L. Rep. (CCH) ¶ 85,502 (March 8, 1985).

13. *See id.* at 77,777.

14. *See id.* at 77,777–77,778.

15. *Id.* at 77,778–77,779, *citing Decision of the Comptroller of the Currency on the Application of Security Pacific National Bank to Establish an Operating Subsidiary to be Known as Security Pacific Discount Brokerage Services, Inc.* (Aug. 26, 1982), *reprinted in* [1982–83 Transfer Binder] Fed. Banking L. Rep. (CCH) ¶ 99,284.

16. OCC Interpretive Letter No. 332 at 77,779–77,780.

17. *Id.* at 77,780–77,782.

Similarly, the OCC has offered no objection to a national bank's plan to sell units in a unit investment trust[18] on a second-tier, agency basis only.[19] The OCC justified its position by analogy to permitted bank discount brokerage activities,[20] since the bank's involvement would be limited to activities as agent on behalf of customers.[21]

The OCC has also approved proposed subsidiary activities of a national bank operating through a third-tier subsidiary as a co-investment adviser to a closed-end municipal fund.[22] The subsidiary would be registered as an investment adviser under the Investment Advisers Act of 1940.[23] The subsidiary would provide investment research, identifying municipal bonds for fund purchase, monitoring market and credit risks of bonds in the portfolio, and identifying trading opportunities.[24] The fund would be sponsored by the other co-investment adviser, and also would serve as the administrator of the fund.[25] In approving the proposal, the OCC reaffirmed its administrative position, adopted at least as early as September 1983, that investment advice was a permissible activity under the incidental powers provision of the National Bank Act.[26]

The Fed has authorized similar mutual fund and unit investment trust activities by bank holding companies through nonbanking discount brokerage subsidiaries.[27] It has also ruled similarly under the BHCA[28] on related activities.

§ 7.13 Investment Securities

Section 16 of the Glass–Steagall Act provides that a national bank "may purchase for its own account investment securities under such limitations and restrictions as the Comptroller of the Currency may by regulation prescribe."[1] Purchasing, underwriting, and dealing in "investment securities"[2] is a longstanding exception to the prohibition against

---

18. On the definition of "unit investment trust," see 15 U.S.C.A. § 80a–4(2).

19. OCC Interpretive Letter No. 363 (May 23, 1986), [1985–86 Transfer Binder] Fed. Banking L. Rep. (CCH) ¶ 85,533 at 77,828.

20. *Id.* at 77,829–77,830, *citing Securities Indus. Ass'n v. Board of Governors*, 468 U.S. 207, 104 S.Ct. 3003 (1984), and *Securities Indus. Ass'n v. Comptroller of the Currency*, 577 F.Supp. 252 (D.D.C.1983), *aff'd* 758 F.2d 739 (D.C.Cir.1985) (per curiam), *cert. denied*, 474 U.S. 1054, 106 S.Ct. 790 (1986), *cert. granted on other grounds and aff'd in part and reversed in part sub nom. Clarke v. Securities Indus. Ass'n*, 479 U.S. 388, 107 S.Ct. 750 (1987).

21. OCC Interpretive Letter No. 363 at 77,830.

22. OCC Interpretive Letter No. 515 (July 9, 1990), *reprinted in* 3 OCC Interpretations and Actions (Aug. 1990).

23. 15 U.S.C.A. §§ 80b–1 *et seq. See* OCC Interpretive Letter No. 515 at 2.

24. OCC Interpretive Letter No. 515 at 1–2.

25. *Id.* at 2.

26. *See id.* at 2 (citing previous interpretations).

27. *See Fed Approves Sovran Plan to Offer Mutual Funds, UITs Through Subsidiary*, 18 Sec. Reg. & L. Rep. 1057 (1986).

28. *See id.* at 1058. *See generally* 12 U.S.C.A. § 1843(c)(8) (authorizing activities "closely related" to banking).

§ 7.13

1. 12 U.S.C.A. § 24(Seventh).

2. The term "investment securities" is defined by Section 16 of the Glass–Steagall Act to mean:

marketable obligations evidencing indebtedness of any person, copartnership, assocommercial bank involvement in securities activities.[3] All other financial institutions that accept deposits are also subject to the Comptroller's regulation of investment securities activities.[4] Essentially a class of high-grade debt securities, investment securities are the core of "bank-eligible" securities that have fueled the development of "Section 20 affiliates" of bank holding companies.[5]

§ 7.14 Municipal Securities

The Glass–Steagall Act permits banks to engage in underwriting of "general obligation bonds"[1] of state and local governments.[2] Revenue bonds, which depend upon revenue of the financed public project and are not backed by the full faith and credit of the governmental issuer, would not be included within this concept. The Comptroller has identified exceptions to this general exclusion, thus permitting underwriting of certain municipal revenue bonds, as early as the 1960s.[3]

The Comptroller's position was challenged in *Baker, Watts & Co. v. Saxon*,[4] and the Federal District Court for the District of Columbia invalidated the Comptroller's interpretations, ruling that permissible underwriting of "general obligations" did not include bonds issued by governmental units lacking general taxing power.[5] On appeal by the governmental issuer of the bonds, the D.C. Circuit affirmed.[6]

Nevertheless, commercial banks can and do *deal* in municipal securities. The Securities Acts Amendments of 1975[7] explicitly required the registration of municipal securities dealers under the 1934 Act,[8] including any department or division of a bank engaged in purchasing and selling municipal securities for its own account.[9]

The pattern of regulation applicable to municipal securities dealers is byzantine. The bank regulatory agencies are to be primarily responsible for enforcement and inspection with respect to the municipal securi-

---

ciation, or corporation in the form of bonds, notes and/or debentures commonly known as investment securities under such future definition of the term "investment securities" as may by regulation be prescribed by the Comptroller of the Currency.
Id.

3. For a discussion of the regulatory implementation and supervision of this exception, see 2 MICHAEL P. MALLOY, BANKING LAW AND REGULATION § 7.3.2 (1994 & CUM. SUPP.).

4. 12 U.S.C.A. § 378.

5. *See supra* § 6.5 (discussing role of "bank-eligible securities" in development of Section 20 affiliate strategy).

§ 7.14

1. On the meaning of the term "general obligations," see 12 C.F.R. § 1.3(g) (1995).

2. 12 U.S.C.A. § 24 (Seventh).

3. *See, e.g.*, 27 Fed. Reg. 10,251 (1962); 28 Fed. Reg. 8280 (1963). *See also* 12 C.F.R. §§ 1.127, 1.167 (1963), *removed* 44 Fed. Reg. 76,264 (1979).

4. 261 F.Supp. 247 (D.D.C.1966), *aff'd sub nom. Port of N.Y. Auth. v. Baker, Watts & Co.*, 392 F.2d 497 (D.C.Cir.1968).

5. *Id.*

6. *See Port of N.Y. Auth.*, 392 F.2d at 504.

7. Pub. L. No. 94–29, 89 Stat. 97 (1975) (codified at scattered sections of 15 U.S.C.A.).

8. *See* 15 U.S.C.A. § 78o–4(a)(1).

9. *See* 15 U.S.C.A. § 78c(a)(30) (defining municipal securities dealer).

ties operations of commercial banks,[10] but the SEC has broad power over the registration of municipal securities dealers.[11] In addition, the Municipal Securities Rulemaking Board ("MSRB") is given authority to regulate the activities of municipal securities dealers.[12] However, registration tests and periodic examinations of *bank* municipal securities dealers are performed by the appropriate bank regulatory agency.[13]

In addition to implementing regulations promulgated by the SEC and the MSRB, the appropriate bank regulatory agencies have also implemented the municipal securities provisions of the 1934 Act by issuing regulations. Those regulations issued by the Comptroller are applicable to national bank municipal securities dealers.[14] Those issued by the Fed apply to state-chartered member bank municipal securities dealers.[15] Those issued by the FDIC apply to state-chartered nonmember insured bank municipal securities dealers.[16]

§ 7.15   Transfer Agent

A commercial bank acting as a transfer agent[1] for purchases and sales of securities may be subject to regulation of its activities both by a clearing agency[2] and by its "appropriate regulatory agency." For pur-

---

10. *See* S. Rep. No. 94–75, 94th Cong., 1st Sess. 52 (1975) (so stating).

11. 15 U.S.C.A. § 78o–4(a)(1).

12. *See id.* § 78o–4(b).

13. *See id.* § 78o–4(b)(2)(A)(iii), (E), (c)(7)(A). *See also id.* § 78c(a)(34)(A)(i)-(iii) (defining "appropriate regulatory agency").

14. *See* 12 C.F.R. Pt. 10.

15. *See* 12 C.F.R. § 208.8(j).

16. *See* 12 C.F.R. Pt. 343.

§ 7.15

1. The term "transfer agent" is defined for these purposes by the 1934 Act as:

any person who engages on behalf of an issuer of securities or on behalf of itself as an issuer of securities in (A) countersigning such securities upon issuance; (B) monitoring the issuance of such securities with a view to preventing unauthorized issuance, a function commonly performed by a person called a registrar; (C) registering the transfer of such securities; (D) exchanging or converting such securities; or (E) transferring record of ownership of securities by bookkeeping entry without physical issuance of securities certificates. . . .

15 U.S.C.A. § 78c(a)(25).

2. For these purposes, the term "clearing agency" is defined as:

any person who acts as an intermediary in making payments or deliveries or both

in connection transactions in securities or who provides facilities for comparison of data respecting the terms of settlement of securities transactions, to reduce the number of settlements of securities transactions, or for the allocation of securities settlement responsibilities. Such term also means any person, such as a security depository, who (i) acts as a custodian of securities in connection with a system for the central handling of securities whereby all securities of a particular class or series of any issuer deposited within the system are treated as fungible and may be transferred, loaned, or pledged by bookkeeping entry without physical delivery of securities certificates, or (ii) otherwise permits or facilitates the settlement of securities transactions or the hypothecation or lending of securities without physical delivery of securities certificates.

Id. § 78c(a)(23)(A). Clearing agencies making use of the mails or any means or instrumentality of interstate commerce to perform a clearing function with respect to securities not exempt under the 1934 Act must register under that Act. *Id.* § 78q–1(b)(1). As to exempted securities under the 1934 Act, see *id.* § 78c(a)(12). (Municipal securities are not exempted securities for purposes of clearing agency registration. *Id.*) The term "clearing agency" does not include

any bank . . . building and loan, savings and loan, or homestead association, or poses of transfer agent regulation of commercial banks, the "appropriate regulatory agencies" are: (1) the Comptroller, for national banks and D.C. banks, and subsidiaries of such banks; (2) the Fed, for state member banks, subsidiaries thereof, bank holding companies, and subsidiaries of bank holding companies that are banks other than banks subject to the authority of the Comptroller or the FDIC; and, (3) the FDIC, for state-chartered nonmember insured banks and subsidiaries thereof.[3]

Regulation of transfer agent activities of commercial banks by the "appropriate regulatory agency" is authorized by Section 17A(c)-(d) of the 1934 Act.[4] Among other things, the appropriate regulatory agency has the authority to review final actions of a clearing agency imposing sanctions or limitations with respect to a bank's participation in the clearing agency.[5] In addition, banks acting as transfer agents may be liable for negligence or conversion with respect to its actions as transfer agent.[6]

Any commercial bank making use, directly or indirectly, of the mails or any means or instrumentality of interstate commerce in connection with transfer agent functions with respect to securities registered under the 1934 Act[7] must register as a transfer agent in accordance with the regulations of the bank's appropriate regulatory agency.[8] The registration requirement is also triggered if transfer agent activities involve securities that would be required to be registered under the 1934 Act but for the exemption provided[9] for certain investment company securities and for certain securities issued by insurance companies.[10]

The appropriate regulatory agencies are given statutory authority to exempt by rule or order any person, security, or class of persons or

---

cooperative bank if such bank ... association, or cooperative bank would be deemed to be a clearing agency solely by reason of functions performed by such institution as part of customary banking, ... association, or cooperative banking activities, or solely by reason of acting on behalf of a clearing agency or a participant therein in connection with the furnishing by the clearing agency of services to its participants or the use of services of the clearing agency by its participants....

Id. § 78c(a)(23)(B). However, the SEC has statutory authority to include such institutions within the term by rule, "as necessary and appropriate to assure the prompt and accurate clearance and settlement of securities transactions or to prevent evasion of [the 1934 Act]." *Id.* Clearing agency regulation of its participants is authorized by Section 17A(b)(4)-(5) of the 1934 Act. 15 U.S.C.A. § 78q-1(b)(4)-(5). A clearing agency's supervisory authority over its participants includes the power to impose such sanctions as summary suspension (*see id.*

§ 78q-1(b)(5)(C)) and denial of participation in the clearing agency, or prohibition or limitation with respect to access to clearing agency services. *See id.* § 78q-1(b)(4)(A)-(B).

3. *Id.* § 78c(a)(34)(B)(i)-(iii).

4. 15 U.S.C.A. § 78q-1(c)-(d). *Cf., e.g.,* 12 C.F.R. § 9.20 (Comptroller's regulations; registration of national bank transfer agents).

5. *See, e.g.,* 12 C.F.R. § 9.22 (applications for review).

6. *See generally Woods v. Bank of N.Y.,* 806 F.2d 368 (2d Cir.1986) (holding duty of bank, acting as mutual fund transfer agent, to follow instructions on check dependent upon obligations assumed by bank under its procedures).

7. *See* 15 U.S.C.A. § 78*l*(a)-(b), (g).

8. *Id.* § 78q-1(c)(1)-(2).

9. *Id.* § 78*l*(g)(2)(B), (G)

10. *See id.* § 78q-1(c)(1).

securities from the transfer agent provisions of the 1934 Act.[11] Such an exemption, resulting from the agency's motion or from an application by the agent, requires a finding by the regulatory agency to the effect that:

(1) the exemption is in the public interest and is consistent with the general statutory goal of protection of investors and the specific goals of prompt and accurate clearance and settlement of transactions and the safeguarding of securities and funds; and

(2) the SEC does not object to the exemption.[12]

The procedure for registration is governed by the regulations promulgated by the regulatory agencies.[13] The regulatory agencies have the statutory authority, by order, to deny registration applications,[14] and to censure,[15] place limitations on,[16] suspend (for periods not exceeding 12 months),[17] or revoke the registration of,[18] registered transfer agents subject to their respective authorities under the 1934 Act.[19]

The imposition of these sanctions requires findings on the record, after notice and opportunity for hearing, that the sanction is in the public interest and that the transfer agent has either willfully violated or is unable to comply with the transfer agent provisions or the recordkeeping, reporting and examinations provisions of Section 17 of the 1934 Act,[20] or any rules or regulations promulgated under these provisions.[21] The regulatory agencies may also enforce compliance with the transfer agent provisions of the 1934 Act by use of the cease-and-desist authority of the FDIA.[22]

---

11. *Id.*

12. *Id.*

13. *See id.* § 78q–1(c)(2). *Cf., e.g.*, 12 C.F.R. § 9.20 (Comptroller's regulations; registration of national bank transfer agents; incorporating SEC rule, 17 C.F.R. § 240.17Ac2–1).

14. 15 U.S.C.A. § 78q–1(c)(3). *See, e.g.*, 12 C.F.R. §§ 19.132(a)(5) (providing for denial of national bank transfer agent registration by Comptroller); 208.8(f)(1) (providing for denial of insured state nonmember bank transfer agent registration by Fed); 341.3(c) (providing for denial of insured state nonmember bank transfer agent registration by FDIC).

15. 15 U.S.C.A. § 78q–1(c)(3). *See, e.g.*, 12 C.F.R. § 19.130(a)(3) (Comptroller's rules for disciplinary proceedings involving the federal securities laws; applying procedures to registered bank transfer agent under § 78q–1(c)(3)(A)); *id.* § 19.132(a)(6) (providing for censure of person associated or seeking to become associated with bank transfer agent). *Cf. Bradford Nat'l Clearing Corp. v. Securities and Exch. Comm'n*, 590 F.2d 1085 (D.C.Cir.1978) (concerning disciplinary actions under § 78q–1 against clearing agent).

16. 15 U.S.C.A. § 78q–1(c)(3). *See, e.g.*, 12 C.F.R. § 19.132(a)(5) (providing for limitations on registered bank transfer agent).

17. 15 U.S.C.A. § 78q–1(c)(3). *See, e.g.*, 12 C.F.R. § 19.132(a)(5)-(6) (providing for suspension of registered bank transfer agent or associated person).

18. 15 U.S.C.A. § 78q–1(c)(3). *See, e.g.*, 12 C.F.R. § 19.132(a)(5) (providing for revocation of registered bank transfer agent).

19. 15 U.S.C.A. § 78q–1(c)(3)(A)-(B).

20. 15 U.S.C.A. § 78q. For a staff interpretation clarifying the transfer agent recordkeeping requirements, see OCC Interpretive Letter No. 473 (Jan. 13, 1989), *reprinted in* [1988–1989 Transfer Binder] Fed. Banking L. Rep. (CCH) ¶ 83,010 (May 26, 1989).

21. 15 U.S.C.A. § 78q–1(c)(3)(A).

22. *See* 15 U.S.C.A. § 78q–1(d)(2), which provides:

[T]he appropriate regulatory agency for such clearing agency or transfer agent may, in accordance with section 8 of the Federal Deposit Insurance Act (12 U.S.C.A. 1818), enforce compliance by such clearing agency or transfer agent with the provisions of this section, sec-

§ 7.16   Underwriting and Placement

The Glass–Steagall Act notwithstanding, banking enterprises have authority to engage in a wide range of securities underwriting activities. Banks and bank holding company securities subsidiaries have been permitted to underwrite "bank-eligible" securities.[1] In addition, so long as it does not account for more than 25 percent of its business, a bank holding company securities subsidiary may also underwrite "bank-ineligible" securities, *i.e.*, corporate equities.[2]

Commercial banks are also involved in the private placement of securities,[3] typically, a non-public offering directly negotiated with large, institutional investors.[4] As such, these distributions are generally exempt from the registration requirements of the 1933 Act.[5] Authority to engage in these activities, in a relatively aggressive manner, was confirmed by the D.C. Circuit in *Securities Industry Association v. Board of Governors*.[6]

§ 7.17   Proposed Reforms

The proposed Financial Services Act of 1998,[1] which was intended to overhaul the U.S. financial services system, is the closest the Congress has come in 65 years to revising the Glass–Steagall Act along contemporary lines. In this regard, the principal feature of the bill was that it would have allowed affiliations among banks, securities firms, and insurance companies through "financial holding companies" that would be

---

tions 17 [concerning recordkeeping, reporting and examinations] and 19 [concerning self-regulatory organizations] of [the 1934 Act], and the rules and regulations thereunder. For purpose of the preceding sentence, any violation of any such provision shall constitute adequate basis for the issuance of an order under [12 U.S.C.A. § 1818(b) or (c)], and the participants in any such clearing agency and the persons doing business with any such transfer agent shall be deemed to be "depositors" as that term is used in [12 U.S.C.A. § 1818(c)].

See, e.g., 12 C.F.R. § 19.130(b) (retaining authority in Comptroller to apply § 1818 to transfer agent violations).

§ 7.16

1. *I.e.,* securities in which banks may deal, purchase and underwrite under section 16 of the Glass–Steagall Act, 12 U.S.C.A. § 24 (Seventh).

2. *See supra* § 6.5 (discussing underwriting of "bank-ineligible" securities by holding company subsidiaries).

3. *See* 3 SECURITIES AND EXCHANGE COMMISSION, REPORTS ON BANK SECURITIES ACTIVITIES 57–60 (1977); FEDERAL RESERVE BOARD, COMMERCIAL BANK PRIVATE PLACEMENT ACTIVITIES 29–31 (1977). *See generally* Miller, *Participation of National Banks in Private Placements of Corporate Securities*, 13 New England L. Rev. 63 (1977).

4. *See, e.g.,* [1978–79 Transfer Binder] Fed. Banking L. Rep. (CCH) ¶ 85,107; OCC Interpretive Letter No. 212, [1981–82 Transfer Binder] Fed. Banking L. Rep. ¶ 85,293.

5. *See* 15 U.S.C.A. §§ 77d(2), 77e (exempting nonpublic offerings). *See also* 17 C.F.R. §§ 230.501–230.503, 230.506 (Regulation D provisions with respect to non public offerings).

6. 807 F.2d 1052 (D.C.Cir.1986), *cert. denied*, 483 U.S. 1005, 107 S.Ct. 3228 (1987).

§ 7.17

1. H.R. 10, 105th Cong., 2d Sess. (1998).

regulated by the Fed.[2] The stated purposes of the bill correspondingly included "enhance[d] competition in the financial services industry, in order to foster innovation and efficiency,"[3] and "reduc[tion] and, to the maximum extent practicable, ... eliminat[ion of] the legal barriers preventing affiliation among depository institutions, securities firms, insurance companies, and other financial service providers."[4]

The bill also contained substantive provisions that would have affected the powers of banks. For example, the bill would have revised the permissible activities of subsidiaries of national banks.[5] It also provided authority for national banks to underwrite certain specified municipal bonds.[6] Finally, it would have established a new regulatory regime for bank investment company activities.[7] The bill was also seen as "enhanc[ing] the competitiveness of United States financial service providers internationally,"[8] by providing broader powers for financial services enterprises.

At the last possible moment in the 105th Congress, the bill failed to reach a Senate vote, largely through the opposition of Senator Gramm to community reinvestment provisions in the bill.[9] Ironically, Gramm, as the new Chair of the Senate Banking Committee, indicated that he expects to send a financial services reform bill to the floor by the end of February 1999.[10]

A new set of financial services reform bills, including one sponsored by Senator Gramm, is now under consideration.[11] The Gramm proposal includes provisions requiring national banks with more than $1 billion in assets to underwrite securities and insurance through holding company affiliates subject to Fed supervision, rather than through direct subsidiaries.[12] Competing bills take differing positions on this issue. A bill sponsored by Representative James A. Leach, the Chair of the House Banking Committee, would allow holding company affiliates, but not direct subsidiaries of banks, to engage in a wide range of new *financial* activities (including securities activities), but not including commercial activities.[13] A bill sponsored by Representative John LaFalce, the ranking Democrat on the Committee, would allow a wide range of new activities for direct bank subsidiaries, except for real estate investment and insurance underwriting, while holding companies would be allowed to engage in commercial (*i.e.*, nonfinancial) activities, not exceeding fifteen percent of a company's annual consolidated gross revenues.[14] With in-

---

2. H.R. 10, §§ 111–117.

3. *Id.* § 1(b)(1).

4. *Id.* § 1(b)(5).

5. *Id.* § 121.

6. *Id.* § 181.

7. *Id.* §§ 211–225.

8. *Id.* § 1(b)(7).

9. *See* Dean Anason, *New Senate Banking Chief Aims To Move Reform Bill Next Month*, Am. Banker, Jan. 13, 1999, at 1, col. 2 (characterizing Gramm as "lawmaker most responsible for killing financial reform").

10. *Id.*

11. *See supra* at 174-175 (discussing competing reform proposals).

12. *See* Jaret Seiberg, *Early March Votes Seen On Financial Reform Bill*, Am. Banker, Feb. 17, 1999, at 1 (reporting on Gramm bill).

13. H.R. 10, 106th Cong., 1st Sess. (1999).

14. H.R. 665, 106th Cong., 1st Sess. (1999).

tensely competing positions being taken within the Congress and between Fed and the Treasury,[15] it is as yet unclear whether an acceptable compromise position can be reached, and what its terms might be.[16] Nevertheless, the reform agenda has already begun to advance in both the House and Senate banking committees.[17]

15. *See* Dean Anason, *Regulators At a Standoff Over Reform Differences*, Am. Banker, Feb. 24, 1999, at 1 (discussing opposing positions).

16. *See* Dean Anason, *House Compromise on Reform Offers a Solution to Turf War*, Am. Banker, Mar. 2, 1999, at 1 (discussing possible compromise proposals).

17. *See, e.g.*, Dean Anason, *House Panel Would Require ATM Owners to Disclose Fees*, Am. Banker, Mar. 11, 1999, at 2, col. 1 (reporting on progress of financial services reform bill in House Banking Committee).

Chapter 8

RESOLUTION OF INSTITUTION FAILURES

Table of Sections

§ 8.1   Introduction

This chapter examines the various ways in which the bank regulatory agencies supervise troubled and failing depository institutions.[1] It begins with an examination of the statutory and regulatory devices available to the agencies to identify, monitor, and rehabilitate institu-

§ 8.1

1. In statutory terms, "troubled" and "failing" institutions are now referred to as "institutions in danger of default" and "in-

stitutions in default," respectively. *See* 12 U.S.C.A. § 1813(x) (definitions relating to default).

tions that are troubled. Some institutions in danger of default may not be susceptible to reasonable efforts to rehabilitate them, however, and these institutions may eventually fail. The chapter therefore continues with a discussion of the statutory and regulatory alternatives available to the agencies to "resolve" the situation of a failing depository institution.

§ 8.2   Institutions in Danger of Default

The federal bank regulatory agencies have a variety of statutory powers available to them to deal with troubled institutions,[1] from relatively informal techniques, through formal, statutorily established enforcement measures, and ending with formal resolution of failed institutions. Any combination of these may come into play with respect to an institution in danger of default. The optimal goal is to activate an appropriate power at an early enough stage to avoid more costly supervisory measures at a more advanced stage of the problem.[2] Figure 8–1, *infra*, illustrates the principal devices found along the continuum of techniques available to the regulators.

§ 8.2

1. *See, e.g.*, Office of the Comptroller of the Currency, The Director's Book 70–75 (1987) (describing supervisory tools available) ("Director's Book").

2. *See, e.g.*, 12 U.S.C.A. §§ 1823(c)(4) (mandating least-cost resolution through use of FDIC financial assistance authority); 1823(c)(8) (concerning least-cost resolution); 1831o (mandating prompt regulatory action for troubled insured depository institutions).

FIGURE 8-1

Supervisory Responses to Troubled Depository Institutions[3]

[3]Excluding financial assistance under, *inter alia*, 12 U.S.C. § 1823(c).

National banks are required by statute to submit periodic reports to the Comptroller of the Currency,[4] which should give early warning of potential problems in the condition of national banks. The Comptroller

4. *Id*. § 161. *See also id*. § 1831m (re-quiring annual report on financial condition   and management).

also has the authority to examine national banks on a periodic basis, generally once a year.[5] The examination process is given teeth by the enforcement powers available to the Comptroller under the Federal Deposit Insurance Act ("FDIA"),[6] to deal with violations of law and unsafe and unsound practices of national banks that may be uncovered in the course of an examination.

Problems that suggest that an institution may be in danger of default may implicate the adequacy of its financial resources.[7] In cases where the capital of a national bank is impaired by losses, there exists— theoretically, but not in current practice—the power to require that any deficiencies in capital be paid in.[8] In addition, where the problem involves capital inadequacy, the statutory provisions for increases in capital may be invoked.[9]

If the problems of a national bank are caused by or are directly related to violations of the National Bank Act ("NBA") by or with the assent of the directors, personal liability provisions of the NBA may be invoked against management.[10] Violations of the NBA may also result in the imposition of civil money penalties under a provision of the NBA that is essentially the same as the general civil money penalty provision of the FDIA.[11] If the troubled condition of the institution is markedly moving towards "failing" status, there exists statutory authority, similar to that found in the general bankruptcy context, to frustrate transfers in contemplation of insolvency.[12]

The Fed has corresponding authority to deal with problem situations involving state-chartered Fed-member banks. Among other things, knowing violations of many bank regulatory provisions of federal law (both civil and criminal) can result in personal liability of participating directors and officers of a member bank for all damages sustained by the bank, its shareholders, and other persons damaged by the violation.[13] Violations of certain provisions of the Federal Reserve Act ("FRA") may also result in the imposition of civil money penalties under a provision of the FRA that is essentially the same as the general civil money penalty provision of the FDIA.[14]

As to insured nonmember state banks, the FDIA also contains reporting provisions that give the Federal Deposit Insurance Corporation ("FDIC") an opportunity to identify potential problems at an early

---

5. *Id.* § 1820(d)(1)–(3).

6. *Id.* § 1818.

7. Some cases have argued that "problem" status is limited to financial considerations. *Cf., e.g., First Nat'l Bank of Bellaire v. Comptroller of the Currency,* 697 F.2d 674 (5th Cir.1983) (limiting concept of "safety and soundness" under § 1818(b) to issues of financial soundness); *Gulf Fed. Sav. & Loan Ass'n v. Federal Home Loan Bank Bd.,* 651 F.2d 259 (5th Cir.1981), *cert. denied,* 458 U.S. 1121, 102 S.Ct. 3509 (1982) (same).

8. *Id.* § 55.

9. *See id.* §§ 57, 3907.

10. *Id.* § 93(a).

11. *Compare id.* § 93(b) (NBA civil money penalty provision), *with id.* § 1818(i)(2) (FDIA provision).

12. *See id.* § 91.

13. *See id.* § 503.

14. *Compare id.* § 504 (FRA provision), *with id.* § 1818(i)(2) (FDIA provision).

stage.[15] The FDIC also has available to it a variety of explicit statutory powers, ranging from denial or termination of insurance[16] to the ability to take enforcement action against the bank to reform its unsafe and unsound practices.[17]

In situations where a bank or savings association is in danger of default, the FDIC has fairly broad authority to act to aid an institution to avoid insolvency.[18] Should insolvency be unavoidable, the FDIC, as the federally designated receiver, has authority to act to resolve the insolvency and liquidate the bank.[19]

As to federally chartered or insured savings associations, the supervisory system administered by the Office of Thrift Supervision ("OTS") parallels that of the other federal regulators.[20] In fact, there is now a more or less unified body of federal enforcement provisions, the enforcement provisions of the FDIA, applicable regardless of the type of depository institution involved.[21] These enforcement provisions include the power to issue administrative cease and desist orders against violations of law or unsafe and unsound banking practices,[22] the power to suspend or remove members of management,[23] and the power to impose civil money penalties.[24]

§ 8.3　The Examination Process

Effective supervision is grounded on the process of annual on-site examinations and other specialized examinations conducted from time to time. A bank may first be apprised of its regulator's concerns over a particular practice or problem at the examiner's exit interview, when the examiner in charge of the periodic examination meets with management to discuss generally the supervisory concerns.[1] At that point, the bank's

---

15. *See id.* § 1817(a)(1). *See also id.* § 1831m (requiring annual report on financial condition and management).

16. *Id.* § 1818(a).

17. *See, e.g. id.* § 1818(b) (providing for cease and desist orders).

18. *See, e.g. id.* § 1823(c) (providing for "open bank" financial assistance).

19. *See, e.g. id.* § 1821(d), (e), (j) (concerning powers of FDIC). *See also id.* § 1823(f) (concerning assisted emergency interstate acquisitions).

20. *See, e.g. id.* §§ 1464(d)(1)(A) (providing authority of Director of OTS under § 1818); 1467(a)–(b) (mandating periodic examinations of savings associations and affiliates); 1831m (requiring annual reports on financial condition and management).

21. This includes not only insured banks but also insured savings associations, primarily regulated at the federal level by the OTS. The Director of the OTS is the "appropriate Federal banking agency" au-

thorized to impose formal enforcement measures with respect to insured savings associations. *Id.* §§ 1813(q), 1818(b)–(n). However, the FDIC has authority to take formal enforce ment action against savings associations, in certain specified circumstances, in the absence of action by the Director of the OTS. 12 U.S.C.A. § 1818(t).

The one exception to this unified body of federal enforcement provisions is the credit union, federally or state-chartered, which is subject to a parallel set of enforcement powers contained in the Federal Credit Union Act, *id.* § 1786, administered by the National Credit Union Administration ("NCUA").

22. *See id.* § 1818(b).

23. *See id.* § 1818(e) (providing for removal authority).

24. *See id.* § 1818(i)(2).

§ 8.3

1. *See* DIRECTOR'S BOOK at 70.

board of directors usually begins to formulate a response and to carry out a reasonable plan to correct any problems noted by the examiners.[2] The bank's regulator generally will encourage it to submit a response indicating the bank's proposed corrective plan with respect to any problems identified by the examination.[3] Most problems can be rectified during the period immediately following the end of the examination through informal discussion and correspondence with the regulator. This is the normal process of regulatory oversight.

§ 8.4   Remedial Actions

Occasionally, the significance of a given problem or the circumstances in which it arises may require more specific action to be taken by the regulator. The usual approach then is remedial action on the part of the regulator short of formal enforcement measures. Remedial action may take a variety of forms: a commitment letter, a memorandum of understanding, or a "formal agreement" between the depository institution and its regulator.[1] In the typical case, the remedial action specifies corrective measures that the institution or individuals affiliated with it need to take with respect to identified problems.

The commitment letter is the least severe remedial action taken by the regulators. The typical commitment letter is initiated by the institution's board of directors or trustees. The letter is signed by the board; identifies problems that require corrective action; and establishes a plan and timetable to remedy the problems.[2] The commitment letter is recommended by the regulator in situations in which the problems do not appear to represent a serious threat to the safety and soundness of the institution.[3]

If the identified problems "do not pose an immediate or serious threat to the [institution] and when the agency expects that the [institution] will cooperate in correcting the problems so that legal enforcement will not be required to achieve compliance,"[4] a memorandum of understanding may be initiated by the regulator.[5] It memorializes the understanding between the regulator and the institution's board or an affiliated individual.[6] The memorandum, which is more formal than the

---

2. *See id.* at 71.

3. *See, e.g., id.*

§ 8.4

1. The terminology varies somewhat from agency to agency, but the three devices discussed in this section are used in the practice of each of the agencies.

2. *See, e.g.,* OCC Quarterly Journal 122–123 (1991) (describing enforcement practices).

3. *See, e.g.,* DIRECTOR'S BOOK at 72 (noting that commitment letter "may be used by a bank that has been responsive and

does not have a history of serious problems and when the problems identified do not pose an immediate or serious threat to the bank's health").

4. *Id.*

5. *See, e.g., Greene County Bank v. Federal Deposit Ins. Corp.,* 92 F.3d 633 (8th Cir.1996), *cert. denied,* 519 U.S. 1109, 117 S.Ct. 944 (1997) (upholding cease and desist order issued on basis of violation of memorandum of understanding regarding futures and securities activities that constituted unsafe and unsound banking practices).

6. DIRECTOR'S BOOK at 72.

commitment letter, is drafted by the regulator and lays out the institution's or individual's agreement to take specified actions within specified time periods to correct violations of law or unsafe and unsound practices.[7]

If the institution has more serious problems, but such problems are not critical and the institution's management is cooperative, the agency may use a "formal agreement."[8] A formal agreement is similar in form to a memorandum of understanding, but it has special statutory significance. Violation of the terms of a formal agreement constitutes grounds for the issuance of a cease and desist order,[9] and judicial enforcement of the order may then ensue.[10]

§ 8.5   Formal Enforcement Actions

In situations in which the problem is serious or the safety and soundness of the institution is threatened, and in situations in which the institution or affiliated individuals have not been cooperative or have already violated the terms of a remedial action, formal enforcement action may ensue.[1] Jurisdiction to take any formal enforcement action against insured depository institutions and persons affiliated with them is divided up among the federal regulatory agencies. This division of authority is illustrated in Figure 8–2, *infra*.

Figure 8–2
Principal Formal Enforcement Powers: Division of Authority[2]

Agency	*Institutions Subject to Agency's Enforcement Authority*
Comptroller of the Currency	▶ national banks ▶ District of Columbia banks ▶ federal branches or agencies of foreign banks
Board of Governors of the Federal Reserve System ("Fed")	▶ state member insured banks (except District of Columbia banks) ▶ branches or agencies of foreign banks, with respect to provisions of FRA, 12 U.S.C.A. §§ 221 *et seq.*, made applicable under International Banking Act of 1978 ("IBA"), 12 U.S.C.A. §§ 3101 *et seq.*, and

7. *Id.*

8. *See generally* Deal, *Bank Regulatory Enforcement—Some New Dimensions*, 40 Bus. Law. 1319 (1985) (discussing status of formal agreements).

9. *See* 12 U.S.C.A. § 1818(b)(1) (providing for issuance of cease and desist order for violation of "any written agreement entered into with the agency"). For cases involving issuance of cease and desist orders based upon violation of formal agreements, see *Rapaport v. United States Dep't of Treasury, Office of Thrift Supervision*, 59 F.3d 212 (D.C.Cir.1995), *cert. denied*, 516 U.S. 1073, 116 S.Ct. 775 (1996); *Groos Nat'l Bank v. Comptroller of Currency*, 573 F.2d 889 (5th Cir.1978). *Cf. CityFed Fin. Corp. v. Office of Thrift Supervision*, 58 F.3d 738

(D.C.Cir.1995) (involving net worth maintenance agreement); *Akin v. Office of Thrift Supervision, Dep't of Treasury*, 950 F.2d 1180 (5th Cir.1992) (same).

10. *See Groos Nat'l Bank*, 573 F.2d at 896–897 (involving cease and desist order issued for violation of written agreement concerning extensions of credit).

§ 8.5

1. *See generally* Michael P. Malloy, *Nothing to Fear but FIRREA Itself: Revising and Reshaping the Enforcement Process of Federal Bank Regulation*, 50 Ohio St. L. J. 1117 (1989) (discussing formal enforcement powers of federal depository institutions regulators).

2. Source: 12 U.S.C.A. § 1813(q).

	with respect to supervisory or regulatory proceedings arising from the authority given to the Fed under Section 7(c)(1) of the IBA, 12 U.S.C.A. § 3105(c)(1) ▶ foreign banks that do not operate insured branches ▶ agencies and commercial lending companies, other than federal agencies ▶ bank holding companies and subsidiaries of bank holding companies (other than a bank)
Federal Deposit Insurance Corporation	▶ state nonmember insured banks (except District of Columbia banks) ▶ foreign banks that operate insured branches
Director of the Office of Thrift Supervision	▶ any savings associations ▶ savings and loan holding companies

For each type of institution covered by each regulatory agency's enforcement authority, "institution-affiliated persons" are also subject to that enforcement authority. The term "institution-affiliated person" is a statutorily broadened concept of "insider" for purposes of formal enforcement authority under the federal banking laws. Figure 8–3, *infra*, illustrates the broad scope of this defined term.

Figure 8–3

Institution–Affiliated Persons of Insured Depository Institutions[3]

Traditional Insiders	▶ directors ▶ officers ▶ employees ▶ controlling stockholders (other than a bank holding company) ▶ agents
Acquiring Individuals	▶ persons who have filed or are required to file change-in-control notice under 12 U.S.C.A. § 1817(j)
Management Participants	▶ any of the following persons who participates in the conduct of the affairs of an insured depository institution: —shareholder (other than a bank holding company) —consultant —joint venture partner —any other person determined by the appropriate federal banking agency (*see supra* Figure 8–2) to be a participant
Independent Contractors	▶ any independent contractor, *including any attorney, appraiser, or accountant,* who *knowingly or recklessly* participates in: —any violation of any law or regulation —any breach of fiduciary duty —any unsafe or unsound practice that caused or is likely to cause more than minimal financial loss to, or significant adverse effect on, insured depository institution

The principal formal enforcement powers that may be applied by the appropriate federal regulatory agency against an insured depository institution or institution-affiliated person are discussed in the sections

---

3. Source: 12 U.S.C.A. § 1813(u).

that follow. Figure 8–4, *infra*, identifies the major, generally applicable enforcement powers available to the regulators.

Figure 8–4

Generally Applicable Enforcement Authorities[4]

Formal Enforcement Power	*Authority*
Termination of Insurance	▶ authority granted to FDIC under 12 U.S.C.A. § 1818(a)(2); termination of insurance for money laundering or cash transaction reporting offenses under 12 U.S.C.A. § 1818(w)
Termination of Federal Reserve Membership	▶ termination required on termination of deposit insurance, *per* 12 U.S.C.A. § 1818(*o*)
Cease-and-Desist Orders	▶ proceedings authorized for each agency, *per* 12 U.S.C.A. § 1818(b) ▶ temporary cease-and-desist orders available under 12 U.S.C.A. § 1818(c)
Capital Directive	▶ § 1818 powers available to remedy unsafe and unsound capital levels, by capital directive *per* 12 U.S.C.A. § 3907(b)
Suspension and Removal of Management, Insiders, and Participants	▶ general authority includes power to prohibition participation, as well as removal from office, under 12 U.S.C.A. § 1818(e) ▶ Summary suspension or removal of institution-affiliated party charged with felony authorized under 12 U.S.C.A. § 1818(g)
Civil Money Penalties	▶ First tier (12 U.S.C.A. § 1818(i)(2)(A)): —applicable to violation of law or regulation, final order or temporary order, condition imposed in writing by agency, written formal agreement —civil penalty of not more than $5,000 per day, per violation ▶ Second tier (12 U.S.C.A. § 1818(i)(2)(B)): —pattern of misconduct that causes or is likely to cause more than a minimal loss, or results in pecuniary gain or other benefit —involves first-tier violation; *recklessly* engages in unsafe or unsound practice; or breaches fiduciary duty; —civil penalty of not more than $25,000 per day per violation, practice, or breach ▶ Third tier (12 U.S.C.A. § 1818(i)(2)(C)): —knowing first-or second-tier violation *and* knowingly or recklessly causes substantial loss or substantial pecuniary gain or other benefit —civil penalty not more than maximum amount, per day, per violation, practice, or breach, of $1,000,000 or (in case of institution) the lesser of $1,000,000 or one percent of total assets

§ 8.6   Cease and Desist Orders

The cease and desist order[1] is the administrative equivalent of an injunction. It is the typical response of the regulator when there is a

---

4. Source: 12 U.S.C.A. §§ 1818, 3907(b).

§ 8.6

1. *See* 12 U.S.C.A. §§ 1786(e) (credit unions); 1818(b) (all other insured depository institutions). *See generally Wachtel v.*

Office of Thrift Supervision, 982 F.2d 581 (D.C.Cir.1993) (holding order for restitution of failed bank's asset deficit requires showing of recklessness or unjust enrichment under § 1818(b)(6)(a)).

need to increase the formality and seriousness of the supervisory response to the problem activities of an institution.[2] The regulators can also issue temporary cease and desist orders.[3] Temporary orders are effective upon service, and they remain in effect (absent court action to the contrary[4]) until the completion of the cease and desist proceedings, or in certain cases, until the regulator determines by examination or otherwise that the books and records are accurate and reflect the institution's financial condition.[5]

Prior to 1989, temporary cease and desist orders were available to deal with such exigencies as violations or threatened violations of law or unsafe or unsound practices that were "likely to cause insolvency or substantial dissipation of assets or earnings" of a depository institution or were "likely to seriously weaken [its] condition . . . or otherwise seriously prejudice the interests of its depositors" during the pendency of a cease and desist proceeding.[6] However, the Financial Institutions Reform, Recovery, and Enforcement Act of 1989 ("FIRREA")[7] amended this authority so that issuance of a temporary order is now possible not only where the violation or practice is likely to cause insolvency of the depository institution involved, but also where (1) the violation or order is likely to cause *"significant,"* rather than "substantial," dissipation of assets or earnings of the depository institution, a change in standard that was intended to "lower the agencies' burden of proof . . . and . . . cover anything more than a minimal or nominal dissipation of assets;"[8] or (2) the violation or practice is likely to *"weaken"* (rather than "seriously weaken") the condition of the bank or otherwise *"prejudice"* (rather than "seriously prejudice") the interests of the institution's depositors.[9]

Temporary cease and desist orders can include an order restricting the growth of the depository institution involved.[10] They are also available where the books and records of an institution are so inaccurate that the enforcing regulator cannot determine, in the normal supervisory

---

2. *See, e.g.,* Director's Book at 73 (noting that such orders issue "most often when the agency is not confident that bank management will take the necessary corrective action or when the problems are so severe that a lesser action cannot be justified").

3. *See* 12 U.S.C.A. §§ 1786(f) (credit unions); 1818(c) (1) (all other insured depository institutions). On the use of temporary cease and desist orders, see *Landmark Land Co., Inc. v. Office of Thrift Supervision,* 990 F.2d 807 (5th Cir.1993).

4. *See* 12 U.S.C.A. §§ 1786(f)(2) (credit unions); 1818(c)(3)(B)(ii) (all other insured depository institutions). On review of temporary cease and desist orders, see *CityFed Fin. Corp. v. Office of Thrift Supervision,* 58 F.3d 738 (D.C.Cir.1995); *Parker v. Ryan,* 959 F.2d 579 (5th Cir.1992).

5. *Id.* §§ 1786(f)(3)(B)(ii)(I)-(II) (credit unions); 1818(c)(3)(B)(ii)(I)-(II) (all other insured depository institutions).

6. 12 U.S.C.A. § 1818(c)(1) (1982).

7. Pub. L. No. 101–73, 103 Stat. 183 (1989) (codified at scattered sections of 12 U.S.C.A.).

8. H. R. Conf. Rep. No. 222, 101st Cong., 1st Sess. 444 (1989).

9. 12 U.S.C.A. §§ 1786(f)(1) (credit unions); 1818(c)(1) (all other insured depository institutions).

10. *Id.* §§ 1786(f)(1) (credit unions); 1818(c)(1) (all other insured depository institutions). *See Spiegel v. Ryan,* 946 F.2d 1435 (9th Cir.1991), *cert. denied,* 503 U.S. 970, 112 S.Ct. 1584 (1992) (discussing § 1818(c) (1)).

process, the financial condition of the involved depository institution, or cannot determine the details or purpose of a transaction that may have a material effect on the financial condition of the institution.[11]

§ 8.7 Suspension and Removal of Management and Affiliated Persons

Suspension and removal of management and affiliated control persons are also specifically authorized.[1] This authority was substantially amended by FIRREA in 1989.[2] Removal or prohibition of participation of an institution-affiliated person requires a determination, *inter alia*, of actual or probable "financial loss or other damage," "prejudice[ ]" to depositors' interests, or "financial gain or other benefit" to such person,[3] rather than "substantial financial loss" or "serious prejudice[ ]" as was the case prior to FIRREA.[4] These changes were intended to "allow[ ] the regulatory agencies to proceed with a removal or prohibition action ... without requiring the agencies to quantify the harm or prejudice."[5]

In situations in which a director, officer, or affiliated person of an insured depository institution has been charged with a felony involving dishonesty or breach of trust, summary suspension or removal is also a possibility.[6] FIRREA expanded this authority to include state criminal proceedings as a ground for initiating summary suspension or removal.[7]

§ 8.8 Civil Money Penalties

Civil money penalties may also be imposed by the regulators in appropriate cases.[1] These penalties were expanded and increased in 1989.[2] Three tiers of civil money penalties against depository institutions

---

11. 12 U.S.C.A. §§ 1786(f)(3)(A) (credit unions); 1818(c)(3)(A) (all other insured depository institutions).

§ 8.7

1. 12 U.S.C.A. §§ 1786(g) (credit unions); 1818(e)(1)-(2) (all other insured depository institutions). There is also authority for the federal regulators to disapprove the proposed addition of any individual to the board of directors or the employment of any individual as a senior executive officer of depository institutions in certain specified circumstances. *See id.* § 1790a (credit unions); § 1831i (all other insured depository institutions).

2. *See id.* §§ 1786(g)(1) (amended FCUA); 1818(e)(1) (corresponding FDIA provisions).

3. *Id.* §§ 1786(g)(1)(B)(i)-(iii) (credit unions); 1818(e)(1)(B)(i)-(iii) (all other insured depository institutions).

4. 12 U.S.C.A. §§ 1786(g)(1), 1818(e)(1) (1982).

5. H. R. Conf. Rep. No. 222, 101st Cong., 1st Sess., at 444.

6. 12 U.S.C.A. §§ 1786(i) (credit unions); 1818(g) (all other insured depository institutions).

7. *See* FIRREA, § 906(a)(1) (codified at 12 U.S.C.A. § 1818(g)(1)) (FDIA provision); *id.* § 906(b)(1) (codified at 12 U.S.C.A. § 1786(i)(1)) (corresponding FCUA provision).

§ 8.8

1. 12 U.S.C.A. §§ 1786(k)(2) (credit unions); 1818(i)(2) (all other insured depository institutions).

2. *See* FIRREA, § 907 (codified at 12 U.S.C.A. §§ 93(b), 481, 504, 505(1), 1467a(i), 1786(k)(2), 1817(j) (16), 1818(i)(2), 1828(j)(4)-(5), 1847, 1972(2)(F)). *See generally Greenberg v. Comptroller of the Currency*, 938 F.2d 8 (2d Cir.1991) (involving OCC suit against director after separation from service).

and institution-affiliated parties now exist. Among other things, the penalties apply to failures to submit timely and accurate reports as required by federal law.[3]

The first tier imposes penalties not exceeding $5,000 per day during the continuation of a violation of any law or regulation, of any order or temporary order, of any written condition imposed in connection with the grant of an application or other request, or of any written agreement between any agency and a depository institution.[4]

The second tier imposes penalties not exceeding $25,000 per day during the continuation of any such violation, recklessly engaging in an unsafe or unsound practice, or breach of a fiduciary duty, where the violation, practice, or breach is part of a "pattern of misconduct," causes more than minimal loss to the depository institution, or results in pecuniary gain or other benefit to such party.[5]

The third tier imposes maximum civil money penalties, which may amount to as much as $1 million per day[6] during the continuance of such a violation, practice, or breach, in situations where the depository institution or institution-affiliated party knowingly or recklessly causes substantial loss to the institution or substantial pecuniary gain or other benefit through the violation, practice, or breach.[7]

§ 8.9 Capital Directives

Because of the critical importance of adequate capital supervision, in appropriate circumstances a regulator may issue to an individual institution a capital directive that establishes higher capital requirements for the individual institution than might otherwise apply under generally applicable regulations.[1] The institution is required by the order to achieve these capital levels within a specified period of time.[2]

§ 8.10 Other Specialized Enforcement Devices

There is a broader range of enforcement authorities available to the federal regulators of depository institutions than the generally applicable devices discussed above.[1] Among the more extreme are such enforcement

---

3. *See* 12 U.S.C.A. §§ 161, 164, 324, 1782(a)(3), 1817(a)(1), 1847(d).

4. *See, e.g., id.* U.S.C.A. § 1818(i)(2)(A) (providing for civil money penalties applicable to insured depository institutions under FDIA).

5. *See, e.g., id.* U.S.C.A. § 1818(i)(2)(B).

6. On the determination of the maximum penalties, *see, e.g., id.* U.S.C.A. § 1818(i)(2)(D). Mitigating factors with respect to the determination of any specific penalty under any of the three tiers are

specified in the statutory provisions. *See, e.g., id.* U.S.C.A. § 1818(i)(2) (G).

7. *See, e.g., id.* § 1818(i)(2)(C).

§ 8.9

1. 12 U.S.C.A. § 3907(a)(1), (b)(2).

2. *See* DIRECTOR'S BOOK at 74.

§ 8.10

1. *See generally* Stephen Huber, *Enforcement Powers of the Federal Banking Agencies*, 7 Ann. Rev. Banking L. 123

powers as charter revocation[2] and deposit insurance termination.[3]

Other more specialized enforcement powers available to these federal regulators include, *inter alia*, (1) civil money penalty provisions for violations of specified provisions of the Federal Reserve Act;[4] (2) criminal and civil penalty provisions for violations of the Bank Holding Company Act ("BHCA");[5] (3) civil money penalties provisions for violations of the antitying provisions of the BHCA;[6] (4) enforcement authority under the Depository Institutions Management Interlocks Act ("DIMIA"),[7] which intersects the authority granted under the FDIA and the NCUA;[8] (5) authority under Section 12(i) of the Securities Exchange Act of 1934[9] with respect to the securities of depository institutions registered under that Act; and, (6) federal criminal penalties for knowing participation in any institution's affairs in violation of a removal or prohibition order,[10] and criminal penalties for knowing unauthorized participation by a convicted person.[11]

§ 8.11   Institutions in Default

The remainder of this chapter explores regulatory problems with respect to the failure of a depository institution, *i.e.*, an "institution in default."[1] As in the case of the bankruptcy of a general business corporation, a depository institution failure usually involves a situation of insolvency.[2] However, the process for failing depository institutions is

---

(1988) (providing exhaustive discussion of state and federal criminal and formal and informal civil enforcement authorities).

2. *See, e.g.*, 12 U.S.C.A. §§ 93 (national bank charters); 1766 (federal credit union charters).

3. *See id.* § 1818(a).

4. *Id.* §§ 504, 505.

5. *Id.* § 1847.

6. *Id.* § 1972(2)(F).

7. *Id.* §§ 3201 *et seq.*

8. *See, e.g. id.* §§ 1786(g)(3) (concerning violations of DIMIA; suspension and removal authority of FCUA); 1818(e)(3) (same; suspension and removal authority of FDIA).

9. 15 U.S.C.A. § 78*l*(i).

10. *See* 12 U.S.C.A. §§ 1786(*l*) (credit unions); 1818(j) (all other insured depository institutions).

11. *See id.* §§ 1785(d) (credit unions); 1829 (all other insured depository institutions).

§ 8.11

1. *See, e.g.*, 12 U.S.C.A. § 1813(x)(1) (defining "default" as adjudication or other official determination under which conservator, receiver, or other custodian is appointed for insured depository institution).

Such a situation should be distinguished from one in which a depository institution decides voluntarily to dissolve. *See, e.g. id.* §§ 181–182 (providing for voluntary dissolution of national bank).

2. *See, e.g. id.* §§ 191(1) (specifying grounds for appointment of receiver of national bank, referring to § 1821(c)(5)); 1821(c)(5)(A) (specifying depository institutions's obligations greater than assets as grounds for appointment of receiver); 1821(c)(5)(F) (specifying inability to meet obligations as they come due as grounds for appointment of receiver); 1821(c)(5)(G) (specifying depletion of capital as grounds for appointment of receiver); 1821(c)(5)(H) (specifying violation of law or regulation, or unsafe or unsound practice or condition likely to cause insolvency as grounds for appointment of receiver). Other grounds for the appointment of a receiver or conservator do not directly relate to a condition of insolvency. These grounds are:

(1) substantial dissipation of assets or earnings due to violation of any statute or regulation or any unsafe or unsound practice (*id.* § 1821(c)(5)(B));

(2) unsafe or unsound condition to transact business (*id.* § 1821(c)(5)(C));

(3) willful violation of a final cease-and-desist order (*id.* § 1821(c)(5)(D));

distinguishable from a general business bankruptcy in two important respects.

First, depository institutions are not subject to the general federal law with respect to bankruptcy.[3] Determination of default by the depository institution's primary regulator in this regard is exclusive, and results in the institution being placed into conservatorship[4] or receivership.[5]

Second, holding companies of depository institutions are themselves subject to the general federal bankruptcy laws.[6] However, since the financial condition of the principal operating subsidiary of such a holding company (*i.e.*, its subsidiary bank or savings association) is likely to be the cause of the parent's insolvency, the situation will naturally be a very complicated one, with the parent subject to the Bankruptcy Code and the principal subsidiary subject exclusively to federal statutes governing the default of depository institutions.[7] For the sake of clarity, the discussion that follows focuses exclusively on the regulatory regime applicable to the failing depository institution.

(4) concealment of the institution's books, papers, records or assets, or any refusal to submit the institution's books, papers, records or affairs for inspection to any examiner or to any lawful agent of the appropriate federal or state supervisor (*id.* § 1821(c)(5)(E));

(5) consent to the appointment by resolution of board of director or of shareholders or members (*id.* § 1821(c)(5)(I); *see also id.* § 1821(c)(12) (directors not liable for such consent or acquiescence));

(6) cessation of insured status of the institution (*id.* § 1821(c)(5)(J));

(7) undercapitalization, under specified circumstances (*id.* § 1821(c)(5)(K)); or,

(8) critical undercapitalization or substantially insufficient capital (*id.* § 1821(c)(5)(L)).

In situations of undercapitalization (grounds (7) and (8), *supra*), additional authority exists for the appropriate federal banking agency to appoint the FDIC as conservator or receiver of any insured state depository institution. *See* 12 U.S.C.A. § 1821(c)(9). *See also id.* § 1821(c)(11) (providing FDIC opportunity to appoint itself as receiver before appropriate federal banking agency may appoint conservator). The FDIC has additional authority to appoint itself as conservator or receiver under any of the grounds identified, if such appointment is necessary to reduce or prevent a loss to the deposit insurance fund. *See id.* § 1821(c)(10).

Appointment of a conservator or receiver does not violate the Fifth Amendment takings clause, since those who enter the banking industry do so voluntarily. *California Housing Sec. v. United States*, 959 F.2d 955, 958 (Fed.Cir.), *cert. denied*, 506 U.S. 916, 113 S.Ct. 324 (1992). Use of the appointment authority is "entitled to a presumption of regularity," and judicial review is narrow. *Franklin Sav. Ass'n v. Director, Office of Thrift Supervision*, 934 F.2d 1127, 1141 (10th Cir.1991), *cert. denied*, 503 U.S. 937, 112 S.Ct. 1475 (1992).

3. *See* 11 U.S.C.A. § 109 (expressly exempting banks and other depository institutions from recourse to bankruptcy protection).

4. *See, e.g.,* 12 U.S.C.A. §§ 202–206, 209, 211 (providing conservatorship rules for national bank).

5. *See, e.g. id.* §§ 191–199 (receivership rules for national bank). *See also id.* § 91 (transfers in contemplation of insolvency).

6. *Cf.* 11 U.S.C.A. § 109 (providing exemption does not explicitly apply to holding company). *See generally MCorp Fin., Inc. v. Board of Governors*, 900 F.2d 852 (5th Cir. 1990), *aff'd in part and rev'd in part on other grounds*, 502 U.S. 32, 112 S.Ct. 459 (1991) (discussing § 109 of the Bankruptcy Code).

7. *See, e.g., MCorp Fin., supra* (illustrating complications inherent in failure of depository institution and holding company parent).

§ 8.12   Insured Deposit Payoff

The ultimate liability of the federal government with respect to a depository institution in default is its obligation for the insured deposits of the institution.[1] However, the resolution of failures by the FDIC has varied, and since 1945 the insured deposit payoff approach has not been favored.[2]

Originally, the FDIC tended to resolve failures by either paying off its deposit insurance obligation or by allowing the failing bank to be acquired by another institution.[3] In a deposit payoff transaction, illustrated in Figure 8–5, *infra*, the FDIC as receiver would hold any net assets of the failed institution, against which uninsured depositors, other unsecured creditors, and the FDIC itself as insurer became general creditors.

FIGURE 8-5
Deposit Payoff

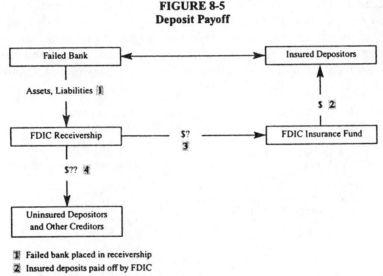

▮ Failed bank placed in receivership
▮ Insured deposits paid off by FDIC
▮ Fund repaid out of net assets
▮ Other obligations repaid out of net assets

The FDIA was amended in August 1993, to provide a national depositor preference for amounts realized from the liquidation or other resolution of FDIC-insured depository institutions.[4] The amendment requires that distributions from all future receivership estates be made in the following order: (1) administrative expenses of the receiver; (2)

§ 8.12

1. *See* 12 U.S.C.A. § 1821(a)(1) (providing for insurance of deposit to maximum of $100,000).

2. *See generally* U.S. DEPARTMENT OF THE TREASURY, MODERNIZING THE FINANCIAL SYSTEM, DISCUSSION CHAPTER I, AT I–30—I–45 (FEB. 1991), *reprinted in* Fed. Banking L. Rep. (CCH) No. 1377, Pt. II (Feb. 14, 1991)

(discussing FDIC treatment of bank failures) ("MODERNIZATION REPORT").

3. MODERNIZATION REPORT at I–30. Between 1935 to 1945, approximately 390 failures were resolved by either payoff or merger. *Id.*

4. Pub. L. No. 103–66, 107 Stat. 312 (1993) (codified at 12 U.S.C.A. § 1821(d)(11)).

deposit liability claims; (3) other general or senior liabilities of the institution, other than subordinated obligations or shareholder claims; (4) subordinated obligations; and, (5) shareholder claims.[5]

The legislation applies to all receiverships of insured institutions established after its enactment date (August 10, 1993),[6] and it supersedes any inconsistent state or other federal distribution provisions.[7]

§ 8.13   Modified Insured Deposit Payoff

In 1984, the FDIC initiated a "modified payoff" approach as a variation on the traditional insured deposit payoff.[1] Under this approach, insured deposits would be paid off, and a sum equal to a relatively conservative estimate of the net realizable assets in the receivership would be paid out to the uninsured deposits, with additional payments to be made in the future if collections exceeded the estimate.[2] This approach eventually led to the development of the "insured deposit transfer,"[3] in which an acquiring bank would pay a premium for insured deposits and certain assets of a failed bank, thus realizing the net asset value up front. These related approaches are illustrated in Figure 8–6, *infra*.

---

5.   12 U.S.C.A. § 1821(d)(11).

6.   *Id.* § 1821 note.

7.   *Id.* § 1821(d)(11). For FDIC rules interpreting and implementing the amendment, see 58 Fed. Reg. 43,069 (1993) (codified at 12 C.F.R. Pt. 360) (interim rule); 58 Fed. Reg. 67,662 (1993) (redesignating 12 C.F.R. §§ 360.1–360.3 as §§ 360.2–360.4) (final rule), *as amended*, 60 Fed. Reg. 35,-487 (1995) (codified at 12 C.F.R. §§ 360.3(f), 360.4).

§ 8.13

1.   MODERNIZATION REPORT at I–32.

2.   *Id.*

3.   *Id.*

FIGURE 8-6
Modified Deposit Payoffs

A. Modified Payoff

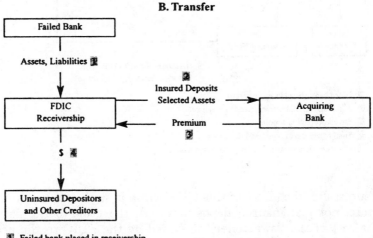

1 Failed bank placed in receivership
2 Insured deposits paid off by FDIC
3 Uninsured deposits paid out of estimated net assets value
4 Fund reimbursed out of liquidated net assets
5 Other obligations (and any remaining uninsured deposits) paid out of liquidated net assets

B. Transfer

1 Failed bank placed in receivership
2 Insured deposits and selected assets transferred to acquiror
3 Premium paid by acquiror
4 Other obligation paid out of liquidated net assets

§ 8.14   Purchase and Assumption

Originally, the typical acquisition transaction involving a failed bank was not a merger, strictly speaking, but a purchase of assets (*i.e.*, loans) and assumption of liabilities (*i.e.*, deposits) of the failing bank by the acquiring bank, with the FDIC making up the shortfall between the value of liabilities assumed and assets purchased.[1] Before the 1960s, these resolutions took place without the creation of a receivership, and so approval of the shareholders and the chartering authority of the acquired bank would be required.[2] During the latter part of the 1960s, the FDIC adopted a different approach to these transactions, by first placing the institution into receivership, so that the FDIC as receiver could approve the transaction directly, without the costly delays of shareholder and chartering authority approval.[3] Figure 8–7, *infra*, illustrates the transaction.

FIGURE 8-7
Purchase and Assumption (post-1964)

■ Failed bank placed in receivership
■ Assets and liabilities transferred to acquiror
■ Sweetener paid to acquiror
■ Fund repaid out of liquidated net assets
■ Other creditors repaid out of liquidated net assets

If successful, the effect of this transaction is similar to a payoff of *all* depositors, not just insured depositors.[4] On the other hand, assuming that the cost of the "sweetener" provided by the FDIC to the acquiror bank is less than its total insured deposits liability, the purchase and assumption method could be less costly to the FDIC.[5] (However, the FDIC as receiver is left, almost inevitably, with a nearly worthless shell

§ 8.14
1. Modernization Report at I–30.

2. *Id.* at I–31.

3. *Id.*

4. *Cf.* Modernization Report at I–31 (describing criticism by Senator Fulbright to this effect).

5. For a discussion of alternative methods for fulfilling the FDIC's obligation to depositors, including deposit payoffs and purchase-and-assumption transactions, see *NCNB Tex. Nat'l Bank v. Cowden*, 895 F.2d 1488 (5th Cir.1990).

within the receivership.) To narrow its exposure still further, since 1968 the FDIC has sought premiums from potential acquiror banks in proposed purchase and assumption transactions through an explicit bidding process.[6]

§ 8.15   "Open–Bank" Assistance

In the various approaches to failed bank resolution adopted by the FDIC, the FDIC has almost invariably sought to avoid the rigors of insured deposit payoff, and the resulting disruption of the local economy that the closing of a bank would cause. An important device in this regard, first seriously used by the FDIC in 1971,[1] is "open-bank assistance,"[2] in which the FDIC lends, contributes, invests, or otherwise utilizes its financial resources to assist an institution in default or in danger of default to regain financial stability. This approach proceeds on the assumption that it will be less costly to the FDIC to lend financial assistance to a troubled institution than to close and liquidate it in receivership.[3] Since 1982 in particular, with the broadening of the FDIC's open bank assistance authority, open-bank assistance has become an extremely important and frequently used option.

One obvious difficulty with this approach is that it sometimes appeared to allow a "walking dead" institution to continue to incur further obligations, followed by a possibly inevitable failure of the institution at a greater net cost to the insurer.[4] With the passage of

---

6. Modernization Report at I–31.

§ 8.15

1. *See* Modernization Report at I–34 (discussing "open-bank" assistance).

2. 12 U.S.C.A. § 1823(c).

3. Previously, § 1823(c) had only authorized loans, deposits, and purchase of assets by the FDIC to prevent closing or to reopen a bank. 12 U.S.C.A. § 1823(c) (1980). Section 111 of the Garn–St Germain Act, Pub. L. No. 97–320, § 111, 96 Stat.1469 (1982), fundamentally amended the formerly narrow option presented by 12 U.S.C.A. § 1823(c). The amended section also explicitly authorized the FDIC to engage in a range of actions in order to facilitate a merger or consolidation of an insured bank, or to arrange a purchase and assumption transaction. *See* 12 U.S.C.A. § 1823(c)(2).

4. Two variations on this "walking dead" approach to failing bank resolution should be mentioned. One was the "capital forbearance" program, in which capital and other supervisory requirements were not enforced against financially troubled institutions viewed as "viable" by the FDIC. Modernization Report at I–37—I–38. *Cf.* 12 U.S.C.A. § 1823(i) (concerning purchase of

"net worth certificates" from troubled depository institution by FDIC as support for institution's capital position). This approach has been severely criticized as increasingly the ultimate cost of unavoided (and possibly unavoidable) collapse of such "viable" but troubled institutions. Modernization Report at I–37. Presumably, this situation is less likely to occur since the FDIC is now required to refrain from invoking Section 1823 unless:

> (i) the [FDIC] determines that the exercise of such authority is necessary to meet the obligation of the [FDIC] to provide insurance coverage for the insured deposits in such institution; and

> (ii) the total amount of the expenditures by the [FDIC] and obligations incurred by the [FDIC] (including any immediate and long-term obligation of the [FDIC] and any direct or contingent liability for future payment by the [FDIC]) in connection with the exercise of any such authority with respect to such institution is the least costly to the deposit insurance fund of all possible methods for meeting the [FDIC's] obligation under [§ 1823].

12 U.S.C.A. § 1823(c)(4)(A)(i)–(ii).

FIRREA[5] and the Federal Deposit Insurance Corporation Improvements Act of 1991 ("FDICIA"),[6] the statutory framework for dealing prospectively[7] with institutions in default was significantly reformed. As to open bank assistance, the current framework is as follows.

To prevent the default of an insured depository institution,[8] to restore a closed insured bank to normal operation,[9] or to lessen the risk to the FDIC from the instability of a significant number of insured depository institutions or of institutions with significant financial resources,[10] the FDIC has the sole authority and discretion to give financial assistance to such institutions.[11] This assistance may take the form of loans to, deposits in, purchase of assets or securities of, assumption of liabilities of, or contributions to any such institution.[12] FDIC financial assistance may also take the form of assistance to facilitate a merger, consolidation, or other acquisition of a troubled or closed insured depository institution by another insured institution.[13] FDIC decisions to render assistance are generally subject to a requirement that the FDIC make a determination that the assistance provided be "necessary to meet the obligation of the [FDIC] to provide insurance coverage,"[14] and that it be the least-cost approach to resolving the problem; *i.e.*, that

> the total amount of the expenditures by the [FDIC] and obligations incurred by the [FDIC] (including any immediate and long-term obligation of the [FDIC] and any direct or contingent liability for future payment by the [FDIC]) in connection with the exercise of any such [assistance] authority with respect to such institution is the least costly to the deposit insurance fund of all possible methods for meeting the [FDIC's] obligation.... [15]

Until 1991, another "walking dead" approach existed that involved an FDIC equity investment in the troubled institution. MODERNIZATION REPORT at I–38—I–39. This often involved extreme, and arguably questionable measures, such as the 75 to 80 percent equity interests assumed by the FDIC in large, failing regional banks such as the MCorp subsidiary and Continental Illinois. *See, e.g., id.* at I–39 (discussing equity investments in failing regional banks). The FDIC is now significantly limited by statute in its use of equity investment as a means of open-bank assistance. *See* 12 U.S.C.A. § 1823(c)(5), (i)(11) (limiting FDIC authority to make equity investments).

5. Pub. L. No. 101–73, 103 Stat. 183 (1989) (codified at scattered sections of 12 U.S.C.A.).

6. Pub. L. No. 102–242, 105 Stat. 2236 (1991) (codified at scattered sections of 12 U.S.C.A.).

7. *See United States v. Winstar Corp.,* 518 U.S. 839, 116 S.Ct. 2432 (1996) (plurality opinion) (rejecting retrospective application of FIRREA capitalization requirements

to savings and loan holding company operating under pre-FIRREA rules).

8. 12 U.S.C.A. § 1823(c)(1)(A).

9. *Id.* § 1823(c)(1)(B).

10. *Id.* § 1823(c)(1)(C).

11. *Id.* § 1823(c)(1). For discussion of the implications of an open bank assistance arrangement, see *Senior Unsecured Creditors' Comm. v. Federal Deposit Ins. Corp.,* 749 F.Supp. 758 (N.D.Tex.1990). In December 1992, the FDIC published a policy statement indicating the circumstances under which it would extend assistance to a troubled insured depository institution that was still open. 57 Fed. Reg. 60,203 (1992). *See also* 61 Fed. Reg. 34,814 (1996) (proposed revision of policy statement).

12. 12 U.S.C.A. § 1823(c)(1). On purchase of assets by the FDIC, see *id.* § 1823(d). On parallel FDIC assistance authority for savings associations, see *id.* § 1823(k)(5).

13. *Id.* § 1823(c)(2).

14. *Id.* § 1823(c)(4)(A)(i).

15. *Id.* § 1823(c)(4)(A)(ii).

The FDIC may not use its assistance authority to purchase voting or common stock of an insured depository institution.[16] The financial assistance provided may be made subordinated to the rights of depositors and other creditors.[17]

§ 8.16 Appointment of Conservator or Receiver

It is generally within the discretion of the chartering authority[1] of a failing depository institution to determine whether or not to place it in conservatorship or receivership.[2] In a conservatorship, the basic statutory assumption is that the institution may well return to the transaction of its business.[3] In a receivership, the basic statutory assumption is that the institution will be liquidated, or that it will be merged with or otherwise acquired by a healthy depository institution.[4] In either event, a

---

16. *Id.* § 1823(c)(5).

17. *Id.* § 1823(c)(9).

§ 8.16

1. *But see* 12 U.S.C.A. § 1821(c)(4) (authorizing FDIC self-appointment as conservator or receiver, notwithstanding other state or federal law, under specified statutory conditions). On judicial review of these FDIC self-appointments, see *id.* § 1821(c)(7). On FDIC replacement of a conservator with itself in such situations, see *id.* § 1821(c)(8). *See also id.* § 1821(c)(10) (providing other grounds for FDIC self-appointment as conservator or receiver of insured depository institution). Heightened involvement of the regulators in the burgeoning thrift crisis beginning in the early 1980s placed additional strains on the regulatory system and raised questions about the discretion and good faith of the regulators themselves. For a case considering a challenge to federal regulatory discretion in the face of claims of basic property rights of thrift owners, see *Biscayne Fed. Sav. & Loan v. Federal Home Loan Bank Bd.*, 720 F.2d 1499 (11th Cir.1983), *cert. denied*, 467 U.S. 1215, 104 S.Ct. 2656 (1984).

2. *See, e.g.,* 12 U.S.C.A. §§ 191 (providing Comptroller with authority to declare conservatorship of national bank); 1464(d)(2)(A) (providing OTS with same authority with respect to federal savings association). On the procedures governing a conservatorship, see generally *In re Conservatorship of Wellsville Nat'l Bank*, 407 F.2d 223 (3d Cir.1969), *cert. denied sub nom. Miller v. Camp*, 396 U.S. 832, 90 S.Ct. 85, *reh'g denied*, 396 U.S. 949, 90 S.Ct. 371. *See also Central W. Rental Co. v. Horizon Leasing*, 740 F.Supp. 1109 (E.D.Pa.1990)

(involving challenge to conservator's actions, notwithstanding § 1464(d)(7)(C) prohibition on judicial action restraining or affecting conservator's power). On the procedures governing the decision to place an institution in receivership, see generally *Federal Deposit Ins. Corp. v. McKnight*, 769 F.2d 658 (10th Cir.1985), *cert. denied sub nom. All Souls Episcopal Church v. FDIC* and *sub nom. Rocket Oil Co. v. FDIC*, 475 U.S. 1010, 106 S.Ct. 1184. The receivership process has primarily been an administrative one, with a limited role for courts. *See Shemonsky v. Office of Thrift Supervision*, 733 F.Supp. 892 (M.D.Pa.1990); *Matter of Receivership of Penn Square Bank, N.A.*, 556 F.Supp. 494 (D.Okla.1983).

3. *See, e.g.,* 12 U.S.C.A. § 205(a)(1) (providing for termination of conservatorship of national bank permitting bank "to resume the transaction of its business subject to such terms, conditions, and limitations as the Comptroller may prescribe"). *See also Minichello v. Saxon*, 337 F.2d 75 (3d Cir.1964), *cert. denied*, 380 U.S. 952, 85 S.Ct. 1084 (concerning Comptroller's authority and minority shareholder rights). *Cf.* 12 U.S.C.A. § 1821(d)(2)(D) (providing general power of FDIC as conservator to put institution on sound and solvent condition and to conserve its assets). But note, as discussed *infra*, conservatorship may become receivership.

4. *See, e.g.,* 12 U.S.C.A. § 1821(c)(2)(A)(ii) (authorizing appointment of FDIC as receiver "for the purpose of liquidation or winding up the affairs of an insured Federal depository institution"). *See also id.* § 1821(d)(2)(E) (providing general power of FDIC as receiver to place institution in liquidation). Despite its startconservator or receiver, respectively, will be appointed. Almost inevitably in either case, this will be the FDIC.[5]

The statutory rules governing the appointment of the FDIC in either capacity override any contrary provision of federal law, state constitution, or state law.[6] In the case of federal depository institutions,[7] appointment of the FDIC as conservator is within the discretion of the institution's supervisor.[8] Appointment of the FDIC as receiver is mandatory whenever the institution's supervisor decides to place it in receivership.[9]

When acting as conservator or receiver, the FDIC is not subject to the direction or supervision of any other state or federal agency in the exercise of its rights, powers, or privileges.[10] However, in the conservatorship context, the institution in conservatorship itself remains subject to the supervision of its appropriate federal banking agency, *i.e.*, the Comptroller (for national banks and District banks) and the Director of the Office of Thrift Supervision (for federal savings associations).[11]

In the case of insured state depository institutions,[12] appointment of the FDIC as conservator or receiver is within the discretion of the appropriate state authority.[13] When acting as conservator or receiver under appointment by the state authority, the FDIC is not subject to the direction or supervision of any other state or federal agency in the

---

ing assumption (*see supra* preceding note), a conservatorship may also ultimately conclude with the liquidation or winding up of the affairs of the institution in conservatorship. *See* 12 U.S.C.A. § 205(a)(2).

5. *See generally* 12 U.S.C.A. § 1821(c) (providing for appointment of FDIC as conservator or receiver).

6. *Id.* § 1821(c)(1).

7. For these purposes, the term "federal depository institution" is defined by the FDIA to mean "any national bank, any Federal savings association, and any Federal branch" of a foreign bank. *Id.* § 1813(c)(4). On the meaning of "Federal savings association," see *id.* § 1813(b)(2). On the meaning of the term "Federal branch," see *id.* § 1813(s)(2).

8. *Id.* §§ 1821(c)(2)(A)(i) (concerning conservatorship in general); 1821(c)(6)(A) (providing for OTS appointment of FDIC as conservator and FDIC acceptance of appointment). *But see id.* § 1821(c)(11) (authorizing FDIC self-appointment as receiver, under certain conditions, before federal agency may appoint a conservator).

9. *Id.* §§ 1821(c)(2)(A)(ii) (receivership in general); 1821(c)(6)(B)(i)-(ii) (providing for OTS appointment of FDIC).

10. *Id.* § 1821(c)(2)(C).

11. *Id.* § 1821(c)(2)(D).

12. For these purposes, the term "insured State depository institution" is derived from two terms defined by the FDIA: "insured depository institution," defined to mean "any bank or savings association the deposits of which are insured by the [FDIC]" and "State depository institution," defined to mean "any State bank, any State savings association and any insured branch which is not a Federal branch" of a foreign bank. *Id.* § 1813(c)(2), (c)(4). On the meaning of the term "State bank," see *id.* § 1813(a)(2). On the meaning of the term "State savings association," see *id.* § 1813(b)(3). On the meaning of the term "insured branch," see *id.* § 1813(s)(3).

13. *Id.* § 1821(c)(3)(A). This discretionary aspect of the appointment of a federal agency as receiver has occasionally created tension between the state authority and the federal agency. *See, e.g., Fidelity Sav. & Loan Ass'n v. Federal Home Loan Bank*, 689 F.2d 803 (9th Cir.1982) (describing tension between California Savings and Loan Commissioner and now defunct FSLIC). For grounds for appointment of FDIC as conservator or receiver of state depository institution by its appropriate *federal* banking agency (after consultation with the state authority), see 12 U.S.C.A. § 1821(c)(9).

exercise of its rights, powers, or privileges.[14] However, in the conservatorship context, the institution in conservatorship itself remains subject to the supervision of its state authority.[15]

As conservator or receiver, the FDIC has a wide range of statutory powers.[16] The FDIC gains control of the entity as its successor by operation of law.[17] As such, the FDIC has full authority to operate the institution.[18] Whether serving as conservator or receiver, it also has the power to effect the merger of the institution with another insured depository institution,[19] or arrange a purchase or assumption transaction with another insured depository institution.[20] The FDIC may, where it determines that it is "practicable, efficient, and cost effective"[21] utilize the resources of the private sector to carry out its responsibilities for management and disposition of the assets of an insured depository institution. In addition to these general powers, there is also a range of specific powers available to the FDIC in either of its capacities.

As conservator, the FDIC has the power to take any action necessary to put the institution in a sound and solvent condition.[22] It also has the power to take any action appropriate to carry on the institution's business and to preserve or conserve the institution's assets.[23]

As receiver, the FDIC has the power to liquidate the institution and realize on the institution's assets, "having due regard [for] the conditions of credit in the locality" of the institution.[24] In this respect, it may organize a new savings association,[25] a new national bank,[26] or transitional "bridge bank"[27] to take over assets and liabilities of the institution in receivership, as it deems appropriate.

14. 12 U.S.C.A. § 1821(c)(3)(C).

15. *Id.* § 1821(c)(3)(D).

16. This grant of authority includes all incidental powers "as shall be necessary to carry out [its] powers" as conservator or receiver. *Id.* § 1821(d)(2)(I). *See also id.* §§ 1821(c)(2)(B), (c)(3)(B) (providing additional powers to FDIC as conservator or receiver); 1821(c)(13) (providing additional powers to FDIC when self-appointed under § 1821(c)(4), appointed by the OTS under § 1821(c)(6), appointed because of undercapitalization under § 1821(c)(9), or self-appointed because of potential loss to deposit fund under § 1821(c)(10)).

17. *Id.* § 1821(d)(2)(A).

18. *Id.* § 1821(d)(2)(B). On the functions of the institution's directors, officers, and shareholders by FDIC regulation or order, see *id.* § 1821(d)(2)(C). In operating the institution, the FDIC also has the responsibility to pay all valid obligations of the institutions, "in accordance with the prescriptions and limitations of [the FDIA]." *Id.* § 1821(d)(2)(H).

19. *Id.* § 1821(d)(2)(G)(i)(I).

20. *Id.* § 1821(d)(2)(G)(i)(II). *See SCFC ILC, Inc. v. Visa USA, Inc.*, 936 F.2d 1096, 1099–1100 (10th Cir. 1991) (interpreting statute). This transaction would be subject to the approval of the appropriate federal banking agency that supervises the acquiring institution. 12 U.S.C.A. § 1821(d)(2)(G)(ii). The FDIC also has the authority to purchase assets of an insured depository institution in default from any conservator, receiver or liquidator, including itself, or to take assets as security for loans from the FDIC. *Id.* § 1823(d).

21. 12 U.S.C.A. § 1821(d)(2)(K).

22. *Id.* § 1821(d)(2)(D)(i).

23. *Id.* § 1821(d)(2)(D)(ii).

24. *Id.* § 1821(d)(2)(E). On the status of the FDIC as receiver, see *id.* § 1822.

25. *Id.* § 1821(d)(2)(F)(i).

26. *Id.* § 1821(d)(2)(F)(ii), (m).

27. *Id.* § 1821(d)(2)(F)(ii), (n). *See generally Bell & Murphy and Assocs., Inc. v. Interfirst Bank Gateway, N.A.*, 894 F.2d 750 (5th Cir.1990) (discussing role of bridge banks).

The FDIC now has authority to determine the validity of claims against the institution in accordance with an administrative procedure created by statute.[28] As was demonstrated in *First Empire Bank–New York v. Federal Deposit Insurance Corporation*,[29] resolving the problems of a failing institution can often be considerably complicated, and the costs markedly increased, by the claims of third parties that have dealt with the institution. In this regard, the now defunct Federal Home Loan Bank Board and the Federal Savings and Loan Insurance Corporation ("FSLIC") experienced great difficulty in attempting to deal with such claims by way of an expedited administrative process for claims resolution created by regulation.[30] The FDIA was subsequently amended to provide an elaborate administrative procedure for the resolution of third-party claims.[31]

28. 12 U.S.C.A. § 1821(d)(3)-(10).

29. 572 F.2d 1361 (9th Cir.1978).

30. *See Coit Independence Joint Venture v. Federal Sav. and Loan Ins. Corp.*, 489 U.S. 561, 109 S.Ct. 1361 (1989) (invalidating administrative claims process). *See also Carrollton–Farmers Branch Indep. Sch. Dist. v. Johnson & Cravens*, 889 F.2d 571 (5th Cir.1989) (rehearing on claims following *Coit*); *Triland Holding & Co. v. Sunbelt Serv. Corp.*, 884 F.2d 205 (5th Cir.1989) (remand under *Coit*); *Central W. Rental Co. v. Horizon Leasing*, 740 F.Supp. 1109 (E.D.Pa.1990) (applying *Coit*). *See generally* Lawrence Baxter, *Life in the Administrative Track: Administrative Adjudication of Claims against Savings Institution Receivers*, 1988 Duke L.J. 422 (discussing *Coit* and making recommendations for reform).

31. *See* Pub. L. No. 101–73, § 212(a), 103 Stat. 183, 225–234 (1989) (codified at 12 U.S.C.A. § 1821(d)), *as amended*, Pub. L. No. 102–242, §§ 123(a), 141(b), 161(a)(1)-(2), 416, 105 Stat. 2236 (1991) (codified at 12 U.S.C.A. § 1821(d)(3)(A), (d)(4), (d)(5)(D), (d)(11)(B), (d)(13)(E)). *See Tuxedo Beach Club Corp. v. City Fed. Sav. Bank*, 737 F.Supp. 18 (D.N.J.1990) (discussing statutory policy and legislative intent of 1989 amendments); *Meliezer v. Resolution Trust Corp.*, 952 F.2d 879 (5th Cir.1992) (discussing administrative claims procedures).

Generally, the 1989 legislation is retroactively applicable to cases pending at the time of its enactment. *Demars v. First Serv. Bank for Sav.*, 907 F.2d 1237 (1st Cir.1990). However, the claims determination provisions, and specifically § 1821(d)(13)(D), do not require dismissal of all pending claims against failed institutions at the time of the enactment of the legislation. *Marquis v. Federal Deposit Ins. Corp.*, 965 F.2d 1148 (1st Cir.1992) (efficiency goal of statute promoted by this approach). Proceedings may be stayed under 12 U.S.C.A. § 1821(d)(12), pending the completion of the administrative claims process. *Marquis, supra* (interpreting § 1821(d) to allow more than one 90–day stay). *But cf. Praxis Properties, Inc. v. Colonial S.B., SLA*, 947 F.2d 49 (3d Cir. 1991) (stay expires 90 days after FDIC appointment); *Hunter's Run v. Arapahoe County Pub. Trustee*, 741 F.Supp. 207 (D.Colo.1990) (stay of proceedings under § 1821(d)(12) inappropriate where FDIC has had sufficient time to prepare case and plaintiff will suffer irreparable harm); *Tuxedo Beach Club Corp. v. City Fed. Sav. Bank*, 729 F.Supp. 1508 (D.N.J.1990) (same result as to RTC as receiver); *Federal Deposit Ins. Corp. v. Taylor*, 727 F.Supp. 326 (S.D.Tex. 1989) (same; FDIC as receiver).

Failure to file a timely claim bars the claim before the administrative agency and the courts. *Althouse v. Resolution Trust Corp.*, 969 F.2d 1544, 1546 (3d Cir.1992). On the relationship between the administrative claims procedure and pending litigation involving the claim, see *Resolution Trust Corp. v. Mustang Partners*, 946 F.2d 103 (10th Cir.1991).

State law claims may be preempted by the administrative claims provisions. *Resolution Trust Corp. v. Elman*, 949 F.2d 624, 627 (2d Cir.1991) (involving attorney retaining lien). *Federal Deposit Ins. Corp. v. Shain, Schaffer & Rafanello*, 944 F.2d 129 (3d Cir.1991) (same). *See also Circle Indus. v. City F.S.B.*, 931 F.2d 7 (2d Cir.1991).

As to standing under the administrative claims procedure, it has been held that a union has standing to represent claims of its members, pursuant to 12 U.S.C.A. § 1821(d)(6). *Transohio S.B. v. Director, Office of Thrift Supervision*, 967 F.2d 598 (D.C.Cir.1992); *Office of Prof'l Employees Int'l Union, Local 2 v. Federal Deposit Ins. Corp.*, 962 F.2d 63, 67 (D.C.Cir.1992).

§ 8.17   Claims Against Third Parties

As conservator or receiver, the FDIC stands in a position to prosecute claims of the depository institution against third parties.[1] The amended FDIA continues, in expanded form, the codification of the *D'Oench, Duhme* rule against secret agreements[2] against the interests of the FDIC.[3] Under this rule, any agreement between a depository institution and a third party that would tend to diminish or defeat the interest

§ 8.17

1. *See, e.g.,* 12 U.S.C.A. 1821(d)(2)(B)(ii) (power of FDIC as conservator or receiver to collect obligation and money due the institution). *See also In re Sunrise Sec. Litig.,* 916 F.2d 874, 889 (3d Cir.1990) (FDIC as receiver has power to pursue derivative claims against officers and directors of failed institution). *But see Hayes v. Gross,* 982 F.2d 104 (3d Cir.1992) (1989 legislation did not amend or subordinate federal securities law cause of action). *See generally Telematics Int'l, Inc. v. NEMLC Leasing Corp.,* 967 F.2d 703 (1st Cir.1992) (FDIC attachment of certificate of deposit as security on loan agreement within FDIC's discretion under § 1821(j)). Under 12 U.S.C.A. § 1821(j), courts are generally prohibited from taking "any action, except at the request of the [FDIC] Board of Directors by regulation or order, to restrain or affect the exercise of power or functions of the [FDIC] as a conservator or a receiver." The provision has been interpreted to restrict injunctions and other equitable relief against the FDIC (or the now-defunct RTC) when it acts as a receiver or conservator, even if it were to violate its own procedures or to behave unlawfully. *281–300 Joint Venture v. Onion,* 938 F.2d 35, 39 (5th Cir.1991), *cert. denied,* 502 U.S. 1057, 112 S.Ct. 933 (1992); *Rosa v. Resolution Trust Corp.,* 938 F.2d 383, 397–400 (3d Cir.), *cert. denied,* 502 U.S. 981, 112 S.Ct. 582 (1991); *In re Landmark Land Co. of Okla.,* 973 F.2d 283 (4th Cir.1992); *Gross v. Bell Sav. Bank PaSA,* 974 F.2d 403 (3d Cir.1992); *Telematics Int'l, Inc. v. NEMLC Leasing Corp.,* 967 F.2d 703, 705–706 (1st Cir.1992); *United Liberty Life Ins. Co. v. Ryan,* 985 F.2d 1320, 1328–1329 (6th Cir.1993); *Harkness Apt. Owners Corp. v. Federal Deposit Ins. Corp.,* 999 F.2d 538 (2d Cir.1993); *National Trust for Historic Preservation v. Federal Deposit Ins. Corp.,* 21 F.3d 469 (D.C.Cir.1994); *Bursik v. One Fourth Street North, Ltd.,* 84 F.3d 1395 (11th Cir.1996).

2. *See D'Oench, Duhme & Co., Inc. v. Federal Deposit Ins. Corp.,* 315 U.S. 447, 62 S.Ct. 676 (1942) (holding such agreements unenforceable against the FDIC). Section 1823(e) codifies but does not preempt the *D'Oench, Duhme* decision. *Federal Sav. and Loan Ins. Corp. v. Griffin,* 935 F.2d 691, 698 (5th Cir.1991), *cert. denied sub nom. Griffin v. First Gibraltar Bank,* 502 U.S. 1092, 112 S.Ct. 1163 (1992); *Adams v. Madison Realty & Dev., Inc.,* 746 F.Supp. 419 (D.N.J.1990). *See also Federal Deposit Ins. Corp. v. Wainer,* 4 Ill.App.2d 233, 124 N.E.2d 29 (1955) (interpreting § 1823(e)); *Central W. Rental Co. v. Horizon Leasing,* 967 F.2d 832, 840 (3d Cir.1992) (doctrine prevents use of "oral undocumented agreements" as defense against enforcement of FDIC judgment); *Federal Deposit Ins. Corp. v. Kasal,* 913 F.2d 487 (8th Cir.1990) (applying § 1823(e)); *Oliver v. Resolution Trust Corp.,* 747 F.Supp. 1351 (E.D.Mo. 1990) (applying 1823(e)); *Morgan v. Heights Sav. Ass'n,* 741 F.Supp. 620 (E.D.Tex.1990) (applying doctrine to alleged pre-insolvency settlement of action on mortgage); *Mery v. Universal Sav. Ass'n,* 737 F.Supp. 1000 (S.D.Tex.1990) (applying § 1823(e) to partner's liability for partnership notes to failed institution); *Carico v. First Nat'l Bank of Bogata,* 734 F.Supp. 768 (E.D.Tex.1990) (applying § 1823(e)). The doctrine applies to affirmative claims as well as to defenses. *Jackson v. Federal Deposit Ins. Corp.,* 981 F.2d 730 (5th Cir.1992). *Accord Bruneau v. Federal Deposit Ins. Corp.,* 981 F.2d 175 (5th Cir.1992); *Federal Deposit Ins. Corp. v. Byrne,* 736 F.Supp. 727 (N.D.Tex.1990) (rule precludes affirmative claims as well as defenses). *See generally Federal Deposit Ins. Corp. v. Kucera Builders, Inc.,* 503 F.Supp. 967, 970 (N.D.Ga.1980) (collecting cases); Frank Skillern, *Federal Deposit Insurance Corporation and the Failed Bank: The Past Decade,* 99 Banking L.J. 292, 295–305 (1982) (discussing cases interpreting § 1823(e)); J. Michael Echevarria, *A Precedent Embalms a Principle: The Expansion of the* D'Oench, Duhme *Doctrine,* 43 Cath. U. L. Rev. 745 (1994) (reviewing and criticizing application of doctrine).

3. 12 U.S.C.A. § 1823(e), *as amended,* Pub. L. No. 101–73, § 217(4), 103 Stat. at 256. *See Timberland Design v. Federal Deposit Ins. Corp.,* 745 F.Supp. 784 (D.Mass. 1990) (applying amended § 1823(e) retroacof the FDIC in any asset acquired by it under the financial assistance provisions of the FDIA[4] or the conservatorship and receivership provisions of the FDIA,[5] either as security for a loan, by purchase, or as receiver, is invalid unless it meets certain specified conditions:[6]

(1) The agreement must be in writing.[7]

(2) The agreement must have been executed by the depository institution and the third party contemporaneously with the acquisition by the institution of the asset in question.[8]

(3) The agreement must have been approved by the institution's board of directors or its loan committee.[9]

(4) The agreement must have been, continuously from the time of its execution, an official record of the institution.[10]

A depository institution's alleged negligence in failing to meet these conditions is not imputable to the FDIC.[11] The doctrine bars defenses and affirmative claims whether characterized as contract or tort.[12] However, a defense of fraud in the inducement on the part of the depository institution may constitute a good defense despite 12 U.S.C.A. § 1823(e).[13]

tively to the benefit of FDIC as receiver); *Federal Deposit Ins. Corp. v. Sullivan*, 744 F.Supp. 239 (D.Colo.1990) (applying amended § 1823(e) retroactively); *Resolution Trust Corp. v. Camp*, 965 F.2d 25, 31 (5th Cir.1992) (avoiding question of retroactivity). *Cf. Resolution Trust Corp. v. Murray*, 935 F.2d 89, 94 (5th Cir.1991) (extension of doctrine to RTC claims); *Olney Sav. & Loan Ass'n v. Trinity Banc Sav. Ass'n*, 885 F.2d 266 274 (5th Cir.1989), *reh'g denied*, 892 F.2d 78 (extension of doctrine to FSLIC claims).

4. 12 U.S.C.A. § 1823(c).

5. *Id.* § 1821.

6. *Id.* § 1823(e). The doctrine may even be raised in the first instance on appeal in exceptional circumstances. *In re 604 Columbus Ave. Realty Trust*, 968 F.2d 1332, 1343–1344 (1st Cir.1992) (discussing circumstances).

7. *Id.* § 1823(e)(1).

8. *Id.* § 1823(e)(2).

9. *Id.* § 1823(e)(3). This approval must be reflected in the minutes of the board or committee. *Id.*

10. *Id.* § 1823(e)(4). In February 1997, the FDIC adopted a policy statement that sets forth circumstances under which the FDIC would assert the *D'Oench, Duhme* doctrine to bar certain agreements or arrangements entered into with an institution prior to its receivership. FDIC, *Statement of Policy Regarding Federal Common Law and Statutory Provisions Protecting FDIC,* *as Receiver or Corporate Liquidator, Against Unrecorded Agreements or Arrangements by a Depository Institution Prior to Receivership, reprinted in* 62 Fed. Reg. 5984 (1997).

11. *Federal Deposit Ins. Corp. v. Alker*, 164 F.2d 469 (3d Cir.1947). *See also Timberland Design, Inc. v. First Serv. Bank for Sav.*, 932 F.2d 46, 50 (1st Cir.1991) (actual knowledge of agreement by FDIC not bar to application of doctrine).

12. *Alker, supra. But see Federal Deposit Ins. Corp. v. Meo*, 505 F.2d 790 (9th Cir. 1974) (third party's defenses valid under § 1823(e) if misrepresentation of bank's records not the result of action or inaction of the third party).

13. *Black v. Federal Deposit Ins. Corp.*, 640 F.2d 699 (5th Cir.1981); *Federal Deposit Ins. Corp. v. Hoover–Morris*, 642 F.2d 785 (5th Cir.1981). *Cf. Federal Deposit Ins. Corp. v. Selaiden Builders*, 973 F.2d 1249, 1254–1255 (challenging ownership by FDIC of notes in question); *Resolution Trust Corp. v. Oaks Apts. Joint Venture*, 966 F.2d 995, 999–1001 (5th Cir.1992), *reh'g denied*, 974 F.2d 1337 (defenses based on obligations contained in integral loan agreement documents); *Federal Sav. and Loan Ins. Corp. v. Mackie*, 962 F.2d 1144, 1150–1151 (5th Cir.1992) (same); *Garrett v. Commonwealth Mortgage Co. of Am.*, 938 F.2d 591, 594–595 (5th Cir.1991) (defenses involving breach of fiduciary duty or negligence not necessarily dependent on "secret agreement").

§ 8.18   Claims Against Directors and Officers

Directors and officers of insured depository institutions in default may be held subject to personal liability in a civil action by or on behalf of the FDIC[1] for gross negligence under applicable state law.[2] Such actions may be brought by or on behalf of the FDIC on the basis of its status as conservator or receiver of the institution, on the basis of a claim purchased from, assigned by, or otherwise conveyed by the conservator or receiver, or on the basis of a claim purchased from, assigned by, or otherwise conveyed by an insured depository institution or its affiliate in connection with financial assistance extended by the FDIC under the "open bank" provisions of the FDIA.[3]

The statute explicitly states that this standard of conduct does not exclude a claim based on action by a director or officer involving a greater disregard of the fiduciary duty of care than gross negligence, such as, for example, intentional torts.[4] Concepts such as "gross negligence," "duty of care," and "intentional tortious conduct" are to be determined under applicable state law.[5]

In *Atherton v. Federal Deposit Insurance Corporation*,[6] the Supreme Court considered the implications of this gross negligence standard. The FDIC as receiver had brought an action against former officers and directors of a failed federal savings association, alleging negligence, breach of fiduciary duty, and gross negligence. The district court dismissed all claims except the gross negligence claim.[7] On interlocutory appeal, the Third Circuit reversed, concluding that the government could pursue any claims for negligence or breach of fiduciary duty available as a matter of federal common law.[8] In an opinion by Justice Breyer, the Court held that there was no federal common law providing a standard of care for officers and directors of federally insured savings institutions.[9] However, the FIRREA provision[10] setting forth a gross negligence standard for directors or officers of federally insured savings institutions provided only a minimum standard of conduct, a floor that guaranteed that officers and directors were required to meet at least a gross negligence standard.[11] Consequently, the FIRREA provision did not bar

---

§ 8.18

1. 12 U.S.C.A. § 1821(k)(1)-(3).

2. *Id.* § 1821(k).

3. *Id.* § 1821(k)(1)-(3). On open bank assistance, see *id.* § 1823.

4. *Id.* § 1823(k).

5. *Id. See Federal Deposit Ins. Corp. v. Canfield*, 967 F.2d 443, 448 (10th Cir.1992), *cert. dismissed*, 506 U.S. 993, 113 S.Ct. 516 (discussing statute's reliance on state law for definition of gross negligence); *Federal Deposit Ins. Corp. v. McSweeney*, 976 F.2d 532 536–537 (9th Cir.1992), *cert. denied*, 508 U.S. 950, 113 S.Ct. 2440 (1993) (citing *Canfield*).

6. 519 U.S. 213, 117 S.Ct. 666 (1997).

7. *Atherton*, 519 U.S. at 216, 117 S.Ct. at 669.

8. 57 F.3d 1231 (3d Cir.1995).

9. *Atherton*, 519 U.S. at 218, 117 S.Ct. at 669.

10. 12 U.S.C.A. § 1821(k).

11. *Atherton*, 519 U.S. at 227, 117 S.Ct. at 674.

the application of any stricter state standard making directors and officers liable for such conduct, as simple negligence.[12]

In a separate opinion joined by Justices Scalia and Thomas, Justice O'Connor concurred in part and concurred in the judgment.[13] She found that "the most natural reading of the savings clause in 12 U.S.C.A. § 1821(k) covers both state and federal rights."[14] Consequently, in light of the plain statutory language, she could not endorse the Court's reliance on admittedly ambivalent legislative history to support the holding.[15]

A cause of action may also be pursued by the FDIC against any director, officer, employee, agent, attorney, accountant, appraiser, or other employee or provider of services for damages for "the improvident or otherwise improper use or investment of an insured depository institution's assets."[16]

§ 8.19   Emergency Interstate Acquisitions

At a time when interstate expansion of banks was subject to significant limitation,[1] the administratively arranged interstate acquisition of a failing depository institution was an important device. From the point of view of the acquiring institution, the transaction had the added attractiveness of giving it access to interstate markets that might otherwise be unavailable.[2]

Such acquisitions are typically arranged through a bidding process. In emergency circumstances an out-of-state acquiror may be the only feasible candidate to take over the failing institution and avoid an expensive regulatory resolution of the institution's eventual default. The FDIA provides for such acquisitions.

§ 8.20   Target Banks in Default

In the case of an insured bank or a holding company, assisted[1] emergency interstate acquisitions by an out-of-state bank, savings associ-

---

12. 519 U.S. at 227, 117 S.Ct. at 675.

13. 519 U.S. at 231, 117 S.Ct. at 676 (O'Connor, J., concurring in part and concurring in the judgment).

14. 519 U.S. at 232, 117 S.Ct. at 677.

15. *Id.*

16. 12 U.S.C.A. § 1821(*l*). Such damages include losses of principal and appropriate interest. *Id.* For a pre-FIRREA cause of action against accountants of a failed savings association, see *Federal Deposit Ins. Corp. v. Cherry, Bekaert & Holland*, 742 F.Supp. 612 (M.D.Fla.1990).

§ 8.19

1. *See, e.g.,* 12 U.S.C.A. §§ 36(c), 1843(d) (1988) (imposing restrictions on national bank branching and on interstate bank holding company acquisitions).

2. *See, e.g.,* Bennett, *Citicorp Acquires Fidelity: New York Bank Allowed into California,* N.Y. Times, Sept. 29, 1982, at D1 (describing Citicorp's entry into California market through acquisition of failing Fidelity Savings and Loan Association).

§ 8.20

1. *I.e.,* financially assisted by the FDIC under 12 U.S.C.A. § 1823(c). *See id.* § 1823(f)(1) (conditioning acquisitions on provision of FDIC assistance).

ation, or holding company are authorized under certain specified conditions.[2] Under certain circumstances, an emergency interstate acquisition may be authorized even though the § 1823(c) financial assistance *preceded* the proposed acquisition, rather than being an integral part of it.[3] The FDIC may require consideration for its previous assistance as a condition for approval of such an acquisition.[4]

If the target insured bank is in default, the target must have total assets of $500 million or more to qualify for an assisted interstate acquisition.[5] The FDIC must consult the target's state bank supervisor before making a determination to take action.[6] The supervisor must be given a reasonable opportunity (not less than 48 hours) to object to the proposed acquisition.[7] If there is an objection, the FDIC may still proceed, but only on an affirmative vote of 75 percent of the FDIC Board of Directors.[8]

Assuming all applicable conditions are met, the FDIC is authorized to arrange a purchase and assumption transaction involving the insured bank in default.[9] Such transactions are also generally subject to the approval of the primary federal or state supervisor of each party to the transaction.[10] However, these transactions are generally not subject to the interstate banking provisions of the Bank Holding Company Act, state law, or the savings and loan holding company provisions of the Home Owner's Loan Act.[11] Any subsidiary created as a result of the

---

2. *Id.* § 1823(f)(1). No assistance is authorized for a holding company subsidiary, other than a subsidiary that is itself an insured depository institution, in connection with any assisted emergency interstate acquisition. *Id.* § 1823(f)(9)(A). However, this does not prohibit an intermediate holding company or an affiliate of an insured depository institution from being a conduit for assistance ultimately intended for an insured bank. *Id.* § 1823(f)(9)(B).

3. *Id.* § 1823(f)(3)(D), which provides:

if—

    (i) at any time after August 10, 1987, the [FDIC] provides any assistance under [§ 1823(c)] to an insured bank; and

    (ii) at the time such assistance is granted, the insured bank, the holding company which controls the insured bank (if any), or any affiliated insured bank is eligible to be acquired by an out-of-State bank or out-of-State holding company under this paragraph,

the insured bank, the holding company, and such other affiliated insured bank shall remain eligible, subject to such terms and conditions as the [FDIC] (in the [FDIC's] discretion) may impose, to be acquired by an out-of-State bank or out-of-State holding company under this paragraph as long as any portion of such assistance remains outstanding.

4. *Id.* § 1823(f)(3)(G).

5. *Id.* § 1823(f)(2)(A). Total assets are determined as of the most recent report of condition. *Id.*

6. *Id.* § 1823(f)(2)(B)(i).

7. *Id.* § 1823(f)(2)(B)(ii).

8. *Id.* § 1823(f)(2)(B)(iii).

9. *Id.* § 1823(f)(2)(A).

10. *Id.*

11. *Id.* § 1823(f)(4)(A), (E), provides:

    (4)(A) Acquisitions not subject to certain other laws

    Section 1842(d) of this title, any provision of State law, and section 1730a(e)(3) of this title shall not apply to prohibit any acquisition under paragraph (2) or (3), except that an out-of-State bank may make such an acquisition only if such ownership is otherwise specifically authorized....

    (E) Certain State interstate banking laws inapplicable

    Any holding company which acquires control of any insured bank or holding company under paragraph (2) or (3) or subparagraph (D) of this paragraph shall not, by reason of such acquisition, be required under the law of any State to transaction may retain existing branches of the target institution,[12] but this does not authorize any move of a principal office or branch.[13] Any subsequent nonemergency interstate acquisitions would be subject to applicable state law.[14]

In determining whether or not to arrange such a transaction, the FDIC is authorized in its discretion to solicit offers or acquisition proposals from any prospective purchasers or merger partners.[15] Intra-industry in-state bidders are favored in this process.[16]

In considering bids, the FDIC is to give consideration to minimizing the cost of its financial assistance and to the maintenance of specialized depository institutions.[17] Generally, a disappointed bidder for bank assets does not have standing to challenge the FDIC's selection of the successful bidder.[18]

In deciding to authorize any particular assisted emergency acquisition, the FDIC is directed to apply the following priorities, in the following order:

(1) Transactions should be authorized, if possible, between depository institutions of the same type within the same state.[19]

(2) Transactions should be authorized between depository institutions of the same type, but in different states that authorize such

divest any other insured bank or be prevented from acquiring any other bank or holding company.

12. *Id.* § 1823(f)(4)(B).

13. *Id.* § 1823(f)(4)(C).

14. *Id.* § 1823(f)(4)(D)(i). This provision does not apply to any out-of-state bank holding company before the end of the earlier of the following two periods:

(1) the end of the two-year period beginning on the date the acquisition is consummated; or

(2) the end of any period established under state law during which the out-of-state bank holding company may not be treated as a bank holding company whose insured bank subsidiaries' operations are "principally conducted" in the state for purposes of acquiring other insured banks or establishing bank branches.

Id. § 1823(f)(4)(D)(ii)(I)-(II). For these purposes, the state where the operations are "principally conducted" means "the State in which the operations of a holding company's insured bank subsidiaries are principally conducted is the State determined under [§ 1842(d)] with respect to such holding company." *Id.* § 1823(f)(4)(D) (iii).

15. *Id.* § 1823(f)(5). Such prospective purchasers or partners must be "both qualified and capable of acquiring the assets and liabilities of the bank in default or in danger of default." *Id.*

16. *See, e.g., id.* § 1823(f)(6)(A):

If, after receiving offers, the offer presenting the lowest expense to the [FDIC]. that is in a form and with conditions acceptable to the [FDIC] (hereinafter referred to as the "lowest acceptable offer"), is from an offeror that is not an existing in-State bank of the same type as the bank that is in default or is in danger of default (or, where the bank is an insured bank other than a mutual savings bank, the lowest acceptable offer is not from an in-State holding company), the [FDIC] shall permit the offeror which made the initial lowest acceptable offer and each offeror who made an offer the estimated cost of which to the [FDIC] was within 15 per centum or $15,000,000, whichever is less, of the initial lowest acceptable offer to submit a new offer.

The FDIC's calculations and estimations of the cost of offers and reoffers are determinative. *Id.* § 1823(f)(6) (D). The FDIC is authorized to set reasonable time limits on offers and reoffers. *Id.*

17. *Id.* § 1823(f)(6)(B). In other words, the FDIC is directed to favorably consider transactions that would not result in a savings association being absorbed by a commercial bank. *Id.*

18. *Gosnell v. Federal Deposit Ins. Corp.*, 938 F.2d 372, 376 (2d Cir.1991).

19. 12 U.S.C.A. § 1823(f)(6)(B)(i).

transactions, or failing that, at least in states that are contiguous.[20]

(3) If not in such states, then transactions should be authorized between depository institutions at least of the same type but in different states.[21]

(4) If not such institutions, then transactions should be authorized between depository institutions of different types in the same state.[22]

(5) If not in the same state, then transactions should be authorized between depository institutions of different types, but in different states that authorize such transactions, or failing that, at least in states that are contiguous.[23]

(6) If not in such states, then transactions should be authorized between depository institutions of different types but in different states.[24]

However, in the case of a minority-controlled target bank, before the FDIC proceeds to these bidding priorities, it is required to seek an offer from other minority-controlled banks.[25] In any event, a transaction is prohibited if it would result in, or further a scheme to create, a monopoly or attempt to monopolize the business of banking in any part of the United States.[26] A transaction is also prohibited if its effect in any section of the country would be anticompetitive, unless the FDIC finds that the anticompetitive effects would be clearly outweighed by the probable effect of the transaction in meeting the convenience and needs of the community to be served by the target institution.[27] Finally, a transaction is prohibited if, in the opinion of the FDIC, the acquisition would threaten the safety and soundness of the acquiror or would not result in the future viability of the resulting institution.[28]

§ 8.21 Target Banks in Danger of Default

If the target is in danger of default, somewhat different conditions apply. In this case, one or more out-of-state banks or holding companies are permitted to acquire and retain shares or assets of an insured bank in danger of default if it has total assets of $500 million or more.[1] In addition, such banks or holding companies may acquire two or more affiliated insured banks in danger of closing if the targets have aggregate total assets of $500 million or more, or if the aggregate total is equal to or greater than 33 percent of the aggregate total assets of all such

---

20. *Id.* § 1823(f)(6)(B)(ii)(I)-(II).

21. *Id.* § 1823(f)(6)(B)(iii).

22. *Id.* § 1823(f)(6)(B)(iv).

23. *Id.* § 1823(f)(6)(B)(v)(I)-(II).

24. *Id.* § 1823(f)(6)(B)(vi).

25. *Id.* § 1823(f)(6)(C). On the acquisition of a minority-controlled bank by a mi-

nority bank holding company, see *id.* § 1823(f)(12).

26. *Id.* § 1823(f)(7)(A).

27. *Id.* § 1823(f)(7)(B).

28. *Id.* § 1823(f)(7)(C).

§ 8.21

1. 12 U.S.C.A. § 1823(f)(3)(A)(i).

affiliated insured banks.[2] In either case, if the 33 percent test is met, the acquirors may also acquire and retain shares or assets of the holding company that controls the affiliated target banks or any other affiliated insured banks.[3]

Assisted emergency acquisitions of banks in danger of default are only permitted if the board of directors or trustees of each target requests FDIC assistance in writing.[4] In addition to any other applicable approval requirements under state or federal law,[5] no final action can be taken by the FDIC unless the state bank supervisor in the state in which the target bank is located approves the acquisition.[6] These acquisitions are subject to the same bidding rules and priorities as apply to acquisitions of banks in default. They are also subject to the same prohibitions with respect to monopoly, anticompetitiveness, and safety and soundness.

§ 8.22   Target Savings Associations

Similar rules apply to emergency acquisitions of savings associations.[1] However, unlike the corresponding provisions with respect to emergency acquisitions of insured banks and holding companies, these provisions do not specifically require that the acquisition transaction involve financial assistance by the FDIC under § 1823(c).[2] They do include specific provisions for financial assistance before grounds exist for appointment of a conservator or receiver.[3]

Notwithstanding contrary state law provisions,[4] the FDIC may authorize certain acquisitions if it determines that severe financial conditions threaten the stability of a significant number of savings associations, or of savings associations with significant financial resources, and that authorization of an emergency acquisition would lessen the FDIC's risk.[5] Eligible transactions under this provision are:

> (1) Merger, consolidation, or purchase and assumption of a savings association eligible for financial assistance under § 1823(c) with any other savings association or any insured bank;[6]

---

2. *Id.* § 1823(f)(3)(A)(ii).

3. *Id.* § 1823(f)(3)(B).

4. *Id.* § 1823(f)(3)(C).

5. *Id.* § 1823(f)(3)(F). However, these transactions are generally not subject to § 1842(d), state law, or the S & L holding company provisions of the Home Owner's Loan Act. *Id.* § 1823(f)(4)(A), (E). Any subsidiary created as a result of the transaction may retain existing branches of the target institution, *id.* § 1823(f)(4)(B), but this does not authorize any move of a principal office or branch. *Id.* § 1823(f)(4)(C). Subsequent nonemergency interstate acquisitions would be subject to applicable state law. *Id.* § 1823(f)(4)(D).

6. *Id.* § 1823(f)(3)(E).

§ 8.22

1. 12 U.S.C.A. § 1823(k).

2. *Id.*

3. *Id.* § 1823(k)(5).

4. Nothing in this authorization overrides or supersedes state laws restricting or limiting the activities of savings associations undertaken on behalf of another entity. *Id.* § 1823(k)(1)(A)(vi).

5. *Id.* § 1823(k)(1)(A)(i).

6. *Id.* § 1823(k)(1)(A)(i)(I). With the concurrence of the OTS, such an acquisition by a federal savings association where the target becomes a subsidiary of the acquiror is permitted without regard to investment

    (2) Acquisition of control of such a savings association by any other savings association;[7] or,

    (3) Acquisition of control, or purchase and assumption of such a savings association by any company.[8]

The FDIC may only authorize such a transaction if it determines that the authorization will not present a substantial risk to the safety and soundness of the target and the acquiror.[9] The transaction may be authorized on such terms as the FDIC provides.[10] The transaction is subject to any required approval of the appropriate federal banking agency of each party to the transaction.[11] Dual service of management officials otherwise prohibited by the Depository Institutions Management Interlocks Act[12] may continue for a period of 10 years after the acquisition, with the approval of the FDIC.[13]

The FDIC must consult the target's state supervisor before making a determination to take action.[14] The supervisor must be given a reasonable opportunity (not less than 48 hours) to object to the proposed acquisition.[15] The FDIC may still proceed, but only on an affirmative vote of 75 percent of the FDIC Board of Directors.[16]

The FDIC is expressly authorized in its discretion to solicit practicable offers and proposals from prospective purchasers or merger partners.[17] Such bidders must be "qualified and capable of acquiring the assets and liabilities of the [target] savings association."[18] However, in the case of a minority-controlled institution, the FDIC is required to seek offers from other minority-controlled bidders before seeking offers from other bidders.[19]

Special provisions exist with respect to the retention of branches.[20] If a merger, consolidation, transfer, or acquisition involves a savings association eligible for FDIC assistance and a bank or bank holding company, the savings association may retain and operate any existing branch or branches or any other existing facilities.[21] If the savings association continues to exist as a separate entity, it may establish and operate new branches to the same extent as any savings association that is not affiliated with a bank holding company, and the home office of which is

---

percentage limitations of § 1464(c)(4)(B). *Id.* § 1823(k)(1)(A)(iv).

7. *Id.* § 1823(k)(1)(i)(A)(II). With the concurrence of the OTS, such an acquisition by a federal savings association where the target becomes a subsidiary of the acquiror is permitted without regard to investment percentage limitations of § 1464(c)(4)(B). *Id.* § 1823(k)(1)(A)(iv).

8. *Id.* § 1823(k)(1)(i)(A)(III).

9. *Id.* § 1823(k)(1)(A)(i).

10. *Id.* § 1823(k)(1)(A)(ii).

11. *Id.* § 1823(k)(1)(A)(iii).

12. *Id.* §§ 3201 *et seq.*

13. *Id.* § 1823(k)(1)(A)(v).

14. *Id.* § 1823(k)(1)(B)(i).

15. *Id.* § 1823(k)(1)(B)(ii).

16. *Id.* § 1823(k)(1)(B)(iii).

17. *Id.* § 1823(k)(2)(A).

18. *Id.*

19. *Id.* § 1823(k)(2)(B).

20. *Id.* § 1823(k)(4). *Cf. Arkansas State Bank Comm'r v. Resolution Trust Corp.*, 911 F.2d 161 (8th Cir.1990) (upholding operation of branches by acquiror despite contrary state law).

21. 12 U.S.C.A. § 1823(k)(4)(A).

located in the same state.[22] Notwithstanding this branching authorization, however, certain limitations apply.[23] If the savings association does not have its home office in the state of the bank holding company bank subsidiary, and it does not qualify as a "domestic building and loan association" for tax purposes,[24] the savings association is subject to the same conditions imposed on a bank seeking to retain, operate, and establish branches in the state in which the insured association is located.[25] The FDIC is authorized, for good cause, to allow the association up to two years to comply with these requirements.[26]

22. *Id.*

23. *Id.* § 1823(k)(4)(B)(i).

24. 26 U.S.C.A. § 7701(a)(19). The same result would apply if the association does not meet the asset composition test imposed by *id.* § 7701(a)(19)(C).

25. 12 U.S.C.A. § 1823(k)(4)(B)(i)(I)–(II).

26. *Id.* § 1823(k)(4)(B)(ii).

Chapter 9

INTERNATIONAL BANKING

Table of Sections

§ 9.1   Introduction

The development of international banking by U.S.-based banks has tended to be reactive.[1] For the most part, U.S. international banking has

---

§ 9.1

1. Nevertheless, a select number of U.S. banks did venture offshore in pursuit of their own strategies by the end of the nineteenth century, such as J.P. Morgan and Company and Lazard Freres among others.

followed the expansion of transnational business interests of U.S. banks' larger customers. By 1914, however, European banks still dominated foreign bank branching over U.S. banks by a margin of almost 100 to 1.[2]

Four developments during the second decade of the Twentieth Century gradually changed the balance of power in international banking. First, in 1913 the Federal Reserve Act ("FRA") was enacted with provisions that for the first time permitted foreign branching by national banks.[3] Second, the beginning of World War I in 1914 began to realign the relative influence of U.S. and European banks.[4] Third, in 1916 the FRA was amended to authorize the Board of Governors of the Federal Reserve System ("Fed") to enter into agreements with state-chartered member banks to incorporate under state law subsidiaries specializing in international and foreign banking, so-called Agreement corporations.[5] Fourth, the Edge Act amended the FRA again in 1919 to permit the Fed to authorize the incorporation under federal law of subsidiaries specializing in international and foreign banking.[6]

The emerging influence of U.S.-based banks in international banking continued through the post-World War II period, in no small part due to the development of the Eurodollar market in offshore dollar-denominated deposits.[7] As the post-war dominance of U.S. commercial and financial strength diminished with reemergence of European economies and the development of newly emerging economies in Asia, and as financial problems of U.S. banks themselves developed in the late 1980s, overall international presence of U.S. banks also diminished.[8] However, during the 1990s, U.S. financial centers have reemerged as stable havens of economic activity,[9] and as a result the strength and influence of those centers have been renewed.[10]

See SARKIS J. KHOURY, DYNAMICS OF INTERNATIONAL BANKING 38 (New York: Praeger Special Studies, 1980) (discussing offshore expansion of certain U.S. banks in the 1800s). Citibank followed this trend after the enactment of international branching provisions in the Federal Reserve Act in 1913, 12 U.S.C.A. §§ 601 *et seq.*, establishing a network of offshore branches by the onset of World War I. *See* Haley & Seligman, *The Development of International Banking by the United States, in* W. H. BAUGHN & D. R. MANDICH, THE INTERNATIONAL BANKING HANDBOOK (1983) (discussing Citibank's expansion into 13 countries).

2. F. JOHN MATHIS, ED., OFFSHORE LENDING BY U.S. BANKS 2–3 (PHILADELPHIA: ROBERT MORRIS ASSOCIATES, 1981).

3. 12 U.S.C.A. §§ 601 *et seq.*

4. Haley & Seligman, *supra* note 1.

5. 12 U.S.C.A. §§ 613 *et seq. See* Neil Pinsky, *Edge Act and Agreement Corporations: Mediums for International Banking, in* Economic Perspective 28 (Federal Reserve Bank of Chicago, September–October 1978) (discussing slow historical beginning of use of state-incorporated "Agreement" corporations and federally incorporated Edge Act corporations).

6. 12 U.S.C.A. §§ 613 *et seq.*

7. *See, e.g.,* WORLD FINANCIAL MARKETS 3, 15 (New York: Morgan Guaranty Trust Co., October 1980) (noting the expanding importance of the Eurodollar market).

8. *See* Kraus, *Overseas Pullback by US Banks Portends Reduced Global Role*, Am. Banker, Sept. 21, 1988, at 1, col. 2 (discussing changes in international role of U.S. banks).

9. *See, e.g.,* Sharon R. King, *Watchful Waiting on Japan*, N.Y. Times, Nov. 26, 1997, at C1, col. 2 (discussing the relative stability of U.S. financial markets).

10. *Cf.* Richard W. Stevenson, *Clinton Presses Asians at Summit To Remedy the Economic Turmoil*, N.Y. Times, at A1, col. 4

§ 9.2   The Regulatory Environment

Permissible international banking activities vary significantly from country to country, largely due to the differing regulatory environments in their respective home states.[1] As a general rule, in less developed countries banking is subject to more severe controls than in developed economies. However, given the increasingly "globalized" nature of the banking markets, the regulatory environment facing a bank involved in international banking tends to be a complex mix of home-state supervision, host-state regulation, and specialized international or multinational rules enforced by both states.

A number of important contemporary trends have shaped the contours of the regulatory environment of international banking. First, an increasingly important role has been taken by the European Union ("EU") in the regulation of banking, and adjustments in the regulatory environment of the individual EU member states have become necessary.[2] Second, the transition from socialist to market economies in central and eastern Europe and the transformation of the former Soviet Union into the loose confederation of the Commonwealth of Independent States has had important consequences for banking and bank regulation.[3] Third, something approaching genuine international regulation has emerged primarily under the auspices of the Bank for International Settlements ("BIS") and the "Group of Ten," the major industrialized democracies. Each of these developments has had a marked impact on the conduct of international banking activities.

§ 9.3   National Supervision of International Banking

One fundamental objective is shared by bank supervisors worldwide: to support the "lender of last resort" function triggered by significant financial instability, in order to maintain public confidence in the depository institutions system.[1] Since domestic banking systems are interlinked—if not integrated—on a transborder basis, significant instability

(discussing relative influence of U.S. economic policy); John M. Broder, *Asia Pacific Talks Vow Tough Action on Economic Crisis*, N.Y. Times, at A1, col. 6 (illustrating effects of U.S. financial and economic strength).

§ 9.2

1. *See* Wendt, *The Role of Foreign Banks in International Banking*, in W. H. BAUGHN & D. R. MANDICH, THE INTERNATIONAL BANKING HANDBOOK (1983) (discussing varying roles of non-U.S. banks in international banking).

2. *See. e.g.*, M. GALY, G. PASTOR & T. PUJOL, SPAIN: CONVERGING WITH THE EUROPEAN COMMUNITY (IMF Occasional Paper 101, Feb. 1993) (discussing effects of ongoing convergence of the Spanish banking system with the EU).

3. *See, e.g.*, Inna Vysman, *The New Banking Legislation in Russia: Theoretical Adequacy, Practical Difficulties, and Potential Solutions*, 62 Fordham L. Rev. 265 (1993) (describing and assessing transformation of banking and bank regulation in the Russian Federation).

§ 9.3

1. In the United States, the lender of last resort function—providing financial assistance to institutions experiencing the in any one market is potentially a problem for other markets. Yet there often appears to be little if any agreement among national regulators as to approaches to regulation and supervision of depository institutions subject to their respective jurisdictions, particularly on a day-to-day basis. In the case of U.S. bank supervision and regulation, the approach has been one of relatively close oversight of the banking system, including maintenance of public confidence and stability by the establishment of restrictions on industry structure (*e.g.*, entry, competition, products,) and operations (*e.g.*, capital adequacy, lending limits, liquidity, interest rates). In other jurisdictions, supervision may be comparatively passive, or it may largely consist of self-regulation, at least on a day-to-day basis.

§ 9.4 U.S. Supervision of International Banking

The regulatory structure governing U.S. domestic banking is extremely complex. That complexity carries over into U.S. regulation of international banking activities. However, additional complications are introduced into the regulatory structure specifically because of the international dimension of these activities. A basic overview of U.S. regulation of international banking activity is provided in Figure 9–1, *infra*.

Foreign-based banks operate in the United States within the same supervisory structure as U.S.-based banks, consistent with the policy of "national treatment" established by the International Banking Act of 1978.[1] (Different modes of operation are explained in § 9.11, *infra*.) A foreign-based bank that wishes to operate a representative office in the United States must obtain the prior approval of the Fed. To operate an agency, branch, affiliate, or subsidiary in the United States it must apply to the Fed, and a U.S. agency or branch of a foreign-based bank must be licensed and supervised either by a state supervisor or the Comptroller of the Currency. In addition, all U.S. agencies or branches must be approved and supervised by the Fed. The FDIC approves deposit insurance coverage for U.S. branches of foreign banks.

In December 1991, the President signed into law the Federal Deposit Insurance Corporation Improvement Act of 1991 ("FDICIA").[2] In brief, the principal features of the FDICIA that affect international banking are as follows.

most significant financial crises—has traditionally been performed by the Federal Reserve System. The National Credit Union Administration also performs a similar function with respect to credit unions, as did the now defunct Federal Home Loan Bank Board, until 1989, with respect to savings associations.

§ 9.4

1. On the concept of national treatment, see *Conference of State Bank Supervisors v. Conover*, 715 F.2d 604 (D.C.Cir.1983), *cert. denied*, 466 U.S. 927, 104 S.Ct. 1708 (1984).

2. Pub. L. No. 102–242, 105 Stat. 2236 (Dec. 19, 1991) (codified at scattered sections of 12 U.S.C.A.).

a. *Capital supervision.* The FDICIA requires the federal banking agencies to revise their risk-based capital standards for insured depository institutions to ensure, among other things, that these standards take account of interest-rate risk, concentration of credit risk, and the risks of nontraditional activities.[3] The agencies are also required to discuss the development of comparable standards with members of the supervisory committee of the BIS.[4]

b. *Payments on foreign deposits.* FDICIA prohibits the agencies from making, directly or indirectly, any payment, or from providing any financial assistance in connection with any insured depository institution that would have the direct or indirect effect of satisfying any claim, in whole or in part, against the institution for its obligations on foreign deposits.[5] This prohibition does not apply to "open bank assistance" provided by the FDIC.[6] Nor does the prohibition bar a Federal Reserve bank from making advances or other extensions of credit consistent with the Federal Reserve Act (so-called discount window lending).[7]

c. *Establishment and operation of federal branches and agencies of foreign-based banks.* Under FDICIA, the Comptroller is required, in considering any application for approval of an initial federal branch or agency, to include any condition imposed by the Fed as a condition for the approval of the application.[8] The Comptroller is also required to coordinate examinations of such branches and agencies with examinations conducted by the Fed, to the extent possible, to participate in any simultaneous examinations of U.S. operations of foreign banks requested by the Fed.[9] Furthermore, in considering any application to establish an additional federal branch or agency of a foreign-based bank, the Comptroller is required to provide the Fed with notice and opportunity for comment on the application.[10]

d. *Broadened Fed supervisory authority.* The Fed is given authority to approve the establishment of any branch or agency, or the acquisition or control of any commercial lending company by a foreign-based bank.[11] The Fed also has the authority, under specified circumstances to order the closing of any state-licensed office of a foreign-based bank,[12] and to recommend to the Comptroller the termination of the license of any federally-licensed office of a foreign-based bank.[13] The FDICIA also gives the Fed broad authority to examine U.S. branches, agencies and affiliates of foreign-based banks, whether state- or federally-approved.[14]

e. *Limitation of powers of state-licensed branches and agencies.* The FDICIA prohibits a state-licensed branch or agency from engaging in any

---

3. FDICIA, § 305(b)(1) (12 U.S.C.A. § 1828 Note).

4. FDICIA, § 305(b)(2).

5. 12 U.S.C.A. § 1831r(a).

6. *Id.* § 1831r(b). On "open-bank" assistance, see *id.* § 1823(c).

7. *Id.* § 1831r(c).

8. *Id.* § 3102(a)(2).

9. *Id.* § 3102(b).

10. *Id.* § 3102(h)(2).

11. *Id.* § 3105(d)(1), (g).

12. *Id.* § 3105(e)(1)–(4), (g).

13. *Id.* § 3105(e)(5).

14. *Id.* § 3105(b)(1).

type of activity that is not permissible for a federally-licensed branch, unless the Fed determines that the activity is consistent with sound banking practice, and (in the case of an insured branch), the FDIC determines that the activity would pose no significant risk to the deposit insurance fund.[15] In addition, such branches and agencies are subject to the same limits on lending to a single borrower that apply to federally-licensed branches and agencies.[16]

f. *Establishment and supervision of representative offices.* Prior to the FDICIA, a foreign bank operating a representative office in the United States was only required to register the office with the Department of the Treasury.[17] Under the FDICIA, establishment of a representative office now requires prior approval of the Fed.[18] The Fed also has the authority to terminate the activities of any representative office.[19] It also has the authority to examine representative offices.[20]

g. *Cooperation with foreign supervisors.* The FDICIA explicitly authorizes disclosure of supervisory information by the federal bank agencies to foreign bank regulatory or supervisory authorities.[21]

h. *Retail deposit-taking by foreign banks.* To accept or maintain deposit accounts with balances of less than $100,000, foreign banks are required to establish one or more U.S. banking subsidiaries for that purpose, and to obtain federal deposit insurance for any such subsidiary.[22] However, if the foreign bank had a U.S. branch that was an insured branch prior to FDICIA, the branch may continue to accept or maintain retail deposits.[23]

i. *New penalties.* The FDICIA established authority for civil money penalties (administrative fines) to be assessed against any foreign bank, and any office or subsidiary of a foreign bank, that violates, and any individual who participates in a violation of, any provision of the International Banking Act, or any regulation prescribed or order issued under the act.[24] In addition, the FDICIA established criminal penalties for the knowing violation of any provision of the International Banking Act or any regulation or order issued by a federal banking agency under the act, with the intent to deceive, to gain financially, or to cause financial gain or loss to any person.[25]

Where do the U.S. state bank regulators fit into this regulatory structure? International Banking Act ("IBA") provisions concerning federal branches and agencies have minimized the role of state bank regulators as policy makers, since entry into the U.S. market through

---

15. *Id.* § 3105(h)(1).

16. *Id.* § 3105(h)(2). In fact, the FDICIA allows the Fed or the state supervisory authority to impose more stringent restrictions than apply to federally-licensed branches and agencies. *Id.* § 3105(h)(3).

17. 12 U.S.C.A. § 3107 (1988).

18. 12 U.S.C.A. § 3107(a). Compliance with any applicable state law requirements is still required. *Id.* § 3107(d).

19. *Id.* § 3107(b).

20. *Id.* § 3107(c).

21. *Id.* § 3109(a).

22. *Id.* § 3104(c)(1).

23. *Id.* § 3104(c)(2).

24. *Id.* § 3110.

25. *Id.* § 3111.

federal licensing of a branch or agency is a preemptive possibility in most cases.[26] FDICIA amendments of the IBA have further affected the relative importance of the state regulators with respect to international banking. The Fed's authority over state-licensed branches and agencies has increased dramatically. Powers of state-licensed branches and agencies are now directly limited by the IBA.[27] The Fed may even impose more stringent restrictions than those that apply to federally-licensed branches and agencies.[28] The establishment of representative offices is also subject to prior Fed approval, and the Fed has the authority to examine and to terminate such offices.[29]

Figure 9–1

Depository Institutions and their Regulators: International Banking Activities[30]

A. Organization & Expansion

Type of Institution	Chartering/ Licensing	Branching Intrastate	Branching Interstate	Acquisitions Intrastate	Acquisitions Interstate
Foreign Branch of U.S. Bank					
National Bank	Federal Reserve	N/A	N/A	N/A	N/A
State Fed–Member Bank	Federal Reserve and States	N/A	N/A	N/A	N/A
Insured State Non–Member Bank	FDIC & States	N/A	N/A	N/A	N/A
Edge Act Corporation	Federal Reserve	Federal Reserve	Federal Reserve	Federal Reserve	Federal Reserve
Agreement Corporation	State and Federal Reserve	Federal Reserve	Federal Reserve	State and Federal Reserve	Federal Reserve
International Banking Facility	N/A	N/A	N/A	N/A	N/A
U.S. Branches & Agencies of Foreign Banks					
Federal	Comptroller & Federal Reserve	Comptroller & Federal Reserve	Comptroller & FDIC	Comptroller & Federal Reserve	Comptroller & Federal Reserve
State	States & Federal Reserve	States & FDIC	States & Federal Reserve	States, Federal Reserve, & FDIC	States & Federal Reserve

26. *Conference of State Bank Supervisors, supra.*

27. 12 U.S.C.A. § 3105(h).

28. *Id.* § 3105(h)(3).

29. *Id.* § 3107.

30. Source: Adapted from Federal Reserve Bank of New York, *Depository Institutions and Their Regulators* (1987).

B. Transactional

Type of Institution	Reserve Requirements	Access to Discount Window	Discount Deposit
Foreign Branch of U.S. Bank			
National Bank	Federal Reserve	N/A	N/A
State Fed– Mem– ber Bank	Federal Reserve	N/A	N/A
Insured State Non–Member Bank	Federal Reserve	N/A	N/A
Edge Act Corporation	Federal Reserve	N/A	N/A
Agreement Corporation	Federal Reserve	N/A	N/A
International Banking Facility	Federal Reserve	N/A	N/A
U.S. Branches & Agencies of Foreign Banks			
Federal	Federal Reserve	Federal Reserve	FDIC
State	Federal Reserve	Federal Reserve	FDIC

C. Supervision & Regulation

Type of Institution	Supervision and Examination	Prudential Limits, Safety & Soundness	Consumer Protection	Enforcement
Foreign Branch of U.S. Bank				
National Bank	Comptroller	Comptroller	N/A	Comptroller
State Fed– Member Bank	Federal Reserve & States	Federal Reserve & States	N/A	Federal Reserve & States
Insured State Non–Member Bank	FDIC & States	FDIC & States	N/A	FDIC & States
Edge Act Corporation	Federal Reserve	Federal Reserve	N/A	Federal Reserve
Agreement Corporation	States & Federal Reserve	States & Federal Reserve	N/A	States & Federal Reserve
International Banking Facility	Federal Reserve	Federal Reserve	N/A	N/A
U.S. Branches & Agencies of Foreign Banks				
Federal	Comptroller & Federal Reserve	Comptroller& Federal Reserve	Comptroller & Federal Reserve	Comptroller & Federal Reserve
State	States, Federal Reserve, & FDIC	States, Federal Reserve, & FDIC	States & Federal Reserve	States, Federal Reserve, & FDIC

§ 9.5 Host State Regulation of International Banking

The international activities of U.S. banks are also affected by the regulation of other host states. International banking is subject to a diverse array of restrictions imposed by host states, in many cases severely limiting and in some cases actually prohibiting entry of nonindigenous banking enterprises into the local market.[1] As a result, the regulatory laws and policies of host states represent a significant factor in the decision to enter the international market and in the determination of the scope and nature of a bank's international operations. In some cases, differential treatment by the host country will impair the competitive position of an international bank.[2]

From the perspective of the United States as a host state, the IBA endorses a policy "national treatment" of foreign banks seeking entry into the U.S. banking market. However, despite the U.S. policy of encouraging "national treatment" for U.S. banks within other local markets, transnational competitive disadvantages remain. Generally, the U.S. policy has resulted in no improvement in most host state markets.[3]

Another approach to the problem of treatment of foreign investment by nonindigenous enterprises is embodied in the concept of reciprocity. As mentioned in *Conference of State Bank Supervisors v. Conover*,[4] U.S. state bank regulatory provisions may include reciprocity as a condition on entry of foreign banks into the state's banking market. As with the national treatment concept, the precise meaning of "reciprocity" will

---

§ 9.5

1. REPORT TO CONGRESS ON FOREIGN GOVERNMENT TREATMENT OF U.S. BANKING ORGANIZATIONS (Washington, D.C.: U.S. Government Printing Office, 1979). In the years since this "National Treatment" study, the range of competitive disadvantages facing U.S. banks in the international market has remained broad. Competitive disadvantages may result from artificially imposed limitations on capital formation, asset growth, and product and market expansion. In addition, host country regulation remains a source of competitive disadvantage, resulting from differential treatment of multinational banking enterprises. Although the 1986 update of the study, DEPARTMENT OF THE TREASURY, NATIONAL TREATMENT STUDY: 1986 UPDATE (1986) indicates improvement in the competitive climate, this improvement is far from complete or uniform. The 1986 Update was intended to examine the improvement, if any, in the competitive climate for U.S. banks and other financial institutions in foreign markets since the issuance of the first update was issued in July 1984. 1986

UPDATE at 1. Senator Garn, then Chairman of the Senate Banking Committee, had requested that the 1986 Update be broadened to include, *inter alia*, the treatment of U.S. securities firms in foreign markets. *See id.* The primary finding of the 1986 Update in this regard was that, overall,

> the degree of national treatment received by U.S. banks abroad has somewhat improved since the 1984 Update. Over the eight years subsequent to passage of the [IBA], the record reflects sporadic and slow improvement in treatment.

Id. at 3.

2. *See* REPORT TO CONGRESS, *supra* (detailing disparate treatment).

3. *See* 1986 UPDATE at 5–9 *passim*. Furthermore, even significant improvement in a particular host state market "do[es] not necessarily mean that national treatment has been approached or achieved—substantial areas of discrimination may still remain." *Id.* at 3.

4. 715 F.2d 604 (D.C.Cir.1983), *cert. denied*, 466 U.S. 927, 104 S.Ct. 1708 (1984).

vary from jurisdiction to jurisdiction, ranging from a strict reciprocity (or "one-for-one") approach, to more flexible approaches.

§ 9.6 International Regulation of International Banking

International banking regulation and supervision is formulated in a domestic context, with certain limited exceptions. The most notable exceptions involve the work of the Bank for International Settlements ("BIS"), and the General Agreement on Trade in Services ("GATS"). Each is intended to produce supervisory initiatives based on multilateral undertakings that respond to the need for regulation of international activities on an international basis. Curiously, the increasing interdependence of international banks and their activities cause domestic regulators to fashion *multilateral* undertakings to secure what are still essentially *domestic* objectives.

§ 9.7 The Bank for International Settlements

The BIS has been a leader in initiating genuine international bank regulation. The BIS, located in Basle, Switzerland, is a multilateral bank for national central banks. It is primarily supported by the "Group of Ten" large industrialized democracies, consisting of Belgium, Canada, France, Germany, Italy, Japan, the Netherlands, Sweden, United Kingdom, and the United States, with Switzerland as an additional significant participant. The BIS assists these central banks in the transfer and investment of monetary reserves and often plays a role in settling international loan arrangements. Of increasing significance is its role as a forum or catalyst for international monetary cooperation and policy development.

§ 9.8 Coordination of International Supervision

The dramatic failure of Herstatt Bank in Germany and Franklin National Bank in New York in 1974—with its financial repercussions throughout the increasingly "internationalized" banking market—led the Group of Ten to sponsor an informal understanding on resolution of international bank failures, now known as the Basle Concordat (1974). The Governors of the BIS acknowledged the need to establish a framework of multilateral bank supervision, and so they formed the Committee on Banking Regulations and Supervisory Practices. The committee consists of foreign exchange and supervisory officials from the Group of Ten, plus Luxembourg and Switzerland.

This standing committee of the BIS is intended to promote cooperation among national regulators. It looks to the establishment of broadly delineated principles to guide the differing national supervisory systems in establishing their own detailed arrangements. Thus, the 1974 Concordat established the following set of broad principles. All foreign banking institutions should be subject to supervision. Supervision should be adequate, judged by the standards of both host and home (parent) authorities. Supervision of a joint venture involving parent institutions in more than one country should be undertaken by the host authorities of the venture. Achievement of these objectives calls for cooperation between host and parent authorities. In general, supervising liquidity (*i.e.*, the ability to meet obligations as they mature) must rest first with the local authorities. Supervision for solvency (*i.e.*, the condition in which assets exceed net liabilities) must rest primarily with the host authority for foreign subsidiaries and joint ventures, while in the case of branches, solvency was principally the concern of the home supervisory authority of the parent bank.

The generality of the guiding principles articulated in the 1974 Concordat encountered harsh reality and lost in 1982, when Banco Ambrosiano failed. The bank was based in Italy and had a subsidiary in Luxembourg. Italian authorities at first indicated that, from the lender of last resort perspective, they would honor only Ambrosiano's domestic (*i.e.*, Italian) obligations. This caused great distress in the banking world, although a large group of creditor banks of the subsidiary did eventually reach a settlement with Italian central bank involving more than $300 million in subsidiary obligations.

One result of the experience of resolving the difficulties of this multinational bank failure was the revision of the Concordat in 1983. The revision articulated in relatively greater detail supervisory responsibilities with respect to multinational banking enterprises. The 1983 Concordat[1] identifies principles for the supervision of the foreign operations of international banking enterprises. It deals exclusively with the responsibilities of banking supervisors for monitoring the prudential conduct and soundness of these foreign operations; it does not address itself to lender-of-last-resort functions of central banks. The "principles" are not, strictly speaking, legally binding. Rather, they are "recommended guidelines of best practices ... , which all members have undertaken to work towards implementing, according to the means available to them."[2] The Concordat established certain basic, thematic principles. First, effective cooperation between home-country and host-country authorities is essential to the supervision of international banking operations. The next two principles follow from the first. Second, no banking establishment should escape supervision. Third, supervision must be adequate.

§ 9.8

1. Bank for International Settlements, Committee on Banking Regulations and Supervisory Practices, Principles for the Supervision of Banks' Foreign Establishments (1983), *reprinted in* Michael P. Malloy, International Banking 55–60 (1998).

2. *Id.* at 55.

Hence, home-country and host-country authorities must keep each other effectively informed of serious problems that arise in or affect a parent bank's foreign operations. The Concordat identified three categories of operation in international banking: branches, subsidiaries, and joint ventures or consortia. As to each of these categories, the Concordat recommends certain principles for the resolution of liquidity and solvency problems. Essentially, these principles attempt to establish relative roles that home-country and host country authorities should undertake.

As to the supervision of a bank's foreign exchange operations, the Concordat takes the position that these should be the joint responsibility of the home-country and host-country authorities. Home-country authorities are expected to monitor the internal controls of their international banking enterprises. Host-country authorities are expected to monitor the foreign exchange exposure of foreign bank operations within their territories.

Since the issuance of the Basle Concordat, the BIS Committee has given further attention to the problems of supervising transnational banking enterprises. An April 1990 Supplement to the Concordat sought to strengthen the principle of effective information flow between home-country and host-country authorities,[3] by making the rules on information transfer more explicit and detailed. Part D of the 1990 Supplement deals with the problem of domestic bank secrecy laws that might otherwise impede information flows necessary for effective transnational regulation and supervision of banking.

The scandal surrounding the collapse of the Bank of Credit and Commerce International ("BCCI")[4] subsequently caused the BIS Committee to review the arrangements for coordination of international bank supervision, which was sorely lacking in the events surrounding the BCCI collapse. Hence, in June 1992, the BIS Committee took the further significant step of issuing a report establishing binding minimum standards on the supervision of international banking enterprises.[5] While the standards are not, on their own terms, binding on states, BIS participating states are expected to implement them, and other states are encouraged to do so. In the United States, implementation has occurred primarily in connection with the enactment of the FDICIA.[6]

---

3. Bank for International Settlements, Committee on Banking Regulation and Supervisory Practices: Supplement to the Basle Concordat Ensuring of Adequate Information Flows between Banking Supervisory Authorities (1990), *reprinted in* Malloy, International Banking, *supra*, at 61–64.

4. For a review of the BCCI scandal and the legislative reaction to the scandal in the United States, see Raj K. Bhala, Foreign Bank Regulation after BCCI (1994).

5. Bank for International Settlements, Basle Committee on Banking Regulation and Supervisory Practices: Report on Minimum Standards for the Supervision of Interna-

tional Banking Groups and Their Cross-Border Establishment (1992), *reprinted in*, Malloy, International Banking, *supra*, at 64–68.

6. *See, e.g.,* 12 U.S.C.A. §§ 3105(d)(2)(1)(A) (approval of U.S. branch of foreign bank; comprehensive supervision of applicant on consolidated basis by home state authorities required); 3105(d)(3)(A) (same; consent of home state to establishment of U.S. branch as standard of approval by U.S. authorities); 3105(e)(1)(A) (termination of U.S. office of foreign bank when foreign bank not subject to comprehensive supervision on consolidated basis by home state authorities).

These issuances are intended to foster better information flows between national regulators and better national controls over the entry of a multinational banking enterprise into the national market supervised by the regulator. If these policies are effective, presumably the supervision of multinational bank failures could be more efficiently anticipated or managed. More recently, the Basle Committee on Banking Supervision, in conjunction with the International Monetary Fund and the International Bank for Reconstruction and Development, has developed a set of core principles for effective banking supervision.[7] The Core Principles consist of twenty-five basic principles, ranging from preconditions for effective banking supervision (Principle 1) to principles for cross-border banking (Principles 23–25).

§ 9.9   Capital Adequacy

The BIS is also responsible for what is perhaps the most significant recent development in terms of substantive international supervision of banking—the formulation of uniform guidelines governing the measurement and enforcement of capital adequacy of banks.[1] In U.S. practice, capital adequacy requirements predate the BIS efforts in this regard.[2] However, the rules developed under BIS auspices are aimed not only at a capital adequacy regime that is effective as a purely regulatory matter, but also one that will encourage a multilateral convergence of regulatory standards.

The guidelines set forth "the details of the agreed framework for measuring capital adequacy and the minimum standard to be achieved which the national supervisory authorities represented on the Committee intend to implement in their respective countries."[3] The guidelines reflect two fundamental objectives: (*i*) "that the new framework should serve to strengthen the soundness and stability of the international banking system;"[4] and, (*ii*) "that the framework should be fair and have a high degree of consistency in its application to banks in different countries with a view to diminishing an existing source of competitive inequality among international banks."[5]

---

7. Basle Committee on Banking Supervision, Basle Core Principles for Effective Banking Supervision (Sept. 22, 1997), *reprinted in* 37 Int'l Leg. Mat. 405 (1998) ("Core Principles"). The principles are, of course, not binding and "serve as a basic reference for supervisory and other public authorities in all countries and internationally." Core Principles, 37 Int'l Leg. Mat. at 407.

§ 9.9

1. Bank for International Settlements, Committee on Banking Regulations and Supervisory Practices, Final Report for International Convergence of Capital Measurement and Capital Standards, *reprinted in* 1 Fed. Banking L. Rep. (CCH) ¶ 5403 (July 29, 1988) ("Final Report"). For discussion of the BIS capital adequacy rules and their implementation in U.S. law, see *supra* § 7.8.

2. *See* Michael P. Malloy, *U.S. International Banking and the New Capital Adequacy Requirements: New, Old and Unexpected*, 7 Ann. Rev. Banking L. 75, 75–76, 81–87 (1988) (discussion of pre-BIS U.S. regulatory practice).

3. Final Report at 3309.

4. *Id.*

5. *Id.*

The basic focus of this multilateral framework is "assessing capital in relation to credit risk (the risk of counterparty failure)."[6] However, the framework acknowledges that "other risks, notably interest rate risk and the investment risk on securities, need to be taken into account by supervisors in assessing overall capital adequacy."[7] Thus, the framework does not represent an exclusive set of rules with respect to capital adequacy regulation, and the rules that it does endorse are "designed to establish *minimum* levels of capital for internationally active banks. National authorities will be free to adopt arrangements that set higher levels."[8] The agreement represented in the framework is generally intended "to be applied to banks on a consolidated basis, including subsidiaries undertaking banking and financial business."[9] The BIS Committee has continued to refine the details and mechanics of risk management and supervision.[10]

§ 9.10   General Agreement on Trade in Services

In April 1994, the Uruguay Round of GATT multilateral trade negotiations finalized the General Agreement on Trade in Services ("GATS").[1] The GATS establishes "a multilateral framework of principles and rules for trade in services with a view to the expansion of such trade under conditions of transparency and progressive liberalization,"[2]

---

6. *Id.*

7. *Id.*

8. *Id.* (emphasis in original).

9. *Id.* at 3310.

10. *See, e.g.,* BIS, Committee on Banking Supervision, *The Treatment of the Credit Risk Associated with Certain Off–Balance–Sheet Items* (July 1994); BIS, Committee on Banking Supervision, *Risk Management Guidelines for Derivatives* (July 1994); BIS, Committee on Banking Supervision, *Amendment to the Capital Accord of July 1988* (July 1994); BIS, Committee on Banking Supervision, *Prudential Supervision of Banks' Derivatives Activities* (December 1994); BIS, Committee on Banking Supervision, *Basle Capital Accord: Treatment of Potential Exposure for Off–Balance–Sheet Items* (April 1995); BIS, Committee on Banking Supervision, *An Internal Model–Based Approach to Market Risk Capital Requirements* (April 1995); BIS, Committee on Banking Supervision, *Public Disclosure of the Trading and Derivatives Activities of Banks and Securities Firms* (November 1995); BIS, Committee on Banking Supervision, *Supervisory Framework for the Use of "Backtesting" in Conjunction with the Internal Models Ap-*

proach to Market Risk Capital Requirements (January 1996); BIS, Committee on Banking Supervision, *Amendment to the Basle Capital Accord to Incorporate Market Risks* (January 1996); BIS, Committee on Banking Supervision, *Interpretation of the Capital Accord for the Multilateral Netting of Forward Value Foreign Exchange Transactions* (April 1996).

§ 9.10

1. General Agreement on Trade in Services, 15 April 1994, Agreement Establishing the World Trade Organization, Annex 1B, 33 Int'l Leg. Materials 1167 (1994) ("GATS"). WTO members are not permitted to derogate from adherence to Annex 1B. Agreement Establishing the World Trade Organization, art. XVI, ¶ 5. For an excellent review of the GATS and its implications for banking, see Kristin Leigh Case, Recent Development, *The Daiwa Wake–Up Call: The Need for International Standards for Banking Supervision*, 26 Ga. J. Int'l & Comp. L. 215 (1996). *See generally* JOHN H. JACKSON, WILLIAM J. DAVEY & ALAN O. SYKES, LEGAL PROBLEMS OF INTERNATIONAL ECONOMIC RELATIONS 893–931 (3D ED. 1995) (offering general discussion of GATS).

2. GATS, preamble.

by applying GATT nondiscrimination principles to trade in services.[3] The GATS specifically applies to financial services.[4] The requirements of nondiscriminatory treatment do not, however, prevent WTO member states from enforcing domestic regulations for "prudential reasons, including for the protection of ... depositors, ... or persons to whom a fiduciary duty is owed by a financial service supplier, or to ensure the integrity and stability of the financial system."[5]

As a transitional matter, a second Annex to the GATS, concerning financial services, permitted temporary withdrawal from the GATS commitments.[6] Nevertheless, it was anticipated that inclusion of financial services under the GATS regime would "likely ... result in increased market access"[7] for international banks. This expectation received a setback when the United States withdrew from the GATS transitional process with respect to the Agreement on Financial Services in June 1995.[8]

In withdrawing from the transitional arrangement, the U.S. Government opted for a policy of measured reciprocity, prospectively limiting access to U.S. markets to financial services firms from home countries that provided reciprocal treatment to U.S. firms.[9] Essentially, the government had decided to seek market-access liberalization through bilateral negotiations, rather than through the multilateral mechanism of the WTO and the GATS.[10]

Matters remained in play, however, because the commitments of WTO member states participating in the transitional arrangement were to expire at the end of 1997.[11] Thereafter, WTO member states were expected to renegotiate GATS financial services commitments.[12] In ad-

---

3. *See, e.g.*, GATS, art. II, ¶ 1 (applying most-favored-nation treatment to services and service suppliers); GATS, art. XVII, ¶ 1 (applying national treatment to services and service suppliers of other WTO member states).

4. GATS, Annex on Financial Services.

5. GATS, Annex on Financial Services, § 2(a).

6. GATS, Second Annex on Financial Services. Case suggests that temporary withdrawal or modification is permitted in the Second Annex to allow for continued negotiation on market liberalization "because at the conclusion of the Uruguay Round, the United States was unsatisfied with other countries' commitments. The United States was not willing to lock in its own liberal policies without reciprocal guarantees of full market access on a most-favored nation basis." Case, *supra* note 1, at 220, n.32 (citing Joel P. Trachtman, *Trade in Financial Services Under GATS, NAFTA and the EC: A Regulatory Jurisdiction Analysis*, 34 Colum. J. Transnat'l L. 37, 54 (1995)).

7. Case, *supra* note 1, at 221.

8. *See* Paul Lewis, *Trade Accord Without U.S. Set in Geneva*, N.Y. Times, July 27, 1995, at D1, col. 6 (reporting U.S. refusal to join transitional arrangement). In July 1995, over 80 states—including Japan, but not the United States—concluded a transitional agreement to liberalize international trade in financial services. *Id.*

9. Bob Davis & John R. Wilke, *Trade Official Is 'Close' to Limited Pact To Liberalize Global Financial Services*, Wall St. J., July 25, 1995 at A2.

10. *See, e.g.*, Frances Williams, *EU Eager to Salvage Financial Services Pact*, Fin. Times, July 1, 1995, at A1 (noting U.S. position).

11. Joel P. Trachtman, *Trade in Financial Services Under GATS, NAFTA and the EC: A Regulatory Jurisdiction Analysis*, 34 Colum. J. Transnat'l L. 37, 55 (1995).

12. *Id.*

vance of the expiration date, however, the United States joined in the signing of a global accord to govern international trade in services.[13] While the United States made no concessions, in light of the relatively open access to U.S. markets already permitted to non-U.S. firms, the initiation of the accord should result in significant opening of banking, insurance and securities service markets in such countries as Argentina, Brazil, India and Indonesia, among others, that have traditionally been relatively opaque.[14] However, other target markets, such as Malaysia and South Korea, have made no concessions for expansion of access.[15] On the other hand, Japan did agree to significant concessions in terms of opening its domestic financial services markets to international competition.[16]

If the accord is successfully implemented,[17] its effect on international trade in financial services could be dramatic. Under the GATS, each WTO member is required to accord most-favored-nation treatment to services and service suppliers of other WTO members.[18] Current restrictions on trade in services of each member must be transparent.[19] Members are also required to administer current restrictions "in a reasonable, objective and impartial manner."[20]

A series of general exceptions do apply to GATS obligations, similar to the general exceptions under the GATT.[21] More importantly, perhaps, the GATS includes a self-judging special exception for essential security interests of member states, similar to the special security exception contained in the GATT.[22] Presumably, this exception would shield U.S. international economic sanctions measures from the requirements and strictures of the GATS.[23]

---

13. *See* Edmund L. Andrews, *Accord Is Reached To Lower Barriers In Global Finance*, N.Y. Times, Dec. 13, 1997, at A1, col. 6 (discussing GATS accord).

14. *Id.*

15. *Id.*

16. *Id.* at B2.

17. *Cf. id.* at A1 (citing possible Congressional criticism of accord, but noting existing authorization for immediate effectiveness of accord under U.S. law).

18. GATS, art. II, ¶ 1.

19. *See* GATS, art. III (requiring publication and reporting of restrictive measures).

20. GATS, art. VI, ¶ 1. *Cf.* GATS, art. X, ¶ 1 (requiring that any emergency safeguard measures be administered in a nondiscriminatory manner).

21. *Compare, e.g.*, GATT, art. XX (excepting from GATT requirements measures undertaken for morals, life or health, precious metals, compliance with certain regulatory laws, products of prison labor, national treasures or patrimony, conservation, certain commodity agreements, world-price

adjustment, and short-supply materials) *with* GATS, art. XIV (excepting from GATS requirements measures undertaken for morals or public order, life or health, compliance with certain regulatory laws, and taxation).

22. *Compare* GATT, art. XXI (providing exceptions from GATT obligations with respect to any measure undertaken that a member "considers necessary for the protection of its essential security interests") *with* GATS, art. XIV *bis*, ¶ 1 (providing exceptions from GATS obligations with respect to any measure undertaken that a member "considers necessary for the protection of its essential security interests"). *But cf.* GATS, art. XIV *bis*, ¶ 2 (requiring reporting of certain excepted measures and of their termination to WTO Council for Trade in Services).

23. *Cf. Panel Report on Nicaraguan Complaint*, GATT Activities 1986 58–59 (1987) (noting that GATT panel examining complaint by Nicaragua concerning U.S. trade sanctions not authorized to examine U.S. invocation of GATT, art. XXI).

§ 9.11   Entry Rules

Rules for entry into the international banking market are complicated by the fact that entry is controlled by two entirely independent jurisdictions, the home country of the entrant and intended host country. Hence, successful entry requires coordination between the regulatory requirements of both home and host. Sections 9.12–9.13 will focus on applicable U.S. rules when the United States is the intended host country and when the United States is the home country of the bank seeking entry into a non-U.S. market.

Available methods for entry vary. The general menu of options is illustrated in Figure 9–2, *infra*. However, specific options may or may not be available from one jurisdiction to the next, depending upon local rules.

FIGURE 9-2
Methods of Entry: Menu of Options

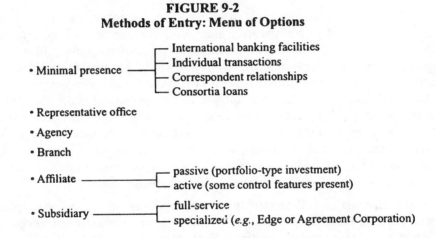

These menu choices reflect varying degrees of intervention into the host-country market. Correspondent banking relationships are similar to domestic correspondent bank relationships, involving virtually no direct contact with the target market. Representative offices typically have significantly limited powers; they cannot take deposits, make loans, accept drafts, or transfer funds.

International deposit facilities are essentially book entry facilities within a bank and are functionally similar to a foreign branch, except that they are located within the bank's home office.[1] For example, in U.S. practice, these facilities are allowed to take time deposits and to grant loans to non-U.S. citizens. Reserve requirements are waived for

---

§ 9.11

1. These facilities, known as international banking facilities ("IBF") in U.S.

practice, are available under the Fed's Regulation K. *See* 12 C.F.R. § 211.8 (authorizing IBFs).

facility deposits.[2] In many states they may be exempted from state and local income taxes.

Alternatively, a bank may establish a locally licensed agency, which operates in the same manner as a branch bank, except it cannot accept deposits from the general public. In contrast, a locally licensed branch offers a full range of banking services. It is not separately chartered, and the home office may be liable for its obligations.[3]

An affiliate bank may represent a passive portfolio-type investment, in which control is not exercised by the outside parent banking enterprise. It may be controlled by local or by other foreign banks. On the other hand, an active affiliate, or consortium bank, may operate as a joint venture, separately incorporated and owned by multiple banks, usually from different countries, often with no majority-controlling shareholder.

Finally, a bank may seek to enter a host-country market through the establishment of a separately chartered subsidiary. In U.S. practice, the possibility also exists for creating a specialized subsidiary limited to international and foreign business. This would be either an Edge Act corporation, chartered under federal law,[4] or an Agreement corporation, chartered under state law but subject to an agreement with the Fed to limit its activities to those of an Edge Act corporation.[5] In either event, the subsidiary would be limited to deposits related to international and foreign transactions. It could also make international-related loans, confirm letters of credit, create bankers acceptances, maintain foreign exchange markets, and act as a collection or disbursement agent.

In contrast, a full-service subsidiary operates as a separate, locally incorporated bank owned or controlled by parent banking enterprise. In either case, the banking enterprise that serves as the parent of the subsidiary bank is generally not subject to liability for subsidiary's obligations.[6]

---

2. 12 C.F.R. § 204.8.

3. *See, e.g., Vishipco Line v. Chase Manhattan Bank*, 660 F.2d 854 (2d Cir.1981), *cert. denied*, 459 U.S. 976, 103 S.Ct. 313 (1982) (so holding); *Garcia v. Chase Manhattan Bank, N.A.*, 735 F.2d 645 (2d Cir. 1984) (so holding; citing, *inter alia, Vishipco Line*). *But cf. Perez v. Chase Manhattan*, 61 N.Y.2d 460, 463 N.E.2d 5, 474 N.Y.S.2d 689 (Ct.App.1984) (liability of foreign branch discharged). *See generally* Heininger, *Liability of U.S. Banks for Deposits Placed in Their Foreign Branches*, 11 Law. & Pol. Intl. Bus. 903 (1979) (discussing foreign branch liability). Other jurisdictions may treat a foreign branch as distinct from its home office for purposes of liability. *Cf. X AG and others v. A bank*, 2 All Eng. L. Rep.

464 (1983) (treating foreign branch as legally distinct from home office); *Libyan Arab Foreign Bank v. Bankers Trust Company*, Queen's Bench, Commercial Court (2 September 1987) (same; citing, *inter alia, X AG*).

4. 12 U.S.C.A. § 613 *et seq.*

5. *See, e.g.*, 12 C.F.R. § 211.4.

6. *See, e.g.*, AMERICAN LAW INSTITUTE, RESTATEMENT OF FOREIGN RELATIONS LAW OF THE UNITED STATES (3D) § 414 (noting subsidiary may be subject to home-country supervision, though generally distinct for purposes of private liability). *But cf. S.E.C. v. Banca Della Svizzera Italiana*, 92 F.R.D. 111 (S.D.N.Y.1981) (claiming jurisdiction over foreign parent of U.S. subsidiary bank).

§ 9.12   Entry into the U.S. Market

The range of options available to foreign banks for entry into the U.S. banking market is essentially the same as that illustrated in Figure 9–2, *supra*. However, at least since the passage of the IBA in 1978, the range of options is somewhat broader, since the dual banking system within the United States makes available many duplicate (federal/state) alternatives. Since the 1970s, foreign banks have increasingly taken advantage of these options. In part, efficient access to U.S. dollar markets may explain some of this growth in interest. Figure 9–1, *supra*, illustrates which regulators are authorized to approve which methods of entry.

Federal policy with respect to branching by non-U.S. banks has become a controversial issue in recent years. The IBA as originally enacted was intended to implement a policy of "national treatment" for foreign banks seeking entry into the U.S. market.[1] However, following the BCCI scandal,[2] the IBA was amended in several significant respects by the FDICIA.[3] Among the effects of FDICIA were the following.

FDICIA significantly altered the rules governing the establishment and operation of federal branches and agencies of foreign-based banks. Under FDICIA, the Comptroller is required, in considering any application for approval of an initial federal branch or agency, to include any condition imposed by the Fed as a condition for the approval of the application.[4] The Comptroller is also required to coordinate examinations of such branches and agencies with examinations conducted by the Fed, to the extent possible, to participate in any simultaneous examinations of U.S. operations of foreign banks requested by the Fed.[5] Furthermore, in considering any application to establish an additional federal branch or agency of a foreign-based bank, the Comptroller is required to provide the Fed with notice and opportunity for comment on the application.[6] The Fed's supervisory authority was substantially expanded,[7] and special examination fees were imposed for examinations of U.S. based operations of non-U.S. banks.[8]

§ 9.12

1. *See Conference of State Bank Supervisors v. Conover*, 715 F.2d 604 (D.C.Cir. 1983), *cert. denied*, 466 U.S. 927, 104 S.Ct. 1708 (1984) (discussing national treatment under IBA).

2. *See* R. K. BHALA, FOREIGN BANK REGULATION AFTER BCCI (1994) (discussing BCCI scandal and its effect on U.S. regulation of international banking). *See also* Note, *Putting the Super Back in the Supervision of International Banking, Post–BCCI*, 60 Fordham L. Rev. S467 (Survey Issue 1992) (discussing effects of FDICIA on U.S. regulation).

3. Pub. L. No. 102–242, 105 Stat. 2236 (December 19, 1991) (codified at scattered sections of 12 U.S.C.A.) ("FDICIA").

4. 12 U.S.C.A. § 3102(a)(2).

5. *Id.* § 3102(b).

6. *Id.* § 3102(h)(2).

7. The Fed implemented its authority to supervise U.S. branches and agencies of foreign banks in regulations published in 1996. 12 C.F.R. § 211.30 (establishing criteria for evaluation of U.S. operations of foreign banks not subject to consolidated supervision).

8. 12 U.S.C.A. § 3105(c)(1)(D) (1994).

The FDICIA also restricted retail deposit-taking by foreign banks. To accept or maintain deposit accounts with balances of less than $100,000, foreign banks are required to establish one or more U.S. banking subsidiaries for that purpose, and to obtain federal deposit insurance for any such subsidiary.[9] However, if the foreign bank had a U.S. branch that was an insured branch prior to FDICIA, the branch was permitted to continue to accept or maintain retail deposits.[10]

The increased burdens placed upon U.S. operations of foreign banks by the FDICIA provoked criticism.[11] These burdens have also exacerbated the uncertainty over the question whether U.S. banking regulation was sufficiently reciprocal to allow entry by U.S. banks into the European Union's Community-wide banking market.

It was against the statutory background of the FDICIA that the Interstate Banking and Branching Efficiency Act of 1994 ("IBBEA")[12] undertook to amend the IBA. Two objectives may be discerned in the amendments: dealing with the practical implications of the 1991 amendments to the IBA,[13] and readjusting the IBA in light of the changes in interstate banking and branching instituted by the IBBEA itself.[14]

The IBBEA amended the IBA rules governing interstate operations of foreign banks.[15] In general, it subjects the establishment of interstate operations of a federal branch or agency of a foreign bank to the same rules that would apply if the foreign bank were a national bank seeking to branch interstate.[16] Similarly, the IBBEA subjects the establishment of interstate operations of a state-licensed branch or agency of a foreign bank to the same rules that would apply if the foreign bank were a state bank seeking to branch interstate.[17] These rules are generally preemptive and exclusive.[18]

---

9. 12 U.S.C.A. § 3104(d)(1). Thus, for any foreign-based bank interested in the U.S. retail deposit market, this provision requires the bank's U.S. operations to be conducted through a subsidiary.

10. *Id.* § 3104(d)(2).

11. *See, e.g.,* Cynthia C. Lichtenstein, *U.S. Restructuring Legislation: Revising the International Banking Act of 1978, For the Worse?,* 60 Fordham L. Rev. S37 (Annual Survey Issue 1992).

12. Pub. L. No. 103–328, 108 Stat. 2338 (Sept. 29, 1994) (codified at scattered sections of 12 U.S.C.A.) ("IBBEA").

13. *See, e.g.,* IBBEA, § 115 (codified at 12 U.S.C.A. § 3105 note) (moratorium on examination fees under § 3105(c)(1)(D)).

14. *See, e.g.,* IBBEA, § 104(a) (codified at 12 U.S.C.A. § 3103(a)(1)) (subjecting U.S. interstate branching and agency operations of foreign banks to rules of 12 U.S.C.A. §§ 36(g), 1831u).

15. For a discussion of the pre-IBBEA rules under IBA for interstate operations of

foreign banks, see *Conference of State Bank Supervisors, supra.*

16. IBBEA, § 104(a) (codified at 12 U.S.C.A. § 3103(a) (1)). On the criteria for determining approval of interstate operations of a foreign bank's federal branch or agency, see 12 U.S.C.A. § 3103(a)(3)(A)–(C).

17. 12 U.S.C.A. § 3103(a)(2). On the criteria for determining approval of interstate operations of a foreign bank's state branch or agency, see *id.* § 3103(a)(3)(A)–(C).

18. *See id.* § 3103(a)(5), which provides:

Except as provided in this section, a foreign bank may not, directly or indirectly, acquire, establish, or operate a branch or agency in any State other than the home State of such bank.

But see id. § 3103(a)(7)(A)–(B) (providing additional authority for interstate operations of foreign banks where a host state expressly permits the operations, and the branch deposit operations are limited to international- or foreign-related deposits). On the definition of "home State" for these

Operation of any interstate branch or agency of a foreign bank is subject to the same IBBEA rules governing domestic branches of national and state banks resulting from interstate merger transactions.[19] However, an additional, potentially controversial requirement may apply to foreign banks. The 1991 FDICIA required foreign banks entering the U.S. retail deposit market to operate through a separately chartered U.S. subsidiary, rather than a direct branch.[20] The IBBEA extends this requirement, under certain specified circumstances, to interstate operations of any foreign bank. If the Fed or the Comptroller finds that, in light of differing regulatory or accounting standards in a foreign bank's home country, adherence by the bank to applicable U.S. capital requirements could only be verified if the foreign bank's U.S. banking activities were carried out in a separate U.S. subsidiary, the agencies[21] have the authority to require that the foreign bank (or the company controlling the foreign bank) establish a U.S. subsidiary to carry out the interstate operations.[22] This provision potentially moves the United States further away from the original policy of national treatment for foreign bank operations in the United States that underlies the IBA.[23] Since most members of the European Union participate in the BIS capital adequacy

purposes, see *id.* § 3103(a)(9). On the rules for determining the home state of a foreign bank for purposes of the interstate branch and agency rules of the IBBEA, see *id.* § 3103(c)(1)–(2).

19. *Id.* § 3103(a)(4). In addition, a U.S. branch or agency of a foreign bank is not permitted to manage, through a managed or controlled office located outside the United States, any type of activity not permitted to be managed by a domestic bank through a branch or subsidiary located outside the United States. *Id.* § 3105(k)(1). This prohibition is effective 180 days after the enactment of IBBEA. IBBEA, § 107(e)(2) (codified at 12 U.S.C.A. § 3105 Note).

20. 12 U.S.C.A. § 3103(a)(6). However, the IBBEA clarifies the impact of the new rules in the following respects. A foreign bank that has a U.S. bank subsidiary is still eligible to establish a direct federal or state branch or agency, in accordance with the IBBEA rules. *Id.* § 3103(d)(1). Similarly, a U.S. bank that is a subsidiary of a foreign bank with a direct federal or state branch or agency is itself still eligible to establish a federal or state branch or agency, in accordance with the IBBEA rules. *Id.* § 3103(d)(2).

21. If the foreign bank intended to carry out interstate branching or agency activities under a federal license, both the Fed

and the Comptroller would have the authority to make the finding. *Id.* § 3103(a)(6). If the foreign bank intended to carry out interstate branching or agency activities under a state license, the Fed alone would have the authority to make the finding. *Id.*

22. *Id.*

23. This movement away from the policy of national treatment is underscored by the IBBEA provisions requiring the agencies to pursue the objective of

affording equal competitive opportunities to foreign and United States banking organizations in their United States operations [and] ensur[ing] that foreign banking organizations do not receive an unfair competitive advantage over United States banking organizations.

Id. § 3104(a) (directive to Comptroller and FDIC under IBA as amended by IBBEA). *See also* IBBEA, § 107(b) (codified at 12 U.S.C.A. § 3104 Note) (requiring review of regulations by federal banking agencies and revision of regulations under § 3104 to equalize competitive opportunities for U.S. and foreign banks). The IBBEA also clarifies that domestic consumer protection laws apply to foreign banks with U.S. operations. 12 U.S.C.A. § 3106a(b) (1)(A), (2)(A).

guidelines, the degree of potential confrontation with our European allies in this regard may be minimized. In addition, IBBEA grandfathers foreign bank operations in place on the day before the enactment of the IBBEA.[24] Nevertheless, depending upon the U.S. agency practice that emerges under this provision, the United States banking market may become significantly less transparent to foreign banks.

One salutary effect of the act was its moratorium on the examination fee provisions included in the IBA by the FDICIA amendments.[25] During a three-year period beginning July 25, 1994, the examination fee provisions of the FDICIA did not apply to examinations of U.S. branches, agencies or affiliates of foreign banks,[26] or to examinations of U.S. representative offices of foreign banks.[27] Before the expiration of this three-year period, the IBA was amended to require that examination fees with respect to each branch or agency of a foreign bank be imposed "only to the same extent that fees are collected by the Board for examination of any State member bank."[28]

IBBEA imposes a continuing requirement on foreign banks with U.S. operations to meet community credit needs, after their initial entry by acquisition in the interstate market.[29] If a foreign bank acquires a U.S. bank or branch in a state in which the foreign bank does not maintain a branch, and the bank is a "regulated financial institution" under the CRA,[30] the CRA continues to apply to each branch of the foreign bank that results from the acquisition.[31]

§ 9.13   Entry into Non–U.S. Markets

Legal and regulatory constraints of both home-country and host-country policy may affect a bank's ability to enter a foreign market.[1] For convenience of discussion, this section focuses on the home-country requirements of the United States. As to host-country restrictions, patterns vary considerably, from relatively familiar chartering or licensing requirements in Group of Ten countries,[2] to virtual exclusion in

---

24. IBBEA, § 104(b) (codified at 12 U.S.C.A. § 3103(b)).

25. *See* IBBEA, § 115 (codified at 12 U.S.C.A. §§ 3105 Note, 3107 Note).

26. IBBEA, § 115(a).

27. IBBEA, § 115(b).

28. Pub. L. No. 104–208, § 2214(a)(4), 110 Stat. 3009–411 (1996) (codified at 12 U.S.C.A. § 3105(c)(1)(D)).

29. 12 U.S.C.A. § 3103(a)(8).

30. *See id.* § 2902.

31. *Id.* § 3103(a)(8)(A). This requirement does not apply to any resulting branch that is limited to international- or foreign-related deposits. *Id.* § 3103(a)(8)(B).

§ 9.13

1. *See, e.g.,* Korsvik, *Legal and Regulatory Constraints Within Other Countries, in* W. H. Baughn & D. R. Mandich, The Interna-

TIONAL BANKING HANDBOOK (1983) (discussing host-country restrictions on entry).

2. The law of the European Union as it affects, among other things, bank regulation, is of considerable interest in this regard. *See generally* Lui, *A Banker's Guide to the European Community's 1992 Program,* 107 Banking L.J. 148 (1990). Certain recent EU developments may significantly restrict or modify entry of U.S. banks into the single integrated EU banking market. *See* Lee, *1992: Promise or Problems for non-EC Companies?,* Int'l Fin. L. Rev. (April 1988) (discussing integration of EU markets). Under the Second Banking Directive (1988), reciprocity of treatment of EU banks is the basis on which U.S. and other non-EU based banks are permitted to enter the single European market. *See* Note, *The Second Banking Directive,* Int'l Fin. L. Rev. 19 (April 1988) (discussing effects of directive). Banks that had not established or many less developed countries.[3]

Entry by U.S. banks into foreign markets is authorized under the FRA subject to Fed approval.[4] For entry by national banks, the authority of the Comptroller of the Currency is limited to notice and filing requirements triggered by submission of an application to the Fed.[5] The Fed's entry approval requirements are contained in Regulation K.[6] Approval of the Fed is required to establish a foreign branch.[7] Separate requirements are applicable to the establishment of an Edge Act or Agreement corporation.[8] Since Agreement corporations are state-chartered, pertinent state law requirements must also be consulted.

Entry into a foreign banking market through the establishment or acquisition of a subsidiary or affiliate also requires approval of the investment by the Fed.[9] These requirements apply whether the investor in the subsidiary is a member bank, a bank holding company, or an Edge Act or Agreement corporation.[10] However, since Edge Act corporations may be primarily engaged either in banking or in investment activities, certain requirements vary slightly between the two types of Edges.[11]

The structure of the regulations would seem to suggest that the decision to enter a foreign market requires a choice of one of the possible methods of operation discussed in the regulations; namely, branch, Edge or Agreement corporation, affiliate, or subsidiary. In fact, there are alternative arrangements that a bank might make in structuring its entry into a foreign market. These arrangements might be particularly useful if the foreign jurisdiction prohibits or significantly restricts a method of entry favored by the bank. For example, if foreign jurisdiction *Nusquam* requires entry through a branch, but the U.S. bank is concerned about possible exposure of home office to the obligations of the Nusquami branch, the bank might create a second-tier subsidiary to branch into Nusquam. Figure 9–3 illustrates this alternative arrangement.

acquired a pre-Directive local subsidiary are required to obtain authorization from the relevant member state, but only after the Commission has determined that such bank's home country would grant reciprocal treatment to EU banks. *See* George Zavvos, *1992: One Market*, Int'l Fin. L. Rev. 7 (March 1988) (discussing Directive requirements).

3. Korsvik, *supra*.

4. 12 U.S.C.A. §§ 601–619.

5. 12 C.F.R. Pt. 28.

6. *Id*. Pt. 211.

7. *Id*. § 211.3.

8. *Id*. § 211.4.

9. *Id*. § 211.5(a).

10. *Id*.

11. *See, e.g., id*. § 211.5(c)(1)(i)(B) (differing investment requirements for general consent procedure applicable to investment by banking and investment Edges).

FIGURE 9-3
Branch Entry through Second-Tier Subsidiary

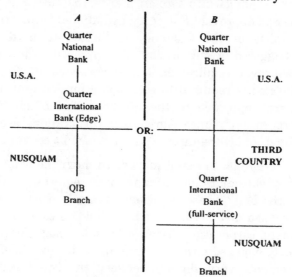

The *A* approach illustrated in Figure 9–3 would involve the incorporation of an Edge Act subsidiary of QNB, which in turn would branch into Nusquam. The creation of the Edge would require compliance with applicable provisions of the Comptroller's notice requirements[12] and of the Fed's Regulation K.[13] In addition, of course, compliance with Nusquami banking law would be required.

The *B* approach illustrated in Figure 9–3 is a variation on the first approach. It might recommend itself to QNB if the geographic area that includes Nusquam were one that QNB expected to exploit as a regional banking market. This investment by QNB in a foreign bank would be subject to applicable provisions of the Comptroller's notice requirements[14] and of the Fed's Regulation K,[15] and any applicable requirements or restrictions of Nusquami law and the laws of the third country involved.

Other further variations on the *B* approach can, of course, be imagined. QNB might create an Edge, QIB, which would in turn coordinate (and directly hold) the investment in the third-country subsidiary. This might recommend itself to QNB, depending on its management style, as a way to coordinate and consolidate its international activities, not only in Nusquam and the third country involved here, but also in other countries in the region as well, where the pattern of indirect ownership and control might repeat itself.

12. *Id.* § 28.3(a)(1)(ii).

13. *Id.* § 211.4(a).

14. *Id.* § 28.3(a)(1)(ii).

15. *Id.* § 211.5(a)–(c).

§ 9.14　International Activities

To the extent that international banking is banking, we may expect that international banking activities include the same range of traditional powers that we encounter in the domestic banking market. A number of features change, however, when a bank moves into the international market. First, there is the obvious fact that international transactions may raise transnational choice of law issues that do not exist in the domestic market. Second, there is the corresponding fact that these transactions may be subject to the constraints of both home-country and host-country regulation. Third, there may be certain activities that do not exist outside of international banking, broadly conceived, or are not as widely permitted in the domestic banking context.

There are certain activities that by their nature are an integral part of international banking. For U.S. banks, some of these activities are delimited by the U.S. regulatory framework that governs international banking. Essentially, this category of international activities is delineated by the Fed's Regulation K. In addition to the core activities of banking (*i.e.*, lending and deposit-taking), foreign branches of member banks, Edge Act and Agreement corporations and other bank subsidiaries are authorized by the Fed to engage in a range of activities in their host market. These activities include: (1) guarantees of third-party debt obligations;[1] (2) underwriting, distributing, and dealing in host-country government obligations[2] and other permitted securities investments;[3] (3) credit extensions to bank officers;[4] (4) real estate loans;[5] (5) acting as an insurance agent or broker;[6] (6) participating in employee benefits programs;[7] (7) securities and commodities repurchase agreements;[8] (8) investing in subsidiaries; and, (9) with Fed prior approval, engaging in other activities that the Fed determines are usual in connection with the transaction of a banking business in the jurisdiction where the branch transacts business.[9]

Though it is limited to international and foreign banking and financial services and investments, an Edge Act corporation may operate through branches within the United States.[10] Beyond core banking activities, an Edge is authorized by the Fed to engage in a range of other activities in its U.S. branches. These activities include: (1) payments and collections in connections with international or foreign transactions;[11] (2) foreign exchange transactions;[12] (3) fiduciary and investment advisory activities;[13] (4) banking services for employees;[14] (5) with Fed prior approval, other U.S. activities that the Fed determines to be incidental to the international or foreign business of an Edge.[15]

---

§ 9.14

1.　12 C.F.R. § 211.3(b)(1).
2.　*Id.* § 211.3(b)(2).
3.　*Id.* § 211.3(b)(3).
4.　*Id.* § 211.3(b)(4).
5.　*Id.* § 211.3(b)(5).
6.　*Id.* § 211.3(b)(6).
7.　*Id.* § 211.3(b)(7).

8.　*Id.* § 211.3(b)(8).
9.　*Id.* § 211.3(b)(10).
10.　*Id.* § 211.4(c).
11.　*Id.* § 211.4(e)(5).
12.　*Id.* § 211.4(e)(6).
13.　*Id.* § 211.4(e)(7).
14.　*Id.* § 211.4(e)(8).
15.　*Id.* § 211.4(e)(9).

Similarly, Agreement corporations are subject to restrictions on their activities within the United States. With prior Fed approval, a member bank or bank holding company is permitted to invest in a corporation that has entered into an agreement or undertaking with the Fed limiting itself to activities permissible for an Edge.[16]

Finally, member banks, bank holding companies, Edge Act and Agreement corporations are permitted to engage in activities outside the United States through investment in foreign subsidiaries and affiliates.[17] Beyond core banking activities, these investors are authorized by the Fed to engage in a range of other activities through their foreign subsidiaries and affiliates. These activities include: (1) leasing real or personal property, or acting as agent, broker, or advisor in leasing real or personal property;[18] (2) fiduciary activities;[19] (3) underwriting credit life insurance and credit accident and health insurance;[20] (4) services for other direct or indirect operations of U.S. banking organizations, including representative functions, sale of long-term debt, name saving, holding assets acquired to prevent loss on debt previously contracted in good faith, and other activities permissible domestically for bank holding companies under the Bank Holding Company Act ("BHCA");[21] (5) holding the premises of a branch of an Edge or a member bank, or the premises of a direct or indirect subsidiary, or holding or leasing the residence of officer or employee of branch or subsidiary;[22] (6) investment, financial, or economic advisory services;[23] (7) general insurance agency and brokerage activities;[24] (8) data processing;[25] (9) organizing, sponsoring, and managing mutual funds, if fund shares are not sold or distributed in United States or to U.S. residents, and the fund does not exercise managerial control over firms in which it invests;[26] (10) management consulting services;[27] (11) underwriting, distributing and dealing in debt securities outside the United States;[28] (12) underwriting, distributing, and dealing in equity securities outside the United States;[29] (13) operating a travel agency;[30] (14) insurance underwriting;[31] (15) acting as a futures commission merchant for financial instruments of the type, and on the exchanges, that the Fed has previously approved;[32] (16) acting as principal or agent in swap transactions, subject to limitations applicable to state member banks;[33] (17) BHCA "closely related" activities;[34] and, (18) with prior specific Fed approval, activities determined to be usual in connec-

16. *Id.* § 211.4(f).

17. *Id.* § 211.5.

18. *Id.* § 211.5(d)(3).

19. *Id.* § 211.5(d)(4).

20. *Id.* § 211.5(d)(5).

21. *Id.* § 211.5(d)(6). *See* 12 U.S.C.A. § 1843(a)(2)(A), (c)(1)(C) (BHCA provisions concerning bank servicing).

22. 12 C.F.R. § 211.5(d)(7).

23. *Id.* § 211.5(d)(8).

24. *Id.* § 211.5(d)(9).

25. *Id.* § 211.5(d)(10).

26. *Id.* § 211.5(d)(11).

27. *Id.* § 211.5(d)(12).

28. *Id.* § 211.5(d)(13).

29. *Id.* § 211.5(d)(14).

30. *Id.* § 211.5(d)(15).

31. *Id.* § 211.5(d)(16).

32. *Id.* § 211.5(d)(17). *See id.* § 225.25(b)(18) (providing Fed rules as to conduct of activities).

33. *Id.* § 211.5(d)(18). *See id.* pt. 208 (limitations applicable to state member banks).

34. *Id.* § 211.5(d)(19). *See id.* § 225.25(b) (providing prior determinations by Fed of closely related activities under BHCA).

tion with the transaction of the business of banking or other financial operations abroad, consistent with the Federal Reserve Act or the BHCA.[35]

In each of these sets of authorizations, the wild card is the "other activities" provision.[36] Since the authorizations focus on what activities are "usual" in connection with banking in a host market,[37] or on what is "incidental" to international and foreign banking,[38] they are highly contextual and must be examined country by country.

§ 9.15   Lending

One essential, traditional role of banking is as a source of funding, *i.e.*, as a commercial lender. Within the international banking context, then, one may expect this role also to be central. Whether international or domestic, certain considerations—like the creditworthiness of the borrower and the adequacy of the spread between cost of funds and rate of return—will be key considerations in the bank's decision to lend. But are there any considerations in the lending decision that are peculiar to *international* lending?

Lending is lending. To some extent, therefore, the considerations that go into the lending decision are the same, whether one is operating in the domestic or international market. However, certain considerations may be peculiar to international banking, or they may have a relatively greater emphasis in the international banking context. Some important features of international lending may be identified as follows. International lending usually involves "cross-national" or transborder risk, a risk to the success of the transaction related not necessarily to the creditworthiness of the borrower, but to the social, political, and economic environment in which the borrower or its project is placed. Components of transborder risk include (*i*) "country risk," taken in its broadest sense to include the complex of socio-political factors that affect success; (*ii*) "regulatory risk," the effect of differing regulatory features in the country of the borrower; and, (*iii*) "jurisdictional risk," the effect of performing and enforcing the lending agreement in a different legal jurisdiction (*i.e.*, the borrower's) or, if the agreement is to be enforced in the lender's home jurisdiction, the indirect effect that the law of the borrower's jurisdiction may have on enforcement. Another important, and fairly obvious feature is exchange rate risk and other attendant problems connected with, for example, foreign currency lending.

These concerns are relevant whether the "bank" involved in international lending is a commercial bank, or an Edge or Agreement corpo-

---

35. *Id.* § 211.5(d)(20).

36. *See, e.g., id.* §§ 211.3(b)(10) (providing for other activities of foreign branches usual in connection with transaction of banking business in host country); § 211.4(e)(9) (providing for other U.S. activities incidental to Edge corporation international or foreign business); § 211.5(d)(20) (providing for other Edge corporation off-shore activities usual in connection with transaction of business of banking or other financial operations).

37. *Id.* §§ 211.3(b)(10) (foreign branch market); 211.5(d)(20) (foreign subsidiary market).

38. *Id.* § 211.4(e)(9) (U.S. activities of Edges).

ration. In addition, special rules apply to credit activities of Edges.[1] Edges may finance: contracts, projects, or activities performed substantially offshore;[2] importation into or exportation from the United States of goods (either directly or through brokers or other intermediaries);[3] domestic shipment or temporary storage of goods being imported or exported (or accumulated for export);[4] and, assembly or repackaging of goods imported or to be exported.[5]

Edges may also finance *domestic* production costs of goods and services for which export orders have been received or which are identifiable as being directly for export.[6] They may also assume or acquire participations in extensions of credit, or acquire obligations arising from other transactions, so long as the extensions or transactions are ones that an Edge corporation could have financed originally (including acquisitions of obligations of foreign governments).[7]

In addition, Edges may guarantee debts, or otherwise agree to make payments on the occurrence of "readily ascertainable events,"[8] if the guarantee or agreement specifies the Edges's maximum monetary liability thereunder and is related to an offshore or export- or import-related transaction.[9] Finally, Edges may provide credit and other banking services, for domestic and foreign purposes, to foreign governments and their agencies and instrumentalities, foreign persons, and other similar foreign entities.[10]

§ 9.16   Lending limits

National banks are subject to limitations on the amount of total loans and extensions of credit to any one borrower at any time, calculated as a percentage of unimpaired capital and surplus.[1] Lending to certain interrelated or commonly controlled groups of borrowers are aggregated for purposes of calculating lending limits.[2] In lending to foreign sovereigns, governmental entities, and other entities owned or controlled by the foreign government, the question may naturally arise whether all such loans should be treated as if they were loan to one "person" for purposes of lending limitations. Some guidance in this regard is offered by the Comptroller's regulations. In general (*i.e.*, for domestic or private foreign borrowers), the basic rule is that loans or extensions of credit to

§ 9.15

1. 12 C.F.R. § 211.4(e)(4).
2. *Id.* § 211.4(e)(4)(i)(A).
3. *Id.* § 211.4(e)(4)(i)(B).
4. *Id.* § 211.4(e)(4)(i)(C).
5. *Id.* § 211.4(e)(4)(i)(D).
6. *Id.* § 211.4(e)(4)(ii).
7. *Id.* § 211.4(e)(4)(iii).
8. "Readily ascertainable events" include, but are not limited to, events such as nonpayment of taxes, rentals, customs duties, or cost of transport and loss or nonconformity of shipping documents. *Id.* § 211.4(e)(4) (iv).

9. *Id.* On offshore and export- or import-related transactions, see *supra* text and accompanying notes 2–6.
10. 12 C.F.R. § 211.4(e)(4)(v).

§ 9.16

1. 12 U.S.C.A. § 84(a)(1) (15 percent of capital and surplus); *id.* § 84(a)(2) (additional and separate 10 percent limit for loans and extensions of credit fully secured by readily marketable collateral). On exemptions from these lending limits, see *id.* § 84(c).
2. *See* 12 C.F.R. § 32.5 (Comptroller's combination rules under § 84).

one borrower should be attributed to another person, with each person deemed the borrower, when either the proceeds of a loan or extension of credit are to be used for the direct benefit of the other person, to the extent so used,[3] or a "common enterprise" is deemed to exist between the persons.[4]

However, in the case of loans to foreign governments, their agencies, and instrumentalities, the generally applicable rules are displaced by special aggregation rules.[5] Loans and extensions of credit to such borrowers are aggregated only if the loans or extensions of credit fail to meet both a "means test" and a "purpose test" at the time the loan or extension of credit is made.[6]

The means test requires that the borrower have resources or revenue of its own, sufficient to service its debt obligations.[7] If the government's support (excluding guarantees by a central government of the borrower's debt) exceeds the borrower's annual revenues from other sources, the Comptroller presumes that the borrower fails the means test.[8] The purpose test requires that the purpose of the loan or extension of credit be consistent with the purposes of the borrower's general business.[9]

The practical consequences of these tests is that, in certain circumstances, loans to interrelated governmental or governmentally controlled entities will not be aggregated, although the same loans to similarly interrelated private borrowers would have been combined as loans to one borrower for purposes of calculating lending limits. Consider the following hypothetical case.

Assume that Quarter National Bank has a general lending limit of $30 million dollars. It has lent $25 million to the Nusquami Port Authority, a governmental corporation controlled by statute by the Ministry of Development of the Republic of Nusquam. NusBank, a commercial bank 90 percent-owned by the Nusquami Ministry of Finance, applies for a $10 million loan from Quarter. NusBank is marginally profitable, and its external debt is guaranteed by investment guarantees provided by the Nusquami Central Bank. NusBank intends to loan the proceeds of the proposed loan to the Ministry of Development, as a project loan to complete renovations of the port facilities managed by the Nusquami Port Authority.

If the proposed loan were combined with the outstanding loan to the Nusquami Port Authority—as it most likely would be if these were private, domestic borrowers with equivalent interrelationships—the pro-

---

3. *Id.* § 32.5(a)(1). For the meaning of "direct benefit" for these purposes, see *id.* § 32.5(b).

4. *Id.* § 32.5(a)(2). On the test for the existence of a "common enterprise" for these purposes, see *id.* § 32.5(c). Special rules for attribution apply to corporate groups, *id.* § 32.5(d), and to partnerships,

joint ventures, and other unincorporated associations. *Id.* § 32.5(e).

5. *Id.* § 32.5(f).

6. *Id.* § 32.5(f)(1).

7. *Id.* § 32.5(f)(1)(i).

8. *Id.*

9. *Id.* § 32.5(f)(1)(ii).

posed loan would exceed Quarter's lending limit. However, under the special rules, the proposed loan probably meets both the means and purpose tests.[10] NusBank has resources or revenue of its own, sufficient to service its debt obligations, since the Central Bank guarantees are excluded from the means test. The purpose test is also met, because *lending*—even to another Quarter borrower—is obviously consistent with the purposes of NusBank's general business.

Imagine this hypothetical case multiplied countless times. Given the potential concentrations of credit that the special rules invite, is it any surprise that U.S. international banks confronted a less-developed-country debt crisis in the 1980s?[11] Ironically, even if the outstanding official debt is later consolidated under a central obligor in a qualifying restructuring,[12] such debt will not be aggregated and attributed to the central obligor, so long as the previously outstanding loans and other extensions of credit qualified for separate lending limit treatment under the special rules.[13] However, when this restructuring rule applies, a national bank's loans and other extensions of credit to a foreign government, its agencies

---

10. Of course, in order to demonstrate that the means and purpose tests are satisfied, Quarter must, at a minimum, retain in its files the following:

(i) A statement (accompanied by supporting documentation) describing the legal status and the degree of financial and operational autonomy of the borrowing entity;

(ii) Financial statements for the borrowing entity for a minimum of three years prior to the date the loan or extension of credit was made or for each year that the borrowing entity has been in existence, if less than three;

(iii) Financial statements for each year the loan or extension of credit is outstanding;

(iv) The bank's assessment of the borrower's means of servicing the loan or extension of credit, including specific reasons in support of that assessment. The assessment shall include an analysis of the borrower's financial history, its present and projected economic and financial performance, and the significance of any financial support provided to the borrower by third parties, including the borrower's central government; and

(v) A loan agreement or other written statement from the borrower which clearly describes the purpose of the loan or extension of credit. The written representation will ordinarily constitute sufficient evidence that the purpose test has been satisfied. However, when, at the time the funds are disbursed, the bank knows or has reason to know of other information suggesting that the borrower will use the proceeds in a manner inconsistent with

the written representation, it may not, without further inquiry, accept the representation.

Id. § 32.5(f)(2)(i)–(v).

11. For representative cases illustrating the difficulties of enforcing loan agreements involving official debt, see, *e.g.*, *Libra Bank Ltd. v. Banco Nacional de Costa Rica*, 570 F.Supp. 870 (S.D.N.Y.1983); *Allied Bank Int'l v. Banco Credito Agricola de Cartago*, 757 F.2d 516 (2d Cir.1985), *cert. dismissed*, 473 U.S. 934, 106 S.Ct. 30; *A.I. Credit Corp. v. Government of Jamaica*, 666 F.Supp. 629 (S.D.N.Y.1987).

12. To qualify, the official debt must be restructured in a sovereign debt restructuring approved by the OCC, upon request by a bank for application of the non-combination rule. The factors used in making this determination include:

(A) Whether the restructuring involves a substantial portion of the total commercial bank loans outstanding to the foreign government, its agencies, and instrumentalities;

(B) Whether the restructuring involves a substantial number of the foreign country's external commercial bank creditors;

(C) Whether the restructuring and consolidation under a central obligor is being done primarily to facilitate external debt management; and

(D) Whether the restructuring includes features of debt or debt-service reduction.

Id. § 32.5(f)(3)(ii)(A)–(D).

13.   *Id.* § 32.5(f)(3)(i).

and instrumentalities—including the restructured debt—is limited in the aggregate to a total equal to 50 percent of the bank's capital and surplus.[14]

Lending limits clearly apply to lending occurring within the United States. In addition, the Federal Deposit Insurance Corporation Improvements Act ("FDICIA")[15] imposes on state-licensed branches and agencies the same limits on lending to a single borrower that apply to federally-licensed branches and agencies.[16] The Fed and the FDIC have each promulgated regulations implementing the FDICIA's limitations on the activities of state-licensed branches and agencies of non-U.S. banks.[17]

The Fed also has lending limit regulations that apply to Edges.[18] These set lending limits and capital requirements covering such activities as acceptances,[19] discussed in § 9.22, *infra*, as well as loans and extensions of credit to one person.[20]

§ 9.17   Lending Supervision

Lending, whether domestic or international, also raises concerns about its effects on the safety and soundness of the lending bank. Such concerns can be dealt with under the generally applicable enforcement provisions of federal banking law.[1] However, in the case of international loans, another statutory enactment, the International Lending Supervision Act of 1983 ("ILSA"),[2] specifically addresses such concerns, and others such as capital adequacy.[3]

§ 9.18   Deposits

Deposit-taking is also a core activity in international banking, particularly given the importance of Eurodollar transactions.[1] International-related deposits raise interesting policy issues concerning the applicability of regulatory regimes such as deposit reserves and deposit insurance.

14.   *Id*. § 32.5(f)(3)(iii).

15.   Pub. L. No. 102–242, 105 Stat. 2236 (December 19, 1991) (codified at scattered sections of 12 U.S.C.A.).

16.   12 U.S.C.A. 3105(h)(1).

17.   59 Fed. Reg. 55,026 (1994) (codified at 12 C.F.R. § 211.29) (Fed rule); 59 Fed. Reg. 60,703 (1994) (codified at 12 C.F.R. § 346.101) (FDIC rule).

18.   12 C.F.R. § 211.6.

19.   *Id*. § 211.6(a).

20.   *Id*. § 211.6(b).

§ 9.17

1.   *See, e.g.*, 12 U.S.C.A. § 1818(b) (administrative cease and desist order available to address unsafe and unsound practices).

2.   Pub. L. No. 98–181, 97 Stat. 1153 (1983) (codified at 12 U.S.C.A. §§ 3901–3912).

3.   *Compare, e.g.*, 12 U.S.C.A. § 1818(b) (general enforcement of safety and soundness) *with id*. §§ 3901–3904, 3907 (specific provisions for lending supervision, including imposition of administratively determined loan loss reserves, known as "allocated transfer risk reserves," or "ATRRs").

§ 9.18

1.   On the legal implications of Eurodollar deposits, see, *e.g.*, *Citibank, N.A. v. Wells Fargo Asia Limited*, 495 U.S. 660, 662–663, 110 S.Ct. 2034, 2036–2037 (1990), *on remand, Wells Fargo Asia Limited v. Citibank, N.A.*, 936 F.2d 723 (2d Cir.1991).

Deposit insurance (§§ 2.10, 5.11) and deposit reserve requirements (§§ 2.11, 5.12) are discussed elsewhere in this hornbook.

Essentially, two rules of thumb should be kept in mind. First, as to deposit reserve requirements, although foreign deposits of U.S. depository institutions can be subjected to reserve requirements,[2] deposits that are payable only outside the United States are currently not subjected to reserve requirements.[3] Deposit reserve requirements apply generally to any deposit payable within the United States, even if also payable elsewhere.[4] U.S. branch and agency deposits are generally subject to the deposit reserve requirements.[5] Inter-office deposits of branches, agencies and Edges are not considered "deposits" for purposes of the reserve requirements.[6] Deposits of international banking facilities are not "demand deposits" for purposes of the reserve requirements.[7]

Second, although foreign deposits of U.S. depository institutions may be covered by federal deposit insurance,[8] resolution of the problems of a failing U.S. depository institution cannot include payments to the benefit of foreign depositors.[9]

A further complication arises under the International Banking Act ("IBA"). Originally the IBA required deposit insurance for "retail deposits" of U.S. branches of non-U.S. banks (*i.e.*, "deposits of less than $100,000"), with some transitional treatment of state branches of such banks.[10] However, the Federal Deposit Insurance Corporation Improvements Act ("FDICIA")[11] added a provision that prospectively requires such retail deposit-taking to be done in separately chartered and FDIC-insured U.S. subsidiaries, rather than through branches.[12]

§ 9.19   Edge Act Corporations

Edge corporations are permitted to engage directly or indirectly in deposit-taking activities within the United States, to the extent that the activities are incidental to international or foreign business.[1] Ordinarily, the Fed considers the following U.S. deposit-taking activities to be "incidental" to international or foreign business: (1) deposits in the form

---

2. *See, e.g.*, 12 C.F.R. §§ 211.3(c) (providing that member bank foreign branch deposits are susceptible to reserve requirements of Regulation D, 12 C.F.R. Pt. 204), 211.4(d) (providing that deposits of Edge and Agreement corporations are subject to Regulations D "in the same manner and to the same extent as if the Edge or Agreement corporation were a member bank").

3. *Id.* § 204.2(a).

4. *See id.* §§ 204.2(a)(1) (definition of "deposit"); 204.2(t) (definition of "payable only at an office located outside the United States"); 204.3(a) (maintenance of reserves).

5. *See* 12 U.S.C.A. § 3105; 12 C.F.R. § 204.3(a)(1).

6. *See* 12 C.F.R. § 204.2(a)(2)(xii).

7. *See id.* §§ 204.2(b)(3)(iv), 204.8(a)(2).

8. *See, e.g.*, 12 U.S.C.A. § 3104 (requiring deposit insurance for retail deposits held by foreign branches and subsidiaries within United States).

9. *Id.* § 1831r(a).

10. 12 U.S.C.A. § 3104 (1978).

11. Pub. L. No. 102–242, 105 Stat. 2236 (December 19, 1991) (codified at scattered sections of 12 U.S.C.A.).

12. 12 U.S.C.A. § 3104(c).

§ 9.19

1. 12 C.F.R. § 211.4(e).

of transaction accounts, savings, and time deposits (including issuing negotiable certificates of deposits) from foreign governments and their agencies and instrumentalities;[2] (2) deposits in the form of transaction accounts, savings, and time deposits (including issuing negotiable certificates of deposits) from foreign persons;[3] (3) deposits from U.S. persons, if the deposits are international- or foreign-related;[4] and, (4) liquid funds not currently employed in the Edge's international or foreign business, if held or invested in the United States, in the form of cash or specified money market instruments.[5]

§ 9.20   Documentary Letters of Credit

The basic structure of a documentary letter of credit transaction in illustrated in Figure 9–4, *infra*. One could argue that a letter of credit ("L/C") is a peculiar form of secured lending. For the brief time that the bank has accepted the documents and paid the beneficiary's draft but has not yet been reimbursed by the account party, there is something not unlike a collateralized loan relationship between bank and account party. On the other hand, the letter of credit is also a payment transfer mechanism. The best approach, of course, may be simply to consider the letter of credit on its own terms.

FIGURE 9-4

Typical Documentary Letter of Credit

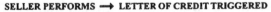

SELLER PERFORMS ➔ LETTER OF CREDIT TRIGGERED

1 Seller ships goods; obtains necessary documents from shipper
2 Seller submits docs and draft to C bank
3 C bank pays Seller on draft
4 C bank submits docs and draft to I bank
5 I bank reimburses C bank
6 I bank makes docs available to Buyer
7 Buyer reimburses I bank in exchange

2. *Id*. § 211.4(e)(1)(i).

3. *Id*.

4.   12 C.F.R. § 211.4(e)(1)(ii).

5.   12 C.F.R. § 211.4(e)(2).

The L/C is primarily governed by transactional rules, embodied in Article 5 of the Uniform Commercial Code,[1] and, for certain international L/Cs, the International Chamber of Commerce's Uniform Customs and Practices for Documentary Credits[2] or other applicable international rules.[3] There is, however, a regulatory dimension to these instruments.

For example, under a former interpretive provision of the Comptroller's regulations,[4] L/Cs were explicitly subject to regulatory considerations concerning sound banking practices. For these purposes, a bank would be required conspicuously to entitle or otherwise indicate that the instrument was an L/C;[5] to condition the L/C by a specified expiration date or definite stated term,[6] and to limit the bank's exposure under the L/C to a stated maximum amount.[7] The bank's liability was required to be limited to presentation of a specified draft or other documentation,[8] and the bank was prohibited from agreeing to undertake the determination of questions of fact or law in dispute between the account party and beneficiary of the L/C.[9] Finally, the bank was required to obtain its customer's unqualified obligation for reimbursement under the L/C.[10]

The Comptroller recently replaced this provision with another, more streamlined interpretation.[11] Under this new interpretation, the Comptroller would not permit a national bank to make its obligation to pay under the L/C to be dependent "upon nondocumentary conditions or resolution of questions of fact."[12] Presumably, a national bank would therefore still be prohibited from performing a physical inspection of goods that were the subject of the transaction for which the L/C was issued.[13]

National banks now have the general authority to issue, confirm or otherwise undertake to honor or purchase L/Cs and other independent undertakings within the scope of the applicable transactional laws or rules of practice recognized by law.[14] The bank's obligation to honor depends upon the presentation of specified documents and not upon nondocumentary conditions or resolution of questions of fact or law at

§ 9.20

1. Uniform Commercial Code, art. 5 (1962, as amended 1990) or revised art. 5 (as amended 1995).

2. Uniform Customs and Practice for Documentary Credits (International Chamber of Commerce, Publication No. 500). *See Bank of Cochin Ltd. v. Manufacturers Hanover Trust*, 612 F.Supp. 1533 (S.D.N.Y. 1985), *aff'd*, 808 F.2d 209 (2d Cir.1986) (discussing Uniform Customs and Practices).

3. United Nations Commission on International Trade Law ("UNCITRAL"), Convention on Independent Guarantees and Standby Letters of Credit (adopted by UNCITRAL 1995); Uniform Rules for Bank-to-Bank Reimbursements Under Documentary Credits (International Chamber of Commerce, Publication No. 525).

4. 12 C.F.R. § 7.7016 (1990).

5. *Id.* § 7.7016(a).

6. *Id.* § 7.7016(b).

7. *Id.* § 7.7016(c).

8. *Id.* § 7.7016(d).

9. *Id. See, e.g., Maurice O'Meara Co. v. National Park Bank of New York*, 239 N.Y. 386, 146 N.E. 636 (Ct.App.1925) (so holding under common law).

10. 12 C.F.R. § 7.7016(e) (1990).

11. 12 C.F.R. § 7.1016.

12. *Id.* § 7.1016(a).

13. *Cf. id.* § 7.1016(b)(1)(i).

14. *Id.* § 7.1016(a).

issue between the account party and the beneficiary.[15] The new interpretation focuses primarily on the safety and soundness considerations involved in a bank's involvement in L/C transactions.[16]

§ 9.21　Standby Letters of Credit

The basic structure of a standby letter of credit transaction in illustrated in Figure 9–5, *infra*. Neither the Comptroller's regulations[1] nor the basic applicable law[2] differentiate between documentary letters of credit, issued to effect payment to a beneficiary-seller for goods under documents, and standby letters of credit, issued to compensate a beneficiary-buyer for the account party's failure to perform services under contract. This lack of distinction may not be surprising, since the power of national banks to issue standby letters of credit was originally justified on the basis of their essential equivalence to traditional documentary letters of credit.[3] Nevertheless, the respective operating assumptions of the two types of letters of credit are diametrically opposed.

FIGURE 9-5

Typical Standby Letter of Credit

SELLER *FAILS* TO PERFORM ⟶ LETTER OF CREDIT TRIGGERED

　1 Seller allegedly breaches contract to provide services to Buyer
　2 Buyer submits demand and draft to C bank
　3 C bank pays Buyer on demand and draft
　4 C bank submits demand and draft to I bank
　5 I bank reimburses C bank
　6 I bank notifies Seller of demand and payment
　7 Seller reimburses I bank

---

15. *Id.*

16. *Id.* § 7.1016(b).

§ 9.21

1. *See* 12 C.F.R. § 7.1016 (making no distinction between documentary and standby letters of credit).

2. *See, e.g., American Bell International, Inc. v. Islamic Republic of Iran*, 474 F.Supp.

420 (S.D.N.Y.1979) (applying traditional letter of credit analysis to standby letter of credit guaranteeing performance).

3. *See, e.g., Legality of Guaranty Letters of Credit*, [1974 Transfer Binder] Fed. Banking L. Rep. (CCH) ¶ 96,301 (July 1, 1974) (equating documentary and standby letters of credit).

In cases like *American Bell International*,[4] courts are essentially applying generally applicable principles (developed in the commercial L/C context) to instruments that, despite their name, are significantly different from traditional commercial L/Cs, and that are more like third-party guarantees. In this regard, consider the effect on a "fraud in the transaction" claim[5] involving a standby letter of credit. In the case of a documentary letter of credit,[6] the stringencies of the "fraud in the transaction" theory can be straightforwardly met by simple facts—have the goods been shipped, or do the boxes contain trash? Do these requirements work out satisfactorily when we are really arguing about the good faith of an undocumented demand under a standby letter of credit, rather than a documented demand? At least in the case of the documented demand, we can assume that there are some goods floating around to secure the bank's risk.

Obviously, *American Bell International* rejects the suggestion that more refined rules should be applied in the case of standby letters of credit. The result is an outcome that, intuitively, seems to be contrary and unsatisfying, since the court assumed that an adequate remedy would exist for the account party in Iran, which at the time was already exhibiting extreme hostility toward Americans and American firms. As the U.S.-Iran crisis of 1979 worsened, however, there were at least some indications that courts were beginning to consider the plight of account parties to standby letters of credit (and their issuing banks) in a more thoughtful fashion.[7]

Eventually, of course, the U.S. Government would intervene and freeze the standby letters of credit, so that potentially fraudulent demands could not be effected.[8] This development means that we lack any definitive judicial resolution of the problem of adapting rules that arose in the documentary letter of credit context to the standby letter of credit context.

§ 9.22 Bankers' Acceptances

A bankers' acceptance is a time draft or bill of exchange drawn on a bank by its customer, and "accepted" by the bank. Acceptance makes the draft an obligation of the accepting bank, much as certification of a check makes the check the bank's own obligation. Because the bank customer or the accepting bank may negotiate the accepted draft or bill in a secondary market in which the Fed itself participates and thus raise

---

4. *Supra* note 2.

5. Uniform Commercial Code, § 5–114(2).

6. *See, e.g., United Bank Ltd. v. Cambridge Sporting Goods Corp.*, 41 N.Y.2d 254, 360 N.E.2d 943, 392 N.Y.S.2d 265 (Ct. App.1976) (involving "fraud in the transaction" claim where mildewed goods had been shipped on a cancelled contract).

7. *See, e.g., Stromberg–Carlson Corp. v. Bank Melli Iran*, 467 F.Supp. 530 (S.D.N.Y. 1979) (finding serious risk of fraudulent or nonauthentic demand sufficient showing for preliminary injunction against payment under standby letter).

8. *See* Michael P. Malloy, *The Iran Crisis: Law Under Pressure*, 1984 Wisc. Int'l L.J. 15 (1984) (discussing standby letter of credit problem).

short-term funds, bankers' acceptances are useful and efficient devices in financing international sales of goods.

The typical acceptance transaction is illustrated in Figure 9–6, *infra*.

FIGURE 9-6
Bankers' Acceptance: Typical Transaction

A Trading Company sells widgets to *XYZ* Import Company (1). To finance these sales, for which it normally receives payment in 180 days, *A* arranges with *B* Bank to accept its drafts. in a predetermined amount, at an agreed discount rate plus an acceptance commission. Pursuant to this arrangement, *B* accepts *A*'s drafts (2), and it credits *A*'s account (3) with an amount equal to the face amount of the drafts, minus the discount (in effect, the interest charged on the financing provided to *A*) and the commission. *B* may then hold the drafts to maturity, or it may rediscount them in the secondary market (4) in order to liquidate its position (5). When the drafts mature (which should be timed for some time shortly after *XYZ* pays *A* (6)), whoever holds them presents them to *B* for payment as the accepting bank (7). *B* will pay the drafts (8), and debit *A*'s account for the amount of the payment (9), *A* having deposited the proceeds of its sale into its account (10).

The key to this market as a financing device is its liquidity, and that depends in large part on the easy negotiability of drafts. Negotiability is enhanced if the acceptance is eligible for rediscount by Federal Reserve banks, consistent with the requirements of the FRA.[1] A member bank, or a federal or state branch or agency of a foreign bank may accept drafts

§ 9.22
1.   12 U.S.C.A. § 372.

drawn upon under the following conditions: (1) The draft must have no more than six months sight to run, exclusive of days of grace.[2] (2) It must "grow out of" an import or export transaction[3] or a transaction involving the domestic shipment of goods,[4] or it must be secured at the time of acceptance by a warehouse receipt or similar document of title, covering readily marketable staples.[5] (3) With certain exceptions,[6] the aggregate amount of acceptances for any institution at any one time must be no more than 150 percent of its paid-up and unimpaired capital stock and surplus (or its dollar equivalent, in the case of a U.S. branch or agency of a foreign bank);[7] however, aggregate acceptances "growing out of" domestic transactions is limited in the aggregate to an amount equal to 50 percent of the aggregate of all acceptances.[8] (4) Institutions are prohibited from accepting bills for any one person at any one time in an aggregate amount greater than ten percent of its paid-up and unimpaired capital stock and surplus, or its equivalent for a U.S. branch or agency of a foreign bank, unless the institution is secured either by attached documents or by some other actual security "growing out of" the same transaction as the acceptance.[9]

Generally, these rules apply to agreements to participate in acceptances as well as to acceptances themselves.[10] However, the limitations do not apply to that portion of one institution's acceptance that is covered by a participation agreement sold to another institution.[11]

Essentially, the FRA restrictions attempt to ensure that a bank's exposure in these transactions is relatively short-term and is linked to goods in commerce, the sale of which is likely to extinguish the obligation of the bank with little risk. The regulatory concerns relevant in this context are not unlike those seen in the letter of credit context. However, a bank's own discounted acceptance is treated as a loan for accounting purposes, and so regulatory policy with respect to lending is also relevant. For example, "ineligible" acceptances (those not qualifying under the FRA) would be included in the lending limit calculations.[12]

§ 9.23 Securities Activities

Securities activities of depository institutions are more fully treated elsewhere in this book. However, distribution of securities and the syndication and distribution of participations in loans are important and cognate activities of international banking. With the increasing interna-

---

2. *Id.* § 372(a).

3. *Id.* § 372(a)(i).

4. *Id.* § 372(a)(ii).

5. *Id.* § 372(a)(iii).

6. The Fed has the authority to permit an institution to accept bills in an aggregate amount not exceeding at any one time equal to 200 percent of its paid-up and unimpaired capital stock and surplus or (in the case of a U.S. branch or agency of a

foreign bank) its dollar equivalent. *Id.* § 372(c).

7. *Id.* § 372(b).

8. *Id.* § 372(d).

9. *Id.* § 372(d).

10. *See, e.g., id.* § 372(b) (applying rules on ratio limit of bills to obligation for participation share therein).

11. *Id.* § 372(f).

12. 12 U.S.C.A. § 84.

tionalization of capital markets,[1] banks are compelled to sustain and broaden their participation in international capital markets if they are to maintain a share of their wholesale customer's business. Participation occurs both in the Eurobond market[2] and the Euroequity market.[3]

Domestically, U.S. depository institutions are not permitted to engage fully in the underwriting of securities,[4] nor can a member bank affiliate with a firm that is principally engaged in securities underwriting and related activities.[5] However, to the extent that underwriting and related activities take place outside the U.S. domestic market, with no "bleed-back" of the underwritten securities into the U.S. market, depository institutions may be authorized to participate.

Typically, U.S. banking enterprises are authorized to participate in securities activities internationally, despite U.S. domestic restrictions, through the invocation of the wild card, or "other activities," provisions of the Fed's Regulation K.[6] In addition, under certain specified circumstances, a bank holding company may engage in debt-for-equity swap investments in firms engaged in activities outside of banking and financial services.[7] These swap investments are subject to the following conditions. A bank holding company may make such investments only through the conversion of sovereign or private debt obligations of a country that has restructured its official debt, either through direct exchange of the debt obligations for the investment or by a payment for the debt in local currency, the proceeds of which are used to purchase investments specified by Regulation K.[8] The specified investments are as follows: (1) Up to and including 100 percent of the shares of, or other ownership interests in, any foreign company located in an eligible country, if the shares are acquired from the government of the eligible country or from its agencies or instrumentalities;[9] or, (2) Up to and

§ 9.23

1. *See, e.g.*, SECURITIES AND EXCHANGE COMMISSION, INTERNATIONALIZATION OF THE SECURITIES MARKETS: REPORT OF THE STAFF OF THE SECURITIES AND EXCHANGE COMMISSION TO THE SENATE COMMITTEE ON BANKING, HOUSING AND URBAN AFFAIRS AND THE HOUSE COMMITTEE ON ENERGY AND COMMERCE (27 JULY 1987) (discussing internationalized capital markets).

2. *See id.* at II-35—II-51 (discussing Eurobond markets, *i.e.*, markets for bonds issued in one country or group of countries, but denominated in currency of another country).

3. *See id.* at II-51—II-62, III-43—III-53 (discussing Euroequity markets, *i.e.*, markets for equity securities underwritten and distributed in one country or group of countries outside issuer's home country by syndicate of international securities firms and banks).

4. 12 U.S.C.A. §§ 24(Seventh), 378(a)(1).

5. *Id.* § 377.

6. *See* 12 C.F.R. §§ 211.3(b)(10), 211.5(d)(20) (authorizing "other" offshore activities by branches, Edges and Agreement corporations).

7. *Id.* § 211.5(f). Upon application, the Fed may permit a swap investment to be made through an insured bank subsidiary of a bank holding company, if the company demonstrates that such ownership is consistent with the purposes of the FRA. In granting its consent, the Fed may impose such conditions as it deems necessary or appropriate to prevent adverse effects, including prohibiting loans from the bank to the company in which the investment is made. *Id.* § 211.5(f)(2).

8. *Id.* § 211.5(f)(1). The proceeds in local currency may include as part of the investment an additional cash investment not exceeding in the aggregate more than 10 percent of the fair value of the debt obligations being converted. *Id.*

9. *Id.* § 211.5(f)(1)(i).

including 40 percent of the shares, including voting shares, of, or other ownership interests in, any other foreign company located in an eligible country[10] subject to certain conditions.[11]

The company is required to divest the shares of, or other ownership interests in, any company acquired through a debt-for-equity swap[12] within ten years from the date of acquisition of the investment[13] or within two years from the date on which the company is permitted to repatriate in full the investment in the foreign company, whichever is longer.[14] However, in either case divestiture must occur within fifteen years of the date of the acquisition.[15] The bank holding company must report to the Fed on its plans for divesting the investment two years prior to the final date for divestiture.[16] In addition, all swap investments are subject to prompt divestiture,[17] if the acquired company engages in impermissible business within the United States that exceeds in the aggregate 10 percent of the company's consolidated assets or revenues calculated on an annual basis.[18]

§ 9.24   Foreign Exchange Transactions

National currencies serve three basic purposes. Domestically, they are legal tender for all debts and other obligations. They are also a measure of value of other property. Internationally, they are a medium of exchange for transactions and investment. Consequently, in the international market they are a commodity. For an Italian importer, for example, the dollar (for example) is a commodity that the importer must purchase, directly or indirectly, to obtain what she really wants—goods for import denominated in dollars. Likewise, for the U.S. importer, the

---

10. *Id.* § 211.5(f)(1)(ii).

11. The conditions are as follows:

(1) The company may invest in more than 25 percent of the voting shares if and only if another shareholder or control group of shareholders unaffiliated with the bank holding company holds a larger block of voting shares of the company.

(2) The company and its affiliates may not lend, or otherwise extend credit to, the foreign company in amounts greater than 50 percent of the total loans and extensions of credit to the foreign company.

(3) The company's representation on the board of directors or on management committees of the foreign company may be no more than proportional to its shareholding in the foreign company.

12 C.F.R. § 211.5(f)(1)(ii)(A)–(C).

12. *Id.* § 211.5(f)(3)(i). The Fed may permit retention of the shares or other ownership interest, if it is otherwise permissible at the time required for divestiture. *Id.* For example, if the activities of the

acquired company was determined to be a permissible "other activity" at the time required for divestiture, *per* § 211.3(b)(10), the Fed might permit retention.

13. *Id.* § 211.5(f)(3)(i)(A). However, the Fed may extend this period if, in its judgment, such an extension would not be detrimental to the public interest. *Id.*

14. *Id.* § 211.5(f)(3)(i)(B).

15. *Id.* § 211.5(f)(3)(i).

16. *Id.* § 211.5(f)(3)(ii).

17. *See id.* § 211.5(b)(4)(i)(A)–(B) (concerning prompt divestiture requirements). The Fed may nevertheless authorize retention, upon application. *Id.* § 211.5(f)(3) (iii).

18. *Id.* § 211.5(f)(3)(iii). In any event, the acquired company is prohibited from engaging in activities in the United States that consist of banking or financial operations, *per* § 211.23(f)(5)(iii)(B), or types of activities permitted under section 4(c)(8) of the Bank Holding Company Act, 12 U.S.C.A. § 1843(c)(8), except with Fed approval. 12 C.F.R. § 211.5(f)(3)(iii).

lira is a commodity that he must purchase, directly or indirectly, to obtain what he really wants—goods for import denominated in lira.

The multifaceted nature of foreign exchange raises some complicated issues for fiscal policy. If the lira, as a commodity, becomes *less* expensive (relative to the dollar), Italian exports ultimately become cheaper for the U.S. importer, but U.S. exports ultimately become more expensive for the Italian importer. The reverse is true, of course, if the lira becomes relatively more expensive in relation to the dollar.

Eventually, these effects will have an impact on the standard of living in Italy. (Consider for example Italian imports of oil and petroleum products, denominated in dollars.) In addition, if consumers and investors (particularly at the high end) believe that the lira is a poor measure of value (because, for example, it tends to decrease in value relative to other currencies), then they will prefer to store their net worth in dollars, or some other currency other than the lira. Complicating this situation will be the activities of "speculators" in currencies, who may sell short or buy long at a current price in international currency markets, depending upon whether they bet that the currency on the date their foreign exchange contract becomes due for "delivery" will be decreasing or increasing in value, respectively.[1] Because currency markets are sensitive to these transactions, the result of this "artificial" demand may be to drive a currency's value further down or up.

The question for the student of international banking policy is: If the monetary authorities in Italy are worried about the effect of speculation on the stable value of the lira, what should they do about it? They could just say, "Speculation in the lira is prohibited," but with what result? Italian monetary authorities would confront the possibility of hidden transactions and difficult questions about whether or not a particular transaction is speculative. If this prohibition is aggressively pursued, possibly calling into question the legality of what are actually legitimate transactions, merchants will move away from lira-denominated goods.

In the alternative, the authorities could ask themselves, what does speculation look like on the books of the currency trader? At the end of a given trading day, it would have sold significantly more than it had bought, or *vice versa*. So, why not prohibit the symptoms of speculation, rather than speculation itself? This is basically the typical approach taken by foreign exchange regulations.[2] What result? Complicated off-shore transactions involving foreign jurisdictions with bank secrecy laws that prevent the authorities from examining the other end of transactions that appear to "square" the books of currency traders within Italy. This is a regulatory problem that confronts even sophisticated currency regulations.

§ 9.24

1. *See, e.g.*, Carley, *Close Encounters*, Wall St. J., Sept. 4, 1982, at 1 (describing speculative currency trading of Citibank).

2. *See id.* (describing Italian foreign exchange restrictions).

In a sense, this situation illustrates a typical problem in international banking. With a host of national authorities each acting independently with respect to *international* transactions, how can national regulatory policy objectives be effectively realized? Of course, this dilemma is present not only in international bank regulatory policy, but in public international fiscal policy as well.[3]

The BIS addressed this problem in the 1983 Concordat.[4] The basic operating principle that it advanced to deal with this problem was one of cooperation and information flow between home-country and host-country regulators. In the view of the BIS Committee, it was particularly important for parent banks to establish internal monitoring systems to supervise overall foreign exchange exposure, and it was equally important for home-country authorities to monitor those systems. Host-country authorities should also monitor the foreign exchange exposure of foreign establishments in their territories.

The BIS Committee has also approached the problems of foreign exchange activities from a more technical perspective. It initiated proposed revisions of the capital adequacy guidelines[5] in July 1994.[6] These would cover such issues as increasing the capital charge for potential future counterparty exposure on exchange rate contracts, and recognition of the effects of bilateral netting arrangements in calculating the potential future exposure for exchange contracts.[7]

§ 9.25   Resolution of Transborder Failures

National and international policy with respect to the resolution of transborder failures has stiffened over the past decade, particularly in the case of the United States. The Federal Deposit Insurance Corporation Improvements Act ("FDICIA")[1] prohibits federal bank regulatory agencies from making, directly or indirectly, any payment or from providing any financial assistance in connection with any insured depository institution, if the payment would have the direct or indirect effect of satisfying any claim, in whole or in part, against the institution for its obligations on foreign deposits.[2] This prohibition excludes foreign deposi-

---

3. On the implications for public international fiscal policy, see Michael P. Malloy, *Shifting Paradigms: Institutional Roles in a Changing World*, 62 Fordham L. Rev. 1911 (1994).

4. BANK FOR INTERNATIONAL SETTLEMENTS, COMMITTEE ON BANKING REGULATIONS AND SUPERVISORY PRACTICES, PRINCIPLES FOR THE SUPERVISION OF BANKS' FOREIGN ESTABLISHMENTS (1983), *reprinted in* MICHAEL P. MALLOY, INTERNATIONAL BANKING 55–60 (1998).

5. BANK FOR INTERNATIONAL SETTLEMENTS, COMMITTEE ON BANKING REGULATIONS AND SUPERVISORY PRACTICES, FINAL REPORT FOR INTER-NATIONAL CONVERGENCE OF CAPITAL MEASUREMENT AND CAPITAL STANDARDS, *reprinted in* 1 Fed. Banking L. Rep. (CCH) ¶ 5403 (July 29, 1988).

6. *See* 61 Fed. Reg. 15,947 (1996) (Fed discussion of 1994 proposals).

7. *Id.*

§ 9.25

1. Pub. L. No. 102–242, 105 Stat. 2236 (December 19, 1991) (codified at scattered sections of 12 U.S.C.A.).

2. 12 U.S.C.A. § 1831r(a).

tors from direct or indirect benefit from a decision by U.S. regulators to place an institution in receivership and resolve its obligations. However, it does not apply to "open bank assistance" provided by the FDIC[3] to a troubled institution.[4] Thus, an institution—even if technically close to receivership—could be revived with open bank assistance, and foreign depositors are permitted to benefit from this process. Similarly, the prohibition does not apply to "discount window lending," Fed bank advances or other extensions of credit consistent with the Federal Reserve Act.[5]

FDICIA also gave the Fed direct authority over U.S. branches, agencies, and commercial lending subsidiaries of foreign-based banks.[6] The Fed has broad authority to examine U.S. branches, agencies and affiliates of foreign-based banks, whether state- or federally-approved.[7] Under specified circumstances, the Fed has the authority to order the closing of any state-licensed office of a foreign-based bank,[8] and to *recommend* to the Comptroller the termination of the license of any federally-licensed office of a foreign-based bank.[9] The Fed can also terminate the activities of any representative office.[10]

Finally, FDICIA broadened the penalties directly applicable to U.S. activities of foreign-based banks. It established authority for civil money penalties (administrative fines) to be assessed against any foreign bank, and any office or subsidiary of a foreign bank, that violates, and any individual who participates in a violation of, any provision of the International Banking Act ("IBA"), or any regulation prescribed or order issued under the act.[11] FDICIA also established criminal penalties for the knowing violation of any provision of the IBA or any regulation or order issued by a federal banking agency under the act, with the intent to deceive, to gain financially, or to cause financial gain or loss to any person.[12]

On the positive side, FDICIA explicitly authorizes disclosure of supervisory information by federal bank regulatory agencies to foreign bank regulatory or supervisory authorities.[13] This is consistent with the objective identified by the BIS Committee to improve the supervision of transborder banking enterprises.[14] With respect to such supervision, the BIS Concordat establishes a two-fold classification system for dealing with problems of troubled or failing international banks. This system is illustrated in Figure 9–7, *infra*.

---

3. *Id.* § 1823(c).

4. *Id.* § 1831r(b).

5. *Id.* § 1831r(c).

6. *Id.* § 3105(d)(1), (g).

7. *Id.* § 3105(b)(1).

8. *Id.* § 3105(e)(1)–(4), (g).

9. *Id.* § 3105(e)(5).

10. *Id.* § 3107(b).

11. *Id.* § 3110.

12. *Id.* § 3111.

13. *Id.* § 3109(a).

14. *See* Bank for International Settlements, Committee on Banking Regulations and Supervisory Practices, Principles for the Supervision of Banks' Foreign Establishments (1983), *reprinted in* Michael P. Malloy, International Banking 55–60 (1998).

Figure 9–7

Supervision under the Concordat

Type of Establishment	Type of Problem	
	Solvency	Liquidity
Branch	primarily matter for home country authority	primary responsibility for host country authority
Subsidiary	joint responsibility of host and home	primary responsibility for host
Joint Venture	primary responsibility with country of incorporation	primary responsibility with country of incorporation

Thus, in deciding on the proper division of responsibility in a transborder problem, we must first ask what type of foreign bank presence are we dealing with. Second, we must ask what kind of problem is the banking enterprise are we actually facing—liquidity (*i.e.*, troubled condition), or insolvency (*i.e.*, failure).

Thus, if the subject enterprise is a joint venture, the host-country regulator is likely to be saddled with the primary responsibility, whether the problem is one of solvency or liquidity. However, if the enterprise is a subsidiary of, for example, a U.S. national bank, and if the host-country authorities determine that it is facing a solvency problem, resolution will be the joint responsibility of host-country and U.S. authorities. If on the other hand it is facing a liquidity problem, this will be the primary responsibility of the host-country authorities.

Of course, only a handful of national supervisors directly participated in the construction of the Concordat. Would it make a difference if the host country involved was not a member of the BIS Committee? First, it should be noted that the Concordat is not, by its own terms, a binding international treaty or agreement. It is at best a statement of principles. Hence, it may be less important that the host country is not a member of the Committee, so long as it endorses the principles.

Second, the Concordat purports to set forth the optimal operating principles endorsed by the members of the Committee. Hence, at the very least the Concordat should be the argumentative focus of discussion between host- and home-country authorities.

Post–Concordat issuances of the BIS have refined the operating assumptions with respect to supervision of multinational banking enterprises.[15] Neither the April 1990 SUPPLEMENT nor the June 1992 MINIMUM STANDARDS affect the basic framework established by the Concordat. However, to the extent that these issuances result in better information

---

15. BANK FOR INTERNATIONAL SETTLEMENTS, COMMITTEE ON BANKING REGULATION AND SUPERVISORY PRACTICES: SUPPLEMENT TO THE BASLE CONCORDAT ENSURING OF ADEQUATE INFORMATION FLOWS BETWEEN BANKING SUPERVISORY AUTHORITIES (APRIL 1990), *reprinted in* MALLOY, INTERNATIONAL BANKING, *supra*, at 61–64;

BANK FOR INTERNATIONAL SETTLEMENTS, COMMITTEE ON BANKING REGULATION AND SUPERVISORY PRACTICES: REPORT ON MINIMUM STANDARDS FOR THE SUPERVISION OF INTERNATIONAL BANKING GROUPS AND THEIR CROSS-BORDER ESTABLISHMENT (JUNE 1992), *reprinted in* MALLOY, INTERNATIONAL BANKING, *supra*, at 64–68.

flows between national regulators and better national controls over the entry of a multinational banking enterprise into the national market supervised by the regulator, presumably the supervision of multinational bank failures could be more efficiently anticipated and managed.

While the MINIMUM STANDARDS are not, on their own terms, binding on states, BIS participating states are expected to implement them, and other states are encouraged to do so. U.S. implementation has occurred primarily in connection with the enactment of FDICIA. The parallels between the MINIMUM STANDARDS and FDICIA provisions are illustrated in Figure 9–8, *infra.*

Figure 9–8

Parallels between BIS MINIMUM STANDARDS and FDICIA

MINIMUM STANDARD	FDICIA	SUBJECT MATTER
1. All international banking groups and international banks should be supervised by a home-country authority that capably performs consolidated supervision	12 U.S.C.A. § 3105(d)(2)(a)	comprehensive supervision of applicant for U.S. branch on consolidated basis by home state required
2. The creation of cross-border banking establishment should receive the prior consent of both host-country supervisory authority and bank's and, if different, banking group's home-country supervisory authority	3105(d)(3)(A)	consent of home state to establishment of U.S. branch required
3. Supervisory authorities should possess right to gather information from cross-border banking establishments of banks or banking groups for which they are the home-country supervisor	3105(d)(3)(B) 3105(d)(3)(C)	foreign bank must furnish information needed to assess application adequacy of foreign bank's assurances that it will make available information on its operations and activities (and those of its affiliates) deemed necessary to determine and enforce compliance with IBA, BHCA, and other applicable Federal law made condition of approval of application
4. If host-country authority determines that any one of the foregoing minimum standards is not met to its satisfaction, that authority could impose restrictive measures necessary to satisfy its prudential concerns consistent with the minimum standards, including prohibition of creation of banking establishments	3105(e)(1)(A)	termination of U.S. office of foreign bank when foreign bank is not subject to comprehensive supervision on consolidated basis by home state authorities

§ 9.26   Foreign Bank Secrecy

This section focuses on what might be called conflicts between extraneous public policy and international banking regulation. By "extraneous" we mean public policy not directly related to the policy values and objectives of banking regulation. Obviously, given the multinational character of banking regulation and the transborder nature of banking itself, conflicts of law and public policy are always a possibility in international banking. By and large, however, we expect to find a relatively high degree of agreement from system to system, at least in principle, over the basic policy values and objectives of banking regulation: maintenance of a safe and sound banking system, maintenance of the public confidence in the system, and the like.

Other public policy concerns and objectives may intersect with, and possibly conflict with, the objectives of banking regulation, however conceived. For example, there is often an obvious conflict between bank secrecy laws and generally applicable criminal and civil enforcement procedures.[1] Frustration may occur in either direction. If bank secrecy is vindicated, legitimate policy interests in the investigation and enforcement of criminal and civil wrongs are frustrated. On the other hand, if the enforcement policy interests are vindicated, this may result in the frustration of legitimate policy values favoring confidentiality between a bank and its customers. Again, the conflict can often be serious and unresolvable.

Bank secrecy is viewed as a fundamental personal right under Swiss law,[2] the classic source of bank secrecy rules, and is protected by criminal penalties in Swiss codes.[3] In contrast, under U.S. law, there is no constitutional right to the privacy of bank records of your transactions,[4] although there are limited notice procedures now available as a matter of statute.[5] Naturally, a high degree of secrecy protection leads to the serious possibility of the abuse of bank secrecy in the service of criminal activity. Accordingly, some limits exist even under Swiss law.[6] There is in fact a growing tendency of Swiss authorities to apply and

---

§ 9.26

1. Bank secrecy laws are not only a feature of havens for money-laundering and insider trading offenses; they are also extremely attractive to depositors seeking to avoid or evade tax consequences in their home jurisdictions. *See, e.g.*, Nash, *Germans in Tax Revolt Embrace Luxembourg*, N.Y. Times, Nov. 25, 1994, at D7 (discussing ways in which bank secrecy laws benefit Luxembourg, as depositors from Germany seek to avoid 1993 German withholding tax on interest income of residents).

2. *See* Honegger, *Demystification of the Swiss Banking Secrecy and Illumination of the United States–Swiss Memorandum of Understanding*, 9 N.C. J. Int'l L. & Com.

Reg. 1 (1983) (discussing fundamental policy bases for Swiss bank secrecy rules).

3. *See* Swiss Banking Law of 1934, art. 47(b) (providing fines and/or imprisonment for willful violation of bank secrecy; fines for negligent violation); Swiss Penal Code, art. 273 (providing imprisonment and fines for eliciting or disclosing business secrets).

4. *See United States* v. *Miller*, 425 U.S. 435, 96 S.Ct. 1619 (1976) (so holding).

5. Right to Financial Privacy Act, 12 U.S.C.A. §§ 3401–3420, 3422.

6. *See* Honegger, *supra* (discussing limits, including contractual understandings between depositor and Swiss bank, and statutory and regulatory limits mandating disclosure to Swiss authorities and courts).

enforce bank secrecy rules in a more restrained fashion, in order to protect significant public policy interest in the avoidance of securities manipulation, fraud and asset conversion, and undesirable activities of foreign states.[7]

Easing of Swiss bank secrecy practices, particularly through such devices as government-to-government or government-to-industry memoranda of understanding on investigative procedures and mutual cooperation treaties, may moderate possible conflicts when Swiss banks are involved. However, the practical effect has been to move transactions to other bank secrecy havens.[8] In that regard, it is important to keep in mind that significant individual variations exist as one moves among the bank secrecy laws of different jurisdictions, and it is dangerous to generalize in this area. The Greek bank secrecy provision, as discussed in *First National Bank of Chicago*,[9] seems very harsh in terms of its penalties, but it seems to be relatively narrow in terms of the scope of possible parties affected by it. In contrast, the Bahamanian bank secrecy provision, considered in *In re Grand Jury Proceedings (Bank of Nova Scotia)*,[10] seems much broader in scope, expressly including even outside advisers. The Swiss bank secrecy provision, considered in *Banca Della Svizzera Italiana*,[11] seems to take the middle ground.

A claim of bank secrecy under the laws of one state triggers a policy conflict only if the information subject to the claim is itself relevant to another state's fundamental policies.[12] Where fundamental U.S. policies are involved, U.S. courts have tended to be intolerant of claims of bank secrecy.[13] U.S. courts have traditionally reached these results in reliance on the policy-balancing test of Section 40 of the *Foreign Relations Restatement (2d)*,[14] starting with the assumption that the conflicting states both have the right to apply their rules.

---

7. *See* Hirsch, *"Dirty Money" and Swiss Banking Regulations*, 8 J. Comp. Bus. & Cap. Market L. 373 (1986) (describing the emergence of "new duties" under Swiss banking law).

8. *See, e.g., In re Grand Jury Proceedings*, 532 F.2d 404 (5th Cir.1976), *cert. denied sub nom. Field v. United States*, 429 U.S. 940, 97 S.Ct. 354 (involving Cayman Islands bank secrecy laws).

9. *United States v. First Nat'l Bank of Chicago*, 699 F.2d 341 (7th Cir.1983).

10. *See, e.g., In re Grand Jury Proceedings*, 691 F.2d 1384 (11th Cir.1982), *cert. denied sub nom. Bank of Nova Scotia v. United States*, 462 U.S. 1119, 103 S.Ct. 3086 (1983).

11. *Securities and Exch. Comm'n v. Banca Della Svizzera Italiana*, 92 F.R.D. 111 (S.D.N.Y.1981).

12. *See, e.g., Trade Dev. Bank v. Continental Ins. Co.*, 469 F.2d 35 (2d Cir.1972) (finding account information not relevant to bank's claim under fidelity bond).

13. *See, e.g., In re Grand Jury Proceedings*, 691 F.2d 1384 (rejecting bank secrecy claim in tax and narcotics investigation); *In re Grand Jury Proceedings*, 532 F.2d 404 (rejecting bank secrecy claim in tax evasion case); *Banca Della Svizzera Italiana, supra* (rejecting bank secrecy claim in securities fraud investigation). *But cf. First Nat'l Bank of Chicago, supra* (upholding bank secrecy claim in tax assessment case, where criminal penalties in secrecy jurisdiction were disproportionately severe).

14. American Law Institute, *Restatement (2d) of the Foreign Relations Law of the United States* § 40, provides:

Where two states have jurisdiction to prescribe and enforce rules of law and the rules they may prescribe require inconsistent conduct upon the part of a person, each state is required by international law to consider, in good faith, moderating the exercise of its enforcement jurisdiction, in light of such factors as

(a) vital national interests of each of the states,

Section 40 has had a significant influence in shaping this area of policy conflict in the U.S. courts. However, they have not necessarily adopted § 40 uncritically. The provisions of § 40 on their own terms, for example, do not give greater emphasis to any one of the factors identified in deciding whether to exercise jurisdiction in the face of inconsistent law of another jurisdiction. Yet Judge Pollack in *Banca Della Svizzera Italiana* appears to give primary emphasis to § 40(a) and (b), while lumping § 40(c)–(e) together with little real attention. On the other hand, in the inverse case—where analysis of the § 40(a)–(b) factors do not appear to counsel application of U.S. law in the face of conflict— Judge Fairchild in *First National Bank of Chicago* analyzes the remaining § 40 factors carefully. If the approaches of Judge Pollack and Judge Fairchild are reconcilable, this would mean that as interpreted and applied by the courts, there is a bias in favor of applying U.S. law in the face of conflicting foreign law.

However, Section 403 of the *Restatement (3d)*,[15] which seems rigged against U.S. enforcement in its balancing test,[16] starts with a different

---

(b) the extent and the nature of the hardship that inconsistent enforcement actions would impose upon the person,

(c) the extent to which the required conduct is to take place in the territory of the other state,

(d) the nationality of the person, and

(e) the extent to which enforcement by action of either state can reasonably be expected to achieve compliance with the rule prescribed by that state.

For cases applying § 40 as the basis for decision, see, *e.g., In re Grand Jury Proceedings, supra; First Nat'l Bank of Chicago, supra.* The Southern District of New York favors an application of § 40 that emphasizes § 40(a)-(b), almost to the exclusion of the other specified factors. *See, e.g., Banca Della Svizzera Italiana, supra.*

15. American Law Institute, *Restatement (3d) of the Foreign Relations Law of the United States*, § 403, provides:

(1) Even when one of the bases for jurisdiction ... is present, a state may not exercise jurisdiction to prescribe law with respect to a person or activity having connections with another state when the exercise of such jurisdiction is unreasonable.

(2) Whether the exercise of jurisdiction over a person or activity is unreasonable is determined by evaluating all relevant factors, including, where appropriate:

(a) the link of the activity to the territory of the regulating state ... ;

(b) the connections ... between the regulating state and the person principally responsible for the activity to be regu-

lated, or between that state and those whom the regulation is designed to protect ... ;

(c) the character of the activity to be regulated, the importance of the regulation to the regulating state, the extent to which other states regulate such activities, and the degree to which the desirability of such regulation is generally accepted;

(d) the existence of justified expectations that might be protected or hurt by the regulation;

(e) the importance of the regulation to the international, political, legal or economic system;

(f) the extent to which the regulation is consistent with the traditions of the international system;

(g) the extent to which another state may have an interest in regulating the activity; and

(h) the likelihood of conflict with regulation by another state.

(3) When it would not be unreasonable for each of two states to exercise jurisdiction over a person or activity, but the prescriptions by the two states are in conflict, each state has an obligation to evaluate its own as well as the other state's interest in exercising jurisdiction, in light of all the relevant factors ... ; a state should defer to the other state if that state's interest is clearly greater.

16. *Cf.* David B. Massey, Note, *How the American Law Institute Influences Customary Law: The Reasonableness Requirement* assumption—that a state lacks jurisdiction to prescribe or enforce if exercising jurisdiction would be unreasonable. Section 403 has been adopted by U.S. courts,[17] but it is sometimes characterized by them as simply an extension or revision of § 40.[18]

The provisions of the *Restatement (3d)* dealing with jurisdictional conflicts were hotly debated over an extended period of time both within and outside the American Law Institute. The compromise text that eventually became § 403 may not significantly change results in bank secrecy cases.[19] As a practical matter, however, there are some areas of congruence between the two sections. Figure 9–9, *infra*, offers some assistance in considering the differences between the two sections.

Figure 9–9

Comparison: § 40 and § 403

Restatement (2d) § 40	*Restatement (3d) § 403*
"is required ... to consider, in good faith, moderating the exercise of its enforcement jurisdiction" under such factors as:	(1) " ... state may not exercise ... jurisdiction ... when the exercise ... is unreasonable."
(c) within	(2) "unreasonable" depends on: (a) within or affecting the regulating state
(d) nationality of person [(a) vital national interest?] [(a)]	(b) state's connection with person regulated or protected (c) character of activity, importance to each state, desirability generally accepted
[(b) hardship of inconsistent rules?]	(d) justified expectation protected or hurt by regulation in question (e) importance of regulation to international political, legal, or economic system (f) regulation consistent with traditions of international system
(a) vital national interest [(e) reasonable expectation of compliance?]	(g) another state's interest in regulating (h) likelihood of conflict with other states

of the Restatement of Foreign Relations Law, 22 Yale J. Int'l L. 419, 437 (1997) (arguing that § 403 did not accurately reflect customary law when published).

17. *See, e.g., Timberlane Lumber Co. v. Bank of Am.,* 749 F.2d 1378 (9th Cir.1984) (adopting seven-factor analysis based on § 403(2)); *Trugman-Nash, Inc. v. New Zealand Dairy Bd.,* 954 F.Supp. 733, 737 (S.D.N.Y.1997) (*citing Timberlane*). *See generally* Massey, *supra,* at 437–439 (surveying U.S. court citation of § 403); Louise Ellen Teitz, *et al., International Litigation,* 31 Int'l Law. 317, 331–334 (1997) (discussing cases).

18. *See, e.g., Filetech S.A.R.L. v. France Telecom,* 978 F.Supp. 464, 477 (S.D.N.Y.

1997), *vacated,* 157 F.3d 922 (2d Cir.1998) (referring to "direct line of succession" between § 40 and § 403 cases); *United States v. Nippon Paper Indus. Co.,* 109 F.3d 1, 7 (1st Cir.1997) (noting § 403 "merely reaffirms"); *In re Grand Jury Proceedings,* 40 F.3d 959, 965 (9th Cir.1994), *cert. denied sub nom. Marsoner v. United States,* 515 U.S. 1132, 115 S.Ct. 2558 (noting § 40 as "revised and ... encompassed within" § 403). *Cf. In re Grand Jury Proceedings,* 709 F.Supp. 192, 195 (C.D.Cal.1989) (invoking § 40).

19. *See, e.g., Filetech S.A.R.L., supra* (applying § 403(2)); *In re Grand Jury Proceedings,* 40 F.3d 959 (applying § 403).

The provisions of Part D of the 1990 Supplement to the BIS Concordat[20] deal with domestic bank secrecy laws that may impede transnational regulation and supervision of banking. The BIS Supplement is not binding, but to the extent its principles are followed, it has the effect of moderating the effect of bank secrecy laws. However, this effect is specialized to the concerns of bank regulators with respect to the availability of information for supervisory purposes. Thus, the BIS Supplement might not alter the outcome in policy conflicts involving the enforcement of nonbanking regulations.

In addition, the provisions of the 1992 BIS Minimum Standards[21] were intended to ensure adequate supervision of transnational banking enterprises through effective coordination among national supervisors, and would also affect the application of bank secrecy laws. The Minimum Standards are "expected" to be implemented by BIS participants, and other states are encouraged to implement them as well. To the extent the standards are implemented, however, their effect is specialized primarily to the concerns of bank regulators considering an application for entry into the domestic banking market. Thus, as with the Concordat Supplement, the standards might not alter the outcome in policy conflicts involving nonbanking regulatory enforcement.

§ 9.27　International Sanctions and Banking

The imposition of international economic sanctions is a traditional, if specialized, technique of foreign affairs, particularly in U.S. practice.[1] Depending upon the form of the sanction, the interests of banks involved in international banking activities may be significantly affected.[2] Given the extensive nature of some of the economic sanctions programs administered by the U.S. Department of the Treasury ("Treasury") in particu-

20. Bank for International Settlements, Committee on Banking Regulation and Supervisory Practices: Supplement to the Basle Concordat Ensuring of Adequate Information Flows between Banking Supervisory Authorities (April 1990), *reprinted in* Malloy, International Banking, *supra*, at 61–64.

21. Bank for International Settlements, Committee on Banking Regulation and Supervisory Practices: Report on Minimum Standards for the Supervision of International Banking Groups and Their Cross-Border Establishment (June 1992), *reprinted in* Malloy, International Banking, *supra*, at 64–68.

§ 9.27

1. *See, e.g.,* Michael P. Malloy, *Remarks* in *Are the U.S. Treasury's Assets Control Regulations a Fair and Effective Tool of*

U.S. Foreign Policy? The Case of Cuba, 1985 Proc. Am. Soc. Int'l L. 169, 188 (varied policy purposes of economic sanctions).

2. For example, in the U.S. "blocking" of assets of the Government of Iran in 1979, it is estimated that approximately $12 billion worth of assets were immobilized (*see* Michael P. Malloy, *The Iran Crisis: Law Under Pressure,* 1984 Wisc. Int'l. L.J. 15, 34) of which some $2.2 billion represented U.S. domestic bank branch deposits, and some $5.5 billion represented deposits and interest in foreign-situs branches of U.S. banks. *Id.* at 85–88. The aftermath of the Iran crisis generated over 400 claims by banks before the Iran–United States Claims Tribunal. *See id.* at 91 & n.453.

lar,[3] the precise effect on those interests may manifest itself in unexpected ways.

§ 9.28   U.S. Statutory Sources of Authority for Economic Sanctions

United States statutory provisions that grant authority for the imposition of economic sanctions are highlighted in this section only to the extent that they provide authority for sanctions significantly affecting banks involved in international banking activities.[1]

Section 5(b) of the Trading With the Enemy Act ("TWEA")[2] provides in pertinent part:

> During the time of war [or during any other period of national emergency declared by the President,[3]] the President may, through any agency that he may designate, or otherwise, and under such rules and regulations as he may prescribe, by means of instructions, license, or otherwise . . .
>
> (B) investigate, regulate, direct and compel, nullify, void, prevent or prohibit, any acquisition, holding, withholding, use, transfer, withdrawal, transportation, importation or exportation of, or dealing in, or exercising any right, power or privilege with respect to, or transactions involving, any property in which any foreign country or a national thereof has any interest, by any person, or with respect to any property, subject to the jurisdiction of the United States.[4]

The specific TWEA programs pertinent to the present discussion are: (1) the Foreign Assets Control Regulations ("FACRs"),[5] which currently impose sanctions on North Korea and nationals thereof;[6] and, (2) the Cuban Assets Control Regulations ("CACRs"),[7] which were originally promulgated in 1963 and currently impose sanctions on Cuba and its nationals. The TWEA authority for the CACRs is augmented by the Cuban Liberty and Democratic Solidarity Act of 1996 ("CLDSA").[8]

---

3. *See, e.g.,* 31 C.F.R. Pt. 500 (1987) (Foreign Assets Control Regulations: commercial and financial prohibitions on specified East Asian countries); 31 C.F.R. Pt. 515 (1987) (Cuban Assets Control Regulations: similar prohibitions applied to Cuba); 31 C.F.R. Pt. 550 (1987) (Libyan Sanctions Regulations: commercial and financial prohibitions applied to Libya); 52 Fed. Reg. 44,076 (1988) (codified at 31 C.F.R. Pt. 560) (Iranian Transactions Regulations: limited trade restrictions applied to Iran).

§ 9.28

1. For a broader discussion of the effects of international economic sanctions, see MICHAEL P. MALLOY, ECONOMIC SANCTIONS AND U.S. TRADE (1990 & 1996 CUM. SUPP.).

2. 50 U.S.C.A. app. § 5(b).

3. This language was deleted by Pub. L. No. 95–223, § 101(a), 91 Stat. 1625, 1625 (1977) (amending 50 U.S.C.A. app. § 5(b) on a prospective basis only). For purposes of then current exercise of emergency powers under Section 5(b) of the TWEA, the bracketed language was not deleted. *See generally Regan v. Wald,* 468 U.S. 222, 104 S.Ct. 3026 (1984), *reh'g denied,* 469 U.S. 912, 105 S.Ct. 285 (1984) (discussing effect of TWEA savings clause).

4. 50 U.S.C.A. app. § 5(b)(1)(B).

5. 31 C.F.R. Pt. 500.

6. *Id.* § 500.201(d) schedule.

7. *Id.* Pt. 515.

8. Pub. L. No. 104–114, 109 Stat. 826 (Mar. 12, 1996) (*codified at* scattered Sections of 22 U.S.C.A.). *See* 22 U.S.C.A.

Section 5 of the United Nations Participation Act of 1945 ("UNPA")[9] is also a statutory source of economic sanctions authority. It authorizes the President to apply economic and other sanctions against a target country or national thereof in accordance with any mandatory decision by the U.N. Security Council under Article 41 of the U.N. Charter.[10]

The UNPA has been invoked by the President many times in recent years. For example, it was invoked in response to the Iraqi invasion of Kuwait in 1990.[11] The UNPA was invoked in 1992 to ban overflight, takeoff, and landing of aircraft flying to or from Libya,[12] and to impose sanctions against the Federal Republic of Yugoslavia (Serbia and Montenegro) (FRY), since suspended.[13] In 1993, the UNPA was invoked as the authority in the second phase of the Haitian sanctions,[14] since suspended,[15] and in the arms embargo against UNITA and Angola.[16] In 1994 it was invoked as to the arms embargo with respect to Rwanda.[17]

The International Emergency Economic Powers Act ("IEEPA")[18] gives the President broad authority over financial transactions and property in which any foreign country or national has any interest, provided that the President first declares the requisite national emergency.[19] The IEEPA essentially recodifies, for peacetime emergency use, the range of powers available to the President under Section 5(b) of the

---

§ 6033(c) (CLDSA; requiring executive branch enforcement of extant CACRs); 22 U.S.C.A. § 6064 (subjecting presidential termination of Cuban embargo to requirements of CLDSA).

9. 22 U.S.C.A. § 287c.

10. Article 41 provides in pertinent part:

The Security Council may decide what measures not involving the use of armed force are to be employed to give effect to its decisions, and it may call upon the Members of the United Nations to apply such measures. These may include complete or partial interruption of economic relations and of rail, sea, air, postal, telegraphic, radio, and other means of communication, and the severance of diplomatic relations.

U.N. Charter, art. 41. Members of the United Nations are required to fulfill in good faith obligations, such as those implicit in article 41, assumed by them under the Charter. U.N. Charter, art. 2, ¶ 2. *See also* U.N. Charter, art. 25, which provides that: "[t]he Members of the United Nations agree to accept and carry out the decisions of the Security Council in accordance with the present Charter."

11. Ex. Order No. 12,724, 55 Fed. Reg. 33,089 (1990) (prohibiting transactions with Iraq under UNPA and IEEPA); Ex. Order No. 12,725, 55 Fed. Reg. 33,091 (1990) (prohibiting transactions with Iraq-occupied

Kuwait); Ex. Order No. 12,817, 57 Fed. Reg. 48,433 (1992) (ordering transfer and consolidation of blocked assets representing proceeds of sale of Iraqi petroleum or petroleum products, *per* U.N. Security Council Resolution No. 778).

12. Ex. Order No. 12,801, 57 Fed. Reg. 14,319 (1992).

13. Ex. Order No. 12,810, 57 Fed. Reg. 24,347 (1992) (imposing sanctions under UNPA and IEEPA).

14. Ex. Order No. 12,853, 58 Fed. Reg. 35,843 (1993); Ex. Order No. 12,872, 58 Fed. Reg. 54,029 (1993).

15. Ex. Order No. 12,932, 59 Fed. Reg. 52,403 (1994).

16. Ex. Order No. 12,865, 58 Fed. Reg. 51,005 (1993).

17. Ex. Order No. 12,918, 59 Fed. Reg. 28,205 (1994).

18. Pub. L. No. 95–223, tit. II, 91 Stat. 1626 (1977) (codified at 50 U.S.C.A. §§ 1701–1706) (1994).

19. *Dames & Moore v. Regan*, 453 U.S. 654, 671–673, 101 S.Ct. 2972, 2982–2983 (1981). *See Chas. T. Main Int'l v. Khuzestan Water & Power Auth.*, 651 F.2d 800, 807 (1st Cir. 1981) (noting that "language of IEEPA is sweeping and broad"); *American Int'l Group v. Islamic Republic of Iran*, 657 F.2d 430, 439 (D.C.Cir.1981).

TWEA. The two statutory authorities differ in that the IEEPA does not contain the following TWEA powers still available to the President during time of war: (1) the power to "vest" (*i.e.*, expropriate) property in which foreign states or their nationals have an interest; (2) the power to regulate purely domestic transactions; (3) the power to regulate gold or silver coin or bullion; and, (4) the power to seize records.[20]

§ 9.29   Extant Programs with an Impact on International Banking

The statutory authorities described above support a range of sanctions programs that affect banks involved in international banking activities. This section examines the pertinent provisions of some of the major programs affecting banks.

    a.   *The Foreign Assets Control Regulations ("FACRs").* The FACRs currently impose a wide range of commercial and financial restrictions on transactions involving property in which North Korea or any national thereof has had any interest since the effective date of the regulations with respect to that country (December 17, 1950).[1] Among other things, the FACRs prohibit the following transactions (unless otherwise licensed): (1) transfers[2] of credit and all payments between, by, through, or to any banking institution[3] or institutions, wherever located with respect to any property[4] subject to the jurisdiction of the United States[5]

---

20. In addition, the IEEPA contained new restrictions on certain other substantive powers that were otherwise available to the President under TWEA. Thus, under the new authority, the President does not have power to: (1) regulate or prohibit personal communications not involving the transfer of anything of value; (2) regulate uncompensated transfers of articles for humanitarian aid, unless he determines that transfers of this type would either (a) seriously impair his ability to deal with the emergency situation; (b) respond to coercion against the potential donor or recipient; or (c) endanger U.S. armed forces. 50 U.S.C.A. § 1702(b). *See generally Veterans Peace Convoy, Inc. v. Schultz [sic]*, 722 F.Supp. 1425 (S.D.Tex.1988) (interpreting humanitarian aid exception to include donation of trucks).

§ 9.29

1. 31 C.F.R. § 500.201.

2. The term "transfer" is defined in 31 C.F.R. § 500.310 as:

any actual or purported act or transaction, whether or not evidenced by writing, and whether or not done or performed within the United States, the purpose, intent, or effect of which is to create, surrender, release, transfer, or al-

ter, directly or indirectly, any right, remedy, power, privilege, or interest with respect to any property....

3. The term "banking institution" is defined for purposes of these regulations as:

any person engaged primarily or incidentally in the business of banking, of granting or transferring credits, or of purchasing or selling foreign exchange or procuring purchasers and sellers thereof, as principal or agent, or any person holding credits for others as a direct or incidental part of his business, or any broker; and, each principal, agent, home office, branch or correspondent of any person so engaged shall be regarded as a separate "banking institution."

Id. § 500.314.

4. The term "property" (as well as the term "property interest(s)") is defined to include "any ... property, real, personal, or mixed, tangible or intangible, or interest or interests therein, present, future, or contingent." *Id.* § 500.311.

5. On the meaning of the term "property subject to the jurisdiction of the United States," for these purposes, the regulations contain a provision, ostensibly definitional but actually interpretive, that provides:

or by any person[6] subject to the jurisdiction of the United States;[7] (2) transactions[8] in foreign exchange by any person within the United States; and, (3) exportation or withdrawal from the United Stated of gold or silver coin or bullion, currency or securities, or the earmarking of any such property, by any person within the United States.[9]

These prohibitions are triggered under the FACRs on either of the following two conditions: (1) the transaction in question is effected by or on behalf of, or pursuant to the instructions of North Korea or national

---

The phrase "property subject to the jurisdiction of the United States" includes, without limitation, securities, whether registered or bearer, issued by:

(1) The United States or any State, district, territory, possession, county, municipality, or any other subdivision or agency or instrumentality of any thereof; or

(2) Any person within the United States whether the certificate which evidences such property or interest is physically located within or outside the United States.

Id. § 500.313(a)(1)–(2). *Cf. id.* § 500.405 (exportation of securities to blocked foreign countries prohibited by § 500.201). Thus, the FACRs contemplate the broadest possible extraterritorial reach whenever securities of any U.S.-situs or government issuer are involved. Aside from the sweeping extraterritorial effects of this "definition," it appears that the term "property subject to the jurisdiction of the United States" is meant to have a territorial meaning, *i.e.,* the term includes any property "physically located within the United States." *Id.* § 500.313(b). For these purposes, the term "United States" is defined to mean the political "United States and all areas under the jurisdiction or authority thereof, including U.S. trust territories and commonwealths." *Id.* § 500.321 (1987).

6. The term "person" is defined for these purposes to mean "an individual, partnership, association, corporation, or other organization." *Id.* § 500.308. For purposes of the particular prohibition under discussion, the term expressly includes any "banking institution." *Id.* § 500.201(a)(1).

7. The term "person subject to the jurisdiction of the United States" is defined for these purposes to include:

(a) Any individual, wherever located, who is a citizen of the United States;

(b) Any person within the United States ... ;

(c) Any corporation organized under the laws of the United States or of any

state, territory, possession, or district of the United States; and

(d) Any corporation, partnership, or association, wherever organized or doing business, that is owned or controlled by persons specified in paragraphs (a) or (c). . . .

Id. § 500.329(a)–(d). In turn, the term "person within the United states," used in § 500.329(b), is defined to include:

(1) Any person, wheresoever located, who is a resident of the United States;

(2) Any person actually within the United States;

(3) Any corporation organized under the laws of the United States, or of any state, territory, possession, or district of the United States; and

(4) Any partnership, association, corporation, or other organization, wheresoever organized or doing business, which is owned or controlled by any person or persons specified in paragraphs ... (1), (2), or (3). . . .

Id. § 500.330(a)(1)-(4).

8. The regulations do not contain a formal definition of the term "transaction." However, as with the term "property subject to the jurisdiction of the United States," the regulations do contain a provision ostensibly definitional but actually interpretive, that bears on the meaning of the term. *See id.* § 500.309 ("transactions involving property in which target country or national thereof has an interest," interpreted to include *payment or transfer* to such country or national; *export or withdrawal* from the United States to such country; or *transfer or payment denominated in currency of such country*). Transactions between principal and agent, when one or the other is outside the United States, may be subject to the prohibitions to the same extent as if the two parties were unaffiliated with each other. *Id.* § 500.404.

9. *Id.* § 500.201(a)(1)–(3).

thereof;[10] or, (2) the transaction involves property in which any target foreign country or national thereof has had, at any time on or since the "effective date" of the prohibition, any direct or indirect interest.[11]

The central provision in the FACRs is paragraph (b) of Section 500.201 of the regulations, which states:

All of the following transactions are prohibited, ... if such transactions involve *property* in which any designated foreign country, or any national thereof, has at any time on or since the effective date of this section had any *interest* of any nature whatsoever, direct or indirect:

(1) All dealings in, including, without limitation, *transfers*, withdrawals, or exportations *of, any property* or evidences of indebtedness or evidences of ownership of property by any *person subject to the jurisdiction of the United States;* and

(2) All *transfers* outside the United States with regard to any *property or property interest subject to the jurisdiction of the United States.*[12]

It is clear that the major effect of the prohibitions of Section 500.201(b) has been the blocking[13] of property, typically bank deposits and other bank-issued instruments and guarantes, subject to the juris-

---

10. The concept of "national" for these purposes is rather broadly defined by the regulations, thereby catching within its meaning a wider category of persons that the term "national" would connote as a matter of customary international law. *See id.* § 500.302(a), which defines the term to include the following:

(1) A subject or citizen of a country or any person who is domiciled in or a permanent resident of that country at any time on or since the "effective date," except persons who were resident or domiciled there in the service of the U.S. government.

(2) Any partnership, association, corporation, or other organization, organized under the laws of, or which on or since the "effective date" had or has had its principal place of business in a foreign country, or which on or since such effective date was or has been controlled by, or a substantial part of the stock, shares, bonds, debentures, notes, drafts, or other securities or obligations of which, was or has been owned or controlled by, directly or indirectly, a foreign country and/or one or more nationals thereof as defined in this section.

(3) Any person to the extent that such is, or has been, since the "effective date" acting or purporting to act directly or indirectly for the benefit of any national of a foreign country.

(4) Any other person who there is reasonable cause to believe is a "national" as defined in this section.

11. *Id.* § 500.201(a). The term "interest" is defined to mean, "when used with respect to property ... an interest of any nature whatsoever, direct or indirect." *Id.* § 500.312.

12. *Id.* § 500.201(b) (emphasis added).

13. The term "blocking" (or "freezing") of assets is not itself a term of art within the regulations, but refers metaphorically to the legal effect of the prohibitions of § 500.201 on property (or persons) affected thereby. *Cf., e.g., id.* § 500.319, defining "blocked account" to mean:

an account in which any designated national has an interest, with respect to which account payments, transfers or withdrawals o[r] other dealings may not be made of effected except pursuant to an authorization or license authorizing such action. The term "blocked account" shall not be seemed to include accounts of unblocked nationals.

Blocked assets are generally required to be held in interest-bearing accounts. *See id.* § 500.205.

diction of the United States.[14] "Blocking" of assets simply means that no transaction of any kind involving the affected assets can occur without a Treasury license.

Because of the expansive way in which they have been defined in the regulations, certain terms are essential to the sweeping application of Section 500.201(b). Such terms as "transfer," "property," and "interest" have been interpreted by the courts to be broad enough to prohibit virtually any direct or indirect transaction involving anything of value when there exists even the most attenuated interest of a designated country or national thereof in the property.[15] For example, in *Welch v. Kennedy*,[16] a case involving both financial and export restrictions, the D.C. District Court held that an attempted donative transfer of funds in favor of Vietnam (blocked at the time under the FACRs) was prohibited under the regulations. The court reached this holding despite the fact that the donee, Vietnam, had no "interest" in the intended but frustrated gift in any legal or equitable sense under traditional property law.

In that case, an American Quaker applied for a license to donate funds to the Canadian Friends Service Committee to be used to purchase medical supplies that were to be sent to Vietnam for the relief of noncombatants. In addressing the question whether Vietnam had an "interest" under the regulations in this donative transfer, the court stated:

> Plaintiff argues that the words "property" and "interest" must be taken as evidencing a congressional intent to regulate only commercial transactions and not donations to international relief organizations. Such an interpretation would be inconsistent with the broad purpose of the [TWEA], which was to give the President full power to conduct economic warfare against belligerent nations in time of war or national emergency.[17]

The provisions of the FACRs also contain a particularly effective enforcement device with respect to banking transactions. On the effective date of the regulations with respect to any of the designated countries to which they have applied from time to time, all transactions, including those in progress, are prohibited unless otherwise licensed by Treasury. Any transfer after the effective date in violation of the regulations is "null and void and shall not be the basis for the assertion or recognition of any interest in or right, remedy, power or privilege with respect to" property blocked under the regulations.[18] The regulations

---

14. Blocking of liquid assets historically has been one of the major effects to the imposition of Treasury controls under Section 5(b) of the TWEA. *See* U.S. Department of the Treasury, 1970 Census of Blocked Chinese Assets; U.S. Department of the Treasury, Census of Foreign Owned Assets in the United States (1945).

15. *See., e.g., Behring Int'l Inc. v. Miller*, 504 F.Supp. 552, 556–557 & n. 8 (D.N.J. 1980).

16. 319 F.Supp. 945 (D.D.C.1970).

17. *Id.* at 946–47 (citations omitted).

18. 31 C.F.R. § 500.203(a). Essentially the same rule of invalidity applies to any unlicensed attachment, judgment, decree, lien, execution, garnishment, or other judicial process entered or effected with respect to property in which a blocked country or national thereof has any interest. *See id.* § 500.203(e). *Cf. id.* § 500.504 (providing also contain a presumption against the asserted validity of putative "pre-effective date" transfers when the fact of the asserted transfer cannot be corroborated by independent evidence. In this regard, § 500.203(b) states:

> No transfer before the "effective date" shall be the basis for the assertion or recognition of any right, remedy, power, or privilege with respect to, or interest in, any property in which a designated national has or has had an interest since the "effective date" unless the person with whom such property is held or maintained had written notice of the transfer or by any written evidence had recognized such transfer prior to such "effective date."[19]

Thus, if a North Korean national entered into a contract for services with a foreign subsidiary of a U.S. national, with payment by means of an irrevocable letter of credit issued by a foreign bank and confirmed by First Credulity, a U.S. domestic bank, a purported transfer to the U.S. national from First Credulity would constitute a transaction involving property (*i.e.*, the letter of credit) in which a foreign national (*i.e.*, the account party) would have an interest.[20] Hence, once the FACRs became effective, any payment in accordance with the letter of credit would be null and void, and First Credulity would be required to establish a blocked account in the name of the North Korean national. It should be noted that the existence of ongoing contractual relationships and commitments would not be a basis in and of itself for Treasury licensing of any particular transfer or transaction after the effective date of the regulations.[21]

The FACRs do contain a limited safe harbor for unlicensed transactions or transfers rendered null and void by Section 500.203. Transactions or transfers otherwise rendered null and void are not deemed so, only as to any person with whom the property in question had been held or maintained, when the person establishes the following: (1) that the transaction or transfer did not represent a willful violation by that person; (2) that the person "did not have reasonable cause to know or suspect, in view of all the facts and circumstances known or available to such person,"[22] that the transaction or transfer was in fact unlicensed and prohibited;[23] and, (3) that, promptly upon discovery of the pertinent facts,[24] the person filed with Treasury a report setting forth the full

---

limited license for judicial proceedings with respect to blocked property).

19. *Id.* § 500.203(b).

20. *See id.* § 500.406. Of course, transfer in the reverse direction (request or authorization from bank or other person within the United States to a person outside the United States to make payment or transfer to blocked person) would also be prohibited by Section 500.201 *See id.* § 500.409.

21. *See id.* § 500.203(b).

22. *Id.* § 500.203(d)(2).

23. *Id.* If under the circumstances, a license or authorization was purported to have covered the transaction or transfer in question, it must be established that the person did not have reasonable cause to know or suspect "that such license or authorization had been obtained by misrepresentation or the withholding of material facts or was otherwise fraudulently obtained." *Id.*

24. For these purposes, the "pertinent facts" are:

(i) Such transfer was in violation of the provisions of [31 C.F.R. ch. V] or any circumstances with respect to the transaction or transfer.[25]

b. *The Cuban Assets Control Regulations ("CACRs")*. The CACRs[26] essentially follow both the structure and the details of FACRs. As a result, the CACRs generally may be expected to have the same impact upon U.S. banks involved in international banking activities as do the FACRs.

The CACRs track the same basic range of commercial and financial restrictions[27] on transfers or transactions involving property in which Cuba or any national thereof has had any interest since the effective date of the regulations.[28] For purposes of these prohibitions, the key terms "transfer",[29] "property,"[30] "interest,"[31] "property subject to the jurisdiction of the United States,"[32] "person,"[33] and "person subject to the jurisdiction of the United States,"[34] all carry the same meaning as they do in the FACRs, with the same results for the scope of the prohibitions.

One noticeable difference between the two sets of regulations is that the CACRs are now frozen in place under the Cuban Liberty and Democratic Solidarity Act of 1996 ("CLDSA").[35] In addition, the CLDSA adds several additional sanctions with respect to Cuba that potentially affect banks involved in international banking activities.

Among other things, the CLDSA prohibits persons subject to U.S. jurisdiction from extending any financing to a foreign or U.S. national "for the purpose of financing transactions involving any property confiscated by the Cuban Government" from a U.S. national.[36] The act also authorizes U.S. nationals (including a former Cuban national who is now a U.S. national) whose property was confiscated by the Cuban Government to bring suit against any person "trafficking" in confiscated

---

regulation, ruling, instruction, license or other direction or authorization thereunder, or

(ii) Such transfer was not licensed or authorized by the Secretary of the Treasury, or

(iii) If a license did purport to cover the transfer, such license had been obtained by misrepresentation or the withholding of material facts or was otherwise fraudulently obtained. *Id.* § 500.203(d)(3)(i)-(iii).

25. *Id.* § 500.203(d)(1)-(3). Filing of the report pursuant to the third requirement does not in itself represent compliance or evidence of compliance with the first two requirements of the safe harbor. *Id.* § 500.203 (d)(3).

26. 31 C.F.R. Pt. 515.

27. *Id.* § 515.201.

28. The effective date of the CACRs is 12:01 a.m., E.S.T., on July 8, 1963. *Id.* § 515.201(d).

29. *Id.* § 515.310 (CACRs definition of "transfer") *Cf. id.* § 500.310 (corresponding FACRs definition).

30. *Id.* § 515.311 (CACRs definition of "property"). *Cf. id.* § 500.310 (corresponding FACRs definition).

31. *Id.* § 515.312 (CACRs definition of "interest"). *Cf. id.* § 500.312 (corresponding FACRs definition).

32. *Id.* § 515.313 (CACRs definition).

33. *Id.* § 515.308 (CACRs definition).

34. *Id.* § 515.329 (CACRs definition of "person subject to the jurisdiction of the United States"). *Cf. id.* § 500.329 (corresponding FACRs definition).

35. 22 U.S.C.A. § 6033(c).

36. *Id.* § 6034(a). This prohibition does not apply to financing by the owner of the property or the U.S. national claiming the property for certain permitted transactions. *Id.*

property.[37] For these purposes, "trafficking" includes: (1) any transaction involving confiscated property;[38] (2) engaging in any commercial activity using or benefiting from the property;[39] or, (3) participating in such trafficking by another person.[40]

For example, a foreign-based bank that financed the purchase of the current crop of a confiscated Cuban plantation formerly owned by a U.S. enterprise might find itself subject to suit in U.S. court for "trafficking" in confiscated property. Liability under this cause of action could equal the current fair market value of the property, plus reasonable cost and attorneys' fees.[41] However, liability could equal treble damages and cost and fees if the defendant had prior notice of the U.S. national's claim to the confiscated property.[42] These liability provisions have been waived for successive six-month periods without exception to the present.[43]

Another major provision of the CLDSA requires the Secretary of State to exclude from the United States any alien whom the Secretary determines to have confiscated or to have trafficked in confiscated property.[44] In the previous example, this exclusion provision would extend to anyone who was a corporate officer, principal, or controlling shareholder of the foreign-based bank.[45] It would also include anyone who was the spouse, minor child, or agent of an excludable person.[46]

c. *The Libyan Sanctions.* The Libyan Sanctions Regulations ("LSRs"),[47] promulgated under the IEEPA and the UNPA, bear more than a passing resemblance to the earlier TWEA programs administered by Treasury. One interesting difference from, for example, the FACRs, is that the LSRs emerged in two successive executive orders, one imposing a set of trade restrictions on 7 January 1986,[48] followed on 8 January 1986 by a second order[49] imposing financial prohibitions in the nature of a blocking[50] of property[51] in which the Government of Libya ("GOL") (including GOL-controlled entities) had an interest.[52]

---

37. *Id.* § 6082(a).

38. *Id.* § 6023(10)(A)(i).

39. *Id.* § 6023(10)(A)(ii).

40. *Id.* § 6023(10)(A)(iii).

41. *Id.* § 6082(a)(1)(A)(i)–(ii).

42. *Id.* § 6082(a)(3).

43. *See, e.g.,* Letter from the President to the Chairmen of the Senate Committees on Foreign Relations and Appropriations and the Chairmen of the House Committees on International Relations and Appropriations, Jan. 15, 1999, *reprinted in,* 1999 WL 18062 (White House) (waiving provisions through 1 August 1999).

44. 22 U.S.C.A. § 6091(a)(1)–(2).

45. *Id.* § 6091(a)(3).

46. *Id.* § 6091(a)(4).

47. 31 C.F.R. Pt. 550 (1998).

48. Exec. Order No. 12,543, 51 Fed. Reg. 875 (1986).

49. Exec. Order No. 12,544, 51 Fed. Reg. 1235 (1986).

50. As with the FACRs and the CACRs, the term "blocking" is not a defined term of art under the LSRs. *But see* 31 C.F.R. § 550.316 (LSRs; defining "blocked account" and "blocked property").

51. The term "property" is given a characteristically broad definition for purposes of the LSRs. *Compare id.* § 550.314 (LSRs; defining property), *with id.* § 500.311 (FACRs; same).

52. Exec. Order No. 12,544, 51 Fed. Reg. 1235 (1986). The term "interest," for purposes of the LSRs, is given the traditionally broad definition. *Compare* 31 C.F.R. § 550.315 (LSRs; defining property "interest" as "an interest of any nature whatsoever, direct, or indirect"), *with id.* § 500.312 (FACRs; same).

The LSRs contain a series of relatively specific transactional prohibitions. "Transportation-related" transactions[53] are prohibited, including: (1) "the provision of transportation to or from the United States by any Libyan person[[54]] or any vessel or aircraft of Libyan registration;"[55] and, (2) the sale in the United States of air passage that includes a stop in Libya.[56] In addition, U.S. persons are prohibited from performing "any contract in support of an industrial or other commercial or governmental project in Libya."[57]

As originally promulgated, the primary impact of the LSRs on U.S. banks is found in two additional prohibitions, one drawn from each of the two successive executive orders that underlie the LSRs. The first prohibits any U.S. person from granting or extending credits or loans to the GOL.[58] The terms "credits" and "loans" are collectively defined in broad terms as follows: "any transfer or extension of funds or credit on the basis of an obligation to repay, or any assumption or guarantee of the obligation of another to repay an extension of funds or credit."[59] The definitional provision gives the following examples of the kinds of "transfers" that would be included under the terms "credits" or "loans":

> overdrafts; currency swaps; purchases of debt securities issued by the [GOL] after January 7, 1986; purchases of a loan made by another person; sales of financial assets subject to an agreement to repurchase; renewals or refinancing whereby funds or credits are transferred to or extended to the [GOL]; and draw-downs on existing lines of credit.[60]

The second prohibition is essentially a blocking of GOL assets. The broad language of the prohibition provides that, except as otherwise authorized:

> no property or interests in property of the [GOL] that are in the United States[,] that hereafter come within the United States or that are or hereafter come within the possession or control of U.S. persons, including their overseas branches, may be transferred, paid, exported, withdrawn, or otherwise dealt in.[61]

The prohibition similarly restricts, absent other authorization, any transaction with respect to securities registered or inscribed in the name

---

53. *See., e.g., id.* § 550.203(a), prohibiting "[a]ny transaction by a United States person relating to transportation to or from Libya," unless otherwise licensed. *See also id.* § 550.207, prohibiting certain transactions relating to travel to and activities within Libya by any "U.S. person," including "unauthorized payment by a U.S. person of his [*sic*] own travel or living expenses to or within Libya."

54. The term "Libyan person" is defined for purposes of the LSRs to mean "any Libyan citizen, any juridical person organized under the laws of Libya, or any juridical person owned or controlled, direct-

ly or indirectly, by a Libyan citizen or the [GOL]." *Id.* § 550.305.

55. *Id.* § 550.203(b).

56. *Id.* § 550.203(c).

57. *Id.* § 550.205.

58. *Id.* § 550.206.

59. *Id.* § 550.312. The term "transfer" is given a characteristically broad definition for purposes of the LSRs. *Compare id.* § 550.313, *with id.* § 500.310.

60. *Id.* § 550.312.

61. *Id.* § 550.209(a).

of the GOL. This restriction applies whether or not the registered or inscribed owner of the security has, or appears to have, assigned, transferred, or otherwise disposed of the security (before, on, or after the prohibition's effective date of January 8, 1986).[62]

The LSRs also contain the familiar provision rendering transfers in violation of the regulations null and void,[63] including the typical safe harbor language found in Treasury's other economic sanctions regulations.[64]

Two subsequent events have markedly expanded the LSRs. First, the UNPA was invoked in the April 1992 banning of overflight, takeoff, and landing of aircraft flying to or from Libya.[65] Second, the Iran and Libya Sanctions Act ("ILSA") was enacted,[66] creating new sanctions that are triggered in one of two ways. First, a foreign company will trigger the sanctions when it provides over $40 million dollars in new investments for the development of the Iranian or Libyan petroleum industry.[67] Second, a foreign company will trigger the sanctions if it violates U.N. prohibitions against trade with Libya for specific goods and services.[68] Once a foreign company has triggered the sanctions, the President is then required to impose two out of seven possible sanctions.[69] The seven sanctions cover a wide spectrum: (1) The President may deny Export–Import Bank assistance with respect to any exports to a sanctioned person.[70] (2) The President may order the denial of export licenses for exports to a sanctioned person.[71] (3) The President may prohibit loans or credits to any sanctioned person from any U.S. financial institutions of over $10 million in any 12–month period.[72] (4) The President may prohibit a financial institution[73] from being designated or continued as a primary dealer for U.S. Government debt instruments.[74] (5) The President may prohibit a financial institution from serving as a

62. *Id.* § 550.209(b).

63. *Compare id.* § 550.210(a)-(c) (LSRs; null-and-void provision), *with id.* § 500.203(a)-(c) (FACRs; same).

64. *Compare id.* § 550.210(d) (LSRs; safe harbor provision), *with id.* § 500.203(d) (FACRs; same).

65. Ex. Order No. 12,801, 57 Fed. Reg. 14,319 (1992).

66. Iran and Libya Sanctions Act of 1996, Pub. L. No. 104–172, 110 Stat. 1541 (1996) (codified at 50 U.S.C.A. § 1701 note) ("ILSA").

67. ILSA, § 5.

68. *Id.*

69. *Id.*

70. ILSA, § 6(1).

71. ILSA, § 6(2).

72. ILSA, § 6(3). This sanction does not apply to loans or credits for projects intended to relieve human suffering. *Id.*

73. For these purposes, the term "financial institution" is defined to include:

(A) a depository institution (as defined in section 3(c)(1) of the Federal Deposit Insurance Act[, 12 U.S.C.A. § 1813(c)(1) (defining "depository institution" as including banks and savings associations)]), including a branch or agency of a foreign bank (as defined in section 1(b)(7) of the International Banking Act of 1978);

(B) a credit union;

(C) a securities firm, including a broker or dealer;

(D) an insurance company, including an agency or underwriter; and

(E) any other company that provides financial services.

ILSA, § 14(5).

74. ILSA, § 6(4)(A).

U.S. fiscal agent or as a repository for U.S. Government funds.[75] (6) The President may deny a sanctioned person U.S. Government procurement opportunities.[76] (7) Finally, the President may ban all or some imports of a sanctioned person.[77]

Not all of these ILSA sanctions are pertinent to banks. However, the third sanction (the loan and credit prohibition) can affect the international lending business of a U.S. bank. In addition, the fourth and fifth sanctions (the U.S. Government debt and U.S. Government funds prohibitions) can affect *any* financial institution.

d. *The Iranian Sanctions*. The Iranian Transactions Regulations ("ITRs")[78] are entirely distinct from the earlier Iranian Assets Control Regulations ("IACRs"),[79] which were originally promulgated in response to the Iranian hostage crisis of 1979–1981.[80] The ITRs were promulgated pursuant to an Executive Order, issued under the authority of Section 505 of the International Security and Development Cooperation Act of 1985,[81] which identified Iran as a state actively supporting terrorism as an instrument of state policy and imposed import restrictions in response.[82]

The ITRs are relatively modest in scope, and their potential effect on U.S. banks involved in international banking activities is correspondingly limited. Essentially, the ITRs are limited to a prohibition on importation into the United States of Iranian-origin goods and services, unless otherwise licensed.[83] The only significant impact of the ITRs with respect to international banks lies in the ban on transactions *related to* prohibited importations. The ITRs provide that "[n]o person may ... finance ... or otherwise service, in whole or in part, any goods or services subject to the prohibitions of [the ITRs]."[84] A violation of the financing prohibition occurs only if the person providing financing acts "with knowledge or reason to know that a violation ... has occurred, is about to occur, or is intended to occur with respect to such goods or services."[85] The ITRs do not contain the traditional "null and void" provision with respect to violations of the regulations, and so these regulations offer no specific "safe harbor" guidance in this regard. Nevertheless, it may be argued that consistent administrative practice would dictate that a similar showing of good faith on the part of a financing person, upon the discovery of a violation, should be sufficient to avoid liability under the ITRs.[86]

75. ILSA, § 6(4)(B).

76. ILSA, § 6(5).

77. ILSA, § 6(6).

78. 52 Fed. Reg. 44,076–44,081 (1987) (codified at 31 C.F.R. Pt. 560).

79. 31 C.F.R. Pt. 535.

80. Exec. Order No. 12,12,170, 44 Fed. Reg. 65,729 (1979).

81. Pub. L. No. 99–83, tit. V. § 505, 99 Stat. 221 (1985) (codified at 22 U.S.C.A. § 2349aa–9).

82. Exec. Order No. 12,12,613, 52 Fed. Reg. 41,940 (1987).

83. 31 C.F.R. § 560.201.

84. 31 C.F.R. § 560.202.

85. *Id*.

86. Thus, the ITRs do provide for reports under oath as may be required by OFAC "relative to any transaction, regardless of whether such transaction is effected pursuant to license or otherwise." *Id*. § 560.602.

The ITRs remained relatively inconsequential, particularly as compared with some of the broader Treasury economic sanctions programs previously discussed. However, the recent promulgation of executive orders with respect to Iran, and the enactment of ILSA have made current sanctions against Iran a more formidable concern for banks involved in international banking activities.

In March 1995, President Clinton issued Executive Order No. 12,-957,[87] imposing a ban on contracts by U.S. persons for the development of Iranian petroleum resources. In May 1995, he issued Executive Order No. 12,959, barring U.S. trade and investment with Iran.[88] The new order, which was expressly intended to supplement the March 1995 order, prohibited all of the following activities, unless licensed: (1) importation into the United States, or the financing of such importation, of any goods or services of Iranian origin;[89] (2) exportation from the United States to Iran, the GOI, or to any entity owned or controlled by the GOI, or the financing of such exportation, of any goods, technology, or services;[90] (3) reexportation to Iran, the GOI, or any entity owned or controlled by the GOI of any goods or technology exported from the United States, the exportation of which to Iran is subject to export license application requirements under U.S. regulations in effect immediately prior to the issuance of the order, with certain specified exceptions;[91] (4) transactions, including purchase, sale, transportation, swap, financing, or brokering transactions, by a U.S. person relating to goods or services of Iranian origin or owned or controlled by the GOI;[92] (5) new investments by any U.S. person in Iran or in property (including entities) owned or controlled by the GOI;[93] (6) approval or facilitation by any U.S. person of the entry into, or performance by an entity owned or controlled by a U.S. person, of a transaction or contract either prohibited as to U.S. persons by the three preceding provisions or relating to the financing of activities prohibited as to U.S. persons by those provisions, or of a guaranty of another person's performance of such transaction or contract;[94] and, (7) transactions by any U.S. person or any person within the United States that evades or avoids, or has the purpose of evading or avoiding, or attempts to violate, any of the preceding prohibitions.[95]

Congress eventually intervened with a broad set of sanctions intended to prevent even non-U.S. firms from participating in investment activities in Iran. As to Iran, ILSA generally requires, on a prospective basis, that the president impose two or more ILSA-specified sanctions, if he determines that the following circumstances exist, on or after the

---

87. Ex. Order No. 12,957, 60 Fed. Reg. 14,615 (1995).

88. Ex. Order No. 12,959, 60 Fed. Reg. 24,757 (1995).

89. Ex. Order No. 12,959, § 1(a).

90. Ex. Order No. 12,959, § 1(b).

91. Ex. Order No. 12,959, § 1(c). The exceptions applied to goods that "have been (i) substantially transformed outside the United States, or (ii) incorporated into another product outside the United States and constitute less than 10 percent by value of that product exported from a third country." *Id.*

92. Ex. Order No. 12,959, § 1(d).

93. Ex. Order No. 12,959, § 1(e).

94. Ex. Order No. 12,959, § 1(f).

95. Ex. Order No. 12,959, § 1(g).

date of enactment of the act: A person, with actual knowledge, has made an investment of $40 million or more (in any combination of at least $10 million each, equaling or exceeding $40 million in any 12 months) that "directly and significantly" contributed to the enhancement of Iran's ability to develop petroleum resources of Iran.[96]

As with the Libyan sanctions, not all of the ILSA sanctions are pertinent to banks. The loan and credit prohibition can affect the international lending business of a U.S. bank. In addition, the U.S. Government debt prohibition and U.S. Government funds prohibition can affect any financial institution, wherever based.

e. *The Iraqi Sanctions.* The scope of the Iraqi sanctions is extremely broad, with a wide range of sanctions being applied, primarily to Iraq, but in the initial stages protective sanctions were also applied to Kuwait as well.[97] The impact of the sanctions is concentrated on governmental assets and transactions.

From the perspective of U.S. practice, the sanctions arrived in two stages: the initial sanctions imposed by the President[98] under the authority of the IEEPA, and the sanctions imposed by the President in compliance with Security Council mandates.[99] The applicability of the sanctions imposed at these two stages was intended to be cumulative, rendering U.S. sanctions consistent with the Security Council mandates.

The realigned U.S. sanctions included, among other things, a continuation of the blocking of the GOI assets.[100] They also prohibited imports of Iraqi origin and the promotion of such imports[101] (with no exception for "informational materials"). The new order prohibited exports "directly or indirectly" to Iraq, or to any entity operated from Iraq, or owned or controlled by the GOI, except for "humanitarian" donations[102] (with no exception for export of "informational materials"). The order

---

96. ILSA, § 5(a). For these purposes, "investment" is defined to mean:

any of the following activities if such activity is undertaken pursuant to an agreement, or pursuant to the exercise of rights under such an agreement, that is entered into with the Government of Iran or a nongovernmental entity in Iran, or with the Government of Libya or a nongovernmental entity in Libya, on or after the date of the enactment of [ILSA]:

(A) The entry into a contract that includes responsibility for the development of petroleum resources located in Iran or Libya (as the case may be), or the entry into a contract providing for the general supervision and guarantee of another person's performance of such a contract.

(B) The purchase of a share of ownership, including an equity interest, in that development.

(C) The entry into a contract providing for the participation in royalties, earnings, or profits in that development, with-

out regard to the form of the participation. The term "investment" does not include the entry into, performance, or financing of a contract to sell or purchase goods, services, or technology.

ILSA, § 14(9).

97. With the liberation of Kuwait, these protective sanctions were rendered moot. 56 Fed. Reg. 12,450 (1991) (lifting of U.S. controls applied to Kuwait).

98. Ex. Order No. 12,722, 3 C.F.R. 294 (1991); Ex. Order No. 12,723, 3 C.F.R. 296 (1991).

99. Ex. Order No. 12,724, 3 C.F.R. 297 (1991); Ex. Order No. 12,725, 3 C.F.R. 299 (1991).

100. Ex. Order No. 12,724, § 1.

101. Ex. Order No. 12,724, § 2(a).

102. Ex. Order No. 12,724, § 2(b).

also expanded a previous prohibition with the respect to performance of contracts, to include an express reference to "financing contracts."[103]

§ 9.30 Impact of Sanctions on International Banking

To illustrate comparatively the regulatory risks that banks undertake in international banking activities across a range of sanctions programs, consider the hypothetical scenarios in Figure 9–10, *supra*.

Figure 9–10
Sanctions: Hypothetical Scenarios

Scenario 1: U.S.-Situs Account of Target

A Bank, a national bank with its principal office in New York, holds a demand deposit account in the name of country *X*. *X* is subsequently added as a target under one of the extant sanctions programs.

> *FACRs*: Account is blocked. *A* will be required to hold the account in interest-bearing status.
>
> *CACRs*: Same result.
>
> *LSRs*: Same result, except no requirement to hold the account in interest bearing status.
>
> *IRAN*: No provision under current regulations, except to the extent that the credit is involved in the financing of a prohibited transaction, in which case it is prohibited.
>
> *IRAQ*: Account is blocked.

Scenario 2: Documentary Letter of Credit

A was the issuer of a documentary letter of credit ("L/C"), opened by *B*, a U.S. based firm, with *C*, a national of *X*, as the beneficiary. *X* is subsequently added as a target under one of the extant sanctions programs.

> *FACRs*: The L/C is blocked. Absent a license, no "transfer" involving the credit may be effected, including acceptance of draft from *C*, modification, or amendment of the terms of the L/C, or extension of the L/C.
>
> *CACRs*: Same result.
>
> *LSRs*: The blocking prohibition only applies to interests of the GOL, its agencies and instrumentalities. If *C* is owned or controlled by the GOL, however, the credit is blocked.
>
> *IRAN*: No provision under current regulations, except to the extent that the credit is involved in the financing of a prohibited transaction, in which case it is prohibited.
>
> *IRAQ*: Blocking provision only applies to interests of the GOI, its agencies and instrumentalities.

---

103. Ex. Order No. 12,724, § 2(f) (prohibiting performance of "any contract, *including a financing contract* . . . "(emphasis added)); *id.*, § 2(g) (prohibiting, *inter alia*, "commitment . . . of funds, or other financial or economic resources . . . ").

Scenario 3: Foreign–Situs Branch Dollar Account

A's London branch holds a dollar-denominated account for D, a national of X. X is subsequently added as a target of one of the extant sanctions programs.

> *FACRs:* The account is blocked. A and its branch are prohibited from engaging in any transfer involving the account, absent a license.
>
> *CACRs:* Same result.
>
> *LSRs:* The blocking prohibition only applies to interests of the GOL, its agencies and instrumentalities. If D is owned or controlled by the GOL, however, the account is blocked.
>
> *IRAN:* No provision under current regulations, except to the extent that the account is involved in the financing of a prohibited transaction, in which case it is prohibited.
>
> *IRAQ:* Blocking provision only applies to interests of the GOI, its agencies and instrumentalities.

Scenario 4: Foreign–Situs Subsidiary Dollar Account

A's subsidiary E, chartered under the banking laws of Y, holds a dollar deposit for D, a national of X. X is subsequently added as a target of one of the extant sanctions programs.

> *FACRs:* The account is blocked. E is a "person subject to U.S. jurisdiction, and is prohibited from engaging in any transfer involving the account, absent a license."
>
> *CACRs:* Same result.
>
> *LSRs:* E is not subject to the blocking prohibition, since it is not a "U.S. person" for purposes of these regulations.
>
> *IRAN:* No provision under the current regulations.
>
> *IRAQ:* E is not subject to the U.S. blocking prohibition, but it is probably subject to a blocking prohibition under Y's laws, to the extent that Y has implemented U.N. resolutions. However, blocking only applies to the GOI, its agencies and instrumentalities. If D is owned or controlled by the GOI, the account is prohibited.

Scenario 5: Foreign Bank Dollar Deposit

F, a bank chartered under the banking laws of country Z, holds a dollar deposit for D, a national of X, X is subsequently added as a target of one of the extant sanctions programs. A itself holds a dollar account for F.

> *FACRs:* The account held by A is blocked, because of the indirect "interest" of D.
>
> *CACRs:* Same result.
>
> *LSRs:* The account held by A is not blocked, because such "cover accounts" are authorized under section 550.514 of the regulations. Even if this license did not exist, the account is not blocked because the regulations only reach interests of the GOL, its agencies and instrumentalities.
>
> *IRAN:* No provision under the current regulations.

> *IRAQ*:   The account is not blocked, because the regulations only reach interests of the GOI, its agencies and instrumentalities.

Further complicating these scenarios is the existence of the investment prohibitions of ILSA, with respect to Iran and Libya, and Executive Orders No. 12,957 and 12,959, with respect to Iranian trade and investment. A foreign bank involved in an investment prohibited by ILSA exposes itself to the specified sanctions of the Act, upon appropriate presidential determination. A U.S. bank exposes itself to potential sanctions under the executive orders if it involves itself in financing activities with respect to Iran that are prohibited by the orders. Prospectively, a foreign bank involved in "trafficking" or the financing of "trafficking" with respect to confiscated Cuban property may subject itself to private litigation under the CLDSA, and to administrative sanctions with respect to entry into the United States by its executives.

The formidable array of economic sanctions administered by the United States is a daunting reality for any U.S. national subject to their reach. Particularly troublesome for a bank involved in international activities is the possibility of having to defend the validity of any of these sanctions programs in a foreign forum. Until recently, there has not been any appreciable body of foreign case law directly challenging U.S. economic sanctions programs. Nevertheless, according to knowledgeable practitioners, U.S. banks today feel the need to take the effect of sanctions into account in their planning, even those not generally involved in international activities.

One particular problem faced by U.S. banks is the applicability of a blocking prohibition to dollar-denominated accounts held by a U.S. bank in the United States in the name of a foreign-situs bank or branch, which in turn holds a dollar-denominated account for a target country or nationals thereof. This is a serious concern for such broadly conceived economic sanctions programs as the FACRs and the CACRs in particular, and would be so especially in the early stages of the implementation of such a program, when ongoing banking relationships are being disrupted.

It is obviously less of a concern for later programs, otherwise similar to the FACRs and CACRs, that have expressly licensed cover account situations out from under the blocking prohibition.[1] Furthermore, this is of virtually no concern for those later programs that are so limited in the scope of their prohibitions as to raise no issue in the first place concerning cover accounts, such as the UNITA/Angola arms embargo or the arms embargo with respect to Rwanda.

From the point of view of the international banker, the potential application of blocking prohibitions to a cover account is perhaps one of

----

§ 9.30

1. *See., e.g.,* 31 C.F.R. § 535.901 (1980) (IACRs provision explicitly authorizing, by general license, transactions in cover accounts).

the more grotesque effects of economic sanctions, working as it does a complete frustration of normal expectations in international transactions. Consider these effects in what may be characterized as virtually a purely extraterritorial transaction.

A wholly foreign bank *G* maintains a dollar-denominated cover account with a New York City bank *H*, in effect partially hedging dollar exposure from its own dollar-denominated accounts held for its own depositors. An office of *G* in a third country issues dollar-denominated irrevocable letters of credit ("L/Cs") for a local depositor, *I*, an importer of foreign goods. Neither *G* nor *I* has any office or other business presence in the United States.

Based on certain information unavailable to *G* or *H*, the Treasury Department determines that *I* is acting as a purchasing agent on behalf of a country blocked under the FACRs. The argument would be made that the cover account held by *H* in New York is blocked because *I* has an indirect—a *very* indirect—interest in the account.

The natural result would be litigation initiated by *I* against the local office of *G* demanding performance of its obligations in accordance with local law. One such case is *China Mutual Trading Co., Ltd. v. Banque Belge*,[2] a 1954 Hong Kong case involving facts similar to those described above, in which the court insisted upon the application of local law. The court's reaction, from the viewpoint of the ordinary expectations of the banking industry, is unremarkable:

> I consider that rights of the plaintiffs re those which ordinarily arise out of the relationship of banker and customer where the latter has made a deposit with the former. . . .
>
> There is no privity of contract between the customer of the bank and that bank's correspondent elsewhere. . . . A debt is situated or localized where it is recoverable. A debt which arises out of the relationship of banker and customer is localized at the branch of the bank where the account is kept.[3]

This straightforward choice of law principle, looking to the place where the account is "kept," prevailed over any suggestion of a cognizable interest on the part of the United States in the application of the economic sanctions. Thus, the court rejected one defense offered by Banque Belge, to the effect that:

> by paying the U.S. dollars, held by [Banque Belge] with their agents [the correspondent bank] in New York, into a blocked account already existing in the name of the plaintiffs with those agents, [Banque Belge had] discharged [its] obligations. I consider that this defence also fails on the ground that payment by a debtor into a blocked account without the consent of the creditor cannot be a good discharge of a debt.[4]

---

2. 39 Hong Kong L. Rep. 144 (1954).   **4.** *Id.* at 152.

3. *Id.* at 151.

A U.S. bank, *J*, agrees to provide short-term financing, possibly through bankers' acceptances, for the manufacture and sale of heavy trucks by a foreign subsidiary *K* of a U.S. manufacturing firm to a trading corporation *L*, incorporated under the local laws of *K*'s host country. None of the parties to this transaction are targets of any U.S. economic sanctions program.

However, as the contract term proceeds, it is discovered that *L* intends to resell to the development agency of a country that is blocked under the FACRs. *K*, being a person subject to U.S. jurisdiction,[5] is informed by Treasury, through its U.S. parent, that it is prohibited from proceeding with the sale and subsequent delivery of the goods.[6] The financing of this transaction might also constitute a prohibited "dealing in" the property subject to the provisions of the FACRs.[7] Under these circumstances, *J* bank would probably still be in a position to claim the benefits of the safe harbor provision of the FACRs[8] and return itself to its original position, but any further action in support of the transaction might well be viewed as a "willful violation," withdrawing the benefits of the safe harbor.[9]

What, then, is *J* to do if *K* is subjected to direct supervision (almost in the nature of a temporary receivership) by its host country, so that the sales transaction with *L* will be completed? Presumably, this would not represent a willful violation for *J* or *K*, but the situation is obviously a precarious one. This situation loosely follows the facts in the famous Freuhauf episode,[10] in which Freuhauf's French subsidiary was subjected to such supervision in connection with a sale of trucks ultimately destined for the Peoples' Republic of China, then blocked under the FACRs. Here again, local host country law prevailed, and reach of U.S. economic sanctions was curtailed. While the subsidiary may be viewed as not acting in a willful manner, and hence ultimately not sanctioned under the FACRs, a considerable amount of expense and uncertainty ensued before the final outcome.

A New York bank *M* has had ongoing relationships with country *W*, which is beginning to experience some foreign policy difficulties with the United States. In particular, *M* maintains an interest-bearing time deposit at its London branch, in the name of *N*, a bank organized under the laws of *W* and owned or controlled by the Government of *W*. The account is denominated in dollars. In addition, some time after the opening of the London branch account, *N* established a demand deposit at *M*'s New York headquarters, also denominated in dollars.

---

5. *See* 31 C.F.R. § 500.329 ("person subject" defined as including foreign subsidiary of corporation organized under laws of any state of the United States).

6. *See id.* § 500.201(b)(1) (prohibition on transfers by any "person subject" of property in which target country has an interest).

7. *Id.*

8. *See id.* § 500.203(d).

9. *See id.* § 500.203(d)(1) (safe harbor conditioned on violation not being willful).

10. *See* Craig, *Application of the Trading With the Enemy Act to Foreign Corporations Owned by Americans: Reflections on Freuhauf v. Massardy* 83 Harv. L. Rev. 579 (1970).

This second account was established only after considerable negotiation between *M* and *N*, and it was ultimately agreed that amounts in the New York account above a specified "peg" amount would be "swept" into the London account as of a specified time each business day. (If the balance in the New York account fell below the peg as of a specified time each business day, funds would be transferred from the London account to make up the difference.)

On a particular day, the difficulties between *W* and the United States reach a crisis, and limited trade sanctions are imposed. By the following day, a considerable balance exists in the New York account, calling for a sweep of the account and a transfer to the London branch. However, during the morning of the second day, *M*'s president is contacted by U.S. Government officials and prevailed upon to delay the requisite sweep. He does so, and at some time after the established time for the sweep, a second set of economic sanctions regulations is put into place, blocking *W* assets that are subject to U.S. jurisdiction. The intended effect of the regulations is to block not only the New York account, but also dollar-denominated accounts held by foreign branches of U.S. banks in the name of *W* and entities controlled by it.

On their own terms, the application of such regulations to accounts held by foreign-situs branches of U.S. banks are vulnerable to attack under local host country law.[11] However, the same choice of law principles that would counsel defeat of the sanctions as to foreign-situs blocked deposits ought to dictate vindication of the sanctions with respect to U.S.-situs assets. The complicating factor in our example is the gratuitous action of *M*'s president in delaying a transfer of funds to the foreign-situs account.

In a case exhibiting features similar to our example, *Libyan Arab Foreign Bank v. Bankers Trust Company*,[12] a British court essentially found the U.S. bank liable for both the amount of the London branch account and the amount that should have been transferred from New York to the London branch prior to the imposition of the blocking of GOL assets. The reasoning is similar to that of the court in *China Mutual*, though perhaps more sophisticated in its analysis.

The *Bankers Trust* court reached the conclusion that the law of the contract governing the overall relationship between the Libyan bank and the U.S. bank was split; English law still governed the London account. Essentially, the court viewed the London branch as distinct from its New York headquarters, and fully subject to English law. The court decisively vindicated the principle of the place were an account is "kept."

---

11. Such challenges were mounted by Iranian banks during the pendency of the blocking under the IACRs in London and elsewhere. *See* Edwards, *Extraterritorial Application of the U.S. Iranian Assets Control Regulations,* 75 Am. J. Int'l L. 870, 876 (1981). However, these challenges were largely mooted by an intervening settlement entered into by the United States and Iran in January 1981.

12. 1 Lloyd's Rep. 259 (1988).

Chapter 10

BANK REGULATION AND
SOCIAL POLICY

Table of Sections

§ 10.1   Introduction

Throughout the preceding chapters of this hornbook, we have been considering the various implications of depository institutions regulatory policy. This policy is grounded on certain objectives. Primary among these policy objectives is the promotion of the safety and soundness of the depository institutions system[1] and, correspondingly, the maintenance of public confidence in that system.[2] Where these objectives are not realized in specific cases, an additional policy objective involves the resolution of troubled or failing institutions with the least risk to the deposit insurance funds,[3] and with preference given to the interests of depositors.[4] Related policy objectives include the encouragement of competitiveness in the provision of depository institution services,[5] and the

---

§ 10.1

1. *See, e.g.,* 12 U.S.C.A. § 1818(b)(1) (identifying safety and soundness as an objective of regulatory enforcement).

2. *See generally* Michael P. Malloy, *Balancing Public Confidence and Confidentiality: Adjudication Practices and Procedures of the Federal Bank Regulatory Agencies*, 61 Temple L. Rev. 723 (1988) (discussing policy objective of maintenance of public confidence).

3. *See, e.g.,* 12 U.S.C.A. § 1823(c)(4)(A)(ii) (providing for least-cost assistance to troubled institution).

4. *Id.* § 1821(d)(11).

5. *See, e.g., id.* §§ 1828(c) (prohibiting anticompetitive mergers); 1842 (prohibiting anticompetitive holding company acquisitions of banks); 1843(c)(8) (prohibiting anticompetitive holding company acquisitions of nonbanking activities).

insulation of depository institution services from other, potentially more risky activities.[6]

There are, however, other public policy objectives applied to depository institutions that may be unrelated, or only indirectly related, to the core objectives of depository institutions regulatory policy. Some of these objectives may focus on the effects of the concentration of economic power and resources within the depository institutions industry, such as nondiscriminatory credit policy.[7] Other objectives may simply use the regulation of depository institutions as a convenient mechanism for achieving other, unrelated objectives, such as the attainment of foreign policy objectives.[8]

This chapter discusses the application of policy objectives to depository institutions. This set of issues is examined through a discussion of selected areas of regulation whose policy objectives are extraneous to the public policies underlying depository institutions. The discussion begins with the issue of privacy of financial information, primarily an enforcement concern for targets of investigation. It then turns to two areas of social policy with significant implications for depository institutions: rules requiring significant community reinvestment by depository institutions, and rules prohibiting discrimination in the provision of credit. The chapter concludes with a survey of other extraneous regulatory concerns that are implemented in part through the regulation of depository institutions.

§ 10.2 Privacy of Financial Information

Under U.S. law, a bank customer has no constitutional right to privacy with respect to the bank records of the customer's transactions.[1] Counterbalancing this, in 1978 Congress enacted the Right to Financial Privacy Act ("RFPA")[2] to regulate the disclosure of such records to the

---

6. *See, e.g., id.* U.S.C.A. §§ 377, 378 (separating banking from securities); 1843(a) (separating bank-related activities of holding companies from nonbanking activities).

7. *See, e.g.,* 15 U.S.C.A. § 1691(a)(1) (prohibiting discrimination in provision of credit based upon race, color, religion, national origin, sex, marital status, or age).

8. *See, e.g.,* 50 U.S.C.A. §§ 1701 *et seq.* (authorizing imposition of economic sanctions in response to threats to U.S. national security, foreign policy, or economy).

§ 10.2

1. *United States* v. *Miller*, 425 U.S. 435, 96 S.Ct. 1619 (1976). *See McDonough v. Widnall*, 891 F.Supp. 1439 (D.Colo.1995) (discussing *Miller* and subsequent enactment of legislation). *See also Rodriguez v. Federal Sav. & Loan Ins. Corp.*, 712 F.Supp. 159 (N.D.Cal.1989) (rejecting cus-

tomer's Fifth Amendment privilege, since customer had neither actual nor constructive possession of records). The appropriate scope of confidentiality accorded to bank records remains a subject of some controversy. *See generally* William C. Hefernan, *Property, Privacy, and the Fourth Amendment*, 60 Brook. L. Rev. 633 (1994); Paul B. Rasor, *Controlling Government Access to Personal Financial Records*, 25 Washburn L.J. 417 (1986); Dan L. Nicewander, *Financial Record Privacy—What are and What Should be Rights of Customer of Depository Institution*, 16 St. Mary's L.J. 601 (1985).

2. Pub. L. No. 95–630, tit. XI, §§ 1101–1121, 92 Stat. 3697 (1978), *as amended*, Pub. L. No. 101–73, §§ 744, 941, 103 Stat. 438, 496 (1989); Pub. L. No. 101–647, § 2596(c), 104 Stat. 4908 (1990) (codified at 12 U.S.C.A. §§ 3401–3422). For legislative history of the RFPA, see H.R. Rep. No. 95–

federal government in specified circumstances.[3] Of course, the protection afforded by the RFPA is susceptible to amendment and revision to a significantly greater extent than a constitutional privacy right would be, and it evinces a level of detail that limits its flexibility. It is nevertheless the only measure of privacy protection currently available to these records.

§ 10.3   Right to Financial Privacy Act

As a general rule, under the RFPA government authorities[1] are prohibited from obtaining access to information contained in financial records[2] of any customer[3] from a financial institution,[4] unless the records

1383, 1978 U.S. Code. Cong. & Admin. News 9273.

3. *See Young v. United States Dep't of Justice,* 882 F.2d 633 (2d Cir.1989), *cert. denied,* 493 U.S. 1072, 110 S.Ct. 1116 (1990) (discussing purpose of RFPA); *McDonough, supra* (discussing purpose in relation to prior decision in *Miller*); *In re Grand Jury Proceedings,* 636 F.2d 81 (5th Cir.1981) (emphasizing RFPA requirement of customer authorization); *In re Porras,* 191 B.R. 357 (Bkrtcy.W.D.Tex.1995) (discussing balance of competing interests in information); *United States v. First Nat'l Bank of Md.,* 866 F.Supp. 884 (D.Md.1994) (discussing same).

§ 10.3

1. For these purposes, the term "Government authority" is defined to mean "any agency or department of the United States, or any officer, employee, or agent thereof." 12 U.S.C.A. § 3401(3). Despite the breadth of this definition, the RFPA has been construed as inapplicable to federal courts and agencies deriving their authority from the courts. *Doe v. Board on Prof'l Responsibility of Dist. of Columbia Ct. of Appeals,* 717 F.2d 1424 (D.C.Cir.1983) (upholding issuance of subpoenas for financial records with respect to transactions in client funds). *Cf. Nichols v. Council on Judicial Complaints,* 615 P.2d 280 (Okla. 1980) (noting that only federal agencies are affected by RFPA).

2. For these purposes, the term "financial record" is defined to mean the "original of, a copy of, or information known to have been derived from, any record held by a financial institution pertaining to a customer's relationship with the financial institution." 12 U.S.C.A. § 3401(2). *See, e.g., Waye v. First Citizen's Nat'l Bank,* 846 F.Supp. 310 (M.D.Pa.), *aff'd,* 31 F.3d 1175 (3d Cir. 1994) (including canceled check in definition); *Neece v. Internal Revenue Serv.,* 922

F.2d 573 (10th Cir.1990) (mortgage and loan application records).

3. For these purposes, the term "customer" is defined to mean "any person or authorized representative of that person who utilized or is utilized any service of a financial institution, or for whom a financial institution is acting or has acted as a fiduciary, in relation to an account maintained in the person's name." 12 U.S.C.A. § 3401(5). "Customer" does not include a corporation. *See id.* § 3401(4) (defining "person" to mean an individual or partnership of no more than five individuals). *See also First Nat'l Bank of Md.,* 866 F.Supp. 884 (so holding); *Jobin v. Resolution Trust Corp.,* 156 B.R. 834 (D.Colo.1993) (so holding); *Collins v. Commodity Futures Trading Comm'n,* 737 F.Supp. 1467 (N.D.Ill.1990) (so holding); *United States v. Theron,* 116 F.R.D. 58 (D.Kan.1987) (so holding); *Pittsburgh Nat'l Bank v. United States,* 771 F.2d 73 (3d Cir.1985) (so holding); *Spa Flying Serv., Inc. v. United States,* 724 F.2d 95 (8th Cir.1984) (so holding). *Cf. Hunt v. Securities and Exch. Comm'n,* 520 F.Supp. 580 (N.D.Tex.1981) (holding that individual customer has right to complete subpoena, even though portions thereof concern request for corporate records not covered by RFPA). The scope of the term "customer" has generated considerable litigation. *See, e.g., In re Porras, supra* (excluding trust from meaning of "customer"); *United States v. Daccarett,* 6 F.3d 37 (2d Cir.1993), *cert. denied sub nom. Confecciones Zuny Ltda. v. United States,* 511 U.S. 1030, 114 S.Ct. 1538 (1994), and *cert. denied sub nom. Creaciones Viviana Ltda. v. United States,* 510 U.S. 1191, 114 S.Ct. 1294 (1994), and *cert. denied sub nom. Abuchaibe Hnos Ltda. v. United States,* 510 U.S. 1191, 114 S.Ct. 1294 (1994), and *cert. denied sub nom. Comercial Samora Ltda. v. United States,* 510 U.S. 1191, 114 S.Ct. 1294 (1994), and

---

4. See note 4 on page 336.

are "reasonably described"[5] and meet one of the following requirements: (1) The customer authorized the disclosure;[6] (2) The records are disclosed pursuant to an administrative subpoena that meets applicable RFPA procedural requirements,[7] including relevance "to a legitimate law enforcement inquiry"[8] and notice to the customer;[9] (3) The records are disclosed in response to a search warrant that meets RFPA procedural requirements;[10] (4) The records are disclosed in response to a judicial

cert. denied sub nom. Industrias Marathon Ltda. v. United States, 510 U.S. 1191, 114 S.Ct. 1295 (1994), and cert. denied sub nom. Manufacturera Del Atlantico Ltda. v. United States, 510 U.S. 1192, 114 S.Ct. 1295 (1994), and cert. denied sub nom. Organizacion JD Ltda. v. United States, 510 U.S. 1191, 114 S.Ct. 1295 (1994) (construing claimants of funds held in custody pursuant to arrest warrants not "customers"); Neece, supra note 2 (construing loan applicant as "customer"); Russell v. Department of Air Force, 915 F.Supp. 1108 (D.Colo.1996) (construing Air Force to be "authorized representative" of military officer, not barred from access to officer's financial records); In re Blunden, 896 F.Supp. 996 (C.D.Cal.1995) (construing loan applicant as "customer"); Inspector Gen. v. Great Lakes Bancorp, 825 F.Supp. 790 (E.D.Mich.1993) (excluding limited partnership with corporate general partner from meaning of "customer"); Ridgeley v. Merchants State Bank, 699 F.Supp. 100 N.D. Tex. 1988) (excluding special interest nonprofit organization); Donovan v. United States Local Plumbers & Pipe Trades Pension Fund, 569 F.Supp. 1488 (N.D. Cal. 1983 (construing individual trustees as "customers" as to pension fund transactions).

4. For these purposes the term "financial institution" is defined to mean:

any office of a bank, savings bank, card issuer . . . , industrial loan company, trust company, savings association, building and loan, or homestead association (including cooperative banks), credit union, or consumer finance institution, located in any state or territory of the United States, the District of Columbia, Puerto Rico, Guam, American Samoa, or the Virgin Islands.

12 U.S.C.A. § 3401(1).

5. Id. § 3402. See In re Blunden, 896 F.Supp. 996 (discussing "reasonable specificity" requirement); Dawar v. United States Dep't of Hous. and Urban Dev., 820 F.Supp. 545 (D.Kan.1993) (discussing "reasonably described" requirement) Ruggles v. Securities and Exch. Comm'n, 567 F.Supp. 766 (S.D.Tex.1983) (finding sufficient specificity).

6. 12 U.S.C.A. § 3402(1). On customer authorization requirements, see id. § 3404. A financial institution cannot require a customer to sign such an authorization as a condition of doing business with the institution. Id. § 3404(b).

7. Id. § 3402(2). On the RFPA requirements for administrative subpoenas, see id. § 3405. See Dawar, supra (discussing requirements).

8. 12 U.S.C.A. § 3405(1). For these purposes the term law enforcement inquiry is defined to mean "a lawful investigation or official proceeding inquiring into a violation of, or failure to comply with, any criminal or civil statute or any regulation, rule, or order issued pursuant thereto." Id. § 3401(8). See, e.g., Breakey v. Inspector Gen., 836 F.Supp. 422 (E.D.Mich.1993) (criticizing "official curiosity" as reason for subpoena); United States v. Wilson, 571 F.Supp. 1417 (S.D.N.Y.1983) (finding legitimate inquiry into transfers of funds from European banks); Donovan, supra (finding legitimate law enforcement inquiry); McGloshen v. United States Dep't of Agric., 480 F.Supp. 247 (W.D.Ky.1979) (finding legitimate inquiry despite paucity of information in affidavit).

9. 12 U.S.C.A. § 3405(2). See, e.g., Botero-Zea v. United States, 915 F.Supp. 614 (S.D.N.Y.1996) (finding violation of RFPA for failure to provide prior notice); Breakey, supra (finding notice to meet RFPA requirements); Pennington v. Donovan, 574 F.Supp. 708 (S.D.Tex.1983) (finding letter notification to customer sufficient); Hunt, supra (requiring complete subpoena to be disclosed to individual customer). This notice requirement does not apply to IRS notice to taxpayers. FitzGerald v. United States, 882 F.Supp. 959 (D.Idaho 1994).

10. 12 U.S.C.A. § 3402(3). On the RFPA requirements for search warrants, see id. § 3406. Notice of the search warrant to the customer may be delayed by court order. Id. §§ 3406(c), 3409. On the requirements for delay orders under § 3409, see Botero-Zea, supra; Matter of Thirty–Nine Admin. Subpoenae, 754 F.Supp. 5 (D.Mass. 1990).

subpoena that meets RFPA procedural requirements;[11] or, (5) The records are disclosed in response to a formal written request that meets RFPA procedural requirements.[12]

The financial institution to which the subpoena, summons, or request for records is made has available whatever rights to challenge normally applied to the subject of a subpoena or summons.[13] The customer's sole judicial remedy to prevent disclosure is an RFPA challenge to access.[14]

Within 10 days of service or 14 days of mailing of a subpoena, summons, or formal written request,[15] a customer may challenge access to the records by filing a motion to quash a summons or subpoena or an application to enjoin the governmental authority from obtaining access.[16] If the court finds that the customer has complied with the filing requirements, it will then order the government authority to file a sworn response.[17] While the court usually will decide the matter on the basis of these filings, it may conduct additional proceedings as appropriate.[18]

In any event, the motion or application must be decided within seven calendar days of the government's response.[19] If the motion or application is denied, the court's decision is not a final order, and no interlocutory appeal is available under the explicit language of the RFPA.[20]

Even if government access to customer records is permissible under the RFPA, the act limits the ability of the government authority that has access to such records to transfer the records to other agencies and

---

11. 12 U.S.C.A. §§ 3402(4), 3407. *See, e.g., Waye, supra* (noting prior notice to customer required for administrative and judicial subpoenae, but forbidden for grand jury subpoenae); *In re Castiglione,* 587 F.Supp. 1210 (E.D.Cal.1984) (concerning grand jury subpoenae). *But cf. United States v. A Residence Located at 218 Third St., New Glarus, Wis.,* 805 F.2d 256 (7th Cir.1986) (rejecting *Castiglione*'s narrow reading of grand jury procedure); *United States v. Kington,* 801 F.2d 733 (5th Cir. 1986), *reh'g denied,* 806 F.2d 261, *cert. denied,* 481 U.S. 1014, 107 S.Ct. 1888 (1987).

12. 12 U.S.C.A. §§ 3402(5), 3408.

13. *Id.* § 3410(f).

14. *Id.* § 3410(e). *See id.* § 3416 (providing for jurisdiction in appropriate federal district court to enforce RFPA provisions). Agencies or departments may, however, be liable to the customer for civil penalties for obtaining or disclosing information in violation of the RFPA. *Id.* § 3417(a). Disciplinary action may be taken against federal agents or employees for willful or intentional violations. *Id.* § 3417(b). These provisions are the exclusive judicial remedies for violations of the RFPA. *Id.* § 3417(d). *But*

cf. id. § 3418 (providing for injunctive relief to require compliance with RFPA).

15. Failure to follow the time requirements for a customer challenge is a jurisdictional defect. *Turner v. United States,* 881 F.Supp. 449 (D.Haw.1995).

16. 12 U.S.C.A. § 3410(a). *See Clark v. Inspector Gen.,* 944 F.Supp. 818 (D.Or.1996) (discussing requirement of service on government authority); *Donovan, supra* (discussing affidavit requirement); *Hancock v. Marshall,* 86 F.R.D. 209 (D.D.C.1980) (discussing affidavit requirement).

17. 12 U.S.C.A. § 3410(b). The government may request *in camera* consideration of its response. *Id. See, e.g., In re Blunden, supra* (upholding government access as relevant to legitimate law enforcement inquiry); *Rodriguez, supra* (upholding FSLIC subpoena); *Grafstrom v. Securities and Exch. Comm'n,* 532 F.Supp. 1023 (S.D.N.Y. 1982) (finding SEC response sufficient to rebut customer challenge).

18. 12 U.S.C.A. § 3410(b).

19. *Id.* On the court's decision, see *id.* § 3410(c).

20. *Id.* § 3410(d).

departments.[21] Records cannot be transferred unless the transferring authority certifies in writing that there exists "reason to believe that the records are relevant to a legitimate law enforcement inquiry within the jurisdiction of the receiving agency or department."[22] The transferring authority must mail a copy of the certification and a notice to the customer.[23] Exchanges of information between supervisory agencies,[24] transfer of records to defend against a customer action, and disclosure of information to duly authorized committees and subcommittees of the Congress are exempt from these requirements.[25]

In addition, there is a wide range of exceptions to the RFPA requirements. RFPA requirements do not apply to: (1) Financial records not identified to particular customers;[26] (2) Records disclosed to any supervisory agency or in connection with supervisory, regulatory, or monetary functions;[27] (3) Records disclosed in accordance with procedures authorized by federal tax law;[28] (4) Records disclosed pursuant to federal statute or rules promulgated thereunder;[29] (5) Records disclosed pursuant to Federal Rules of Civil or Criminal Procedure;[30] (6) Records disclosed under a subpoena issued by an administrative law judge;[31] (7) Records containing only customer name, address, account number, and type of account or as to an ascertainable group of customers, under specified circumstances;[32] (8) Records disclosed pursuant to a lawful

21. *Id.* § 3412(a).

22. *Id.*

23. *Id.* § 3412(b). The notice may be delayed by court order in appropriate circumstances. *Id.* § 3412(c).

24. *See Adams v. Board of Governors,* 855 F.2d 1336 (8th Cir.1988) (upholding transfer of records from OCC to Fed).

25. 12 U.S.C.A. § 3412(d). Exchanges of financial records and other information among and between the five member agencies of the Federal Financial Institutions Examination Council ("FFIEC") (*i.e.,* OCC, Fed, FDIC, OTS, and NCUA) and the SEC are also exempt from these requirements. *Id.* § 3412(e). Transfer or disclosure of financial records to the Attorney General or to the Secretary of the Treasury are subject to separate procedures. *Id.* § 3412(f)(1)–(2).

26. *Id.* § 3413(a). *See, e.g., Donovan v. National Bank of Alaska,* 696 F.2d 678 (9th Cir.1983) (seeking information with respect to employee benefit plans).

27. 12 U.S.C.A. § 3413(b). *See, e.g., United States v. Davis,* 953 F.2d 1482 (10th Cir.1992), *cert. denied,* 504 U.S. 945, 112 S.Ct. 2286 (upholding exchange of information among Fed, FHLBB, and OCC); *Adams, supra* (upholding exchange under Change in Bank Control Act).

28. 12 U.S.C.A. § 3413(c). *See, e.g., Neece, supra* (criticizing access not in compliance with RFPA or tax law); *United*

States v. McKay, 608 F.2d 830 (10th Cir. 1979) (applying summons authority of tax laws); *King v. United States,* 684 F.Supp. 1038 (D.Neb.1987) (same); *McTaggart v. United States,* 570 F.Supp. 547 (E.D.Mich. 1983) (same); *United States v. Hill,* 537 F.Supp. 677 (N.D.Tex.1982) (same).

29. 12 U.S.C.A. § 3413(d). *Cf. Coronado v. BankAtlantic Bancorp, Inc.,* 951 F.Supp. 1025 (S.D.Fla.1997) (upholding disclosure pursuant to Anti–Money Laundering Act).

30. 12 U.S.C.A. § 3413(e).

31. *Id.* § 3413(f).

32. *Id.* § 3413(g). This exemption only applies to the RFPA notice requirements, customer challenges, and transfer of information to other agencies. *Id.* The records must involve either a particular financial transaction or class of transactions, *id.* § 3413(g)(1); *see In re Request for Assistance from Ministry of Legal Affairs of Trinidad and Tobago,* 648 F.Supp. 464 (S.D.Fla. 1986), *aff'd,* 848 F.2d 1151 (11th Cir.1988), *cert. denied sub nom. Azar v. Minister of Legal Affairs of Trinidad and Tobago,* 488 U.S. 1005, 109 S.Ct. 784 (1989) (so holding), or transactions with a foreign country or subdivision thereof in the case of a government authority administering economic sanctions under applicable federal law. *Id.* § 3413(g)(2). In contrast, special procedures apply to disclosure of financial records in connection with either intelligence activities proceeding, examination, or the like with respect to a financial institution, a legal entity, or with respect to government loan or guarantee programs;[33] (9) Records disclosed pursuant to grand jury subpoenae or judicial orders in connection with grand jury proceedings;[34] (10) Records disclosed pursuant to a General Accounting Office proceeding, investigation, or the like, directed at a government authority;[35] (11) Records disclosed as necessary for administration of federal old-age or retirement benefits programs;[36] (12) Records disclosed in connection with possible crimes by insiders against a financial institution;[37] (13) Records disclosed to employees or agents of the Federal Reserve Board ("Fed") or any Federal Reserve Bank in connection with extensions of credit to a financial institution or others;[38] (14) Records disclosed to the now defunct Resolution Trust Corporation or its employees or agents in connection with a financial institution conservatorship, receivership, or liquidation;[39] (15) Records disclosed to the Federal Housing Finance Board ("FHFB") or any Federal Home Loan Bank ("FHLB") in connection with extensions of credit to a financial institution or others;[40] and, (16) Records disclosed as necessary for administration of federal veterans benefits programs.[41]

§ 10.4   Effect on Financial Institutions

While there can be considerable burdens for a depository institution that is the subject of a subpoena, summons, or request for customer records,[1] the RFPA does provide for reimbursement to a financial insti-

---

or Secret Service protective functions. *Id.* § 3414.

33. 12 U.S.C.A. § 3413(h). The confidentiality of customer records must still be maintained by the financial institution under § 3402, and the civil penalty and injunctive relief provisions of §§ 3417 and 3418 still apply to these records. *Id.* § 3413(h).

34. *Id.* § 3413(i). *See generally In re 1980 U.S. Grand Jury Subpoena Duces Tecum,* 502 F.Supp. 576 (E.D.La.1980) (permitting access to customer records pursuant to grand jury subpoena); *In re Grand Jury Subpoena (Connecticut Sav. Bank),* 481 F.Supp. 833 (D.Conn.1979) (permitting access to customer records notwithstanding Connecticut statute). The cost reimbursement provision of the RFPA, 12 U.S.C.A. § 3415, and specific provisions concerning grand jury proceedings, *id.* § 3420, still apply to these records. *Id.* § 3413(i). *But see McDonough, supra* (rejecting as impermissible under RFPA use of grand jury records in administrative proceeding). *But cf. Theron, supra* (permitting transfer of grand jury records to trustee in bankruptcy). On application of the specific RFPA provision with respect to grand jury proceedings, see *United States v. Jackson,* 11 F.3d 953 (10th

Cir.1993) (permitting use of subpoenaed records to obtain search warrant prior to returning records to grand jury); *United States v. A Residence Located at 218 Third Street, New Glarus, Wis.,* 805 F.2d 256 (7th Cir.1986) (concerning presentation of records to grand jury, rejecting *In re Castiglione) supra; United States v. Kington, supra* (same); *United States v. Mosko,* 654 F.Supp. 402 (D.Colo.1987), *aff'd sub nom. United States v. Pinelli,* 890 F.2d 1461 (10th Cir.1989), *cert. denied,* 495 U.S. 960, 110 S.Ct. 2568 (1990) (rejecting motion to suppress records on alleged improper presentation to grand jury).

35. 12 U.S.C.A. § 3413(j).

36. *Id.* § 3413(k).

37. *Id.* § 3413(*l*).

38. *Id.* § 3413(m).

39. *Id.* § 3413(n).

40. *Id.* § 3413(o).

41. *Id.* § 3413(p).

§ 10.4

1. Financial institutions have a statutory duty to comply with a request for customer records in accordance with the procetution of reasonably necessary costs for assembling or providing customer records.[2] The cost reimbursement provision does not apply to records with respect to the institution's perfection of a security interest, claims in bankruptcy, debt collection or application processing,[3] or to records with respect to the first eight exemptions discussed above.[4] Since the RFPA does not apply to records of corporate customers of a financial institution, the cost reimbursement provision has been held inapplicable to costs with respect to assembling and providing records of such customers.[5]

In general, there is no direct cause of action for damages under the RFPA for an institution's improper release of records.[6] However, financial institutions are directly subject to an RFPA requirement that they maintain the confidentiality of customer records absent a government inquiry that complies with the RFPA.[7] Financial institutions are prohibited from releasing such records until the government authority certifies in writing to the institution that it has complied with the applicable requirements of the RFPA.[8]

However, this does not prohibit an institution from notifying an appropriate government agency that it has information that may be relevant to a possible violation of statute or regulation.[9] Nor is an institution prohibited from providing copies of financial records to a court or government authority "as an incident to perfecting a security interest, proving a claim in bankruptcy, or otherwise collecting a debt."[10] Likewise, an institution is not prohibited from providing any financial record necessary to a government authority "as an incident to processing an application for assistance to a customer in the form of a Government loan, loan guaranty, or loan insurance agreement, or as an incident to

dures and requirements of the RFPA. 12 U.S.C.A. § 3411. *See Waye v. First Citizen's Nat'l Bank*, 846 F.Supp. 310 (M.D.Pa.), *aff'd*, 31 F.3d 1175 (3d Cir.1994) (discussing RFPA duty).

2. 12 U.S.C.A. § 3415.

3. *Id.* § 3403(d).

4. 12 U.S.C.A. § 3415. In addition, where the financial institution is itself the target of a grand jury investigation, at least one court has held that the cost reimbursement provision does not apply to the target's costs in complying with a grand jury subpoena. *In re Grand Jury Proceedings*, 636 F.2d 81 (5th Cir.1981).

5. *Pittsburgh Nat'l Bank v. United States*, 771 F.2d 73 (3d Cir.1985).

6. *Neece v. Internal Revenue Serv.*, 922 F.2d 573 (10th Cir.1990).

7. 12 U.S.C.A. § 3403(a). Presumably, failure to comply with this duty of confidentiality would constitute a "violation of law" for purposes of federal administrative en-

forcement provisions. *See, e.g., id.* § 1818(b)(1) (providing for cease and desist orders for violation of law).

8. *Id.* § 3403(b).

9. *Id.* § 3403(c). The institution cannot be held liable, under U.S. or state law, for any such notification, or for failure to notify a customer of such notification. *Id. See, e.g., Waye, supra* (reporting of check-kiting scheme); *Waye v. Commonwealth Bank*, 846 F.Supp. 321 (M.D.Pa.1994) (bank exempt from customer claim for negligence and bad faith, in light of § 3403(c)). *Cf. Nikrasch v. State*, 698 S.W.2d 443 (Tex.App.1985) (reporting information concerning lessee of safe deposit box to police). *But cf. Velasquez–Campuzano v. Marfa Nat'l Bank*, 896 F.Supp. 1415 (W.D.Tex.1995), *aff'd*, 91 F.3d 139 (5th Cir.1996) (suggesting that voluntary disclosure did not preempt liability under state law).

10. 12 U.S.C.A. § 3403(d)(1). The debt may be owed to the institution, or in its capacity as a fiduciary. *Id.*

processing a default on, or administering, a Government guaranteed or insured loan."[11]

A word of caution is warranted. Financial institutions may be liable to the customer for statutorily specified *civil penalties* for "obtaining or disclosing financial records or information ... in violation of" the RFPA.[12] While rarely pursued successfully to date, the civil penalties can be potentially significant. They may consist of: (1) $100.00, without regard to the volume of records at issue;[13] (2) The customer's actual damages sustained as a result of the disclosure;[14] (3) Punitive damages determined by the court, if the violation was willful or intentional;[15] and, (4) Costs and reasonable attorneys' fees.[16]

A good faith defense is available. A financial institution, or any agent or employee, acting in good faith reliance on certification by a government authority of compliance with the RFPA,[17] or pursuant to the exception for reporting crimes against an institution by an insider,[18] is given a complete affirmative defense against a claim by the customer under the RFPA and any state constitution, law, or regulation.[19] These provisions are the exclusive judicial remedies for violations of the RFPA.[20]

§ 10.5 Effect on State Law

By its own terms, the RFPA does not apply to inquiries from state and local government agencies.[1] Uncertainty remains, however, about the extent to which the RFPA overrides state law requirements and procedures.

Some courts have at least suggested that state law barring disclosure of financial records of a customer would be inapplicable in situations where the RFPA authorizes disclosure, though the courts routinely construe such state provisions as not creating conflict with federal law.[2] In addition, there is case law finding that contrary state law restricting

11. *Id.* § 3403(d)(2). *See, e.g., Bailey v. United States Dep't of Agric.,* 59 F.3d 141 (10th Cir.1995) (concerning food stamp program).

12. 12 U.S.C.A. § 3417(a).

13. *Id.* § 3417(a)(1). *See Duncan v. Belcher,* 813 F.2d 1335 (4th Cir.1987) (finding proof of actual damages unnecessary for recovery under RFPA).

14. 12 U.S.C.A. § 3417(a)(2). *See Neece, supra* (discussing proof of damages). *Cf. Duncan, supra* (finding proof of actual damages unnecessary).

15. 12 U.S.C.A. § 3417(a)(3).

16. *Id.* § 3417(a)(4). Fees and costs are available only in successful customer actions. *Id.*

17. *Per id.* § 3403(b).

18. *Per id.* § 3413(*l*).

19. *Id.* § 3417(c).

20. *Id.* § 3417(d).

§ 10.5

1. *United States v. Zimmerman,* 957 F.Supp. 94 (N.D.W.Va.1997); *Nichols,* 615 P.2d 280 (Okla.1980); *Austin v. Old Nat'l Bank in Evansville,* 656 N.E.2d 886 (Ind. App.1995) (holding RFPA inapplicable to state agencies); *Matter of Grand Jury Applications for Court–Ordered Subpoenas and Nondisclosure Orders,* 142 Misc.2d 241, 536 N.Y.S.2d 939 (N.Y.Sup.Ct.1988) (holding RFPA inapplicable to state court).

2. *See, e.g., United States v. Wilson,* 571 F.Supp. 1417 (S.D.N.Y.1983) (construing Texas Civ. St. art. 342–705).

or prohibiting access to customer records is preempted by the RFPA in certain instances.[3] Other courts have indicated that the RFPA does not have a broad preemptive effect.[4]

The better view is probably that the RFPA is only selectively preemptive of contrary state law, in fairly explicit terms. For example, it is clear from the text of the RFPA that any state constitution, law, or regulation that would prohibit an institution from notifying an appropriate federal government agency that it has information that may be relevant to a possible violation of statute or regulation is explicitly preempted by the RFPA.[5] Likewise, the good faith defense against customer claims for civil penalties expressly preempts contrary state law.[6] Thus, where the RFPA intends preemptive effect, it is quite explicit. Courts should therefore be hesitant to expand the scope of RFPA preemption beyond what the text appears to indicate is necessary.

§ 10.6   Community Reinvestment Rules

Few areas of depository institutions regulation have engendered the commentary and controversy that has accompanied the Community Reinvestment Act ("CRA").[1] One central feature has been the continuing debate over whether state and federal CRAs can effectively achieve their objectives. Recent empirical studies, focusing on the Texas market, have suggested that CRA regulations have not increased the availability of banking services in low-income communities, and that the number of branches in low-income areas actually decreased in the period following the relevant regulatory changes.[2] Other commentators have tentatively argued that it remains to be seen whether the state and federal CRAs and related policies can offset the effects of current federal interstate banking and branching policy and the emerging industry consolidation that has resulted from the interstate policy.[3] The regulatory apparatus

3. *See, e.g., In re Grand Jury Subpoena (Connecticut Sav. Bank)*, 481 F.Supp. 833 (D.Conn.1979) (permitting access pursuant to federal grand jury subpoena without compliance with state law).

4. *See, e.g., Foxworth v. Trustmark Nat'l Bank*, 934 F.Supp. 218 (S.D.Miss. 1996) (taking selective approach to preemption issue).

5. 12 U.S.C.A. § 3403(c).

6. *Id.* § 3417(c).

§ 10.6

1. Pub. L. No. 95–128, tit. VIII, 91 Stat. 1147 (1977), *as amended* (codified at 12 U.S.C.A. §§ 2901–2907). For legislative history of the CRA, see H.R. Rep. No. 95–128, 95th Cong., 1st Sess. (1977); H.R. Conf. Rep. No. 95–634, 95th Cong., 1st Sess. (1977), *reprinted in* 1977 U.S. Code Cong. & Admin. News 2884. *See generally Symposium Issue*, 143 U. Pa. L. Rev. 1285–1593

(1995) (assorted articles on CRA); David Evan Cohen, *The Community Reinvestment Act—Asset or Liability?*, 75 Marquette L. Rev. 599 (1992); Michael E. Schrader, *Competition and Convenience: The Emerging Role of Community Reinvestment*, 67 Ind. L.J. 331 (1992).

2. Leonard Bierman, Donald R. Fraser, Javier Gimeno & Lucio Fuentelsaz, *Regulatory Change and the Availability of Banking Facilities in Low–Income Areas: A Texas Empirical Study*, 49 S.M.U. L. Rev. 1421 (1996). *See also* Leonard Bierman, Donald Fraser & Asghar Zardkoohi, *Community Reinvestment Act: A Preliminary Empirical Analysis*, 45 Hastings L.J. 383 (1994).

3. Dwight Golann, Fred H. Miller, Alvin C. Harrell, *Introduction to the 1996 Annual Survey of Consumer Financial Services Law*, 51 Bus. Law. 825 (1996). *See generally* John H. Huffstutler, *Bank Holding Compa-*

has responded to these market changes with a heightened focus on reinvestment transactions and new data collection and reporting obligations,[4] increasing the CRA burden on insured institutions, but in the view of some commentators these developments are unlikely to satisfy advocates of CRA public policy.[5]

Nevertheless, revitalized by 1994 amendments intended to retool the act to deal with the increasingly interstate depository institutions market,[6] the CRA is undoubtedly here to stay. The discussion that follows will analyze the statutory provisions that implement the CRA public policy of encouraging depository institutions "to help meet the credit needs of the local communities in which they are chartered consistent with the safe and sound operation of such institutions."[7]

§ 10.7   Requirements and Procedures

The impetus of the CRA is explicitly based upon Congressional findings that embody the following loose syllogism:

Major Premise: In order to be chartered, and for other regulatory approvals, depository institutions[1] are required to demonstrate that their deposit facilities serve the convenience and needs of the community in which they are chartered to do business.[2]

Minor Premise: The convenience and needs of the community includes the need for credit services as well as deposit services.[3]

Conclusion: Therefore, depository institutions have a continuing and affirmative duty to help meet the credit needs of the local communities in which they are chartered.[4]

ny *Restructuring Alternatives Following the Enactment of the Riegle–Neal Interstate Banking and Branching Efficiency Act of 1994*, Practicing Law Institute, Corporate Law and Practice Course Handbook Series (Dec. 1996) (noting three layers of CRA review applicable to interstate banks, as well as state regulation); Mark D. Rollinger, *Interstate Banking and Branching Under the Riegle–Neal Act of 1994*, 33 Harv. J. on Legis. 183 (1996) (surveying potential effect of interstate banking legislation on banking industry).

4. *See* 12 C.F.R. §§ 25.42, 228.42, 345.42, 563e.42 (imposing data collection, reporting, and disclosure requirements).

5. David E. Teitelbaum & John M. Casanova, *Regulatory Reform or Retread? The New Community Reinvestment Act Regulations*, 51 Bus. Law. 831 (1996). *Cf.* Charles R. Whitt, *Eleven Accuse NationsBank of Bias in Mortgages*, 8 Loy. Consumer L. Rep. 6 (1996) (noting lawsuit against interstate-

expanding NationsBank Corp., alleging mortgage-lending discrimination).

6. Pub. L. No. 103–328 §§ 10, 108 Stat. 2364 (1994) (codified at 12 U.S.C.A. § 2906).

7. 12 U.S.C.A. § 2901(b). *See Hicks v. Resolution Trust Corp.*, 970 F.2d 378 (7th Cir.1992) (seeking to balance CRA obligations and safety and soundness and limiting effect of CRA accordingly).

§ 10.7

1. The CRA actually uses the term "regulated financial institution" as its basic reference point. This term is defined to mean "an insured depository institution (as defined in [12 U.S.C.A. § 1813])." 12 U.S.C.A. § 2902(2).

2. *Id.* § 2901(a)(1).

3. *Id.* § 2901(a)(2).

4. *Id.* § 2901(a)(3).

Taken in the abstract, there is nothing particularly remarkable about this conclusion. The CRA explicitly links itself to the traditional banking factor of "convenience and needs," which is routinely applied by regulators in deciding a wide variety of applications. However, on the basis of this rather vague and flexible concept, the CRA imposes some relatively specific and arguably inflexible expectations about serving the credit needs of low-income segments of an institution's local market. Furthermore, in an increasingly interstate market, determining what the "local" market of a given institution is can often be problematic.

The basic tools used to implement CRA policy are the assessment and evaluation. In examining an insured depository institution, the institution's appropriate federal financial supervisory agency[5] must assess its record of "meeting the credit needs of its entire community, including low- and moderate-income neighborhoods, consistent with the safe and sound operation of such institution."[6] The assessment is based upon a set of tests implemented in the agencies' CRA regulation. The data that is plugged into these tests is derived from a number of sources specified in the regulations.[7] In effect, these sources establish the context within which CRA performance is assessed and evaluated.

At the conclusion of a CRA examination, the agency is required to prepare a written evaluation of the examined institution's CRA record,[8] consisting of a public section and a confidential section.[9] The public section of the CRA written evaluation is required to include: (1) The agency's conclusions for each CRA factor assessed, as identified in its regulations;[10] (2) Discussion of facts and data supporting its conclu-

---

5. For these purposes, the term "appropriate Federal financial supervisory agency" is defined as follows:

(1) the Office of the Comptroller of the Currency ("OCC"), with respect to national banks;

(2) the Federal Reserve Board ("Fed"), with respect to state-chartered member banks and bank holding companies;

(3) the Federal Deposit Insurance Corporation ("FDIC"), with respect to insured state-chartered nonmember banks and savings banks; and

(4) the Office of Thrift Supervision ("OTS") with respect to insured savings associations and savings and loan holding companies.

Id. § 2902(3)(A)-(D).

6. *Id.* § 2903(a)(1). In assessing an institution's record, the CRA discriminates between "majority-owned institutions" on the one hand, and "minority-" or "women-owned institutions" on the other. *Id.* § 2903(b). In assessing a majority-owned institution's record, the agency may consid-

er the institution's capital investment in, and loan participation and other joint ventures with, minority- and women-owned financial institutions and low-income credit unions. *Id.* These activities may be considered only if they "help meet the credit needs of local communities in which such institutions and credit unions are chartered." *Id.* On operation of branch facilities by minorities and women, see *id.* § 2907.

7. 12 C.F.R. §§ 25.21(b) (OCC regulations) 228.21(b) (Fed regulations), 345.21(b) (FDIC regulations), 563e.21(b) (OTS regulations).

8. 12 U.S.C.A. § 2906(a)(1).

9. *Id.* § 2906(a)(2).

10. *Id.* § 2906(b)(1)(A)(i). *See, e.g.,* 12 C.F.R. §§ 25.21–25.24, 228.21–228.24, 345.21–345.24, 563e.21–563e.24 (lending, investment and service tests of OCC, Fed, FDIC, and OTS, respectively). *See also id.* §§ 25.25, 228.25, 345.25, 563e.25 (community development test for a wholesale or limited purpose bank of OCC, Fed, FDIC and OTS, respectively); 25.26, 228.26, 345.26, 563e.26 (small bank performance sions;[11] and, (3) The examined institution's CRA rating, together with an explanation of the basis for the rating.[12]

The confidential section of the written evaluation contains any references that identify customers, institution officers or employees, or any other person who has provided information to a state or federal supervisory agency in confidence.[13] It also contains any statements considered in the judgment of the agency to be too sensitive or speculative to disclose to the examined institution or to the public.[14]

The emergence of interstate banking and branching as a matter of federal depository institutions policy has complicated CRA assessment and evaluation. Special procedures now apply to the assessment and evaluation of a depository institution with interstate domestic branches.[15] For such institutions, the agency must prepare a written evaluation of the entire institution's CRA record of performance,[16] and a separate written evaluation for each state in which the institution maintains a domestic branch.[17] In addition, in situations in which the examined institution maintains domestic branches within one multistate metropolitan area, the agency is required to prepare a separate written evaluation

standards of OCC, Fed, FDIC, and OTS, respectively). The conclusions must be presented separately for each metropolitan area in which the institution maintains a domestic branch office. 12 U.S.C.A. § 2906(b)(1)(B). For these purposes, "metropolitan area" is defined to mean:

any primary metropolitan statistical area, metropolitan statistical area, or consolidated metropolitan statistical area, as defined by the Director of the Office of Management and Budget, with a population of 250,000 or more, and any other area designated as such by the appropriate Federal financial supervisory agency.

Id. § 2906(e)(2).

11. 12 U.S.C.A. § 2906(b)(1)(A)(ii). This discussion must be presented separately for each metropolitan area in which the institution maintains a domestic branch office. *Id.* § 2906(b)(1)(B).

12. 12 U.S.C.A. § 2906(b)(1)(A)(iii). The CRA requires the use of the following ratings:

(1) Outstanding record of meeting community credit needs;

(2) Satisfactory record of meeting community credit needs;

(3) Needs to improve record of meeting community credit needs; and

(4) Substantial noncompliance in meeting community credit needs.

Id. § 2906(b)(2)(A)–(D). *See, e.g.,* 12 C.F.R. §§ 25.28, 228.28, 345.28, 563e.28 (providing for assigned CRA ratings under OCC, Fed,

FDIC, and OTS regulations, respectively). The ratings must be disclosed to the public. 12 U.S.C.A. § 2906(b)(2).

13. 12 U.S.C.A. § 2906(c)(1).

14. *Id.* § 2906(c)(2). The agency may disclose the confidential section, in whole or in part, to the examined institution if the agency determines that disclosure will promote CRA objectives. *Id.* § 2906(c) (3). However, such disclosure may not identify a person or organization that has provided information in confidence to a state or federal supervisory agency. *Id.*

15. For these purposes, the term "domestic branch" is defined to mean "any branch office or other facility of a regulated financial institution that accepts deposits, located in any State." *Id.* § 2906(e)(1).

16. *Id.* § 2906(d)(1)(A).

17. *Id.* § 2906(d)(1)(B). This state-by-state evaluation is specifically required to include information required by § 2906(b)(1)(A)-(B) separately for each metropolitan area in which the examined institution maintains a domestic branch office, and separately for the remainder of the non-metropolitan area of the state, if the institution maintains any domestic branch offices in the non-metropolitan area. *Id.* § 2906(d)(3)(A). *But cf. id.* § 2906(d)(2), discussed in following note (noting that state-by-state evaluation is to be adjusted where separate evaluation is done of multistate metropolitan area). The state-by-state evaluation must also describe how the agency performed the examination, including a of the institution's CRA record of performance within the metropolitan area.[18]

The agency is also required to take a depository institution's CRA record into account in its evaluation of any application by the institution for a "deposit facility."[19] The CRA definition of this term is the key to the act's potentially broad effect. The term "application for a deposit facility" is defined for these purposes to mean any application for: (1) A charter for a national bank or federal savings and loan association;[20] (2) Deposit insurance, in the case of a newly chartered state bank, savings bank, savings and loan association, or similar institution;[21] (3) The establishment of a domestic branch or other facility that can accept deposits;[22] (4) The relocation of a home or branch office;[23] (5) The merger, consolidation or purchase/assumption requiring approval under the Bank Merger Act ("BMA");[24] or, (6) The acquisition of shares in, or the assets of, a depository institution requiring approval under federal holding company law.[25]

Obviously, if vigorously implemented[26] and administered by the agencies,[27] these CRA requirements may have a significant impact on an institution's credit and asset-management policies. Most commentators have not found that administration of the CRA has had any marked effect on the availability of credit to low- and moderate-income neighborhoods within institution's "local" community, however defined.[28] Effective or not, however, the CRA presents institutions with a significant supervisory challenge and a potentially substantial regulatory cost. Fail-

list of the individual branches examined. *Id.* § 2906(d)(3)(B).

18. *Id.* § 2906(d)(2). If the agency prepares a multistate metropolitan area evaluation, the scope of the state-by-state evaluation, *per id.* § 2906(d)(1)(B), should be adjusted accordingly. *Id.* § 2906(d)(2).

19. *Id.* § 2903(a)(2). In evaluating an institution's record, the CRA discriminates between "majority-owned institutions" on the one hand, and "minority-" or "women-owned institutions" on the other. *Id.* § 2903(b). In evaluating a majority-owned institution's record, the agency may consider the institution's capital investment in, and loan participation and other joint ventures with, minority- and women-owned financial institutions and low-income credit unions. *Id.* These activities may be considered only if they "help meet the credit needs of local communities in which such institutions and credit unions are chartered." *Id.* On operation of branch facilities by minorities and women, see *id.* § 2907.

20. *Id.* § 2902(3)(A).

21. *Id.* § 2902(3)(B).

22. *Id.* § 2902(3)(C). *See, e.g., Corning Sav. & Loan Ass'n v. Fed. Home Loan Bank Bd.*, 571 F.Supp. 396 (E.D.Ark.1983), *aff'd*, 736 F.2d 479 (8th Cir.1984) (upholding

FHLBB approval of branch application in light of CRA).

23. 12 U.S.C.A. § 2902(3)(D).

24. *Id.* § 2902(3)(E). On approval of mergers and similar acquisition transactions under the Bank Merger Act, see *id.* § 1828(c).

25. *Id.* § 2902(3)(F). The text of this provision refers to 12 U.S.C.A. § 1842, the appropriate Bank Holding Company Act provision, but it also continues to refer to the repealed savings and loan holding company provision of 12 U.S.C.A. § 1730a(e) (1988), which has been replaced by 12 U.S.C.A. § 1467a.

26. *See id.* § 2905 (mandating promulgation of regulations). The agencies have promulgated substantially identical CRA implementing regulations. 12 C.F.R. Pts. 25, 228, 345, 563e, (CRA regulations of OCC, Fed, FDIC, and OTS, respectively).

27. *See* 12 U.S.C.A. § 2904 (requiring annual report to Congress by agencies outlining CRA actions taken).

28. *See, e.g.,* Leonard Bierman, Donald R. Fraser, Javier Gimeno & Lucio Fuentelsaz, *Regulatory Change and the Availability of Banking Facilities in Low–Income Areas: A Texas Empirical Study*, 49 S.M.U. L. Rev. 1421 (1996) (discussing empirical findings).

ure to take the CRA into account in formulating credit and asset-management policies can result in frustration in corporate planning.[29]

Institutions may take advantage of an alternative mechanism for CRA assessment and evaluation offered by the agencies' CRA regulations—the development and implementation of a CRA strategic plan.[30] With an approved plan[31] in effect and operating for at least one year,[32] an institution's CRA record is assessed under the criteria of the plan developed by the institution, rather than under the lending, investment, and service tests imposed by agency regulations.[33]

The plan may have a term of no more than five years, and any multi-year plan must include annual interim measurable goals under which the institution's appropriate agency will evaluate the bank's performance.[34] Institutions with more than one assessment area may prepare a single plan for all assessment areas, or one or more plans for one or more of assessment areas.[35] In addition, affiliated institutions may prepare a joint plan if the plan provides measurable goals for each institution.[36] Activities may be allocated among institutions at their option, provided that the same activities are not considered for more than one institution.[37]

The finalized plan must be submitted to the appropriate agency at least three months prior to its proposed effective date.[38] The institution must submit with the plan a description of its informal efforts to seek suggestions from members of the public, any written public comment received, and, if the plan was revised in light of comments received, the initial version plan released for public comment.[39] The agency applies the following criteria in evaluating the plan and deciding whether or not to approve it: (1) Extent and breadth of lending or lending-related activities, including distribution of loans among different geographies, businesses and farms of different sizes, and individuals of different income levels, extent of community development lending, and use of innovative or flexible lending practices to address credit needs; (2) Amount and innovativeness, complexity, and responsiveness of institution's qualified investments; and, (3) Availability and effectiveness of institution's systems for delivering retail services, and extent and innovativeness of institution's community development services.[40]

---

29. *See, e.g.,* 12 C.F.R. §§ 25.29, 228.29, 345.29, 563e.29 (effect of CRA performance on applications).

30. 12 C.F.R. §§ 25.27, 228.27, 345.27, 563e.27.

31. *See, e.g.,* 12 C.F.R. § 25.27(g) (OCC Regulations; providing for approval of CRA strategic plan).

32. *See, e.g., id.* § 25.27(a)(1)–(4).

33. *See, e.g., id.* § 25.27(a). Agency approval of a plan does not affect an institution's obligation to report data as required by the regulations. *Id.* §§ 25.27(b), 25.42.

34. *See, e.g., id.* § 25.27(c)(1).

35. *See, e.g., id.* § 25.27(c)(2).

36. *See, e.g., id.* § 25.27(c)(3).

37. *Id.*

38. *See, e.g., id.* § 25.27(e).

39. *Id.*

40. *Id.*   §§ 25.27(g)(3)(i)–(iii), 228.27(g)(3)(i)–(iii),   345.27(g)(3)(i)–(iii), 563e.27(g)(3)(i)–(iii).

The approved plan may be amended during its term, subject to approval by the agency, on the grounds that there has been a material change in circumstances.[41] Development of an amendment to a previously approved strategic plan requires the same public participation procedures as development of an original plan.[42]

There are several advantages to the use of a CRA strategic plan that may be beneficial to an institution. First, and most important, development of strategic plan allows an institution to fine-tune the performance criteria and goals to its particular situation, rather than subject itself to generally applicable criteria and goals contained in the CRA regulations. Second, the development process, requiring public participation and comment, gives the institution an opportunity to solicit, identify, and resolve community concerns with respect to it CRA activities and services outside of the formal supervisory process. Third, the development of the plan allows the institution to take a more proactive and positive approach to its CRA responsibilities, which may have the beneficial effect of building a rapport with the local communities.

§ 10.8   Equal Credit Opportunity Rules

Under the Equal Credit Opportunity Act ("ECOA"),[1] it is unlawful for any creditor[2] to discriminate against any applicant[3] for

---

41. *Id.*   §§ 25.27(h),   228.27(h), 345.27(h), 563e.27(h).

42. *Id.* §§ 25.27(d), (h), 228.27(d), (h), 345.27(d), (h), 563e.27(d), (h).

§ 10.8

1. Pub. L. No. 93–495, tit. V, 88 Stat. 1521 (1974), *as amended* (codified at 15 U.S.C.A. §§ 1691–1691f). For legislative history, see Sen. Rep. No. 93–902, 93d Cong., 2d Sess. (1974), H. Conf. Rep. No. 93–1429, 93d Cong., 2d Sess. (1974), *reprinted in*, 1974 U.S. Code Cong. & Admin. News 6119. *See Brothers v. First Leasing*, 724 F.2d 789 (9th Cir.1984), *cert. denied*, 469 U.S. 832, 105 S.Ct. 121 (discussing purposes of ECOA); *Anderson v. United Fin. Co.*, 666 F.2d 1274 (9th Cir.1982) (same); *Riggs Nat'l Bank v. Linch*, 829 F.Supp. 163 (E.D.Va.1993), *aff'd*, 36 F.3d 370 (4th Cir. 1994) (discussing spousal creditworthiness); *Diamond v. Union Bank and Trust of Bartlesville*, 776 F.Supp. 542 (N.D.Okla.1991) (discussing credit discrimination against married women). *See generally* Stephen M. Dane, *Eliminating the Labyrinth: Proposal to Simplify Federal Mortgage Lending Discrimination Laws*, 26 U. Mich. J. L. Reform 527 (1993) (discussing ECOA); Ann Fagan Ginger, *Enforcing the Hidden U.S. Equal Rights Law*, 20 Golden Gate U. L. Rev. 385 (1990) (same).

2. For these purposes, the term "creditor" is defined to mean "any person who regularly extends, renews, or continues credit; any person who regularly arranges for the extension, renewal, or continuation of credit; or any assignee of an original creditor who participates in the decision to extend, renew, or continue credit." 15 U.S.C.A. § 1691a(e). *See, e.g., In re Brazil*, 21 B.R. 333 (Bkrtcy.N.D. Ohio 1982) (finding utility, regularly providing gas to customers prior to payment, to be "creditor").

3. For these purposes, the term "applicant" is defined to mean "any person who applies to a creditor directly for an extension, renewal, or continuation of credit, or applies to a creditor indirectly by use of an existing credit plan for an amount exceeding a previously established credit limit." 15 U.S.C.A. § 1691a(b). *Cf. Cragin v. First Fed. Sav. and Loan Ass'n*, 498 F.Supp. 379 (D.Nev.1980) (finding oral request for credit not credit "application" for purposes of ECOA). On meaning of "applicant" for purposes of ECOA, see *Midlantic Nat'l Bank v. Hansen*, 48 F.3d 693 (3d Cir.1995), *cert. dismissed*, 515 U.S. 1184, 116 S.Ct. 32 (discussing spouses as joint applicants); *Federal Deposit Ins. Corp. v. Medmark, Inc.*, 897 F.Supp. 511 (D.Kan.1995) (finding wife required to join husband in guaranty of corcredit,[4] with respect to any aspect of a credit transaction,[5] on the basis of race,[6] color, religion, national origin, sex or marital status,[7] or age.[8]

porate indebtedness "applicant" for ECOA purposes). *But cf. Delta Diversified, Inc. v. Citizens & S. Nat'l Bank*, 171 Ga.App. 625, 320 S.E.2d 767 (1984) (*contra*); *Mercado Garcia v. Ponce Fed. Bank*, 779 F.Supp. 620 (D.P.R.1991), *aff'd*, 979 F.2d 890 (1st Cir. 1992) (former bank employee/borrower not "applicant" under circumstances of special loan program).

4. For these purposes, the term "credit" is defined to mean "the right granted by a creditor to a debtor to defer payment of debt or to incur debts and defer its payment or to purchase property or services and defer payment therefor." 15 U.S.C.A. § 1691a(d). *See, e.g., Roberts v. Walmart Stores, Inc.*, 736 F.Supp. 1527 (E.D.Mo. 1990) (finding tendered check in payment for goods not "credit" for purposes of ECOA); *Dunn v. American Express Co.*, 529 F.Supp. 633 (D.Colo.1982) (finding express teller card not "credit").

5. *See Shaumyan v. Sidetex Co., Inc.*, 900 F.2d 16 (2d Cir.1990) (holding home improvement contract not "credit transaction" for purposes of ECOA); *Butler v. Capitol Fed. Sav.*, 904 F.Supp. 1230 (D.Kan. 1995) (application to open savings account not "credit transaction").

6. *See, e.g., Cherry v. Amoco Oil Co.*, 481 F.Supp. 727 (N.D.Ga.1979) (addressing racial discrimination in credit transaction); *cf. Douglas County Nat'l Bank v. Pfeiff*, 809 P.2d 1100, 1104 (Colo.App.1991) (*citing Cherry*). *But cf. Higgins v. J.C. Penney, Inc.*, 630 F.Supp. 722 (E.D.Mo.1986) (declining to follow *Cherry* analysis as to specificity requirements with respect to denial of credit).

7. *See, e.g., Silverman v. Eastrich Multiple Investor Fund, L.P.*, 51 F.3d 28 (3d Cir.1995) (permitting creditor to obtain signature of guarantor's spouse where guarantor not considered independently creditworthy); *Mayes v. Chrysler Credit Corp.*, 37 F.3d 9 (1st Cir.1994) (addressing sex discrimination in credit transaction); *Anderson, supra* (same); *Miller v. American Express Co.*, 688 F.2d 1235 (9th Cir.1982) (finding credit card company policy of automatic cancellation of surviving spouse's supplementary account upon death of basic card-holder discrimination on basis of marital status); *Haynes v. Bank of Wedowee*, 634 F.2d 266 (5th Cir.1981) (permitting creditor's consideration of husband's bankruptcy in accelerating loan to wife); *Carroll v. Exxon Co.*, 434 F.Supp. 557 (E.D.La.1977) (permitting inquiry concerning number of dependents).

However, for purposes of the ECOA it is not considered prohibited discrimination for a creditor to make an inquiry concerning marital status if the inquiry is for the purpose of ascertaining the creditor's rights and remedies applicable to a particular extension of credit, and not to discriminate in a determination of credit-worthiness. 15 U.S.C.A. § 1691(b)(1). *See id.* §§ 1691d(a) (providing for requests for signature of husband and wife for creation of valid lien, and the like); 1691d(b) (concerning state property laws affecting creditworthiness); 1691d(c) (concerning state laws prohibiting separate extension of consumer credit to husband and wife); 1691d(d) (permitting combination of credit accounts of husband and wife with same creditor to determine permissible finance charges or loan ceilings under federal and state laws). *See also United States v. ITT Consumer Fin. Corp.*, 816 F.2d 487 (9th Cir.1987) (concerning required signature of spouse in equal management community property state); *Evans v. Centralfed Mortgage Co.*, 815 F.2d 348 (5th Cir.1987) (permitting creditor to require spouse to sign deed of trust and be included as grantee on warranty deed); *In re Farris*, 194 B.R. 931 (Bkrtcy.E.D. Pa. 1996) (finding debtor-spouse's signature necessary to encumber residence and provide creditor with legal right to proceed against property in event of default under loan). *Cf. Markham v. Colonial Mortgage Serv. Co.*, 605 F.2d 566 (D.C.Cir.1979) (finding state laws attaching in the event of marriage no justification for creditor's refusal to aggregate incomes of unmarried joint applicants); *In re DiPietro*, 135 B.R. 773 (Bkrtcy.E.D. Pa. 1992) (finding no ECOA violation in required wife's signature on term note as condition of creditworthiness); *Bank of Am. v. Hotel Rittenhouse Assocs.*, 595 F.Supp. 800 (E.D.Pa.1984) (permitting bank to obtain spouse's signature on joint credit application). *See generally* Richard J. Wirth & Jonathan B. Alter, *Spousal Defenses Based in Equal Credit Laws*, 99 Com. L.J. 93 (1994) (discussing ECOA).

8. 15 U.S.C.A. § 1691(a)(1). The prohibition with respect to age discrimination is modified by the proviso that the credit applicant must, of course, have the capacity to contract. *Id. Cf. Restatement (Second) of Contracts* § 14 (concerning capacity of infants to contract). Furthermore, for purposes of the ECOA, it is not considered prohibited discrimination for a creditor to

Likewise, creditors are prohibited from discriminating on the basis of the fact that all or part of a credit applicant's income derives from a public assistance program.[9] Finally, creditors are prohibited from discriminating against a credit applicant because the applicant has exercised in good faith any right under the ECOA or related laws.[10]

Certain programmatic activities do not constitute "discrimination" under the ECOA.[11] It is not an ECOA violation for a creditor to refuse to extend credit offered pursuant to any of the following types of programs: (1) A credit assistance program expressly authorized by law for an economically disadvantaged class of persons;[12] (2) A credit assistance program administered by a nonprofit organization for its members or for an economically disadvantaged class of persons;[13] or, (3) A special-purpose credit program offered by a profit-making organization to meet special social needs, provided the program meets standards prescribed in Fed regulations.[14] These exceptions are available if refusal to provide credit is required by, or made pursuant to, the requirements of such a program.[15]

The ECOA requires that a creditor notify an applicant of its action on the credit application within a specified period of time.[16] Failure to

make an inquiry of an applicant's age if the inquiry is for the purpose of determining the amount and probable continuance of income levels, credit history, or other pertinent elements of credit-worthiness, as provided in regulations promulgated by the Fed. 15 U.S.C.A. § 1691(b)(2). On the authority of the Fed to promulgate regulations under the ECOA, see *id.* § 1691b. *See also id.* §§ 1691d(g) (authorizing exemption from ECOA, by Fed regulation, of credit transactions covered by state law; failure to comply with state law deemed violation of ECOA); 1691e(e) (providing that good faith compliance with Fed rule, regulation, or interpretation, or interpretation or approval by duly authorized Fed official or employee shields creditor from ECOA liability). *See generally Miller, supra* (upholding Fed's rule-making authority).

In addition, a creditor may use an empirically derived credit system that considers age, if the system is "demonstrably and statistically sound," in accordance with Fed regulations, except that in the operation of such system the age of an elderly applicant may not be assigned a negative factor or value. 15 U.S.C.A. § 1691(b)(3). However, a creditor may make an inquiry concerning or consider the age of an elderly applicant, if the age of the applicant is to be used by the creditor in the extension of credit in favor of such applicant. *Id.* § 1691(b)(4).

9. 15 U.S.C.A. § 1691(a)(2). For purposes of the ECOA, it is not considered prohibited discrimination for a creditor to make an inquiry of whether an applicant's

income derives from any public assistance program if the inquiry is for the purpose of determining the amount and probable continuance of income levels, credit history, or other pertinent elements of credit-worthiness, as provided in regulations promulgated by the Fed. *Id.* § 1691(b)(2).

10. *Id.* § 1691(a)(3). *See, e.g., Bryson v. Bank of N.Y.,* 584 F.Supp. 1306 (S.D.N.Y. 1984) (finding ECOA cause of action for bank's denial of credit because of applicant's inquiries under Truth-in-Lending Act); *Owens v. Magee Fin. Serv. of Bogalusa, Inc.,* 476 F.Supp. 758 (E.D.La.1979) (finding violation in creditor's requirement that applicant sign document settling and releasing claims).

11. 15 U.S.C.A. § 1691(c).

12. *Id.* § 1691(c)(1).

13. *Id.* § 1691(c)(2).

14. *Id.* § 1691(c)(3). *But see United States v. American Future Sys., Inc.,* 743 F.2d 169 (3d Cir.1984) (ECOA violation in designing and administering credit program discriminating on prohibited basis, not related to social need program sought to address).

15. 15 U.S.C.A. § 1691(c).

16. *Id.* § 1691(d)(1) (action on application is typically within 30 days of receipt of completed application). *See Jochum v. Pico Credit Corp. of Westbank, Inc.,* 730 F.2d 1041 (5th Cir.1984) (discussing notice requirement); *Williams v. Mid–Am. Fed. Sav.*

notify may constitute an ECOA violation even in the absence of prohibited discrimination.[17] Where adverse action[18] is taken, the ECOA requires the creditor to provide a statutorily specified statement of reasons for the such action.[19] If an appraisal report was used in connection with the application for a loan to be secured by a lien on residential real property, upon written request of the applicant (within a reasonable time of the application) the creditor must promptly furnish the applicant with a copy of the appraisal.[20]

While the ECOA is implemented through regulations promulgated by the Fed,[21] it is enforced under the authority of a variety of federal

and Loan Ass'n, 624 F.Supp. 160 (S.D.Ohio 1985) (same). On the running of the period of time for notification, see *Dufay v. Bank of Am.*, 94 F.3d 561 (9th Cir.1996); *Riggs Nat'l Bank v. Webster*, 832 F.Supp. 147 (D.Md.1993); *Howard Oaks, Inc. v. Maryland Nat'l Bank*, 810 F.Supp. 674 (D.Md. 1993); *High v. McLean Fin. Corp.*, 659 F.Supp. 1561 (D.D.C.1987). ECOA notification is post-credit-decision only. *Cartwright v. American Sav. & Loan Ass'n*, 880 F.2d 912 (7th Cir.1989); *Vander Missen v. Kellogg–Citizens Nat'l Bank*, 481 F.Supp. 742 (E.D.Wis.1979).

17. *Sayers v. General Motors Acceptance Corp.*, 522 F.Supp. 835 (W.D.Mo.1981).

18. For these purposes, "adverse action" if defined to mean:

a denial or revocation of credit, a change in the terms of an existing credit arrangement, or a refusal to grant credit in substantially the amount or on substantially the terms requested. Such term does not include a refusal to extend additional credit under an existing credit arrangement where the applicant is delinquent or otherwise in default, or where such additional credit would exceed a previously established credit limit.

15 U.S.C.A. § 1691(d)(6). *See, e.g., O'Dowd v. South Cent. Bell*, 729 F.2d 347 (5th Cir. 1984) (discussing meaning of "adverse action"); *Jochum, supra* (same).

19. 15 U.S.C.A. § 1691(d)(2). According to the ECOA, this obligation can be satisfied by:

(A) providing statements of reasons in writing as a matter of course to applicants against whom adverse action is taken; or

(B) giving written notification of adverse action which discloses (i) the applicant's right to a statement of reasons within thirty days after receipt by the creditor of a request made within sixty days after such notification, and (ii) the identity of the person or office from

which such statement may be obtained. Such statement may be given orally if the written notification advises the applicant of his right to have the statement of reasons confirmed in writing on written request.

Id. § 1691(d)(2)(A)-(B). A statement of reasons meets these requirements only if it contains the specific reasons for the adverse action taken. *Id.* § 1691(d)(3). *See, e.g., Pierce v. Citibank (South Dakota), N.A.*, 843 F.Supp. 646 (D.Or.1994), *on reconsideration*, 856 F.Supp. 1451, *aff'd*, 92 F.3d 1193 (9th Cir.1996) (excusing inadvertent error in notification and statement); *Higgins v. J.C. Penney, Inc.*, 630 F.Supp. 722 (E.D.Mo. 1986) (finding reasons given by creditor sufficient); *O'Dowd, supra* (discussing requirement of statement of reasons); *Fischl v. General Motors Acceptance Corp.*, 708 F.2d 143 (5th Cir.1983) (criticizing insufficiency of statement); *Cherry v. Amoco Oil*, 481 F.Supp. 727 (N.D.Ga.1979) (same); *Carroll v. Exxon Co.*, 434 F.Supp. 557 (E.D.La. 1977) (finding violation in failure to provide sufficient statement of reasons).

If the creditor is requested by a third party to make a specific extension of credit directly or indirectly to an applicant, the notification and statement of reasons may be made directly by such creditor, or indirectly through the third party, provided in either case that the creditor's identity is disclosed. 15 U.S.C.A. § 1691(d)(4). These requirements may be satisfied by verbal statements or notifications in the case of any creditor who did not act on more than 150 applications during the calendar year preceding the calendar year in which the adverse action was taken, as determined under Fed regulations. *Id.* § 1691(d)(5).

20. 15 U.S.C.A. § 1691(e). The creditor may require the applicant to reimburse it for the cost of the appraisal. *Id.*

21. *See id.* 1691b (noting Fed authority). *Cf. id.* § 1691c(d) (authorizing regulations by other designated agencies with respect to ECOA enforcement procedures).

agencies, depending upon the creditor involved. Figure 10–1, *infra*, illustrates the division of enforcement authority under the ECOA.

Figure 10–1
ECOA: Division of Enforcement Authority[22]

Agency	*Authority*[23]	*Scope*
Office of the Comptroller of the Currency ("OCC")	12 U.S.C.A. § 1818	> national banks > Federal branches and Federal agencies of foreign banks
Federal Reserve Board ("Fed")	12 U.S.C.A. § 1818	> state-chartered member banks > state-licensed, noninsured branches and agencies of foreign banks > commercial lending companies owned or controlled by foreign banks > foreign branches of U.S. banks > Edge Act and Agreement Corporations
Federal Deposit Insurance Corporation ("FDIC")	12 U.S.C.A. § 1818	> insured state nonmember banks > insured state-licensed branches of foreign banks
Office of Thrift Supervision ("OTS")	12 U.S.C.A. § 1818	> insured savings associations
National Credit Union Administration ("NCUA")	12 U.S.C.A. §§ 1751 *et seq.*	> federal credit unions
Secretary of Transportation	49 U.S.C.A. subtit. IV 49 U.S.C.A. subtit. VII	> carriers subject to jurisdiction of Surface Transportation Board > air carriers and foreign air carriers subject to Part A
Secretary of Agriculture	7 U.S.C.A. §§ 181 *et seq.*	> except as provided in 7 U.S.C.A. §§ 226, 227, with respect to activities subject thereto
Farm Credit Administration	12 U.S.C.A. §§ 2001 *et seq.*	> federal land banks > federal land bank associations > federal intermediate credit banks > production credit associations
Securities and Exchange Commission ("SEC")	15 U.S.C.A. §§ 78a *et seq.*	> securities brokers and dealers
Small Business Administration	15 U.S.C.A. §§ 661 *et seq.*	> small business investment companies
Federal Trade Commission ("FTC")	15 U.S.C.A. §§ 11 *et seq.*	> overall enforcement authority as to all other "creditors" under ECOA[24]

Agencies may also seek ECOA enforcement by request to the Attor-

22. Source: 15 U.S.C.A. § 1691c.

23. Violations of the ECOA are deemed to be violations of the identified authorities. *Id.* § 1691c(b), (c).

24. *See, e.g., United States v. Blake*, 751 F.Supp. 951 (W.D.Okla.1990) (discussing ECOA two-year limitation and FTCA five-year limitation); *United States v. Landmark Fin. Servs., Inc.*, 612 F.Supp. 623 (D.Md. 1985) (upholding FTC authority under ECOA).

ney General for a civil action against a creditor.[25] The Attorney General is authorized to bring a civil action enforcing the ECOA whenever he or she has reason to believe that a creditor is engaged in a pattern or practice in violation of the ECOA.[26] The Attorney General may seek any relief deemed appropriate, including actual and punitive damages, as well as injunctive relief.[27]

As an alternative to referring the matter to the Attorney General, an agency authorized to enforce the ECOA may, under certain circumstances, notify the Department of Housing and Urban Development ("HUD") of violations.[28] Such notification is appropriate in situations in which the agency does not refer the matter to the Attorney General,[29] and: (1) The agency has reason to believe, as a result of a consumer complaint, a consumer compliance examination, or otherwise, that an ECOA violation has occurred;[30] and, (2) It has reason to believe that the alleged violation would also be a violation of the Fair Housing Act.[31]

Under these circumstances, the agency is required to notify the HUD Secretary of the violation.[32] The agency must also notify the applicant that the Secretary has been notified of the alleged violation and that remedies for the violation may be available under the Fair Housing Act.[33]

Any creditor that violates the requirements of the ECOA may also be liable to the aggrieved applicant[34] for any actual damages sustained, either individually or as a member of a class.[35] In addition, a non-

25. 15 U.S.C.A. § 1691e(g).

26. *Id.* § 1691e(h).

27. *Id. Cf. United States v. Beneficial Corp.*, 492 F.Supp. 682 (D.N.J.1980), *aff'd*, 673 F.2d 1302 (3d Cir.1981) (finding Attorney General not authorized to seek money damages on behalf of nonparties).

28. 15 U.S.C.A. § 1691e(k).

29. *Id.* § 1691e(k)(3).

30. *Id.* § 1691e(k)(1).

31. *Id.* § 1691e(k)(2). *See* 42 U.S.C.A. §§ 3601 *et seq.* (Fair Housing Act).

32. 15 U.S.C.A. § 1691e(k).

33. *Id. Cf. id.* § 1691e(i):

No person aggrieved by a violation of [the ECOA] and by a violation of section 3605 of Title 42 shall recover under [the ECOA] and section 3612 of Title 42, if such violation is based on the same transaction.

34. *See generally Integra Bank/Pittsburgh v. Freeman*, 839 F.Supp. 326 (E.D.Pa. 1993) (finding co-guarantor, whose wife was not required to sign, lacked standing to assert ECOA claim for creditor's alleged discrimination in requiring other guarantor's spouse to sign); *Riggs Nat'l Bank v. Linch*, 829 F.Supp. 163 (E.D.Va.1993), *aff'd*, 36 F.3d 370 (4th Cir.1994) (same);

Ford v. Citizens and S. Nat'l Bank, 700 F.Supp. 1121 (N.D.Ga.1988) (finding person signing deed to secure promissory note could be aggrieved party with standing to bring ECOA action); *Morse v. Mutual Fed. Sav. & Loan Ass'n of Whitman*, 536 F.Supp. 1271 (D.Mass.1982) (finding wife signing as guarantor of husband's note not "aggrieved applicant" under regulations).

35. 15 U.S.C.A. § 1691e(a). *See Fischl, supra* (noting that actual damages under ECOA may include out-of-pocket monetary losses, injury to credit reputation and mental anguish, humiliation or embarrassment); *Anderson, supra* (same); *Shuman v. Standard Oil Co. of Cal.*, 453 F.Supp. 1150 (N.D.Cal.1978) (finding harm to reputation for creditworthiness compensable as actual damages); *Integra Bank/Pittsburgh, supra* (finding permissibly bound debtor may suffer ECOA-cognizable injury resulting from being impermissibly required to secure spouse's or other party's signature). *Cf.* 15 U.S.C.A. § 1691e(f) (concerning jurisdiction of courts in ECOA suits; two-year limitation for maintenance of action). *See Farrell v. Bank of New Hampshire–Portsmouth*, 929 F.2d 871 (1st Cir.1991) (discussing limitation of ECOA action); *Sony Elecs., Inc. v. Putnam*, 906 F.Supp. 228 (D.N.J.1995) (same); *Silverman v. Eastrich Multiple In-*

governmental creditor may be liable to the aggrieved applicant for punitive damages in an amount not greater than $10,000, in addition to any actual damages.[36] In determining the amount of punitive damages, the court is required to consider, among other relevant factors: (1) The amount of any actual damages; (2) The frequency and persistence of failures in ECOA compliance by the creditor; (3) The resources of the creditor; (4) The number of persons adversely affected; and, (5) The extent to which the creditor's failure of compliance was intentional.[37]

Equitable and declaratory relief is also available to an aggrieved applicant in the appropriate U.S. district court, or any other court of competent jurisdiction, "necessary to enforce the requirements imposed" under the ECOA.[38]

In any successful action for damages, punitive damages, or equitable or declaratory relief, the ECOA requires that costs of the action, together with reasonable attorneys' fees as determined by the court, are to be added to any damages awarded by the court.[39]

---

vestor Fund, L.P., 857 F.Supp. 447 (E.D.Pa. 1994), rev'd, 51 F.3d 28 (3d Cir.1995) (same); Pierce v. Citibank (South Dakota), N.A., 856 F.Supp. 1451 (D.Or.1994), aff'd, 92 F.3d 1193 (9th Cir.1996) (same); Riggs Nat'l Bank of Washington, D.C. v. Webster, 832 F.Supp. 147 (D.Md.1993) (same); Stern v. Espirito Santo Bank of Fla., 791 F.Supp. 865 (S.D.Fla.1992) (same); Blake, supra (discussing ECOA two-year limitation and FTCA five-year limitation); In re Remington, 19 B.R. 718 (Bkrtcy.D. Colo. 1982) (finding recoupment claim for alleged ECOA violation not barred). See generally Owens v. Magee Fin. Serv. of Bogalusa, Inc., 476 F.Supp. 758 (E.D.La.1979) (discussing jurisdiction).

An ECOA violation may also constitute a compulsory counterclaim in a collection action, and, if proven, it would entitle the debtor to recoupment of damages, as a set-off against amount owed under the loan. CMF Va. Land, L.P. v. Brinson, 806 F.Supp. 90 (E.D.Va.1992); In re Remington, supra this note.

No showing of specific intent to discriminate or statistical showing of adverse impact on a protected class is necessary to establish prima facie case of violation under the ECOA. Miller, supra. But see Moore v. United States Dep't of Agric., 857 F.Supp. 507 (W.D.La.1994), vacated, 55 F.3d 991 (5th Cir.1995) (requiring showing that aggrieved party was member of protected class, and that party was denied credit though qualified); Mercado Garcia v. Ponce Fed. Bank, 779 F.Supp. 620 (D.P.R.1991), aff'd, 979 F.2d 890 (1st Cir.1992) (same); Gross v. United States Small Bus. Admin., 669 F.Supp. 50 (N.D.N.Y.1987), aff'd, 867 F.2d 1423 (2d Cir.1988) (same).

A jury trial is required in a damages action brought under the ECOA. Vander Missen v. Kellogg–Citizens Nat'l Bank of Green Bay, 83 F.R.D. 206 (E.D.Wis.1979).

36. 15 U.S.C.A. § 1691e(b). However, in the case of an ECOA class action, the total punitive damages award may not exceed $500,000 or one percent of the net worth of the creditor, whichever is less. Id. See Fischl, supra (noting punitive damages may be awarded, regardless of proof of actual damages, where creditor's conduct is wanton, malicious, or oppressive, or creditor acted in reckless disregard of applicable law); Anderson, supra (same); Ricci v. Key Bancshares of Me., Inc., 662 F.Supp. 1132 (D.Me.1987) (same); Sayers v. General Motors Acceptance Corp., 522 F.Supp. 835 (W.D.Mo.1981) (concerning reckless disregard of legal duty owed to plaintiff); Vander Missen, supra (discussing punitive damages); Smith v. Lakeside Foods, Inc., 449 F.Supp. 171 (N.D.Ill.1978) (noting that, even in absence of actual damages, punitive damages may be available under ECOA).

37. 15 U.S.C.A. § 1691e(b).

38. Id. § 1691e(c). See Smith, supra (noting that, even in absence of actual damages, equitable relief may be available under ECOA). Cf., e.g., Integra Bank/Pittsburgh, supra (creditor violating ECOA not be permitted to look for payment to party who, but for violation, would not have incurred personal liability on underlying debt).

39. 15 U.S.C.A. § 1691e(d). See Anderson, supra (discussing attorneys' fees); Markham, supra (denying interim fee award); Owens, supra (discussing attorneys' fees).

One innovation in the enforcement scheme under the ECOA is the provision for incentives for self-testing and self-correction by creditors.[40] A creditor may conduct, or authorize an independent third party to conduct, a self-test of any aspect of a credit transaction by a creditor, in order to determine the level and effectiveness of its ECOA compliance.[41] To maintain this self-test as privileged, the creditor must identify any possible ECOA violations and take appropriate corrective action to address any such possible violations.[42]

If a creditor meets these conditions,[43] any report or results of that self-test shall remain privileged,[44] and such results may not be obtained or used by any applicant, department, or agency in any proceeding or civil action in which one or more ECOA violations are alleged.[45] In addition, they may not be obtained or used in any examination or investigation relating to ECOA compliance.[46]

However, an applicant, department, or agency can obtain and use a report or the results of a self-test in a proceeding or civil action, or in an examination or investigation in a situation where: (1) The creditor or any person with lawful access to the report or results voluntarily releases or discloses all, or any part of, the report or results to the applicant, department, agency, or the general public;[47] (2) The creditor or person with lawful access refers to or describes the report or results as a defense to charges of ECOA violations against the creditor to whom the self-test relates;[48] or, (3) The report or results are sought in conjunction with an adjudication or admission of an ECOA violation for the sole purpose of determining an appropriate penalty or remedy.[49]

§ 10.9　Other Regulatory Initiatives

Given the pervasiveness of the regulation of depository institutions, it should not be surprising that the regulatory system has often been harnessed to implement other extraneous policy objectives. The preceding sections have discussed some of the major regulatory initiatives in that regard, but it must be emphasized that federal law is replete with such unrelated uses of the depository institutions regulatory system. Figure 10–2, *infra*, illustrates a selective sample of these other regulatory initiatives.

---

40. 15 U.S.C.A. § 1691c–1.

41. *Id.* § 1691c–1(a)(1)(A).

42. *Id.* § 1691c–1(a)(1)(B).

43. *Cf. id.* § 1691c–1(c) (providing for adjudication challenging asserted privilege).

44. *Id.* § 1691c–1(a)(2)(A).

45. *Id.* § 1691c–1(a)(2)(B)(i).

46. *Id.* § 1691c–1(a)(2)(B)(ii).

47. *Id.* § 1691c–1(b)(1)(A)(i).

48. *Id.* § 1691c–1(b)(1)(A)(ii).

49. *Id.* § 1691c–1(b)(1)(B). On disclosures with respect to determination of a penalty or remedy, see *id.* § 1691c–1(b)(2).

Figure 10–2
Selected Statutory Provisions

Enactment	Citation	Policy Objective
Anti–Money Laundering Act	Pub. L. No. 102–550, tit. XV, 106 Stat. 4044 (1992) (*codified at* scattered sections of 12, 18, 31 U.S.C.A.)	Criminal investigation and enforcement
Bank Secrecy Act	Pub. L. No. 91–508, tit. I, II, 84 Stat. 1114–1124 (1970), *as amended* (31 U.S.C.A. §§ 321, 5311–5314, 5316–5322)	Criminal investigation and enforcement
Community Development Banking and Financial Institutions Act	Pub. L. No. 103–325, § 102, 108 Stat. 2163 (1994) (*codified at* scattered sections of 5, 12, 15, 18 U.S.C.A.)	Economic revitalization and community development
Consumer Credit Protection Act	Pub. L. No. 90–321, 82 Stat. 146 (1968), *as amended* (15 U.S.C.A. §§ 1601–1649, 1661–1667e, 1671–1681u, 1691–1693r; 18 U.S.C.A. §§ 891–896)	Consumer protection
Consumer Leasing Act	Pub. L. No. 94–240, 90 Stat. 257 (1976) (15 U.S.C.A. §§ 1667–1667e)	Consumer protection
Credit Card Fraud Act	Pub. L. No. 98–473, tit. II, ch. XVI, 98 Stat. 2183 (1984)	Consumer protection
Credit Repair Organizations Act	Pub. L. No. 104–208, § 2451, 110 Stat. 3009 (1996) (15 U.S.C.A. §§ 1679–1679j)	Consumer protection
Cuban Liberty and Democratic Solidarity Act (Helms–Burton)	Pub. L. No. 104–114, 110 Stat. 785 (1996) (U.S.C.A. §§ 1643*l*–1643m, 6021–6024, 6031–6046, 6061–6067, 6081–6085, 6091)	Foreign Affairs
Electronic Fund Transfer Act	Pub. L. No. 95–630, tit. XX, 92 Stat. 3728 (1978) (15 U.S.C.A. §§ 1693–1693r)	Consumer protection
Emergency Low Income Housing Preservation Act	Pub. L. No. 100–242, tit. II, 101 Stat. 1877 (1988), *as amended* (12 U.S.C.A. §§ 4101–4124, 4141–4147)	Housing policy
Fair Credit Billing Act	Pub. L. No. 93–495, tit. III, 88 Stat. 1511 (1974) (15 U.S.C.A. §§ 1666–1666i)	Consumer protection
Fair Credit Reporting Act	Pub. L. No. 91–508, § 601, 84 Stat. 1128 (1970) (15 U.S.C.A. §§ 1681–1681u)	Consumer protection
Fair Debt Collection Practices Act	Pub. L. No. 95–109, 91 Stat. 874 (1977) (15 U.S.C.A. §§ 1692–1692o)	Consumer protection
Home Equity Loan Consumer Protection Act	Pub. L. No. 100–709, 102 Stat. 4725 (1988) (15 U.S.C.A. §§ 1637a, 1665b, 1647)	Consumer protection
Home Mortgage Disclosure Act	Pub. L. No. 94–200, tit. III, 89 Stat. 1125 (1975) (12 U.S.C.A. §§ 2801–2810)	Consumer protection
International Emergency Economic Powers Act	Pub. L. No. 95–223, tit. II, 91 Stat. 1626 (1977), as amended (50 U.S.C.A. §§ 1701–1706)	Foreign affairs
Iran and Libya Sanctions Act (D'Amato Act)	Pub. L. No. 104–172, 110 Stat. 1541 (1996)	Foreign affairs
Money Laundering Control Act	Pub. L. No. 99–570, tit. I, 100 Stat. 3207 (1986) (18 U.S.C.A. §§ 981–982; 31 U.S.C.A. § 5324)	Criminal investigation and enforcement
Money Laundering Prosecution Act	Pub. L. No. 100–690, tit. VI, 102 Stat. 4354 (1988) (31 U.S.C.A. §§ 5325–5326)	Criminal investigation and enforcement
Money Laundering Suppression Act	Pub. L. No. 103–325, tit. IV, 108 Stat. 2243 (1994) (31 U.S.C.A. § 5330)	Criminal investigation and enforcement

Enactment	*Citation*	*Policy Objective*
National Consumer Cooperative Bank Act	Pub. L. No. 95–351, 92 Stat. 449 (1978), *as amended* (12 U.S.C.A. §§ 3001, 3011–3026, 3041–3051)	Consumer credit
Real Estate Settlement Procedures Act ("RESPA")	Pub. L. No. 93–533, 88 Stat. 1724 (1974) (12 U.S.C.A. §§ 2601–2610, 2614–2617)	Consumer protection
Removal of Regulatory Barriers to Affordable Housing Act	Pub. L. No. 102–550, tit. XII, 106 Stat. 3938 (1992) (42 U.S.C.A. §§ 12705a–12705d)	Housing policy
Trading With the Enemy Act § 5(b)	Act of Oct. 6, 1917, ch. 106, 40 Stat. 411 (1917), *as amended* (50 U.S.C.A. app. § 5(b))	Foreign affairs
Truth-in-Lending Act	Pub. L. No. 90–321, tit. I, 82 Stat. 146 (1968), *as amended* (15 U.S.C.A. §§ 1601–1608, 1610–1613, 1631–1635, 1637–1646, 1648–1649, 1661–1667f)	Consumer protection
Truth-in-Savings Act	Pub. L. No. 102–242, tit. II, 105 Stat. 2334 (1991) (12 U.S.C.A. §§ 4301–4313)	Consumer protection
United Nations Participation Act § 5	Pub. L. No. 264, 59 Stat. 619 (1945), *as amended* (22 U.S.C.A. § 287c)	Foreign affairs

Many of these initiatives concern consumer protection, and they may seem unavoidable in a regulatory system that countenances such significant concentration of economic power within one specialized industry.[1] Others, however, are more obviously extraneous to the depository institutions system; they simply take opportunistic advantage of the fact that these institutions are optimally placed to assist in the attainment of a particular policy objective.

For example, various initiatives apply specialized rules to money-transfer transactions of depository institutions, among other entities.[2] The objective here is primarily the identification of criminal activity by persons engaged in the laundering of proceeds of illicit activity, not the maintenance of safety and soundness in the banking system. Depository institutions simply represent a convenient vehicle for federal investigators to test for symptoms of illegal activity that generates significant funds in need of laundering. Nevertheless, compliance with such initiatives is extremely important for depository institutions. Regardless of the attenuated relationship between these extraneous rules and the objectives of depository institutions regulation, an institution is well advised to comply.

Another example of the attenuated relationship between depository institutions regulatory policy and extraneous policy objectives is afforded by various foreign policy provisions of federal law.[3] Under the broad

§ 10.9

1. 15 U.S.C.A. §§ 1601–1649, 1661–1667e, 1671–1681u, 1691–1693r; 18 U.S.C.A. §§ 891–896 (codifying Consumer Credit Protection Act).

2. *See, e.g.*, 31 U.S.C.A. §§ 321, 5311–5314, 5316–5322 (codifying Bank Secrecy Act); 18 U.S.C.A. §§ 981–982; 31 U.S.C.A. §§ 5324–5326, 5330 (prohibiting money laundering).

3. *See, e.g.*, 22 U.S.C.A. § 287c (authorizing imposition of economic sanctions in compliance with U.N. Security Council resolutions); 50 U.S.C.A. §§ 1701 *et seq.* (authorizing imposition of economic sanctions authority granted by these provisions, depository institutions are often drafted into the service of U.S. economic warfare, regardless of the effect on the policy objectives of depository institution regulation.[4] Yet the mandatory nature of these foreign policy sanctions programs makes compliance unavoidable.

It should be clear from the preceding chapters that the regulation of depository institutions is an extremely complex undertaking. This undertaking is rendered all the more complicated by the intersection of so many varying, and often unrelated policy initiatives. Perhaps this situation is ultimately a testament to the extremely significant position that depository institutions occupy in contemporary society—what touches these institutions affects and is affected by a congeries of social, political, and economic aspects of our modern society.

in response to foreign threat to U.S. national security, foreign policy, or economy).

4. *See supra* § 9.30 (discussing effects of U.S. economic sanctions on depository institutions).

APPENDIX

RESEARCHING THE LAW OF BANK REGULATION ON WESTLAW®

Analysis

Section 1.   Introduction

Bank Regulation provides a strong base for analyzing even the most complex problem involving bank regulation. Whether your research requires examination of statutes, regulations, case law, administrative decisions, expert commentary or other materials, West books and Westlaw are excellent sources of information.

To keep you abreast of current developments, Westlaw provides frequently updated databases. With Westlaw, you have unparalleled legal research resources at your fingertips.

Additional Resources

If you have not previously used Westlaw or have questions not covered in this appendix, see the *Westlaw Reference Manual* or call the West Group Reference Attorneys at 1–800–REF–ATTY (1–800–733–2889). The West Group Reference Attorneys are trained, licensed attorneys, available 24 hours a day to assist you with your Westlaw search questions.

Section 2. Westlaw Databases

Each database on Westlaw is assigned an abbreviation called an *identifier*, which you use to access the database. You can find identifiers for all databases in the online Westlaw Directory and in the printed *Westlaw Database Directory*. When you need to know more detailed information about a database, use Scope. Scope contains coverage information, lists of related databases and valuable search tips. To access Scope, click the **Scope** button while in the database.

The following chart lists Westlaw databases that contain information pertaining to bank regulation. For a complete list of bank regulation databases, see the online Westlaw Directory or the printed *Westlaw Database Directory*. Because new information is continually being added to Westlaw, you should also check the Welcome to Westlaw window and the Westlaw Directory for new database information.

Selected Westlaw Databases

Database	Identifier	Coverage
Federal Finance and Banking–Combined Financial Materials	FFIN–ALL	Varies by source
Federal and State Case Law Combined		
Federal & State Case Law	ALLCASES	Begins with 1945
Federal & State Case Law–Before 1945	ALLCASES–OLD	1789–1944
Federal Case Law		
Federal Finance & Banking–Federal Cases	FFIN–CS	Begins with 1789
Federal Finance & Banking–Supreme Court Cases	FFIN–SCT	Begins with 1790
Federal Finance & Banking–Courts of Appeals Cases	FFIN–CTA	Begins with 1891
Federal Finance & Banking–District Courts Cases	FFIN–DCT	Begins with 1789

State Case Law

Multistate Finance & Banking Cases	MFIN–CS	Varies by state
Individual State Finance & Banking Cases	XXFIN–CS (where XX is a state's two-letter postal abbreviation)	Varies by state

Federal Statutes and Regulations

Federal Finance & Banking–U.S. Code Annotated	FFIN–USCA	Current data
Federal Finance & Banking–Code and Regulations	FFIN–CODREG	Varies by source
Federal Finance & Banking–Final, Temporary and Proposed Regulations	FFIN–REG	Varies by source
Federal Finance & Banking–Code of Federal Regulations	FFIN–CFR	Current data
Federal Finance & Banking–Federal Register	FFIN–FR	Begins with July 1980
Federal Finance & Banking–Federal Reserve Board–Federal Register	FFIN–FRBFR	Begins with July 1980
Arnold & Porter Riegle Community Development and Regulatory Improvement Act of 1994	RIEGLE94–LH	Full history
Arnold and Porter Riegle–Neal Interstate Banking and Branching Efficiency Act of 1994	IBANK94–LH	Full history
FIRREA Legislative History	FIRREA–LH	Full history
United States Public Laws	US–PL	Current data

Federal Administrative Materials

Federal Finance & Banking–Administrative Materials	FFIN–ADMIN	Varies by source
Federal Finance & Banking–Federal Deposit Insurance Corporation (FDIC) Decisions and Interpretive Letters	FFIN–FDIC	Decisions: begins with February 1981; letters: begins with January 1979

Federal Finance & Banking–Federal Deposit Insurance Corporation (FDIC) Enforcement Decisions	FFIN–FDICED	Begins with February 1981
Federal Finance & Banking–Federal Deposit Insurance Corporation (FDIC) Interpretive Letters	FFIN–FDICIL	Begins with January 1979
Federal Finance & Banking–Federal Deposit Insurance Corporation (FDIC) Financial Institution Letters	FFIN–FDICFIL	Begins with January 1989
Federal Finance & Banking–Federal Reserve Board Materials Combined	FFIN–FRB	Varies by source
Federal Finance & Banking–Federal Reserve Board Actions	FFIN–FRBACT	Begins with May 1990
Federal Finance & Banking–Federal Reserve Board Agreements	FFIN–FRBAGR	Begins with May 1990
Federal Finance & Banking–Federal Reserve Board Interpretive Letters	FFIN–FRBIL	Begins with June 1928
Federal Finance & Banking–Federal Reserve Board Speeches	FFIN–FRBSP	Begins with October 1992
Federal Finance & Banking–Federal Reserve Bulletin	FFIN–FRBBUL	Begins with January 1970
Federal Finance & Banking–Federal Reserve Regulatory Service	FFIN–FRRS	Current data
Federal Finance & Banking–News Releases	FFIN–NR	Varies by agency
Federal Finance & Banking–Office of the Comptroller of the Currency	FFIN–OCC	Varies by source

Federal Finance & Banking–Office of the Comptroller of the Currency–Banking Issuances	FFIN–OCCBI	Banking circulars: begins with June 1968; OCC Alerts: begins with February 1994; banking bulletins: begins with December 1981; advisory letters: begins with July 1987
Federal Finance & Banking–Office of the Comptroller of the Currency–Enforcement Actions	FFIN–OCCEA	Begins with 1977
Federal Finance & Banking–Office of the Comptroller of the Currency–Interpretations and Actions	FFIN–OCCIA	Begins with March 1986
Federal Finance & Banking–Office of the Comptroller of the Currency–Interpretive Letters	FFIN–OCCIL	Varies by source
Federal Finance & Banking–Office of the Comptroller of the Currency–Quarterly Journal	FFIN–OCCQJ	Begins with 1982
Federal Finance & Banking–Office of the Comptroller of the Currency–An Examiner's Guide to Consumer Compliance	FFIN–OCCEG	Begins with January 1993
Federal Finance & Banking–Office of the Comptroller of the Currency–Comptroller's Handbook for National Bank Examiners	FFIN–OCCHNBE	Begins with June 1994
Federal Finance & Banking–Office of Thrift Supervision Materials Combined	FFIN–OTS	Varies by source
Federal Finance & Banking–Office of Thrift Supervision Director's Orders	FFIN–OTSDO	Begins with August 1989
Federal Finance & Banking–Office of Thrift Supervision Letters, Memoranda and Opinions	FFIN–OTSL	Federal Home Loan Bank Board: February 1964–August 1989; Office of Thrift Supervision: begins with September 1989

Federal Finance & Banking–Office of Thrift Supervision Regulatory Bulletins, Thrift Bulletins and Legal Alert Memos	FFIN–OTSB	Regulatory bulletins and thrift bulletins: begins with July 1988; legal alert memos: October 1989–August 1990

State Statutes and Regulations

State Statutes–Annotated	ST–ANN–ALL	Varies by state
Individual State Statutes–Annotated	XX–ST–ANN (where XX is a state's two-letter postal abbreviation)	Varies by state
State Administrative Code Multibase	ADC–ALL	Varies by state
Individual State Administrative Code	XX–ADC (where XX is a state's two-letter postal abbreviation)	Varies by state

Texts, Periodicals and Research Tools

Finance & Banking–Law Reviews, Texts & Bar Journals	FIN–TP	Varies by publication
Andrews Bank & Lender Liability Litigation Reporter	ANBLLLR	Begins with November 1996
Annual Review of Banking Law	ANNRBL	Selected coverage begins with 1991 (vol. 10); full coverage begins with 1993 (vol. 12)
The Banking Law Journal	WGL–BLJ	Full coverage begins with 1987 (vol. 104)
Banking Policy Report	BNKPR	Full coverage begins with 1992 (vol. 11, no. 5)
Electronic Banking Law and Commerce Report	GLEBLCR	Begins with January 1997
Fordham Finance, Securities & Tax Law Forum	FDMFSTLF	Full coverage begins with 1997 (vol. 2)
NAAG Financial Crimes Report	NAAGFCR	Begins with January 1995
North Carolina Banking Institute	NCBNKI	Full coverage begins with 1997 (vol. 1)

Stanford Journal of Law, Business and Finance	STNJLBF	Full coverage begins with 1994 (vol. 1)

News, Current Events and Directories

Finance & Banking News	FINNEWS	Varies by source
BNA Banking Daily	BNA–BBD	Begins with September 1987
BNA International Business & Finance Daily	BNA–IBFD	Begins with January 1991
BNA's Finance & Banking Database	BNA–FIN	Begins with January 1986
Financial Regulation Report	FINRR	Begins with July 1992
International Banking Regulator	INTLBR	Begins with August 1993
Westlaw Topical Highlights–Finance & Banking	WTH–FIN	Current data
West Legal Directory™ –Banking and Finance	WLD–FIN	Current data

Section 3. Retrieving a Document with a Citation: Find and Jump

3.1 Find

Find is a Westlaw service that allows you to retrieve a document by entering its citation. Find allows you to retrieve documents from anywhere in Westlaw without accessing or changing databases. Find is available for many documents, including case law (state and federal), the *United States Code Annotated*®, state statutes, regulations (state and federal), administrative materials, and texts and periodicals.

To use Find, simply access the Find service and type the citation. The following list provides some examples:

To Find This Document	Access Find and Type
Connelly v. Comptroller of the Currency, 876 F.2d 1209 (5th Cir. 1989)	**876 f2d 1209**
12 U.S.C.A. § 3303	**12 usca 3303**
12 C.F.R. § 5.50	**12 cfr 5.50**
O.C.C. News Release 98–123	**occ nr 98–123**

For a complete list of publications that can be retrieved with Find and their abbreviations, consult the Find Publications List. Click the **Pubs List** button after accessing Find.

3.2 Jump

Use Jump markers (> or f) to move from one location to another on Westlaw. For example, use Jump markers to go directly from the statute, case or law review article you are viewing to a cited statute, case or article; from a headnote to the corresponding text in the opinion; or from an entry in a statutes index database to the full text of the statute.

Section 4.   Searching with Natural Language: WIN—Westlaw is Natural

Overview: With WIN, you can retrieve documents by simply describing your issue in plain English. If you are a relatively new Westlaw user, Natural Language searching can make it easier for you to retrieve cases that are on point. If you are an experienced Westlaw user, Natural Language gives you a valuable alternative search method.

When you enter a Natural Language description, Westlaw automatically identifies legal phrases, removes common words and generates variations of terms in your description. Westlaw then searches for the concepts in your description. Concepts may include significant terms, phrases, legal citations or topic and key numbers. Westlaw retrieves the 20 documents that most closely match your description, beginning with the document most likely to match.

4.1   Natural Language Search

Access a database, such as Federal Finance & Banking–Federal Cases (FFIN–CS). If the Terms and Connectors Query Editor is displayed, click the **Search Type** button and choose **Natural Language**. At the Natural Language Description Editor, type a Natural Language description such as the following:

are national banks allowed to sell insurance

4.2   Next Command

Westlaw displays the 20 documents that most closely match your description, beginning with the document most likely to match. If you want to view additional documents, click your right mouse button and choose **Next 10** Documents from the pop-up menu, or choose **Next 10 Documents** from the Browse menu.

4.3   Natural Language Browse Commands

Best Mode: To display the best portion (the portion that most closely matches your description) of each document in your search result, click your right mouse button and choose **Next Best** from the pop-up menu or click **Best f**.

Standard Browsing Commands: You can also browse your Natural Language search result using standard Westlaw browsing commands, such as citations list, Locate, page mode and term mode. When you browse your Natural Language search result in term mode, the five portions of each document that are most likely to match your description are displayed.

Section 5.   Searching with Terms and Connectors

Overview: With Terms and Connectors searching, you enter a query, which consists of key terms from your issue and connectors specifying the relationship between these terms.

Terms and Connectors searching is useful when you want to retrieve a document for which you know specific details, such as the title or the fact situation. Terms and Connectors searching is also useful when you want to retrieve documents relating to a specific issue. If the Natural Language Description Editor is displayed when you access a database, click the **Search Type** button and choose **Term Search**.

5.1   Terms

Plurals and Possessives: Plurals are automatically retrieved when you enter the singular form of a term. This is true for both regular and irregular plurals (e.g., **child** retrieves *children*). If you enter the plural form of a term, you will not retrieve the singular form.

If you enter the nonpossessive form of a term, Westlaw automatically retrieves the possessive form as well. However, if you enter the possessive form, only the possessive form is retrieved.

Automatic Equivalencies: Some terms have alternative forms or equivalencies; for example, 5 and five are equivalent terms. Westlaw automatically retrieves equivalent terms. The *Westlaw Reference Manual* contains a list of equivalent terms.

Compound Words, Abbreviations and Acronyms: When a compound word is one of your search terms, use a hyphen to retrieve all forms of the word. For example, the term **along-side** retrieves *alongside, alongside* and *along side*.

When using an abbreviation or acronym as a search term, place a period after each of the letters to retrieve any of its forms. For example, the term **f.d.i.c.** retrieves *fdic, f.d.i.c., f d i c* and *f. d. i. c.* Note: The abbreviation does not retrieve federal deposit insurance corporation, so remember to add alternative terms to your query such as **"federal deposit insurance"**.

The Root Expander and the Universal Character: When you use the Terms and Connectors search method, placing the root expander (!) at the end of a root term generates all other terms with that root. For example, adding the ! to the root *encrypt* in the query

encrypt! /5 message transmission signal

instructs Westlaw to retrieve such terms as *encrypt, encrypted, encryption* and *encrypting*.

The universal character (*) stands for one character and can be inserted in the middle or at the end of a term. For example, the term

withdr*w

will retrieve withdraw and withdrew. Adding three asterisks to the root elect

elect* * *

instructs Westlaw to retrieve all forms of the root with up to three additional characters. Terms such as *elected* or *election* are retrieved by this query. However, terms with more than three letters following the root, such as *electronic*, are not retrieved. Plurals are always retrieved, even if more than three letters follow the root.

Phrase Searching: To search for an exact phrase, place it within quotation marks. For example, to search for references to *federal reserve*, type **"federal reserve"**. When you are using the Terms and Connectors search method, you should use phrase searching only if you are certain that the terms in the phrase will not appear in any other order.

5.2 Alternative Terms

After selecting the terms for your query, consider which alternative terms are necessary. For example, if you are searching for the term *constitutional*, you might also want to search for the term unconstitutional. You should consider both synonyms and antonyms as alternative terms. You can also use the Westlaw thesaurus to add alternative terms to your query.

5.3 Connectors

After selecting terms and alternative terms for your query, use connectors to specify the relationship that should exist between search terms in your retrieved documents. The connectors are described below:

Use:	To retrieve documents with:	Example:
& (and)	both terms	**financ! & privacy**
or (space)	either term or both terms	**stock security**
/p	search terms in the same paragraph	**internet /p encrypt!**
/s	search terms in the same sentence	**insured /s deposit**
+s	the first search term preceding the second within the same sentence	**burden +s prov* * * proof**
/n	search terms within "n" terms of each other (where "n" is a number)	**deposit! /3 direct!**
+n	the first search term preceding the second by "n" terms (where "n" is a number)	**letter +3 credit**
" "	search terms appearing in the same order as in the quotation marks	**"bank holding company act"**

Use:	To exclude documents with:	Example:
% (but not)	search terms following the % symbol	**adequate /s capital % sy,di("credit union")**

5.4   Field Restrictions

Overview: Documents in each Westlaw database consist of several segments, or fields. One field may contain the citation, another the title, another the synopsis and so forth. Not all databases contain the same fields. Also depending on the database, fields with the same name may contain different types of information.

To view a list of fields for a specific database and their contents, see Scope for that database. Note that in some databases not every field is available for every document.

To retrieve only those documents containing your search terms in a specific field, restrict your search to that field. To restrict your search to a specific field, type the field name or abbreviation followed by your search terms enclosed in parentheses. For example, to retrieve a case in the Federal Finance & Banking–Supreme Court Cases database (FFIN–SCT) entitled Plant City v. Dickinson, search for your terms in the title field (ti):

ti("plant city" & dickinson)

The fields discussed below are available in Westlaw databases you might use for researching banking regulation law issues.

Digest and Synopsis Fields: The digest (di) and synopsis (sy) fields, added to case law databases by West's attorney-editors, summarize the main points of a case. The synopsis field contains a brief description of a case. The digest field contains the topic and headnote fields and includes the complete hierarchy of concepts used by West's editors to classify the headnotes to specific West digest topics and key numbers. Restricting your search to the synopsis and digest fields limits your result to cases in which your terms are related to a major issue in the case.

Consider restricting your search to one or both of these fields if

● you are searching for common terms or terms with more than one meaning, and you need to narrow your search; or

● you cannot narrow your search by using a smaller database.

For example, to retrieve cases that discuss cease and desist orders in the context of FIRREA, access the Federal Finance & Banking–Federal Cases database (FFIN–CS) and type the following query:

sy,di(ceas! /3 desist! /p f.i.r.r.e.a. "financial institutions reform recovery")

Headnote Field: The headnote field (he) is part of the digest field, but does not contain topic numbers, hierarchical classification information or key numbers. The headnote field contains a one-sentence summary for each point of law in a case and any supporting citations given by the author of the opinion. A headnote field restriction is useful when you are searching for specific statutory sections or rule numbers. For example, to retrieve headnotes from federal cases that cite 12 U.S.C.A. § 1817(j), access the Federal Finance & Banking–Federal Cases database (FFIN–CS) and type the following query:

he(12 +5 1817(j))

Topic Field: The topic field (to) is also part of the digest field. It contains hierarchical classification information, including the West digest topic names and numbers and the key numbers. You should restrict search terms to the topic field in a case law database if

- a digest field search retrieves too many documents; or

- you want to retrieve cases with digest paragraphs classified under more than one topic.

For example, the topic Banks and Banking has the topic number 52. To retrieve federal cases that discuss mergers or acquisitions in the context of banks, access the Federal Finance & Banking–Federal Cases database (FFIN–CS) and type a query like the following:

to(52) /p merg! aquisition

To retrieve cases classified under more than one topic and key number, search for your terms in the topic field. For example, to search for cases discussing penalties for usurious interest rates, which may be classified to Banks and Banking (52), Consumer Credit (92b), Consumer Protection (92h) or Usury (398), among other topics, type a query like the following:

to(interest /5 rate /p penalty)

For a complete list of West digest topics and their corresponding topic numbers, access the Key Number Service: click the **Key Number Service** button or choose **Key Number Service** from the Services menu.

> *Note:* Slip opinions, cases not reported by West and cases from topical services do not contain the digest, headnote and topic fields.

Prelim and Caption Fields: When searching in a database containing statutes, rules or regulations, restrict your search to the prelim (pr) and caption (ca) fields to retrieve documents in which your terms are important enough to appear in a section name or heading. For example, to retrieve federal regulations regarding mutual savings banks, access the Federal Finance & Banking–Code of Federal Regulations database (FFIN–CFR) and type the following:

pr,ca("mutual savings bank")

5.5   Date Restrictions

You can use Westlaw to retrieve documents decided or issued before, after or on a specified date, as well as within a range of dates. The following sample queries contain date restrictions:

da(1998) & community /s reinvest!

da(aft 1995) & community /s reinvest!

da(9/23/1997) & community /s reinvest!

You can also search for documents *added to a database* on or after a specified date, as well as within a range of dates. The following sample queries contain added-date restrictions:

ad(aft 1995) & community /s reinvest!

ad(aft 2–1–1998 & bef 2–17–1998) & community /s reinvest!

Section 6.   Searching with Topic and Key Numbers

To retrieve cases that address a specific point of law, use topic and key numbers as your search terms. If you have an on-point case, run a search using the topic and key number from the relevant headnote in an appropriate database to find other cases containing headnotes classified to that topic and key number. For example, to search for federal cases containing headnotes classified under topic 52 (Banks and Banking) and key number 6 (Authority or license to do business), access the Federal Finance & Banking–Federal Cases database (FFIN–CS) and enter the following query:

52k6

For a complete list of West digest topic and key numbers, access the **Key Number Service**: click the **Key Number Service** button or choose **Key Number Service** from the Services menu.

> *Note:* Slip opinions, cases not reported by West and cases from topical services do not contain West topic and key numbers.

Section 7.   Verifying Your Research with Citator Services

Overview: A citator service is a tool that helps you ensure that your cases are good law; helps you retrieve cases, legislation or articles that cite a case, rule or statute; and helps you verify that the spelling and format of your citations are correct.

7.1   KeyCite

KeyCite is the citation research service from West Group that integrates all case law on Westlaw. KeyCite helps you trace the history of a case, retrieve a list of all cases and selected secondary sources that cite a case, and track legal issues decided in a case.

KeyCite provides both direct and negative indirect history for any case within the scope of its coverage. The History of the Case window displays a case's direct appellate history and its negative indirect history, which consists of cases outside the direct appellate line that may have a negative impact on its precedential value. The history also includes related references, which are opinions involving the same parties and facts but resolving different issues.

In addition to case history, the Citations to the Case window in KeyCite lists all cases on Westlaw and secondary sources, such as law review articles and ALR® annotations, that cite the decision. These citing references are added to KeyCite as soon as they are added to Westlaw. All citing cases on Westlaw are included in KeyCite—even unpublished opinions.

For citation verification, the KeyCite result provides the case title; parallel citations, including many looseleaf citations; the court of decision; the docket number; and the filing date.

7.2 Westlaw As a Citator

For citations not covered by the citator services, including persuasive secondary authority such as restatements and treatises, use Westlaw as a citator to retrieve cases that cite your authority.

Using Westlaw as a citator, you can search for documents citing a specific statute, rule, regulation, agency decision or other authority. For example, to retrieve federal cases citing 12 C.F.R. § 225.7, access the Federal Finance & Banking–Federal Cases database (FFIN–CS) and type a query like the following:

12 +5 225.7

Section 8.   Researching with Westlaw—Examples

8.1 Retrieving Law Review Articles

Recent law review articles are often a good place to begin researching a legal issue because law review articles serve 1) as an excellent introduction to a new topic or review for a stale one, providing terminology to help you formulate a query; 2) as a finding tool for pertinent primary authority, such as rules, statutes and cases; and 3) in some instances, as persuasive secondary authority.

Suppose you need to gain more background information on bank insolvency regulation.

Solution

● To retrieve recent law review articles relevant to your issue, access the Finance & Banking–Law Reviews, Texts & Bar Journals database (FIN–TP). Using the Natural Language search method, enter a description like the following:

bank insolvency regulation

● If you have a citation to an article in a specific publication, use Find to retrieve it. For more information on Find, see Section 3.1 of this appendix. For example, to retrieve the article found at 76 Tex. L. Rev. 723, access Find and type

76 tex l rev 723

● If you know the title of an article but not which journal it appeared in, access the Finance & Banking–Law Reviews, Texts & Bar Journals database (FIN–TP) and search for key terms from the title in the title field. For example, to retrieve the article "Bank Insolvency Law Now That It Matters Again," type the following Terms and Connectors query:

ti(insolvency & matters)

8.2 Retrieving Statutes and Regulations

Suppose you need to retrieve federal statutes and any proposed, final or temporary regulations dealing specifically with truth in savings in the context of credit unions.

Solution

- Access the Federal Finance & Banking–Code and Regulations database (FFIN–CODREG). Search for your terms in the prelim and caption fields using the Terms and Connectors search method:

  pr,ca(truth /s savings & "credit union")

- When you know the citation for a specific section of a statute or regulation, use Find to retrieve it. For example, to retrieve 12 C.F.R. 1 707.3, access Find and type

  12 cfr 707.3

- To look at surrounding regulatory sections, use the Table of Contents service. Select a Jump marker in the prelim or caption field. You can also use Documents in Sequence to retrieve the section following § 707.3, even if that following section was not retrieved with your search or Find request. Click the **Docs in Seq** button.

- When you retrieve a statute on Westlaw, it will contain an Update message if legislation amending or repealing it is available online. Similarly, a regulation codified in the *Code of Federal Regulations* will contain an Update message if information in the *Federal Register* amends or repeals it. To display this updating information, select the Jump marker in the Update message.

> Because slip copy versions of laws are added to Westlaw before they contain full editorial enhancements, they are not retrieved with Update. To retrieve slip copy versions of laws, access the United States Public Laws database (US–PL) or a state's legislative service database (XX–LEGIS, where XX is the state's two-letter postal abbreviation). Then type **ci(slip)** and descriptive terms, e.g., **ci(slip) & "credit union"**. Slip copy documents are replaced by the editorially enhanced versions within a few working days. Update also does not retrieve legislation that enacts a new statute or covers a topic that will not be incorporated into the statutes. To retrieve this legislation, access US–PL or a legislative service database and enter a query containing terms that describe the new legislation.

8.3   Retrieving Case Law

Suppose you need to retrieve New York case law dealing with civil actions for usury.

Solution

- Access the New York Finance & Banking Cases database (NYFIN–CS). Type a Natural Language description such as the following:

elements needed to prove usury

- When you know the citation for a specific case, use Find to retrieve it. (For more information on Find, see Section 3.1 of this appendix.) For example, to retrieve *Freitas v. Geddes Savings and Loan Association*, 481 N.Y.S.2d 665 (N.Y. 1984), access Find and type

481 nys2d 665

- If you find a topic and key number that is on point, run a search using that topic and key number to retrieve additional cases discussing that point of law. For example, to retrieve cases containing headnotes classified under topic 398 (Usury) and key number 12 (Intent, knowledge, and mutual assent of parties), type the following query:

398k12

- To retrieve cases written by a particular judge, add a judge field (ju) restriction to your query. For example, to retrieve cases written by Justice Mahoney that contain headnotes classified under topic 398 (Usury), type the following query:

ju(mahoney) & to(398)

8.4   Retrieving Administrative Decisions

Suppose you need to retrieve recent FDIC decisions that discuss the termination of FDIC insurance.

Solution

- Access the Federal Finance & Banking–Federal Deposit Insurance Corporation (FDIC) Enforcement Decisions database (FFIN–FDICED). Type a Terms and Connectors query such as the following:

da(aft 1997) & terminat! /s insurance

8.5   Using KeyCite

Suppose one of the cases you retrieve in your case law research is *Lester v. Levick*, 376 N.Y.S.2d 619 (N.Y.A.D. 1975). You want to determine whether this case is good law and to find other cases that have cited this case.

Solution

- Use KeyCite to retrieve direct history and negative indirect history for *Lester v. Levick*. While viewing the case, click the **KeyCite** button.

- Use KeyCite to display citing references for Lester. From the History of the Case, click the **Citations to the Case** button.

Table of Cases

377

C

*

INDEX